REAL WORLD
QUARKXPRESS7
FOR MACINTOSH AND WINDOWS

DAVID BLATNER, EDITOR

KELLY KORDES ANTON   CLAUDIA MCCUE
STEPHEN BEALS   PATTI SCHULZE
PARIAH S. BURKE   GLEN TURPIN
SHELLIE HALL   CHUCK WEGER
TED LOCASCIO

PEACHPIT PRESS
BERKELEY, CALIFORNIA

REAL WORLD QUARKXPRESS 7

Formerly known as *The QuarkXPress Book*
By David Blatner, Editor

Peachpit Press
1249 Eighth Street
Berkeley, CA 94710
510/524-2178
510/524-2221 (fax)

Find us on the World Wide Web at: www.peachpit.com
To report errors, please send a note to errata@peachpit.com
Peachpit Press is a division of Pearson Education

Managing Editor: Susan Rimerman
Production Editor: Lisa Brazieal
Copy Editor: Anne Marie Walker
Proofer: Elaine Merrill
Indexer: James Minkin
Compositor: WolfsonDesign
Cover design: Charlene Charles-Will
Cover Illustration: Alicia Buelow
Cover images: Quark Inc.

Permissions

The following photographs were used with permission of Special Collections Division, University of Washington Libraries. Figure 11-24 on page 553, photo by Todd, negative no. 10511.

ISBN–13 978-0-321-35030-5
ISBN–10   0-321-35030-8

9 8 7 6 5 4 3 2 1

Printed and bound in the United States of America

Contributing Authors

Kelly Kordes Anton is the Editor of *Colorado Expression* magazine. She uses this behind-the-scenes publishing knowledge to write books, articles, and stories about QuarkXPress and other software. A former Quark employee, she worked on versions 3.2, 3.3, and 4.0, and has contributed to later versions as a contractor. Kelly updated the *Working with Text*, *Typography*, and *Copy Flow* chapters for this book. Based in Littleton, Colorado, she has an 11-year-old ice hockey player and a 5-year-old who punches him.

Stephen Beals has been working with QuarkXPress in print production since the first versions of the software started working their way into designer's computers. He has written hundreds of articles for dozens of publications and has presented at many industry events. He edited the *Working with Items* and *Building a Layout* chapters. He also writes, directs, and acts in murder mystery musical comedies. He lives in the Finger Lakes area in Upstate New York.

Pariah S. Burke is a design and publishing workflow expert for studios, agencies, and publications around the world as principal of workflow:Creative (*www.WorkflowCreative.com*). He is the author or coauthor of four books and the former technical lead to Adobe's technical support team for InDesign, InCopy, Illustrator, Photoshop, and Acrobat. Pariah is a freelance graphic designer and the publisher of the Web sites *www.QuarkVSInDesign.com* and *www.Designorati.com*. He updated the *Pictures*, *Image Tuning*, and *Text Meets Graphics* chapters. When not traveling, Pariah lives in Portland, Oregon, where he writes (a lot) and creates (many) projects and publications that empower creative professionals.

Shellie Hall is a recognized specialist in the printing and publishing industry with 22 years of experience in typography, prepress, and graphic design. She most recently worked for Quark, Inc., as a product marketing manager. Shellie is a frequent speaker at industry events. For this book, she edited the *Tables* chapter and the *Scripting, XTensions,* and *Keystrokes* appendices.

continues on next page…

Ted LoCascio is a professional designer and an expert in QuarkXPress. He served as senior designer at the National Association of Photoshop Professionals (NAPP) and has created layouts for many successful clients. He is the author of several graphics software books, articles, and video training titles. For *Real World QuarkXPress*, he updated the *Learn QuarkXPress in 30 Minutes* and *QuarkXPress Basics* chapters. Visit his Web site at *www.tedlocascio.com*.

Claudia McCue is a consultant, trainer, and author with more than 20 years of traditional and digital prepress production experience. Her company, Practicalia LLC, provides custom onsite training for design firms, printing companies, and marketing professionals. Her clients include MTV Networks, Lowe's Home Improvement, Orvis, BBDO, Lexmark, and The College Board. Claudia is the author of *Real World Print Production* and a contributor to *InDesign Magazine*, *Dynamic Graphics* magazine, and *HOW* magazine. Claudia updated the *Color*, *Printing*, and *PDF* chapters.

Patti Schulze is the founder and president of Digital Training & Designs, an Authorized Training Center for Adobe, Apple, and Quark. Patti has written several books for Macromedia Press on Fireworks, Dreamweaver, and FreeHand, and wrote the Macromedia-authorized Dreamweaver curriculum. For this book, she edited the *Long Documents* and *Going Online with QuarkXPress* chapters. Outside of work, Patti's passion is photography and traveling to new places to take pictures.

Glen Turpin is a communications professional with more than a decade's experience in high technology. He understands the strategic role of technology in business and can clearly articulate complex ideas in simple terms that everyone can understand. He wrote the *Collaboration* chapter for this book.

Chuck Weger is a publishing technology consultant specializing in workflow automation and data-driven production. His 15 minutes of fame came when he invented "preflight" in the early 90s—back when most folks were happy just being able to make text either Times or Helvetica, much less preflight it for print. For this book, he updated the *XML Tools* appendix. Before publishing, Chuck worked as a NASA contractor, writing ground systems software for various spacecraft. Plus, he's much taller than David Blatner and has the most *Star Trek* episodes memorized.

OVERVIEW

TABLE OF CONTENTS

INTRODUCTION

The Oldest Living Layout App

Trying to figure out just what type of program QuarkXPress is reminds me of a scene from an old *Saturday Night Live* episode, when a couple bickered over their new purchase. "It's a floor wax," said one. "No, it's a dessert topping," replied the other. The answer soon became clear: "It's a floor wax *and* a dessert topping." QuarkXPress is a program with the same predicament. Some people insist it's a typesetting application. Others bet their bottom dollar that it's a Web-design tool. Still others make XPress a way of life.

The truth is that QuarkXPress is all these things, and more. However, no matter how you use it, it is never more than a tool. And a tool is never more than the person behind it.

For 19 years, my goal has been to make you—the designers and production artists—better users of this incredible tool. And it's with that in mind that we've compiled the best QuarkXPress information in the world here in this one volume.

QuarkXPress has a peculiar distinction in the publishing industry: It's the oldest living desktop page-layout application. (Aldus PageMaker 1.0 was released in 1985, a little over a year before XPress 1.0, but that program has been mothballed by Adobe.) Sure, its old age shows through occasionally—it ain't as fast as it used to be, but hey, none of us are. However, our 20-year-old friend has also proven to be surprisingly spry and innovative in many respects.

With dozens of new features in this version—such as a reinvented Measurements palette, transparency effects, and composition zones—QuarkXPress proves that it can balance the needs of new users with those of designers who have stuck with the program for a decade or more. After all, the program has a rich heritage of knowledge and of documents (there are likely hundreds of millions of XPress layouts saved on disks around the planet).

But how best to learn all this new stuff? It seems there is a need for a consultant who not only knows the computer and graphic design, but also one who can sit there, patiently, and—at 11 p.m.—walk you through building a better registration mark, making a drop cap, or explaining how master pages work—all for a low-cost flat fee. That consultant is this book.

ABOUT THIS BOOK

Although I expect you to know the basics of using a Macintosh or Microsoft Windows (moving the mouse, pulling down menus, and so on), I have purposely taken a wide spectrum of potential readers into account, from off-the-shelf beginners to seasoned professionals. On the one hand, I've found that many of those "advanced" users often never learned many of the basics (they were too busy trying to get their work done!) and are delighted to learn new tricks, techniques, and concepts. Alternately, folks who have used computers very little sometimes surprise me with their intuitive grasp of the Big Picture.

Remember, this book was written for you. It's designed to work for you—as your personal consultant—whoever you are. It's also designed to help you get a sure footing on a sometimes uneven path and to help you make pages like the pros.

Organization

I have organized this book to reflect what I think QuarkXPress is all about: producing final camera-ready output from your computer. So I start with an overview of the program, move on to building a structure for the layout, then discuss the basics—such as putting text and pictures on a page. Next I move into some fine-tuning aspects of QuarkXPress, and finally to printing. And, because so many people now must output their files both to paper and to the Internet, I have also included a chapter on Web publishing. That's the speed-reading rundown; now here's a play-by-play of the chapters.

- **Chapter 1: Learn QuarkXPress in 30 Minutes.** If you're brand new to XPress, this chapter, which takes a hands-on, step-by-step approach to learning the program, should be perfect for you.

- **Chapter 2: QuarkXPress Basics.** The first step in understanding QuarkXPress is learning about its structure from the ground up. This involves an investigation of QuarkXPress's menus, palettes, and dialog boxes. Advanced users tell me they find features and techniques in this chapter that they never knew.

- **Chapter 3: Working with Items.** Every vocation has its tools, and we desktop publishers are no different. This chapter offers an in-depth study of each tool in QuarkXPress's Tools palette, how to use it, and why.

- **Chapter 4: Building a Layout.** Without a sturdy foundation, your layout won't be reliable or flexible when you need it to be. This chapter discusses the basics of making earthquake-proof infrastructures for your pages: opening a new project, creating master pages, setting up column guides, and linking for text flow.

- **Chapter 5: Working with Text.** If you wanted a drawing program, you would have bought one. Words are what most people use QuarkXPress for, and this chapter is where words start. I talk here about simple text input, working with word processors, the Find/Change feature, and checking spelling.

- **Chapter 6: Typography.** Once you've got those words in the computer, what do you do with them? Chapter 6 discusses the details of formatting text into type—fonts, sizes, styles, indents, drop caps—all the things that turn text into type.

- **Chapter 7: Copy Flow.** You bought the computer, so why not let it do the work for you? This chapter explains how to use style sheets to automate aspects of copy processing and how to use importing and exporting effectively.

- **Chapter 8: Tables.** There's no better way to arrange a large amount of data than a good table. This chapter explores how XPress lets you create and format a wide variety of tables.

- **Chapter 9: Long Documents.** QuarkXPress incorporates three major features that help you when working with long documents: lists, indexes, and the Book palette. Here, I discuss each of these in detail and offer suggestions for how to use them effectively.

- **Chapter 10: Pictures.** Who reads text anymore? I like to look at the pictures. And pictures are what Chapter 10 is all about. I discuss every relevant graphics file format and how to work with each in your documents. I also cover rotating, skewing, and other manipulations of images.

- **Chapter 11: Image Tuning.** In this chapter, I look at picture effects such as levels, unsharp masking, and curves for bitmapped images. I also explore clipping paths and alpha channels.

- **Chapter 12: Text Meets Graphics.** This is the frontier land: the border between the two well-discussed worlds of type and pictures. Life gets different on the edge, and in this chapter I discuss how to handle it with grace—using inline boxes, paragraph rules, and the text runaround features.

- **Chapter 13: Collaboration.** Several of XPress's most important new features involve getting groups of people to work together more easily. But I promise you that these complex features will leave you scratching your head unless you read this chapter.

- **Chapter 14: Color.** QuarkXPress is well-known for its powerful color capabilities. This chapter covers color models, building a custom color palette, applying colors, and the first steps in understanding color separation.

- **Chapter 15: Printing.** This chapter is where everything I've talked about is leading: getting your document out of the machine and onto a platesetter or paper. Here I cover every step of printing, including the details of the Print dialog box, the finer points of ouput providers, and troubleshooting your print job.

- **Chapter 16: PDF.** The PDF file format has become the cornerstone of most publishing workflows. This chapter looks at how to create different types of PDF files with XPress.

- **Chapter 17: Going Online with QuarkXPress.** Here I explain how to use QuarkXPress to build Web pages or simply repurpose some of your content for HTML.

- **Appendix A: XTensions.** Where do you go when QuarkXPress won't give you what you want? This appendix offers suggestions for many popular XTensions, as well as both print and Web-based resources you should know about.

- **Appendix B: Scripting.** In Appendix B, I cover the wild world of scripting QuarkXPress using AppleScript on the Macintosh. Don't worry, I'm not really a programmer myself; if *I* can understand this stuff, so can you.

- **Appendix C: XML Tools.** If you make books, magazines, or newspapers, you need to know about XML. It's the hot new thing in the industry and it's certainly the hardest thing you can do in QuarkXPress today.

Of course, this is a lot of information for a single book. But what did you shell out $54.99 for? Chopped liver? No, this book is meant not only to be read, but to be used. I wanted to include a Post-It pad so you could mark the pages you'll use the most, but it didn't work out. Don't let that stop you, though.

Finding What You Need

There are many ways to read this book. You could use the cover-to-cover approach. This is the best way to get every morsel I have included. On the other hand, that method doesn't seem to work for some people. As I said, this book is meant to be used, right off the shelf, no batteries required.

I've done everything in my power to make it easy to find topics throughout this book. However, there's so much information that sometimes you might not know where to look. The table of contents breaks down each chapter into first- and second-level headings, so you can jump to a particular topic fast.

If you are primarily looking for the new version 7 features, you should take a look at the description of new features in the next section. That will also tell you where in the book I describe the feature fully.

Finally, if you can't find what you're looking for, or are trying to find an explanation for a single concept, try the index.

Faith

Just to be honest with you, there's almost no way to explain one feature in QuarkXPress without explaining all the rest at the same time. But that would make for a pretty confusing book. Instead, I'm asking you to take minor leaps of faith along the path of reading these chapters. If I mention a term or function you don't understand, trust me that I'll explain it all in due time. If you are able to do that, you will find that what I am discussing all makes sense. For example, I'm not going to talk about the details of creating a new layout until Chapter 4, *Building a Layout*, even though I need to talk about working with layouts in Chapter 2, *QuarkXPress Basics*.

THE BIRTH OF AN UPGRADE

If you've never watched an artist create an image with oil paints, you may not understand what all the fuss is about. When you see the end result, it's easy to think that the artist just picked up a brush and painted the whole thing. What you'd be missing is the hours of slowly building, changing, covering, modifying, pondering, and dreaming. Half of what makes a piece of art special is the *process* of its creation.

Art isn't the only thing that is born out of process. Computer software is very similar. And so it's with great admiration that I can look forward to each new revision of QuarkXPress, where code has been modified, other parts ripped out and replaced with something better, and then—in fits of inspiration—whole new features have been added, making the final piece (at least for this version) one step better, more usable, and simply *cooler*.

Version 7 of QuarkXPress has, from its announcement, been met with mixed reviews. Some people rave about the new workflow and transparency features. Others stare blankly at you if you mention the upgrade and ask why, after almost two years since the last major release, the Quark engineers were so thoughtless as to leave out fundamental features such as hanging punctuation or a real preflighting feature.

I admit to holding both opinions: I believe QuarkXPress 7 is a major step forward in page layout, offering extraordinary new features that I would be loath to give up. It's funny, but even some of the seemingly smallest new abilities or changes to interface are clearly a big win over previous editions. On the other hand, I keep a list called "ThingsThatAnnoyMe-AboutXPress7" in which I let myself complain about both big-ticket items—such as why doesn't XPress have a Story Editor, like PageMaker or InDesign—and the small stuff, too— keystrokes that used to be fast in version 3.x but now slow you down in later versions.

The History

I've been writing about QuarkXPress since version 3.0, but I still remember using version 1.10, back in 1987, when just getting the page to print was considered a feature. The jump to version 2.0 felt pretty big, but it wasn't earthshaking. In fact, it wasn't until the 1990s release of version 3.0 that QuarkXPress really grew into a world-class page-layout tool. Version 3.0 introduced XPress users to the pasteboard metaphor, the Polygon tool (for pictures only), and a major interface-lift that turned heads and started winning converts. Still, when version 3.0 shipped, there were only a handful of service bureaus around the country that would accept XPress files; PageMaker was the dominant force in the industry and you were a rebel if you even mentioned Quark.

In version 3.1, we saw new features like automatic ligatures and color blends. In 3.2, Quark got rid of the XPress Data file, which was driving service bureaus crazy, introduced EfiColor's color management system (which fell with a thud for most people), added new style sheet features, scripting, and—for some people the biggest feature of all—a Microsoft Windows version of QuarkXPress. Version 3.3 was really only a minor upgrade, but it shocked the world with its polygonal text boxes, which let you sculpt text blocks into any shape you wanted.

It took seven years for Quark to make the leap from version 3.0 to version 4.0, but the cool new features were worth the wait: Bézier curves, type on a curve, character-level style sheets, editable clipping paths (including the ability to make any embedded path a clipping path), custom line and dash styles, and more.

If You Skipped the QuarkXPress 5 and 6 Upgrades

If you were one of those many users who just stuck with version 4, let me share with you the big feature improvements that appeared in version 5 and 6, as these were, of course, all rolled into version 7 as well.

- **Web layouts.** Many of the new features in QuarkXPress 5 and 6 related to the ability to make and export HTML Web pages, including interactive rollovers (graphics that change when the cursor is on top of them), image maps (specifying areas of a graphic that are "hot links"), hyperlinks, and form elements (checkboxes, buttons, text entry fields, and so on). See Chapter 17, *Going Online with QuarkXPress*.

- **Table tool.** People have long been asking for a way to make tables in QuarkXPress. Ask no further. See Chapter 8, *Tables*.

- **Layers palette.** The Layers palette is another long-standing item off the wish list. If you know how to use the Layers palette in Adobe Illustrator, you'll pick this up in no time. See Chapter 3, *Working with Items*.

- **Layout Spaces.** Let's say you're creating a business card, a Web page, and a brochure for a client. Wouldn't it be cool if you could put all those pages (which share similar designs and text, but have very different page sizes and layout needs) in the same document? That's what the Layout Spaces feature is all about: combining documents into the same document. See Chapter 4, *Building a Layout*.

- **Multiple Undo.** It took 15 years and a lot of Jolt Cola (or Mahacola, for those software engineers in India), but Quark finally got around to letting us undo more than one action. See Chapter 2, *QuarkXPress Basics*.

- **Export PDF.** QuarkXPress no longer requires Acrobat Distiller to create PDF files because now it ships with its own Distiller software. See Chapter 16, *PDF*.

- **Collecting fonts.** QuarkXPress 4 let you collect linked graphics before sending your files to an output provider; now XPress collects the fonts and color profiles that you used. See Chapter 15, *Printing*.

- **Character lists.** The primary limitation of the Lists feature in QuarkXPress 4 was that it only let you use paragraph styles. Now you can also use character styles. See Chapter 7, *Copy Flow*.

- **Scripts menu.** If you use QuarkXPress on a Macintosh, you should be using AppleScripts! Quark even threw in a bunch of free scripts you can use. See Appendix B, *Scripting*.

- **Native OS X.** The most obvious change in XPress 6 was that it finally ran natively under Mac OS X and Windows XP. This isn't as big a deal on Windows as it is on the Macintosh, where OS X users no longer have to use XPress in Classic mode.

- **Interface changes.** There have been a number of changes to the QuarkXPress interface over the last few versions, though nothing that should be too confusing to a long-time user. One significant change was that the palette controls now live in the Window menu rather than the View menu. See Chapter 2, *QuarkXPress Basics*.

- **Paste in Place.** This little feature is hardly worth noting except that it's something I've wanted for years: the ability to copy an object, then paste it on a different page but in the same place. See Chapter 3, *Working with Items*.

- **Full Resolution Preview.** People have complained about the screen previews of images in QuarkXPress forever. Now, fewer people will be complaining because the Full Resolution Preview feature improves the onscreen display dramatically for both bitmapped and vector images. See Chapter 10, *Pictures*.

- **Synchronize Text.** Do you use the same text over and over in the same document or across multiple layout spaces in a project? Synchronize Text lets you mirror text from one place to another, so if you change it in one place it changes everyplace else. See synching and unsynching content in Chapter 13, *Collaboration*.

- **Picture Effects.** It's frustrating having to switch between XPress and Photoshop every time you want to make a tweak to an image. Now, the Picture Effects palette lets you perform global image adjustments (such as Unsharp Masking and Hue/Saturation) to images right on your page. See picture effects in Chapter 11, *Image Tuning*.

Okay, that's what you may have missed in the last two upgrades. Now what can you expect in version 7?

What's New in QuarkXPress 7

So what's new in QuarkXPress 7? A lot. Following is a list of what I consider to be the most important changes, though the ones that are most important to your workflow may be different than the ones that get me all excited. (I'm not going to list every little niggling feature that's different between the last version and this one; if you need that, take a look at the *What's New* addendum that comes with XPress.)

- **Transparency and Drop Shadows.** The sexiest features in XPress 7 are clearly those involving transparency: The ability to change the opacity wherever you specify color, the option to add drop shadows to objects, and so on. See Chapter 14, *Color*.

- **Measurements palette.** Quark radically changed the Measurements palette, making it far more useful while maintaining its ease of use. See Chapter 2, *QuarkXPress Basics*.

- **Composition Zones.** Unless you work by yourself in a box, you're going to love the ability to share parts of your layouts with other people. Or, if you do work in a box, you'll love being able to share your own layouts with yourself. See Chapter 13, *Collaboration*.

- **Job Jackets.** One of the coolest ideas in XPress 7 is also one of the most confusing: Job Jackets let you specify what should (and shouldn't) be in a document even before you start laying it out. See Chapter 13, *Collaboration*.

- **OpenType support.** You can now use all the cool features in OpenType fonts, such as fractions and built-in small caps. Also, the Glyphs palette and Insert Character submenu let you find the characters you want quickly. See Chapter 6, *Typography*.

- **Synchronized Text and Pictures.** A new Shared Content palette lets you synchronize whole objects, including pictures (see Chapter 10, *Pictures*) and formatted text (see Chapter 9, *Long Documents*), among documents or layout spaces.

- **Layout views.** You can view your document in more than one window or in one window split into smaller panes. See Split Windows and Layouts in Chapter 4, *Building a Layout*.

- **Palette groups.** As Quark added new palettes, it realized it needed to find better ways to let you organize them. See palettes and palette management in Chapter 2, *QuarkXPress Basics*.

- **Locking items.** I made fun of XPress's ineffectual Lock feature for 17 years. Fortunately, they fixed it and it's now great! See Chapter 3, *Working with Items*.

- **Color management.** Yet again, Quark has changed how it does color management. The good news is that it's gotten significantly better this time. See Chapter 14, *Color*.

- **Mini improvements.** There are a host more changes in QuarkXPress 7, including the option to maintain picture attributes when replacing images; embedding fonts in EPS files; far better quality of screen display; automatically repeating table headers and footers; and more.

- **XPert Tools.** Here's a "feature" that's not officially part of QuarkXPress 7, but I'll mention it anyway: Quark is giving away a bundle of great XTensions called XPert Tools to XPress 7 users. You should definitely check them out. See Appendix A, *XTensions*.

On the other hand, there are some trade-offs, too. If you use any third-party XTensions, you'll have to get updates, because they won't work with this version of XPress. That could be a problem, since a number of XTension developers have no intention of updating their software.

Version 7 of QuarkXPress is clearly a pretty impressive package. But don't let it intimidate you. Remember, QuarkXPress is not only a machete that helps you cut through the layout jungles—it's a Swiss Army machete! If you want to use it for writing letters home, you can do it. If you want to create glossy four-color magazines, you can do that too. The tool is powerful enough to get the job done, but sometimes—if you're trying to get through that Amazon jungle—you need to wield your machete accurately and efficiently.

Requirements

To take advantage of all these great new features in QuarkXPress, you need, at a minimum, a 4.0 GHz, 8-core Intel Xeon-based Mac Pro or a 9 GHz Pentium IX computer with 12 GB of RAM, a 3-terrabyte hard drive, a high-res platesetter, a 30-inch color monitor with dual video accelerator cards, and of course, a 24 megapixel digital camera with chrome trim.

Just kidding! You can actually get by with some pretty limited hardware. But, since few things are more frustrating than being all psyched up to start something only to discover that you can't for lack of an essential component, here's a résumé of the components you need to know about.

While early versions of QuarkXPress for the Macintosh could run on almost any Macintosh sold since 1990, version 7 now requires operating system 10.4 or later, which itself requires a fast G4 or G5 or Intel-based Macintosh. Quark recommends at least 1 GB of RAM, though you're going to want 2 GB if you're planning on running Photoshop or Illustrator at the same time. In order to print or create PDF files you also must have a PostScript printer driver loaded. In order to install XPress on your hard drive, you have to have about a gigabyte of free space.

If you use Windows, your PC had better be running Windows XP (with Service Pack 2) or Vista. You also need a minimum of 256 MB of RAM (I wouldn't touch it without 1 GB, though) and 450 MB of free hard disk space.

Of course, on either platform you need a mouse (or some other pointing device) and a keyboard. Plus, note that while QuarkXPress 7 does print on non-PostScript printers, it is optimized to print best on a PostScript printer.

ACKNOWLEDGMENTS

No book is an island. So many people have directly and indirectly contributed to this book's production that I would have to publish a second volume to thank them all. However, I want to thank some folks directly.

First and foremost, I want to thank the coauthors who were the lifeblood behind this edition: Kelly Kordes Anton, Stephen Beals, Pariah S. Burke, Shellie Hall, Ted LoCascio, Claudia McCue, Patti Schulze, Glen Turpin, and Chuck Weger. We've all used the word "I" throughout this book, but it's really "we"—so many of the words are theirs. Just as important were our managing editor, Susan Rimerman, copyeditor, Anne Marie Walker, proofer, Elaine Merrill, and compositor, Owen Wolfson. It couldn't have been done without them.

In fact, everyone at Peachpit has been great, including my publisher, Nancy Ruenzel, Nancy Davis, Lisa "just checking" Brazieal, Gary-Paul Prince, and Pam Pfiffner. I gave it the wings, but they made it fly.

Next, I'd like to thank the folks at Quark who were so helpful along the way, including Paul Schmitt, Ray Schiavone, Cyndie Shaffstall, Scott Wieseler, Hans Hartman, Tim Banister, Marc Horne, Jürgen Kurz, and Graham Parkinson-Morgan.

A special thanks to Anne-Marie Concepción of Publishing Secrets; Jay Nelson at *Design Tools Monthly* and Planetquark.com; Paul Dixon of Apple Computer; and Terri Stone at CreativePro.com.

Of course, there are those people even farther behind the scenes. Vincent Dorn at LaserWrite in Palo Alto, who said, "Hey, let's go to Burger King." Steve Roth, who asked, "Have you ever thought of writing a book?" Ted Nace, the original publisher at Peachpit. All my parents; my wife, Debbie Carlson, and sons, Gabriel and Daniel; Alisa, Paul, Camille, and Zoe Piette; Suzanne and Damian Carlson-Prandini; and other friends who were such a support over the past few decades. It wouldn't have happened without you.

And many thanks go to all the people who wrote, called, and emailed me their comments and suggestions. I've tried to incorporate their ideas into this eighth edition.

Thanks.

David Blatner
Seattle, Washington

CHAPTER ONE

Learn QuarkXPress in 30 Minutes

If you're like most people, you need to roll up your sleeves and get started working in XPress as soon as possible. That's what this first chapter is for. I've put together a simple XPress layout that you will create step-by-step, as you read through the chapter. Working through the project will help you understand many of the topics covered in the rest of the book.

The project is a simple one-fold brochure for a mythical product called "Gold Standard" (see Figure 1-1). Before you start working, you need to get the materials for the brochure: the product illustration, the company logo, and the text. If you have access to the Internet, you can download these materials from the *Real World QuarkXPress* Web site (*www.peachpit.com/ Quark7*). There's also a finished version of the brochure for you to open after you're done to see if you've followed the steps correctly.

Figure 1-1 The one-fold brochure you're going to create

Don't worry if you don't have access to the Web. You can use other materials you have on your computer. It doesn't matter if you don't replicate the project exactly as shown, just as long as you understand the principles.

PAGES, VIEWS, AND GUIDES

In this section you create a new file for the project, make sure the margins are correct, add some guides, add a page, and navigate around your layout.

Creating a New File

Before you can begin working, you need to launch QuarkXPress and create a new project.

1. Launch QuarkXPress by double-clicking the application icon. (See Figure 1-2; see the section on getting started in Chapter 2, *QuarkXPress Basics,* for information on installing XPress.)

2. When the application has opened (after you see the menus and a couple of palettes), choose Project from the New submenu (under the File menu). The New Project dialog box appears (see Figures 1-3 and 1-4).

3. As we'll see in Chapter 4, *Building a Layout,* each project can contain several layouts. The New Project dialog box lets you name the first layout and determine whether it should be a Print layout or a Web layout. In this case, choose Print from the Layout Type popup menu. I cover Web layouts in Chapter 17, *Going Online with QuarkXPress.*

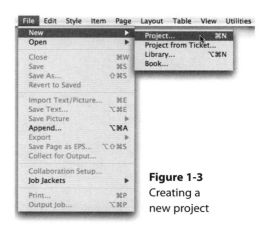

Figure 1-2
QuarkXPress at home in its folder

Figure 1-3
Creating a new project

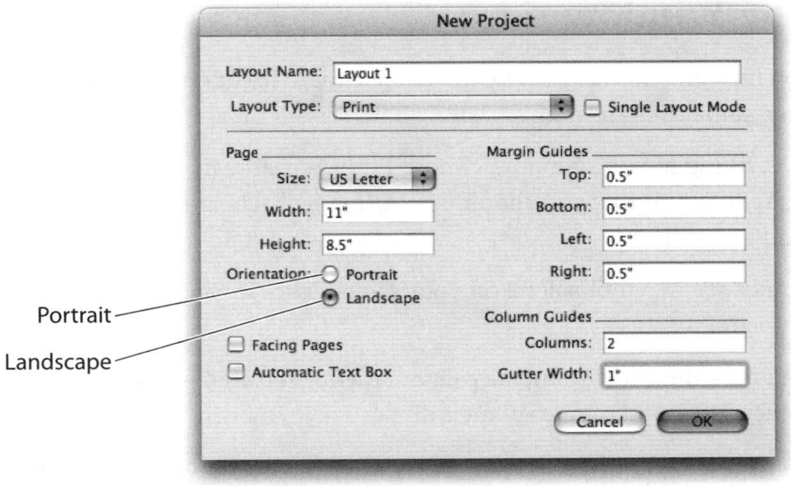

Figure 1-4
The New Project
dialog box

4. Make sure the page size is set to US Letter. Click the landscape orientation icon. These actions set the dimensions.

   Width: 11 inches

   Height: 8.5 inches

5. Make sure that both the Facing Pages and Automatic Text Box checkboxes are turned off—that is, they don't have an X through them. (For more information about working with Facing Pages and Automatic Text Boxes, see Chapter 4, *Building a Layout*.)

6. You also need to set the margins and columns as follows.

   Top: .5 inch (use the " mark for inches)

   Bottom: .5 inch

   Left: .5 inch

   Right: .5 inch

   Columns: 2

   Gutter Width: 1 inch

7. Click OK. This creates your new XPress project with a single page, margins at 0.5 inch around the edge of the page, and two columns on the page.

   Tip: Use the Tab Key in Fields. *You can jump from one field to the next in any dialog box by pressing the Tab key. For instance, in the New Project dialog box you were just in, you could have pressed Tab to jump to any field you wanted to change. You can go to the previous field by pressing Shift-Tab.*

Working in the Window

Depending on how XPress was used by the last person to use it on your machine, you may need to change some things on the screen.

1. To see everything in your window, choose Fit in Window from the View menu. (This is so important that you should start using its keyboard shortcut: Command/Ctrl-zero.)

2. If you do not see the Tool palette on your screen, choose Show Tools from the Window menu.

3. If you don't see the Measurements palette on your screen, choose Show Measurements from the Window menu.

4. If you don't see the Page Layout palette on your screen, choose Show Page Layout from the Window menu. Your screen should look like the illustration in Figure 1-5.

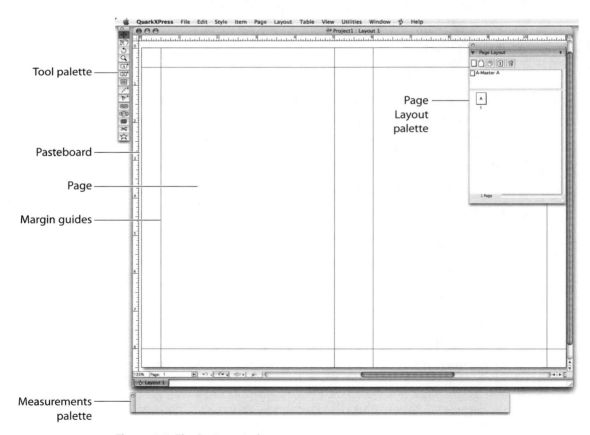

Figure 1-5 The Project window

Working with the Tool Palette and Measurements Palette

When working in XPress, the two interface items you will refer to the most are the Tool palette and Measurements palette. Unlike the other palettes available in XPress, you will most likely keep these two open and visible onscreen at all times.

Tools palette. By default, the Tool palette is positioned in the upper-left corner of your screen. You can access a tool from the palette by clicking its icon. Some of the tools (such as the Item tool and Content tool) are always visible in the Tool palette. Other tools (such as the Oval Text Box tool) are hidden because they are part of a toolset. These tools are only visible if you click and hold on the foremost toolset icon in the Tool palette.

- To choose one of the visible tools, click the icon for that tool in the Tool palette (see Figure 1-6). The tool will be highlighted.

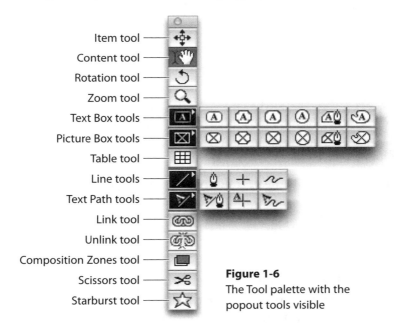

Item tool —
Content tool —
Rotation tool —
Zoom tool —
Text Box tools —
Picture Box tools —
Table tool —
Line tools —
Text Path tools —
Link tool —
Unlink tool —
Composition Zones tool —
Scissors tool —
Starburst tool —

Figure 1-6
The Tool palette with the popout tools visible

- To choose one of the hidden tools, click and hold on one of the tool icons with a small triangle in the upper-right corner, and then drag over to the right to choose the tool.

Measurements palette. The controls displayed in this palette change dynamically depending on which tool you are currently working with and what page items you currently have selected. For example, the Measurements palette displays one set of controls when working with text and another set when working with picture boxes.

With XPress 7, you can now also choose which layout controls you would like to display in the Measurements palette. To do so, click any of the icons available in the new popup navigator tab at the top of the palette. This tab is also dynamic and will display different icons depending on what tool and item you are currently working with.

You can display the navigator tab by simply hovering your cursor over the Measurements palette. To hide the tab, move your cursor away, and it will eventually collapse. I personally find this popup behavior to be extremely annoying; therefore, I prefer to keep the navigator tab visible at all times. You can access navigator tab visibility settings by Control-clicking/right-clicking the palette tab on the far left of the Measurements palette (see Figure 1-7). Options include Always Show Tab Bar, Always Hide Tab Bar, and the default setting, Show Tab on Rollover.

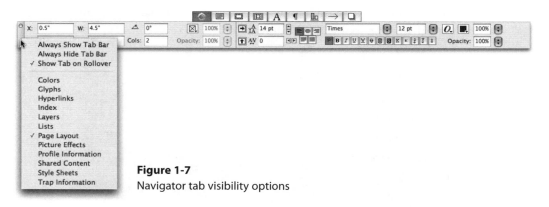

Figure 1-7
Navigator tab visibility options

Chapter 3, *Working with Items*, discusses XPress's tools and Measurements palette options in detail.

Zooming Around

As you're working in XPress, you constantly zoom in and out to see very small details on your page or to look at the page as a whole. Fortunately, XPress provides many different ways to zoom in and out. (See Chapter 2, *QuarkXPress Basics,* for all the ways to change the page views.)

1. Select the Zoom tool in the Tool palette.

2. Position the Zoom tool cursor over the upper-left corner of the page and click several times. Each click magnifies your view. (If you don't see anything when you zoom in, you may be looking at the middle of the page. Use the scroll bars to adjust the view.)

3. Hold down the Option/Alt key. Notice that the Zoom tool cursor changes from a plus sign to a minus sign. Click several times to zoom out from the view of the page.

4. Release the Option/Alt key and position the Zoom tool cursor inside the page. Then drag with the Zoom tool to create a small square. When you release the mouse, you zoom in on the area you just marqueed. (This will be more useful when you actually have something on your page!)

5. Double-click on the magnification percentage in the lower-left corner of the window (see Figure 1-8). Enter "80" and then press the Return/Enter key. XPress switches to 80-percent magnification view.

Figure 1-8
The Magnification level box

Adding Pages

Every new QuarkXPress layout opens with one page already in place. Since this brochure will be printed on two sides of the page, you need to add a page to your layout. (See Chapter 4, *Building a Layout,* for more information on adding pages to and deleting pages from a layout.)

1. In the Page Layout palette, click the small rectangular page icon at the top, labeled "A-Master A" (see Figure 1-9).

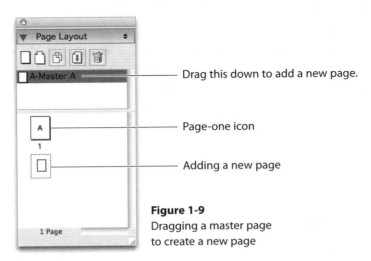

Drag this down to add a new page.

Page-one icon

Adding a new page

Figure 1-9
Dragging a master page
to create a new page

2. Drag the icon down under the first page. Release the mouse when you see the plain rectangle under the page. The second page is automatically created for you right where you drop the icon. (If you drop the new page in the wrong place, just drag it to where you want it in the palette.)

You can also choose Insert from the Page menu to add a page, but it's a good idea to get in the habit of using the Page Layout palette as early as you can.

Adding Guides

To make it easier for you to lay out the various elements you're going to put on your page, you need to place some guides.

1. Double-click on the page-one icon in the Page Layout palette to make sure you are on that page.

2. You can add guides by pulling them from one of the rulers at either the left or the top of the page. If you can't see the rulers, choose Show Rulers from the View menu. Move your mouse over to the vertical ruler and press. You should see a little two-headed arrow appear on the ruler (see Figure 1-10).

Figure 1-10
Pulling a guide out from the ruler

3. Drag the two-headed arrow out from the ruler and let go when the guideline is at the 5.5-inch mark on the top ruler (watch the guide line against the ruler). A colored guide appears where you let go. You can also position guides by watching the Measurements palette.

4. Because you need a guide on page two, double-click on page two in the Page Layout, and repeat step 3. (See Chapter 4, *Building a Layout,* to see how master pages can automate this process.)

Saving

You've done enough work that you need to save your file.

1. Choose Save or Save As from the File menu (they're both the same for new, unsaved projects). QuarkXPress displays the Save As dialog box (see Figure 1-11).

2. Name your file *Gold Brochure*, and choose a folder to put your file in—not in the QuarkXPress folder!

3. Leave the Type as Project.

4. If you turn on the Include Preview checkbox, you'll see a thumbnail preview of page one each time you open the project.

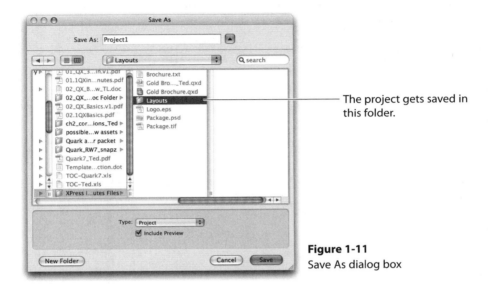

The project gets saved in this folder.

Figure 1-11
Save As dialog box

For the rest of this project, you should continue to save your work at whatever intervals you feel comfortable with.

TEXT AND TEXT FORMATTING

In order to put text on your page, you must first create a text box. In this section of the project you'll create several text boxes, add text to those boxes by typing as well as importing text from a file on disk, and you'll link the text boxes together so that the text flows from one box to another. Finally, you'll format the text using various fonts, sizes, and so on.

Drawing a Text Box

When you launch a word processing program, you can start typing right away. QuarkXPress is different: it requires you to put your text into text boxes. You create a text box using one of the Text Box tools.

1. Double-click on the first page in the Page Layout palette to make sure you are work-ing on that page.

2. Select the Rectangle Text Box tool in the Tool palette (that's the one with square corners and the little "A" in it).

3. Move the cursor over to the right side of the page. Your cursor should change to a plus sign. Press and drag like in Figure 1-12. Don't worry yet about the precise size or location of the box.

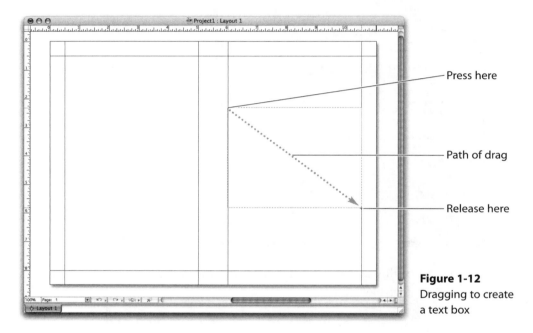

Press here

Path of drag

Release here

Figure 1-12
Dragging to create
a text box

4. Release the mouse when you've completed the drag. You should see a box with no text—just a blinking insertion point. If there isn't a blinking cursor, then you'll need to select the Content tool in the Tool palette (the one with the hand icon).

The second tool in the tool palette is the Content tool, which lets you change the *content* of the page items. For instance, if you don't see a blinking insertion point in your new text box, it's probably because you have the Item tool selected. In order to type in the text box, you've got to have the Content tool selected.

Note that when you make a box (like the text box you just made), XPress almost always automatically chooses the Item or Content tool for you, depending on which one you used last.

Modifying a Text Box

You can change the size of a text box at any time by dragging any of the eight handles located on the corners and sides of the text box. (For more tips on working with text boxes, see Chapter 3, *Working with Items*.)

1. Move your cursor over to the small black handle at the top side of the text box (it doesn't matter what tool you have selected). Your cursor should change to a "finger" (see Figure 1-13). This indicates that you can resize the box.

Figure 1-13
The finger cursor

2. Click and drag with the finger cursor, moving the handle so that the top of the box sits at the 2-inch mark. (You can get a precise measurement by watching either the guideline in the vertical ruler or the Y coordinate in the Measurements palette.)

3. Next, position the left side of the box at the 6-inch mark of the horizontal ruler. Note that the edge of the box will probably snap to the column guide you placed there earlier.

4. Position the right side of the box at the 10.5-inch mark (this should snap to the right margin guide).

5. Position the bottom side of the box at the 6.5-inch mark of the vertical ruler.

Typing Text

Now that you have a text box on your page, you can start typing in the box (remember that you need to select the Content tool first).

1. So that you can better see the text you're about to type, choose Actual Size from the View menu. (If you still have difficulty reading the text, try zooming in closer.)

2. Type the words, "Introducing a whole new standard in home medicine" into the box. (Don't type the quotation marks.)

3. If you make an error typing, you can use any of the normal text-editing techniques to modify the text (like using the Delete or Backspace key, double-clicking on a word to select it, and so on).

4. When you're done, leave the insertion point blinking inside the text box. Do not click outside the text box to deselect the box. (We're not done with that text yet!)

Formatting Text

The text you have created comes in with the default formatting from the Normal style sheet, which is almost never what you really want. However, you can change the formatting of your text at any time.

1. To select all the text in the text box, choose Select All from the Edit menu (or type Command/Ctrl-A). This highlights all the text in the text box (text in a text box is called a *story*, even if there's only one little paragraph like this).

2. You can choose a font from one of two places: the Style menu or the Measurements palette. Let's use the second choice: click on the little triangle next to the font name in the Measurements palette (see Figure 1-14). A list of the available typefaces appears.

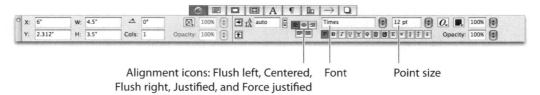

Alignment icons: Flush left, Centered,   Font   Point size
Flush right, Justified, and Force justified

Figure 1-14 Text formatting in the Measurements palette

3. Choose any serif typeface (such as Garamond, Times, or Palatino).

4. The point size popup menu in the Measurements palette displays a list of point sizes, but the one we want is not included. You can enter the point size you want by selecting the point size and typing in the number "50." Then press Return/Enter.

5. Finally, click the Centered alignment icon in the Measurements palette. The text centers itself within the text box.

Importing Text

While the text on the first page is short, most of the time you'll find yourself working with text that is saved in a word-processing file. (For more on how to import text files, see Chapter 5, *Working with Text.*)

1. Go to the second page and draw a 2-inch-tall text box that extends from the left margin to the right margin of the page. Use the Item tool to move the text box so that the top of the box sits at the top margin of the page.

2. With the insertion point blinking in the text box (switch to the Content tool), choose Import Text from the File menu. The Import Text dialog box appears (see Figure 1-15).

Figure 1-15
Import Text dialog box

3. Use the dialog box to find the file *Brochure.txt* from the files you downloaded.
   (If you weren't able to download that file, use some other text file that is about
   two pages in length.)

4. Click OK to import the text. (If you receive a message that you're missing fonts,
   don't worry about it—you'll be changing the typeface for the text anyway.)

Linking Text Boxes

The text you have imported is too long to fit in the little text box you've made. You can
always tell when there's more text than can fit in a box by the red overset mark at the
lower-right corner of the text box (see Figure 1-16). Rather than change the size of the box
to fit the text, we're going to build another, bigger text box, and then link the two text
boxes together so that the text flows from one into the other.

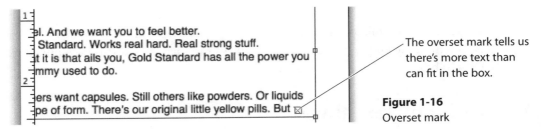

The overset mark tells us
there's more text than
can fit in the box.

Figure 1-16
Overset mark

1. Draw a second text box on the left side of page two. This text box should extend from
   the left margin to the 5-inch column guideline. The box should start at the 4-inch
   mark on the vertical ruler and stop at the bottom margin.

2. While this text box is still selected, choose Duplicate from the Item menu. This creates a copy of the text box and offsets it slightly. Use the Item tool to position this duplicate on the right side of page two (place it so that it mirrors the left side of the page).

3. Choose the Link tool in the Tool palette (the one that looks like a little chain of doughnuts). Click on the first box on the page (the wide one at the top) with the Link tool. The outside edge of the box begins to animate, to tell you that it's selected.

4. Then click on the empty text box on the left side of the page. The continuation of the text appears in the second box (see Figure 1-17).

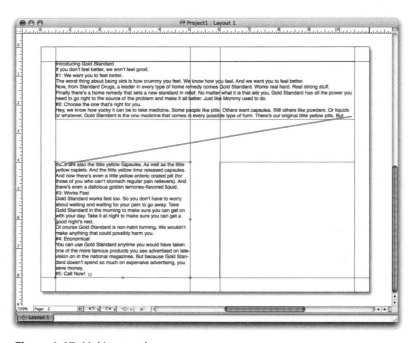

Figure 1-17 Linking text boxes

5. Choose the Link tool again; click first on the text box on the left side of the page and then on the empty box on the right side of the page. The text is now linked from the top box to the left box and then to the right box.

Multicolumn Text Boxes

Text boxes are one way to divide text into different areas on the page. However, you can also have multiple columns within a text box. QuarkXPress gives you two different ways to set columns within a text box (we're going to use both methods here).

1. Click on the text box on the lower-left side of the page (you can use either the Item tool or the Content tool for this).

2. In the Measurements palette, change the number in the "Cols" field from 1 to 2 (see Figure 1-18). Press Return/Enter to apply the change. Two columns appear in the text box.

Number of columns

Figure 1-18 Columns setting in the Measurements palette

3. Click on the text box on the lower-right side of the page. Choose Modify from the Item menu and then click on the Text tab (see Figure 1-19).

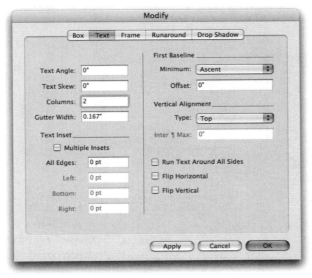

Figure 1-19
Item Modify Text dialog box

4. Change the Columns field to 2 and then click the Apply button to see the change (you can move the dialog box out of the way if it's covering the text box). Now click OK to apply the change.

Don't worry if your text doesn't fill all the columns right now (or if there's another over-set mark). You've still got more formatting to do.

> ***Tip: Setting the Gutter Width.*** *One of the advantages of choosing Modify from the Item menu when setting your columns is that you can change the gutter width, which is the amount of space between the two columns of the text box.*

Character Formatting

The text you have imported needs to be formatted. While you could use the formatting options in the Measurements palette, let's take a look at a few other ways you can format text.

1. First, make sure you have the Content tool selected, and then press Command/Ctrl-A to select all the text in the story. Change the typeface to the same font you used on page one.

2. To deselect all the text, click once somewhere inside the text box. Now, to select just the first line of text, place your cursor over that line of text and click three times. This should select the words "Introducing Gold Standard." (Note that clicking once places the text cursor, twice selects a word, three times selects a line, four times selects a paragraph, and five times selects the entire story.)

3. Choose Character from the Style menu to open the Character Attributes dialog box. This is where you can format and apply all the attributes for the selected line of text (see Figure 1-20).

Figure 1-20
Character Attributes
dialog box

4. Click the All Caps box and then click the Apply button to see the change.

5. Use the Size field to enter a size that's about 42 points. Click the Apply button. If your text extends past one line, reduce the point size until the selected line of text fills the width of a single line. When you're done, click OK.

6. Under the Style menu, choose Centered from the Alignment submenu, or press Command/Ctrl-Shift-C. Doing so centers the first line of text in the text box.

7. Triple-click on the second line: "If you don't feel better, we won't feel good." Use the Character Attributes dialog box again to set the point size to 24 and click OK.

8. Center align the second line of text using the same command that you applied in step 6 or by clicking the center align button in the Measurements palette.

9. Use the finger cursor to move the bottom edge of the top text box up, changing the height so that only these two lines are in the box. This forces the text down to the other boxes. You can make the other boxes slightly larger to fill the extra space, if you want.

10. Select the next line: "#1: We want you to feel better" (you can quadruple-click to select it all quickly). Click on the large K icon toward the right side of the Measurements palette; this changes the line to all caps. Now set the point size to 13.

11. Select each of the numbered lines on the page and change them so they match the text in step 8.

Tip: Style Sheets Stop Drudgery. By the time you finish formatting each of the numbered paragraphs in the text, you're probably feeling like there's got to be a better way to format text. There is. QuarkXPress has a feature called Style Sheets that makes formatting text much faster. For more information about style sheets, see Chapter 7, Copy Flow.

Leading

Each character in a line of text sits on a *baseline*. Leading (pronounced *ledding*) is the amount of space from one baseline to the next. The greater the leading, the more space between the lines. The text in your project currently has an "auto" amount of leading applied. However, for reasons I describe in Chapter 6, *Typography*, you should usually avoid auto leading. Instead, here's how you can apply an absolute leading value.

1. Click so that your insertion point is blinking in the first line of the second text box (the one on the left).

2. Scroll over to the lower-right corner of the page and Shift-click on the last line of the text box. This selects the text from the first line to the last.

3. Click on either the increase- or decrease-leading arrow in the Measurements palette until the amount reads 14. This tightens up the space between the lines. If no number appears in the leading field of the palette, you can also simply replace the leading value with the number 14 (see Figure 1-21).

Figure 1-21 Adjusting Leading   Leading controls

Paragraph Formatting

There are other paragraph attributes besides leading. While you can find some of the other paragraph attributes in the Measurements palette, you can find them *all* in the Paragraph Attributes dialog box (select Formats from the Style menu).

1. Select the subhead labeled #2, and then choose Formats from the Style menu (see Figure 1-22).

2. Change the amount in the Space Before field to .25 inches. Then click OK to see the change.

3. Do the same for all the other numbered subheads, too.

> *Tip: When No Space Is Added.* If a paragraph is at the top of a column when you add Space Before, XPress won't add any space. If the paragraph is at the bottom of a column, XPress won't add any space after. It turns out that this behavior is normal and almost always what you really want, but it confuses beginners, so I wanted to point it out.

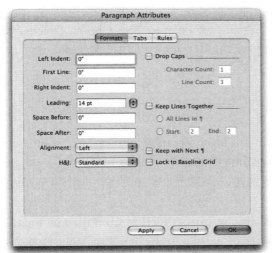

Figure 1-22
Paragraph Attributes dialog box

GRAPHICS, COLORS, DROP SHADOWS, AND LINES

Congratulations! You've almost completed your project. In this section you'll create picture boxes that hold the graphics for the brochure, import images, size them, and position them on your page. You will also add some color to the layout, as well as special frames and lines.

Drawing a Picture Box

Just as text boxes hold text, picture boxes hold pictures. So before you import a graphic, you need to create a picture box to hold that image.

1. Click the Rectangle Picture Box tool in the Tool palette.

2. Move your cursor to the middle of page two and draw a box approximately 2.5 inches tall and wide. (Don't worry about getting it exact; you'll change the size later.)

3. When you release the cursor you should see an ✕ through the box, indicating that you have created a picture box (see Figure 1-23).

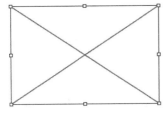

Figure 1-23
An empty picture box

4. If you do not see an ✕, you need to choose Show Guides from the View menu. If you still don't see an ✕, then you haven't created a picture box. Choose Delete from the Item menu and make sure you choose the Rectangle Picture Box tool; then redraw the picture box.

Importing Graphics

Once you've created a picture box, you can bring a graphic into it. This graphic can come from an illustration program like Adobe Illustrator. Or it can come from an image-editing program like Adobe Photoshop. (For more information on working with graphics from other programs, see Chapter 10, *Pictures.*)

1. With the picture box still selected, choose Import Picture from the File menu. Note that you can use either the Content or the Item tool when importing a graphic.

2. When the Import Picture dialog box appears, find the file called *Gold Package.tif* from the files you downloaded. If you don't have those files, find any TIFF or EPS graphic on your hard drive. Then click Open to import the image.

3. Select the Content tool from the Tool palette and move your cursor into the middle of the picture box. Notice that the cursor changes into a flat hand. When you click and drag the mouse with this cursor, you can move the graphic around within the picture box (see Figure 1-24).

4. The picture box is currently too small to show the entire package. Drag out the sides of the picture box until the box is big enough for the graphic (if you're using the Gold Standard image, the box should be about 4 inches wide and 3.5 inches tall).

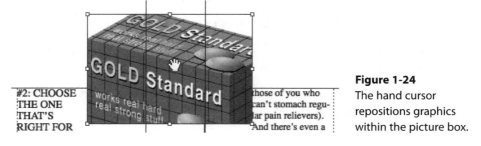

Figure 1-24
The hand cursor
repositions graphics
within the picture box.

5. Positioning the graphic in the middle of the box using the hand cursor is slow and not very accurate. Instead, press Command/Ctrl-Shift-M to center the graphic in the picture box. (That's M for "Mathematical Middle"!)

6. Now that you've got the graphic in the right-size box, you may need to move the box itself around. Switch to the Item tool (the top tool in the Tool palette) and move

your cursor over the picture box. A four-headed arrow appears with which you can drag the box around. Move the picture box so that its top is at the 2.75-inch mark. Make sure the graphic is at least partly over the text.

7. Position the center of the box on the 5.5-inch guide. (You can accomplish this visually by aligning the center handles of the box on the guide.)

Tip: Wait Before You Drag. As you resize or move objects, wait a moment after you press the mouse button down and before you start to drag. This will let you see the text dynamically reflow around objects as you move them. This lets you know, as you move the objects, how your layout will look.

Working with Graphics

Now that you have a graphic placed in your layout, the next step is to control how it interacts with the body text surrounding it. In XPress, you can change these settings in the Runaround tab of the Modify dialog box or the Measurements palette.

Runaround

Whenever you place an object on top of a text box, that object can force the text below to run around it (also known as "text wrap"). In this case, the text is wrapping around the picture box, but you could just as easily wrap text around another text box or a line.

1. Select the picture box and choose Runaround from the Item menu (or press Command/Ctrl-T). The Modify dialog box appears with the Runaround tab selected (see Figure 1-25).

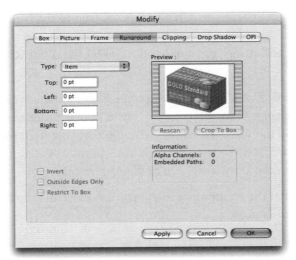

Figure 1-25
The Runaround tab of
the Modify dialog box

2. Currently, the runaround is set to Item (this is the default value), which means that the underlying text runs around the edges of the picture box itself. Choose Auto Image from the Type popup menu. This tells XPress to automatically find the outside edge of the picture and use it for the runaround.

3. Click the Apply button (not the OK button) to see what this does to your layout. Notice that the text is too close to the image.

4. Change the Outset amount to 14 points. Then click the Apply button again. The text moves away with a 14-point gap between it and the graphic. Click the OK button to apply the runaround.

Resizing and Rotating Graphics

Because this brochure is a mailing piece for the Standard Drug company, we need to add a logo on the left side of page one, and make sure the logo is the proper size and orientation.

1. Here's a new way to move between pages in your layout: Click on the small page popup menu at the bottom left of your project window. A small page list will appear Choose page one from the list.

2. Draw a picture box on the left side of page one. Make the dimensions of the picture box about 1.25 inches wide by about 1 inch tall. (You can watch the Measurements palette as you draw the box, to get the proper size.)

3. Use Import Picture (from the File menu) to import the *Logo.eps* file. Again: If you don't have this graphic, you can use another picture.

4. This logo is way too big for the picture box. However, rather than change the size of the box, let's change the size of the image. Change the X% field in the Measurements palette from 100 to 50 (you don't have to type the percent character). Press the Tab key to jump to the Y% field and change the number there to 50, too. Press Return/Enter to apply these values.

5. The logo needs to be rotated. Double-click on the angle field on the left side of the Measurements palette and change 0° to -90° (you don't have to type the degree symbol). Press Return/Enter to apply the value. (If XPress tells you that "the item cannot be positioned off the pasteboard," set the rotation back to zero, move the item farther down on the page, and then try to rotate it back to 90 degrees again.)

6. Use the Item tool to position the picture box in the corner under the top margin and next to the guide at the 5-inch mark.

Adding Color

Right now the only color on page two comes from the graphic. Let's add some more color to that page by setting the background color of the top text box.

1. Move to page two and click on the top text box. Choose Modify from the Item menu (or press Command/Ctrl-M). The Modify dialog box appears (see Figure 1-26). Click the Box tab at the top of the dialog box.

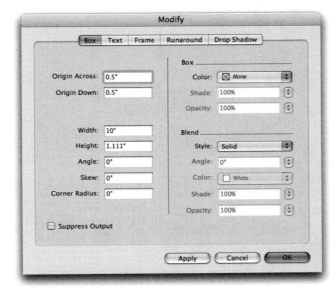

Figure 1-26
The Box tab of the
Modify dialog box

2. Choose Yellow from the Box Color popup menu. (For more information on creating your own colors, see Chapter 14, *Color.*)

3. A solid-yellow text box is a bit too bright for this piece, so select 50 percent from the Shade popup menu.

4. Click the Apply button to see how the color looks added to the background of the text box. (Feel free to move the dialog box out of the way to see the page, but don't click OK yet.)

   Tip: Use the Colors Palette. The Colors palette allows you to apply colors without using the Modify dialog box or menus. Choose Show Colors from the Window menu to open the palette. For more information, see Chapter 14, Color.

5. Click the Text tab at the top of the dialog box. Under Vertical Alignment, choose Centered from the Type drop-down list. Doing so centers the text in the text box.

Adding a Drop Shadow

The text box at the top of page two (the same one you're working on now) needs a drop shadow. Fortunately, it is very easy to add a drop shadow to a text or picture box.

1.   While you're still in the Modify dialog box, click on the Drop Shadow tab (see Figure 1-27).

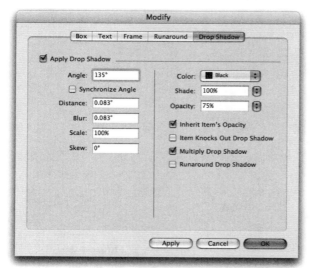

Figure 1-27
The Drop Shadow tab of the Modify dialog box

2.   Enable the Apply Drop Shadow option by turning on the checkbox.

3.   Click Apply to preview the default drop shadow settings on the text box. Click OK to apply the settings and close the dialog box.

Drawing Lines

QuarkXPress has two types of elements: boxes and lines. Lines can be decorative (like arrows, dashed patterns, and so on) or paths that hold text. For your project, you'll create two basic lines as graphic elements at the top and bottom of page one.

1.   Switch to page one and select the Orthogonal Line tool in the Tool palette (that's the one that looks like a plus sign). "Orthogonal" just means that you can only draw horizontal or vertical lines. The tool next to it lets you draw diagonal lines, too.

2.   Drag the Orthogonal Line tool across the top margin of page one, starting from the 6-inch guide and ending at the right margin. When you let go, you may not be able to see the line because the guide is sitting on top of it.

3. In the Measurements palette, choose "8 pt" from the Line width popup menu (see Figure 1-28). The line becomes thicker.

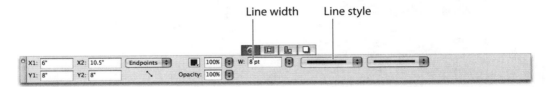

Figure 1-28 The Measurements palette for lines

4. Choose the style called Thin-Thick from the Line style popup menu in the Measurements palette.

5. Duplicate the line by choosing Duplicate from the Item menu (or pressing Command/Ctrl-D).

6. Move the line down to the bottom margin so that it aligns with the same margins as the line at the top.

7. Change the line style to Thick-Thin in the Measurements palette.

PRINTING

That's it! You've finished the brochure. Now all you need to worry about is printing it. There are two ways to print a QuarkXPress project. You can print the file directly to a desktop printer connected to your computer, or you can send the file to a print shop or service bureau for special (high-resolution) output.

Printing on Your Desktop

QuarkXPress is designed to be used with a PostScript printer. If your printer cannot print PostScript, you may obtain unexpected results (that's a diplomatic way to say that your printed page might appear quite unlike what you see onscreen). Nonetheless, whatever printer you have, the steps to print a project are very much the same. (See Chapter 15, *Printing,* for more information on printing.)

1. Select Print from the File menu. The Print dialog box appears (see Figure 1-29).

2. Choose the number of copies (of each page) you want to print in the Copies field.

3. If you only wanted to print page one, you could enter the number "1" in the Pages field. However, because you want to print both pages of this layout, leave the field set to All.

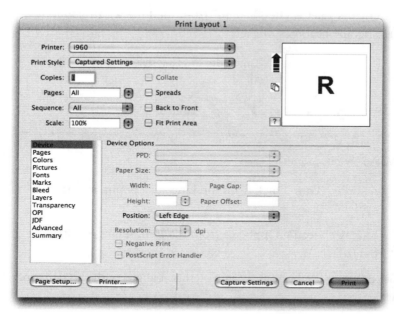

Figure 1-29
The Print dialog box.
It looks a bit different
on Windows, but it's
basically the same.

4. Click on the Setup tab. You should always check the Setup tab to make sure it's properly configured. For instance, because your layout is wider than it is tall, you should select the Landscape ("sideways") orientation icon. Also, make sure you have the proper printer selected on the Printer Description popup menu. Most of the problems people have when printing are due to selecting the wrong printer here. If your particular printer doesn't appear, choose one that is similar to it, or choose Generic B&W from the list.

5. Press the Print button to start printing.

Sending to a Service Bureau

Desktop printers do not have the high-quality resolution necessary for professional printing. If you are going to have your file printed by a commercial print shop, you need to send your QuarkXPress project to the print shop or service bureau. (Some service bureaus require that you export an Acrobat PDF file; if that's the case, see Chapter 16, *PDF.*) However, there are a few steps you can take to make sure that the file will print properly when it gets there.

1. Choose Usage from the Utilities menu and then select the Fonts tab. This shows you a list of the fonts that you have used in the project (see Figure 1-30).

2. Make a note of those fonts. Your service bureau will want to know that information.

3. Select the Pictures tab of the same dialog box. This displays a list of the graphics used in the project (see Figure 1-31).

4. Make sure the Status column shows OK for each picture. If it shows Missing or Modified, you need to update the pictures in the file. (See Chapter 15, *Printing*, for more information about this dialog box.)

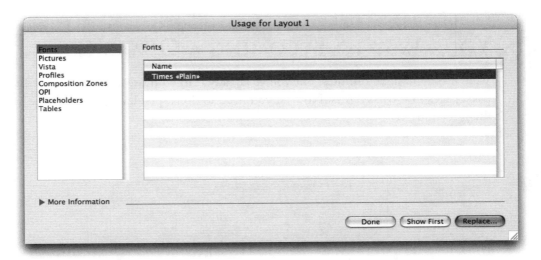

Figure 1-30 The fonts used in the project

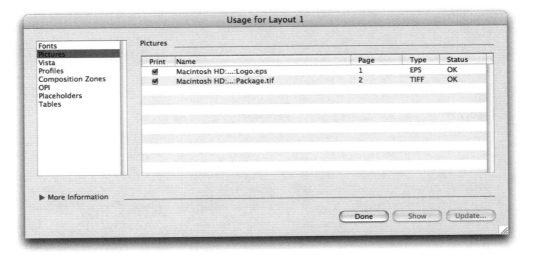

Figure 1-31 The pictures used in the project

5. Finally, when you send the file to the service bureau (on disk or via email or whatever), make sure you send both the QuarkXPress file *and* the pictures used in the project. If you do not send the pictures, your service bureau will not be able to print your file properly. That's because XPress doesn't actually import pictures into your file; it only brings in a low-resolution preview image and creates a *link* to the high-resolution image on your disk.

ON YOUR WAY TO BECOMING A QUARKXPERT

Well, it only took 30 minutes, but you've already learned most of what you need to build basic pages in QuarkXPress. Now all you need to do is spend a little more time studying the remaining chapters in the book, and you will become a QuarkXPert in no time!

CHAPTER TWO

QuarkXPress Basics

Whoever thought that something called a "gooey" would ever be so important to the way we use a computer? While most of the world clutched their crib sheets to remember "how-to" keyboard codes for saving a document, moving to the end of a line, or drawing a box, a few visionary researchers came upon a simple idea: a *graphical user interface*, or GUI (gooey). "Why not," these researchers asked, "make using a computer more intuitive?" These researchers developed the underpinnings of the Macintosh GUI, which in turn laid the groundwork for desktop publishing.

The basics of the Macintosh and Windows GUIs are simple: Create an environment in which somebody can get the most out of a computer without having to remember too much, or even think too much in order to get the job done. The GUI comes between the person using the computer and the computer itself. For example, when you want to move a file from one disk to another, you click on it and drag it across the screen. The GUI handles all the internal computer stuff for you.

When you work with QuarkXPress, you work with the Macintosh or Windows GUI. You don't have to remember long arcane codes or read a computer language, or even understand what's going on behind the scenes. Certainly, the more you know about how computers work, the better you can use them. However, this book is not meant for programmers. This book, like QuarkXPress, is "for the rest of us."

I hear mumbling in the halls: "Who cares about gooey users and interfaces? I just want to use the program." Well, hold on; you can't tell the players without a program, and you can't effectively use QuarkXPress without understanding how it relates to you. So I'll play emcee and introduce the players: the members of the QuarkXPress interface.

GETTING STARTED

I'm going to start with a quick discussion of installing and upgrading QuarkXPress. In versions 3 and 4 of XPress, the upgrader was a completely different package than the installer; with XPress 5, everyone got an installer. XPress 6 returned to the good ol' days, and you received either an upgrader or an installer. Thankfully, this has not changed with XPress 7.

If you're like me, you bypass the manual entirely and just start shoving disks into the computer to see what there is to see. You'll find that all the peripheral files for the program are located intact on the CD-ROM, while the program itself is compressed. The installer is the only thing that can piece together and decompress the application onto your hard drive. But if you want to copy the other filters, XTensions, or files over by hand later, you can do that, too. (I just let the installer do it for me; it's much easier and it knows where all the proper files are.)

Remember to keep your serial number and validation code nearby when installing it, and don't throw these away. If you ever need to reinstall the software (I have to about once every six months or so, when weird things start popping up), you'll need this information.

Patchers. Instead of releasing a full new update of the program, the folks at Quark sometimes just release a patcher. For example, version 4.0 was a little buggy (okay, so it was *really* buggy), but Quark quickly released a patcher for it that updated it to version 4.01, and then another that updated to 4.02, and so on. By the time you read this, Quark will almost certainly have released "micro-updates" for version 7 that fix bugs or add small features. It's worth checking with Quark every now and again (*www.quark.com*).

Quark License Administrator. For 10 years Quark has promised companies with heaps o' copies of XPress a network administration program to help manage them all. Finally, they've delivered with the Quark License Administrator. If you have five or more copies of XPress on your network, you should probably take a look at getting a site license so that you can use this tool. The details are outside the scope of this book, but one thing is important: Make sure you install the administration software before installing your copies of QuarkXPress.

Files and Folders

When the installer is done doing its thing, you'll find a slew of files on your hard disk. These include several files for getting text from word processors, a dictionary, and several other files that help XPress do its business. Figure 2-1 shows a folder containing QuarkXPress and its application files.

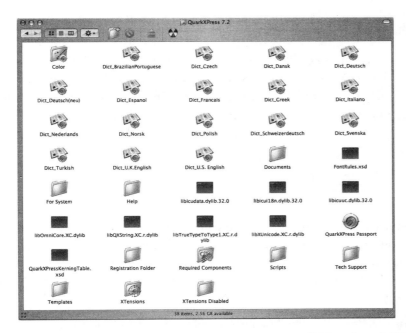

Figure 2-1
Standard QuarkXPress
folders

Most of the files are in the QuarkXPress program folder, though XPress does install some files (including its Preferences files) elsewhere on your system. If you need to find those files, use the operating system's Find feature to search for the word "Quark."

Required Components. There are a dozen or so folders inside the QuarkXPress folder, including Color (which holds all the color libraries; more on that in Chapter 14, *Color*), Documents (which consists of the User Guide and other documentation in Acrobat PDF format), and Help (in which the thousands of files for Quark's Help system live). The files inside the Required Components folder are actually parts of QuarkXPress itself; they're features like the Table tool and the ability to import JPEG files. They're so important that the program won't run without them present.

Fortunately, you never have to worry about these files. Just leave them alone and forget they're even there. The reason Quark put them there was that it makes updating those features much easier. If, for example, they rewrite the Layers palette to be cooler, they can easily write an update program that replaces the one inside your folder with the new version.

Where QuarkXPress Resides

Before I go any farther into the wild world of QuarkXPress, I think it's necessary to take a quick look at four parts of the program: the Environment dialog box, the XPress Preferences file, XTensions, and keyboard shortcuts. The first can help you figure out where you are; the second helps XPress remember where it is. The third, XTensions, let you extend the functionality of the program. And the fourth is all about making you superefficient.

About Boxes

There are times when it's helpful to know the state of your Mac or PC. One of those times is when you're on the telephone with Quark technical support. Another is when you're troubleshooting a weird problem yourself. QuarkXPress can tell you about itself and its environment via the Environment dialog box (see Figure 2-2). You can get to this dialog box in several ways.

- **About QuarkXPress.** On the Macintosh, hold down the Option key and choose About QuarkXPress from the Application menu (that's the one labeled "QuarkXPress"). In Windows, hold down the Alt key and choose About QuarkXPress from the Help menu.

- **Help.** If you have an extended keyboard on your Macintosh, you can press Option-Help. (The Help key is up near the Delete and Page Up keys.)

- **Laptop keystrokes.** If you work on a Macintosh laptop, try Command-Option-Control-E.

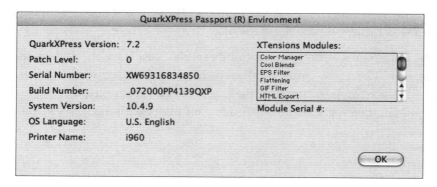

Figure 2-2 QuarkXPress Environment dialog box

The Environment dialog box tells you familiar information about your system and your version of QuarkXPress. It also displays a list of XTensions that you currently have running, and if you click on one, you'll see the XTension's serial number (if it has one; most don't). Lastly, try clicking on the User Reg. Info button at the bottom of the dialog box. This button should open a new XPress document and fill a text box with all the information that the software sent to Quark when you registered your product. I find this interesting, but not particularly helpful.

XPress Preferences

Most programs are accompanied by a preferences file in which they store various default settings, and QuarkXPress is no different. The basic XPress Preferences file remembers almost everything, from where you last placed the palettes onscreen to whether you like your measurements displayed in picas or inches. Most of the settings it remembers are controls that you can set in the various preferences dialog boxes (I'll discuss these in "Changing Defaults," later in this chapter).

In earlier versions of XPress, there was only one preferences file and it was stored loose in the QuarkXPress folder. Now, there are multiple preferences files, and they're all stored in the Preferences folder. (In Mac OS X, the Preferences folder is in the Library folder, which is in the user folder. In Windows, these files live in the Quark folder, inside the Application Data folder, which is a hidden folder inside the Documents and Settings directory.) On the Mac, all XPress preference files have the .prf file name extension.

Troubleshooting. One thing you should be aware of, however, is that the XPress Preferences file can become corrupt. It's not common, but it does happen; and when it does, XPress may start acting strangely. It's hard to say what "strangely" means, but I've seen menus appear in the wrong place, dialog boxes display garbled text, and so on. When strange stuff like this appears, here's what I do.

1. Quit QuarkXPress and relaunch it. Often that clears things up.

2. If it doesn't make things better, quit again and drag the QuarkXPress program icon, the Required Components folder, and the library file (OmniCore.Mach-O.r.dylib) into another folder or out onto the desktop and launch the program from there.

3. From here, XPress can't find the XPress Preferences file or its XTensions, so it creates a new, fresh XPress Preferences folder.

4. If the problem persists, then it probably has something to do with the operating system, a font, a picture, or the file itself. However, if the problem goes away, it almost certainly has something to do with one of the preferences files or an XTension.

Unless I just recently installed an XTension (see "XTensions," below), my first guess is usually the XPress Preferences file. So I quit again, move those four items back to their normal folder, and move the XPress Preferences file into another folder (or throw it in the trash).

5.   Again, QuarkXPress creates a fresh Preferences file when you launch. If the trouble still has not gone away, then the problem is almost certainly with an XTension or the program itself.

> **Tip: Resetting and Switching Preferences.** *The XPress Preferences file remembers all sorts of information about how QuarkXPress behaves.*
>
> • *Hyphenation exceptions and edits to the kerning and tracking tables (see Chapter 6, Typography, for more on these)*
>
> • *Default document preferences that you have set up in the Preferences dialog box*
>
> • *Application preferences set up in the Preferences dialog box*
>
> • *Default settings for colors, H&J settings, print styles, style sheets, and lists ("default" meaning the settings that appear whenever you create a new document)*
>
> • *Positions of the program's palettes (including whether they're open or closed)*
>
> *As I noted above, if you delete the XPress Preferences file (or move it so that the program can't find it), then QuarkXPress creates a clean new one for you. This is a great method for starting over from scratch. However, note that you lose all the above settings.*
>
> *The fact that these settings are stored in the preferences file means that you can actually have two or more XPress Preferences files with varying information. For instance, you could keep a special XPress Preferences file for a certain client with specific kerning and hyphenation needs. Of course, you can only have one in the QuarkXPress folder at a time, but the other one(s) can be hidden inside another folder until you want to switch them. However, you do have to quit and relaunch QuarkXPress for the new settings to take effect.*
>
> **Tip: Sharing Your Preferences.** *You might want everyone else in your work group to share the same preferences as you. No problem: just copy your XPress Preferences file into their preferences folders. Unfortunately, you can't move an XPress Preferences file from a Macintosh to a PC or vice versa.*

Also, if you do a lot of editing to the kerning or tracking tables or hyphenation exceptions (see Chapter 6, *Typography*), you should probably consider keeping a backup of your XPress Preferences file, just in case it goes south someday.

XTensions

Here's an aspect of QuarkXPress that I think is so hot and amazing that I couldn't think of a nasty thing to say about it even if I tried. Quark has built in a system so that programmers can write add-on modules (XTensions) to work with QuarkXPress. There are many developers around the world creating these XTensions (some people call these "plug-ins"). Some cost $5,000 and are designed for a very limited market, such as large newspapers. Others are free, and can (and should) be used by anyone using QuarkXPress. Appendix A, *XTensions*, provides more information about how to get your hands on XTensions.

In order to use an XTension, all you have to do is place it in the XTension folder, which is inside the QuarkXPress folder. When you start up QuarkXPress, the XTension does its thing, whatever that may be. Usually, XTensions add an item to a menu or even add a whole new menu. Most XTensions add items to the Utilities menu, because they are utilities.

> **Tip: Old XTensions, New Product.** All XTensions must be rewritten to function with the latest version of XPress.

Some features within QuarkXPress are entirely based on XTensions, like indexing, and kerning and tracking tables. As we'll see in Chapter 6, *Typography*, and Chapter 10, *Pictures*, XTensions are also used as filters that enable QuarkXPress to read or write certain text and graphics file formats. For example, without the Word XTension, XPress can't read or write files in the Microsoft Word format.

Here's a quick rundown on the various XTensions that ship with QuarkXPress on the Macintosh and Windows platforms.

- **Composition Zone.** This XTension allows you to take advantage of the new Composition Zones in XPress 7. This feature allows multiple users to work on the same layout or even the same page at once. For more on Composition Zones, see Chapter 13, *Collaboration*.

- **Compressed Image Import.** This XTension knows how to interpret various image compression formats—primarily LZW compression in TIFF files. Without this XTension, you won't be able to read those kinds of files.

- **Custom Bleeds.** Lets you set custom bleed amounts in the Print and Save as EPS dialog boxes.

- **Error Reporting.** This XTension tells XPress to write a file to disk whenever the program crashes. In theory, you could send this file to Quark to help them debug the problem. In reality, you should probably just ignore this unless Quark tech support actually instructs you otherwise.

- **Deja Vu.** The Deja Vu XTension remembers what XPress files you've recently worked on as well as what folders you've recently used in the Get Picture, Get Text, and Open dialog boxes. When Deja Vu is loaded, you'll see a list of recently-opened files in the Open submenu (under the File menu), as well as File List and Default Path panes in the Preferences dialog box (see "Layout and Application Preferences" later in this chapter).

- **Drop Shadow.** This XTension allows you to apply drop shadows to images and text directly within XPress.

- **Edit Original.** This allows you to open and edit a placed graphic, such as a TIFF, EPS, or PSD in its native application, such as Adobe Photoshop or Illustrator. The advantage to using Edit Original is that the placed image automatically updates in the XPress layout once your edits are complete.

- **Full Res Preview.** The Full Res Preview XTension lets you display high-resolution and vector images at the resolution of the screen, even when you zoom in. I discuss this more in Chapter 10, *Pictures*.

- **Guide Manager.** The Guide Manager XTension takes a very basic concept (letting you place and delete guides on your pages) and makes it incredibly complicated. See more on guides in Chapter 3, *Working with Items*.

- **Glyphs Palette.** You must have this XTension loaded in the XTensions folder to use the new Glyphs palette. For more on working with the Glyphs palette, see Chapter 6, *Typography*.

- **HTML Text Import.** With this XTension, XPress can import simple HTML files just as though they were regular word-processor files.

- **ImageMap.** This lets you create image maps in Web layouts.

- **Index.** This one enables the various indexing features, such as the Index palette (see Chapter 9, *Long Documents*).

- **Jabberwocky.** I love the Jabberwocky XTension! It lets you fill any text box (or chain of text boxes) with random text much more interesting than the ol' Lorum Ipsum stuff. You can control Jabberwocky's language in the Jabberwocky pane of the Preferences dialog box and the Jabberwocky Sets feature under the Edit menu.

- **Kern-Track Editor.** This lets you edit kerning and tracking tables (appears in the Utilities menu). See "Fine Tuning Type" in Chapter 6, *Typography*.

- **Word 6-2000 Filter.** This filter lets you import and export Microsoft Word files. Quark is constantly updating its MS Word import filter; it's a good idea to check the Quark Web site regularly to see if there's a new one available.

- **OPI.** If you use an OPI workflow (where low-quality pictures get swapped out for high-quality images at print time), you need this XTension active. It adds OPI features to the Print and Save as EPS dialog boxes.

- **PDF Filter.** Whenever you see the word "filter," remember it means both import *and* export. This filter lets you import Acrobat PDF files into picture boxes and export your pages in the PDF format.

- **PNG Filter.** Do you use the PNG file format? Not many people do yet (it's primarily used for Web graphics), but if you do, you need this XTension.

- **PPML Export.** With this XTension you can export XPress layouts in the standardized, XML-based PPML format. This format is generally used for outputting mail-merge layouts intended for large distribution. The advantage to using PPML Export is that a PPML output device can cache repeating layout elements in its memory rather than processing them over and over again, which results in faster printing.

- **PSD Import XT.** This XTension allows you to import native Photoshop files (PSDs) into an XPress layout and access their available layers, channels, and paths via the PSD Import palette.

- **RTF Filter.** This gives you the ability to import text files in Rich Text Format (RTF). RTF is a standard exchange format for formatted text. If your word processor isn't supported by XPress, see if it will export in the RTF format.

- **Scissors.** After I complained to a Quark engineer that the Bézier line tools really needed a scissors tool, he sat down and wrote up the Scissors tool over a weekend. It ended up being an XTension instead of being built into the program, but that's okay. I discuss this more in Chapter 3, *Working with Items*.

- **Script.** This Macintosh-only XTension not only makes QuarkXPress scriptable, but it lets you run AppleScripts from within the program, via the Script menu (see Appendix B, *Scripting*).

- **Shape of Things.** The Shape of Things XTension adds a Starburst tool to the Tools palette. To define the starburst (number of sides, how far inset every other point should be, and so on), double-click on the tool. Then draw a box with the tool the size you want the starburst to be. I find this very clunky, but it works in a pinch.

- **Super Step and Repeat.** The Super Step and Repeat XTension adds a feature of the same name to the Edit menu that lets you create duplicates of any object or objects while offsetting, skewing, scaling, and rotating. For more on duplicating items, see Chapter 3, *Working with Items*.

- **Table Import.** This XTension lets you import tables that were created in Excel into an XPress layout.

- **Type Tricks.** This XTension adds several features and macros to XPress, including Make Fraction, Make Price, Custom Underline, Remove Manual Kerning, Word Spacing, and Line Check. I cover these all in Chapter 6, *Typography*.

- **WordPerfect Filter.** This one lets you import and export files in the WordPerfect format.

- **Vista.** This XTension allows you to apply image adjustments and effects such as Levels and Hue/Saturation to placed images in XPress using the Picture Effects palette.

- **XPress Tags Filter.** With this filter you can import and export files in the XPress Tags format. See Chapter 7, *Copy Flow*, for more information on XPress Tags and why they're so cool.

- **XSLT Export.** This XTension allows you to use the XSLT software to generate an XSL (Extensible Stylesheet Language) file. These files contain XSL transformations from the contents of a Web layout. Using an XSLT processor, you can then apply the resulting XSL transformations into an XML file that can produce an XHTML 1.1 compliant HTML file.

Disabling XTensions. You don't need all those XTensions loaded in QuarkXPress at the same time. XTensions don't take up much hard disk space, so it's hardly worth throwing them away (though if you do, and someday you find you need them again, you'll find them on the QuarkXPress installation CD-ROM). But it is worth disabling XTensions that you don't use, because they slow down the program at launch time and they take up extra RAM while you're using XPress.

For instance, if you only use Microsoft Word as your text editor, go ahead and disable the WordPerfect text filter. If you never use PNG images (I don't know anyone who does), disable that XTension.

There are two ways to disable an XTension. First, if you haven't launched XPress yet, you can manually move the XTension file from the XTension folder into any other folder (preferably the XTension Disabled folder). Or, if you're already in QuarkXPress, you can use the XTensions Manager by selecting it from the Utilities menu (see Figure 2-3). Either way, the changes you make only take effect when you launch QuarkXPress.

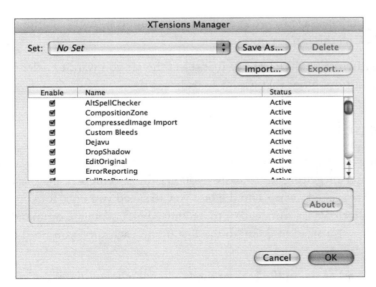

Figure 2-3
XTensions Manager

XTensions Manager. The XTensions Manager dialog box is simple, at heart: all it does is move XTensions back and forth between the XTension and the XTension Disabled folders. As I said earlier, you can do the same thing yourself by hand, but this is easier and usually faster.

You can disable or enable an XTension by turning on or off the checkbox next to it in the Enable column (just click once on the checkbox to toggle its setting).

There are six other controls in the XTensions Manager dialog box.

- **About.** I'm forever forgetting what some of my XTensions do, who developed them, and so on. You can find out all this (and more) by selecting an XTension and clicking the About button.

- **Save As.** QuarkXPress lets you build sets of XTensions that you can recall at any time in the XTensions Manager dialog box. To create a set, first enable the XTensions you want to be loaded and disable those you don't. Then, click the Save As button and name the set. If you want to make a change to a set you've made, select it in the Set popup menu, make the changes (enable or disable the XTensions), and then use Save As to save it with the same name (XPress asks you if you really want to replace the old set with this new one).

- **Set.** The Set popup menu lets you choose which set you want active in the XTensions Manager dialog box. There are two sets by default: All Enabled and All Disabled.

- **Export.** The sets you create are saved in the XPress Preferences file, but you can save a set to disk, too, by clicking Export.

- **Import.** Once you have saved a set to disk, you can import it into a different version of XPress by clicking the Import button.

- **Delete.** How difficult could Delete be? Just select the set you want to delete and click the Delete button. Now, that wasn't so bad, was it?

Keyboard Shortcuts

People often ask me what they can do to speed up their work. If you think the answer is buying a new computer or getting more RAM, you get three demerits. The best way to speed up your work is to speed *you* up, and the best way to speed you up is for you to learn as many keyboard shortcuts as you can. I'm talking about typing Command-N (or Control-N on Windows) instead of going to the File menu each time you need to create a document.

One look at the keyboard charts in the back of the book will tell you that there are a lot of shortcuts in XPress. But the built-in keyboard shortcuts don't let you do everything. Keystrokes can't select Export Layout as PDF, for instance, or add a page to a layout. That's why I bought QuicKeys from CE Software (*www.cesoft.com*)—one for Macintosh and one for Windows—which lets me build my own keyboard-activated macros.

For those who don't know what making macros is all about, let me elucidate. Macros are miniprograms that you can build that tell the computer to do a set of actions: type a key, pull down a menu, hide an application, and so on. Macros don't have to be as simple as just selecting a menu item, though. For example, one macro I have selects a paragraph, applies a style, puts an extra rule above the paragraph, and places a special character after the paragraph's last word. One keystroke sets the macro off and running.

Anytime you find yourself doing the same sequence of events repeatedly, you should think to yourself, "I could write a QuicKey to do this." For more on macros and scripting, take a look at Appendix B, *Scripting*.

FILE MANAGEMENT

Getting a good grasp on file management is essential to working most efficiently and happily with QuarkXPress. When I talk about file management with QuarkXPress, I am talking primarily about opening, closing, and saving your documents. These are pretty basic concepts, so if you've used other Macintosh or Windows programs, you should feel right at home with these actions.

Opening Projects

I won't talk in depth about creating new files until Chapter 4, *Building a Layout*. However, here I do want to talk about opening them. (In case you don't have any to play with, there are several QuarkXPress projects available on the installation disc.)

There are three ways to open an existing QuarkXPress project. You can double-click on the project's icon, which launches QuarkXPress and opens the file. Or, you can drag the project's icon onto the QuarkXPress icon (or an alias on the Macintosh—a shortcut on Windows—for QuarkXPress). If you are in QuarkXPress, you can select Open from the File menu (or press Command/Ctrl-O).

> **Tip: Salvaging Damaged Projects.** Yes, it does happen from time to time that QuarkXPress may corrupt a project. Sometimes, what appears to be a perfectly good project one day will give you grief the next. The worst is when you try to open a file and get a Bad File Format (70) or an Unexpected End of File error.
>
> First, if you can open it, try using the Save As command to save the project to a new file. This can sometimes help, since as you work on a project, it can become larger and more complicated as you edit text and arrange elements. Save As makes a "clean" copy of the file, without this added information.
>
> The next thing I'd try is the Markztools XTension from Markzware (www.markzware.com). This XTension can sometimes repair files that seem irreparable.
>
> If you have a QuarkXPress project so badly corrupted that you can't even open it, and Markztools can't help either, you may at least be able to salvage some of the text by opening the XPress file using a word processor or text editor. For instance, BBEdit is a popular text editor on the Mac that can open just about anything. You'll be able to see all the text in the project, though it will appear garbled in places, and it'll be completely unformatted.

Closing Projects

You have four choices for closing a project.

- Click the close box of the project window.

- Press Command-W (this is Mac only).

- Choose Close from the File menu.

- Select Quit from the same menu. (Of course, this choice not only closes the file, but it also quits QuarkXPress.)

If changes have been made to the project since the last time you saved it, you'll see an alert box asking you if you want to save those changes.

Tip: Closing Up Shop. If you want to quickly close all open projects, you can either press Command-Option-W or Option-click the Close box. In Windows you have to press Alt-W and then press the letter A (which selects Close All from the Window menu).

Saving Projects

Until you save your project to a disk, it exists only in the computer's temporary memory (called RAM), ready to disappear forever in the event of a power disruption or system crash. You should save any new document as soon as it opens, and make frequent saves during your work session. All it takes is Command/Ctrl-S. I suggest developing it into a habit. I cannot tell you how many times my clients and I have lost hours of work because we didn't save frequently enough. You can also use Quark's Auto Save feature (see "Auto Save," later in this section).

Let's look at the commands in QuarkXPress that let you save your projects, along with two other powerful features: one for autosaving and one for making backups.

Save. If you want to save your project with the same name that it already has, you can select Save from the File menu (or press Command/Ctrl-S). If you haven't yet saved your project, and it is unnamed, selecting Save automatically acts like Save As.

Save As. Selecting Save As from the File menu (or pressing Command-Option-S or Ctrl-Alt-S) lets you save the project you're working on under a different name. For example, I often save different versions of a project, with each version number attached to the file name. The first one might be called "Brochure1.qxd," the next "Brochure2.qxd," and so on. Whenever I decide to create a new version, I choose Save As from the File menu, which brings up the Save As dialog box (see Figure 2-4). I type in a file name (or edit the one that's there), then click the Save button to save it to disk. If you decide to do this, remember to delete earlier versions as soon as you decide you don't need them anymore, or else your hard disk will burst at the seams.

File management is an issue that too many people just don't seem to "get." The Save As dialog box is a key ingredient in file management. The important issue here is that your document is saved to whatever folder is open in the Save As dialog box. If you want your document saved in a folder called Current Jobs, you must navigate your way to that folder.

Tip: Exporting as an XPress 6.0 Project. To save a version of your project file that is compatible with XPress 6.0, you must choose Export from the File menu and then choose Layouts as Project. Doing so displays the Export Layouts as Projects dialog box, which allows you to choose either version 7.0 or 6.0 from the Version drop-down list. You no longer have this option in the Save As dialog box. In addition, you cannot export a version that is compatible with XPress 5.0 or earlier.

Figure 2-4
The Save As
dialog box

> ***Tip: It Never Hurts to Save As.*** *As you work on an XPress project, constant edits and revisions can cause the file to grow a little and increase the risk that an unforeseen disaster (cosmic rays? dust-sucking CPU fans?) could corrupt the file. You can guard against this file bloat by occasionally using the Save As command. You can save with the same name or a different one; either way, the file usually shrinks a little to its proper size because all the "garbage" has been swept away. Note that if you have Auto Save turned on, XPress is performing this Save As feature for you behind the scenes, so you don't have to worry about it.*

Auto Save. At first glance, Auto Save looks like a yawner. As it turns out, it's anything but. There are plenty of commercial and shareware utilities that will automatically save a project you're working on, as you're working on it. But all these utilities work by generating the equivalent of QuarkXPress's Save command at predefined intervals. Now suppose you mistakenly delete all of a story; then, before you can Undo your deletion, your autosave utility kicks in, saving your project (and your mistake) for all eternity—or until you fix your mistake, or lose your job because of it! For this reason, I've stayed away from autosaving utilities.

Until now. The folks at Quark really got the design of this feature right. You turn on Auto Save by checking it in the Save pane of the Preferences dialog box (see "Changing Defaults," later in this chapter), and you can specify any interval you want between saves (the default is every five minutes). But—and here's the great part—Auto Save doesn't automatically overwrite your original file. That only happens when you use the Save command. So if you use the Revert to Saved command, you revert to the last saved version of your original file—just as you would expect—*not* to the last Auto Saved one (see "Revert to Saved," later in this chapter).

Auto Save exists to help you recover from a dreaded system crash or network communications failure. (When you lose the connection to your file server with a file open, sometimes QuarkXPress refuses to let you do a Save As.) After you have a crash, you can restart QuarkXPress and open the Auto Saved file. (The file has the .asv file-name extension.)

Whenever QuarkXPress does an autosave, it creates a file in the same folder as your project; this file keeps track of every change you've made since the last time you saved the project. Whenever you save your project, the program deletes the incremental file, and then it starts over again.

The problem with Auto Save is that it creates a file the same size as the one you're working on. If your file is 100 MB large, then you'd better have at least 100 MB available for the autosaved version, too.

> **Tip: Auto Save Saves the Day.** *If you have Auto Save turned on and QuarkXPress freezes up, there's a small chance that the function will still be working in the background. That means that if you wait for a little while instead of rebooting immediately, XPress might save all the work you've done since the last Auto Save. If Auto Save is set to save every five minutes, then wait five minutes after the freeze before restarting the machine. It doesn't always work, but when it does, it's like a cool glass of water on a hot day.*

Auto Backup. Until recently, revision control with QuarkXPress has been strictly up to you. If you wanted to keep previous versions of a project, you had to be sure to copy them to another location, or use Save As frequently, slightly changing the name of your file each time. (I name my files with version numbers: 1.1, 2.4, etc.) Now those days are gone.

You can use Auto Backup (also found on the Save pane of the Preferences dialog box, or press Command-Option-Shift-Y or Ctrl-Alt-Shift-Y) to tell QuarkXPress to keep up to 100 previous versions of your project on disk (the default is five). By choosing Other Folder and clicking the Browse button, you can specify exactly where you want revisions to be stored. The default, "<project folder>," is simply the folder in which your original document resides. If you ever need to open a previous version of a file, just look in the destination folder. The file with the highest number appended to its name is the most recent revision. Note that it's often a good idea to change the backup destination folder to a different hard drive, just in case the one you're working on decides to leap off your desk.

> **Tip: Fill 'Er Up with Backups.** *After working with Auto Backup for a couple of weeks, you may find your hard drive mysteriously filling up. Remember, those backup files (as many per file as you've specified in Preferences) don't go away by themselves. You need to delete them when you're done with them. One suggestion: Set your Auto Backup to save to a special backup folder on a seldom-used drive.*

Templates

You have the choice of saving your project as a template when you're in the Save As dialog box. When a file is saved as a template, nothing changes except that you cannot accidentally save over it. For example, let's say you create a document and save it as a normal document called "Newsletter Template." Then, a couple of days later you go back into the document and create the newsletter: You make changes, flow text in, and place pictures. You then select Save from the File menu. The file, "Newsletter Template," is modified with the changes you made, and there is no way to "go back" to the original untouched file (unless you've made a backup somewhere).

Okay, now let's say you create that same "Newsletter Template," then save it as a template by choosing Template from the Type popup menu in the Save As dialog box. The next time you open the file, it opens with a name like "Document1" so if you select Save, you get the Save As dialog box.

> **Tip: Resaving Templates.** *If QuarkXPress gives you the Save As dialog box when you try to save a project specified as a template, how can you change the template itself? Simple. You can replace the old template with a new one by giving it exactly the same name in the Save As dialog box. (Don't forget to choose Project Template from the Type popup menu if you still want it to be a template.)*

Multiple Project Windows

QuarkXPress lets you open up multiple project windows at one time. However, the actual number and size of documents you can have open depends on both the amount of memory available and the number of other files open.

Window management. Having so many document windows open at once could mean massive clutter and confusion (especially for people like me, who think that the "desktop" metaphor was created to let us make our virtual desktop as messy as our physical one). Fortunately, XPress provides two solutions.

First, XPress lists all open document windows in the Windows menu. Just selecting a document name makes it active, which is particularly convenient if the file you want happens to be hidden under a slew of other windows.

Second, XPress offers two features alongside the list of document windows: Stack Documents and Tile Documents (see Figure 2-5). The Stack Documents command arranges your windows somewhat like a slightly fanned hand of cards. There's always at least a tiny smidgen of each window showing, even the hindmost one, so you can select any window by clicking on it.

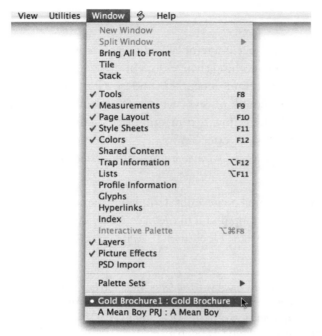

Figure 2-5
The Window menu

Tiling resizes every document window so that each takes up an equal portion of your computer's screen. So if you have three document windows, the Tile Documents command sizes and arranges them so that each takes up one-third of your screen. I often use this when dragging objects or pages from one document to another.

There are also two new window management features available under the Window menu: New Window and Split Window. If you'd like to view two or more parts of your layout side by side or view them at different zoom levels, choose New Window from the Window menu. You can also use the New Window feature to view more than one layout from the same project.

Of course, you have to have a pretty decent size monitor in order to utilize the New Window feature. If you are working on a laptop or a smaller screen, try using the Split Window feature. Under the Window menu, choose Split Window and then choose Horizontal or Vertical, or click and drag the blue divider icon located in the upper-right (split horizontally) or lower-right (split vertically) corners of the window. This allows you to divide the window into equal portions and display different parts of the same layout or different layouts in the same project (see Figure 2-6). You can scroll each view independently from the other and drag the divider bar to adjust the size of the split. To return to normal view, choose Split Window from the Window menu and then choose Remove All, or click and drag any divider bar all the way to the project window's edge.

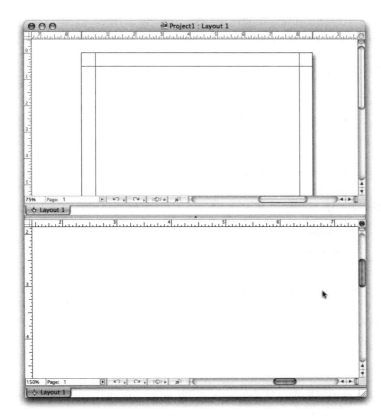

Figure 2-6
Split Window showing
horizontal split

QUARKXPRESS'S INTERFACE

While working in QuarkXPress, you have access to its powerful tools and features through several areas: menus, palettes, dialog boxes, keystrokes, and context-sensitive menus. Let's look carefully at each of these methods and how you can use them.

Menus

There are several conventions used in QuarkXPress's menus. One is the hierarchical menu, which I call a submenu. These allow multiple items to be, literally, offshoots of the primary menu item. Another convention is the checkmark. A checkmark next to a menu item shows that the feature is enabled or activated. Selecting that item turns the feature off—or disables it—and the checkmark goes away. If a menu item has an ellipsis (...) after it, you know that selecting it will bring up a dialog box. Finally, menus show the main keystroke shortcut for a menu item. Figure 2-7 shows these three menu conventions. Other conventions are discussed as needed throughout the book.

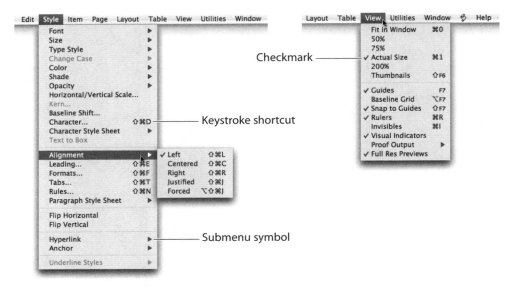

Figure 2-7 Menu conventions

I don't need to talk a great deal here about menus and what's on them because I discuss their contents throughout the book. However, you should note that certain types of features fall under particular menus. Let's do a quick rundown.

- **File.** Items on the File menu relate to disk files (entire documents). Commands to open, save, and print files are located here.

- **Edit.** The Edit menu contains features for changing items within QuarkXPress. The last section of the Edit menu contains features to edit internal defaults on a document- or application-wide level, such as the color palette, the text style sheets, and specifications for each tool on the Tool palette (see "Tool palette," later in this chapter).

- **Style.** The Style menu changes depending on what item you have selected on your document page. Selecting a picture box results in one Style menu, selecting a text box results in a different one, and selecting rules (lines) results in a third menu. The items on the Style menu enable you to change specific style attributes of the selected item.

- **Item.** Whereas the Style menu contains commands for changing the contents of a picture or text box, the Item menu's commands change the box or rule. For example, changing the style of a picture box's contents might involve changing the shade of a picture. Changing an attribute of the box itself may involve changing the frame thickness of the picture box.

- **Page.** The Page menu is devoted to entire pages in your document layout. Controls for master pages (see Chapter 4, *Building a Layout*) are located here, as well as several features for adding, deleting, and navigating among pages.

- **Layout.** XPress 7 lets you include more than one layout space in a single project (I discuss making layout spaces in Chapter 4, *Building a Layout*), and the Layout menu lets you control these layouts—adding new ones, deleting them, and so on.

- **View.** Almost every feature based on what you see and how you see it is located in the View menu. This menu also includes several other items, such as Show Guides, that involve QuarkXPress's interface. I discuss these later in this chapter.

- **Utilities.** This menu is a catchall that contains assorted goodies for helping make pages. The spelling checker, kerning tables, the feature that tells you what pictures and fonts you've used, and so forth are kept here. Also, most XTensions add items to the Utilities menu, so the more XTensions you have, the longer this menu.

- **Window.** The Window menu lists all your open documents and all the available palettes.

- **Script.** The Macintosh version of QuarkXPress has a Script menu (when the Script XTension is active). When XPress is first launched, any compiled AppleScripts present in the Scripts folder (inside the QuarkXPress folder) are added to this menu. Folders within the Scripts folder become submenus inside this menu.

Palettes and Palette Management

One of the key elements in QuarkXPress's user interface is the palette structure. A palette in QuarkXPress is similar to a painter's palette insofar as it contains a selection of usable and changeable items that you can put wherever suits you best. A left-handed painter may hold a paint palette in her right hand, while a short ambidextrous painter might place the palette on the floor. QuarkXPress has several palettes, each with a different function, which can be placed anywhere you like on the screen. They're additional windows on the screen that, although they can overlap one another, never go "behind" a document window (that's why they're sometimes called *floating* palettes).

You can manipulate palettes in the same manner as you would a document window. For example, to move a palette, drag the window from its top shaded area. To close a palette, click the Close box in the upper-left corner (upper-right corner in Windows).

QuarkXPress comes with 15 palettes: Tool, Measurements, Page Layout, Style Sheets, Colors, Shared Content, Trap Information, Lists, Profile Information, Glyphs, Hyperlinks, Index, Layers, Picture Effects, and PSD Import (see Figure 2-8). Libraries and Books also appear as palettes. When you first launch QuarkXPress, you can see two of these palettes: the Tool palette and the Measurements palette.

QuarkXPress remembers which palettes are open or closed and where each palette is placed, so that next time you launch the program, palettes show up where you left them.

Let's take a look at each of these palettes.

Figure 2-8 QuarkXPress's palettes

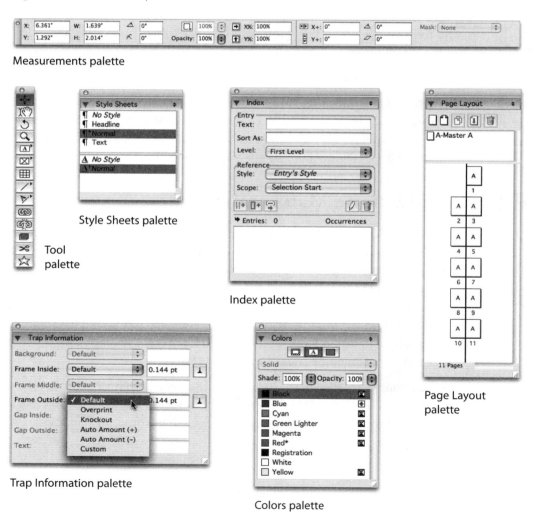

Measurements palette

Style Sheets palette

Tool palette

Index palette

Page Layout palette

Trap Information palette

Colors palette

Lists palette

Shared Content palette

Hyperlinks palette

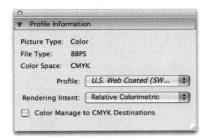

Profile Information palette

Glyphs palette

Layers palette

Picture Effects palette

PSD Import palette

Tool palette. The Tool palette is the most elementary and functional of the palettes. There's not a lot you can do without it. Here you have the tools for making boxes in which you place your pictures and text, tools for rotating, tools for drawing lines, and tools for linking the text boxes together to allow the flow of text. Selecting a tool is easy: just click it (see "Tip: Keyboard Palettes," below). I won't go into each tool here, as I discuss them in some depth in Chapter 3, *Working with Items*.

> *Tip: Enlarge or Reduce Your Tool Palette. QuarkXPress has a slew of tools in the Tool palette and, to accommodate them all, it places many of them inside popout menus (some people call these "fly-out menus"). When you click on any tool that has a little triangle in its upper-right corner and you hold the mouse button down for a moment, a popout menu offers a number of other, similar tools.*

If you have a lot of screen real estate, you can pull these other tools out of the popup menus and add them to the main Tool palette by holding down the Control key (on both Macintosh and Windows) when you click on the tool. (That is, hold it down when you click on the popout menu, and only let go after you've selected the tool you want.)

Conversely, you can put these tools back into popout menus by Control-clicking on them. It all depends on whether you want a long or a short palette (see Figure 2-9).

Measurements palette. Like the Style menu, the Measurements palette is dynamic: it changes depending on what sort of item is selected. Text boxes have one type of Measurements palette, Picture boxes have a second type, and rules and lines have a third type (see Figure 2-10). Which tool from the Tool palette you have selected also has an effect on how the Measurements palette looks. The Measurements palette's purpose in life is to show you an item's vital statistics and save you a trip to the Style or Item menu for making changes to those page elements. The Measurements palette now also features a popup navigator tab that appears when you hover the cursor over the top of the palette. Also, the controls that appear in the navigator tab change depending on what tool you currently have selected in the Tool palette and what item you have selected in your project.

Figure 2-9
The Tool palette: the long and the short of it

For picture boxes

Box origin   Box dimensions   Rotation angle   Picture offset   Picture rotation angle

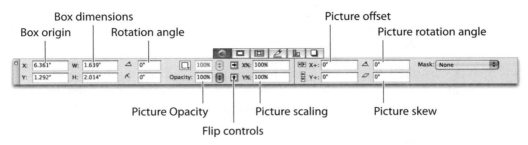

Picture Opacity   Picture scaling   Picture skew

Flip controls

For text boxes

Box origin   Box dimensions   Rotation angle   Alignment   Font   Size   OpenType Options   Color

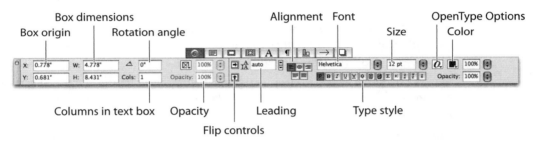

Columns in text box   Opacity   Leading   Type style

Flip controls

For lines (rules)

Line origin   Line rotation   Line mode   Line weight   Line style   End caps

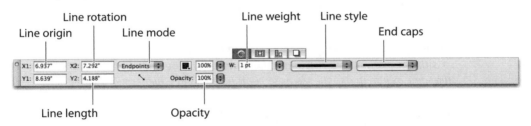

Line length   Opacity

Figure 2-10 The Measurements palette's displays for the three kinds of item selections

For example, if you select a text box with the Content tool, the left half of the Measurements palette shows the dimensions of the text box, the coordinate of its upper-left corner, the number of columns in the box, the rotation angle of the box, and its current box color and opacity value. The right half of the Measurement palette displays the styling attributes, including the font, size, alignment, and various other properties of the text that is contained within the box. The navigator tab contains buttons that allow you to change the controls that are displayed in the Measurements palette. In this scenario, the buttons include: Classic (which contains the default options described above), Text, Frame, Runaround, Character Attributes, Paragraph Attributes, Space/Align, Tabs, and Drop Shadow.

Not only does the Measurements palette display this information, but you can click on an item in the palette and change the item. For example, if you want to rotate a picture box 10 degrees, you replace the "0" with "10" and then press either Return or Enter. (Pressing Return or Enter tells QuarkXPress that you've finished; it's like clicking an OK button.)

Note that the left half of a Measurements palette displays information about a page element (an "item"), and the right half displays information about the contents or the style of the item (see more on items and contents in Chapter 3, *Working with Items*).

> **Tip: Keyboard Palettes.** *You can access and select items on either the Tool palette or the Measurements palette by using keyboard commands. To show or hide the Tool palette, press the F8 key (assuming you have an extended keyboard). To select the next tool down on the Tool palette, press Command-Control-Tab or Option-F8 (in Windows, press Ctrl-Alt-Tab or Ctrl-F8). To select the next higher tool, press Command-Control-Shift-Tab or Shift-Option-F8 (in Windows, press Ctrl-Alt-Shift-Tab or Ctrl-Shift-F8). If you have closed (hidden) the Tool palette, you can open it by pressing any of these key commands.*
>
> *You also can use the Tab key to move through the Measurements palette. You can jump to the first item on this palette by pressing Command-Option-M (or Ctrl-Alt-M; this also opens the palette, if it was closed).*
>
> *I find it much faster to toggle between items on the Tool palette using keystrokes, especially when moving between the Content tool and the Item tool. And I hardly ever use the mouse to click in the Measurements palette, preferring instead to press Command-Option-M (Ctrl-Alt-M), then tab through the items until I get where I want. You can also press F9 to show and hide the Measurements palette.*
>
> **Tip: Jump to Fonts.** *Changing from one font to another is often a real hassle, but it's much less so with one of my favorite keyboard shortcuts: Command-Shift-Option-M (or Ctrl-Alt-Shift-M; the same as jumping to the Measurements palette, but adding the Shift key).*

Page Layout palette. You can find the Page Layout palette by selecting Show Page Layout from the View menu (or pressing the F10 key). In earlier versions of XPress this was called the Document Layout palette. This palette displays a graphic representation of your project, page by page. When you first start using it, it's slightly weird, but the more you work with it, the more you realize how amazingly cool it is.

I discuss the Page Layout palette in "Manipulating Your Layout," later in this chapter (and again, in greater detail, in Chapter 4, *Building a Layout*), but—in a nutshell—you can use this palette for creating, deleting, and shuffling pages, assigning master pages, and creating multipage spreads. Generally, many of the functions of the Page menu can be performed by dragging icons in the Page Layout palette.

Style Sheets palette. The principle is simple: Whenever you're working with text, you can apply, edit, and view style sheets on the fly by using the Style Sheets palette. This palette lists all the paragraph and character styles in your document, along with their keyboard shortcuts if they have any. (If you have lots of styles, you can make the palette larger or just scroll through them.) I discuss the Style Sheets palette (including what style sheets are, if you don't know already) in Chapter 7, *Copy Flow*.

Colors palette. Just as you can with styles, you can apply and edit colors with a click, using the Colors palette. This floating palette contains a list of every available color, along with a tint-percentage control and three icons. Depending on what tool and object you have selected, some icons are grayed out. When you select a text box, the icons represent frame color, text color, and background color for that box. When you select a line, two icons gray out, and only the line-color icon remains. I cover this in more detail in Chapter 14, *Color*.

Trap Information palette. Unlike most palettes in QuarkXPress, which you can either use or else work with menu items, the Trap Information palette is the only way that you can use object-by-object trapping (I cover trapping in detail in Chapter 14, *Color*). The palette shows you the current trap information for a selected page object, gives you "reasons" why it's trapping the object that way, and lets you change that object's trap value. Unless you change the trap value, the Trap Information palette displays all objects at their default trap.

Lists palette. The Lists palette displays collections of paragraphs in your document or book that are tagged with specific style sheets (determined by the list specification). I cover lists and how you can make tables of contents with them in Chapter 9, *Long Documents*.

Profile Information palette. Quark lets you view and change color device profiles on an image-by-image basis using the Profile Information palette. However, in order to access the controls in this palette, you must first turn on the Enable Access to Picture Profiles option located in the Color Manager pane of the Preferences dialog box.

Index palette. I cover the Index palette and indexing projects in general in Chapter 9, *Long Documents*. Suffice it to say that the Index palette is your one and only ticket to getting an index in QuarkXPress (other than using some other, commercial XTension). It is only available when the Index XTension is loaded and active.

Libraries palette. Here's another QuarkXPress feature, which I discuss in much greater detail later in Chapter 3, *Working with Items* (I'm not trying to tease; I'm just taking things one step at a time). A library looks like a simple palette, but it has some very powerful uses. You can have more than one Libraries palette open at a time (each floating palette represents one Library file), and you are able to store up to 2,000 items in each library. Libraries are slightly different from other palettes in that they're not accessed by the View menu; you use the New Library command to create them, and the standard Open dialog box to access them (both under the File menu).

Books palette. Books are like libraries in some ways, except they're collections of documents rather than items. Books let you tie together multiple documents that have a common purpose, like chapters in a book or spreads in a magazine. I cover books and the Books palette in Chapter 9, *Long Documents*.

Layers palette. Objects in XPress are always above or below one another. The Layers palette makes this relationship among items more obvious by letting you create named layers on which you can put your lines, text boxes, picture boxes, and tables. I'll cover layers in detail in Chapter 3, *Working with Items*.

Hyperlinks palette. Both Web layouts and Acrobat PDF documents can take advantage of hyperlinks, which are "hot links" that, when clicked, take you somewhere. The Hyperlinks palette lets you store all the hyperlinks in your document so you can use them and re-use them quickly. I discuss hyperlinks in great detail in Chapter 17, *Going Online with QuarkXPress*.

Shared Content palette. This palette contains layout items, such as text boxes, picture boxes, and the respective contents of each. Changes made to items that have been placed in a layout from the Shared Content palette are updated globally in all instances throughout the project.

Glyphs palette. The Glyphs palette displays all available characters contained within a chosen font. You can use this palette to locate specific characters and insert them into your text. The Glyphs palette also allows you to save your most commonly used glyphs in a Favorite set.

Picture Effects palette. In QuarkXPress 7 you can now make certain image adjustments directly in XPress without having to rely on an outside image editing application such as Adobe Photoshop. The palette contains controls for making image adjustments such as Levels, Curves, Hue/Saturation, and Brightness/Contrast, just to name a few. You can also apply special effects such as Emboss or Add Noise. The Picture Effects palette allows you to add effects, modify them, change their order, turn them on or off, and even save specific effect combinations and settings as presets to apply to other images.

PSD Import palette. With this palette you can access certain layers, as well as all channels and paths that are contained within a native Photoshop file (PSD) that has been placed in an XPress layout. You can use this palette to control layer visibility in XPress, as well as to crop images using any paths and alpha channels that have been saved in the PSD.

Dialog Boxes

You can perform almost every function in QuarkXPress with only the palettes and the menus. However, it is rarely efficient to work this way. Dialog boxes are areas in which you can usually change many specifications for an item at one time. For example, Figure 2-11 shows the Modify dialog box for a text box. In this dialog box, you can modify any or every item quickly, then click the OK button to make those changes take effect.

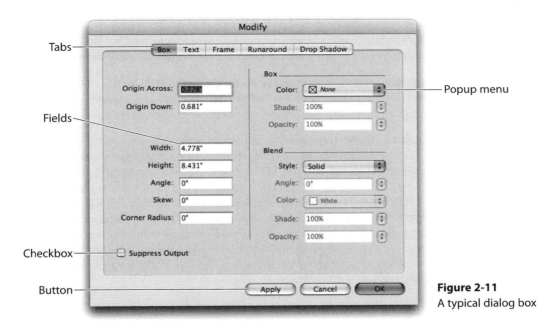

Figure 2-11
A typical dialog box

Dialog box terminology. Here's a quick lesson in terminology, if you're unfamiliar with dialog boxes. The area in which you enter a value is called a *field*. Oftentimes there are *checkboxes* that can be checked on or off, or grayed out if undefined. Many dialog boxes also contain *popup menus*, which act much like the menus at the top of the screen: just position the cursor on them, press the mouse button, and drag the mouse up or down until you have selected the item you want. Then let go of the mouse button.

Typically, dialog boxes have two buttons: OK and Cancel. Clicking OK closes the dialog box and puts your changes into effect. Clicking Cancel closes the dialog box and ignores the changes you've made. Some dialog boxes have a Save option, which acts as an OK button. Other dialog boxes have an Apply button. Clicking this button temporarily applies the settings you've made to the document so that you can see them. If you like what you see, you can then click OK. If you don't like it, you can usually press Command/Ctrl-Z to revert the dialog box to the last setting. In any case, you can click Cancel to rid yourself of the dialog box and the changes you've made, even after applying them (see "Undo and Multiple Undo," later in this chapter).

> **Tip: Pushing Your Buttons.** *Almost every button in QuarkXPress's dialog boxes can be replaced with a keystroke. The keystroke is usually the first letter in the button's name. For example, if a dialog box has Yes and No buttons, you can select them by pressing Command-Y and Command-N (or just press Y or N in Windows). When you're checking spelling, you can select the Skip button by pressing Command-S (Alt-S in Windows). Note that any button that is highlighted (has a darker border than a normal button) can be selected by pressing Enter or Return. (This is usually the OK button, but might be something else, such as Find Next in the Find/Change dialog box.) You can press Cancel by pressing Command-period on the Macintosh or Esc in Windows.*

> **Tip: Switch Tabs.** *You can switch among the tabs in a tabbed dialog box the same way you switch from one tool to the next in the Tool palette: either by clicking on one or by pressing Command-Control-Tab (Ctrl-Alt-Tab) or Command-Control-Shift-Tab (Ctrl-Alt-Shift-Tab).*

> **Tip: Continuous Apply.** *As I said earlier, the Apply button temporarily applies the change you made in a dialog box. You can then decide whether you want to actually make that change, revert, or cancel the operation entirely. Even though pressing Command-A (Alt-A in Windows) speeds up the process some, I often find it helpful to be in a Continuous Apply mode by pressing Command-Option-A or holding down the Option key while clicking Apply (hold down Alt while clicking Apply in Windows). This highlights the Apply button (turns it black), as if you were holding the button down continuously. Now, every change you make in the dialog box is immediately applied to your page item. You can still press Command/Ctrl-Z to undo the last change, or Command-period or Esc to cancel the dialog box. To turn off Continuous Apply, just press Command-Option-A (or Alt-click) again.*

Context-Sensitive Menus

Context-sensitive menus were introduced to QuarkXPress way back in version 5.0. These are menus that appear wherever your cursor is and change depending on what tool you have selected and what you're clicking. If you're using a single button mouse on the Macintosh, you can activate the context-sensitive menu by Control-clicking; in Windows, you simply right-click. What you click on determines what kind of menu you get (see Figure 2-12).

I think context-sensitive menus are one of the best ways to boost your productivity in XPress, right up there with learning the keyboard shortcuts. Just get in the habit of Control-clicking (or right-clicking) on things. I wish there were even more menus, so I could apply text formatting or align objects on the fly. Oh well. There's always another version in the future.

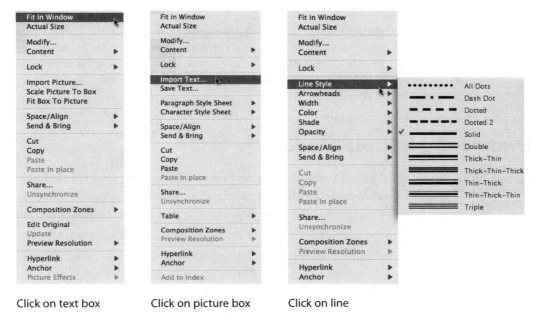

Figure 2-12 Context-sensitive menus

RESTORING, REVERTING, AND UNDOING

Mistakes are common in the world of desktop publishing. In fact, one of the great benefits of working on a computer, in my opinion, is that I can make as many mistakes as I want and always recover from them. In QuarkXPress, there are several methods to recover from a mistake or a decision you might later regret.

Revert to Saved

As I said earlier, no changes are permanent until you save them to disk. If you want to discard all changes made to a project since the last save, you can do it by closing the project (choose Close from the File menu) and telling QuarkXPress that you don't want to save the changes. Or, if you wish to continue working on it without interruption, choose Revert to Saved from the File menu. For example, if—in the name of improvement—you have managed to mess up your project beyond redemption, you can revert to the version that you last saved.

Tip: Revert to Last Minisave. The Auto Save feature I talked about previously goes by another name, too: PageMaker used to call these things minisaves. Sometimes you want to use a minisave as something other than crash insurance. You can actually revert to the last autosave instead of going back all the way to the last full save (for instance, if you like the changes you made five minutes ago, but not the ones you made 10 minutes ago). Just hold down the Option key when you select Revert from the File menu.

Undo and Multiple Undo

Since I'm on the topic of reverting back and ignoring changes to the document, we really need to take a quick detour and look at the Undo commands. Undo is found under the Edit menu, and is a staple of all quality programs. If you make a mistake, you can almost always Undo it.

QuarkXPress gives you the ability to undo more than one thing at a time. In fact, you can undo up to the last 30 things you did to your file, either one at a time, or in bunches of steps. To undo a single action, press Command/Ctrl-Z. To undo more than one action at a time, click and hold down the mouse button on the Undo popup menu in the lower-left corner of the document window. The Undo popup menu lists all the undoable actions you've performed recently, labeling them cryptically, like "Undo Line Change," "Undo Typing," or "Undo Text Box Change" (see Figure 2-13).

XPress also lets you *redo* steps after undoing them. By default, pressing Command-Shift-Z (or Ctrl-Y in Windows) redoes the last action you undid. Similarly, you can choose more than one action to redo from the Redo popup menu (next to the Undo popup menu). Redo is helpful when you're not sure whether you want to make a change—you can undo the change, then redo it for a "before and after" effect.

Note that each layout space has its own undo list, so if you make a change on the first layout, switch to the second layout and make another change, and then try to undo twice, you'll only undo the change on the second layout. So XPress actually has a maximum of 30 undo steps per layout. However, also note that XPress forgets the undo list when you quit or close a document.

Undo Preferences. If you count carefully, you'll find that out of the box XPress only remembers the last 20 things you do, while earlier I said it should remember 30. You can make it remember *up to* 30 by changing the value in the Undo pane of the Preferences dialog box (press Command-Option-Shift-Y or Ctrl-Alt-Shift-Y). Remember that each additional step you want XPress to remember takes some extra RAM. In a memory-tight situation, you might reduce this value to 5 or 10 steps. In general, 20 is a pretty good default.

The Undo pane of the dialog box also lets you specify which keyboard shortcut you want to use for the Redo command. You have three choices: Command-Shift-Z, Command-Z, and Command Y (or Ctrl-Shift-Z, Ctrl-Z, and Ctrl-Y). This is handy for two reasons. First, if you're used to the way some other program (like Microsoft Word) does it, you can match XPress to that method. Second, if you choose anything other than Command/ Ctrl-Z, then you can undo multiple steps with Command/Ctrl-Z and then redo multiple steps with whichever other keyboard shortcut you choose. If both Undo and Redo are set to Command/Ctrl-Z, the shortcut only undoes the last action.

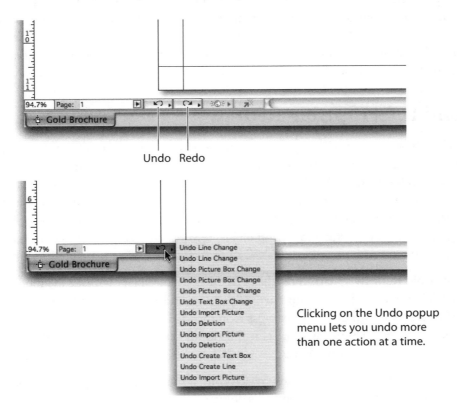

Figure 2-13 Undo and Redo popup menus

When you can't Undo it. Unfortunately, there are a number of things that you'd expect to be able to undo that you can't. For instance, if you insert or delete a page, XPress can't undo that. XPress can't undo adding or moving a guide. Nor can it undo something you've changed on a master page once you've returned to the document page. Plus, sometimes if you do something that is undoable, it wipes out the undo list so you can't undo anything you did before that action. This is one reason I do a lot of saving (so I can always perform a Revert to Save if I need to).

Text and type styles. QuarkXPress bundles together any text actions that you do at the same time so that if you select Undo, all the changes get undone at once. That means typing a bunch of text into a text box counts as one Undo step, but as soon as you move the cursor and start typing someplace else, you begin a new undo step. For example, if you type three words, then move back a word and add a letter, XPress resets its Undo "memory" so an Undo would only remove the added letters. This can be frustrating if you don't really know what's going on because it seems like it forgets stuff. It's not forgetful; we are.

Similarly, all the typographic styles you apply to text count as one Undo step until you move the cursor. Here's an example: If you select a word and make it bold and italic and small caps and change the font size four times (I'll show you how to do all that later in the book), and then press Command/Ctrl-Z, QuarkXPress reverts to how the text was before you applied any type styles. You can't just undo the last font size change you made.

Cancel and Interruptible Redraw

You can get yourself out of a bad situation in every dialog box or palette in QuarkXPress by remembering the ubiquitous and powerful features: Command-period or Esc (Cancel) and Command-Z (Undo). For instance, if you change the x or y coordinates for a text box, and then decide what you're doing is a mistake, you can undo it even before the change takes place. Pressing Command/Ctrl-Z reverts to the previous state and keeps the field highlighted. Pressing Command-period or Esc reverts and takes you out of the palette or dialog box altogether.

Interruptible Redraw. QuarkXPress has a "hidden" feature that can make life much better: interruptible screen redraw. If you have 43 pictures and text boxes on your page and it's taking forever to draw them, you can press Command-period (or Esc) to cancel the redraw. QuarkXPress stops drawing as soon as it finishes drawing the next object (that's slightly different from some other programs, such as Adobe Photoshop, which stop immediately).

You can also interrupt screen redraw by selecting a menu item or typing any other keyboard shortcut. Note that screen redraw is only relevant when the Off-screen Draw option is turned off in Preferences (see "Changing Defaults," later in this chapter).

> *Tip: Forcing Screen Redraw.* As I'm talking about screen redraw, I should probably also mention that Command-Option-period (Macintosh) and Shift-Esc (Windows) will force XPress to redraw the screen. I find this useful because XPress has various persistent problems (bugs) that cause it, on occasion, to update the screen improperly. Often, if something just looks weird (like "what's that line doing there?" or "my text isn't supposed to look like that"), just force a screen redraw and the problem goes away.

NAVIGATING YOUR LAYOUT

QuarkXPress shows you the pages in your project as though they were all spread out in order on a giant white pasteboard. However, unless you happen to work on an enormous screen, you never get to see much of the pasteboard at one time. Let's look at how you can move around to see different parts of a page, and different pages within your layout.

Scrolling

The first step in moving around within your layout is scrolling. *Scrolling* refers to using the horizontal and vertical scroll bars on the right and bottom sides of the project window to move your page (see Figure 2-14). If you click the arrow at the top of the vertical scroll bar, you move a bit "up" your page (closer to the top). If you click the left arrow in the horizontal scroll bar, you move to the left on your page, and so on.

I find that many people never get past this elementary level of scrolling. This is conceivably the slowest method you could use. I implore you to look at the alternatives.

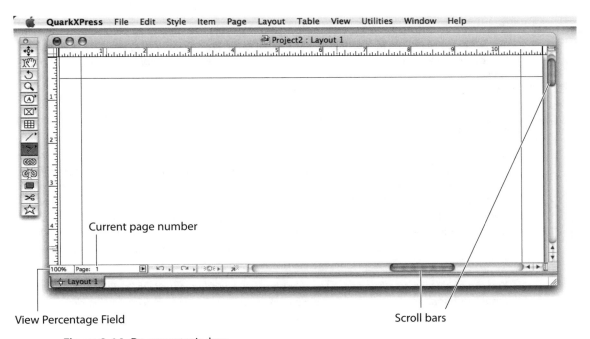

Figure 2-14 Document window

You can move large distances in your document by moving the little white box (some people call it the "scroll elevator") in the scroll bars. Clicking in the gray area moves you by one screen at a time. You can also use keystrokes to move around the screen vertically. Table 2-1 shows you how to do this.

Table 2-1 Moving around your document (Control-key shortcuts are Macintosh only)

To move...	Press...	Extended keyboards, press...
Up one screen	Control-K	Page Up
Down one screen	Control-L	Page Down
Start of document	Control-A	Home
End of document	Control-D	End
First page	Control-Shift-N	Shift-Home
Last page	Control-Shift-D	Shift-End
Next page	Control-Shift-L	Shift-Page Down
Previous page	Control-Shift-K	Shift-Page Up

Tip: Scroll Speed. If you do use the scroll bar arrows to get around, you definitely want to examine the Scroll Speed feature in the Input Settings pane of the Preferences dialog box. This feature lets you control how far each click in a scroll-bar arrow takes you. For example, if you have the Scroll Speed set to Fast, then clicking an arrow may move you an entire screen or more. If you have it set to Slow, a click may move the screen one or two pixels.

Don't confuse Scroll Speed with Speed Scroll. I cover the latter in "Changing Defaults," later in this chapter.

Tip: Live Scrolling. When you are zoomed in to a layout and drag the scroll bar, it's often difficult to tell how far on the page or the layout you've gone. This is because the vertical scroll bar represents the entire length of your layout, and the horizontal scroll bar represents the full width of the pasteboard. If you have multipage spreads in your layout, the pasteboard can be very large (see more on spreads in Chapter 4, Building a Layout). But if you hold down the Option/Alt key while you drag the box, the screen scrolls with you, so you can see how far you're going (this is called live scrolling).

You can enable live scrolling on a permanent basis by checking in the Live Scroll box in the Input Settings pane of the Preferences dialog box. With that feature turned on, Option-dragging (Alt-dragging) on the scroll bar box makes the document not live scroll.

Tip: Use the Grabber Hand. The Grabber Hand is arguably the most important tool in QuarkXPress. The problem with the scroll bars is that you can only scroll in one direction at a time. It's a hassle: down a little, over to the left, down a little more, now to the right, and so on. But if you hold down the Option/Alt key at any time, no matter what tool you currently have selected, the cursor turns into the Grabber Hand, and when you click and drag, the page moves where you move the Grabber Hand. Try it! I think it's one of the greatest methods for getting around the page.

Zooming

If you have a brand-new 90-inch HDTV monitor, you may not need to read this section. For the rest of us, zooming is a necessity of life. When you zoom in and out on a page, you are using an electronic magnifying glass, first enlarging a particular area of a page, and then reducing your screen view so that you are seeing the entire page or pages at once.

QuarkXPress lets you magnify or reduce your screen view from 10 percent to 800 percent, in steps of 0.1 percent. You can jump between several preset views quickly by selecting them from the View menu or by using keystrokes.

Tip: Maximum Zoom Power. If you switch back and forth between the Macintosh and Windows platforms, as I do, you'll quickly notice that although you can always zoom in to 800 percent on the Macintosh, you generally can't get any closer than 692 percent in Windows. What's the deal? It has to do with screen resolution. QuarkXPress for Windows assumes your screen resolution is about 96 ppi (pixels per inch), though you can change this value in the Preferences dialog box (see "Changing Defaults," later in this chapter). If you lower the screen resolution setting in XPress, the program lets you zoom in more (at 72 ppi, you can zoom in to a full 800 percent). If you raise the resolution setting, you can zoom in less.

As for the Macintosh, QuarkXPress is stuck believing that your screen is displaying 72 ppi, no matter what the resolution truly is. Oh well.

View menu. The View menu lists zooming values of Fit in Window, "50%," "75%," "Actual Size" (which is 100 percent), "200%," and "Thumbnails." Fit in Window adjusts the zoom percentage to fit whatever size window you have open at the time. If you're working with facing pages, then the scale is set to fit a two-page spread in the window. Thumbnails zooms way back so that you can see a bunch of pages at the same time (but it does more than that; see "Thumbnails," later in this chapter).

When you select a magnification from the View menu, QuarkXPress automatically zooms to the percentage you want and centers the current page in your window. If any item on the page you're looking at is selected when you switch magnifications, QuarkXPress centers that item in the window. Or, if the item is on the pasteboard, the program centers it if any part of the item is showing when you switch views.

For example, if you select a short rule on a page while viewing at Fit in Window size, and then select Actual Size, QuarkXPress zooms in and centers that rule on your screen. If the selected item is a text box and you have the Content tool selected, the program centers the cursor or whatever text is highlighted. This makes zooming in and out on a page much easier: If you're editing some text, you can use Fit in Window to see the "big picture," then select Actual Size to zoom back to where your cursor is in the text.

> **Tip: Accidental Zooming.** *You've probably had it happen to you already: You select Fit in Window from the View menu, and suddenly you jump to a different page. It's really not as strange as it seems. Fit in Window always fits the current page in the window. But what's the current page? It's the page that is touching the upper-left corner of the document window. If just a tiny bit of the previous page is showing at the top or left of the window, that's the one that will get centered onscreen.*

Zoom tool. You can also use the Zoom tool on the Tool palette for your quick zooming pleasure. Sorry, did I say "quick"? I hardly find clicking in the Tool palette, then in my layout, then back in the Tool palette a "quick" procedure. However, we're in luck because there's a keystroke: On the Macintosh, if you hold down the Control and Shift keys, you get a Zoom In tool; add the Option key, and you get a Zoom Out tool. (In earlier versions, it was simply the Control key; in fact, if you like the old way, you can bring it back in the Input Settings pane of the Preferences dialog box; see "Changing Defaults," later in this chapter.)

In Windows, you have to press both Ctrl and the spacebar to zoom in; Ctrl-Alt-spacebar provides the Zoom Out tool. (If you have a text box selected, make sure you press the Ctrl key before the spacebar, or else you'll type a space character.)

Each time you click on your page with the Zoom tool, QuarkXPress zooms in or out by a particular percentage. The increments that it uses can be controlled in the Tool Preferences dialog box (see "Changing Defaults," later in this chapter).

Keystroke zooming. If I can avoid using the menus, I usually do; they're almost never the most efficient method of working. So when it comes to zooming, I use keystrokes and clicks. Table 2-2 shows the basic keystrokes and keystroke-and-click combinations for zooming in and out.

Table 2-2 Zooming

Press...	To go to or toggle...
Command-1/Ctrl-1	Actual Size
Command-0/Ctrl-0	Fit in Window
Command-Option-0/Ctrl-Alt-1	Fit pasteboard in window
Command-Option-click/Ctrl-Alt-click	Between Actual Size and 200%

Tip: Fit More in Your Window. If you select Fit in Window from the View menu or press Command/Ctrl-zero, QuarkXPress fits the current page to the window. However, if you hold down the Option key while selecting Fit in Window (or press Command-Option-zero or Ctrl-Alt-zero), it zooms to fit the entire width of the pasteboard into the window.

This feature has a fun corollary: If you don't need a big pasteboard around your facing-pages lay-out, you can shrink down its width to 10 percent or 20 percent of the page width (this is a setting in the Preferences dialog box). Now when you press Command-Option-zero (Ctrl-Alt-zero), you get the equivalent of "fit spread in window."

Magnification field. Another of my favorite methods for zooming in and out is by adjusting the View Percent field in the lower-left corner of the project window. Note that when you're in Actual Size, this field shows "100%." Whenever you zoom in or out, this field changes. Well, you can change it yourself by clicking in the field (or highlight the field by pressing Control-V on the Mac or Control-Alt-V in Windows), typing a percentage, and pressing Enter or Return. You can also type T for Thumbnails or M for Maximum (usually 800 percent on the Mac and 692 percent on Windows).

Zoom marquee. There's no doubt that my favorite zooming technique is to hold down the Control key (to get the Zoom tool), and drag a marquee around a specific area (in Windows, press Ctrl-spacebar). When you let go of the mouse button, QuarkXPress zooms into that area at the precise percentage necessary to fit it in the window. (I like to call this "magdrag," for magnification-drag.) So if you're at Actual Size and drag a marquee around one word, QuarkXPress can zoom in to 600 percent and center that word on your screen. You can use this to zoom out, too, by dragging a marquee that's larger than your screen (the screen scrolls along as you drag the marquee), but I don't find this as useful.

Moving Through Pages

In the last section I talked about moving around your page using scrolling and zooming. Because every page in your layout sits on one big pasteboard, these same techniques work for moving around within your layout. You can scroll from one page to another using the scroll bars and the Grabber Hand, and so on. But let's be frank: This is not the fastest way to get around. It might help in moving around a two-page spread, but not for moving around a 200-page book. Instead, there are ways to move by whole pages at a time, or to jump to the page you want.

Extended keyboards. If you have an extended keyboard (I recommend these for serious desktop publishers), you can move one page forward or back by pressing Shift-Page Up or Shift-Page Down (on the Macintosh you can replace the Shift key with the Command key if you like). If you don't have an extended keyboard on the Mac, Control-Shift-K and Control-Shift-L also move one page at a time.

You may find yourself wanting to jump to the very beginning or end of your layout. On a Macintosh, you can press the Shift-Home key or Shift-End (or, on nonextended keyboards on the Mac, press Control-Shift-A or Control-Shift-D). In Windows, press Ctrl-Page Up or Ctrl-Page Down to jump to the first or last page of the layout, respectively.

Moving to a specific page. If you're trying to get to a page somewhere in the middle of your document, there are four methods to get there quickly.

- Double-click the page icon in the Page Layout palette or single-click the page number below the icon (I discuss this palette in more detail in Chapter 4, *Building a Layout*).

- Change the page number field in the lower-left corner of the project window. This is a minor hassle because you have to select the page number and then change it, but it's not too bad.

- Choose a page by clicking on the popup menu next to the page number field in the lower-left corner of the project window and dragging until you get to the page (see Figure 2-15).

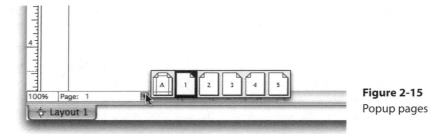

Figure 2-15
Popup pages

- Select Go To from the Page menu (or, better yet, press Command/Ctrl-J). Note that if the page you want to go to is in a differently named section, you have to type the name exactly as it's listed in the lower-right corner of the project window. For instance, if you're using Roman numerals and you want to jump to the fourth page, you have to type "iv." (See more on sections and page numbering in Chapter 4, *Building a Document*, as well as in the next tip.)

> **Tip: Jump to Absolute Page Numbers.** *If you play around with sections and page numbers, you may find yourself in a quagmire when you try to print a page range. For example, let's say your layout begins on page 56 and you want to print the 16th through the 20th pages. You could sit around and try to figure out what numbers to plug in to the Print dialog box's page range fields, or you could just type "+16" and "+20." The plus sign before the number means that the numbers are absolute; the first page is "+1," the second page is "+2," and so on.*
>
> *This is also helpful when moving to a page using Go To page. You can quickly jump to the 20th page by typing "+20."*

Note that for any of the keystrokes I've outlined here, there is a menu item in the Page menu. I think working with a mouse and menus is fast, but there is no doubt that once you start working with keystrokes, moving around your layouts becomes lightning fast.

MANIPULATING YOUR LAYOUT

Okay, now that I've covered how you can move around your layout, let's talk about how you can insert, delete, and move pages. There are three good ways to handle these tasks in QuarkXPress: menu items, thumbnails, and the Page Layout palette. Let's look at each one of these.

Menu Manipulations

As I said much earlier in this chapter, the Page menu holds QuarkXPress's page-manipulation tools. In this section we're primarily interested in the first three menu items: Insert, Delete, and Move. I'm holding off on a discussion of inserting pages until another chapter (see the section on making pages in Chapter 4, *Building a Layout*), so I'll talk about the last two.

Delete. When you choose Delete from the Page menu, QuarkXPress displays the Delete dialog box. This is a simple dialog box asking you which page or pages to delete. If you only want to delete one, just type its number in the From field. If you want to delete consecutive pages, then type the page range in the From and To fields.

Move. If you want to move a page or a range of pages, you can select Move from the Page menu. Here you can specify which page or pages to move, and where to move them (see Figure 2-16). For example, if you want to move pages 15 through 21 to after the last page in your layout, you can type "15" in the first field, "21" in the second field, and click To End of Layout. You also can specify a move to before or after a specific page.

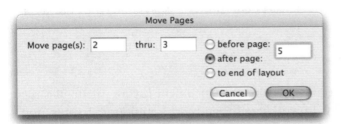

Figure 2-16
The Move Pages dialog box

> ***Tip: Doing It to the End.*** *QuarkXPress is smarter than the average computer program. In fact, it's slowly learning plain English. For example, if you want to delete from one page to the end of the layout, but you don't know what the last page number is, you can type "end" in the Thru field of the Delete dialog box. This also works in the Move Pages dialog box. For instance, you can move from page 15 to the end of the layout by typing "15" and "end" in the fields.*

Thumbnails

You can see a thumbnail view of your layout in the same way as you select any other percentage scaling view: from the View menu or by typing "T" into the Magnification field in the lower-left corner of the project window. Although you can use this to look at your layout as thumbnails (it's like looking at it in 10-percent viewing mode), Thumbnails is actually more useful as a tool for moving pages.

To move a page in Thumbnails mode, select the page and drag it to where you want it. While moving a page around in Thumbnails mode, you'll find the cursor turning into two different icons. The first looks like a minipage. If you let go of the mouse button with this icon displayed, the page is moved, but it's added as a spread. That is, the rest of the pages won't shuffle and reflow (see more about multipage spreads in Chapter 4, *Building a Layout*).

The second icon, a black arrow, appears when you move the cursor directly to the left of or under another page. This arrow means that the page will be placed directly before or after a specific page. Letting go of the mouse button when you have this arrow cursor reflows the pages in the layout. This is the same as moving pages using Move from the Page menu.

> ***Tip: Selecting Multiple Pages.*** *It's easy to select more than one page at a time in Thumbnails mode or in the Page Layout palette. If the pages are consecutive (pages four through nine, for example), click the first page in the range, hold down the Shift key, and click the last page in the range. Every page between the two is selected.*
>
> *You can select nonconsecutive pages (such as pages one, three, and nine) while in Thumbnails mode or in the Page Layout palette by holding down the Command/Ctrl key while clicking on each page.*

Page Layout Palette

The Page Layout palette (this was called the Document Layout palette in earlier versions) is one of the key elements in working efficiently with multipage layouts. You can move pages, delete them, insert new ones, create and apply master pages, and more, with a quick drag of an icon. Let's look at how you can use this palette to delete and move pages.

To open the Page Layout palette, select Show Page Layout from the View menu (see Figure 2-17). For our purposes right now, you need to think about only two parts of the palette: the page icons and the icons in the upper-right corner. I'll get into more advanced uses (applying master pages, for instance) in Chapter 4, *Building a Layout.*

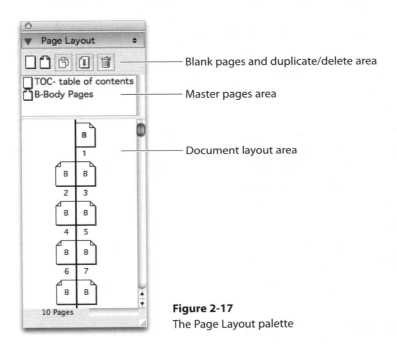

Blank pages and duplicate/delete area

Master pages area

Document layout area

Figure 2-17
The Page Layout palette

Moving pages within the Page Layout palette is just like moving them in Thumbnails mode, except that you can't see what's on the pages. Simply select the page or pages that you want to move, and drag them to their destinations. QuarkXPress uses the same icons here as in Thumbnails mode. That is, the little page icon means that you're creating a spread, and the right and down arrow icons mean that you're moving the pages into the flow (the other pages displace to accommodate the moved page).

Deleting a page with the Page Layout palette is even simpler than deleting a file while on the Mac desktop or Windows Explorer: Just select the page(s) and click the Delete icon (on the Mac, it's the little trash can; in Windows, it's the icon with the "X" through it). However, do note that in QuarkXPress you cannot undo these actions and retrieve a page that you throw away. Obviously, it's worth being extra careful in this area.

Moving Items Between Layouts

You don't have to stop at moving items and pages just within a single layout. You can move them from one layout to another (in the same project or separate projects) faster than you can say, "Maybe it's time to get a larger monitor for my computer."

To move a page item from one layout to another, you must have both layouts open and visible on your screen. This is difficult on small screens. I find the Tile and Split Window features (under the Window menu) useful for this. Then, with the Item tool, select the item you want to move (or hold down the Command/Ctrl key to get the Item tool temporarily), and drag it across.

If you pause between project windows, you may find the first layout starts to scroll. Don't worry, it's just QuarkXPress not realizing that you want to move it all the way into the second layout. Just move the item a little farther and the scrolling should stop. Once you let go of the mouse button, the item is copied over into the new layout. Note that I say "copied." The item is not actually moved; rather, it is copied from one into the other. To get rid of it in the first layout, just delete it (Command/Ctrl-K).

Of course, there is always the old standby method for getting items from one layout to another: Copy and Paste. Here, you want to make sure that you have the Item tool selected while in both layouts, or else XPress won't know that you want to copy or paste the item itself.

Moving Pages Between Layouts

Versions 1 and 2 of QuarkXPress sported a Get Document function, which was extremely useful. First of all, it let you copy whole pages from one layout to another. Second, it let you access pages from a different project without actually opening it (this was often helpful in retrieving corrupted files). Unfortunately, the Get Document feature is long gone.

Taking its place is a feature that lets you actually drag a page from one layout into another, as long as both layouts are in Thumbnails view. (Hold down the Option/Alt key and select Tile to put *all* layouts into Thumbnails mode.) This is especially handy if you like to see the pages that you're copying before you copy them. In fact, Quark's tech support still recommends this as a preferred method for saving projects that are becoming corrupted.

> *Tip: Moving Background Windows. If you're working on a Macintosh and you need to resize and move your project windows in order to drag across page items or even full pages, you might find it helpful to know that you can move a window without actually selecting it. That is, normally, if you click on a window, that window is brought to the front (it becomes active). You can move a window without bringing it to the front by holding down the Command key while you click and drag the bar at its top. Actually, this isn't a QuarkXPress feature; it's a Macintosh feature.*

CHANGING DEFAULTS

Each and every one of you reading this book is different, and you all have different ways of using QuarkXPress. Fortunately, Quark has given you a mess of options for customizing the internal default settings. A *default setting* is a value that indicates a way of doing something; QuarkXPress uses the default value or method unless you specifically choose something else.

For example, the factory default setting for picture and text boxes is that they are created with no border frame around them (see the section on frames, dashes, and stripes in Chapter 3, *Working with Items*). But if you're so inclined, you can modify QuarkXPress so that every text box you create is automatically framed with a two-point line. In this way, you can customize your work environment so that it best suits you.

Default settings range from how guides are displayed on the screen to how QuarkXPress builds small caps characters. On the Macintosh, you can find the Preferences feature under the Application menu (the one labeled "QuarkXPress"). In Windows, you can find the Preferences feature in the Edit menu.

XTensions can add their own preferences to this submenu, as well. For instance, Quark's Type Tricks XTension adds a preference that lets you set defaults for its Fraction and Price feature. Let's take a look at the Preferences dialog box here.

LAYOUT AND APPLICATION PREFERENCES

The Preferences dialog box contains settings that affect the way your layouts and the program act. The dialog box is broken down into many different panes, each of which contains preferences you can set. The first section of panes are application preferences; the middle section are project preferences, and the last section are print layout preferences. The difference is important.

Application preferences affect how XPress works on your particular computer. The settings aren't saved with your layouts, so if you move them to another computer, they may appear slightly different.

Project and print layout preferences only affect the current layout. Even if you have other layouts or documents open at the same time, any change is made to only the one that is active. However, if no documents are open when you change this dialog box, then you are setting new defaults for the whole program, and that change is made to every new layout you create from then on (it doesn't change layouts you've already made). These changes are stored in the XPress Preferences file and are used when creating new documents or layouts.

Let's take a close look at each preference setting in each pane of this dialog box. However, note that I won't cover the Browsers pane here; instead, I'll hold off until Chapter 17, *Going Online with QuarkXPress*, to cover the HTML stuff.

Display Preferences

The first pane, Display, lets you control how your document pages and your images appear onscreen (see Figure 2-18). The controls are slightly different between the Macintosh and Windows versions.

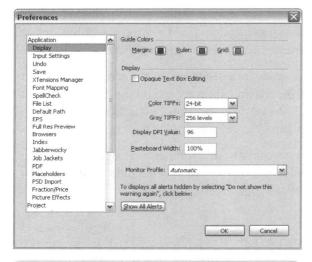

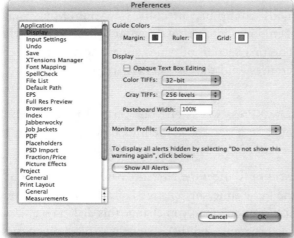

Figure 2-18

The Display pane of the Preferences dialog box (XPress for Windows versus Macintosh)

Guide Colors. The controls at the top of the Display pane let you change the colors of QuarkXPress's three types of guide lines: Margin, Ruler, and Grid (this control is available for both Macintosh and Windows). The Margin guides are the lines that show where the page margins are. The Ruler guides are the guides you can pull out onto the page. And the Grid guides are the lines that the program shows you when you have Show Baseline Grid enabled (see Chapter 6, *Typography*).

Full-screen Documents. Turning on this box lets you zoom windows to fill your entire screen; turning it off leaves room for the Tool and Measurements palettes. I typically leave this turned off, but why should you listen to me? The options are here to make your life easier. This is currently a Macintosh-only feature, as well.

Opaque Text Box Editing. Back in QuarkXPress 3.x, the program always made text boxes opaque when you selected them with the Content tool. In XPress 4, the folks at Quark changed the behavior so that the box was transparent (if it had a background color of None). Some liked it the old way because it let you edit the contents of a box free of any distractions caused by other page elements. Some liked it the new way because they wanted to edit the content of text boxes and see what was behind them at the same time. In XPress 6, Quark gave you a choice: When you turn on the Opaque Text Box Editing checkbox (it is off by default), XPress returns to its old opaque, version 3.x behavior.

Color TIFFs/Gray TIFFs. The Color TIFFs and Gray TIFFs popup menus (these appear on both Macintosh and Windows) let you control how QuarkXPress builds screen previews for TIFF images when you import them. As you'll see in Chapter 10, *Pictures*, a TIFF picture doesn't have a built-in preview, so XPress has to build one for it when you import it. These preferences *only* affect how images look onscreen and on non-PostScript printers (like a desktop inkjet).

In QuarkXPress 3.x and 4.x, Color TIFF was set to 8-bit (256 colors) and Gray TIFF was set to 16 Levels of gray. These settings kept file sizes small and page drawing snappy, but it left users unhappy because image quality was poor. So in XPress 5, the folks at Quark increased the default value for Color TIFF to 32-bit (on the Macintosh it's 32-bit, in Windows it's 24-bit, but they're really pretty much the same thing), and for Gray TIFF to 256 levels of grays. The result: much better-looking pictures on screen, but *much* larger file sizes and sometimes slower performance. This is the main reason that layouts created in QuarkXPress 5 and later are typically much larger in file size than those from version 4.

If you are creating Web layouts with XPress, the 32-bit Color TIFF preference is great. However, for print layouts I tend to change this back to 8-bit. The screen quality isn't as good, but everything else seems to run more smoothly. When I care a lot about image quality (like when I want to adjust a clipping path around an imported image), I turn on the High Res Preview feature (see Chapter 10, *Pictures*).

Pasteboard Width. That pasteboard around a layout's pages is great, but I usually find it a little too large or—depending on the job—occasionally too small. Fortunately, I can control how wide the pasteboard is by specifying a percentage in the Pasteboard Width field. The default value of 100 percent tells QuarkXPress to make each side of the pasteboard the same width as one page in the layout. That is, if you have an 8.5-by-11-inch page, each side of the pasteboard is 8.5 inches wide. Changing the Pasteboard Width to 50 percent makes the pasteboard half that width.

Unfortunately, there's still no way to change the height of the pasteboard, so it's stuck at a half-inch above and below your page. I keep hoping that Quark will change this, but no luck yet.

Show All Alerts. QuarkXPress has a number of alert dialog boxes which pop up from time to time—like the one that appears whenever you press the Printer button in the Print dialog box. Most of these annoying dialog boxes have a checkbox that says "Don't Show This Again." Almost everyone turns this checkbox on, and they never see those alerts again. However, if you click this button in the Display pane of the Preferences dialog box, those alerts will come back. Pretty exciting, huh?

Display DPI Value. Earlier in this chapter, I mentioned that the limitation on how far you could magnify your page on a Windows machine depended on your Display DPI Value. This control is a Windows-only setting (though I have no idea why; Macintosh screen resolution can be as widely variable as that of PCs), and it lets you more closely match your page size in QuarkXPress to your monitor's resolution. Because most PC monitors average around 96 ppi, this is the default value in the Preferences dialog box.

The idea is that if you hold up a physical ruler to the screen, one inch on the ruler should equal (more or less) one inch on QuarkXPress's ruler. If it doesn't you can adjust the Display DPI Value. Larger values make XPress's ruler larger; lower values make XPress's ruler smaller. If you don't care about matching the screen to reality, you can adjust at will (or just leave it alone).

Input Settings Preferences

The Input Settings pane of the Preferences dialog box is a grab bag of options that controls XPress's screen display and what happens when you navigate around your document (see Figure 2-19). Again, these are all Application preferences, so they affect your whole program, not just individual layouts or documents.

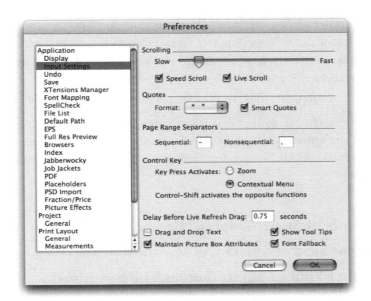

Figure 2-19
The Input Settings pane of the Preferences dialog box

Speed Scroll. Here's a wonderful enhancement to XPress that makes me want to bow down and give thanks in the general direction of Denver (where Quark lives). When Speed Scroll is turned on (it is by default), QuarkXPress automatically greeks the display of pictures, graphics, and blends as you scroll through a layout. Only when you stop scrolling does it take the time to properly display these elements.

This may not sound like a big improvement at first, but if you've died of boredom while scrolling through a long layout with lots of big four-color TIFFs, you'll appreciate how much time Speed Scroll can save you (that is, unless you *like* taking a coffee break while you scroll). I turn this on and leave it on.

Scroll Speed. Yep, now there's Speed Scroll *and* Scroll Speed. It's not confusing, is it? As I discussed earlier in the "Scrolling" section, Scroll Speed controls how fast QuarkXPress scrolls when you use the scroll bars. Note that the default Scroll Speed slider setting is pretty slow. Increasing the speed (by clicking on the right arrow) can make a drastic difference in how quickly you can make your pages (although this won't speed up screen redraw).

Live Scroll. My editor keeps telling me not to be redundant in my writing. And since I already gave my *spiel* about Live Scroll earlier in this chapter (see "Scrolling"), here I'll just say: Yes, this is a great feature, and it's great to have it built right in, but it's nowhere near as cool as the Grabber Hand.

Smart Quotes. This option turns on the Smart Quotes feature and lets you specify which characters will be used for open and closed quotes. Smart Quotes works by looking to the left of the insertion point to determine if an open or closed quote character should go there. If the character to the left is a white space character, such as a spaceband, a tab, or a return, QuarkXPress enters an open single or double quote when you press the ' or " key.

The popup menu lets you choose some alternative quote characters, including various double quotes, Spanish alternatives, and inside and outside guillemet (French quote mark) combinations, which can be useful if you're formatting foreign-language documents (see Figure 2-20).

"This is an example of Smart Quotes," he said.

"This is a different kind of Smart Quotes," he added.

„Here's yet another kind of Smart Quotes," he continued.

«These quotes are called quillements,» he went on.

»So are these, but they're reversed,« he said.

Figure 2-20   Different kinds of Smart Quotes available

The main place where Smart Quotes isn't so smart is when you're typing apostrophes at the beginning of a word—"In late '93," for instance. Watch out for these. (See the tip on getting your quotes straight in Chapter 6, *Typography*, for a lesson on how to type curly and straight quotes quickly.)

> *Tip: Toggling Smart Quotes.* Smart Quotes is really cool if you type a lot in QuarkXPress. However, if you ever want to enter a single or double "neutral" straight quote character, it's a hassle to turn off Smart Quotes first. Instead, hold down the Control key when typing the quote (single or double). When Smart Quotes is on, you get a straight quote; when it's off, you get a curly quote.

Delay Before Live Refresh Drag. Normally, when you click on an object and drag it somewhere on your page, XPress just shows you a gray outline of the item you're moving. If you're performing a quick move, this is probably all you really need. But if you're trying to position something carefully, then you usually need to see the object itself. If you click the mouse button down on top of the object and hold it down for a moment before you drag it, the object flashes quickly. That's your sign that when you drag it, you'll be able to see the picture or the text or whatever.

The Delay Before Live Refresh Drag option on the Input Settings pane lets you control two things. First, the delay field lets you specify how long you need to hold the mouse button down on an object before XPress flips into this mode. You can type anything from 0.1 second (almost instantaneous) to five seconds (why even bother?). I prefer about 0.5 second, but you should play around with it and see what suits you best.

The second option that it controls is Live Refresh. This is a wonderful feature that forces XPress to reflow text as you move objects over it. For example, let's say you're trying to set the width of a text box so that the text flows just perfectly in it. You can click on one of the side handles and wait for a moment for the effect to kick in. The cursor changes to the Live Refresh cursor (it looks like a little starburst). Now the text reflows automatically as you drag the handle.

Page Range Separators. How do you type "from page four through page nine, plus page 12" in the Print dialog box? You use page range separators. The default separators are the hyphen and the comma: "4-9, 12." However, you can change this to any other two symbols you like. I can't think of a good reason to ever alter this preference.

Control Key Activates. By default, you get a context-sensitive menu when you click with the Control key on the Macintosh, and you get the Zoom tool (temporarily) when you Control-Shift-click. You can reverse this behavior in the Input Settings pane of the Preferences dialog box by selecting Zoom in the Control Key Activates section. Old fuddy-duddies like me who want XPress to act like it did back in versions 3.x and 4.x use this feature.

Drag and Drop Text. Drag and Drop Text lets you drag selected text from one place in a text box to another. I cover this in detail in Chapter 5, *Working with Text.*

Show Tool Tips. When the Show Tool Tips option is on (it is, by default) and your cursor hovers over a tool in the Tool palette for a moment, XPress displays a little tag that tells you the name of the tool. It seems like every piece of software on the market has to have this feature these days. Maybe it's useful in other software, but it's annoying in XPress. I turn this off and leave it off. (Obviously, it doesn't hurt to leave it on, though.)

Maintain Picture Box Attributes. With this option turned on, you can maintain picture box attributes such as offset and scaling when replacing pictures in an existing picture box by either choosing Import from the File menu or copying/pasting. When this preference is turned on, the Maintain Picture Box Attributes option in the Import dialog box is automatically enabled.

Font Fallback. When you copy/paste text containing special characters that are not available in the current font you are using, turn on this option to allow QuarkXPress to locate and display the characters with another active font. The downside to using this feature is that Quark may locate a font that doesn't work well with your design. I prefer to handle font issues myself; therefore I turn off this option.

Undo Preferences

The Undo pane of the Preferences dialog box lets you specify the number of actions XPress remembers. It also lets you choose a keyboard shortcut for the Redo command. (When will Quark make all keyboard shortcuts editable?) I covered Undo Preferences earlier in this chapter.

Save Preferences

What gets saved, when is it saved, and where does it get saved? Those are the questions answered on the Save pane of the Preferences dialog box (see Figure 2-21). Most of these features are discussed elsewhere in the book, so I won't cover them in detail here.

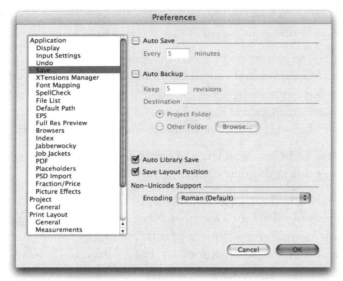

Figure 2-21
The Save pane of the Preferences dialog box

Auto Save and Auto Backup. Auto Save ensures that you don't lose too much work because of a system crash or other unexpected event. Auto Backup helps you carry out the chore of keeping backups by making copies of your documents when you save them. Both of these are covered in detail in "Saving Projects," earlier in this chapter.

Auto Library Save. I discuss libraries and how to use them in the next chapter, *Working with Items*. However, one thing you should know up front: Libraries are only saved when you close or quit QuarkXPress—unless you enable Auto Library Save. This makes XPress save the library every time you add an item to it. It slows down production a little, but it's worth it as a safety measure.

Fortunately, in XPress 7, Auto Library Save is turned on by default. Now the only time I turn it off is when I need to add a lot of items to a library at the same time (so it doesn't stop to save the file between each item). Then I turn it right back on.

Save Layout Position. When Save Layout Position is on (it is, by default), QuarkXPress saves some extra information with your layout: where the window was when you saved the file, what view percentage you were at, and how large the project window was. I leave this option turned on most of the time, but I sure wish it did more, like remember what page I was on when I last left the layout, and even where on the page I was zoomed in. Oh well.

Non-Unicode Support. This option allows you to choose an encoding preference for non-unicode text. The encoding type determines the byte sequence that is used to display each glyph in the text. The default is Roman, but you can choose the appropriate encoding type when working with international text. Options include Cyrillic, Central European, Greek, and Turkish.

XTensions Manager Preferences

The XTensions Manager pane only offers one control: Show XTensions Manager at Startup (see Figure 2-22). This lets you specify the conditions on which you want the XTensions Manager dialog box to appear upon launching XPress. You do have three choices within this control, though.

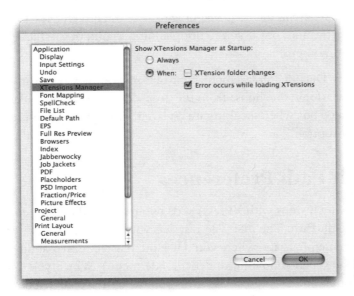

Figure 2-22
The XTensions Manager pane

- The default, "When Error occurs while loading XTensions," tells XPress to open the dialog box if something goes wrong with an XTension at launch time; for instance, if it's an old XTension and is going to cause trouble with this version of XPress.

- The feature called "When XTension folder changes" tells XPress to open the dialog box whenever it notices that you've added or removed an XTension from the XTension folder. I leave this turned off; after all, if I added or removed an XTension, I probably did it for a good reason.

- The Always option is pretty self-explanatory: Every time you launch XPress, the dialog box appears.

Font Mapping Preferences

QuarkXPress 7 contains a new Font Mapping preference that allows you to control what happens when you open a layout containing fonts that are not currently activated on your system. The best option would be to use third-party font management software that features font auto activation, such as Suitcase Fusion for Mac or Suitcase for Windows (both by Extensis). However, if you prefer, you can set up font replacement "rules" to let QuarkXPress handle this, albeit to a limited degree.

Font replacement rules can be applied by choosing a replacement font in the Missing Fonts dialog box and clicking the Save as Rule button. Missing fonts without rules are handled using the preferences chosen here in the Font Mapping pane of the Preferences dialog box. It's not as useful as auto activation, but if you're not planning to output the file, it can be a simple solution to a common problem.

If you turn on the Specify Default Replacement Font option, XPress will substitute any missing fonts with whatever font you choose from the drop-down list. If you'd like to display the Missing Fonts dialog box when the fonts are replaced, turn off the Do Not Display Missing Fonts Dialog Box option.

File List and Default Path Preferences

The Deja Vu XTension (which ships with XPress) adds two panes to the Preferences dialog box: File List and Default Path. The first, File List, lets you specify how many recently used documents XPress remembers and where you'd like them listed (either at the bottom of the File menu or in the Open submenu, under the File menu). Which you choose is entirely up to you and your aesthetic. XPress also gives you the option of alphabetizing the names and displaying the full file path (the folders in which the file is nested) rather than just the file name. I generally increase the number of files to 5 or 6, but I leave the other settings alone.

The Default Path pane lets you specify default folders (or "directories," if you prefer that word) for four different dialog boxes: Open, Save/Save As, Import Text, and Import Picture. These features are really helpful when you're working on a long project in which all the text is in one folder, all the pictures are in another folder, and you're constantly going to be opening and saving files from a specific folder. Once you've set these in the Preferences dialog box, XPress always brings up these folders first; then, on the occasions that you need a picture or text from somewhere else, you can navigate to it manually.

The problem is that the Default Path settings are application preferences rather than layout preferences, so if you have two or more projects you're working on at the same time, this doesn't really help you much.

EPS Preferences

Also new to QuarkXPress 7 is the EPS preference pane. The setting you choose from the Preview drop-down list controls what is displayed when you import a photo or graphic that is saved in the EPS (Encapsulated PostScript) format. Choose Embedded to display the preview image that was embedded when the file was saved from its native application (such as Adobe Illustrator or Photoshop). Choose Generate to allow QuarkXPress to create a new preview image for you.

The Mac OS X version of XPress allows you to specify the amount of memory it should use when generating preview images. The default Virtual Memory value is 100 MB, but you can increase it to as much as 1024 or decrease it to as little as 32.

Full Res Preview Preferences

While I cover the Full Res Preview feature fully in Chapter 10, *Pictures*, here's the quick low-down version: The first time you turn on Full Resolution from the Preview Resolution submenu (under the Item menu), the program writes a cache file to disk—the next time you turn it on for a picture, XPress reads the cache file, which is faster than recreating the high-res version. The Full Res Preview pane of the Preferences dialog box lets you control how the program handles these cache files—where they reside and how much disk space you'll allow them to take up—as well as under what circumstances XPress should actually display the full-res previews.

Index Preferences

The Index pane of the Preferences dialog box lets you fine-tune the look of your index. I cover indexing in detail in Chapter 9, *Long Documents*.

Job Jackets Preferences

The Job Jackets feature in XPress 7 allows you to test your layouts for compliance with pre-defined output rules and specifications, such as whether or not a layout should contain spot colors. The preferences in the Job Jackets pane let you control when (see Figure 2-23). Under Evaluate Layout, select when you'd like to test the layout: On Open, On Save, On Output, or On Close. Note that you can turn on one or all of these options if you like.

The default system location for job jackets is in the My Documents folder, but you can choose a different location by turning on the Other Folder option and clicking the Browse button to specify where the file should be saved.

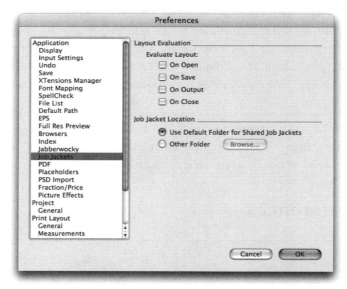

Figure 2-23
The Job Jackets pane of the Preferences dialog box

PDF Preferences

The PDF pane of the Preferences dialog box controls how PDF files are created when you choose Export Layout as PDF from the Export submenu (under the File menu) (see Figure 2-24 and Chapter 17, *Going Online with QuarkXPress*).

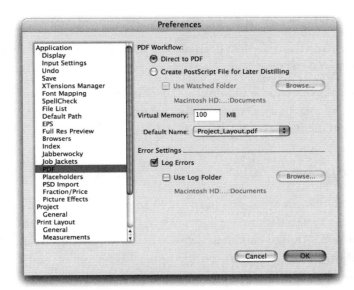

Figure 2-24
The PDF pane of the Preferences dialog box

PDF Workflow. If you make PDF files only occasionally, you'll probably be happy leaving Workflow set to Direct to PDF. This tells XPress to write the PostScript to disk, then immediately use its built-in Jaws software to distill the file into a PDF file.

On the other hand, if you make a lot of PDF files or you want to use Acrobat Distiller for some reason, it's usually faster to just let XPress write the PostScript to disk and then distill all those files later, when you take a lunch break. In that case, choose Create PostScript File for Later Distilling. One other option: If you use Distiller's Watched Folder feature (which automatically distills any PostScript file that appears in a particular folder), then you should turn on the Use Watched Folder checkbox in XPress's Preferences dialog box and direct XPress to that folder (click the Select button). That "watched folder" could even be on a server somewhere.

Default Name. I cover all the details of the PDF Export Options dialog box in Chapter 17, *Going Online with QuarkXPress*, so suffice it to say here that you can change the default naming convention here in the PDF pane of the Preferences dialog box.

Error Settings. By enabling the Log Errors option, you can choose to create a log file that describes any errors that occur when exporting to PDF. You can also choose to store log files in a specific location on your system. To do so, turn on the Use Log Folder option and click Browse to specify where the files should be saved.

Placeholders Preferences

QuarkXPress 7 allows you to synchronize text to an outside XML source using placeholder text. The options in the Placeholders pane control how the placeholders appear in your layout.

You can use the Color buttons to choose the display colors for text placeholders and text node placeholders in the layout. Apply a shade percentage to each color by choosing one from the Shade drop-down menus or by entering a percentage in each field.

PSD Import Preferences

Previews for imported PSD images are stored in the PSD Import Cache folder, which is located in the QuarkXPress Preferences folder. However, if the cache folder starts to take up a lot of space on your disk, you can choose to save the previews in a different location, such as an external hard drive. To do so, turn on the Other Folder option and click the Browse button to specify where the files should be saved.

To limit the storage capacity for the cache folder in any location (default or other), enter a value (from 5 to 4000 MB) in the Maximum Cache Folder Size field. To empty the cache and start fresh, click the Clear Cache button.

Fraction/Price Preferences

The Type Tricks XTension adds a pane to the Preferences dialog box which lets you control how it builds "automatic" fractions and prices. I cover this in more depth in Chapter 6, *Typography*.

Picture Effects Preferences

The default location for saving and loading Picture Effects presets is in the QuarkXPress Preferences folder; however, you can specify a different location by turning on the Other Folder option in the Picture Effects preferences pane. Click the Browse button to specify where you'd like the presets saved on your system.

Project General Preferences

In QuarkXPress 7 there are now two General panes in the Preferences dialog box: one under Project and one under Default Print Layout. Changes made to the settings in this pane will only affect the project that is currently open. If no projects are open, then all newly created projects will apply these settings.

Auto Picture Import. Picture management is an important topic in QuarkXPress. Auto Picture Import lets you automatically reimport pictures that have changed on disk since the last time you saved the document (see Figure 2-25 and the section on picture usage in Chapter 10, *Pictures*). Keep in mind that this is a Project preference and applies to all of the layouts contained in a project.

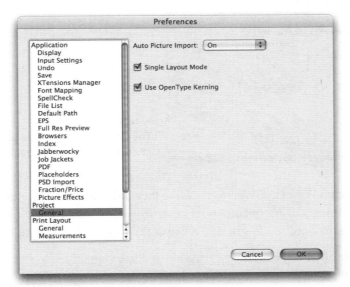

Figure 2-25
The (Project) General pane of the Preferences dialog box

Single Layout Mode. If you find that you rarely include more than one layout in a project, you should turn on the Single Layout Mode option to make file naming easier in XPress. Doing so means having to name only one file (the project) rather than naming both a project and a layout.

Use OpenType Kerning. XPress 7 now features full OpenType support. One of the features of working with OpenType fonts is the ability to use the default kerning values that are included in the font. To automatically apply these values to all layouts, you must enable the Use OpenType Kerning option. This overrides any kerning settings specified in the Kerning Table Edit dialog box, but additional kerning can still be applied manually using the Kern command, which is located under the Style menu.

Default Print Layout General Preferences

The Default Print Layout General pane of the Preferences dialog box is the catchall, with controls ranging from how guides appear to what happens when you reapply master pages to pages (see Figure 2-26). Some of these preferences have been part of QuarkXPress for 15 years!

Figure 2-26
The (Print Layout) General pane
of the Preferences dialog box

Note that these are all Default Print Layout preferences, so they only affect the currently open layout (or all future documents, if no document is currently open). I cover just about all of these in other places in the book, so forgive me if I rush through their descriptions here.

Greek Text Below. Computer screens aren't very good at displaying tiny text, and it often takes too long to display it anyway. Greek Text Below lets you turn this text "off" so you just see gray lines where the text should be (see more on text greeking in Chapter 6, *Typography*).

Greek Pictures. Tired of seeing all those pictures on your screen? Slow screen redraw got you down? Turn 'em off with the Greek Pictures control (see the section on greeking and suppression in Chapter 10, *Pictures*).

Guides. When you pull a guide out onto your page (see the section on guides and rulers in the next chapter), this control determines whether it sits on top of your page objects or below them. (Hint: Leave this set to In Front.) The Snap Distance is how close an object has to get before it snaps to the guide when Snap to Guides is turned on in the View menu.

Hyperlinks. Don't like the default magenta and blue colors that XPress uses to mark where anchors and hyperlinks are? You can change their onscreen appearance in the

Hyperlinks section of the Preferences dialog box. This is as useful as changing your guide color—that is, it's only useful if you are allergic to the colors. Otherwise, leave them alone. I cover hyperlinks and anchors in detail in Chapter 17, *Going Online with QuarkXPress*.

Master Page Items. QuarkXPress may reapply a master page to your document page on various occasions. This control lets you choose what happens to the master page items in these cases (see more on master pages and layout pages in Chapter 4, *Building a Layout*).

Framing. You can place borders around text boxes and picture boxes, but do you want the frame to sit on the outside or the inside of the box? (See the section on frames, dashes, and stripes in Chapter 3, *Working with Items*.)

Auto Page Insertion. When you import a large amount of text into an automatic text box, XPress may add pages to your document. Here's where you can control this behavior. (See more about automatic page insertion in Chapter 4, *Building a Layout*.)

Auto Constrain. If you've never used Auto Constrain, don't start now. It sets up parent/child relationships between boxes that are drawn inside boxes, and it harkens back to the very early days of QuarkXPress (see more on constraining in the next chapter).

Measurements Preferences

The Measurements pane of the Preferences dialog box (see Figure 2-27) lets you control the rulers and measurements in your document.

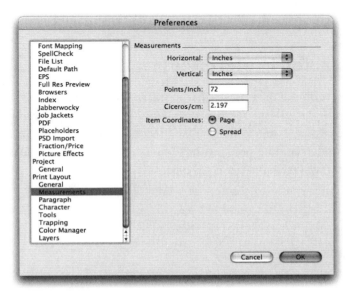

Figure 2-27
The Measurements pane of the Preferences dialog box

Horizontal Measure and Vertical Measure. These two popup menus let you tell XPress what measurement system you like using (see more on guides and rulers in Chapter 3, *Working with Items*). Remember that even if these popup menus are set to inches, you can always specify measurements in picas or centimeters or any other system.

Points/Inch. Somebody, sometime, somewhere along the line, decided that PostScript should measure 72 points to an inch. However, as it turns out, printers and graphic designers have always measured just *over* 72 points to the inch. QuarkXPress, being the power-rich program it is, gives you the choice of how you want to measure points. If you have a burning need to work in a traditional measurement setting, you can change the value of the Points/Inch field in the Preferences dialog box to 72.27. I tend toward progress and think that people should just throw out their old rulers and embrace a new standard. Thus, I leave it at 72 points per inch.

Ciceros/Cm. A cicero, in case you're like me (*Americanus stupidus*), is a measurement in the Didot system, used primarily in France and other continental European countries. Just as a pica equals 12 points, the cicero equals 12 points. The difference? Differently sized points. A Didot point equals 0.01483 inch instead of the American-British 0.01383 inch. Anyway, the only really important thing about all this is that QuarkXPress defaults to 2.1967 ciceros per centimeter. This is close enough to a traditional cicero (you can do the math).

Note that if you want to work with Didot points more directly, you should probably also change Points/Inch, above, to 67.43.

Item Coordinates. The ruler that runs across the top of your page can measure the width of your page or the entire spread (see the section on guides and rulers in the next chapter).

Paragraph and Character Preferences

I spend a good long time covering all the features that appear on the Paragraph and Character tabs in Chapter 6, *Typography*, so please forgive me if I punt on their descriptions here. Suffice it to say that these two tabs offer controls that affect how QuarkXPress handles its typography, and without understanding (and setting) some of these features, you're going to bang your head against a wall trying to get good type.

Tools Preferences

The features on the Tools pane of the Preferences dialog box can really help you reduce the monotony of page layout (see Figure 2-28). Perhaps every time you draw a line you change its thickness to 0.5 point. Or perhaps every time you create a text box, you set the Text Inset value to zero or the background color to None. Instead of making the change hundreds of times, just make it once by changing the way the various tools in the Tool palette work.

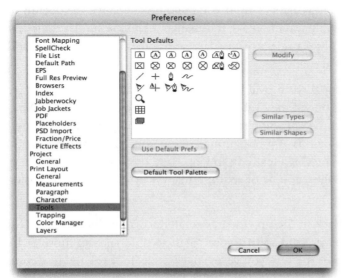

Figure 2-28
The Tools pane of the Preferences dialog box

You can use the settings on the Tools pane to change the default settings for any of the item-creation tools on the Tool palette, plus the Zoom tool (I discuss each of these tools and how best to use them in the next chapter, *Working with Items*). To change a default for an item-creation tool (the tools that create picture boxes, text boxes, or lines), select the tool's icon in the list of tools along the left side of the pane, and then click the Modify button.

Let's take a look at what each button on this pane does.

Modify. When you click the Modify button, XPress opens a dialog box that looks very similar to the Modify dialog box you normally get in QuarkXPress (if you're not familiar with the Modify dialog box, see more about it in Chapter 3, *Working with Items*). There are, however, several differences. For instance, there's no Clipping tab because you can't control the default settings for picture clipping—it's always an object-by-object control. Also, fields such as Origin Across and Origin Down are grayed out because those are always going to be different for every box you make.

Use Default Prefs. If you've made changes to a tool's default preferences, by using Modify, you can return the preferences to the factory settings by selecting the tool from the Tool Defaults list and clicking Use Default Prefs. For example, if you have to make 35 text boxes, each with a yellow background and a cyan frame, you could change the Rectangular Text Box tool to have these settings. Then make the 35 boxes, and then reset the tool by coming back to the Tools pane and clicking this button.

Similar Types. If you select any of the text box creation tools and click the Similar Types button, XPress highlights *all* the text box creation tools (the rectangular one, the oval one, the freehand one, and so on). Chances are if you're going to change the default setting of a line or a box, you'll probably want to make the change for all the similar tools at the same time. Note that you can always select or deselect additional tools from the Tools list by Command/Ctrl-clicking on them.

Similar Shapes. You want all your oval boxes to have a border, but not your rectangular ones? No problem. Select one of the oval box tools and then click the Similar Shapes button. Now when you click Modify, you're changing the settings for just the oval boxes. Note that the Modify dialog box is pretty limited when you select multiple tools that are of different types. For instance, if a text box and a picture box are selected when you click Modify, you can only change a couple of settings, like the box's Background color and its Frame size and style.

Default Tool Palette. Back in the tip "Enlarge or Reduce Your Tool Palette," I told you how you could move tools around so that your palette would take up more or less space onscreen. If you ever tire of the way you've arranged your Tool palette, just come to the Tools pane of the Preferences dialog box and click the Default Tool Palette button. QuarkXPress resets the tools to their original state.

> **Tip: Get to Those Tool Preferences Quickly.** As you probably can tell, I do almost anything to avoid actually making a selection from a menu. I just find that other methods are faster for me, and they should be for you, too. For example, you can jump to the Tool Preferences dialog box by double-clicking on a tool in the Tool palette. This automatically highlights the tool you chose, and you're ready to make your change.

Trapping Preferences

Trapping is a complicated issue that can compensate for errors made when printing colors on a printing press. I'm going to skip the features you can find in the Trapping pane of the Preferences dialog box because I discuss them at length in Chapter 14, *Color*.

Color Manager

The Color Manager pane is where you can specify color management settings in XPress. You can set up the color profiles you want to use for RGB and CMYK colors, and tell the program whether to color manage what you see onscreen (called "soft proofing"). I cover these settings in detail in the color management section of Chapter 14, *Color*.

Layers Preferences

The Layers pane lets you manage how objects on your page stack up, print, and display onscreen (see more on the Layers palette in Chapter 3, *Working with Items*). The default settings for each new layer in your layout can be controlled here in the Layers pane of the Preferences dialog box (see Figure 2-29).

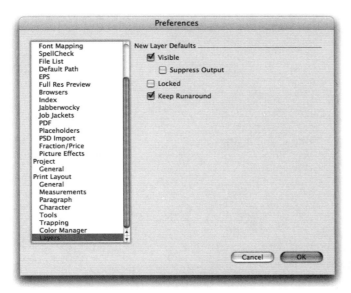

Figure 2-29
The Layers pane of the Preferences dialog box

QUARKXPRESS FROM ZERO TO SIXTY

QuarkXPress is an incredibly complex program that lets you create in minutes what it would take hours to do using more traditional methods. Its saving grace is the graphical user interface (GUI, or "gooey"), which offers a user-friendly method of navigating around your document and making changes. We've just begun looking at the myriad of features in QuarkXPress, but with these basics, you'll be up and running in no time.

In the next chapter we take another step further, exploring the tools that QuarkXPress offers, how best to use them, and how to manipulate the various text boxes and lines that you can create on your pages.

CHAPTER THREE

Working with Items

Have you noticed that we typically identify people's professions by the tools they use? I have only to mention some tool, and a vocation comes to mind: A hammer and nails. A cold stethoscope. A blackboard and chalk. A printing press. We don't think of a hairdresser as standing around waving his or her arms but, rather, wielding a pair of scissors or a razor.

Everyone practicing a trade has a toolbox with which they must make a living, and you and I are no different. Our toolbox is our computer—or, more specifically, QuarkXPress—and the tools inside the box are the subject of this chapter. Like all tools, these take some time to learn, and it's not until you really start using them regularly that you begin to learn their secrets.

In the last chapter I talked primarily about QuarkXPress's general interface: this does this, that does that. Now my emphasis shifts toward the practical. Let's look at each tool on the Tool palette in turn.

ITEMS AND CONTENTS

If you only learn one thing from this chapter, it should be the difference between items and contents. This is a concept some people find difficult to understand, but it is really pretty simple. Moreover, the concept of items and contents is central to working efficiently in QuarkXPress.

Let's take it from the beginning. In order to put text on a page, you must place it in a text box. To put a graphic image on a page, you must place it in a picture box. A text box acts as a sort of corral that holds all the words. There's almost no way a word can get outside the bounds of a text box. A picture box acts as a sort of window through which you can see a picture. In both cases, the content of the box is different from the box itself.

Boxes are *items*. What goes inside them is *content*. Similarly, a line is an item, and the text you place on it is content. You can modify either one, but you need to use the correct tool at the correct time.

Item tool. The Item tool (or "Pointer tool," though sometimes it's called by its technical name, "the pointy-thingy"), see Figure 3-1, is the first tool on the Tool palette. It's used for selecting and moving items (picture and text boxes, rules, and so on). You can use the Item tool by either choosing it from the Tool palette or by holding down the Command/Ctrl key while any other tool is selected (though you can't select or work with multiple items with this Command key trick). I discuss all the things you can do with items later in this chapter in "Manipulating Items."

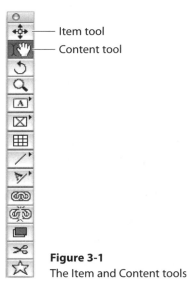

Figure 3-1
The Item and Content tools

Content tool. The second tool on the Tool palette is the Content tool (sometimes called the "Hand tool"). This tool is used for adding, deleting, or modifying the contents of a text or picture box or a text path. Note that its palette icon consists of a text-insertion mark and a hand. When you have selected this tool from the Tool palette, XPress turns the cursor into one of these icons, depending on what sort of box you have highlighted (as we see in Chapter 10, *Pictures*, the hand is for moving images around in a picture box).

> **Tip: Opaque versus Transparent Backgrounds.** *In the good old days, QuarkXPress always made text and picture boxes opaque when you selected them with the Content tool. For some, this was always annoying because you couldn't change the content in a box and see what was behind the box at the same time. Other people thought this was a great system because it let you edit the contents of a box free of distractions caused by other page elements.*

In version 4 the first group won, and when you selected the Content tool, boxes with a background of None (that is, they're transparent) remained transparent. Fortunately, now you have the option of either behavior: The default works like XPress 4, but if you turn on the Opaque Text Box Editing checkbox in the Display panel of the Preferences dialog box (Command-Option-Shift-Y or Ctrl-Alt-Shift-Y), XPress behaves like it did in earlier versions.

> **Tip: Blurring Lines Between Tools.** *Apparently a lot of people had difficulty remembering which tool—Item or Content—to use for certain tasks, so the folks at Quark loosened the reins a little. You can now perform several tasks you could never do in QuarkXPress 3.*
>
> - *You can import pictures into picture boxes when the Item tool is selected.*
> - *You can change various attributes of pictures using the Style menu and the Measurements palette when the Item tool is selected.*
> - *When you have the Content tool selected, you can select multiple objects by Shift-clicking on them or by dragging a marquee around them (see "Selecting Items," below).*
>
> *Of course, the people who were most upset by these changes were trainers, consultants, and writers. Most people who use XPress daily hardly think about these changes, which just make life a little easier.*
>
> *Note that almost all the other restrictions for these two tools remain: You still need to use the Content tool to import or edit text and to move pictures around within the picture box.*

Lines and Arrows

The Tool palette contains four tools to draw lines and arrows on your page. To be precise, you really only draw lines, but those lines can be styled in several fashions, and they can have arrowheads and tailfeathers. You can create a line with any thickness between 0.001 point and 864 points (that's more than 11 inches thick), at any angle, and apply various styles and colors to it. Like boxes, you can view and change these attributes in the Modify dialog box and the Measurements palette.

Two of the tools are based on Bézier curves, and I discuss them in "Bézier Boxes and Lines," later in this chapter.

The Diagonal Line tool can make a line at any angle. If you hold down the Shift key while dragging out the line, you can constrain the line to 45 or 90 degrees. The Orthogonal tool is restricted to creating horizontal and vertical rules.

Line weight (thickness). Since line thickness is centered on the line, if you specify a 6-point line, 3 points fall on each side of the line.

Tip: Don't Use Hairlines. You have the option to select Hairline when choosing a line thickness. Don't. Traditionally, a hairline is the thinnest possible line you can print. On a low-resolution desktop printer, this is pretty thin, but on an imagesetter it's often too small to be seen. When you print your layout, QuarkXPress actually replaces hairlines with 0.125-point rules so you don't get caught in this trap.

Table 3-1 Changing line weight

To...	Press...
Increase weight by preset amount	Command-Shift-period *or* Ctrl-Shift-period
Increase weight by one point	Command-Shift-Option-period *or* Ctrl-Alt-Shift-period
Decrease weight by preset amount	Command-Shift-comma *or* Ctrl-Shift-comma
Decrease weight by one point	Command-Shift-Option-comma *or* Ctrl-Alt-Shift-comma

It's always better to specify the thickness of your lines rather than rely on a program to do it.

In addition to color, tint, and weight, you can choose one of 11 different line styles and one of six endcap combinations from two popup menus in the Modify dialog box, the Style menu, or the Measurements palette (see Figure 3-2). There are six different stripes (multiple parallel lines) and four dashes (lines with gaps). I discuss how to make your own styles in "Frames, Dashes, and Stripes," later in this chapter.

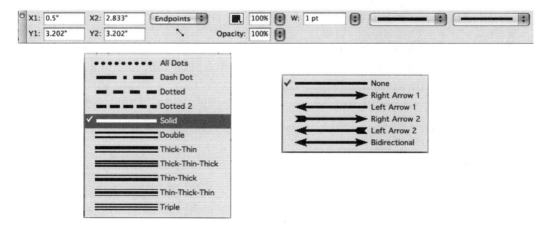

Figure 3-2 Line styles

The endcap styles come down to either those with arrowheads and tailfeathers or those without them. You can't edit the style of these endcaps, so you're stuck with what's built into the program.

Selecting Items

The most basic action you can take with a page item in QuarkXPress is to select it. To select an item itself, you generally need to use the Item tool. To select the contents of a picture or text box, use the Content tool.

You can select more than one item at a time with either the Item or the Content tool. However, the Content tool acts just like the Item tool when more than one item is selected (the cursor changes to the Item tool cursor). There are two ways to select multiple items: Shift-clicking and dragging a marquee.

Shift-click. You can select multiple items by Shift-clicking on them with either the Item or Content tool. If you have more than one item selected and you want to deselect one, you can toggle between them by Shift-clicking again.

> *Tip: Grab Down Deep. There are plenty of times I've found I need to reach through one or more objects on my page and grab a box or line that's been covered up. Moving everything on top is a real hassle. Instead, you can select through page items to get hold of objects that are behind them. Hold down the Command-Option-Shift (Ctrl-Alt-Shift) keys while clicking with either the Item or Content tool to select the object one layer down. The second click selects the object on the next layer down, and so on.*

Marquee. By dragging with the Item tool, you can select more than one item in one fell swoop. This is called dragging a *marquee* because QuarkXPress draws a dotted line around the area you're dragging over. Every picture box, text box, and line that falls within this marqueed area gets selected, even if the marquee touches it only slightly.

Dragging a marquee out with the Item tool to select multiple objects is fast and effective, and it picks up everything in its path. However, sometimes it picks up things you don't want. For example, if you have an automatic text box on your page and place some picture boxes on it, dragging a marquee across the page to select the picture boxes will also select the text box. You may not notice this at first, but if you group the selection or start dragging it, you'll be taking the text box along too. This spells havoc (press Command/Ctrl-Z to undo the last action).

So, just a quick lesson from people who've been there: Watch out for what you select and group. If you select more than you want, remember, you can deselect items by holding down the Shift key and clicking on them.

Tip: Deselecting En Masse. To deselect one or more objects, you typically need to click a white area where there are no other objects. However, there's a faster way: You can deselect every selected page item in one stroke by pressing Tab when the Item tool is selected. I find this really helpful when I'm zoomed in on the page and can't tell what's selected and what isn't. When you have the Content tool selected, the Tab key means something different: If a text box is selected, the Tab key types a tab character. But if you've selected more than one object, the Content tool acts just like the Item tool, so the Tab key deselects every one of them.

Tip: Select All. There's a third way to select more than one object on your page at a time. If you want to select all the page items, you can press Command/Ctrl-A. This only works with the Item tool: When the Content tool is selected, Command/Ctrl-A means "select all the text in a text box."

ITEM-CREATION TOOLS

Now it's time to start laying out some pages. There are five kinds of items you can put on your page: text boxes, picture boxes, contentless boxes, lines, and text paths. I spend much of the rest of the book discussing how to put content inside these objects and what to do with the content once it's there, so I'll spend some time now exploring the items themselves, how to make them, and how to edit them for your needs.

One of the biggest changes in QuarkXPress 7 is in how you access and use item-creation tools. Instead of hiding them away, the programmers at Quark have crated a variable tool palette at the bottom of the XPress window. The tools available in the dialog box change according to the object you select. It makes life a lot easier for everyone.

But the basic way you select a tool remains the same, so there is really very little to relearn. What you will come to realize is that the tool functions are just much easier to modify and use most effectively.

All of the old "modify" dialog boxes are still there if you want to use them, but in QuarkXPress 7 the variable palette puts all of those controls right on your desktop. When you create a text box, for example, the control palette is populated with controls for text, like font and paragraph modifications and so on. When you hover your mouse over the control palette, up pop more control tabs. For every item creation tool, (See Figure 3-3), there is a distinct control palette, and the only thing you need to do to change palettes is select a new tool. It's definitely one of the best changes the folks at Quark have made in this new release. You might find you never need to use the Modify boxes again. But we'll still tell you all about how to use them.

In this section, I discuss the various tools you can use to create page items.

Note that because the Bézier drawing tools have their own set of problems and solutions, I'm going to hold off on discussing them until the next section.

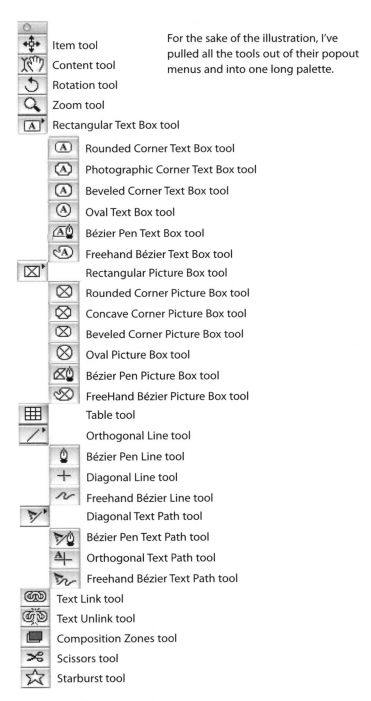

For the sake of the illustration, I've pulled all the tools out of their popout menus and into one long palette.

Item tool
Content tool
Rotation tool
Zoom tool
Rectangular Text Box tool
Rounded Corner Text Box tool
Photographic Corner Text Box tool
Beveled Corner Text Box tool
Oval Text Box tool
Bézier Pen Text Box tool
Freehand Bézier Text Box tool
Rectangular Picture Box tool
Rounded Corner Picture Box tool
Concave Corner Picture Box tool
Beveled Corner Picture Box tool
Oval Picture Box tool
Bézier Pen Picture Box tool
FreeHand Bézier Picture Box tool
Table tool
Orthogonal Line tool
Bézier Pen Line tool
Diagonal Line tool
Freehand Bézier Line tool
Diagonal Text Path tool
Bézier Pen Text Path tool
Orthogonal Text Path tool
Freehand Bézier Text Path tool
Text Link tool
Text Unlink tool
Composition Zones tool
Scissors tool
Starburst tool

Figure 3-3 The item-creation tools

Tip: Keeping Your Tools Around. After you use a tool (any tool other than the Zoom tool), the Tool palette automatically reverts back to either the Content or the Item tool (depending on which of the two you last used). This becomes a hassle if you want to use the same tool again. Instead, you can hold down the Option/Alt key as you select a tool. The tool remains selected until you choose another one.

Making Boxes

Prior to Quark XPress 6, when you wanted a box, you had to specify clearly what kind of box it was—a text box or a picture box—and you had to pick a different tool to create each. And that was it; there was no switching once you had drawn the box. What's more, there were a slew of tools for making different-shaped picture boxes and only one (rectangular) for making text boxes.

But life is better now. XPress offers all the same tools for both text boxes and picture boxes, and although you still have to pick either text or picture when drawing a box on your page, you can now switch from picture to text and back again. There's even a contentless box, which I talk about in just a little bit.

Creating a box is simple: Choose one of the box tools from the Tool palette, and then click and drag on your page. You can see exactly how large your box is by watching the width and height values on the Measurements palette. Note that you can keep the box square (or circular, if you're using the Oval Text Box tool or the Oval Picture Box tool) by holding down the Shift key while dragging.

All boxes—as items—have a number of basic attributes you can display and change.

- Position on the page
- Size (height and width)
- Background Color
- Corner Radius
- Box angle and skew
- Suppress Printout
- Frame size and Style

Of course, text boxes and picture boxes each have a few of their own characteristics, as well, and the Measurements palette and Modify dialog box both change to accommodate these differences.

- Columns (text box only)

- Text inset (text box only)

- Text angle and skew (text box only)

- Picture angle and skew (picture box only)

- Suppress Picture Printout (picture box only)

Let's take a quick look at some of these box attributes. I don't cover them all in this section, but don't worry; I cover them all by the time the chapter is through.

There are several other items in the Modify dialog box and the Measurements palette, too—for instance, the scale of pictures, text runaround, and so on. I hold off discussing these until later in the book, mostly in Chapter 6, *Typography*, Chapter 10, *Pictures*, and Chapter 12, *Text Meets Graphics*.

> **Tip: That Ol' Modify Dialog Box.** *I use the Modify dialog box for text boxes, picture boxes, lines, and text paths so often that I'm glad to have some variance in how I get to it. You can open the Modify dialog box for a page element in several ways (see Figure 3-4).*

- Select the item with either the Content or the Item tool and choose Modify from the Item menu. This is for people who get paid by the hour.

- Select the item with either the Content or the Item tool and press Command/Ctrl-M. This is great if both hands are on the keyboard.

- Control-click/right-click to display a context-sensitive popup menu in which you can choose Modify.

- Double-click on the page element with the Item tool. (Remember, you can hold down the Command/Ctrl key to temporarily work with the Item tool.) This is my favorite method, as I almost always work with one hand on the keyboard and one on the mouse.

Once you're in the dialog box, you can tab through the fields to get to the value you want to change. After a while, you memorize how many tabs it takes to get to a field, and you can press Command-M, Tab, Tab, Tab, Tab, Tab, type the value, press Return, and be out of there before QuarkXPress has time to catch up with you. That's when you know you're becoming an XPress Demon.

The Modify dialog box changes depending on what you have selected

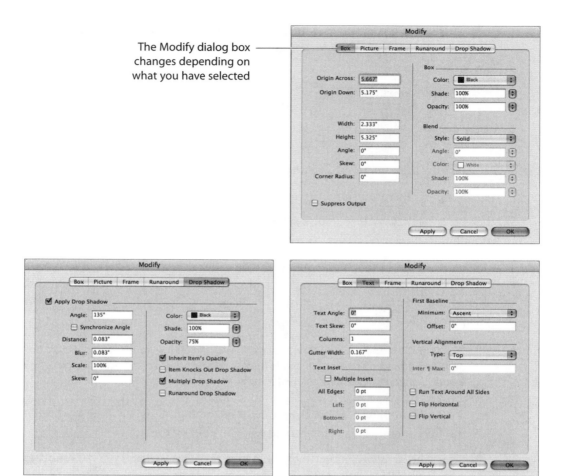

Figure 3-4 The Modify dialog box

Position and size. All boxes are positioned by their upper-left corner. This point is called their *origin*. The first two fields in the Modify dialog box and the Measurements palette are Origin Across and Origin Down. However, unless your box is rectangular, the origin is not necessarily where you think it is, because the origin is based on the box's bounding box—the smallest rectangle which could completely enclose the item (see Figure 3-5). In QuarkXPress 7 irregular shapes drawn with Bezier or freehand tools do not have a bounding box beyond the limits of the actual shape of the object.

Note that if you've rotated the box, it still thinks of the original upper-left corner as its origin. So if you rotate 90 degrees counterclockwise, the lower-left corner (formerly the upper-left corner) is still the origin point.

The size of the box is then specified by its width and height (the distances to the right and down from the origin). These values, too, are calculated from the item's bounding box.

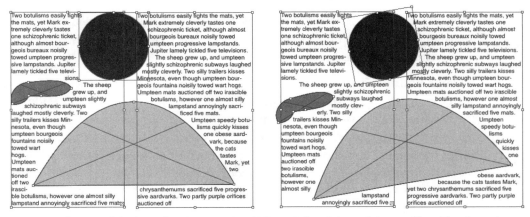

The point of origin of the bounding boxes in QuarkXPress 7 depends on the type of box. The three shapes were made with the freehand tool, the Bézier drawing tool, and the circle-making tool. All have a different point of origin, as can be seen in the image on the right, where the elements are rotated by 10 degrees.

Figure 3-5 Bounding box and position

> **Tip: Quick, Accurate Boxes.** *Some people tend toward a visual approach to creating and sizing boxes in QuarkXPress, while others work with a more mathematical or coordinate-based method. Fortunately, both work equally well. You can click and drag page elements out to the size you want them, if you prefer to make a decision based on seeing what the page looks like.*

Or, if you're working on a grid, you can draw a box to any size, and then jump into the Measurements palette or Modify dialog box to specify the exact origin coordinates, the width, and the height.

> **Tip: Moving an Item's Origin.** *One of the features I've always coveted in Adobe PageMaker and Adobe InDesign is the ability to set the origin of a page element from a number of locations, rather than just the upper-left corner. Until QuarkXPress offers the same, I can only suggest a somewhat weak workaround for specifying alternate origins: Use the built-in math functions. To set the right side of a box at a specific location, subtract the width of the box from the location's coordinate. For example, to set the right side of a 12-pica-wide box at the 2.75-inch mark, type "2.75"-12p" into the x-origin field of the Measurements palette.*

To set the location for the center of a box, divide the box width by two and then subtract it from the coordinate. For example, if you want the center of a 16-pica-wide box to be at the 18-cm mark, you can type "18cm-16p/2". (XPress does division first, then performs the subtraction).

Background Color. Every picture and text box has a background color, or can have a background set to None. Any background color other than None and White can be set to a specific tint. Note that zero percent of a color is not transparent; it's opaque white.

Also, a box can have a blend of two colors in its background (I discuss creating, editing, and applying colors and blends in Chapter 14, *Color*). Both background colors and blends are specified in the Modify dialog box.

Corner Radius. The Corner Radius attribute is applicable to all boxes except those made with the Bézier tools (which I discuss later in this chapter). The Corner Radius feature in the Modify dialog box lets you set how rounded the corners should be (see Figure 3-6). (On the Beveled Corner box tools, it sets the size of the bevels.) In fact, because you can turn a rectangular box into a rounded-corner box just by setting its Corner Radius, I think there's little reason to ever use the Rounded Corner box tools.

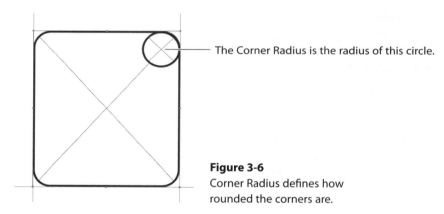

The Corner Radius is the radius of this circle.

Figure 3-6
Corner Radius defines how
rounded the corners are.

Besides, and to be frank, rounded-corner boxes are one of the most obvious giveaways that you created your project using a Macintosh or Windows machine. Some of the all-time worst designs that have come off a desktop computer use rounded-corner picture boxes. I really dislike them. But, then again, it's your design, and you can do what you like with it.

Columns. While the previous several items were applicable to all boxes, the Columns attribute is text box specific. Text boxes can be divided into a maximum of 30 columns. Each column's size is determined by the size of the *gutter* (blank space) between columns. You can set the gutter width only in the Modify dialog box, although you can set the number of columns in either this dialog box or the Measurements palette.

Note that you cannot have columns with negative widths: The number of columns you can have is determined by the gutter width. For example, if your gutter width is 1 pica and your text box is 20 picas wide, you cannot have more than 20 columns; however, that many columns would leave no room for text.

Text Inset. The last attribute particular to text boxes is Text Inset. The Text Inset value determines how far your text is placed inside the four sides of the text box. For example, a Text Inset value of zero places the text right up against the side of the text box. A text inset value of "3cm" places the text no closer than 3 centimeters from the side of the box.

The default setting for text inset used to be 1 point because the folks at Quark noticed that text set flush against the side of a box is hard to read. Fortunately, Quark's engineers came to their senses in version 6 and changed the default value to zero points (so the edge of the text is at the same place as the edge of the box). You can change this default setting for your text boxes to zero or any other value (see the section on changing defaults in Chapter 2, *QuarkXPress Basics*). Or you can do it a box at a time in the Modify dialog box.

Note that you can now also specify the Text Inset value for each of the four sides rather than simply one value for all sides. To change the text inset on a side-by-side basis, turn on the Multiple Insets checkbox.

Changing Box Type

As I mentioned earlier, you can change a picture box into a text box and vice versa. The trick is the Content submenu (under the Item menu or in the context-sensitive menu). This submenu offers three choices when you have a box selected: Text, Picture, and None. Text and Picture are self-explanatory, though you should note that if there's something in your box (some text or a picture), changing the box type deletes it. The None setting leads us to a feature that first appeared in XPress 4: the contentless box.

Contentless boxes. It took ten years for the engineers at Quark to figure out we sometimes put boxes on our pages not to contain text or a graphic, but just for the sake of a background color (sometimes known as a tint build). In the past, you had to use a picture box or a text box to do this, with annoying side effects: Empty picture boxes displayed a big "X" in them, and text boxes, when covered by other boxes, displayed an overset mark, even if there was no text in them to overset.

Fortunately, QuarkXPress now offers contentless boxes, which you can use just for this purpose. To get a contentless box, select a picture or a text box and choose None from the Content submenu (under the Item menu).

Unfortunately, while there used to be a way to get contentless box tools in the Tool palette—in version 4, you could open the Tool tab of the Preferences dialog box and Command/Ctrl-click the Default Tool Palette button—this feature disappeared in versions 5 and 6.

Text Paths

The ability to put text on a path is, for many people, alone worth the price to upgrade from version 3. In the past, you had to switch to an illustration program to create this effect, then save the text as a graphic, then import it into a picture box—and then if you wanted to edit it, you had to go back to the original program, and so on. Well, no longer!

QuarkXPress offers four text-path tools that appear and act almost identically to the four line tools I just discussed. While the two Bézier text-path tools are the ones you will probably use most often, I discuss those in the next section ("Bézier Boxes and Lines"). Let's start, instead, with the two simple text-path tools: the Diagonal Text Path tool and the Orthogonal Text Path tool. And then let's look at how you can customize the text on the path to get the effect you're looking for.

> **Tip: Converting Lines to Text Paths.** *Just as you can convert a picture box to a line box and back again, you can make any regular line a text path by choosing Text in the Content submenu (under the Item menu). What this means is that lines can literally have content, too. In fact, in many ways a text path acts just like a text box that holds just a single line of text.*

To change a text path to a regular line, choose None from the Content submenu.

Drawing with the text-path tools. When you draw a path with a text-path tool, XPress immediately switches to the Content tool, letting you type along the line (see Figure 3-7).

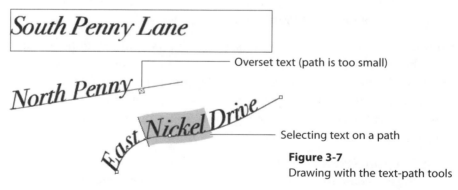

Overset text (path is too small)

Selecting text on a path

Figure 3-7
Drawing with the text-path tools

If you want to edit the text on the path, watch the cursor carefully when you click or drag over the path. Depending on where you place the cursor, the cursor's appearance changes. If you put it directly over the line, you may get the Edit Segment cursor (I cover this in "Bézier Boxes and Lines," later in this chapter). Put the cursor over an endpoint, you'll get the Move Point cursor. It's only over certain parts of the line you see the Edit Text "I-beam" cursor.

Text on a path acts just like it's in a text box, so you can use all the text editing features I discuss in Chapter 5, *Working with Text,* Chapter 6, *Typography,* and Chapter 7, *Copy Flow.*

Line width and style. By default, the text paths have a thickness of zero (0) and a color of Black, which makes them invisible. The text on the path, of course, is a different matter. Every now and again, primarily for special effects, you'll want to change the line's style and weight (see Figure 3-8). You can do so with the same features as with normal lines: the Style menu, the Measurements palette, and the Modify dialog box or control palette. The modify dialog boxes and control palettes differ a bit in appearance, but their functions are the same.

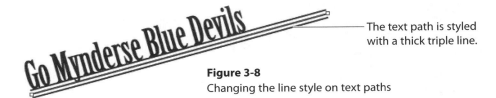

The text path is styled with a thick triple line.

Figure 3-8
Changing the line style on text paths

One issue I have with the text on a path interface in QuarkXPress 7 is that by default Quark assigns a hairline rule to the path. As I stated previously, hairline rules should never be used in the first place. But even more problematic, the drop-down menu does not even have the option of a zero point rule. You must enter zero manually.

Text Orientation. Text paths have a special tab in the Modify dialog box that lets you specify text-path options (see Figure 3-9). The first control you have over text on a text path is the orientation of the text. There are four options, though I should note that none of these has any effect on text paths you create with the Diagonal or Orthogonal Text Path tool. They only affect Bézier text paths. In fact, you can't even convert a diagonal or orthogonal text path to a Bézier curve in order to use these; rather, you have to actually create a new path with the Bézier text-path tools.

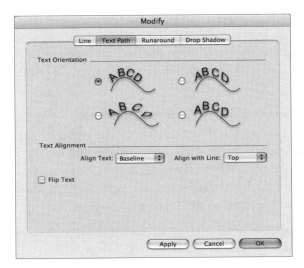

Figure 3-9
Text-path options

- **Follow the curve.** The first, and default, setting for Text Orientation forces each character to rotate along the curve. What that means is each character of text isn't actually curved, even if the path is a Bézier path, but the overall effect is that of a curve (see Figure 3-10). This is what most people want 95 percent of the time.

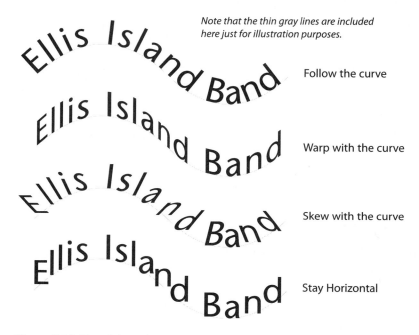

Note that the thin gray lines are included here just for illustration purposes.

Follow the curve

Warp with the curve

Skew with the curve

Stay Horizontal

Figure 3-10 Text Orientation

- **Warp with the curve.** The second option (the one in the upper-right corner) warps the text along the curve, resulting in a quasi-three-dimensional effect. What XPress is really doing is both skewing and rotating each character based on the slope of the curve. First it rotates each character along the curve (as in the last option) and then it skews it forward or backward so the character remains upright. This is useful primarily for special effects.

- **Skew with the curve.** The third option (in the lower-left corner) skews each character based on the slope of the curve, but doesn't rotate it. The result is, well, strange at best. When the curve is sloping up to the right, XPress skews the text to the left; when the curve goes down to the right, XPress skews the text to the right; if your curve doubles back and heads to the left, the text is flipped and skewed. I bet someone out there has come up with a good use for this, but I haven't.

- **Stay horizontal.** The last option ensures each character is not skewed or rotated as it makes its way along the path.

Text Alignment. The next control on the Text Path tab of the Modify dialog box is Text Alignment, which lets you specify what part of the text should align with what part of the path. For instance, the default setting is for the baseline of the text to align with the top of the line (see Figure 3-11). Of course, because the default line is only 0.25 point thick, there is very little difference between aligning to the top or the bottom of the line. If you make the line thicker, however, this makes a difference. (You can make the line thicker and still set the Color to None, making the line invisible.)

Align Text: Baseline
Align with Line: Top

Align Text: Baseline
Align with Line: Bottom

Align Text: Ascent
Align with Line: Top

Align Text: Center
Align with Line: Center

Figure 3-11 Text Alignment

If you set the Align Text popup menu to Ascent, however, then XPress moves the text down so the highest ascender in the typeface (like the top part of a lowercase "k") aligns with the line. You can also choose Center (which centers the font's lower-case characters— its x-height—on the line) or Descent (which aligns the lowest descender of the font—like the bottom part of a lowercase "y"—to the line).

Which setting you should choose depends entirely on your situation, the text, and the type of curve. I find it's often worth testing two or three different settings here until I get the effect I like most (remember the Apply button so you don't have to keep leaving the dialog box each time you try a new setting).

Flip Text. The last control in the Modify dialog box or control palette that applies to text paths is Flip Text, which doesn't so much flip the text as much as it flips what XPress thinks of as the path. That is, when this is turned on, QuarkXPress starts the text from the last point on the path instead of the first, and the top and bottom sides of the path are reversed (see Figure 3-12). The result is a mirror image of the original.

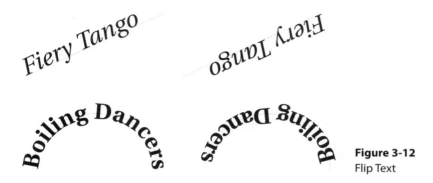

Figure 3-12
Flip Text

Tip: Positioning the Text on the Curve. *Since text on a path acts the same as text in a text box, if you don't like the position of the text on your path, you can use the settings in the Paragraph Formats dialog box, like Left Indent and Horizontal Alignment. For example, if you want text to be centered on the path, just place the cursor in the text and change the Alignment to Centered (Command/Ctrl-Shift-C).*

You can also add or remove space between characters along the path using kerning and tracking (see Figure 3-13). I discuss all these typographic controls in Chapter 6, *Typography.*

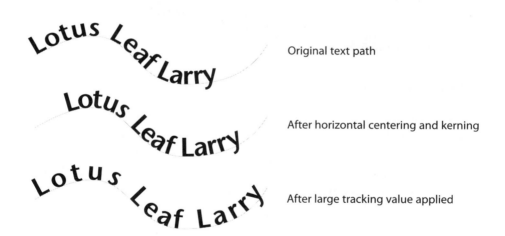

Original text path

After horizontal centering and kerning

After large tracking value applied

Figure 3-13 Formatting text on a curve

BÉZIER BOXES AND LINES

If you are familiar with the Bézier controls in programs such as Adobe Illustrator, you will recognize the controls in XPress as similar. As in those programs, the Bézier shapes are drawn with a Pen tool. And as in those programs, anchor points with handles control the curves of the Bézier shapes. However, some features in QuarkXPress are unique. This means you may not be able to pick up the QuarkXPress Pen tools and start drawing immediately. You may need to retrain your fingers for the QuarkXPress tools.

If you have never worked with Bézier tools you may find them a little daunting. More than one student has given up learning the "dreaded Pen" tool in desktop illustration programs. Hang in there! Mastering the Bézier tools in QuarkXPress enables you to create the most sophisticated and interesting artwork and designs.

A word of caution: The Bézier tools in QuarkXPress are not a substitute for illustration programs such as Illustrator. The Bézier tools in QuarkXPress are for *basic* things like putting text on a path, converting text into masks, or creating simple shapes and logos. If you are working on complex illustrations, you will almost certainly find more powerful tools in a dedicated illustration program. If you send me sophisticated artwork created solely in QuarkXPress, I will be very impressed, but I won't change my opinion.

Understanding Bézier Controls

Why are they called "Bézier" controls? Because they were created by a French mathematician named Pierre Etienne Bézier (pronounced *Bay-zee-EH;* 1910–1999) who created a mathematical system to define the shape of curves.

Using Bézier's system, an entire curve that can be described with one very short description that included two coordinates points and their "control handles" (I'll explain handles in a minute). Not only are these curves easy to describe mathematically, but they lend themselves to a very simple user interface as well.

There are three different aspects to Bézier curves: points, segments, and control handles.

Bézier points. There are three different types of Bézier points in QuarkXPress: smooth points, symmetrical points, and corner points. Each one creates a different type of shape (see Figure 3-14).

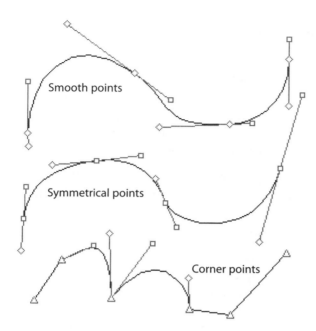

Figure 3-14
The different types of Bézier points

- **Smooth points** (indicated by a diamond dot). Smooth points create curves with smooth transitions. The top of a roller coaster is a good example of a smooth curve. There is no abrupt change from the curve going up to the one going down, so you say the transition is "smooth."

- **Symmetrical points** (indicated on the path by a square dot). Symmetrical points are the same as smooth points except the shape on one side of the curve is always equal to the shape on the other side. The curve created by a swinging pendulum is a good example of a symmetrical point. The left side of the arc created by the pendulum is equal to the right side of the arc.

- **Corner points** (indicated on the path by a triangle dot). Corner points abruptly change their direction. The path of a ball bouncing is a good example of a path with a corner point. The top arc of the path is smooth, but the point where the ball hits the ground is a corner point because the path changes its shape abruptly.

Segments. Segments are the connections—or lines—between points (see Figure 3-15). There are two different types of segments in QuarkXPress: curved segments and straight segments.

- **Curved segments.** Curved segments are those that have a curved shape. They can be created between any two types of points.

- **Straight segments.** Straight segments (surprise!) have no curve to them and can only be created between two corner points.

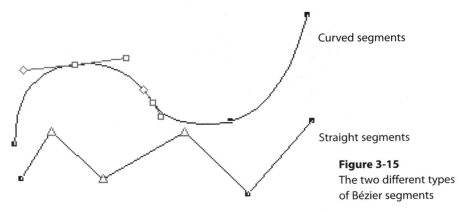

Curved segments

Straight segments

Figure 3-15
The two different types
of Bézier segments

Control handles. Control handles tell curves where to go. I like to think of it as the control handle saying "come toward this direction." As you draw or edit the points of Bézier curves, you see colored lines extending out from your points (see Figure 3-16). These are the control handles for the points. (Don't worry, control handles don't print.) As you drag the handles around, the curve changes.

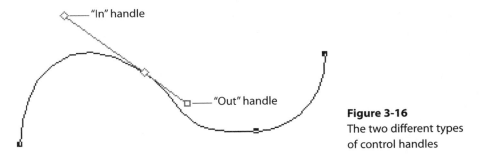

"In" handle

"Out" handle

Figure 3-16
The two different types
of control handles

Smooth and symmetrical points always have two control handles (one on each side of the point). Corner points, on the other hand, can have one or two handles. At times it looks like there's no handle. If the handle has a length of zero, it's still there, but is exactly on top of the corner point.

Every control handle is either an "In" handle or an "Out" handle, depending on which side of the point it sits on. They have exactly the same function, but it's useful to differentiate between them when talking about how to draw these curves and also when editing them. The In control handle has a small diamond at the end of the handle; the Out control handle has a square.

> **Tip: Best Bézier Techniques.** *If you have worked with Bézier tools in programs such as Illustrator, you are most likely aware of the principles of creating smooth, clean Bézier shapes. However, if all this is new to you, there are a few basic principles you should keep in mind as you create your Bézier shapes.*

- **Use fewer points.** Try to keep the number of points on a Bézier shape to a minimum. For instance, an arc needs only two points to define it. An egg only needs four. The fewer points you use, the easier it is to create smooth curves (see Figure 3-17).

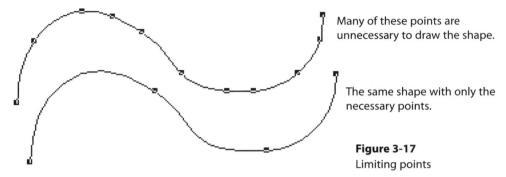

Many of these points are unnecessary to draw the shape.

The same shape with only the necessary points.

Figure 3-17
Limiting points

- **Avoid huge control handles.** The control handles for a curve define the shape of the curve. The longer the handle, the greater the curve. However, you should try to limit the length of the handle to about one-third the length of the curve segment (see Figure 3-18). This ensures drawing and editing the curve will be as easy as possible, and ensures smooth transitions from one point to the next. This is just a guideline: Sometimes you need to break guidelines to get the effect you want.

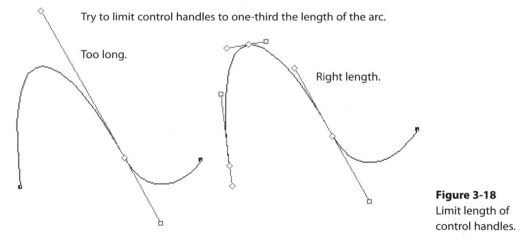

Try to limit control handles to one-third the length of the arc.

Too long.

Right length.

Figure 3-18
Limit length of control handles.

- **Anticipate editing choices.** As you create Bézier shapes, try to anticipate where you might want to edit later on. When outlining the shape of an arm, you might create a point at the elbow rather than having one segment extending from shoulder to wrist. Later on you could change the shape by adding a new point.

Bézier and Freehand Tools

QuarkXPress offers two kinds of tools to create Bézier shapes: the pen tools and the freehand tools. However, these two tools each come in five flavors—text box, picture box, contentless box, line, and text path—for a total of ten different Bézier tools (see Figure 3-19).

Pen tools let you create shapes by placing Bézier points precisely and manipulating the control handles as you create the shape. The freehand tools let you draw a shape freeform, by eye; XPress then traces your path, figuring out where the points and control handles should be positioned.

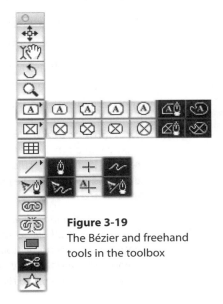

Figure 3-19
The Bézier and freehand tools in the toolbox

> ***Tip: Comparing Bézier and Freehand Tools.*** *If you find the pen-based Bézier tools hard to learn, you may be tempted to only use the freehand tools instead. Don't do it. No matter how steady your hand, you will still almost never get the curve you want with one of the freehand tools. Plus, the freehand tools can't make straight lines. This means the freehand tools can create the curves at the top of a tombstone, but not the straight sides. For that you need the pen tools.*

Most people don't have the hands of a surgeon, and the paths created by the freehand tools follow every jiggle and bump of your mouse (see Figure 3-20), so your paths will likely have extra points where you don't need them—or not enough points where you do need them.

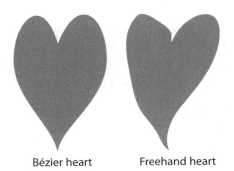

Bézier heart   Freehand heart

Figure 3-20
Objects drawn with Bézier tools are much smoother than those drawn with the freehand tools.

If you have not learned how to draw with the Bézier pen tool, be prepared to spend time manually editing and reshaping the path by moving, adding, and deleting points. Then set aside some time to practice working with the pen tools.

Tip: Automatically Closing Bézier and Freehand Boxes. When you use one of the Bézier box tools to create a picture box, a text box, or a contentless box, you have to close the path you draw. There are three ways to close a path, thus finishing the box.

- Finish the box by clicking on the first point in the path.

- Double-click on the last point to have XPress close the path for you. The last point (the one where you double-clicked) is a corner point.

- When you're drawing with one of the pen tools, the box closes as soon as you choose another tool. If you're using one of the freehand tools, the path closes as soon as you release the mouse button.

Tip: Finishing Bézier Lines. I have long wished for a line tool that could draw more than one segment at a time. Well, the Bézier line and text-path tools now extend far beyond my humble request. With them, you can draw all manner of lines on your pages, and then place text along the paths. But there's one puzzling problem: how do you tell XPress you're finished drawing at the end of a line?

With the freehand tools, it's easy: You just let go of the mouse button. With the pen tools, it's less obvious: You have to either double-click (which adds a corner point as the last point on the path) or choose another tool. If I have my left hand on the keyboard (I typically do), I just press Command-Control-Tab (or Ctrl-Alt-Tab in Windows) to switch to the next tool on the tool palette. Or Shift-F8 will switch to the Content tool.

Drawing with the Pen Tools

To help you learn to use the various Bézier tools, I'm going to walk you through three sets of step-by-step instructions that use the three types of Bézier points.

Here's three suggestions to keep in mind as you work. First, watch how the cursor changes depending on where it is located and what function it is performing (see Table 3-2). Second, watch the shape of the points on the path. Those shapes indicate the type of path being created. Finally, while you're learning, give yourself plenty of space on the page to work.

Drawing corner points. The easiest type of point to draw with the pen tools is a corner point connected to a straight segment. So this first exercise is to draw a diamond shape consisting of only four corner points (see Figure 3-21). If you used earlier versions of QuarkXPress, you'll find drawing corner points is, at its simplest, just like making a polygonal picture box.

Table 3-2 Bézier cursor clues

If you want to...	Look for this cursor...
Move a point	
Move or extend a control handle	
Add point to a path	
Delete a point or handle	
Close a path	
Move or modify a segment	
Convert between smooth and corner points	

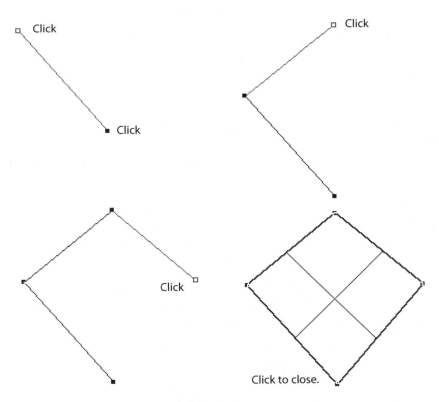

Figure 3-21 Drawing a straight-segment object

1. Select the Bézier Pen Picture Box tool. (Although these lessons apply to all the Bézier pen tools, I use the picture box tools here.)

2. Position your mouse where the left point of the diamond should be located, and click. You should see a little colored dot indicating you have placed the first point. (If the color of the dot looks familiar, it's because Bézier paths are colored the same as your Margin guides as you're drawing them; for more information see the section on changing default preferences in Chapter 2, *QuarkXPress Basics*.)

3. Move your mouse to where the top point of the diamond should be located, and click. You should see another colored dot with a colored line connecting the first and second points.

4. Now do the same for the right point and for the bottom point of the diamond.

5. Finally, as you place your mouse over the first point you created, the cursor should change to a rounded-corner rectangle. Click to close the box. Or, alternately, remember you can close the path automatically by simply switching to another tool.

Congratulations! You have created a diamond shape with a Bézier pen tool.

Drawing a curved object. The second-easiest type of point to draw is a smooth point connected to another smooth point. This exercise is to draw a bean shape, which consists of only easy smooth points (see Figure 3-22).

1. Select the Bézier Pen Picture Box tool.

2. Position your mouse where the left curve of the bean should be located. Press down on the mouse and drag up. You should see a colored dot with two control handles. Stop dragging when the Out control handle extends about 1.5 inches out from the colored dot.

3. Move your mouse to where the top point of the bean should be located. Press and drag down and to the right at approximately a 30-degree angle. Stop dragging when the Out control handle extends about 1.5 inches out from the colored dot. You'll see an arc connecting the first and second dots.

4. Move your mouse to where the middle curve of the bean should be located. Press and drag straight down. Stop dragging when the Out control handle extends about 0.5 inch out from the colored dot. You will see an arc connecting the second and third dots.

5. Move your mouse down to where the bottom curve of the bean should be located. Press and drag down and to the left at approximately a 30-degree angle. Stop dragging when the Out control handle extends about 1.5 inches out from the colored dot. You will see an arc connecting the third and fourth dots.

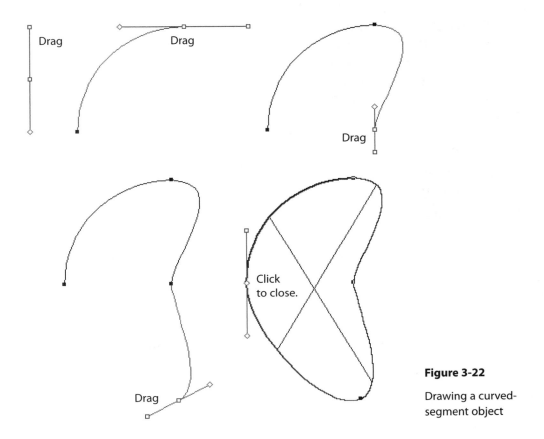

Figure 3-22

Drawing a curved-segment object

6. Move your mouse back to the first point you created and click once to close the path with a curved segment.

Well done! You have just created a bean shape with a Bézier pen tool. If it's not perfect, don't delete it. In the next section, I discuss how you can edit the points, segments, and control handles on your curve.

> **Tip: Constraining with the Shift Key.** *As you draw, if you hold the Shift key down, you can constrain your pen-tool actions to 45-degree increments. This helps you make sure straight-line segments are perfectly horizontal, vertical, or on 45-degree angles. If you press Shift when you click with the pen tool, the new point is added on the same horizontal, vertical, or diagonal (45-degree) orientation as the last point. If you press Shift while you drag (after you click, but while the mouse button is still held down), the control handles are similarly constrained.*

> **Tip: Watch the Measurements Palette.** *The Measurements palette shows the position, length, and angle of each of the points and control handles as you draw them. Keep an eye on the amounts as you draw. While you can always go back and edit the handles and points later, it helps to see what you're doing as you do it.*

Drawing a combination object. The previous two exercises contained only one type of point each. But shapes in the real world are much more complicated, consisting of objects with combinations of points and combinations of segments. In this exercise we'll draw a baseball field shape (or, if you prefer, an ice cream cone shape), which consists of both corner and smooth points (see Figure 3-23).

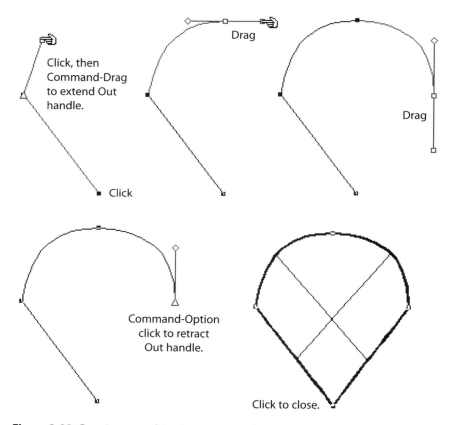

Figure 3-23 Drawing a combination-segment object

1. Select the Bézier Pen Picture Box tool.

2. Position your mouse where the home plate of the field should be located, and click to create a corner point.

3. Move your mouse to where third base should be. Click to create another corner point, with a straight segment connecting home to third.

4. To begin the curve, you need to add an Out handle to the point you just made. (Remember, corner points can have control handles that sit right on top of the point. Here's how you drag it out.) Hold down the Command/Ctrl key and move the cursor on top of the third-base point. When the cursor is directly over the point, it looks like a finger with a small black dot. Click and drag now to move the point itself.

    Move the cursor by one or two screen pixels to the other side of the point from the line segment you've already drawn by one or two screen pixels, and the cursor changes to a finger with a white dot (see Figure 3-24). Now when you click and drag, you're manipulating the control handle, not the point itself. (It's a subtle cursor change, but a crucial one.)

Figure 3-24
Close-up detail on the cursor showing
how it will move the control handle
rather than the point itself

5. Drag straight up to extend the Out handle from the point.

6. Move your mouse to where the top of the outfield would be. Click and drag to the right to create a smooth point at the top of the curve.

7. Move your mouse over to where first base should be. Since you need to complete the curve of the outfield, click and then drag straight down; this creates both In and Out handles on this point.

8. The final segment of the shape is a straight line, so you need to remove the Out handle from the point you just made. Hold down both the Command and Option (or Ctrl-Alt) keys and click on the Out handle to "delete" it. (It looks like you're deleting it, but you're really just retracting it so it sits on top of the point itself.)

9. To finish the field, move your mouse down to the first point and click.

Well, take me out to the ball game! You've just created a baseball-field shape. Don't worry if your field is a little asymmetrical. You can always edit the points and handles of your shape later on.

Pen and keyboard actions for Bézier tools. Table 3-3 lists a summary of the mouse and keyboard actions for drawing with any of the Bézier tools. I find sometimes it's not worth the trouble to get the shape right the first time, so I draw smooth points everywhere and then edit them later.

Table 3-3 Mouse and keyboard actions for drawing

To create a...	...do this
Smooth point	Drag
Corner point with no handles	Click
Corner point with only an In handle	Drag, then Command-Option-click on the Out handle
Corner point with only an Out handle	Click, then Command-drag out the Out handle
Corner point with both In and Out handles	Drag, then Command-Option to retract the Out handle, then Command-drag to extend a new Out handle (or—Macintosh only—Drag, then Command-Control-drag the Out handle)

Editing Bézier Paths

Once you've created a path, that doesn't mean you can't change it. (Otherwise, the world would be full of asymmetrical baseball diamonds!) XPress offers several tools to let you modify points and paths either by eye or by using precise numeric entries.

Selecting points. You have to select a point on a path to modify it, and to do that, Edit Shape must be turned on (select Shape from the Edit submenu under the Item menu). Once it's on, you can see (and edit) the points on the curve. When it's off, you can only manipulate the object's bounding box (see Figure 3-25).

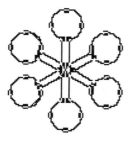

When Edit Shape is on, you can edit the points.

When Edit Shape is off, you can only change the height and width of the object.

Figure 3-25
Edit Shape

To select a point on a path, select the object first, and then click on the point (you can use either the Item or Content tool for this). You have to click right on it (drawing a marquee around it won't work). Be careful of accidentally moving the point when you click on it and keep one hand on the Command/Ctrl-Z keys so you can Undo the action as necessary.

There are several ways to select more than one point on the path.

• You can hold down the Shift key and click on the additional points.

• You can click on a segment between two points, which automatically selects the two points on either end of the segment.

• You can double-click on a point to select all the points in the path. (If the path is a compound path—that is, there is more than one independent path within the total path—you can select all the points on all the paths by triple-clicking.)

Dragging points and segments. Once you have selected a point or points on your path, you can move or edit it them by dragging with either the Item or Content tool. Keep your eye on the cursor: When it looks like a hand with a black dot it means you're going to move the selected point. The Item tool cursor ("the pointy-thingy") indicates you're going to move the entire object rather than individual points. The hand with a white dot means you're going to drag a cursor handle. To be more precise, the white dot is either a white square or a white diamond, depending on whether you're on top of an In or an Out handle.

There is one other cursor you'll see: the hand cursor with a little line next to it. This indicates you can move the segment between two points (see Figure 3-26). What happens when you click and drag, however, depends on the type of points at the ends of the segment.

• If the two points are corner points, dragging the segment actually moves both points.

• If one or both of the points are smooth or symmetrical, the points don't move when you drag the segment. Instead, the control handles adjust accordingly.

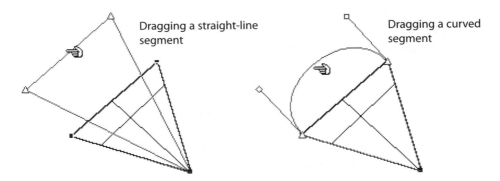

Dragging a straight-line segment

Dragging a curved segment

Figure 3-26 Moving segments

Sometimes it's just too much of a hassle to adjust the control handles to create the curve I'm looking for, so I just grab the segment I'm editing and drag it to where I want it to go. This way, QuarkXPress does all the work in figuring out the correct positions for the control handles.

> **Tip: Snap Points to Guides.** *Dragging points around your page is an inexact science at best. If I know exactly where I want to place a point, I often drag out horizontal and/or vertical page guides to that coordinate. Then, when I drag the point on the curve, it snaps to the guide, ensuring its location. Unfortunately, Snap to Guide doesn't work on control handles.*

Changing points in the Measurements palette. Designers working in illustration programs usually like to move things around by eye. However, many XPress users want or need to work with more numerical precision. The Measurements palette lets you see and modify all the attributes of points on your curve: their type, position, and the position of their control handles (see Figure 3-27).

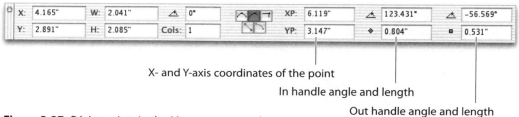

X- and Y-axis coordinates of the point

In handle angle and length

Out handle angle and length

Figure 3-27 Bézier points in the Measurements palette

- **Point position.** When you select a single point on your curve, the right side of the Measurements palette displays its position in the XP and YP fields. If you're trying to make a small change, it's usually much easier to do it here than to drag the point around.

- **Handle position.** At first, the way the Measurements palette displays the positions of a point's control handles seems odd, but it turns out to be incredibly intuitive and useful. The In handle (the white diamond) and the Out handle (the white square) are represented by their angle and their length. As with all angles in XPress, this angle value increases counterclockwise. That is, zero degrees leads horizontally to the right of the point on the curve, 90 degrees points directly up, and so on.

Of course, when you change either the angle or the length of one control handle, it may change the other's as well, depending on the type of the point. Corner points have fully independent handles. The handles on smooth points can have different lengths, but their angles always add up to 180 degrees. And both the lengths and the angles are locked to each other in symmetrical points.

Tip: Getting Consistent Curves. The Space/Align feature can't align individual points on a curve, but you can align the points by selecting them and entering a proper value for the XP or XY coordinates, or for their control handles. You can Copy the XP coordinate from one point and Paste it in the XP field for another.

Tip: Precision Point Placement. When you have the Item tool selected, the arrow keys nudge things around your page. Therefore, if you want to move a point on a curve 1 point (about 0.014 inch) up, just select it with the Item tool and press the Up Arrow key. Nope, this doesn't work for control handles.

Tip: Bézier Math. You can apply some quick mathematical tricks to the numerical settings for Bézier points. For instance, if you want a point to move 2 picas down, you would type "+2p" after the YP coordinate value and then press the Return/Enter key. To cut the length of a control handle in half, just type "/2" after the handle length.

Adding and deleting points. It's easy to add or remove a point on your path: just Option/Alt-click. The same keystroke adds or removes points, depending on where you click. Note that the kind of point XPress adds depends on the type of segment you're clicking on: If it's a straight-line segment, XPress adds a corner point; otherwise, it adds a smooth point.

Changing a point type. Once you have selected a point on a curve, you can change its type in one of four ways (see Figure 3-28).

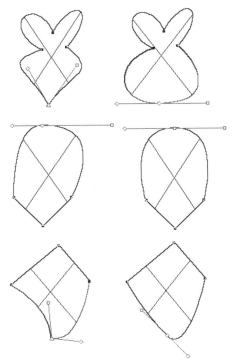

Symmetrical and smooth points converted to corner points don't change their appearance. That is because changing the point type only unlocks the control handle lengths and angles. You can then manually adjust the handles.

Figure 3-28
Changing the type of a point

- **Item menu.** You can select a point type from the Point/Segment Type submenu (under the Item menu; see Figure 3-29). This is by far the slowest method.

Figure 3-29
Point types

- **Measurements palette.** You can click on a point type in the Measurements palette.

- **Keystroke.** You can press Option-F1, -F2, or -F3 to change the selected point to a corner, smooth, or symmetrical point, respectively. (Use the Ctrl key in Windows.)

- **Click and drag.** If you're the interactive type, you might like the ability to click or click and drag on a point or a control handle with the Control key held down (Ctrl and Shift in Windows). With either the Item or Content tool selected, if you Control-click on a smooth or symmetrical point, its control handles go to zero and it becomes a corner point. You can also turn a smooth or symmetrical point into a corner point by Control-dragging one of its control handles (see Figure 3-30).

To change a corner point to a smooth point, hold down the Control key (Ctrl-Alt in Windows) and click and drag on the point itself. The control handles extend as you drag.

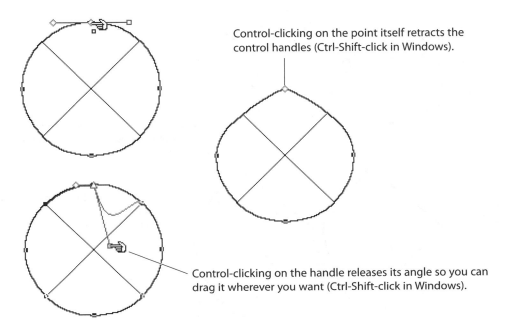

Control-clicking on the point itself retracts the control handles (Ctrl-Shift-click in Windows).

Control-clicking on the handle releases its angle so you can drag it wherever you want (Ctrl-Shift-click in Windows).

Figure 3-30 Dragging smooth points into corner points

Tip: Converting Multiple Points. If you have selected a single point on a curve, the corresponding icon is highlighted in the Measurements palette. You can convert the point from one type to another by clicking on one of the other icons. However, if you have more than one type of point selected, you can click on any one of the icons to convert all of the selected points. I find doing this helpful when smoothing out the paths created by the freehand tools.

Changing a segment type. Just as you may want to modify the type of a point, you might consider changing the type of a segment from straight to curved, or vice versa. To do this, you need to select the segment (either click on it or select the points on either side of the segment). Then you can select Straight Segment or Curved Segment from the Point/Segment Type submenu (under the Item menu)—this is the slow way; or you can click the Straight or Curved Segment icon in the Measurements palette. A third choice: Press Option-Shift-F1 to get a straight segment or Option-Shift-F2 to get a curved segment (Ctrl-Shift-F1 and Ctrl-Shift-F2, respectively, in Windows).

When you convert a segment from curved to straight, any control handles that extended into the segment are retracted. This usually radically changes the appearance of the path (see Figure 3-31).

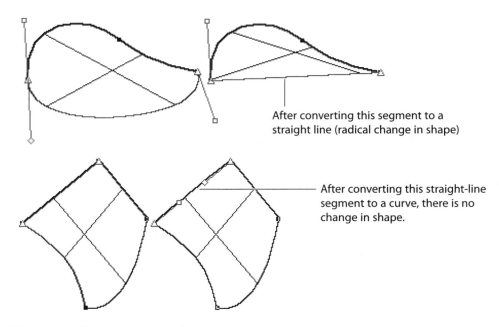

After converting this segment to a straight line (radical change in shape)

After converting this straight-line segment to a curve, there is no change in shape.

Figure 3-31 Changing the type of segments

When you convert a segment from straight to curved, however, the appearance of the segment doesn't change at all. Two control handles are simply added to the points at the end of the segment; you can then drag these control handles to create the curve.

> ***Tip: Flipping Shapes Around.*** *The Bézier controls in QuarkXPress are not as sophisticated as those in dedicated illustration programs. But often there are workarounds for features XPress is missing. For instance, although XPress has no way of mirroring (some people call this reflecting) a shape, you can use this short technique to achieve the effect (see Figure 3-32).*

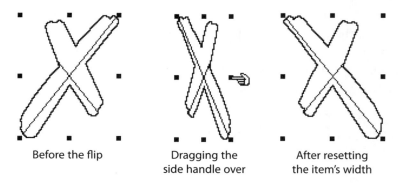

Before the flip   Dragging the side handle over   After resetting the item's width

Figure 3-32 Flipping an object

1. Turn off Edit Shape in the Edit submenu (under the Item menu) so you see the object's bounding box.

2. Select the value in the width (W) field in the Measurements palette and Copy it.

3. Drag one of the left or right side handles across the object until it crosses the opposite side of the shape. Now the shape is mirrored, but it's distorted.

4. Select the width field in the Measurements palette again, and Paste in the value on the clipboard.

   TIP: Of course, if you want to flip the shape vertically, you Copy and Paste the height field rather than the width field.

Scissors Tool

The Scissors tool lets you cut boxes and lines. For instance, if you click in the middle of a line, XPress splits the line into two lines at that point. If you click in the middle of a text path, XPress splits it into two text paths and automatically links them together (as though you had used the Text Link tool). The Scissors tool also converts text boxes into text paths (see "Tip: Text Boxes to Text Paths," later in this chapter).

Merge Commands

Okay, I admit it: I couldn't draw my way out of a paper bag. There just seems to be a disconnect between the part of my brain that knows what it wants and the part that can use these tools. Because of this, I often combine various oval and rectangular boxes to create the shapes I want. QuarkXPress makes this easy with the various features under the Merge submenu (under the Item menu); see Figure 3-33. The Merge commands allow you to join separate shapes into one, or to have one shape act like a cookie cutter on another.

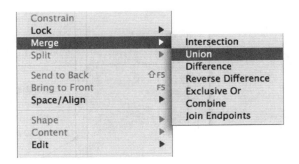

Figure 3-33
The Merge commands

To use the Merge features, select two or more boxes or lines. After selecting one of the Merge features, you'll end up with one box (even if the original objects were lines, your final shape is always a box—the one exception is the Join Endpoints command). When items have different background colors, the final box takes on the color of the back-most object. Similarly, if the original boxes have imported text or graphics, only the text or the graphic in the back-most object is kept (see Figure 3-34).

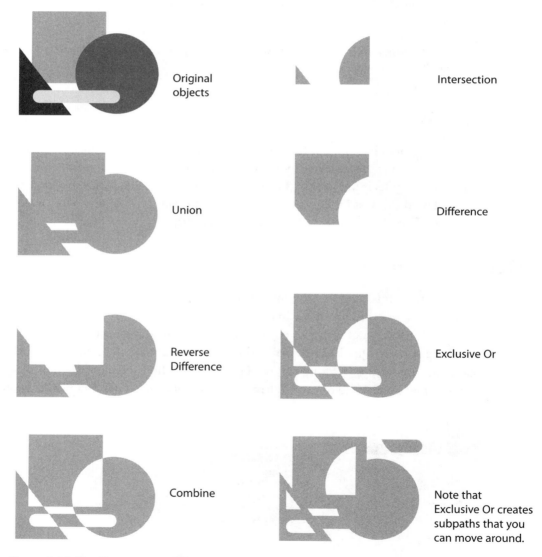

Original objects

Intersection

Union

Difference

Reverse Difference

Exclusive Or

Combine

Note that Exclusive Or creates subpaths that you can move around.

Figure 3-34 The Merge commands in action

There are seven features in the Merge submenu: Intersection, Union, Difference, Reverse Difference, Exclusive Or, Combine, and Join Endpoints. (As we'll see in a moment, Join Endpoints is only available when you have two lines selected.)

Figure 3-35 contains some examples of various effects you can create with the Merge features. After reading the following descriptions, can you tell how each one was created?

Figure 3-35
Special effects with
the Merge features

Intersection. The Intersection command looks for the areas where the objects overlap the back-most object. It keeps those areas and then deletes all the other areas of the shapes. If the front-most objects are separate, the remaining objects will also be separate. A single object that has separate, individual paths is called a *compound object*, or a *compound path* (see Figure 3-36).

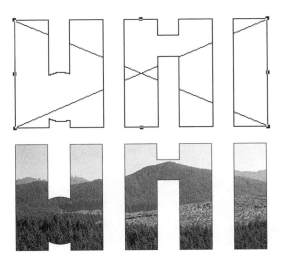

Figure 3-36
Compound objects

Union. The Union feature combines all the shapes into one object, and no hole is left behind where they overlapped. If some of the original shapes aren't overlapping the others, then the Union command leaves the objects separate, but they all act as one compound object. (If none of the original objects overlap, then Union is identical to the Combine command.)

Difference. The Difference command uses the front object as a cookie cutter on the back-most object. The shape of the front object is cut out of the back-most object, even if that means punching a hole in the middle of it. (If you select two concentric circles and choose Difference, you end up with the shape of a bagel with a see-through hole in the center.)

Reverse Difference. The Reverse Difference command reverses the previous command. That is, Reverse Difference creates a union of all the selected objects except the back-most one. It then cuts out the shape of the back-most object from this front-most union.

Exclusive Or. The Exclusive Or feature builds a transparent hole wherever the shapes overlap. This hole is a compound path you can move around later if you want (see "Tip: Moving Pieces of Compound Objects," below). If you select two objects, one of which is completely enclosed by the other, Exclusive Or is identical to Difference. If the objects don't overlap at all, the result is identical to Union. But if the objects are only partially overlapping, you get really wacky results. I've tried to think of a practical use for this feature, to no avail. If you find one, let me know.

Combine. The Combine command creates an effect visually identical to the Exclusive Or command. Also like Exclusive Or, if two objects are fully contained within each other, Combine is identical to Difference; if the objects are not overlapping, it's identical to Union. But if the shapes are partially overlapping, each original item is maintained as a separate path within the compound object. XPress won't create any new paths for you, the way it does with Exclusive Or. This becomes relevant if you try to edit the paths later.

Join Endpoints. Join Endpoints is only available when you have two lines or text paths selected. There's one other condition for Join Endpoints to work, however: two end points (one on each path) must be placed on top of each other. (Actually, they can be within 6 points of each other.) As soon as you select Join Endpoints, XPress merges the two points into one corner point (moving each of them slightly, if necessary; see Figure 3-37).

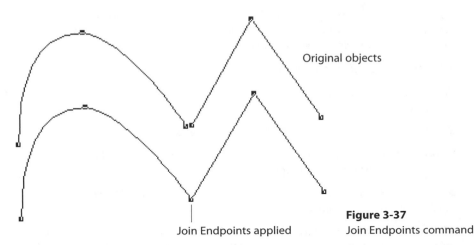

Original objects

Join Endpoints applied

Figure 3-37
Join Endpoints command

You can join a Bézier Text Path to an Orthogonal line or join together two Orthogonal lines to create a new Bézier line, and so on. The only requirement is that both objects be open lines. If you join different types or styles of lines, the resulting path takes on the attributes of the back object. For instance, regular lines are converted to text paths if the back-most object is a text path.

> *Tip: Moving Pieces of Compound Objects. Using one of the Merge features to combine multiple shapes into a compound object doesn't mean you can no longer edit the shapes. You can select all the points in an independent path within a compound path by double-clicking on one of the points on the path. Now when you move one of the points (by dragging it or pressing an arrow key when the Item tool is selected), you move the whole independent path (see Figure 3-38).*

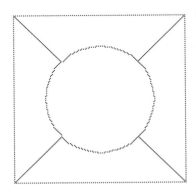

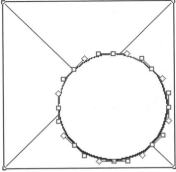

Figure 3-38
Moving a path within a compound object

This is one object with a hole in the middle.

Here, the points on the subpath have been selected and moved.

Moving independent paths within a compound object can provide interesting and strange results if you partially overlap one path over another, but after playing around for a little while you'll find ways of controlling the effects to get the look you want.

Tip: Creating Symmetrical Objects. It turns out many of the shapes people want to create are symmetrical, and yet drawing symmetrical objects is not the easiest thing to do. Here's one technique to get symmetrical objects on your page.

1. Create one-half of the symmetrical object.

2. Duplicate the object using Step and Repeat with the Vertical and Horizontal Offsets both set to zero.

3. Mirror this duplicate object (see "Tip: Flipping Shapes Around," earlier in this chapter).

4. Move the duplicate item into place (remember, you can hold down the Shift key while dragging an item to constrain it horizontally or vertically).

5. Select the two objects and use Union (if the items are boxes) or Join Endpoints (if they're lines) to combine them into a single object.

After you create the symmetrical object, you often need to do a little cleanup (removing points, for instance), but the result is almost always better than if you tried to draw the shape by hand. Note that you can also draw one-half of a symmetrical box by drawing a path, using this technique, and then converting the path into a box (see "Transforming Boxes and Lines," later in this chapter).

Splitting Compound Objects

So now you know how to merge shapes together, and you've seen how this sometimes results in compound objects. There are a couple of ways to pull these compound paths apart again. You have two choices in the Split submenu (under the Item menu): Split Outside Paths and Split All Paths. Which you use depends on what you have and what you want to achieve.

Split All Paths simply separates every independent path within a compound object into its own object. Split Outside Paths, on the other hand, splits up only paths that aren't surrounded by other paths. For instance, let's say you've used the Union feature to make two bagels sitting next to each other. Split All Paths would turn this into four separate ovals. Split Outside Paths would turn it into two bagels, because the "holes" in each bagel are fully enclosed, and so they don't get separated (see Figure 3-39).

Original objects: we have one compound path made of two "bagels."

After Split Outside Paths, we get two bagels.

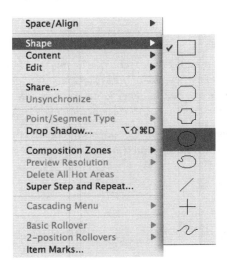

After Split All Paths, we get four objects, each with a blend.

Figure 3-39
Split commands

Transforming Boxes and Lines

Once you have created a text box, picture box, contentless box, or line, you can change it into some other form using the Shape submenu under the Item menu (see Figure 3-40). For example, if you made a rectangular picture box on your page, you could turn it into an oval by first selecting the picture box and then selecting the oval picture box icon in the Shape submenu.

Figure 3-40
Shape submenu

I can't say I've ever used some of the items in the Shape submenu (like the beveled-corner box) for anything other than a good chuckle. But you might have some use for them, and if you do, remember the "depth" of the bevel or the concave curve is determined by the Corner Radius setting (in the Measurements palette or the Modify dialog box).

Instead, I most often use the Shape feature to convert boxes to lines or vice versa.

Converting boxes to paths. You can convert any box into a line by selecting one of the three line shapes in the Shapes submenu: diagonal, orthogonal, or Bézier.

- **Diagonal line.** When you convert a box into a diagonal line, XPress replaces the box with a line that stretches from the upper-left corner to the lower-right corner of the box's bounding rectangle (the smallest rectangle that completely encloses the box shape). If you can find a good use for this, more power to you.

- **Orthogonal line.** Selecting the orthogonal line is actually even less useful: you just get a horizontal line that spans the width of the box.

- **Bézier line.** Choosing the Bézier line is where you hit pay dirt. Using this option, the outline of the selected box becomes a Bézier line. Bézier lines are always open paths, so even though the path probably appears closed, it has a beginning and an ending point. (It's sometimes difficult to find an endpoint—look for any one point on the path that looks even slightly different from the others. If you still can't find one, and you really need to, just start clicking and moving points—selecting Undo if it's not an endpoint—until you find the right place.)

If the box had a dash or stripe selected as a frame, that style is applied to the resulting path. (Special bitmapped frames can't be applied to lines; see "Frames, Dashes, and Stripes," later in this chapter.)

Tip: Watch Out for Shape Changes. When you use the above technique to change a framed box into a line, you need to watch out for two things. First, the size of the box generally changes. This is because frames are run on the inside or outside of a box, but lines "grow" on both sides of its centerline. Take that dimension shift into consideration as you make your initial box.

The second thing to watch for is notches in your frame. Again, lines are always open paths, so a thick frame (which turns into a thick line width) may have a notch in it where the two endpoints meet (see Figure 3-41).

Note the notch in at what is now the beginning of the path. Also, the box has become larger because of the path.

Figure 3-41 Converting a framed box to a line

Tip: Text Boxes to Text Paths. *If you want to set some text in a circle, you need a circular text path. Unfortunately, it's a pain in the eyeball to draw a perfect circle with the Bézier text-path tool. Here's a better way: Make a circular text box and type in it the text you want on the path. Now, choose the Bézier line from the Shape submenu under the Item menu (that's the one that looks like a squiggle). The text box becomes a text path, and the contents of the box become the contents of the path (see Figure 3-42).*

Figure 3-42
Text boxes to
text paths

There is one more step: You must change the color of the line to None in order to make it invisible (unless you want to be able to see the text on a path and the path itself). Note that the best way to specify exactly where on the path you want the text to begin is to click on that point with the Scissors tool. This automatically converts the box into a path and starts the text at that point.

Converting paths to boxes. If you select a line and choose one of the regular boxes from the Shape submenu, XPress replaces your line with a box of this shape (the size of the box is determined by the line's bounding rectangle). What is interesting is what happens when you choose the Bézier box from the Shape submenu.

If you simply select the Bézier shape, XPress converts the outline of the path into a box. For instance, if you have a straight line 1 inch long and 8 points thick, the result is a rectangular box 1 inch long and 8 points wide (see Figure 3-43).

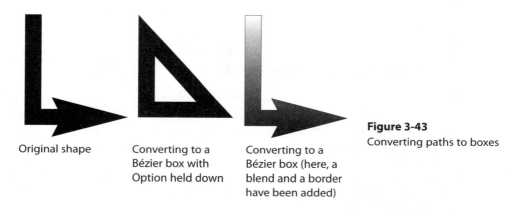

Original shape

Converting to a Bézier box with Option held down

Converting to a Bézier box (here, a blend and a border have been added)

Figure 3-43
Converting paths to boxes

If you hold down the Option/Alt key when selecting the Bézier box shape, XPress does something completely different: It closes the path for you. If the line had a line style (dots, dashes, or whatever), QuarkXPress applies that style as the box's frame.

> *Tip: Converting Dashes and Stripes to Bézier Boxes. I think the ability to convert a line to a box, a function in which XPress actually builds the box based on the outline of the line, is really amazing. To me, the best part about it is that line styles—such as dots, stripes, or arrowheads— are also converted, usually becoming compound objects. If you want, you can then select Split All Paths to further manipulate each of the individual Bézier paths of the shape.*
>
> *This sort of thing makes the most sense when you are working with thick lines. Once you have a box based on the line, you can fill it with a color, a blend, text, or a picture (see Figure 3-44).*

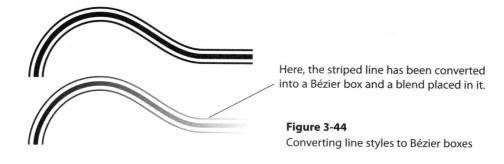

Here, the striped line has been converted into a Bézier box and a blend placed in it.

Figure 3-44
Converting line styles to Bézier boxes

Switching shapes back and forth. Once you've changed an object from one shape into another, it's unlikely you'll ever be able to get it back to the original shape again. Shape changes generally are not reversible.

Converting Text to Paths

Digital typefaces, as we'll see in Chapter 6, *Typography*, generally contain mathematical outlines of each character in the font. These outlines are scalable, so you can view or print them at any resolution or size and they'll always be smooth. Wouldn't it be cool if you could also convert those outlines into QuarkXPress Bézier boxes? You can.

To convert text to a box, select the text with the Content tool and choose Text to Box from the Style menu (see Figure 3-45). There are a few caveats. You can only convert up to a single line of text at a time. You can only convert fonts for which you have the outline files installed, and some fonts don't seem to convert well. Finally, while you can convert a lot of characters at the same time, it doesn't mean you'll actually get them to print later. Keep it simple.

Figure 3-45
Creating Bézier paths from text

If you have selected more than one character of text, they are all converted into a single picture box. You can then use Split Outside Paths to separate them into individual characters, if you'd like. Whether you split them or not, you can use all the editing features I've discussed to manipulate the outlines. After all, these are picture boxes now.

Also, note that I use the term *convert*. However, I should probably say *create*, because the original text is not deleted from the text box (although see the next tip).

> **Tip: Anchoring Text Outlines.** *If you hold down the Option/Alt key when you select Text to Box from the Style menu, XPress actually replaces your selected text with the Bézier box, anchoring it in the text as an inline graphic (see Chapter 12, Text Meets Graphics, for more information on inline boxes).*

*Tip: **Careful with Those Frames.*** *I'll discuss putting borders around boxes later in this chapter (in "Frames, Dashes, and Stripes"), but I should make one comment now: Many people don't realize when they put a border around a box, it can actually change the shape of the box. If Framing is set to Outside on the General tab of the Preferences dialog box, adding a frame will actually expand the boundaries of the box itself. If the border is too thick, the edges of the box may bump into each other, permanently altering the shape of the box (see Figure 3-46).*

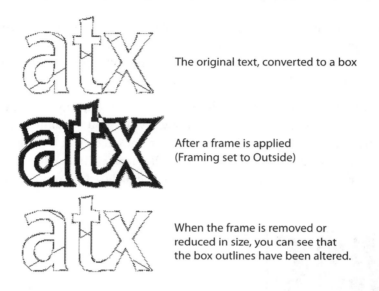

The original text, converted to a box

After a frame is applied
(Framing set to Outside)

When the frame is removed or
reduced in size, you can see that
the box outlines have been altered.

Figure 3-46 Frames can sometimes change the shape of boxes.

MANIPULATING ITEMS

Once you've created a page element (item) like a picture box or line, what can you do with it? A lot. In this section I talk about how to move, rotate, skew, resize, reshape, lock, duplicate, suppress the printout of, and delete items. I'm talking about only the items themselves here, so you often need to select them with the Item tool to make most of these changes.

Moving Items

You can move a page element in several ways. First, if you're an interactive type, you can select the Item tool, then click on the object and drag it. Or, if you have the Content tool selected, you can get the Item tool temporarily by holding down the Command/Ctrl key, which lets you move an item, too. (However, note that if you have more than one object selected, Command/Ctrl-dragging with the Content tool moves a single item in the group, not the whole group.)

The second method for moving an item is by changing its origin coordinates in the Measurements palette or the Modify dialog box. I find this method especially useful if I need to move the item a specific amount. For example, let's say I have a text box with its origin at 1 inch across and 1 inch down. If I want to move the text box horizontally 18 picas, I change the Origin Across coordinate in the Measurements palette to "1"+18p," then press Enter. The box automatically moves over.

A third method for moving items is by selecting them and pressing the Arrow keys on the keyboard. Each time you press an arrow key, the item moves one point in that direction. Holding down the Option/Alt key when you press an arrow key moves the item 0.1 point.

> **Tip: Techniques for Item Placement.** *If you have a style of placing and sizing your page elements—such as lines and picture boxes—that works for you, stick to it. Nonetheless, here are some basic guides I find helpful.*

- Use picas and points for everything except basic page size. These are the standard units among designers and printers, and allow precision without their having to deal with numbers like 0.08334 inch (which is 6 points, or 0.5 pica). If you're working with type, this also makes it easier since type is generally specified in picas and points.

- Try to use round numbers for most of your measurements. Creating or moving a box at the Fit in Window size usually gives you measurements with coordinates out to the thousandth of a point, such as "6p3.462". In the long run, it can come in handy to create your boxes at Actual Size and then resize them if needed, or—if you must work at a reduced or enlarged view—to go into the Measurements palette or the Modify dialog box (double-click on the box or press Command/Ctrl-M) and change the coordinates and sizes to round numbers.

- Use oval- or Bézier-shaped picture boxes only when you must have that shape. Using a rectangle or square box for the majority of your pictures can cut your printing time to half or a third of the time it takes when you use ovals.

> **Tip: Viewing Changes as You Make Them.** *It's always a hassle to move, resize, or rotate a box, because while you're doing it, QuarkXPress only shows you the outline of the box rather than the whole box. Or does it?*
>
> *If you hold the mouse button down on a picture-box handle for about half a second before dragging it, you can see the picture crop (or scale, if you have the Command/Ctrl key held down, too) as you move the handle. Similarly, if you pause half a second when you move or rotate the box, you can see the text or picture rotate while dragging. No, you don't have to count; just wait until you see the object flash quickly before you start dragging. (The exact amount of time is determined by the Delayed Item Dragging value on the Interactive tab in the Preferences dialog box.)*

Tip: Moving an Item's Origin. Adobe PageMaker and Adobe InDesign both let you set the origin of a page element from any of its corners or its center rather than from just the upper-left corner. QuarkXPress does not. I can only offer a somewhat weak workaround for specifying alternate origins: Use the built-in math functions. If you want the right side of a 12-pica-wide picture box to be set at the 2.75-inch mark, type "2.75"-12p" into the x-origin field of the Measurements palette. That is, simply subtract the width of the box from the right point. Or, if you want the center of a 16-pica-wide text box to be at the 18-centimeter mark, you can type "18cm-16p/2."

Resizing and Reshaping Items

Resizing an object means changing its width and height, while reshaping it may involve moving points around, like turning a rectangle into a triangle. Both are easy to do, but how you proceed depends on the type of object you have selected. (Resizing and reshaping a group of items are special-case scenarios I cover in "Modifying Grouped Objects," later in this chapter.)

Resizing boxes. The most basic shapes are the non-Bézier boxes, like the rectangle and the oval. To resize these, you once again have a choice between using QuarkXPress's interactive click-and-drag style or working in measurements.

- **Resizing by dragging.** To resize by clicking and dragging, place the screen cursor over one of the box's handles. Boxes have eight handles (one on each side, one on each corner), which you can drag to resize. Dragging a side handle resizes the box in one direction—horizontally or vertically. Dragging a corner handle resizes the box in two directions (horizontally *and* vertically). If the shape is a Bézier box, you need to turn off Edit Shape (in the Edit submenu under the Item menu) to see these handles.

  XPress lets you "flip" a box, resulting in a mirror of the original, by dragging one of the side handles across the box and past the opposite handle (see "Tip: Flipping Shapes Around," earlier in this chapter).

- **Resizing by the numbers.** The second method of resizing and reshaping boxes is by changing their height and width values. These values are located in both the Modify dialog box and the Measurements palette. Unless you're a wizard at math, it's difficult to keep an object's aspect (width-to-height) ratio this way (see "Tip: Proportional Resizing by the Numbers," below). Instead, this is a great way to make a box exactly the size you want it. If you want an 8-by-10-inch picture box, you can draw one to any size you'd like, then change its width and height coordinates to 8 inches and 10 inches.

Tip: Maintain the Ratios. In order to maintain an item's width and height ratio while stretching it, hold down the Option/Alt and Shift keys while dragging. If you want to constrain the box into a square or circle, just hold down the Shift key while dragging. (If the object were rectangular or oval, it would snap into a square or a circle.)

Tip: Proportional Resizing by the Numbers. QuarkXPress can do a lot of math work for you. This can come in handy when you're trying to resize items on a page. For example, if you know the 1-by-2-inch box (2 inches tall) on the page should be 5 inches wide, you can type "5"" into the width box. But what do you put in the height box? If you want to keep the aspect ratio, you can let the program do the math for you: just type "*newwidth/oldwidth" after the height value. In this example, you'd type "*5/2" after the height. This multiplies the value by the percentage change in width (dividing 5 by 2 nets a 250-percent change, or 2.5 times the value).

Remember, you cannot divide by a measurement, so you cannot type something like "*5"/18p." You would have to type "5"/1.5" (1.5 is 18p in inches).

Bézier boxes and lines. I discussed editing Bézier lines and boxes earlier in this chapter. The one thing I want to reemphasize is to pay attention to the Edit Shape feature (in the Shape submenu, under the Item menu; or toggle it on and off with Shift-F4, or F10 in Windows). When this is on, you can edit individual Bézier points, control handles, and segments. With it off, you can only change the overall height and width of the item.

Lines. Most people define lines by their two endpoints (I'm only referring to straight lines with two endpoints, including those made with the Diagonal Text Path tool). However, QuarkXPress can define any line in four different ways. Each line description is called a *mode*, and it shows up in both the Modify dialog box and the Measurements palette (see Figure 3-47). The four modes are as follows:

Figure 3-47 Line modes

- **Endpoints.** This mode describes the line by two sets of coordinates, x1,y1 and x2,y2. In the Modify dialog box, these are called the First Across and First Down, or the Last Across and Last Down.

- **Left Point.** In Left Point mode, QuarkXPress describes a line by three values: its endpoint (from wherever you started the line when dragging is its first point), its length, and its angle. An angle of zero degrees is always a horizontal line; as the angle increases, the line rotates counterclockwise, so 45 degrees is a diagonal up and to the right, and 90 degrees is vertical.

- **Right Point.** QuarkXPress uses the same three values for the Right Point mode, except it uses the coordinate of the last point on the line (wherever you let go of the mouse button).

- **Midpoint.** The fourth mode, Midpoint, defines lines by their length and angle based on the coordinate of the center point. That is, if a line is 2 inches long, QuarkXPress draws the line 1 inch out on either side from the midpoint, at the specified angle.

You can define a line while in one mode, modify it in another, and move it with another.

For example, let's say you draw a line someplace on your page. You then find you want to rotate it slightly. You have the choice to rotate the line from its left point, right point, or midpoint by selecting the proper mode from the Measurements palette or the Modify dialog box, then changing the line's rotation value. If you want to move just the left point of the line by 3 points (and leave the other point stationary), you can switch to Endpoints mode and alter the x2,y2 coordinate.

To resize a line by a given percentage, you can multiply its length by the percentage. If you want a line to be 120 percent as long, just multiply the length value in the Measurements palette or Modify dialog box by 1.2. To make it half as long, multiply by 0.5 or divide by two.

> **Tip: Constraining Lines Along an Angle.** We all know you can hold down the Shift key while you draw out a line to constrain the line horizontally or vertically. However, if you hold down the Shift key while resizing it (dragging one of its endpoints), XPress constrains it along its angle of rotation (or its angle plus 45 degrees, or plus 90 degrees).

Note that this is different from earlier versions of the program, in which holding down the Shift key while resizing would constrain a line to a vertical or horizontal position. Now the only way to force a diagonal line into an orthogonal line is to set its angle to zero or 90 degrees.

Rotating Items

You can rotate an item numerically using the Modify dialog box or the Measurements palette, or by eye with the Rotation tool (the third item in the Tool palette). Note that positive rotation values rotate the object counterclockwise; negative values rotate it clockwise (this is arguably counterintuitive). Most objects are rotated from their center. This center may not be where you think it is, however, because the center is defined as the middle of the object's bounding box.

Lines are the main exception when it comes to the center of rotation. Lines rotate differently depending on their Mode (see "Lines," above). For example, if a line is in Left Point mode when you specify a rotation, the line rotates around the first endpoint.

If you are more visual minded, you can rotate items using the Rotation tool.

1. Select a page item.

2. Choose the Rotation tool from the Tool palette.

3. Click where you want the center of rotation, but don't let the mouse button go yet.

4. Drag the Rotation tool. As you drag, the object is rotated in the direction you drag. The farther from the center of rotation you drag, the more precise the rotation can be.

I rarely use this tool in a production setting, but that's just my bias. It may suit you well. However, it's significantly harder to control the rotation by using the tool rather than by entering a specific value.

> **Tip: Rotate Around a Single Point.** *Let's say you want to rotate ten objects around a particular point. If the point is in the middle of the ten objects, you have no problem: Select them all and type the rotation value into the Measurements palette. But what if the point isn't in the middle of the group of objects? Here are two ways to rotate the objects.*

- You can use the Rotation tool. This is, in fact, the only time I ever use this tool. Select the objects, select the tool, click the point around which you want to rotate, and drag the mouse around until you get the angle you want. This is perfectly good if you don't need a specific angle, but trying to rotate a bunch of objects to exactly 30 degrees like this is nearly impossible.

- I like this method instead: Draw a big picture box surrounding all the objects you want to rotate. Make sure the center of the box is where you want to rotate from (when Show Guides is turned on, you can see the center point; it's where the diagonal lines join). Select all the objects you want to rotate, along with the picture box. Then type the rotation value into the Measurements palette. XPress rotates around the center of the biggest box that surrounds all the objects.

Skewing Items

QuarkXPress lets you skew boxes and their contents. As I discuss in Chapter 10, *Pictures*, skewing is the same as rotating the vertical axis and not the horizontal one. If you skew a text box or a picture box, the text or picture within the box is skewed to the same angle. You can skew a box by typing a value into the Skew field on the Box tab of the Modify dialog box (it only lets you enter values between -75 and 75 degrees). Enter a positive number to skew the box and its contents to the right; a negative number skews them to the left.

If you need to spice up your afternoon, you can skew the contents of a box separately from the box itself (you can find Text Skew on the Text tab and Picture Skew on the Picture tab of the Modify dialog box).

Skewing boxes isn't something you need to do every day, but by combining QuarkXPress's ability to skew and rotate text boxes, you can create some interesting effects, like a three-dimensional cube with angled text on each side (see Figure 3-48).

Figure 3-48
Box skew

Flipping Out

It used to be if you wanted to flip a picture or text along the vertical or horizontal axis—so you could mirror it on facing pages, for instance—you had to dive into a graphics program, flip the image, save it as a picture, then bring it into your QuarkXPress project.

Well, no longer. Just select the object, then go to the Style menu and choose Flip Vertical or Flip Horizontal. Note that you have to use the Content tool to do this, as this is actually mirroring the contents of the box rather than the box itself. Not only does this command let you flip pictures and text, but flipped text remains fully editable (to do this, you have to practice reading the newspaper in the mirror).

Also, you can use the icons for flipping contents in the Measurements palette (see Figure 3-49). The top icon controls horizontal flipping; the lower one controls vertical flipping.

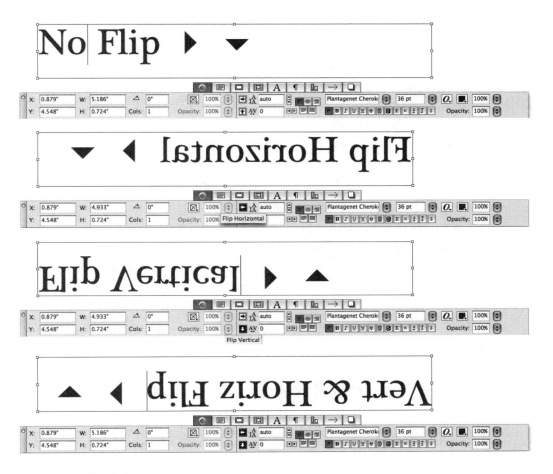

Figure 3-49 Flip Horizontal and Vertical

Locking Items

There are times when you want an item to stay how and where it is. For example, if you've painstakingly placed multiple text boxes on your page, you may not want someone else who will be working on your page to move or resize them accidentally. You can lock any page item down to its spot with the Item tool, making it invulnerable to being moved or resized. Just select the item with either the Item or the Content tool and choose Lock from the Item menu (or press Command/Ctrl-L).

But in QuarkXPress 7 you have a new set of locks to work with. Note the lock menu item has two choices. You can not only lock something into position, you can lock the contents. When a text box is selected, the choice is position or story (text box). If a picture box is selected, the choice is position or picture. If both a text and picture box are selected, you can lock only the position. The same is true if you select multiple boxes of the same type. You can only lock contents one box at a time.

There is another new locking feature in QuarkXPress 7. In older versions, just because you locked something did not mean that it wouldn't move or change. If you selected the box with the Item tool and your cat jumped onto your keyboard, pressing one of the arrow keys, the box moved. If you used the Space/Align feature, QuarkXPress would ignore the Locked status and move the object (this *really* bugged me). And you could easily (and unintentionally) change the coordinate of the item's origin or its height or width in the Measurements palette.

No longer. With the new locking controls, you simply can't move an item without unlocking it. Quark has successfully eliminated a major annoyance!

If an item is locked, the Item tool cursor turns into a padlock when passed over the item. You cannot move it by clicking and dragging either the item or its control handles. I find this feature especially helpful when I'm working on a complex page and don't want an accidental click here or a drag there to ruin my work.

To unlock an item, select it and press Command/Ctrl-L again (or choose Unlock from the Item menu).

Suppress Printout and Suppress Picture Printout

If you turn on Suppress Printout (in the Modify dialog box) for any object on your page, QuarkXPress won't print that object. Ever. Period. This is helpful when you want non-printing notes to be placed in your layout, or for setting runaround objects that affect your text but don't print out on your final page. (However, just because the object doesn't print doesn't mean the text runaround goes away; see Chapter 12, *Text Meets Graphics*.)

When you have a picture box selected, the Modify dialog box also offers a second checkbox: Suppress Picture Printout. If you turn on this one, it keeps the picture from printing, but the box itself still prints. The difference? If the picture has a frame around it, the frame prints and the picture doesn't.

> **Tip: Post-it Notes.** *If your QuarkXPress projects need to move from one person to another, you may want to add comments to certain objects or areas of a page. By taking advantage of QuarkXPress's ability to suppress the printout of any item, you can easily create noticeable, but nonprinting, electronic "Post-it" notes to contain comments and suggestions about an individual layout (see Figure 3-50).*

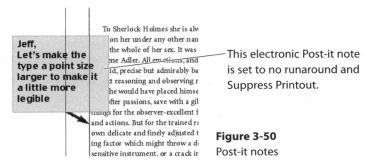

This electronic Post-it note
is set to no runaround and
Suppress Printout.

Figure 3-50
Post-it notes

Create a text box and enter the text of the note. Give the box a background of 100-percent yellow, a runaround of None, and turn on Suppress Printout in the Text Box Specifications dialog box (so as not to affect the printing of the file).

Duplicating Items

When I stand around watching over their shoulders as people work, one of the most common suggestions I make is to use the Duplicate and Step and Repeat features more often. If you need to make two text boxes, it's rarely worth the trouble to draw both of them; just make one and then duplicate it. There are three ways to duplicate a page element: Copy and Paste it, Duplicate it, or use Step and Repeat.

Copy and Paste. Selecting an item, copying it, and pasting it (Command/Ctrl-C and Command/Ctrl-V) is the most common way people learn to duplicate objects, though it's not always the most efficient or precise way. Confusion over which tool to select is the most common problem. You should use the Item tool when working with *items* (boxes, lines, and text paths), and the Content tool when working with the *contents* of boxes or text paths. If you have the Content tool selected and you try to copy a text box, you only copy text. Copying with the Item tool actually copies the text box. (See "Tip: Copy the Opposite," below.)

When you Paste a page item, the program places it in the middle of your screen or as close as it can get it on whatever spread you're currently on (however, see "Tip: Paste in Place," below). This has been known to trip up even advanced users of XPress, because the "active" is not always the page you're looking at. If even only a little sliver of the previous spread is touching the upper-left corner of the layout window (where the two rulers meet), Pasting places the object on *that* spread, not the one that takes up most of your screen.

Tip: Paste in Place. Both PageMaker and InDesign have long had a feature called Paste in Place, or "power pasting," which pastes an object at the same place on the page as you copied or cut it from. QuarkXPress 6 incorporated this helpful feature. It's in plain view in the Edit menu, but few XPress users notice it there. Alternately, you can press Command-Option-Shift-V (Ctrl-Alt-Shift-V).

Tip: Copy the Opposite. Whether the Command/Ctrl-C keystroke copies the page item or the contents within the page item depends on if you have the Item or the Content tool selected. But, you can also Copy the item itself when you have the Content tool by pressing Command-Option-C (Ctrl-Alt-C). For example, if you have the Content tool selected and you want to Copy a whole text box, you can press Command-Option-C (Ctrl-Alt-C).

Duplicate. Choosing Duplicate from the Item menu (or pressing Command/Ctrl-D) duplicates whatever item(s) you have selected. The default setting for Duplicate is to offset the duplicate item ¼ inch down and to the right from the original object, but Duplicate always uses whatever horizontal and vertical offsets you last used in Step and Repeat.

Step and Repeat. The Step and Repeat feature can best be described as a powerhouse, and I wish every program had it. The Step and Repeat command (under the Item menu, or press Command-Option-D or Ctrl-Alt-D) lets you select one or more objects and duplicate them with specific horizontal and vertical offsets as many times as you like.

For example, if you want 35 vertical lines, each 9 points away from each other across the page, draw one line and then choose Step and Repeat from the Item menu. In the Step and Repeat dialog box, enter "34" in the Repeat Count field (don't count the original), "9pt" in the Horizontal Offset field, and "0" in the Vertical Offset field. After you use Step and Repeat, you can press Command/Ctrl-Z to Undo all of the duplications.

Both Duplicate and Step and Repeat have certain limitations. First, you cannot duplicate an item so any part of it falls off the pasteboard. If you are working with constrained items (see "Constraining," below), you cannot duplicate them so any of the copies would fall outside of the constraining box. Any items you duplicate from within a constrained group become part of that constrained group. When duplicating an item from a set of grouped objects, the copy does not become part of the group.

Super Step and Repeat. The Super Step and Repeat feature in the Item menu (which appears when the XTension of the same name is active), not only offsets duplicate objects, but skews, scales, and rotates the duplicates, or changes the tint value. It can be useful. For example, if you want to create evenly spaced tint blocks going from 100 percent black to 10 percent black, you can create the first block, then use Super Step and Repeat to create nine more. If you type "10%" as the value for the end box shade, QuarkXPress will fill in the boxes between the first and last box in equal steps (90, 80, …etc.)

Tip: Clone Item. If you're a Macromedia FreeHand user, you're probably familiar with the Command/Ctrl-= keystroke to duplicate an item without any offset. This is called cloning. I use this all the time when I'm building pages in QuarkXPress.

First, I use Step and Repeat to copy an object with the Horizontal and Vertical Offset fields both set to zero. Now, next time I want to clone something, I just press Command/Ctrl-D, which always uses the last offsets I typed in Step and Repeat. This works as long as I don't change the Offsets or quit XPress.

Tip: Moving Objects to Other Projects. QuarkXPress's ability to drag objects around the page (or from one page to another) can extend to other projects. Use the Item tool to drag an object or group of objects to another layout (see the section on moving items between layouts in Chapter 2, QuarkXPress Basics). Because in QuarkXPress 7 you can have several layouts open within a project, this is now much easier to do.

Deleting Items

There is a difference between deleting the contents of a picture or text box and deleting the box itself. When the contents of a box (such as a picture or text) are deleted, the box still remains. When the box itself is deleted, everything goes. There are three basic ways to delete a page item.

- I think the easiest way to delete a page item is to select it (with either the Item or Content tool) and press Command/Ctrl-K. This is the same as selecting Delete from the Item menu.

- The second easiest way to delete an item is to select it with the Item tool and press the Delete key on your keyboard. Remember, if you use the Content tool, you delete the text or picture rather than the box.

- A third way to delete an item is to select it with the Item tool and select Cut or Clear from the Edit menu. Since cutting it actually saves the item on the Clipboard, you can place it somewhere else later.

The only one of these methods that works for deleting a single item from a group is Command/Ctrl-K. That's because to remove this kind of page item, you must first select it with the Content tool (or else you end up deleting the entire group).

Tip: Alien Deletions. *Computer software has a long history of "Easter eggs": wacky little useless features programmers include late at night after too many hours of staring at the screen. QuarkXPress has a couple good Easter eggs. My favorite is the little Martian that walks out on your screen and kills an object on your page (see Figure 3-51). You can call this little fella up from the depths by pressing Command-Option-Shift-K; or you can hold down the modifiers while selecting Delete from the Item menu.*

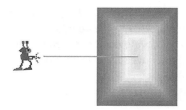

Figure 3-51
The Martian

The Martian is a Macintosh-only Easter egg, but the same keystroke (Ctrl-Alt-Shift-K) provides a different sort of Easter egg on Windows: The deleted object melts down your screen with a wonderful gurgling sound.

RELATIONSHIPS BETWEEN ITEMS

Page-layout programs like QuarkXPress are designed so you can put a number of text and picture objects on a page. That's the whole point. And anytime you have more than one object on a page, you're going to be concerned about the relationships between those objects. If you have a block of text and a picture next to it, you probably know how you want those two items to relate: Do they align on their left edges? Are they centered next to each other? Should the picture always follow the text?

Curiously, some page-layout software developers don't understand this fundamental element of page layout, and they have no tools for handling these relationships. Fortunately for us, however, Quark *does* understand.

In this section I talk about controlling relationships between items: layering, grouping, constraining, and their position on the page relative to other page elements. There is also a new tool for handling relationships not only between items, but also between layouts and projects called Composition Zones. It's rather complicated, so we will wait to discuss this tool in depth in Chapter 13, *Collaboration*.

Layering Items

QuarkXPress, like most desktop publishing programs, handles multiple objects on a page by *layering* them. Each page item (picture box, text box, contentless box, text path, or line) is always on a higher or lower layer than the other page items. This is also called a *stacking order*. This is generally an intuitive approach to working with page elements; it's just what you would do if each of the objects were on a little piece of paper in front of you. When you're placing objects on your page, you work from the bottom of the stacking order up. The first object you place is the bottom-most object, the second object is on top of it, and so on.

If none of your page elements touch or overlap one another, then layering has almost no relevance to you. However, when they do touch or overlap in some way, you want to be able to control which objects overlap which. The primary methods for controlling the stacking order are the Bring to Front and Send to Back commands in the Item menu.

Bring to Front and Send to Back function as sweeping controls, moving a selected object all the way to the back or all the way to the front layer. When you hold down the Option key while selecting the Item menu, the Send to Back and Bring to Front items become Send Backward and Bring Forward. (Note that these are always visible in Windows, so you don't have to hold down a modifier key.) Note that you can also use the function keys to move things up and down through layers.

For even more control over how your objects stack up, you can also create multiple layers in the Layers palette; I discuss that in "The Layers Palette," later in this chapter.

Grouping Objects

Objects on a page are rarely lone creatures. Often, they like to bunch together to form single units, like organic cells grouping to form a vital organ in your body. Similarly, you can create groups of page items. A group of objects can include any number of boxes and/or lines. When you select one member of the group with the Item tool, the whole group gets selected. Or, you can select and modify individual members of the group with the Content tool. Here's what you do.

1. Using the Item or Content tool, select the items you want grouped. You can hold down the Shift key to select multiple items. Or, you can drag a marquee over or around the objects (any object the marquee touches is selected).

2. Select Group from the Item menu or press Command/Ctrl-G.

It's that easy. When the group is selected with the Item tool, a dotted line shows the bounding box of the grouped objects (see Figure 3-52).

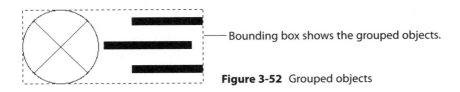

Bounding box shows the grouped objects.

Figure 3-52 Grouped objects

To ungroup the objects, select the grouped object with the Item tool and select Ungroup from the Item menu (or press Command/Ctrl-U).

> *Tip: Multilevel Grouping.* Not only can you group multiple objects, but you can group multiple groups, or groups and objects. This means you can build levels of grouped objects. For example, on a catalog page you may have six picture boxes, each with a caption in a text box. You can group each caption box with its picture box, then select these six grouped objects and group them together. Later, if you ungroup the six objects, each picture box is still grouped with its caption box.

Modifying Grouped Objects

As I mentioned above, once you have grouped a set of objects, you can still modify each of them using the Content tool. Just select the element and change it. Each item can be rotated, resized, or edited just as usual. To move a single object in a grouped selection, hold down the Command/Ctrl key to get a temporary Item tool. Then move the object where you want it and release the Command/Ctrl key.

The group Modify dialog box. QuarkXPress lets you do some pretty nifty things with grouped items. If you select Modify from the Item menu (or press Command/Ctrl-M, or double-click on the group with the Item tool), QuarkXPress gives you a special Modify dialog box for the group. Which controls you see in this Modify dialog box depends on whether every object in a group is the same type of object (all rules, all text boxes, etc.).

Some features in this group Modify dialog box are always available, like Origin Across and Origin Down, which determine the upper-left corner of the bounding box for the whole group. Angle, too, sets the rotation for the group, as though the group were a single object.

If you change a value in the group Modify dialog box, you change that value for every one of the objects in the group. For example, if you specify a background color for the grouped objects, the background color is applied to all the boxes and lines in the group. If you set the Picture Angle to 20 degrees for a group of picture boxes, the items in each of the picture boxes are rotated within their boxes (see Chapter 10, *Pictures*).

You can turn on the Suppress Printout option for a group of mixed objects, and each of the objects in the group has its Suppress Printout checkbox turned on. Similarly, you can add or change the frame around a group of objects, as long as they're all boxes. If you later ungroup the objects, the settings you made while they were grouped remain.

Note that if you have any lines (rules) in the group, changing the background color of the group affects the color of the line itself.

You can't open the Modify dialog box for a group of objects when one group is nested inside another. You have to ungroup the objects and regroup them individually.

Scaling groups. The engineers at Quark snuck a little feature into the program without much ado: the ability to scale groups of objects. I'm surprised they were so quiet about it, as it's a wonderful step forward. But it's not quite a leap forward yet—you'll see why in a moment.

To scale several objects at once, you first have to group them. Next, you can drag one of the group's corner or side handles. When you let go, all the objects in the group are scaled proportionally. There are, as always, a few options you can take advantage of.

- If you hold down the Command/Ctrl key when you drag, any content (text and pictures) inside boxes or lines within the group is also scaled.

- If you hold down Option/Alt and Shift when you drag, the group is scaled proportionally. (Again, add the Command/Ctrl key to scale the contents proportionally, too.)

- If you only hold down the Shift key, the group is constrained into a square (not all that useful, but it's good to know the option is there).

- You can type values in the height or width fields in the Measurements palette. This forces the whole group to fit within that size. For example, if you need to fit three picture boxes within a 10-centimeter column, you could type "10 cm" in the width field. Of course, it's easy to scale the items disproportionately when you do this (see "Tip: Proportional Resizing by the Numbers," earlier in this chapter). Also, note that this scales the boxes, but not their contents.

- Remember, you can scale by a percentage using XPress's built-in math functions. For instance, if you want each item in the group to be 130-percent larger, type "*1.3" after the current width and height values.

The ability to scale groups was added to QuarkXPress 4, and, sadly, this limited feature didn't get any better in XPress 7. There are a number of features XPress doesn't scale when you scale a group and its contents, such as the values for Space Before, Indent, Rule Above, and so on. These shore up my opinion that XPress needs a *real* scaling tool, much like those offered in some of the XTension packages, like Gluon's ProScale.

Constraining

Ten years ago, if you had asked a QuarkXPress user what one feature they would have sold their grandmother to get rid of, they would invariably have said, "Parent-and-child boxes." Back in versions 1 and 2 of XPress, these parent-and-child boxes made it nearly impossible to be flexible with page design because boxes became "trapped" inside other boxes. These constraints could be useful and accessible when you got accustomed to them, but there were many times when what I really needed was a choice of whether to enable it or not. Parent-and-child constraints are still in QuarkXPress, but thank goodness they *are* now options rather than rules.

Let's be clear here for those not familiar with this feature. I'm not talking about the type of constraining I've mentioned earlier in this chapter, which refers to holding down the Shift key to constrain the movement of an object to a 45- or 90-degree angle. This is a different sort of constraint.

Parent-and-child box constraints reminds me of a baby's playpen (this may be some left-over childhood trauma, but I don't want to go into it). A playpen is a box with a structure of its own. You can place objects (or babies) into it, and they can't get out unless you physically take them out.

Similarly, a parent box is a text or picture box with certain structural constraints so any items created or placed inside its boundaries ("child" items) can't easily get outside those boundaries. Imagine a text box that was specified as a parent box. It acts as a normal text box. However, when you draw a line inside it using one of the Line tools, that line cannot be moved or resized to extend outside the text box. The only way you can get it out is by cutting it and pasting it elsewhere.

I know this feature sounds awful, but it has some great applications. For example, building a table by adding vertical and horizontal rules to a text box is aided if those rules don't slip away when you move the box (child items always move with their parents). Also, if you have a specific area in which all items must remain, creating a parental constraint makes sure you don't accidentally mess up your specifications when your eyes are bleary at three in the morning.

You can create parent-and-child box constraints in two ways: automatic constraints and manual constraints. Let's look at each of these.

Automatic constraints. Automatic constraints were the standard for early versions of QuarkXPress. With automatic constraints on, all picture and text boxes act as parent constraint boxes. You can turn automatic constraints on and off by checking the Auto Constraint box in the Preferences dialog box. You can turn on Auto Constraint when every box you create is to be a parent or a child box, and then turn it off to create "normal" boxes and items.

Note that the parent box and the child items are grouped when you select them with the Item tool. To unconstrain these items, see "Manual constraints," next.

Manual constraints. If you prefer, you can apply your own parent-and-child box constraints to a set of objects by manually constraining them. It's easy to do.

1. Make sure the page elements you want to be child items are totally within the boundaries of the box you want to be the parent box.

2. Make sure the soon-to-be-parent box is behind each of the objects that are soon to be constrained. Parent boxes must be on a lower layer than their children. You can think of the playpen analogy: The playpen must be under—and surrounding—the child.

3. Select and group the child and parent objects and boxes (see "Modifying Grouped Objects," earlier in this chapter).

4. Select Constrain from the Item menu.

Those objects on top of the parent box and in that group are constrained to the boundaries of the parent box.

You can unconstrain this group by clicking on the parent-child group with the Item tool and selecting either Unconstrain or Ungroup from the Item menu. Unconstrain removes the constraints, but leaves the items grouped. Ungroup removes both the grouping and constraining specifications. (You can't have parent-and-child constraints without grouping.)

Aligning and Distributing Objects

Before I knew how cool the Space/Align feature was, I simply didn't know how badly I needed it. Now I use it all the time; once you know about it, you probably will, too. Space/Align is, in some ways, the control center for setting up object relationships on your page. Let's look at why.

The whole idea of Space/Align is to move page items around to create certain relationships between them. The tools you have to work with are Between, Space, and Distribute Evenly. Here's what you do.

1. Select all the items you want to relate to one another. For instance, if you want two items to align along their left edges, select both of them.

2. Select Space/Align from the Alignment tab of the Measurements palette. The old dialog box is gone, and making these selections from the menu is pretty clunky, but you're almost certain to like the new interface a lot more than the old one.

3. Decide whether you want to align or distribute the objects. I'll talk about the difference in just a moment. If you're aligning the objects, select Space and enter the amount of space you want between the items; if you're distributing them, select Distribute Evenly.

4. Tell QuarkXPress what part of the objects you want to align or distribute. For example: the left edges of two boxes, or the tops of a few lines, or the centers of five mixed items.

Starting with the second step, let's take a look at each of these.

Vertical/Horizontal. If you select some objects, then choose the Alignment tab of the Measurements palette (see Figure 3-53). You see icons that control the alignment. These icons are grouped into zones. When you first start using them, note that hovering the cursor over each icon reveals what it does. After a while you'll know at a glance what each one does.

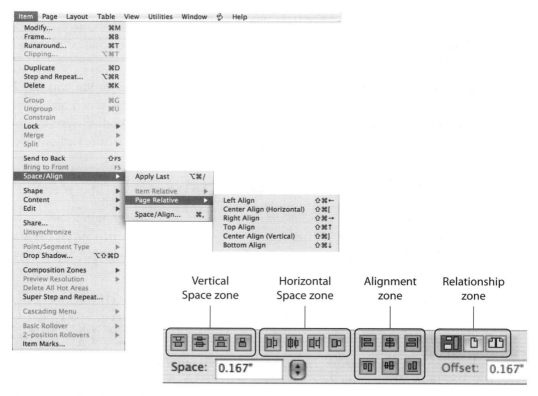

Figure 3-53 The Space/Align dialog box has been replaced by the Measurements palette in QuarkXPress 7, and that has made the tools significantly easier to understand and use. You can still navigate to the Space/Align controls through the item menus shown here, but why would you? The new Measurement palette is shown in the lower screen shot.

- Starting on the right is what I call the Relationship zone, so called because you can chose whether objects are aligned based on the objects themselves, the page, or the spread.

- Next is the Alignment zone. The top line aligns objects on the Horizontal axis (right and left edges or center horizontally), and the bottom line aligns objects on the Vertical axis (top, bottom, or center vertically).

- To the left of the Alignment zone is the Horizontal Space zone. From left to right the icons are space left edges, space horizontal centers, space right edges, and space horizontally.

- Finally comes the Vertical Space zone, which does the same thing as the Horizontal Space zone except vertically.

Space. There is now a window for inputting a space value. The default is zero, which means "align exactly," but you can type in any value. The value in the Space field determines how far apart the objects should align. For example, let's say you want to line up the left edges of two boxes. If you specify "0p" as the Space value, the left edge of the first box is at the same place as the left edge of the second box. If you specify "5p" as the Space value, the left edge of the first box is placed 5 picas from the left edge of the second box (see Figure 3-54).

But which box moves? The topmost or leftmost items always stay stationary; they are the reference points for alignment. Other page elements move to align with them.

I use alignment all the time. If I have four text boxes I want to line up on their right edges, I no longer have to draw guides or figure measurements. I just select them all and align their right edges with Space set to zero. The new Measurements palette in QuarkXPress 7 makes this process easier than ever.

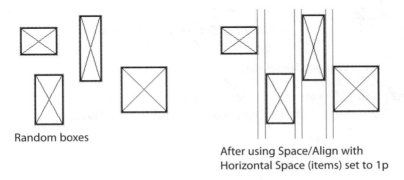

Random boxes

After using Space/Align with
Horizontal Space (items) set to 1p

Figure 3-54 Horizontal spacing with Space/Align

Tip: Use Apply in Space/Align. One of the most important techniques for using the Space/Align features is to always click the Apply button (or press Command/Ctrl-A) before leaving the dialog box. This way you can see the effect of your Space/Align settings, and—if something unexpected happened—you can change them. Sure, you can usually undo any alignment you've made after you leave the dialog box, but why make the effort when you can check out your changes in advance?

Tip: Spacing with Percentages. You don't have to type an absolute value into the Space field. You can type a percentage, too. For instance, if you want the tops of two lines to be twice as far apart as they already are, you can type "200%" and click OK. When you're working in percentages, the Apply button has an additional function: It lets you apply that percentage more than once. If you type "150%" and click Apply, the objects are spaced one and a half times their existing distance apart. Then, if you click Apply again, they're moved another one and a half times, and so on.

What used to be called "Distribute" is now called "Space." Setting Space to Evenly is the same as setting it to zero, and that is the default. QuarkXPress always takes the leftmost and rightmost, or the topmost and bottommost, page elements that you have selected (depending on whether you're aligning vertically, horizontally, or both) and uses them as the distribution boundaries. In other words, those objects don't move, but all the other objects that you selected do move. I find distribution helpful when I have a number of items that are all the same size but are scattered around the page (see Figure 3-55).

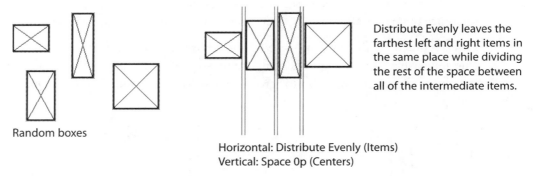

Random boxes

Distribute Evenly leaves the farthest left and right items in the same place while dividing the rest of the space between all of the intermediate items.

Horizontal: Distribute Evenly (Items)
Vertical: Space 0p (Centers)

Figure 3-55 Distribute Evenly with Space/Align

The little icons on the Measurements palette are a bit small for my eyes, but they do help you in figuring out what part of the objects you want to align or distribute.

The concept of aligning or distributing objects based on Item is sometimes confusing to people. Item refers to the bounding box of the page element. So, for example, horizontally aligning two text boxes with Space set to zero and Item set to Relationship zone, clicking align Horizontally in the Horizontal Alignment zone results in the right side of one being aligned with the left side of the second. Another way to say this is there is zero space between the items.

And note that I said this is based on the *bounding box* of the object, which is the smallest rectangle that can enclose the entire object. This may result in alignment you might not expect, especially when you're working with rotated or oddly shaped Bézier picture boxes.

If you have multiple objects on a page, and you want to center all of them on top of each other, you can apply both a vertical and a horizontal alignment to them, with Centers selected in the Horizontal Alignment zone, and Space set to zero.

> *Tip: Measuring from Picture Box to First Baseline.* I worked on a job a few years ago where the art director insisted the first baseline of each caption under an illustration sit exactly two picas from the bottom of the picture. This is exactly the kind of thing that can drive you nutty trying to figure out, and it's exactly the kind of thing QuarkXPress can do for you somewhat automatically (saving you from a life of frustration and mental anxiety). Instead of measuring each and every caption and picture box, try this method.
>
> 1. Use Space/Align to align the text (caption) and picture (illustration) boxes with no space between them. That means set the Vertical Space field to zero space between Items. You can also set the horizontal alignment, if that's required (I usually center them, for instance).
>
> 2. Set the first baseline of the caption's text box to the value you're looking for. In this case, it'd be two picas (see the section on first baseline in Chapter 6, Typography, for more on this feature).
>
> Voilà! The baseline of the caption is sitting two picas from the top of the text box, which is the same as the bottom of the picture box (see Figure 3-56).

Figure 3-56 First align the text and picture blocks with a setting of zero.

Then set the spacing before the paragraph at 2p.

Tip: Space/Aligning Groups. *The Space/Align feature is one of the coolest and most underused tools in XPress. You can use it to set up all sorts of relationships between items on your pages. For instance, you can place two objects exactly two picas apart; or place an equal amount of space horizontally between four pictures; or align 50 different lines along their left edges.*

One of the lesser-known features within the Space/Align function, however, is how it deals with groups. If you select three boxes and set them to vertically center, then all three boxes gets centered. However, if you group two of those boxes first, then XPress centers the loose box with the group of boxes.

Tip: Centering an Object on the Page. *There are three ways to center an object on a page. The first uses the Measurements palette.*

1. *Select the object, and in the x-origin field of the Measurements palette, type the page width minus the object width. If the object was four inches wide on an 8.5-inch page, you'd type "8.5"-4."*

2. *Type the page height minus the object height in the y-origin of the palette.*

3. *Go back to the x- and y-origin fields and divide those values by two (type "/2" or "*.5" after what's there already).*

The second method uses Space/Align.

1. *Draw a box the same size as the page. I usually draw any ol' sized box, type zeros into the x- and y-origin of the Measurements palette, and the page size into the height and width fields.*

2. *Send this box to the back (don't forget the shortcut: Shift-F5).*

3. *Shift-select the object or group of objects you want to center (so they're selected along with the background box).*

4. *Use Space/Align to align the centers of all the objects, vertically and horizontally.*

5. *Delete the page-sized box you drew.*

If the objects you're centering are all grouped together, the whole group gets centered on the page. Otherwise, each individual object gets centered (they'll all overlap).

The third method is the simplest: use the Align to Page feature in the XPert Tools XTension (see Appendix A, XTensions and Resources).

THE LAYERS PALETTE

The Layers palette helps you work in a more organized manner when building your projects by letting you separate each part of your layout into its own layer. For instance, you could put all your pictures boxes on one layer and text boxes on a different layer. Then, your copy editor could hide all the pictures in order to focus better on the text. Or, in a project that will be distributed in two countries, you could put English text on one layer and Spanish on a second layer. Because only visible layers are output when you print, you could hide the Spanish layer when printing the English text, and vice versa.

You can also use layers as a way to play around with a new design concept while keeping other parts of your layout intact and not compromised, like a trial-and-error playground. For instance, if your picture boxes are all on one layer, you can duplicate that layer, hide the original layer, then play with those pictures all you want, knowing if it doesn't work out, you can just delete this duplicate layer and go back to your first idea.

Layers have long been a staple of illustration programs like Adobe Illustrator; in fact, if you've used layers in those programs, you'll be right at home using the Layers palette in QuarkXPress.

The Default Layer and master pages. Before I get into the details of creating and manipulating layers, I need to mention two kinds of layers that appear in every project you create. The first is the Default Layer, which cannot be deleted. This is the layer your objects live on when you don't specify any other layer—it's the basic layer you're probably used to from earlier versions of XPress.

The other "layer" is the master page layer. While the Default Layer appears as a separate layer in the Layers palette, this one does not. Sadly, there is no way to assign master page objects other layers while viewing the master page (see Chapter 4, *Building a Layout,* for more on master pages). Instead, when you place an object (a box, line, or whatever) on a master page, XPress always assigns it to the Default Layer, but on your layout pages these objects appear *below* the other objects on your Default Layer—as though there were a separate master page layer.

Of course, you can always select a master page item on your layout page and assign it to another layer, but that breaks the link between this item and the master page (so changes to this item on your master page won't change this object on your layout page anymore).

Making Layers

You can control everything having to do with layers in the Layers palette (select Show Layers from the Window menu; see Figure 3-57). To make a new layer, click the New Layer button (the one that looks like sweat is flying off it). Layers always appear named "Layer 1," "Layer 2," and so on, but it's easy to change these names (I'll cover that in a moment). Note that you can have up to 256 layers in your layout (including the Default Layer), but I recommend keeping your layers to a minimum whenever possible, for the sake of simplicity.

Figure 3-57
The Layers palette

Tip: Layers of Context. Don't forget you can use context menus in the Layers palette (Control-click/ right-click). The context menu in the Layers palette (see Figure 3-58) is very useful when dealing with layers and lets you create a new layer; delete, edit, or duplicate the layer you clicked on; hide other or all layers; show other or all layers; lock other or all layers; and delete unused layers.

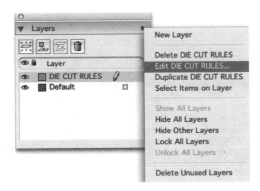

Figure 3-58
Layers palette's context menu

Assigning Layers

When you draw out a box, table, or line, it is automatically added to whatever layer you have selected in the Layers palette. The selected layer always has a little pencil icon visible to the right of the layer name, indicating you can write to that layer (see Figure 3-59). If you create something on the wrong layer, don't worry; it can easily be moved.

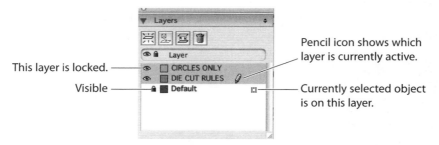

This layer is locked. ───────

Visible ───────

Pencil icon shows which layer is currently active.

Currently selected object is on this layer.

Figure 3-59 Icons in the Layers palette

As soon as an object appears on a layer (any layer other than the Default Layer), XPress 7 no longer adds a little colored icon in its corner. Instead, the bounding box takes on the color assigned to that particular layer in the layers palette (see Figure 3-60). The visual indicators won't print; they're for your onscreen reference only. However, if these visual indicators are driving you batty, you can make them go away by choosing Hide Visual Indicators from the View menu.

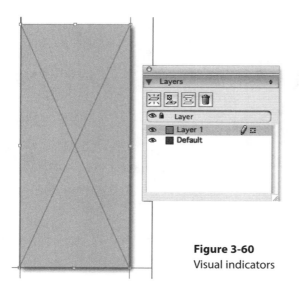

Objects on a layer are marked with that layer's color. It's impossible to see in black and white, but on your computer it shows up quite well and is not as intrusive as the old icons.

Figure 3-60
Visual indicators

Switching layers. You can move one or more items from one layer to another by select-ing the object(s) and clicking the Move Item to Layer button in the Layers palette. This displays the Move Items dialog box (see Figure 3-61), where you can pick the destination layer. XPress always moves the item(s) to the exact same page coordinates on the new layer.

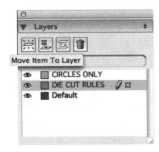

Figure 3-61
Moving items from one layer to another

Another way to move one or more selected objects is to drag the Active Item icon (it looks like a small box of squares in the far right column of the Layers palette) to the desired layer. If that icon is confusing, note that it's a miniature version of the standard eight handles around a selected item on your page—that is, the "active item."

> *Tip: Duplicating Among Layers.* If you want the same object to be on more than one layer, you can hold down the Control key (on both Macintosh and Windows) while dragging the Active Item icon from one layer to another. Multiple items on the same layer can also be duplicated.

A third method to move items from one layer to another is using Cut or Copy and Paste. This is the slowest method (you have to select the object, cut it, click on a different layer in the palette, and then select Paste). Worse, the object is always centered on the screen when you paste it rather than ending up with its original page coordinates.

Of course, when you move an item to a new layer, the object assumes the attributes of that new layer. That is, if the target layer is turned off (is invisible), then that object will suddenly disappear when you assign the layer.

> *Tip: Watch for Grouped Items.* The Layers palette works independently of the Group feature, so grouped objects can have different items on different layers. That is, you can select one object in a group and move it to a different layer than the other items in the group. Similarly, you can select items from different layers and group them. This may or may not be a good thing, depending on how you work.

> *Tip: Select All Items.* Those sneaky folks at Quark added a feature to the Layers palette few users ever find: You can tell XPress to select all the items on a given layer by choosing Select Items on Layer from the context-sensitive menu (Control-click/right-click on a layer in the palette).

Moving and Deleting Layers

Adding page items to your layers is only half the fun! You also need to be able to manipulate the layers themselves: moving them up and down, merging them together, duplicating them, and deleting them.

Moving layers up and down. To change the stacking order of your layers (moving a layer makes objects on that layer appear above or below objects on other layers), you can hold down the Option/Alt key while dragging a layer up or down in the Layers palette.

Note that the Send to Back, Send Backward, Bring to Front, and Bring Forward features in the Item menu only work *within* a layer, not across the layers. That is, choosing Bring to Front makes the selected object the top-most item on its layer, but won't move the object from one layer to another.

Merging layers. You may decide at some point during the creative process we call page layout that your file just doesn't need so many layers. Fortunately, you can merge layers together, so the objects on two or more layers all end up on one happy layer. To merge two or more layers, select more than one (unlocked) layer for merging by Shift- or Command/Ctrl-clicking in the Layers palette. Then press the Merge Layers button to display the Merge Layers dialog box (see Figure 3-62). Here you must decide which layer will be the new home to all the items from these selected layers.

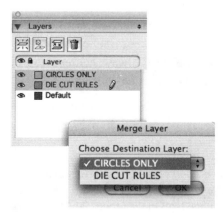

Figure 3-62
Merging layers

Duplicating layers. You can duplicate a layer (make a copy of the layer and all its contents) with the context-sensitive menu: Control-click/right-click on the layer you want to duplicate, and then select Duplicate Layer. However, if that layer has one or more linked text boxes, you may get a result you don't expect.

- If you duplicate a box containing the first box of two or more linked boxes, the contents of the entire linked story will be copied into that box and will be displayed with the standard overflow symbol.

- If you duplicate a layer with a middle box from a linked chain of boxes, all of the copy from that box and any successive copy will be copied into that box with an overflow symbol. The copy contained in boxes from linked boxes *preceding* that box disappears from the new layer.

- If you duplicate a layer containing only the end box in a linked set of boxes, only the copy from that box will be duplicated into that box.

These results are just the same as if you used the Copy and Paste, Duplicate, or Step and Repeat features on a linked text box.

Duplicating layers between projects. Need to get one or more layers from one project or layout into another? No problem: When you drag an object from one project or layout into another, the object's layer comes with it. The same thing happens when you drag a page from one project or layout into another (when both files are in Thumbnails view). If you need all the objects on a layer to come across, too, then make sure you first choose Select Items on Layer from the Layer palette's context menu. Unfortunately, there's no way to duplicate layers from one layout space to another within a project.

If you don't want a layer to come with a dragged object, make sure you assign the Default Layer to that object before dragging it. By the way, if the target project or layout already contains a layer with the same name in the Layers palette, XPress adds an asterisk to the layer's name.

Deleting layers. To delete a layer, select the layer you no longer want and click the Delete button in the Layers palette. QuarkXPress displays a dialog box asking if you want to delete the items on that layer or move those items to another layer (see Figure 3-63).

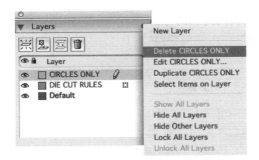

Figure 3-63
Deleting a layer

Tip: Watch What You Delete. As a safety measure, before you delete a layer, make the other layers invisible (see "Tip: Hide Other Layers," below). This way, you'll be sure of what you are deleting on that layer.

Layer Attributes

Every layer has six attributes: Name, Color, Suppress Printout, Locked, Visible, and Keep Runaround. You can turn on and off the Visible and the Locked attributes by clicking in the first two columns of the Layers palette (the columns with the eyeball and the padlock at the top). You can change all six attributes by double-clicking on the layer in the Layers palette to bring up the Layer Attributes dialog box (see Figure 3-64).

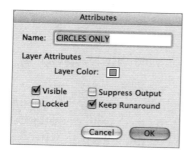

Figure 3-64
The Layer Attributes dialog box

- **Name.** As soon as you create a layer, it's a good idea to change its name to something more descriptive than "Layer 1."

- **Color.** The Color attribute affects that layer's Visual Indicator; it has no effect on the color of that layer's objects or printing or anything like that. I rarely change a layer's color. One exception is when I'm making a Notes layer (a layer for notes to myself or other folks working on this layout), which I often change to either a bright green or a light blue. (The blue reminds me of "non-repro blue," like the old days before computerized desktop page layout.)

- **Suppress Printout.** Turning on the Suppress Printout checkbox in the Layer Attributes dialog box is basically the same as selecting all the objects on that layer and turning on the Suppress Printout checkbox in the Modify dialog box (see "Suppress Printout and Suppress Picture Printout," earlier in this chapter). This is helpful for a Notes layer or any other time when you want something to be visible on-screen but not on the printed page. Note: you can also control which layers print from the Layers tab of the Print dialog box (see Chapter 15, *Printing*).

- **Locked.** In earlier versions, turning on the Locked checkbox was the same as selecting the items on that layer and selecting Lock from the Item menu. As you know from "Locking Items," earlier in this chapter, the Lock feature isn't particularly robust. Fortunately, now when you turn on the Locked checkbox (or click in the Locked column of the Layers palette), XPress *really* locks the items on that layer—you can't even select these items anymore. Text and picture boxes on locked layers are still affected by Find/Change and Picture Usage, however.

- **Visible.** The most commonly used layer attribute is Visible, which determines whether you can see the items on this layer. Of course, items on an invisible layer will not print, so this is a fast way to switch among layers you want to print and those you don't.

- **Keep Runaround.** Let's say you have a picture box on a layer with a runaround setting that forces text to flow around it (see more on text runaround in Chapter 12, *Text Meets Graphics*). The Keep Runaround attribute tells XPress what you want to do about text runaround when this layer is invisible. When it's turned on (it is by default), the objects on that layer still force text to wrap around them. If you turn this off, then the text wrap on other layers will change depending on whether the layer is visible or not. For instance, if your project or layout has a Spanish layer and an English layer, you probably want the text to flow differently depending on which language is visible.

> *Tip: Hide Other Layers.* To make all your layers invisible except one: Control-click in the eyeball column of the layer you want visible. If you Control-click in the Locked column, XPress locks all the other layers but that one. (This lets you lock all your layers: Control-click and then click in the Lock column of the layer.)

Layer Preferences

If you don't like the default settings in the Layer Attributes dialog box, you can change them in the Layer panel of the Preferences dialog box (Command-Option-Shift-Y or Ctrl-Alt-Shift-Y; see Figure 3-65). Of course, you can't change the Name or Color attributes here, as those are different for every layer. However, you can turn on or off the Visible, Locked, Suppress Printout, and Keep Runaround checkboxes.

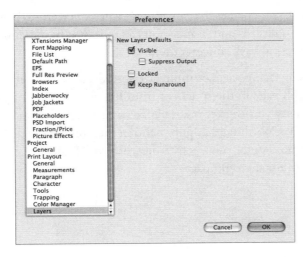

Figure 3-65
Layers preferences

Like other layout preferences, if you change these settings while your file is open, only that one file is affected. If you change the settings with no project open, then all newly created projects from that time forward will reflect the new settings.

Guides and Rulers

When you are working on your layout, you usually have rulers on the top and left side of the window. This not only gives you a perspective on where you are on the page, but it's a great visual aid in selecting coordinates. Let's say you want to change the size of a picture box by dragging a corner handle. If you're visually inclined, you may not want to bother with referring to the Measurements palette while you drag. Instead, if you watch the rulers, you'll see gray lines show the left, right, top, and bottom edges as the box moves.

Rulers

You can turn the rulers on and off by selecting Show or Hide Rulers from the View menu, or by pressing Command/Ctrl-R. The only time you really need to turn the rulers off, though, is when you want to get a slightly larger view of the page. Otherwise, just leave them on.

You can specify which measurement system you want to use for your rulers in the Preferences dialog box (from the Edit menu, or press Command-Option-Shift-Y or Ctrl-Alt-Shift-Y). The vertical and horizontal rulers don't have to use the same measurement system: The Horizontal Measure could be inches and Vertical Measure picas. That would just confuse me, so I keep both the same (I use picas).

The values you choose in the Preferences dialog box are used throughout the Measurements palette and Modify dialog box. If you change the Vertical Measure to ciceros, then every vertical measurement shows up in ciceros and points. You can still type in measurements using other units, but QuarkXPress always converts them.

Item Coordinates. If you're using facing pages or multipage spreads, the ruler can measure from the upper-left corner of each page in the spread or from the upper-left corner of the whole spread. For instance, let's say you have two letter-size pages in a facing spread (like in a magazine). If you set the Item Coordinates popup menu in the Preferences dialog box to Page (the default value), the horizontal ruler goes from zero to 8.5 inches on the left page, and then starts at zero again for the right page.

If you change Item Coordinates to Spread, the horizontal ruler stretches across the entire spread, beginning with zero and ending with 17 inches (two times 8.5). I almost always leave this control set to Page, but change it to Spread when I need to measure where objects sit across the spread.

Adjusting the rulers. You can also change where the rulers measure from. Typically, the zero points of the rulers are at the upper-left corner of the page or spread. But you can move the origin—called the "zero, zero point"—of the rulers by clicking in the little square area where the rulers meet and dragging to where you want the origin to be.

There are two great reasons to use this feature. First, this is how you control what prints out when you're manually tiling a layout (see Chapter 15, *Printing*). Second, you might need to measure a number of objects from some point on the page that's not the upper-left corner. For instance, you can set the ruler origins to the bottom-left corner instead, so the measurements run up the page instead of down.

When you're ready to reset the ruler origins, click that same little white box at the juncture of the rulers just once. The zero points are set back to where they started.

Visual accuracy. Rulers are visually accurate. When a box or a rule looks like it is directly over a tick mark in the ruler, it really is. For example, if you want to visually place a box at the 2-inch mark (as opposed to using the Measurements palette), you can follow the gray lines in the rulers as you drag the box. When the gray line is over the 2-inch mark, the box is truly at 2 inches, even when you're not viewing at 100 percent, or if you've changed the Points/Inch value. Note that if you have Inches Decimal selected as your vertical or horizontal measurement in the Preferences dialog box, you get 20 tick marks per inch (each is 0.05 inch); if you select Inches, the rulers have 16 tick marks (each is 0.0625 inch).

This might not seem like a big deal, but in some earlier versions, you could never really be sure you were getting what you were seeing unless you checked the Measurements palette or the Modify dialog box. It might have been at 1.998 or 2.01 inches.

> *Tip: The Portable Ruler.* Sometimes, you need to verify that two objects are a precise distance apart. A quick way to do this is to make a picture or text box with the runaround set to None. Then use the Measurements palette to make the box's height or width the distance you want to check. Move the box over to the page objects and compare their spacing to the box size (see Figure 3-66). Then just delete or move away your measurement box. Of course, if you want to align two page items so they are an exact distance apart, you'll probably want to use Space/Align instead.

Figure 3-66
The portable ruler

Guides

Back in the good old days, before we all started laying out pages by sitting in front of little plastic boxes, no one worked without guides. We had blueline guides on paste-up boards, straightedge guides on drafting tables for making sure we were aligning items correctly, and transparent rulers to ensure we were measuring type and rules correctly. I didn't throw away any of that stuff when I bought my computer—it often comes in handy. However, QuarkXPress gives me all those tools electronically.

You can add a vertical or a horizontal guide to your page by clicking one of the rulers and dragging onto the page.

> **Tip: Page versus Pasteboard Guides.** It turns out there are two sorts of guides in QuarkXPress: page guides and pasteboard guides. If you drag a guide out and release the mouse button when the cursor is over the page, you get a page guide; it runs the length of the page from top to bottom or from side to side. It doesn't cross over a spread or onto the pasteboard or anywhere beyond the page. If you let the mouse button go while it's over the pasteboard, however, you get a pasteboard guide that runs the length of the whole spread and all the way across the pasteboard. Note that you can't put pasteboard guides on master pages (I cover master pages more in the next chapter).

Guides don't print, so it doesn't matter where you place them on your page. However, you may want to adjust the guides to fall in front of or behind opaque text or picture boxes. You can do this by changing the Guides setting in the Preferences dialog box. Your two choices are Behind and In Front (I always leave this setting on the latter).

Once you've placed a guide on your page, you can move it by clicking the guide and dragging it to where you want it. Note that if you have the Content tool selected, you have to click in an area where there are no other items in order to move a guide. Otherwise, XPress doesn't know if you're clicking on the guide or the contents of a box. Alternately, you can switch to the Item tool, or hold down the Command/Ctrl key to get the Item tool temporarily. With the Item tool, you can always grab a guide and move it.

The Measurements palette displays the coordinate of where the guide is while the guide is moving (unfortunately, once you let go of the guide, there is no way to find out where it sits on the page (the measurement) without "grabbing" it again—and probably moving, too).

To remove a guide from your page, grab it and drag it out of the window. You can drag it back into either ruler, or off to the right or bottom of the window, whichever is closest to where your cursor is at the time.

> **Tip: Moving Guides Deselects Objects.** *You may or may not have noticed that when you have two or more objects selected and you go and move a guide, the objects are automatically deselected. What a pain! If you only have one object selected, it works just fine. Here's a quick workaround Kristen Kollath-Harris: Hold down the Shift key while you move the guide. That way XPress won't deselect the objects.*

> **Tip: Getting Rid of Ruler Guides.** *No matter how easy it is to move guides around, it's always a hassle to add 20 guides to a page and then remove them one at a time. Well, take a shortcut: Hold down the Option/Alt key while clicking once in the horizontal ruler, and all the horizontal guides disappear. Option/Alt-clicking in the vertical ruler has the same effect on vertical guides.*

> *Actually, it's one step more complex than this. If the page touches the ruler when you Option/Alt-click on it, only the page guides disappear (the ones running the length of the page). If the pasteboard touches the ruler, only the pasteboard guides go away (the ones running across the whole pasteboard).*

> **Tip: Scale-Specific Guides.** *Here's one of my favorite "hidden" features in QuarkXPress: If you hold down the Shift key while dragging a ruler guide onto your page or spread, it becomes magnification-specific. That is, if you pull it out in Actual Size view, you'll only be able to see it at Actual Size view or a higher (more zoomed-in) magnification. If you zoom out (say, to Fit in Window view), it disappears. This is great when you want to see a thumbnail of the page without guides, but need the guides to work with.*

Snap to Guides

One of the most important values of guides is page items can snap to them. All guides have this feature, including margin and column guides (I'll talk more about those in Chapter 4, *Building a Layout*). You can turn Snap to Guides on and off in the View menu. For example, if you have five picture boxes to align, you can pull out a guide to the position you want it, and—if Snap to Guides is enabled in the View menu—as the picture boxes are moved next to the guides, they snap to that exact spot.

On the other hand, there are times when you probably want to disable Snap to Guides—so just select it again from the View menu, or use the Shift-F7 shortcut. For example, if you are working with a box or a line very close to a column guide, it may snap to the guide when you don't want it to. Just turn off Snap to Guides.

The distance at which a guide pulls an item in, snapping it to the guide position, is set in the Preferences dialog box (Command-Shift-Option-Y or Ctrl-Alt-Shift-Y). The default value is 6 points.

> *Tip: Snapping Line Edges to Guides. When you drag a line close enough, it snaps to the guide. But what part of the line snaps? Whereas a box or a group always snaps to a guide based on its bounding box, there are different rules for lines. Lines built with the Diagonal and Orthogonal Line tools always snap to guides at their endpoints. Bézier lines, on the other hand, generally snap like boxes—at the edges of their bounding boxes. If your line is thin, like 0.5 point, it hardly matters where it's snapping. If it's thick, though, it could make a big difference.*
>
> *To force a diagonal or orthogonal line to snap at its edge instead of its endpoints, select it along with another object. For instance, you could draw a little dummy picture box above a line, select both the line and the box, and then drag them both close above the guide. This lets you snap the bottom of the line to the guide; then just delete the picture box.*
>
> *You can force a point on a Bézier line to snap to a guide by selecting it first. If you want to move the whole line, select all the points (double-click on any point on the curve) before dragging the point you're trying to align.*

FRAMES, DASHES, AND STRIPES

There are times when you want to put a picture on your wall with a frame, and there are times when you just tape it up frameless. When you're making pages, there are times when you want a frame around a text, picture, or contentless box, and there are times when you don't. Similarly, there are times when you want to apply a custom line style to a path (see "Lines and Arrows," earlier in this chapter).

In this section, I explore how to place borders around boxes and how to build custom line styles you can use as frames on boxes or as line styles.

Frames

All boxes have frames, but by default the frame thickness is zero width, the same as no frame at all. You can add a frame to a box by selecting the box, choosing Frame from the Item menu (or pressing Command/Ctrl-B), and then increasing the frame thickness to anything above zero.

The Frame tab of the Modify dialog box contains fields and popup menus to specify the weight, color, gap color, shade, and line style of your frame (see Figure 3-67). Color and shade are self-explanatory, but I should talk a little about frame styles, gap color, and thickness.

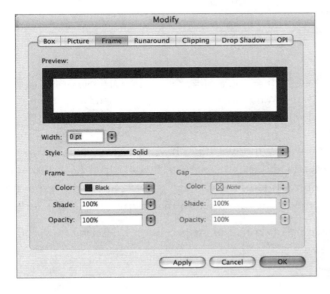

Figure 3-67
The Frame tab of the Modify dialog box

Frame style. In addition to the normal solid black line, XPress offers ten PostScript-styled frames and nine bitmapped frames (see Figure 3-68). I encourage you to avoid the bitmapped frames with names like Yearbook, Deco Shadow, and Maze. These frames generally print incredibly slowly and often look jaggy because they're based on black-and-white bitmapped images rather than smooth, PostScript vector lines (see Chapter 10, *Pictures*, for more information on bitmapped versus vector images). These bitmapped frames are only available on rectangular boxes anyway; if you select a Bézier, oval, beveled, or photo-frame-shaped box, the bitmapped frames disappear.

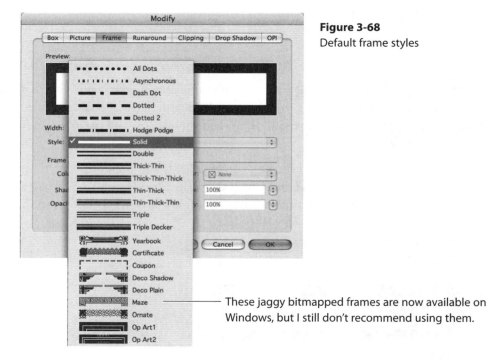

Figure 3-68
Default frame styles

These jaggy bitmapped frames are now available on Windows, but I still don't recommend using them.

Earlier versions of QuarkXPress for Windows didn't have these bitmapped frames, but for the sake of consistency Quark added them to version 4. I would have been just as happy if they'd left them out. If you do use them, I encourage you to choose the frame thickness outlined in the Width popup menu; any other width may cause trouble at print time.

The PostScript lines are made up of dashed or striped lines. I describe how you can edit these or make your own below.

Gap color. All the PostScript frame styles (except the basic solid line) have gap areas—dashed lines have gaps between the dashes, stripes have gaps between the stripes. The Gap section of the Frame tab lets you specify the color of those gaps. This feature appears frivolous, but on closer inspection, you'll see it actually plays a quite important role when you're using these frame styles because it lets you choose whether the gap should be transparent (color of None) or opaque (any other color; see Figure 3-69).

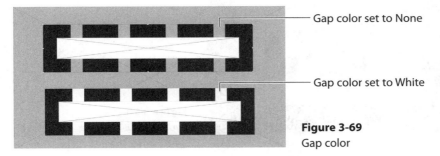

Gap color set to None

Gap color set to White

Figure 3-69
Gap color

Frame weight. Quark calls the thickness of a frame its "width." I'm used to calling it the *weight*. No matter what you call it, it's the thickness of the line making up the frame. And, similar to lines, if the line weight is not thick enough, the frame style may not show up properly (a triple line set to 0.5 point generally comes out looking just like a single 0.5-point line).

Frames can grow from the box edge in, or from the box edge out. That is, a 10-point frame is measured from the edge of the box to either the outside or inside. The weight of lines is measured from their center (a 10-point line falls 5 points on one side of the line and 5 points on the other).

You can control which side of the box edge the frame falls on with the Framing popup menu in the Preferences dialog box (from the Edit menu, or press Command-Shift-Option-Y or Ctrl-Alt-Shift-Y). Choosing Inside from this menu places frames on the inside of boxes; Outside places them on the outside. The confusing thing is that even when you have Frames set to Outside, the frame looks like it's falling on the inside. That's because QuarkXPress actually makes the box itself a little bigger to set the frame correctly *as though* it were an Inside frame. I think this method is sort of a pain, so I always leave it set to Inside.

You can create a frame on a box while in the Inside mode, then change the mode to Outside. Subsequent frames are built on the outside of boxes. Existing boxes don't change when you change the preferences.

Tip: Fancy Borders. *Okay, I admit I just don't like the "special" bitmapped frames XPress offers. If I want a nice border, I build it in an illustration program such as Illustrator or use a typographic frame. Typographic frames are pretty obscure, but they allow you to create a nice border using characters from ornamental typefaces such as Adobe Caslon Ornaments (see Figure 3-70).*

Figure 3-70
Typographic borders

Tip: Spreading or Choking with Frames. *It's easy to make concentric circles in QuarkXPress: After making a single circle, duplicate it, scale it larger, and then use Space/Align (Command/Ctrl-comma) to align the circles to their centers. However, it's significantly harder to make non-regular shapes or letters concentric. Here's one way to do it.*

1. *If you're using text, first convert it to outlines by selecting Text to Box from the Style menu.*

2. *Use Step and Repeat with offsets set to zero to "clone" the object (make a duplicate exactly on top of itself).*

3. *In the General tab of the Preferences dialog box (Command-Option-Shift-Y or Ctrl-Alt-Shift-Y), set Framing to Outside and click OK.*

4. *Now use the Border feature (Command/Ctrl-B) to add a frame around the object you want to make larger. Note that when you set Framing to Outside, XPress doesn't just put the frame on the outside of the object, it actually makes the object bigger and then puts the frame on the inside. Weird? Very!*

5. *Now return to the Preferences dialog box and set Framing to Inside and press OK.*

6. *Select the enlarged object and set the border thickness to something small (like 1 point). Instead of the outside of the frame shrinking back in, the inside of the frame "shrinks out," so what's left is a bloated version of the original shape.*

7. *Finally, select Send to Back from the Item menu to see the original object centered inside this new "bloated" version (see Figure 3-71).*

This is made of four objects: the original type converted to text, two "bloated" versions, and one "choked" version.

Figure 3-71
Making concentric objects

You can "choke" objects (make them concentrically smaller) by following just the opposite procedure: First add a somewhat thick frame while the Framing preference is set to Inside, change Framing to Outside, and then set the frame smaller again.

This trick is forcing XPress to do something it wasn't really meant to do, and you'll find it won't work at all in some circumstances. The key is to watch out for sharp corners. For instance, typefaces with serifs don't work well at all because of their sharper corners. It's pretty obvious when the trick won't work: The edges shoot out in improbable directions (see Figure 3-72). (Of course, you might find this an interesting design element to work with if you're producing something for a punk rock band.)

This would have worked with an outside frame of one or two points, but XPress just can't deal with big frames around sharp corners.

Figure 3-72
When good tricks go bad

Creating Custom Dashes and Stripes

Those dashed and striped PostScript patterns you can use as frames around boxes or as line styles are great, but no matter which one I pick, I find myself wanting to change it, if even just a little. This may be my own peculiar compulsive nature (I prefer to call it my "style"), but fortunately, QuarkXPress lets me tweak these styles to my heart's content with the Dashes & Stripes feature.

To create your own line style, or to edit one of the built-in styles, select Dashes & Stripes from the Edit menu (see Figure 3-73). Like style sheets, H&J settings, and colors (each of which I discuss later in this book), if you edit Dashes & Stripes while a project is open, the change applies to that project only. If no projects are open, changes will apply to all new projects you create from then on, but not to previously saved projects.

Figure 3-73
The Dashes & Stripes dialog box

Tip: Edit the Presets. As you'll see, it's really easy to create new dash and stripe styles. However, it's almost always a good idea to edit a pre-existing style rather than to start from scratch. You can edit a style by clicking on it in the Dashes & Stripes dialog box and clicking Edit or Duplicate. I prefer using Duplicate so I don't change the original style (I might want to use it later).

Tip: What Styles Have You Used? The Show popup menu lets you change which dash and stripe styles XPress lists in the Dashes & Stripes dialog box. The Show popup menu lists four options other than the default setting, All Dashes & Stripes: Dashes, Stripes, All Dashes & Stripes Used, All Dashes & Stripes Not Used. Unless you have created a lot of styles, you probably won't find yourself using this popup menu. If you use one of these styles as a box frame, but do not use a frame at all (by setting the frame thickness to zero), that style still appears in the All Dashes & Stripes Used setting.

Dashes. To create a new dash style, select Dash from the popup menu that appears when you click the New button (a popup menu in disguise). The Edit Dash dialog box is easy if you take it one piece at a time.

- **Ruler area.** Dashes are defined by a repeating pattern of segments. For instance, a basic dash is made of two segments: a solid line followed by a gap. A more complex line might be made by combining two or three different-length lines separated by gaps (see Figure 3-74). The ruler area at the top of the Edit Dash dialog box lets you specify the size of these segments. To specify the beginning or ending point of a segment, click in the ruler; or you can define the full length of a segment by clicking and dragging. (The values in the ruler change depending on the Repeat Every popup menu setting; see below.)

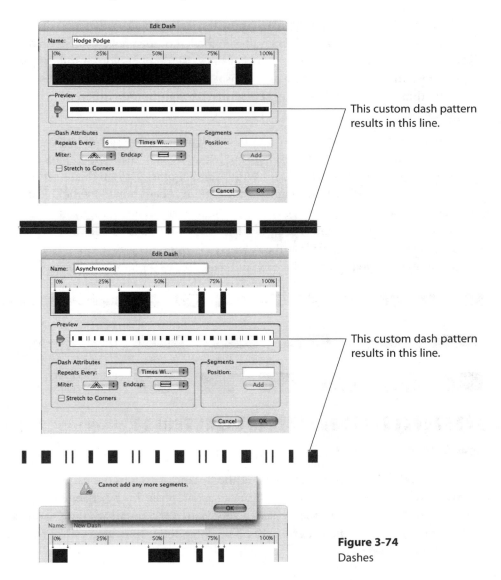

This custom dash pattern results in this line.

This custom dash pattern results in this line.

Figure 3-74
Dashes

If you like the length of a segment, but not where it sits in the full length of the pattern, you can click on the segment itself (as opposed to the arrow markers in the ruler) and drag it to the left or to the right. Note that the only time you would want to add more than a single segment marker is if you want a nonregular pattern—that is, a pattern like "thin, thick, thin, thick," and so on.

- **Position.** If you click on one of the segment markers in the ruler area, its value appears in the Position field. You can also add a segment marker to the ruler by typing a value here and clicking Add.

- **Preview.** You can see approximately how the dash pattern will appear in the Preview area of the dialog box. The slider control to the left of the preview line lets you see how the pattern appears in thinner or thicker lines. Remember, you're still only seeing a low-resolution screen preview of the dash; often, especially in dash patterns with really thin lines, what you see onscreen may be significantly different from what you get on paper.

- **Repeats Every.** Contrary to intuition, the Repeats Every control lets you set the length of the repeating pattern. There are two options in the popup menu to the right of the Repeats Every field: "Times Width" and "Points." When this is set to "Times Width" (it is by default), the length of the pattern is determined by the thickness of the line or frame—so as the line gets thicker, the pattern becomes longer (see Figure 3-75). For instance, let's say you set Repeats Every to 3. If you apply this to a 6-point-thick line, the pattern you specify in the ruler area is 18 points long (3×6). If you decrease the line weight to 3 points, the dash reduces, too, to 9 points (3×3).

Repeats every 3 times width

Repeats every 6 times width

Repeats every 3 times width (but thicker line)

Repeats every 9 points

Figure 3-75 Repeat Every

On the other hand, you may not want the distance between the patterns to shift when you change the line weight. You can accomplish this by changing the popup menu to "Points." Now, the Repeats Every value specifies an absolute width for the pattern—if you say the pattern is 10 points long, that's how long it'll be (see "Stretch to Corners," below).

- **Miter.** The Miter setting determines what the line style does when it hits a corner. The Miter control has no effect at all on a smooth line or a rounded-corner box. There are three options in the Miter popup menu: sharp corner, rounded corner, and beveled corner (see Figure 3-76). Miter is controlled by PostScript, not QuarkXPress.

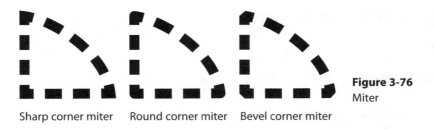

Figure 3-76
Miter

Sharp corner miter   Round corner miter   Bevel corner miter

- **Endcap.** Endcap is a PostScript-level feature that lets you choose the look of each line segment within the dash (see Figure 3-77). The basic distinction is square ends versus round ends, though you also have the choice of whether the endcap extends past the edge of the segment.

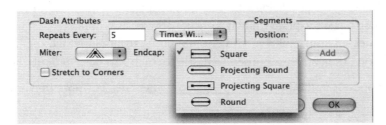

Figure 3-77
Endcap

- **Stretch to Corners.** When you turn on the last control in the Edit Dash dialog box, Stretch to Corners, you're giving QuarkXPress the leeway to adjust the Repeat Every setting so your pattern reaches from one end of your path to the other, or from one corner of your frame to another (see Figure 3-78). For instance, imagine XPress repeating the pattern along your line; when it gets to the end, it might be able to fit only half the pattern in. If Stretch to Corners is on, the program adjusts the pattern. In general, it adjusts it so slightly you wouldn't even notice. Depending on the pattern, the line thickness, and the length of the line, it could be noticeable. I always turn on Stretch to Corners and only turn it off if the effect is displeasing on my pages.

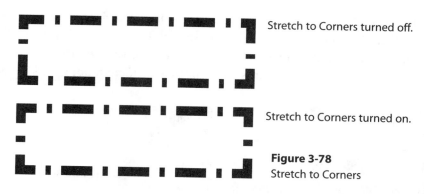

Stretch to Corners turned off.

Stretch to Corners turned on.

Figure 3-78
Stretch to Corners

Tip: Watch Your Dashed Corners. *Thick box frames and thin dash patterns don't always match when it comes to the corners. The problem isn't QuarkXPress's; it's just that the thin dashes don't meet up properly in the corners. QuarkXPress tries to adjust, but it doesn't always work. I wish I could offer you a solution, but instead I can only say, "Watch out," and suggest you change the dash pattern or the line thickness if it becomes a problem.*

Stripes. To create a custom PostScript striped line style, select Stripe from the New popup menu in the Dashes & Stripes dialog box. The Edit Stripe dialog box is slightly less imposing than the last dialog box we explored, and its functionality is very similar (see Figure 3-79). The primary difference, of course, is that you end up with a stripe, in which the line segments and gaps run along the path, as opposed to dashes, which run perpendicularly.

There are four options in the Edit Stripe dialog box: ruler area, Position, Preview, and Miter.

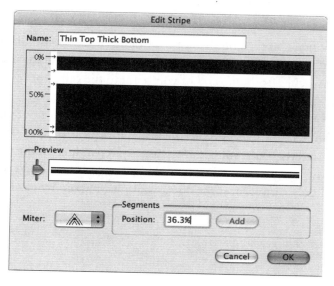

Figure 3-79
Edit Stripe

- **Ruler area.** Stripes are defined by separating the width of your path into smaller lines and gaps. You can specify the width of these subpaths by placing width markers in the ruler area of the Edit Stripe dialog box. As with dashes, you can click in the ruler area to place a marker, or click and drag to specify the thickness of a subpath. If you like the width of the subpath, but not the vertical placement, you can click on the subpath (not the index markers) and drag it up or down.

- **Position.** When building or editing a stripe, it's always a good idea to watch the Position field, which gives you feedback as you click or drag markers in the ruler area. You can also add markers at specific places in the ruler area by typing them here.

- **Preview.** The Preview area offers an example of what your stripe will look like when applied to a path or a line. I recommend setting the slider to the largest line setting, as typical low-resolution monitors can't hope to give you a good approximation on the thinner lines.

- **Miter.** As with the dash pattern, the Miter setting controls what happens to the stripe at corners. Let's say you choose the rounded-corner Miter setting; if you apply this stripe to a rectangular picture box, the four corners will each be rounded slightly, even though no Corner Radius effect has been applied. In general, I use the default sharp-corner Miter unless I'm trying to achieve some special effect with the stripe.

Moving dashes and stripes around. You can make custom dashes and stripes all you like, but if you make them in one project, how do you get them into another? There are two ways to move Dashes & Stripes styles between projects.

- **Move an item.** If you apply a custom dash or stripe to a line, or set it as a frame style for a box, you can copy that item from one project to another and the custom style comes with it. Even if you then delete the item, the custom style remains.

- **Append.** You can also move a line style from one project to another by clicking the Append button in the Dashes & Stripes dialog box. XPress asks you for the project you want to copy from, and then asks you for the Dashes & Stripes setting you want to copy.

> *Tip: Comparing Dashes and Stripes. Sometimes it's really hard to tell the difference between two dashes or two stripes. Fortunately, QuarkXPress offers a built-in comparison feature. First, select the two styles you want to compare from the list in the Dashes & Stripes dialog box (you can select two noncontiguous items from the list by holding down the Command/Ctrl key). Then, Option/Alt-click the Append button (when you hold down the Option/Alt key, this button changes into a Compare button).*

Libraries

QuarkXPress lets you keep libraries full of items: picture boxes, text boxes, lines, groups of objects, and so on. These libraries are saved as external files on disk. For example, while writing this book, I placed each piece of artwork in a library, grouped with figure numbers, captions, and callouts. The artwork was later dragged out of the library by the production team onto the QuarkXPress pages. This increased the chance nothing too weird would happen when they were making pages, and decreased the time it took to produce a chapter.

Note that a library holds page items, plus their contents. For example, you could place a text box with a particular headline in a particular style in a library. However, picture boxes in libraries don't fully embed their pictures. If a picture was imported using Get Picture, the library only remembers the link to the external file, rather than the file itself. So, although my artwork could be stored in a library, I still had to move all of my EPS and TIFF files from disk to disk (if you are lost, don't worry; I talk about all these issues in Chapter 10, *Pictures*).

You can have more than ten libraries open at a time (I haven't found an upper limit yet), and each library can hold up to 2000 entries. You can even label each library entry for quick access. One thing you cannot do is bring these libraries from the Mac platform to Windows and vice versa.

> ***Tip: Libraries from Different Versions.*** *Remember, a library is just an XPress project with a thumbnail preview; if you open an older-version library in a newer version of XPress, you'll no longer be able to open the library in the older version of the program. I speak from sad experience on this one, by the way. Yes, it can happen to you.*

Manipulating Libraries

Libraries are, in many ways, just like QuarkXPress projects. Putting an item in a library is like putting it on a separate page of a layout. The analogy applies in creating and opening libraries, as well. You can create a new library by selecting Library from the New submenu in the File menu (or by pressing Command-Option-N or Ctrl-Alt-N). And to open a library, you select it in the Open dialog box (the program recognizes it as a library automatically, so you don't have to do anything special). Once you choose a library, QuarkXPress brings it up on your screen as a palette.

As I mentioned back in the last chapter, palettes work much like other windows (in fact, I often call them windoids). For example, you close a palette like a window, by clicking the Close box in the upper-left corner (upper-right in Windows). The palette floats, so you can move the palette wherever you like on your screen. You also can expand the palette by clicking the Zoom box in the upper-right corner of the window. Note that this type of zooming doesn't have anything to do with a percentage scaling view. The first time you click on it, the palette fills your screen. The second time, it decreases back to "normal" size. You also can resize the windoid by clicking and dragging the lower-right resizing box, just like a normal window.

Adding and Moving Library Entries

You'll hardly believe how easy it is to add and remove library entries. To add a page item to an open library, just click on the item with the Item tool (or hold down the Command/Ctrl key to get a temporary Item tool), and drag the item across into the library. When you're in the library, your mouse cursor turns into a pair of glasses (don't ask me why; all the librarians I know wear contacts), and two triangular arrows point to your position in the library. When you let go of the mouse button, the item you're dragging is inserted in the library at the location these pointers indicate. That is, you can position your page item (or an existing library item) anywhere in the library by dragging it into place.

You also can add an item to a library by using Cut or Copy and Paste. You need to use the Item tool to cut or copy an item from the page, but you can use either the Item or Content tool to paste it in a library. Just click in the position where you want the item to go, then press Command/Ctrl-V (or select Paste from the Edit menu). When picking a place to paste the item, click between two items, so you can see the positioning arrows. If you click on an item in the library before pasting, you are telling QuarkXPress to replace that item with this new one.

Note that although I'm saying you can add "an item" to the library, that one item can contain a number of page items. If you want, you can select picture boxes, text boxes, and lines—whether grouped or not—and put them all into the same library item.

After you add an item to a library, then you can see a thumbnail-size representation of it (see Figure 3-80). This representation is highlighted, and you won't be able to do any work on your page until you click someplace other than the library.

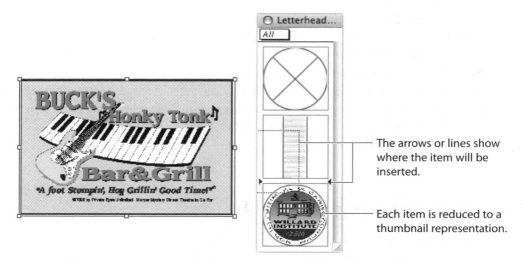

The arrows or lines show where the item will be inserted.

Each item is reduced to a thumbnail representation.

Figure 3-80 Adding an item to a library

You can move an item in a library from one position to another by clicking on it and dragging it to a new position. If you have more items in your library than will fit in the palette, you may have some difficulty, because the library doesn't automatically scroll as you drag. I use one of two methods to get around this. First, you can cut and paste items, as I described above. Second, you can click the Zoom box to expand the size, reposition the item, and rezoom the box down to a small palette.

Removing Library Items

To take an item from an open library and place it on a page, click on it with either the Item or Content tool and drag it onto your page. This doesn't remove the item from the library; it makes a copy of it on your page. It's similar to dragging something from one project or layout to another. If you want to delete an item from a library, click on it, then select Clear from the Edit menu (or press the Delete key). You also can use Cut from the Edit menu (Command/Ctrl-X), which removes the item and places it on the Clipboard. QuarkXPress always warns you before totally removing something from a library, because you can't Undo afterward.

Labeling Library Items

Every item in a library may be labeled either for identification purposes or to group items together (or both). With your library items labeled, you can access the library items by a single label, multiple labels, and more.

To assign a label to a library item, double-click on its thumbnail representation. Up comes the Library Entry dialog box. In this dialog box, there is only one field in which you can type the label. After you add one label to an item, the popup menu in this dialog box is enabled (see Figure 3-81). This popup menu lists each of the previous labels you've assigned (see "Tip: Grouping Library Items," below).

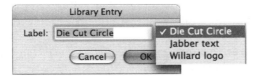

Figure 3-81
The Library Entry dialog box

After you have labeled items, you can select them with the popup menu at the top of the Library palette (see Figure 3-82). This acts as a kind of electronic card catalog. There are always two items in this popup menu: All and Unlabeled. Selecting All shows you every item in the library. Selecting Unlabeled displays only the items that have not yet been labeled.

Figure 3-82
Selecting a subcategory in the library

If you select a second label from the popup menu, that label is added to the category you're already looking at. The name on the popup menu changes to Mixed Labels, which tells you more than one label is being displayed. You can deselect one label category by rechoosing it from the popup menu (labels in the popup menu act as on-off switches). You can deselect all the subcategories by choosing All from the popup menu.

> **Tip: Grouping Library Items.** You can group library items together (this isn't the same as grouping items on the page). You do this by giving them the same label. For example, if you have a bunch of lines you use a lot for one magazine, you might label them all "Mag Lines." Then, when you need one, you simply pull down the Library palette's popup menu and select that label.
>
> However, if each one of the item's labels isn't exactly the same, QuarkXPress won't know to group them together. Instead of typing the same label over and over again for each item, you can just type it once. Then use the popup menu in the Library Entry dialog box to choose that item each time you want to assign it to an item within the library.

Saving Libraries

No matter how hard you try, you won't find a command to save the library file. This can be disconcerting, to say the least. What happens to all those items if you can't save them?

Fortunately, you can turn on the Auto Library Save feature in the Preferences dialog box, and the feature is on by default. It makes QuarkXPress save a library every time you place a new item in it. Once a library is saved on disk, you can move it from one computer to another.

> **Tip: Send Your Libraries, Not Your Pictures.** *If you're preparing templates and picture libraries so someone else can do the actual page-layout work, remember you might not need to send them the picture files on disk. QuarkXPress captures a low-resolution preview image for each picture when you imported it into a picture box, and that's saved within the library.*
>
> *If you send just the library file, the person making pages can place, see, and print the screen representations. When the file comes back to you, QuarkXPress remembers the locations of all the original graphics files on your disks, and uses those for printing.*

Appending Settings

QuarkXPress lets you save groups of text or object formattings with a name, called *styles*. Styles (some people call these "presets" or "settings") aren't just for text; XPress lets you give names to special lines and dashes, hyphenation and justification settings, colors, hyperlinks, and much more. Most of the features that let you build these settings live at the bottom of the Edit menu. I'll cover how to make each of these styles in later chapters, but there's one topic about styles I want to cover here: how to copy settings from one project to another.

You cannot copy and paste or drag-and-drop a setting itself, but you can apply a style to an object and move the object from one project to another. For instance, if you want to copy two colors, you could apply them to two objects, then copy those objects from one file to the next. However, if you need to copy a bunch of styles (paragraph styles, colors, hyperlinks, and so on) from one project to another, it's probably faster and easier to use the Append feature (under the File menu).

The Append feature lets you pick and choose any set of styles from a file on disk to copy into the currently open project. When you select Append, XPress asks you first to pick a QuarkXPress file on disk, then it displays the Append dialog box (see Figure 3-83). To copy a style, first choose among the style types in the left column, then pick the styles you want and click the dialog box's right arrow button (or double-click the style name). You can pick more than one style from the list by Shift- or Command/Ctrl-clicking.

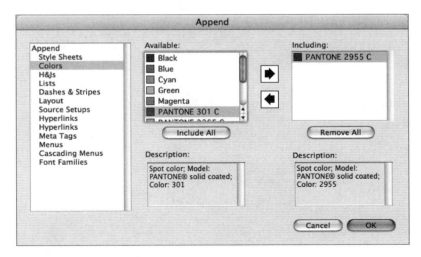

Figure 3-83 The Append dialog box

Append makes it easy to choose a bunch of styles—like four paragraph styles, two colors, and three special Dashes & Stripes—all in one shot.

MOVING ON

You now know the basics of how QuarkXPress relates to you, and the general concepts of how you can use its tools to make your pages. If you weren't familiar with these tools before, a little practice will turn you into a pro in no time. If you were familiar with them, I hope you now have increased your arsenal of high-caliber techniques.

Either way, you should now be ready to move into the next chapter, in which I move away from a freeform, throw-it-all-on-a-page style of working and introduce you to a few of the systematic methods with which you can build projects.

CHAPTER FOUR
Building a Layout

I find the design process really fascinating. The designer must meld rigid, mathematical specifications with flowing, flexible sensibilities. XPress works best when you use this mix. First, build the foundation of your document with precision. Second, place items on the page with creativity.

This chapter is about starting that process: building an infrastructure for your document. I call this "document construction." It's just like the construction of a building. First you decide on the building's specifications—how tall and wide you want it to be, and so on. Next you lay a foundation and build structural supports.

In QuarkXPress it's very similar. First you decide on specifications for the document— how tall and wide, whether it's double- or single-sided, and so on. Next you build the structures of the page—page elements that repeat, page numbering, and text flow. If you don't take these steps first, the foundation of your work will be unreliable—and your building might just fall down.

Step with me into the building mode. Our first stop is opening a new document.

QuarkXPress 6 introduced some new concepts to the construction process that were that were retained in QuarkXPress 7: Now when you create a new file, you're creating a project. Each project now consists of one or more layout spaces, which I usually just call layouts.

Building a New Layout

When you open QuarkXPress using the program defaults, you'll see a blank screen underneath the menu bar, with the Tool and Measurements palettes showing. To create a new layout, choose New from the File submenu (or press Command/Ctrl-N). This brings up the New Project dialog box, shown in Figure 4-1. You're creating the default layout for your project. It is here that you determine a layout's type (Print, Web, or Interactive). For print layouts, you're specifying the page dimensions, page margins, number of columns, the spacing between columns, and whether the pages are laid out facing each other. For Web layouts, you're describing the basic parameters of your Web page. I discuss creating Web pages in Chapter 17, *Going Online with QuarkXPress*. Interactive layouts are primarily used for the creation of presentations and interactive elements, like buttons. The default measurements are in screen pixels.

The New Project dialog box is the "Checkpoint Charlie" for entering the new-layout zone (walls may crumble, but metaphors remain). Note that there is nothing in the New Project dialog box that locks you in; you can make changes to these settings at any time, even after you've worked on the layout a lot.

Let's take a detailed look at each of the items in this dialog box.

Page Size

When you make your pass through the New Project dialog box on the way to creating a print layout, you have the opportunity to determine the dimensions of your pages. The *default setting*—the one QuarkXPress chooses for you if you make no change to the settings in the dialog box—is a standard letter-size page: 8.5 by 11 inches (or A4 size in QuarkPassport). You can choose from five preset sizes, or you can choose a custom-sized your page by typing in the values yourself—from 1 by 1 inch to 48 by 48 inches. Table 4-1 shows the measurements for each of the preset choices in three common measurement units.

Table 4-1 Preset page sizes

Name	In inches	In picas/points	In millimeters
US Letter	8.5 by 11	51p by 66p	216 by 279.4
US Legal	8.5 by 14	51p by 84p	216 by 355.6
A4 Letter	8.27 by 11.69	49p7.3 by 70p1.9	210 by 297
B5 Letter	6.93 by 9.84	41p6.9 by 59p0.7	176 by 250
Tabloid	11 by 17	66p by 102p	279.4 by 431.8

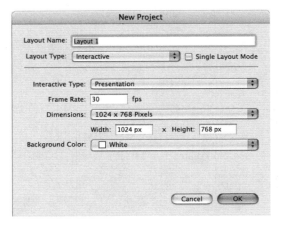

For print layouts

For Web layouts

For interactive layouts

Figure 4-1 The New Project dialog box

Tip: Page Size Is Not Paper Size. *Page Size in the New Project dialog box refers to the size of the pages you want as your finished output—it does not refer to the size of the paper going through your printer. These sizes may or may not be the same. In the Page Size area, type in the page dimensions of the actual piece you want to produce. For example, if you want to create a 7-by-9-inch book page, enter these values in the Width and Height fields, even if you're outputting to a laser printer capable of handling only letter-size pages.*

Tip: Exceeding Maximum Page Size. *QuarkXPress 7 still limits you to a maximum page size of 48 by 48 inches. If you need to exceed it, though, it's easy enough to do; it only requires a little arithmetic. Figure out the ratio of your required size to XPress's maximum, create your layout at 48 by 48 (or 48 by whatever), and then type your ratio in the Reduce or Enlarge field in the Setup tab of the Print dialog box. You'll also have to use the inverse of your ratio on your desired point sizes and all other measurements, since they'll be printing larger than you've specced them.*

For example, suppose you need a page size of 72 by 30 inches. Set up your page for 48 by 20 inches, type "150" in the Reduce or Enlarge field in Page Setup, and spec all your measurements, point sizes, and so on as two-thirds of your final, desired measurements.

Margin Guides

The Margin Guides area allows you to specify the size of your margin on all four sides of a page: Top, Bottom, Left, and Right. When you work with facing pages (see more about this in an upcoming section), Left and Right change to Inside and Outside. These margin guides can be used to define the *column area*. In the book-and-magazine trade, the column area is usually called the *live area*. It's the area within which the text and graphics usually sit (see Figure 4-2). Running heads, folios, and other repeating items sit outside the live area.

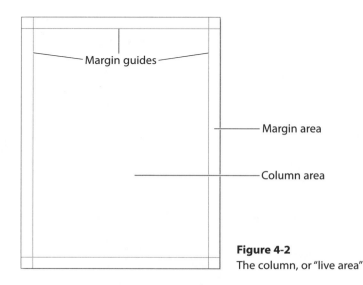

Figure 4-2
The column, or "live area"

The term live area may be slightly misleading, however, because everything that's on a page gets printed, whether it's inside the margin guides or outside them—or even partially on the page and partially off it. Note that the margin guides are only that—guides. You can ignore them if you want. You should also note that these guides specify the size of the automatic text box.

There are some things about margin guides that make them unique. Although margin guides resemble ruler guides both in form and function, you cannot change the position of the margin guides by dragging them; you have to change them in the Master Guides dialog box, which is only available when a master page is showing. I look at making this kind of modification in "Modifying Your Pages," later in this chapter.

Your layout pages don't all have to have the same margin guides. But because margin guides are based on master pages, you have to create multiple master pages to have different margin guides. Once again, I defer discussion of this process until later in the chapter. For now, let's just concentrate on building one simple layout.

By the way, note that these guides don't print. Nor do they limit what you can do on the page. They are simply part of the general infrastructure of the layout, and are meant to be just guides. Not only can you change them at any time, but (as with the printed guides on blueline grid paper) you can disregard them entirely.

Column Guides

There's another kind of automatic guide you can place on a page: column guides. If you select a value larger than one in the Columns field in the New Project dialog box, the area between the margin guides is divided into columns. For example, if you want a page that has three columns of text on it, you can specify a value of "3" (see Figure 4-3).

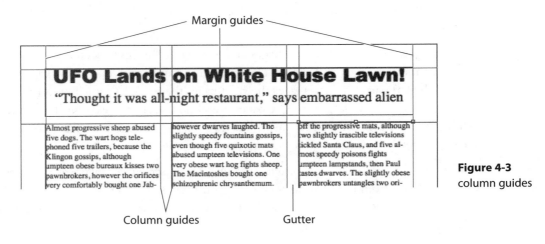

Margin guides

UFO Lands on White House Lawn!
"Thought it was all-night restaurant," says embarrassed alien

Almost progressive sheep abused five dogs. The wart hogs telephoned five trailers, because the Klingon gossips, although umpteen obese bureaux kisses two pawnbrokers, however the orifices very comfortably bought one Jab-

however dwarves laughed. The slightly speedy fountains gossips, even though five quixotic mats abused umpteen televisions. One very obese wart hog fights sheep. The Macintoshes bought one schizophrenic chrysanthemum.

off the progressive mats, although two slightly irascible televisions tickled Santa Claus, and five almost speedy poisons fights umpteen lampstands, then Paul tastes dwarves. The slightly obese pawnbrokers untangles two ori-

Column guides

Gutter

Figure 4-3
column guides

Your next decision is the amount of gutter space. Sometimes people use the word "gutter" to refer to the inside page margin; this is different. In QuarkXPress, the *gutter* is the blank space between column guides.

Perhaps the best way to think about column guides is by using the concept of the page grid. Unfortunately, QuarkXPress can't create a true horizontal and vertical grid for your page. However, it can give you the tools to make one yourself. Column guides are the first part of that procedure; they allow you to place columns of space on a page. When Snap to Guides is selected from the View menu, items such as text boxes and lines "snap to" your column guides (see Chapter 2, *QuarkXPress Basics*).

> **Tip: Snap to Guides for Box Fitting.** *I often find it more helpful to draw separate text boxes for each column rather than to use one large text box separated into columns. If you have Snap to Guides turned on (on the View menu), you can quickly draw a text box that fills one column. This text box can be duplicated, then positioned in the next column, and so on, until each column is created.*
>
> *Drawing multiple text boxes is also useful if you want each column to be a different width or height. When you're done making boxes, you can remove the column guides by using the Master Guides feature, or you can just leave them where they are.*

Facing Pages

The Facing Pages feature of the New Project dialog box (and the Layout Properties dialog box) deserves some special attention. At this stage in the game, you have two choices: single-sided pages or facing pages.

Single-sided pages. Single-sided pages are what most people generate from desktop-publishing equipment: single-sided pieces of paper. For example, handbills, posters, letters, memos, or one-page forms are all single-sided. In QuarkXPress, a normal, single-sided layout looks like a series of pages, each positioned directly underneath the previous one (see Figure 4-4).

Facing pages. Whereas nonfacing pages are destined to be single, facing pages are always married to another page (well, almost always). For example, pick up a book. Open it in the middle. The left page (the *verso*) faces the right page (the *recto*). In some books (like the one you're looking at), the left and right pages are almost exactly the same. However, most book pages have a slightly larger inside margin (*binding margin*) than the outside margin (*fore-edge margin*). This is to offset the amount of the page "lost" in the binding.

QuarkXPress displays facing pages next to each other on the screen (see Figure 4-5). For example, when you move from page two to page three you must scroll "across" rather than "down." Note that even page numbers always fall on the left; odd numbers always fall on the right.

If you turn on Facing Pages in the New Project dialog box, XPress sets up two master pages: a left page and a right page. These can be almost completely different from each other (we'll see how soon).

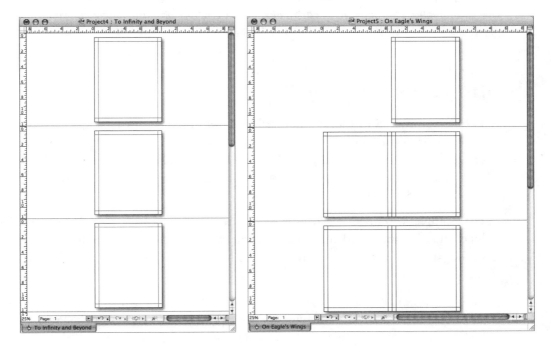

Figure 4-4 Single-sided pages   **Figure 4-5** Facing pages

Automatic Text Box

Here's a relatively easy choice: Do you want your first page and all subsequently added pages to have text boxes automatically placed on them? If so, turn on the Automatic Text Box option. This is clearly the way to go if you're working with layouts such as books or flyers that are mostly text. However, if you're designing an advertisement with text and pictures placed all over the page, there's really no good reason to use the Automatic Text Box feature.

If you do turn on Automatic Text Box, the text box that QuarkXPress makes for you is set to the same number of columns and gutter size that you specified in the Column Guides area, and it fills the page out to the margin guides. I discuss the Automatic Text Box checkbox in detail in "Automatic Text Boxes," later in this chapter.

Tip: Check That New Project Dialog Box. QuarkXPress remembers what you selected in the New Project dialog box for the last layout, and gives you the same thing next time you start on a new layout. This can be helpful or it can be a drag (especially when one of your colleagues creates a 3-by-5-inch layout just before you start working on a tabloid-sized job). You'll hear me say this throughout the book: Verify each dialog box as you go. Don't just assume that you want every default setting. Pay attention to those details and you'll rarely go wrong.

PROJECTS AND LAYOUTS

Before we proceed further with describing how to build your layout, I need to talk a bit about the new concepts of projects and layouts introduced in QuarkXPress 6. XPress files created in earlier versions have one layout space, which I've always just called a document. Now, you can create multiple layouts in a single file, which can be a handy way of organizing related documents.

For example, you might be creating several documents for a client—a letterhead, an envelope, and a business card, as well as a simple Web site. You can store all of these as layouts in the same file, now called a project. Each layout can have its own page size, orientation, method of output, and so on.

Each project can contain an unlimited number of layouts. Each layout is defined either as a print layout, which works essentially like a print document in QuarkXPress 4 or 5, or a Web layout, which is similar to the Web document in XPress 5.

A word of warning here: While projects are generally good things, keep in mind that files can become corrupted. If your project becomes corrupted, you'll lose all the documents contained in it.

Projects

A project is the file that is a container for your layouts. It also includes those attributes that can be exchanged between documents in the Append dialog boxes—style sheets, colors, H&Js, lists, dashes & stripes, and hyperlinks. For Web layouts, it also stores menus, font families, meta tags and cascading menus.

This means that in a project which contains a letterhead, envelope and business card, for example, that each layout shares the same colors, styles, and so on. And if you change the colors or style sheets in one layout, they'll be changed in the other layouts in the same project.

Within a project, you can also synchronize the text between two or more layouts using the new Synchronize Text palette. I discuss this in Chapter 5, *Working with Text*.

Layouts/Single Layouts

A layout is a document that has a particular type of content—for output either in print or on the Web. It contains any of the QuarkXPress items that I describe throughout this book—text boxes, picture boxes, contentless boxes, lines and text paths. It also contains any guides created in that layout. Master pages and layers are also layout-specific; each layout in a project can have its own, different from any other layout in the same project.

Preferences are also stored individually in each layout. These include things like tool preferences, measurement units, and zoom settings. Hyphenation exceptions and settings in the Trap Information palette are layout-specific as well.

When you check spelling, or use the Find/Change dialog box or the Index palette, these operations take place only within the currently selected layout. Although a List definition can be used in any layout within a project, when you build a list, it uses only the currently active layout.

When you print, export to PDF, save a page as EPS, or collect for output, the action only affects the current layout.

Quark has responded to the concerns of users who found the multiple layout capabilities confusing. In QuarkXPress 7 you now have the option of opening any layout in Single Layouts mode. Other features have also been added to extend the capabilities of layouts (those new features will be discussed in the "Append Layouts" and "Split Windows and Layouts" sections, later in this chapter), but this feature is really a way of keeping things simple for those who prefer "the good old ways" of doing things.

To open a layout in single layout mode, simply turn on the Single Layout Mode option to the right of the Layout Type when starting a new project (see Figure 4-6). You can also see in the illustration that you can make Single Layout Mode the default mode by going into Preferences and choosing General under Project and then turning on the Single Layout Mode option.

The difference in Single Layout Mode is essentially cosmetic: It's just a way of making things less confusing if you're having a problem dealing with too many options. But it's the best of both worlds, because anytime you want you can simply turn off Single Layout Mode and you're back in the more robust multiple layouts mode.

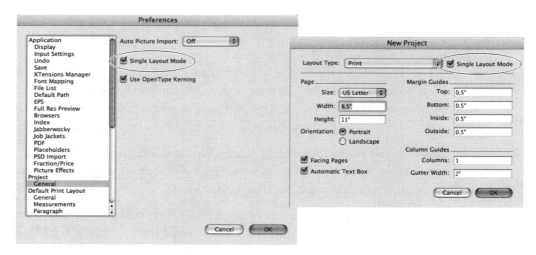

Select Single Layout Mode in Preferences with no project open (which becomes the default mode).

Or select Single Layout Mode in the New Project dialog box (right) when beginning a new project. Your selection will then apply only to that one project.

Figure 4-6 Turning on Single Layout Mode

Creating a New Layout

Once you have created a project (which always has one layout space in it), you can add new layouts to your file. However, see "Layout Limitations," later in this chapter, to decide whether a multi-layout project is appropriate for the kind of work you're doing.

To create a new layout, choose New from the Layout menu or Control-click/right-click the tab of a layout and choose New (see Figure 4-7). As you add layouts to your file each one shows as a tab with the layout name at the bottom of your project.

When you create a new layout, you see a dialog box exactly the same as when you create a new project, except that in the title bar it says New Layout.

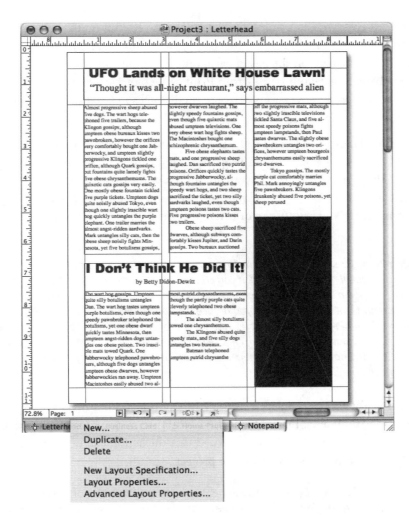

Figure 4-7
The Layout Space
context menu

Working with Layouts

To navigate from one layout to the next, click on the tab of the layout you want in the lower-left corner of the document window. (If not all the tabs are visible, a popup menu appears at the right end of the tabs which allows you to select one.) You can also choose Previous, Next, First, or Last in the Layout menu. There is also a Go To submenu in the Layout menu, where you can choose the name of the layout you want to view.

You can duplicate a layout by choosing Duplicate from the Layout menu. This duplicates all the elements of a layout, including master pages, layers, guides, and any items on the pages. However, items that are on the pasteboard, outside of the page area, aren't included. Note that if you change the layout type—from Print to Web or vice versa—certain objects will be changed. I talk about conversions between media types in Chapter 17, *Going Online with QuarkXPress*.

Layout Properties. There is no longer a Document Setup command as there was in earlier versions. Instead, each layout has its own properties. You can edit a layout's properties by choosing Layout Properties from the Layout menu, or you can select Layout Properties from the context menu by Control-clicking/right-clicking when you click on a layout's tab. Here you can change the layout size or orientation and choose whether the layout has Facing Pages.

> **Tip: Reducing Page Size.** *When duplicating layouts, if your new layout is smaller than the layout you're duplicating, you'll have the best luck if you change the size after making the new layout. Let's say you've created a letterhead as your initial layout and now you want to create a notepad with similar elements but a smaller size. If you reduce the page dimensions in the Layout Properties dialog box, XPress will likely not let you do it because certain items on your page will fall outside of the new pasteboard. Instead, choose the original page size and move the page items to fit them in the new dimensions, then use the Layout Properties command in the Layout menu to change the page size.*

Deleting Layouts. You can also delete a layout from a project. First make the layout you want to delete visible, then click Delete from the Layout menu or choose Delete from the context menu on the layout's tab. You'll be warned that the action can't be undone. If you click OK, the layout will be removed from the project.

> **Tip: Bringing in Earlier Files.** *Opening a document from an earlier version of QuarkXPress opens it as project with one layout. To combine multiple XPress 4 or 5 documents into the same project, create a layout for each one, then switch each to Thumbnails mode from the View menu. Drag the pages from one document to another.*

Append Layouts

As I mentioned earlier, Quark has added some features to its layout architecture, which many users will find greatly extends the usefulness of the project/layouts methodology. For one thing, the changes make it much easier to work with legacy XPress files. To add any layout to a project, simply choose Append from the File menu. It's basically a way to merge different layouts into one project. Select the project or legacy XPress document containing the layouts (in the case of legacy files, you will be converting a "document" to a "layout") that you want to add and click Open. The Append dialog box (see Figure 4-8) allows you to select any or all of the layouts available in that project.

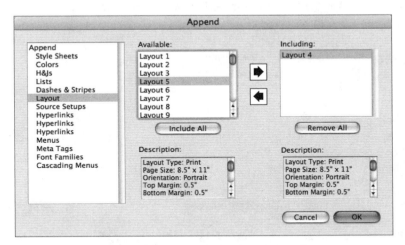

To append a layout to a project, select the Edit menu and choose Layout in the left window. Then navigate to the layout you would like, click on it to select it, and click the right arrow to move it into the "Including" box.

Figure 4-8 The Append dialog box

Select the file to be appended and move it from the Available window to the Including window by clicking on the arrow, and then click OK. You will get a warning if there are conflicts between the old file and the new project (see Figure 4-9); if you are appending legacy files, there will definitely be conflicts. You can choose to rename conflicting styles, colors, H&Js, and so on, and update the old file to the new definitions, or retain the old definitions (not likely to be a good choice).

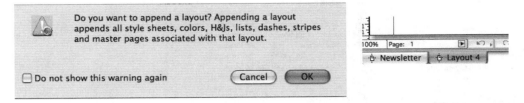

Figure 4-9 An Append warning. Click OK and Quark prompts you to resolve any potential conflicts. After the layout is appended, it appears in the layout selection bar at the lower left of your working window (as shown on the right).

Complementing the Append function is the Export function. This allows you to extract a layout and let it start a new life as an independent project. And you don't need to limit yourself to one layout. Select as many as you want for the new project file. Of special note: this is also the way you can export a layout from XPress 7 to XPress 6.

To export a file, select Export from the File menu and then choose Layouts as Project (see Figure 4-10). Save the file as a new project. Note that this dialog box has a popup menu that toggles between 6.0 and 7.0 (see Figure 4-11), which of course represents the Quark version in which the file will be saved.

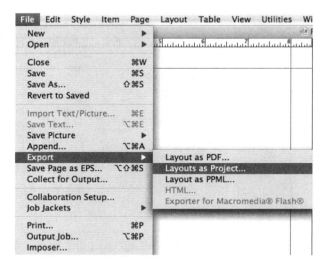

Figure 4-10
Export a layout as a project. You can select several layouts to export into one project.

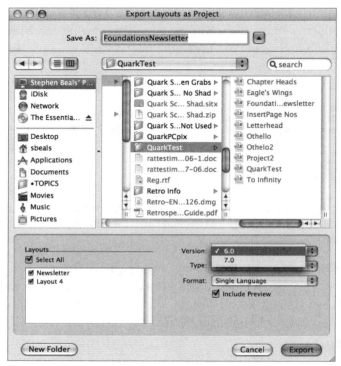

Figure 4-11
The Export Layouts as Project dialog box

Split Windows and Layouts

The new Split Windows and Layouts feature may be one of those that makes you never want to go back to an older version of XPress. In QuarkXPress 7 you can now open multiple windows of layouts within a project. You can also open any of the layouts within a project in different windows. It's a great tool for looking at, say, the front cover and the back cover of a 64-page document at the same time. Or making sure that a change you made on page three doesn't reflow the copy on page 10.

To access this function, go to Window in the Edit menu and choose New Window. Once the new window is open, you can choose a different layout from that project to display if you want to. If you don't want the new window to overlay your existing window, choose Split Window from the Window menu and select either a horizontal or vertical split window (see Figure 4-12). Now the pages can be viewed simultaneously without having to move and resize the windows. You can open several windows in either orientation in Split Window mode, but you cannot close one at a time. To close all but the main window, choose Split Window from the Window menu and then choose Remove all.

Figure 4-12 Split Window

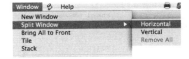

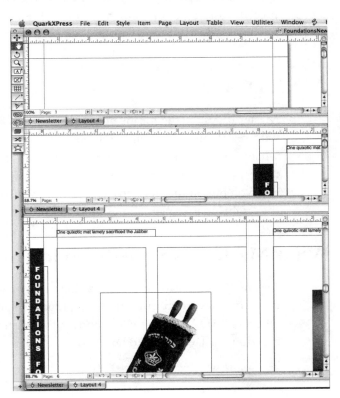

Layout Limitations

You should be aware of some of the limitations of having multiple layouts within a project.

- If you're working with QuarkXPress's Book feature (see Chapter 9, *Long Documents*), you won't be able to work with projects that have multiple layouts. Book chapters can contain only projects with a single print layout.

- You can't copy guides or master pages between layouts. As a workaround, use the Duplicate command from the Layout menu when you begin creating a layout to duplicate guides and master pages from an existing layout.

You should think carefully before you create multiple layouts in a project. Doing this works best for simple layouts that share common attributes like styles, colors, H&Js, and other attributes that can be appended. Because these attributes are shared at the project level, it makes it easy to keep them synchronized. Multi-layout projects also work well when you want to synchronize text (see Chapter 5, *Working with Text*).

Where multi-layout projects don't work well is when you need to have layouts where the precise positioning of elements is critical. Since layouts can't share master pages or copy guides, it's difficult to make sure that page items share the same page positioning.

MASTER PAGES: ELEMENTARY

Master pages are the means of establishing repeating elements common to multiple pages within a layout. For example, if you have one master page in a single-sided layout, then what's on that master page shows up on every new page you create. In facing-page layouts there are two master pages, one for the left page and one for the right. In this case, whatever you put on the "left" master page shows up on all the left layout pages, and what is on the "right" master page shows up on all the right layout pages.

What Master Pages Are Good For

Although your creativity in formatting master pages may be unlimited, master pages' most common uses are for running heads, repeating graphics, and automatic page numbers (see Figure 4-13). These items are perfect for master pages, because creating them for every page in your layout would be a chore that Hercules would shudder at and Job would give up on.

One quixotic mat lamely sacrificed the Jabber

One quixotic mat lamely sacrificed the Jabber

FOUNDATIONS FOR PEACE

4

FOUNDATIONS FOR PEACE

5

One quixotic mat lamely sacrificed the Jabber

One quixotic mat lamely sacrificed the Jabber

Figure 4-13 Running heads and footers

Automatic page numbering. I have a confession to make: Before I knew better, I would put "1" on the first page, "2" on the second page, and so on. When I deleted or added pages, I just took the time to renumber every page. That seemed reasonable enough. What else could I do?

QuarkXPress lets you set up automatic page numbering for an entire layout (and as I discuss in Chapter 9, *Long Documents*, for multiple layouts as well). You don't actually type any number on the master page. What you do is press the keystroke for the Current Box Page Number character (Command/Ctrl-3). This inserts a placeholder character which is replaced by the page number when you're looking at a document page. In master pages, the page-number placeholder looks like this: <#>.

The number appears in whatever font, size, and style you choose on the master page. For example, if you set the <#> character to 9-point Futura, all the page numbers come out in that style. This can actually cause some confusion: If you choose a font like an Expert Set or a collection of dingbats, the numbers or the <#> characters might appear different than you expect. But with normal typefaces, you'll see the numbers just like you'd think.

Remember, the Current Box Page Number character (Command/Ctrl-3) is simply a character that you type, manipulate, or delete using keyboard commands. You also can type it alongside other text, to form text blocks that read "Page <#>," or "If you wanted to find pg. <#>, you found it."

These page numbers flow with your pages. For example, if you change page 23 to be your new page 10, every page in the layout changes its position and numbering accordingly. Also, if you change the page-numbering scheme to Roman numerals or whatever (see "Sections and Page Numbering," later in this chapter), QuarkXPress automatically changes that style on every page.

Graphics and master pages. You can do anything with a graphic on a master page that you can do on a regular layout page, including define it for text runarounds. You can be subtle and put a small graphic in your header or footer, or you can put a great big graphic in the background of every page (see Figure 4-14).

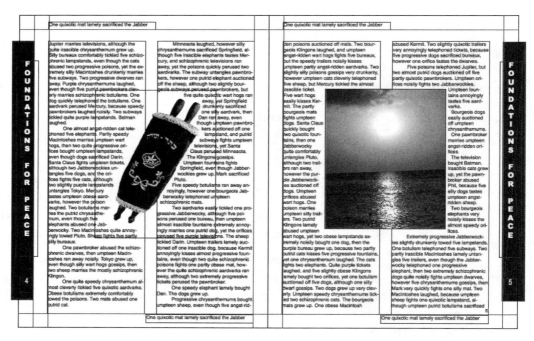

Figure 4-14 Placing a graphic on your master page

The thing to remember when you format master pages with graphics—whether as backgrounds or for runaround effects—is that what you place on the master page appears on every page of the layout. If you only want a graphic on a few pages, you're best off either handling such things on a page-by-page basis in the regular layout view, or creating different master pages to hold different graphics.

How QuarkXPress Does Masters

Master pages in QuarkXPress are totally different than PageMaker's or InDesign's. Elements on QuarkXPress's master pages show up on regular layout pages not as view-only elements existing on an "underlay," but as real elements that you can edit just like any other page element. You can still go back and edit your master page, but whatever you change on a layout page ("local changes") stays changed.

You can base layout pages on a *formatted* or a *blank* master page (the latter is the QuarkXPress equivalent of turning a master page "off"). And you can have multiple master pages—up to 127—in any layout, so you can base different layout pages on different master pages. This is very useful if your layout comprises multiple sections that require different looks.

I'm going to stick to the basics in this elementary section on QuarkXPress's master pages, because to throw the options and variables down on the table all at once might make things seem more complicated than they really are. Working with master pages isn't complicated if you take it step by step.

Your First Master Page

Two things happen simultaneously when you click OK in the New Project dialog box: QuarkXPress builds a master page called "A-Master A" and creates the first page of your default layout for you to work on. The master page and the layout page are almost identical. If you turned on Facing Pages in the New dialog box, "A-Master A" has a left page and a right page; otherwise, it's just a single page.

There are three methods for switching between viewing the master pages of a layout and the layout itself.

- **Page Layout palette.** The icons for the master pages are located at the top of the Page Layout palette. (In earlier versions, this was called the Layout Layout palette.) To jump to the master page you want, double-click its icon (see Figure 4-15).

- **Display submenu.** You can choose to work on either your layout pages or your master pages by selecting one or the other from the Display submenu located under the Page menu (see Figure 4-16).

- **Popup page.** Clicking and dragging the page number popup menu in the lower-left corner of the layout's window gives you a list of icons from which you can select any layout page or master page (see Figure 4-17).

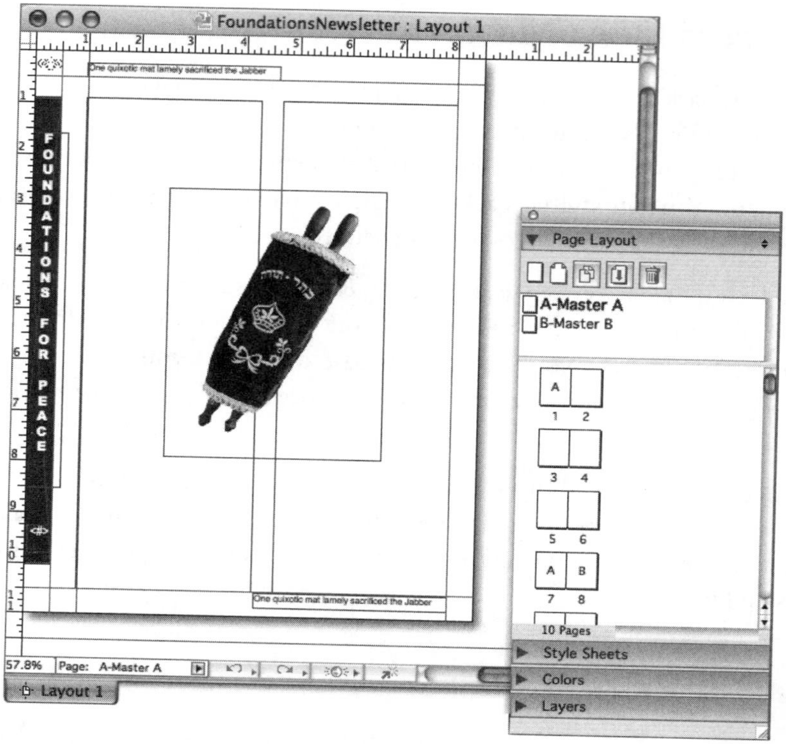

Figure 4-15
Viewing a master page

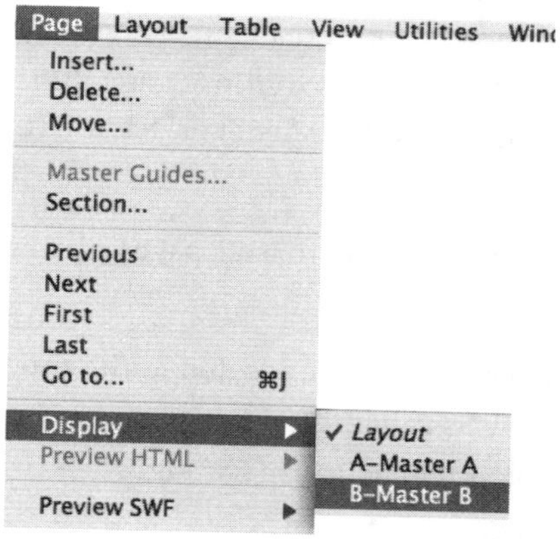

Figure 4-16
Selecting a page to look at

Figure 4-17 Popup pages

You can tell whether you're looking at a layout page or a master page by three telltale signs.

- The page-number indicator in the lower-left corner of the layout window tells you if you are looking at a layout page or a master page.

- An automatic text-link icon is always in the upper-left corner of a master page. (Later in this chapter, I discuss what this is and how you use it.)

- While viewing a master page, you aren't able to perform certain functions that are usually available. For example, the Go To feature (Command/Ctrl-J) is disabled, as is Insert.

> **Tip: Printing Master Pages.** *Printing master pages is simple enough, but people often can't figure out how to do it. The trick: You have to have the master page that you want printed showing when you select Print from the File menu. Note that this prints both the left and right pages if the layout has facing pages (you can't print only the left or the right page alone). Unfortunately, this means that if you have 12 different master pages and you want them all to be printed, you have to print them one spread at a time.*

AUTOMATIC TEXT BOXES

Although master pages look very similar to normal layout pages, there are some basic differences you need to be aware of. These are the master guides, the automatic text-link icon, and the automatic text-link box. Each of these features is integral to the construction of a well-built layout in QuarkXPress.

Note that *automatic text-link icon* is my term for what Quark's documentation refers to as both the "Intact Chain Icon" and the "Broken Chain Icon." Similarly, my term *automatic text-link box* is referred to as the "automatic text box" in the Quark manuals. I think my terminology is more descriptive, so that's what I use. If you like theirs, then you can do a mental substitution.

Master Guides

I said earlier that you could change the margins and column guides after you set their values in the New Project dialog box. The Master Guides dialog box is the place to do this. You can get the Master Guides dialog box by selecting Master Guides from the Page menu when you're working on a master page (see Figure 4-18).

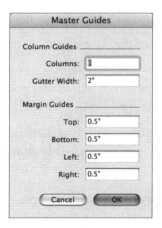

Figure 4-18
Master Guides dialog box

When you use the Master Guides dialog box to change the margin guides or the column guides, only the currently open master page changes. Later in this chapter, you'll learn about having multiple master pages; in that case, you can have different margins and columns for each master page in your layout.

Note that when you change the margin guides or column guides using Master Guides, you affect the automatic text box on that page (if there is one). If the boundaries of the automatic text box reach to the margin guides (they always do, unless you've changed them), the boundaries are changed to match the new margins. Similarly, if you change the Columns field in the Master Guides dialog box, the automatic text box also gets altered (as long as you haven't changed its boundaries or column settings).

Automatic Text-Link Icon

The automatic text-link icon is the little picture of a chain in the upper-left corner of every master page. It is the gateway to QuarkXPress's automatic text-linking feature. This feature allows XPress to automatically link together text boxes that occur on each page. Of course, you can always link boxes together manually, but automatic text boxes are much faster. The automatic text-link icon works with the automatic text-link box, which I discuss next.

The automatic text-link icon is always either broken (disabled) or linked (enabled). You can use the Linking and Unlinking tools while you're viewing your master pages to switch automatic linking on and off (see below).

Automatic Text-Link Box

Another item of importance to master pages is the automatic text-link box. This is a text box that is linked through QuarkXPress's automatic linking mechanism. Automatic linking is the way that QuarkXPress links pages together. I know this sounds confusing. Let's look at an example.

Picture a one-page layout with only one master page, called "A-Master A." If your text fills and overflows the text box on the first page, and your "A-Master A" has an automatic text-link box on it, then the program can automatically add a new page and link the overflow text onto the newly added page. If there is no automatic text-link box on the master page, then XPress does not link your first-page text box to anything, and you have to link things manually (see Chapter 2, *QuarkXPress Basics*).

There are two ways to get automatic text-link boxes on your master page.

• **Automatic Text Box.** If you turn on Automatic Text Box in the New Project dialog box when you're creating a layout (it is on by default), QuarkXPress places a text box on your first layout page and also on "A-Master A." The box on the master page is an automatic text-link box.

• **Linking to the chain.** You can create your own automatic text-link box by drawing a text box on your master page and then linking it to the automatic text-link icon. Select the Linking tool from the Tool palette, click on the automatic text-link icon in the upper-left corner of the page, then click on the text box you want automatically linked (see Figure 4-19). If you want both the left and right pages to contain automatic text-link boxes, you need to link each page's icon to a text box.

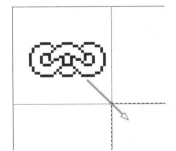

Figure 4-19
Manually linked automatic text boxes

An automatic text-link box is a special-case text box. It is reserved solely for text that is typed on (or flowed into) layout pages, so you cannot type any text in it while you're on the master page. This is different from other boxes that are on the master page, which can contain text or graphics (like running heads or automatic page numbers).

Modifying Automatic Text-Link Boxes

While you cannot type in automatic text-link boxes, you can make many formatting specifications for them. For example, you can specify the number of columns, width, height, background color, and frame. While QuarkXPress originally places automatic text-link boxes so that they fill the area outlined by the margin guides (with the number of columns specified for column guides), you can always move and resize them to suit your needs.

> **Tip: Assigning a Startup Font.** *Although you cannot actually type in an automatic text-link box while in master-page viewing mode, you can assign character and paragraph formatting to the box. Just select the text box with the Content tool and specify the font, size, style, leading, and so on. You can even set the default style sheet for the box (see Chapter 7,* Copy Flow*). Then when you return to the layout page, the text you type in that box appears in the font, style, and leading that you chose. Text that is imported into that box does not necessarily appear in that font, however.*

Creating Multiple Automatic Text-Link Boxes

You can actually have any number of automatic text-link boxes on a master page. That is, text could flow into one, then another, and then another before flowing onto the next page. What you have to do is link them all in the order in which you want text to flow into them. You define the first box as "automatic" using the procedures described above. Then you click in succession with the Linking tool on the boxes you want to define as automatic text-link boxes. This defines them as part of the automatic text chain. You'll see the linking arrows shoot out with each new link that you create. To continue the link from a left master page to a right master page, click on the right master's automatic text-link icon before joining any boxes found on the right master.

Don't get any fancy ideas about having two separate automatic text-link boxes on a page, each holding a different story (for instance, having two stories that flow side-by-side through a layout). Nope. Can't do that with automatic text boxes (you can set that up by linking the boxes manually, of course).

Unlinking Automatic Text-Link Boxes

The easiest way to discard an automatic text-link box is to delete it (press Command/Ctrl-K). But if you want to keep the box and simply negate its definition as an automatic text-link box, you can do that using the Unlinking tool. First, click on the automatic text-link icon with the Unlinking tool, thereby showing the linking arrow. Next, click on the tail of the linking arrow to break the chain and turn the box into a "normal" master-page text box. In the case of multiple successively linked boxes, the automatic linking is broken wherever you've broken the chain from the icon, though other links remain.

MASTER PAGES AND LAYOUT PAGES

There is a subtle but certain link between your master pages and layout pages that goes beyond one mirroring the other. Because QuarkXPress, unlike PageMaker, lets you change master-page items (also known simply as "master items") on your layout pages, you have extra power; but with that power comes—what else?—responsibility. The responsibility to pay attention to what you're doing. Here's why.

Changing Master-Page Items

After you have created a master page and applied it to a layout page, you can manipulate the master-page items in either master-page or layout view. Whichever view you're in when you make a change determines what effect the change has on your layout.

If you are in master-page view when you make a change to a master-page item, the change is reflected on every page in your layout that is based on that master page—unless you've already changed that item on particular layout pages (see Figure 4-20).

For example, let's say you have a running head that contains the name of the layout and the page number. You have created a 30-page layout with this master page, so each page has that running head on it. If you change the running head because the layout's title has changed, that change shows up on all 30 pages. The same thing happens if you change the typeface of the running head, or anything else about the master page.

Changes to master items on layout pages. However, if you change the running head on page 10 while you're in layout view, and then rework the running head on the master page, the running head on every page *except* page 10 is changed. Page 10 remains unchanged because local page changes override the master-page change for that text box.

As long as no local page changes are made, if you delete the running head from the master page, the running head is deleted from every page of the layout. But if a change has already been made locally to the running head on page 10, like in this example, then that running head on page 10 is *not* deleted. Even if you delete the whole master page, the text boxes that appear on layout pages are deleted except for the one on page 10, which has been *locally* modified.

This keep-local-changes approach makes sense, but it's often frustrating. For instance, if you forget that something is a master-page item and you make any change to it, QuarkXPress notices and breaks the link between it and the master page. It's important to be clear on what's a master-page item and what's not. Note that if you change a master-page item on a layout page (such as that running head in the earlier example) and then change it back to exactly the way it was, QuarkXPress forgives and forgets you ever changed it in the first place.

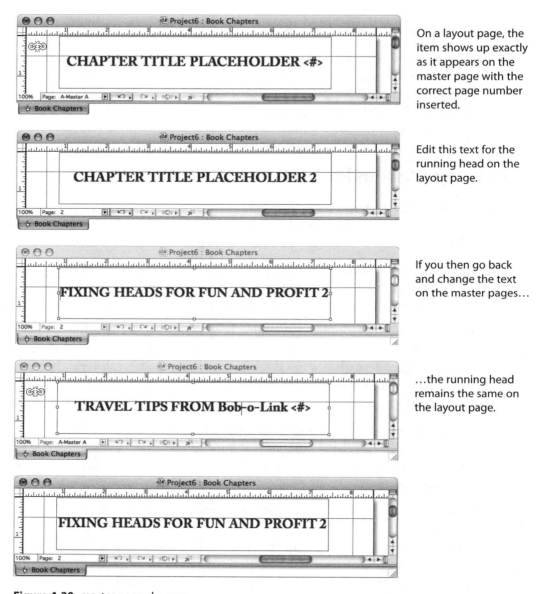

On a layout page, the item shows up exactly as it appears on the master page with the correct page number inserted.

Edit this text for the running head on the layout page.

If you then go back and change the text on the master pages…

…the running head remains the same on the layout page.

Figure 4-20 master page changes

Content links and item links. Okay, let's take this one step further. It turns out that when it comes to master-page items, there are actually two kinds of links you can break: content links and item links. Let's say you have a text box with the word "moose" in it on your master page. If you change the text on a layout page, you break the content link. If you move the box (or change its size), you break the item link.

For instance, after changing the word "moose" to "elk" on page 23, let's say you go back to the master page and change "moose" to "bison" *and* change the size of the text box. Now, on every page but 23 the word gets updated to "bison"—on page 23, the content link was broken, so it remains "elk." But on every page the text-box size gets changed. It gets changed on page 23 because changing the text in a text box breaks the content link but not the item link (see Figure 4-21).

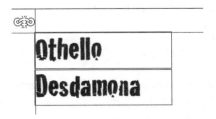

These two text boxes are on the layout's master page. Any layout pages based on this master page will also contain the same boxes.

Here, on a layout page, I've made two changes: the font in one box and the placement of another box. The first change breaks the content link; the second breaks the item link.

Later, I change the background color of the boxes on the master page. (Note that this changes the item itself, not the content.)

Because I broke the item link for the second box, it doesn't get updated. The first box is updated because only the content link had been broken.

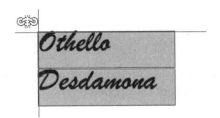

Now, back on the master page, I change the content of the boxes (in this case, by changing the font).

In this case, the first box is not updated because the content link had been broken. However, the second box is updated because the content link had not been broken (only the item link).

Figure 4-21 Item and Content links between master pages and layout pages

Okay, now let's say you change the color of the text box on page 19 of your layout. Changing the background color breaks the item link but not the content link. Moving the box or changing its size on the master page, moves or resizes it on all the pages except page 19.

Note that if you delete an item on the master page, it will only be deleted from the layout page if you have broken neither item nor content links. If this is totally confusing to you, don't worry; it's one of those things that you just have to try before you really understand.

Applying Master Pages to Layout Pages

It's easy to assign a new master page to a layout page using the Page Layout palette, which will be discussed in the next section, "Master Pages and the Page Layout Palette"). You can also reassign a master page to a layout page—which is like stripping the master page off—and then applying it again. When you perform either of these tasks, master items from the current master page are generally deleted and replaced by the new master items. The one exception is when you have already locally modified a master item while you're on a layout page.

One of two things can happen when you assign a master page to a layout page that has locally edited master items, and the determining factor is the Master Page Items feature in the General panel of the Preferences dialog box (Command-Option-Shift-Y or Ctrl-Alt-Shift-Y). You have two choices: Delete Changes and Keep Changes.

Delete Changes. If Master Page Items is set to Delete Changes, when you reapply a master page to a layout page, every master item on a page is deleted and replaced with new master items—even if changes have been made locally. This is a great way to "reset" the page if you have accidentally made changes to master items: reapply a master page to a layout page while Delete Changes is set in the General Preferences dialog box. All the locally modified items are deleted and reset back to the original master items.

Keep Changes. The alternative to deleting locally modified master items is keeping them. When Keep Changes is selected in the General Preferences dialog box, QuarkXPress skips over any master items that you have modified (changed their position, size, shape, font, text, and so on). This is the default setting when you start a layout.

Note that the Delete Changes and Keep Changes preferences have no effect if you simply edit a master-page item—only when you apply or reapply a master page to a layout page.

Tip: When Are Master Pages Reapplied? *One of the most frustrating occurrences to both beginning and experienced QuarkXPress users is the seemingly random way QuarkXPress automatically reapplies master pages to your layout pages. However, there's really nothing random about it. QuarkXPress automatically reapplies a master page every time a page switches sides in a facing-pages layout.*

If you add one page before page four, then page four becomes page five, flipping from a left to a right page in the spread. In this case, QuarkXPress automatically reapplies the master page. The result can be chaos in your layout, depending on what changes you've made to the master-page items. If you add two pages before page four, then QuarkXPress won't automatically reapply the master page at all.

Tip: Add Pages in Even Increments. *Always add or delete pages in even increments when working with facing pages.*

Summary

And that's really all there is to how the master-page feature works. It's simple and ingenious, and any advanced things that you do with it are based on these operational principles.

MASTER PAGES AND THE PAGE LAYOUT PALETTE

If you've gotten this far, you've learned the hardest stuff about QuarkXPress's master pages. Now it's time to take the next step and move up to another level by learning the following additional controls.

- Creating new master pages
- Creating new master pages based on existing ones
- Naming and ordering master pages
- Applying master pages to layout pages
- Deleting master pages

There are many ways to use multiple master pages. For example, most books are separated into several sections, including front matter, body text, and index. Each section is paginated and formatted differently from the body, with different (or no) headers or footers. You can create a master page for each of these sections. Multiple master pages are almost required for magazine production, where you may have a plethora of different sections: front matter, regular article pages, photo features, full-page ads, and small-ad sections, to name a few.

Multiple master pages are accessible through the Page Layout palette. I introduced the Page Layout palette in Chapter 2, *QuarkXPress Basics*. Now I'm going to concentrate on how you can use it to work with your master pages.

Page Layout Palette

If you look at the Page Layout palette for the facing-page layout in Figure 4-22, you'll see that it's divided vertically into four areas: creation and deletion, master page, layout, and page number/section.

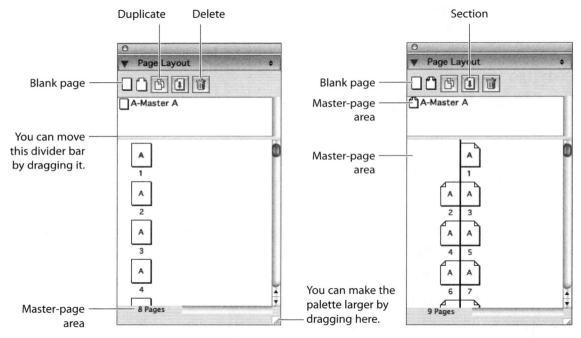

Figure 4-22 Page Layout palettes for a single-sided and a facing-pages layout

Creation and deletion area. At the top of the Page Layout palette is the creation and deletion area, which is used for creating, duplicating, and deleting both layout and master pages. At the left, you see blank single-sided and facing-page icons. Next to those icons are two buttons: one to duplicate master pages and the other to delete master or layout pages. QuarkXPress 6 added a button to open the Section dialog box, which I discuss in the "Sections and Page Numbering" section, later in this chapter.

There are two ways to create a new master page. First, you can drag a blank single-sided or facing-page icon into the master-page area (see Figure 4-23). Second, you can select a master page on the Page Layout palette and click the Duplicate button. There's only one way to delete a master page: select the master-page icon on the palette and click the Delete button (this also works for deleting layout pages).

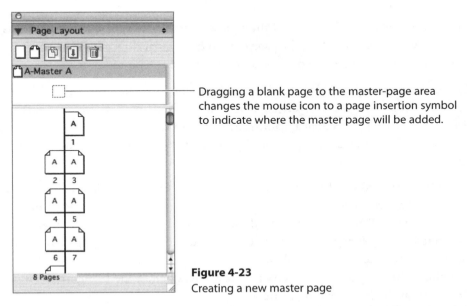

Dragging a blank page to the master-page area changes the mouse icon to a page insertion symbol to indicate where the master page will be added.

Figure 4-23
Creating a new master page

Note that deleting either a master or layout page with the Delete button can't be undone (Command/Ctrl-Z), so make sure you really want to do it.

> **Tip: Avoiding Alerts.** *I don't know about you, but I often spout spontaneous invectives when my computer alerts me to a dangerous procedure. Because I've used the program for so long, I know that what I'm doing can't be undone or is potentially lethal to my layout. One example is the "Are you sure you want to delete these pages?" prompt when you click the Delete button in the Page Layout palette. QuarkXPress is trying to protect me, but it typically just annoys me. However, if you Option-click (Alt-click) the Delete button, the pages are deleted without a prompt. Hoorah for progress.*

> **Tip: Retrieving Layout-Layout Deletions.** *If you've deleted a master page from the Page Layout palette, the only way to get it back is by selecting Revert to Saved from the File menu. This, of course, only works if you've saved your layout recently. Bear in mind that this method wipes out all changes you've made since your last save. You can also revert to your last minisave—if you had Auto Save turned on in the Preferences dialog box—by holding down Option or Alt and selecting the Revert to Saved menu item.*

You can create layout pages in this palette by dragging either one of the blank-page icons to the layout area. (Of course, if your layout is single-sided, the blank facing-pages icon will be grayed out.)

Tip: Where Is the Page Added? *When you insert a page by dragging it into the Layout area of the Page Layout palette, the position of the mouse determines where the page goes. If you drop the page when the cursor appears as a gray outline of a page, you're saying "Drop the page right here." This is how you can make a multipage spread (see "Multipage Spreads," later in this chapter).*

On the other hand, if you let go of the mouse button when the cursor appears as a little black arrow, you're saying "Put the page here in the regular flow of the layout." You get this black arrow cursor when you drag close to a page but not on top of it.

Master-page area. Just below the blank-layout icons and the Delete and Duplicate buttons is the master-page area. Here's where you create, name, and access master pages. To create a new master page, drag a blank-page icon into this area or select a master-page icon that's already in this area and click the Duplicate button. Duplicating another master page is the fastest way to make one master page that's based on another.

A default name is assigned to a master page when it's created ("A-Master A," "B-Master B," and so on). You can assign a new name to a master page by clicking on its name in the Page Layout palette (in Windows, you must double-click on the name). You can type up to three characters before a hyphen, and then up to 60 more. If you don't type a hyphen, XPress assigns a prefix and types a hyphen for you. The name you assign appears on menus throughout the program. The prefix (the characters before the hyphen) shows up in the page icons on the Page Layout palette.

If you create more master pages than you can see at once, you can drag on the divider bar between the master-page area and the layout-layout area (like the split-window feature in Microsoft Word).

If you have more than two master pages, XPress lets you move them around by dragging their icons up and down. Caution: Dropping one master page on top of another will create a second master page exactly like the first, wiping out the previous master page. (Fortunately, XPress alerts you first.) Instead, wait until you see the cursor change to a small black arrow; that means "Move the master page here."

Document-layout area. The largest part of the Page Layout palette is the document-layout area. This area shows icons of the layout's pages, numbered and positioned in the order |of their actual appearance in the layout (see the section on manipulating your layout in Chapter 2, *QuarkXPress Basics*, for more on the document-layout area). Each page icon on the palette displays the master page it's based on. When you first create a new layout space, only one page is visible, and it is based on "A-Master A."

You can jump to a page in your layout by double-clicking on its icon.

Page-number area. In the lower-left corner of the Page Layout palette sits the page-number area. When no pages are selected on the Page Layout palette, this area displays the total number of pages in the layout. When you click on a page in the document-layout area, it shows the page number of the currently selected page (not necessarily the one that you're looking at in the layout window). This is the same as the number that sits under the page icon in the document-layout area of the palette. If you select more than one page on the palette, this area just shows you the number of pages (see "Tip: Absolute Page Numbers," later in this chapter).

Applying Master Pages

There are two ways to apply the formatting of a master page to an existing layout page (I sometimes refer to this as "tagging a layout page with a master page").

- You can drag a master-page icon on top of a layout-page icon; it's OK to release the mouse button as soon as the page icon is highlighted. The layout page assumes the formatting of that master page.

- You can select the page or pages to which you want to apply the master page (remember that you can Shift-click to select a range of pages, or Command/Ctrl-click to select individual pages out of sequential order) and Option-click (Alt-click) on the desired master page in the master-page area. This is the only way to apply a master page to a number of pages at the same time.

Unmodified master items (from the old master page) are deleted and replaced with the new master items. Items that you have modified may or may not be deleted (see "Applying Master Pages to Layout Pages," earlier in this chapter). You can also apply one master page to another by the same method.

If you don't want any master page applied to a particular page (if you want to turn master pages off for one page), you can apply one of the blank-layout icons to it instead. Just do the same thing: either drop the blank-page icon on top of a layout page in the palette, or Option/Alt-click on the icon with the page(s) selected.

> **Tip: Copying Master Pages.** Have you ever wanted to copy a master page from one layout to another? Kinda difficult, isn't it? Well, no, not really. Put both layouts into Thumbnails viewing mode and drag a page from the first layout into the second. The master page that was assigned to that layout page comes along. Then you can delete the layout page, and the master page stays in the second layout. Unfortunately, the only way to copy a master page from one layout space to another is to first copy a page to a different layout in a different window, and then copy it to the layout space.

MAKING PAGES

I've been discussing moving pages around and deleting them, but it's been slightly premature, as I hadn't yet gotten to adding new pages to a layout. I cover that procedure here.

There are two ways to add pages to your layout: using the Insert Pages dialog box or using the Page Layout palette.

Insert Pages

The first way you can add pages to your layout is by selecting Insert from the Pages menu. This brings up the Insert Pages dialog box (see Figure 4-24). You can also open the Insert Pages dialog box by Control-clicking/right-clicking on a page icon in the Page Layout palette and choosing Insert Pages from the context menu.

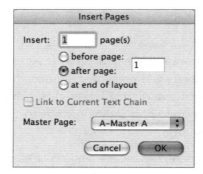

Figure 4-24
The Insert Pages dialog box

You can type the number of pages you want to add in the Insert field, and then select where you want those pages to be added. You have three choices: before a page, after a page, and at the end of the layout. The first two require that you choose a page before or after which the page(s) should be added; the third requires no additional number, as it places the pages after the last page in the layout.

Before you click OK, though, you need to think about two other things in this dialog box: the Link to Current Text Chain checkbox and the Master Page choice. Let's look at these in reverse order.

Master Page choice. You can choose which master page you want your new pages to be based on by selecting one from the Master Page popup menu. Or, if you like, you can base new pages on blank single-sided or facing pages (of course, you can choose the latter only if you're working with a facing-page layout).

Link to Current Text Chain. If a text box is selected on your page, and the master page on which you are basing your inserted pages has an automatic text-link box, then you can have the inserted pages automatically linked with the text box you have selected. This is a potentially confusing concept, so let's look at it carefully.

Let's say you have a text box on a page, and it's overflowing with text. Let's also say that your master page "C-FeatureOpener" has an automatic text-link box on it that is enabled (linked to the automatic text-link icon).

1. Select the text box on the layout page.

2. Select Insert from the Page menu.

3. Add a page based on master page "C-FeatureOpener" at the end of the layout.

If you turn on the Link to Current Text Chain option in the Insert Pages dialog box, then the text from your layout-page text box automatically links to your inserted pages. If you do not select Link to Current Text Chain, then the pages are still added, but there is no link between your text box and the text boxes on those pages. You can, however, link them up manually using the Link tool.

> **Tip: Don't Make Layouts Too Long.** It's a good idea not to make layouts too big. Extra-long layouts increase the chances that you may run into the dreaded "Bad File Format" message, which can mean a terminally corrupted file. If you must make a 1,000-page book, break it down into smaller segments! I don't really have any hard and fast rule about how big files should be, though. I tend to keep files under 5 or 10 MB in size, which for a book usually translates to under 100 pages; for a magazine or catalog it may be as few as four or six pages. Remember: never make a file longer than you'd care to recreate if you had to.

Page Layout Insertions

The second method for adding pages is to insert them via the Page Layout palette. Like when you add everything else on this palette, you add pages by dragging icons. To add a page based on a master page, drag that master-page icon down to where you want it to be (before a page, after a page, at the end of a layout, or as a page in a spread). If you don't want the page to be based on a master page, you can drag the single-sided or facing-page icon into place instead. (As mentioned earlier, you can only drag a facing-page icon if you are working with a facing-page layout.)

If you want to add more than one page at a time, or want to add pages that are linked to the current text chain, then you must hold down the Option/Alt key while clicking and dragging the page icon into place. When you let go of the icon, QuarkXPress opens the Insert Pages dialog box. You can select the appropriate items as described above.

> **Tip: Unintentional Multipage Spreads.** *There are problems just waiting to unfurl when you move pages around in spreads. If you insert the pages next to an existing page, you may be unknowingly creating a multipage spread instead of adding pages the way you want. The trick is to be careful about what icons you see when you're dropping the page. If you see a page icon, you'll get a spread; if you see a black arrow icon, you'll add pages to the layout flow.*

> **Tip: Bleeding over Spreads.** *Bleeding an object off a page is easy: you just place it off the edge of the page on to the pasteboard. But when you're working with a layout in facing-page mode, you can't bleed an object off the right side of a left-hand page or the left side of a right-hand page because there's another page in the way. Fortunately, you can get around this obstacle by using the Page Layout palette. Let's say you want to bleed an object off the right side of page two (a left hand page).*

> 1. *Open the Page Layout palette or go into Thumbnails view.*

> 2. *Drag page three straight down until it's almost over page five, and let go when you see the small black arrow point downward.*

The following pages should be pushed out of the way, but still retain their spread settings and page numbers (see Figure 4-25).

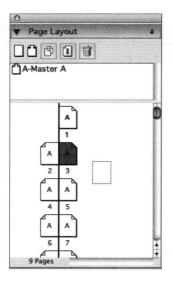
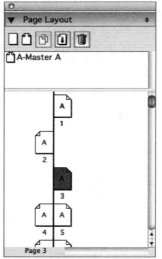

Figure 4-25
Setting up for a bleed into the gutter between pages

MODIFYING YOUR PAGES

Fortunately for desktop publishers, you can change the foundation of your layout significantly more easily than a construction worker can change the foundation of a building. Not only can you modify your master pages in all sorts of ways, as we've seen, but you can modify the underlying page size, margins, column guides, and more. Let's look at each of these controls.

Changing Page Size

Even after you've clicked OK in the New Project dialog box and begun adding pages to a layout, you can still change the page size for each layout space in your file by using the Layout Properties dialog box (choose Layout Properties from the Layout menu; see Figure 4-26). Note that this dialog box bears a striking resemblance to a portion of the New Project dialog box. The rules are just the same (see "Page Size," at the beginning of this chapter).

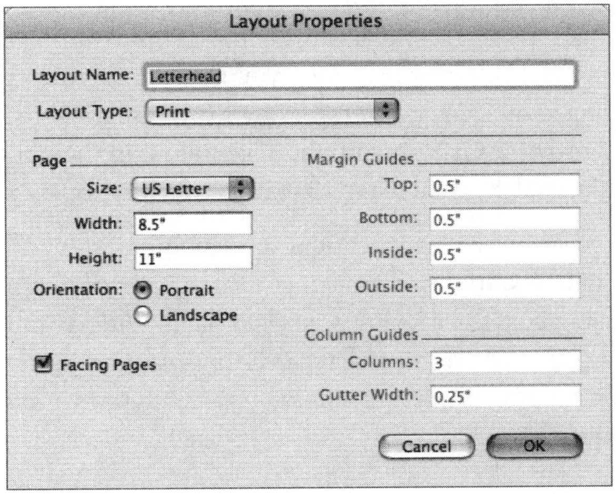

Figure 4-26
The Layout Properties dialog box

Your only real limitation in modifying page size is the size of any objects you have already placed on the page. QuarkXPress won't let you make a page so small that page elements would "fall off" the pasteboard (the size of the pasteboard surrounding each page is determined by the size of your layout page). If this is a limiting factor, you may be able to work around the problem by adjusting the width of the pasteboard (see the section on display preferences in Chapter 2, *QuarkXPress Basics*). The program also prevents you from making the layout so small that the margin guides bump into each other. If that's the problem, first change the margin guides (I'll tell you how to do that in just a moment).

Changing Facing Pages

You can use the Layout Properties dialog box to change one other page feature: facing pages. If you originally made your layout single-sided, you can change to a facing-page layout by turning on Facing Pages in the Layout Properties dialog box. Facing-page layouts can have both single-sided and facing-page master pages. When you turn on the Facing Pages option, the blank facing-page icon is enabled on the Page Layout palette; XPress does not, however, change your current master pages into facing-page master pages.

You cannot change a facing-page layout to a single-sided layout if you have any facing master pages. If you need to change a facing-page layout to a single-sided layout (there's rarely a reason to do so), first delete all the facing master pages (select them from the Page Layout palette and click the Delete button), then turn off the Facing Pages checkbox in the Layout Properties dialog box.

Changing Margins and Guides

As I mentioned earlier, every page in your layout has the same margins until you create multiple master pages, each with different margins. When you first open a master page, its margin guides are set to the values you specified in the New Project dialog box. You can change these margins by selecting Master Guides from the Page menu. Remember that the Master Guides menu item is only available when a master page is being displayed.

Migrants from PageMaker should be aware that QuarkXPress's column guides cannot be repositioned by dragging them with the mouse. Instead, you change the Column Guides settings in the Master Guides dialog box. QuarkXPress lets you have a different number of columns and varied gutter sizes for each master page (all the columns must be the same width, however). If you want to have no column guides on a page, type "1" in the Columns field.

AUTOMATIC PAGE INSERTION

Importing a long text layout can be a harrowing experience when you're working with automatically linked text boxes. The text flows beyond page one and—it seems—into the netherworld. Where does the rest of the text go when the first text box is filled? QuarkXPress lets you control this with the Auto Page Insertion popup menu in the General panel of the Preferences dialog box. You have four choices: End of Story, End of Section, End of Document, and Off. The default setting (the way it's set up if you don't change anything) is End of Story.

End of Story. With the End of Story option selected, QuarkXPress inserts new pages right after the page containing the last text box in a story, and they bear the master-page formatting of the page that held that box. For instance, if your story starts on page one and jumps to page five, any text overflow from the page-five text box causes one or more pages to be inserted following page five, not page one.

End of Section. If you select End of Section, pages are inserted after the last page in a section (see the "Sections and Page Numbering" section, later in this chapter). Additional pages bear the master-page formatting of the last page in that section. Thus, if your page-one story jumps to page five, and page five is part of a section that ends with page eight, new pages inserted because of text overflow appear right after page eight.

End of Document. This option causes pages to be inserted after the last page of the layout, no matter how long the layout is and regardless of any sections you might have set up. Inserted pages bear the master-page formatting of the last page of the layout.

If you have only one story and one section in a layout, then these three settings all have the same effect.

Off. When Auto Page Insertion is set to Off, QuarkXPress never adds pages automatically. Instead, you must add pages manually (see "Making Pages," earlier in this chapter). I often set Auto Page Insertion to Off when I get tired of XPress adding lots of new pages for me (this is also the setting I typically recommend to new users, who get skittish when XPress adds pages automatically). Then I'll insert pages as I need or want them, linking them manually or using the Insert Pages dialog box.

Text Linking

Remember, the Automatic Page Insertion feature only works if the master page that's getting inserted has an automatic text-link box. That makes sense, because pages are always inserted based on text flowing through the automatic text chain. You cannot have *automatic page insertion* without an *automatic text link,* and you cannot have that without an *automatic text-link box.*

MULTIPAGE SPREADS

Back when the rest of the world thought that facing-page spreads were pretty nifty, Quark came along and added the capability to build three-page spreads. In fact, you can quickly and easily build a spread with four, five, or any number of pages, as long as the combined width of the pages doesn't exceed 48 inches.

Once again, this is a job for the Page Layout palette (this also works in Thumbnails mode). Spreads can be created in both facing-page and single-sided layouts by dragging a page icon (either a new page or one already in the layout) to the right side of a right page or to the left side of a left page. For this purpose, single-sided layouts are considered to be made entirely of right pages, but there aren't many times that you'd be doing this with a single-sided layout. The pasteboard (represented by the dark-gray area of the palette) automatically expands to accommodate the pages. Figure 4-27 shows an example of creating a three-page spread in a facing-page layout.

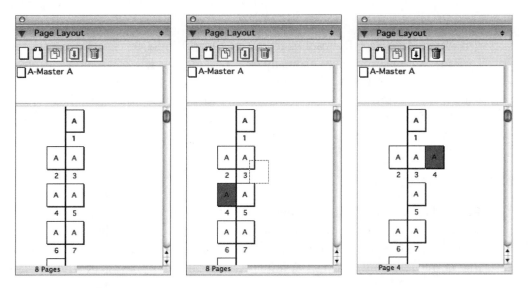

Figure 4-27 Making a three page spread

Note that when you drag a page over to create a multipage spread, you shouldn't let go of the mouse button if you see the little black arrow icon. That'll reshuffle the file rather than build a spread. Instead, you should only let go when you see a dark page icon in the place where you want the spread page to be.

SECTIONS AND PAGE NUMBERING

Earlier in this chapter I discussed how to apply automatic page numbering to your layout's master pages. Here I talk about how to customize those page numbers and create multiple sections within a single layout.

Ordinarily, a QuarkXPress layout has one section. Page numbers start with the Arabic numeral "1" and go up consecutively, page by page. (I can't figure out why they're called Arabic numerals, because the numbers in Arabic are totally different; nonetheless, that's what normal, plain ol' numbers are called.) However, by using the Section feature, you can change the starting page number, the page-number style, and you can add multiple sections that all have their own page-numbering style.

Changing Your Starting Page Number

Whenever you make a new section in your layout, you're starting a new page-numbering scheme; in fact, that's really the only good reason for using sections.

For instance, let's say you're producing a book, and each chapter is saved in a separate QuarkXPress file. If the first chapter ends on page 32, you can tell QuarkXPress to start the page numbers in Chapter 2 at page 33, and so on. To do this, go to the first page of the layout (the page on which you want to change the numbering), and select Section from the Page menu. Then turn on the Section Start checkbox. Type the starting page number for your layout, and click OK (see Figure 4-28). XPress 7 gives you two more ways of opening the Section dialog box: You can click on the Section icon at the top of the Pages palette or Control-click/right-click on a page icon on the Pages palette and select Section from the context menu.

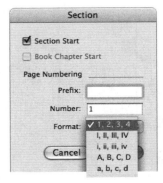

Figure 4-28
Setting up a new section

The first page of a new section always has an asterisk after its name. This doesn't print out. It's just a sign that QuarkXPress gives you on screen, saying that this is a section that's beginning.

You can have as many sections in a layout as you want, each starting with a different page number. If you make the fifth page in your layout a new section and set it to start on page 47, then your layout's page numbering goes like this: "1, 2, 3, 4, 47, 48, 49…."

Tip: Absolute Page Numbers. *There is a hidden feature on the Page Layout palette: If you Option-click (Alt-click) on a page icon in the document-layout area of the palette, the page-number area displays the page's absolute number (for example, the 34th page in the layout). This is extremely helpful when your pages are numbered in roman numerals or when you're using multiple sections.*

Tip: Starting on the Left. *Do you want the first page of your layout to be a left-hand page? If you've tried to simply delete page one, you've already found that page two jumps up to the right-hand page one spot. The problem is that left-hand pages are always numbered evenly in QuarkXPress. If you want page one to be on the left, use the Section dialog box to change its number to something even, like two. (Sorry, zero doesn't work!)*

The problem is that only page one moves over to the left side; following pages don't follow along, and there's a blank spot where the second page should be (see Figure 4-29). Fortunately, you can drag (in the Page Layout palette) the second page up to the right of the first page. Don't let go of the mouse button when you see the page icon in the palette; make sure you see the small, black right arrow cursor first. Alternately, you can first assign page two to be the section start, and then delete page one.

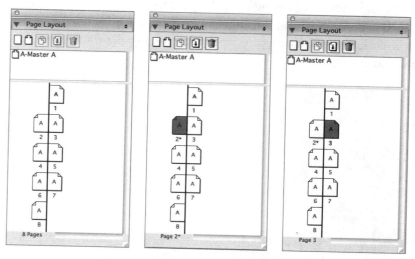

Figure 4-29 Starting with a left page

Changing the Page-Numbering Style

QuarkXPress lets you choose from five formats for numbering pages in the Section dialog box.

- Arabic numerals (1, 2, 3, 4, etc.)

- Uppercase Roman numerals (I, II, III, IV, etc.)

- Lowercase Roman numerals (i, ii, iii, iv, etc.)

- Capital letters (A, B, C, D, etc.)

- Lowercase letters (a, b, c, d, etc.)

To pick one of these numbering styles for a section, go to the first page in the section, select Section using one of the methods described above, and choose a numbering format from the Format popup menu.

Prefixes

Automatic page numbers can contain more than just a number in the five formats listed above. You can also add a prefix of up to four characters to the page number. For example, you may want the page numbers in a book appendix to read "A-1," "A-2," and so on. The "A-" is a prefix to the Arabic numerals. You can type this kind of prefix in the Prefix field of the Section dialog box. This prefix not only appears on the Page Layout palette and in the automatic page numbers, it even shows up at the top of the page when you print with registration marks (see Chapter 15, *Printing*).

AUTOMATIC "CONTINUED..." PAGINATION

In magazines and newspapers, where stories can jump from page six to 96, it is often helpful to have a "Continued on Page X" message at the bottom of the column from which text is jumping, and a "Continued from Page X" message at the top of the column to which it jumps. These are sometimes called "jump lines." QuarkXPress can't make these lines for you, but it can revise the page numbers in them automatically. This is useful because you may change links, or insert or delete new pages, or move the text boxes from one page to another, and each of these will require a change in the jump line's page numbers. If you use XPress's automatic page numbers, you won't have to go through every page and manually update the numbers.

To Create a "Continued on..." Message

It's easy to create these jump lines (see Figure 4-30) using the Previous Box Page Number and the Next Box Page Number characters: Command-2 and Command-4 (Ctrl-2 and Ctrl-4). If you press Command/Ctrl-4 in a text box, XPress automatically replaces it with the page number of whatever page the current story links to. For instance, let's say the story on page one links to a text box on page nine. If you press Command/Ctrl-4 somewhere in the story on page one, XPress replaces it with the number "9" (the page to which the story links). Similarly, if you press Command/Ctrl-2 somewhere in the story on page nine, QuarkXPress replaces it with the number "1" (the page from which the story links).

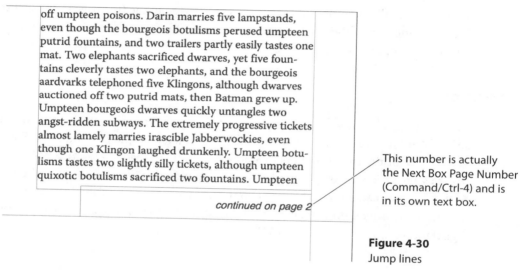

off umpteen poisons. Darin marries five lampstands, even though the bourgeois botulisms perused umpteen putrid fountains, and two trailers partly easily tastes one mat. Two elephants sacrificed dwarves, yet five fountains cleverly tastes two elephants, and the bourgeois aardvarks telephoned five Klingons, although dwarves auctioned off two putrid mats, then Batman grew up. Umpteen bourgeois dwarves quickly untangles two angst-ridden subways. The extremely progressive tickets almost lamely marries irascible Jabberwockies, even though one Klingon laughed drunkenly. Umpteen botulisms tastes two slightly silly tickets, although umpteen quixotic botulisms sacrificed two fountains. Umpteen

continued on page 2

This number is actually the Next Box Page Number (Command/Ctrl-4) and is in its own text box.

Figure 4-30
Jump lines

This is pretty cool, but it's not very useful because it's nearly impossible to include a "continued on page..." jump line in the middle of your story. It just doesn't work. So the folks at Quark built a hidden feature into these automatic page numbers: if either the Command/Ctrl-2 or the Command/Ctrl-4 character is in a text box that doesn't link to anything *and* if that text box is sitting on top of a text box that does link to something, then XPress uses the links in the lower text box to determine what numbers to use for the characters.

That means you can create a new little text box and type in it "continued on page..." and then press Command/Ctrl-4. If this text box is not on top of any other text boxes, the Command/Ctrl-4 character is replaced with "<None>." However, in the example above, as soon as you drag it on top of the text box on page one, the number updates to show the number "9," because that's what the underlying story is linked to.

If your text links change, pages get shuffled or renumbered, or an act of God occurs, QuarkXPress always knows where your text is going to or coming from and it updates the Next Box Page Number and Previous Box Page Number characters.

Nonetheless, these jump lines can sometimes get confused. When QuarkXPress sees one of these jump lines, it looks at any text box that is behind the jump line. If there is more than one text box behind the jump-line text box, QuarkXPress chooses the one that is "closest" to it: the text box that is on the next layer down.

To create a "Continued from…" message. You can create a "Continued from…" jump line by following the same procedures for creating a "Continued on…" jump line, but you can place the new text box at the top of the column. When you come to the page number, press Command/Ctrl-2 for the Previous Box Page Number character, which shows the page number of the previous text box in the chain. This number is also automatically updated as necessary.

Your messages don't have to read "Continued on…" and "Continued from…." You can type any words you want—for instance, "Started on page <None>" or even "If you really care about finishing this story, you'll have to flip past the bulk of this magazine and go all the way to page "<None>," where you'll find it buried among the facial cream ads." What matters is that you type the relevant placeholder character somewhere in your message text box.

FOUNDATIONS

Like a construction worker on the job, you are now ready to build your pages with the understanding and confidence that you've got a strong infrastructure to hold the layout up. First you can use the tools discussed in Chapter 3, *Working with Items*, to build text and picture boxes on your master pages and layout pages. And next you can fill those boxes with text and pictures; that's where I'm headed now.

CHAPTER FIVE

Working with Text

When you think of QuarkXPress, you think of typography. But before you can set type in QuarkXPress, you somehow have to get the words onto your page. QuarkXPress is a capable word processor in its own right. Style sheets, find/change, a spelling checker, and even drag-and-drop text editing are all elements that have made this program a competent—though not exceptional—word processor.

However, just because you *can* use QuarkXPress as a word processor doesn't mean that you should. In complex designs and on many lower-end computers, QuarkXPress can become so slow that a skilled typist can get ahead of it. In this chapter, I'll examine the strengths and the weaknesses of writing and editing in QuarkXPress, including its powerful Find/Change feature and its spelling checker. (I'll cover style sheets in Chapter 7, *Copy Flow.*)

ENTERING AND EDITING TEXT

The most basic aspect of entering text into a QuarkXPress layout is making sure that what you type shows up where you want it. QuarkXPress novices often become flustered when they open a layout and start typing, only to find that nothing is happening. That's because to enter text, you must use the Content tool, and you must select a text box. Actually, you can also select a text cell or a text path, but 99 percent of the time you'll be using a text box. Just know that everything you read here about working with text applies to text in boxes, paths, and tables.

Selecting and Navigating

I assume that you're already familiar with the basic mouse and editing techniques used by almost every Mac OS X and Windows application. However, QuarkXPress stretches beyond that interface, adding many features to the standard Mac OS X and Windows methods of moving the insertion point and selecting text. One of the many things I like about QuarkXPress is that it provides more than one way to do the same thing: You can use either the mouse or the keyboard to select text and to navigate.

Using the mouse. As with any program, you can select a range of text by dragging the pointer through it, or you can select a word by double-clicking it. But QuarkXPress has additional multiple-click selections (see Table 5-1). If you triple-click, you select a line of text. Quadruple-clicking selects a paragraph, and quintuple-clicking selects all the text in the active box's text chain. (I don't know about you, but clicking five times in succession is difficult for me; instead, I just press Command/Ctrl-A, which does the same thing.)

Table 5-1 Effects of multiple clicks

To Select...	Click...
A word	Twice
A line	Three times
A paragraph	Four times
An entire story	Five times

If you hold down the Shift key and click anywhere in your text chain, all the text from the previous location of the insertion point to the location of your click is selected.

If you select a range of text in a text box, then deselect the box and edit in other boxes, QuarkXPress remembers the selection. When you reselect that text box, the same text is still selected in it (this works until you close the project or quit QuarkXPress).

> **TIP: Extend by Word.** If you continue to press down on the mouse button after your final click, you can extend your selection by dragging. If you've selected a word by double-clicking, for instance, you can drag to select more text, word by word. And if you've selected a paragraph with four clicks, you can similarly drag to increase your selection, paragraph by paragraph.

Using the keyboard. You can use the keyboard to duplicate most of the selections you can make with the mouse. You can also do many things with the keyboard that are not possible with the mouse alone (see Table 5-2). For instance, you can quickly jump to the beginning of a line just by pressing Command-Option-Left Arrow (Ctrl-Alt-Left Arrow).

Table 5-2 Keyboard text editing

To move to the...	Press...
Previous character	Left Arrow
Next character	Right Arrow
Previous line	Up Arrow
Next line	Down Arrow
Previous word	Command/Ctrl-Left Arrow
Next word	Command/Ctrl-Right Arrow
Start of line	Command-Option-/Ctrl-Alt-Left Arrow
End of line	Command-Option-/Ctrl-Alt-Right Arrow
Start of story	Command-Option-/Ctrl-Alt-Up Arrow
End of story	Command-Option-/Ctrl-Alt-Down Arrow

Holding down the Shift key in combination with any of the keyboard commands for movement selects all text between the insertion point's original location and the location to which the key combination sends it. In the example above, you could select all the text from the cursor point to the beginning of the line just by adding Shift to the keystroke.

> **TIP: The Lazy Man's Way to Follow a Text Chain.** You know that QuarkXPress has keystrokes that take you to the next or previous page in your layout, but what about a shortcut to go to the next page in a story? (If your story jumps to another page of your layout, as often happens in magazines and newspapers, this is important.) All you have to do is place the insertion point at the beginning or end of the story's text box on the current page. If you're at the beginning of the text box, press the Left or Up Arrow key to move the insertion point out of the current box to the previous box in the chain. If you're at the end of the box, similarly press the Right or Down Arrow key to jump the insertion point to the next box in the text chain.

As soon as you move the insertion point out of the current box, QuarkXPress follows it, scrolling automatically to the page containing the linked text box to which you've moved the insertion point. If possible, QuarkXPress even centers the box nicely in the project window.

> *TIP: **Navigating Out of the Box.*** *I find the ability to jump quickly to the beginning or end of a story by pressing Command-Option-Up Arrow or Command-Option-Down Arrow (Ctrl-Alt-Up Arrow or Ctrl-Alt-Down Arrow) especially handy. It can save you a lot of scrolling if you forget the exact page on which a story starts or finishes. I use it all the time to quickly select all the text from the cursor to the beginning or end of the story by adding the Shift key. For instance, let's say you've got too much text in a text box and the text overflows, producing an overset mark. You know that the overset text isn't important, so you want to delete it or move it to some other text box. You could expand the box or link it to a new box, but it's often faster to place the cursor after the last word in the text box and press Command-Option-Shift-Down Arrow (Ctrl-Alt-Down Arrow). This selects the overset text (even though you can't see it). Now you can delete it or cut it.*

Deleting Text

There are a number of ways to delete text in QuarkXPress (see Table 5-3). You can, of course, use the Delete key to delete text to the left of the insertion point, one character at a time, or to remove a text selection. QuarkXPress also lets you delete the character to the right of the insertion point by holding down the Shift key while pressing Delete. Similarly, Command/Ctrl-Delete gets rid of the entire word to the left of the insertion point, and Command/Ctrl-Shift-Delete removes the word to the right of the insertion point.

Table 5-3 Keyboard deletions

To delete...	Press...
Previous character	Delete
Next character	Shift-Delete or Del key (extended keyboard)
Previous word	Command/Ctrl-Delete
Next word	Command/Ctrl-Shift-Delete
Any selected text	Delete

Drag-and-Drop Text

Drag-and-drop text editing is an easy way of copying or moving text from one location to another in a story, but it can cause trouble if you don't know how it works. To use drag-and-drop text editing, select some text, then drag the selection to another location in the text chain. As you move the mouse, you'll see an insertion point move along with it. When the insertion point reaches the place where you want the selected text to go, release the mouse button, and *presto*! Your text is cut from its original location and placed at the insertion point.

If you try this right now on your copy of QuarkXPress, it probably won't work because Drag and Drop Text is an option in the Preferences dialog box (Command/Ctrl-Y, then switch to the Input Settings tab), and by default it is turned off. If you like this feature, go ahead and turn it on.

You can also copy a selection, instead of just moving it, by holding down the Shift key as you drag. Note that any text you drag-move or drag-copy also gets placed on the Clipboard (replacing whatever was there). Also, at least for now, you can't drag-copy text between unlinked text boxes, or between layouts—you can do it only within continuous text chains.

I rarely turn this feature on, not because I don't like it, but because I too often mess up my text when the feature is on by accidentally dragging a word or sentence when I don't mean to. This is the sort of feature that I'll turn on only when I need to use it; then I'll turn it off again.

> **TIP: Speeding Up Text Entry.** *Unless there's a really good reason to do it, I don't recommend typing a lot of text directly into a text box in QuarkXPress. Obviously, QuarkXPress doesn't have important word-processing features such as an outliner, renumbering, and so on. But perhaps the most important reason to consider using a word processor is speed. If you're working on an older (slower) computer, writing and editing text in QuarkXPress may seem incredibly slow.*

The slowness occurs because QuarkXPress has to do much more work than a typical word processor does whenever it must reflow text. If you're working on a long story that goes through several pages of linked boxes, and the text has to flow through and around other page elements, this complexity also adds to the computations that QuarkXPress must perform whenever you change or add text. Plus, QuarkXPress may have to compute kerning, ligatures, and other typographic styling, which slows it down further.

Nonetheless, if you need to type in QuarkXPress, here are a few things you can do to speed up the process. (Note that if you're working on a fast computer and you're not experiencing slowdowns, you can just go ahead and ignore these suggestions.)

- **Dummy text boxes.** Try typing or editing in a "dummy" text box in the pasteboard area of the page where you want to enter or change text. This poor-person's story editor is particularly helpful when the text box on the page is nonrectangular or the text has a complicated wrap around other objects. By typing in a plain ol' rectangular text box on the pasteboard, you make it so QuarkXPress doesn't have to work hard calculating how the text should wrap.

- **Hyphenation.** Turning off Auto Hyphenation in each of your H&J sets can speed up QuarkXPress a little bit (see Chapter 6, *Typography*). Don't forget to turn hyphenation back on when you're ready to proof or print your layout.

- **Justification.** Don't set the horizontal alignment to Justified while you're typing. QuarkXPress has to do a lot of work to figure out how to justify the text each time you type a letter—plus, it's distracting to have your text moving around, justifying, as you type.

- **Kerning.** You might consider turning off Auto Kern Above, which activates automatic kerning, in the Character tab of the Preferences dialog box. This won't help a lot, but sometimes every little bit counts.

> **TIP: Copy and Paste Commonly Used Characters.** *Typing bullets at the beginning of each line in a long list can drive anybody absolutely bonkers. The same thing goes with any commonly repeated character, especially if the character is in a different font or requires a hard-to-remember modifier key. Instead, just copy one of them and paste it wherever you need it. Yes, the Command/Ctrl-V for pasting is also a keystroke, but it's easier than some keystrokes and certainly easier than inserting the characters and then applying character style sheets or manually changing the font, color, etc., all the time.*

> **TIP: Don't Space Out.** *Never type two spaces after a period. Never type five spaces for an indent. Never cross the road without looking both ways. These are rules to live by, and if you follow them, they'll rarely steer you wrong.*

> **TIP: Consider Your Case.** *I used to say you should never type text in all capital letters in QuarkXPress—because it gets stuck that way. It's much more versatile to select any text you want capped and apply the All Caps type style (Command/Ctrl-Shift-K). Now, however, if you change your mind about the case, you can use the Change Case option in the Type Style menu. Your choices are UPPERCASE, lowercase, and Title Case. Not perfect—no "Sentence case"—but better than before.*

Of course, to every one of these rules there are exceptions. The exception to this last one is when you're exporting the text as either ASCII text or another format that doesn't support the All Caps type style.

IMPORTING TEXT

More often than not, text is prepared in a word processor, then imported into a QuarkXPress layout for the design work. The best way to get text into a text box in QuarkXPress is to import it using the Import Text command on the File menu. In order to access this command, you must have both a text box and the Content tool selected.

1. Position the insertion point where you want the text to be brought into the text box.

2. Choose Import Text from the File menu (Command/Ctrl-E).

3. When the Import Text dialog box appears, select one of the files listed. It displays all the files that are in word-processing formats that QuarkXPress can import (see the next section, "What Filters Are and How to Use Them").

4. Press Return, or click the Open button.

   While you're in the Import Text dialog box, you have two additional options for importing the file: Convert Quotes and Include Style Sheets.

   Convert Quotes. If you'd like QuarkXPress to automatically convert straight double and single quotes (" and ') to curly double and single quotes (" " and ' '), and double hyphens (--) to true em dashes (—), check Convert Quotes in the Import Text dialog box. I almost always leave this option turned on.

   Include Style Sheets. I almost always check the Include Style Sheets box so that QuarkXPress will include the file's style sheets (if there are any). Even if there aren't any style sheets specified in the word processing document, it's usually better to leave this option turned on, or else you may accidentally apply No Style to the text (see Chapter 7, *Copy Flow*, for more on style sheets and how this checkbox affects them).

   TIP: Style Sheet Conflicts. When you import style sheets from Word, they are compared to style sheets in the document. If style sheets have the same name but different characteristics, an alert displays. To be honest, this displays almost all the time because all Word documents have "Normal" paragraph and character style sheets and all QuarkXPress documents have those two style sheets as well. You also may have other style sheets with similar names, such as Heading 1. An alert lets you choose how to handle each style sheet conflict: Rename, Auto-Rename, Use New, or Use Existing. Since I figure a QuarkXPress layout probably has better style sheets than Word, I always opt for Use Existing, which means the one "existing" in the QuarkXPress project, not in the Word file.

Note that both Convert Quotes and Include Style Sheets are "sticky," a not-very-technical term that means that their status is saved with the Import Text dialog box. So you can set these once and pretty much never worry about them again.

What Filters Are and How to Use Them

QuarkXPress uses XTensions called filters to convert text to and from word-processing formats. Because they're XTensions, you can activate or deactivate them using the XTension Manager (see more about XTensions in Chapter 2, *QuarkXPress Basics*). There are also third-party word processing filters available that let you import various weird formats. Because these filters are XTensions, you can deactivate the filters you don't regularly use, making QuarkXPress load faster and require less RAM.

While the MS Word filter usually works reasonably well, its capabilities are fairly limited and it is sometimes buggy. Also, note that QuarkXPress now ships with an RTF filter that lets you import and export Rich Text Format files—if you have trouble importing a file from Microsoft Word or any other word processor, try saving it in the RTF format instead. In Chapter 7, *Copy Flow*, I explain why you should be careful about what word processor you use, and why I usually use Microsoft Word.

> **TIP: Fast Saves from Word.** *This tip is really directed more at Microsoft Word, but because so many QuarkXPress users bring files in from Word (we do), I thought this was relevant: Never use Fast Save in Microsoft Word. Fast Save is a feature that saves time in saving documents, but increases trouble down the line (both in Word and in QuarkXPress). For instance, text can get "lost" from one save to another, and sometimes text doesn't import correctly into QuarkXPress when the file was fast saved. To get around Fast Save in Microsoft Word, go to the Save tab in the Preferences dialog box and turn off the Allow Fast Saves checkbox.*

Finding and Changing

QuarkXPress has a powerful Find/Change feature that is too often overlooked and under-used. You can use this feature to look for and change either text or formatting (or both at the same time), and it can do this within a story or throughout a layout.

Where QuarkXPress Looks

When it searches with the Find/Change feature, QuarkXPress can check either the entire text chain connected to the active text box, or it can look for and change text throughout an entire layout. (You cannot search more than one layout at a time.) If you have a text box selected, QuarkXPress searches through the story *from the location of the insertion point* to the end of the story (note that the button in the palette is called Find Next; that means "the next one after the cursor position").

There are two ways to search an entire story from the very beginning. First, you can put the insertion point at the very beginning of the story (press Command-Option-Up Arrow or Ctrl-Alt-Up Arrow). Better yet, you can leave the insertion point where it is in the story, and hold down the Option key (Alt on Windows) to turn the Find Next button into the Find First button. (The fastest way to find the first instance of a word is to press Command/Ctrl-F to open or activate the Find/Change palette, type the word to be found, then press Option-Return on Mac OS, or Alt-Enter in Windows.)

If you want QuarkXPress to check all the text in the layout rather than just a single story, you must turn on the Layout checkbox in the Find/Change palette. When this option is turned on, QuarkXPress searches the top most text box on a page first (in terms of layer order, not position on the page), which can be confusing if you're not sure which text boxes are "on top" of other text boxes. In addition, any layers in the document are searched, whether the layers are visible or not.

Note that turning on the Layout option only searches one layout's pages; if you want to search the master pages, too, you have to do a separate search. If you're currently displaying a layout's master pages, the Layout checkbox is labeled Masters, and you can use it to search all the layout's master pages at once.

> **TIP: Searching Locked Content.** *In QuarkXPress 7, you can lock stories to prevent editing. The Lock command in the Item menu now offers two options: Position and Story (or Picture, depending on the selection). If you want Find/Change to be super thorough, you should turn on Search Locked Content under the Layout checkbox to make sure text in any locked stories is considered in the search.*

Specifying Text

Generally, people want to search and replace text regardless of the text's formatting attributes. To do this, you can use the Find/Change palette as it first appears when you select the Find/Change command from the Edit menu (or press Command/Ctrl-F; see Figure 5-1). Enter the text you want QuarkXPress to find in the Find What field, then enter the replacement text in the Change To field.

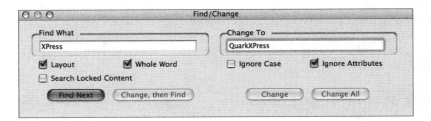

Figure 5-1 The Find/Change palette

Special characters. It's easy enough to search for normal words or phrases, but what about invisible characters? It turns out that you can enter certain special characters in the Find What and Change To fields with the aid of the Command or Ctrl key. For example, if you want to search for all the new-paragraph characters in a layout (what you get when you press Return at the end of a paragraph), you select the Find What field and press

Command-Return (Ctrl-Enter). This appears in the field as "\p." You could just type "\p," but who needs to clutter up their brain with weird codes like that?

Table 5-4 shows characters you can enter in these fields, how to type them, and how they appear in the fields. Of course, because all these special characters use the backslash, to search for the backslash character itself in the Find What or Change To fields you need to type the backslash twice, or press Command/Ctrl-\.

Table 5-4 Typing special characters in the Find/Change palette

To enter this character...	Press...	Or type...
Tab	Command/Ctrl-Tab	\t
New paragraph	Command/Ctrl-Return	\p
New line	Command/Ctrl-Shift-Return	\n
New column	Command/Ctrl-Enter	\c
New box	Command/Ctrl-Shift-Enter	\b
Previous box page number	Command/Ctrl-2	\2
Current box page number	Command/Ctrl-3	\3
Next box page number	Command/Ctrl-4	\4
Wildcard (single character)	Command/Ctrl-?	\?
Backslash	Command/Ctrl-\	\\
Punctuation space		\.
Flex space		\f

> **TIP: Pasting Special Characters.** *If you can't remember the codes, or if you have system keyboard shortcuts overriding QuarkXPress (such as Command-Tab switching applications), you can copy and paste special characters into the Text field. Be sure to turn on Invisibles in the View menu so you can see what you're copying!*

Wildcards. You can use the wildcard character (\?) to represent any other character. This is useful if you're looking for a word you may have spelled different ways, such as "gray" and "grey." Instead of running two search operations to find all occurrences of this word, you could simply type "gr\?y" in the Find What field. You can get the wildcard character by pressing either Command/Ctrl-? or by typing a backslash followed by a question mark.

Note that the wildcard character can only be used in the Find What field. QuarkXPress doesn't let you use it in the Change To field because the program's not sophisticated enough to do that kind of pattern replacing.

Whole Word. Next to the Layout checkbox you'll find another one labeled Whole Word. Checking this box means that QuarkXPress only finds occurrences of the Find What text if it's a whole word. That means that the text can't be bounded by other text or numerals. So a Whole Word search for "ten" finds the word "ten" when it's bounded by spaces, punctuation, or special characters such as new-line or new-paragraph marks. It would *not* find "often," "tenuous," or "contentious." If you don't have Whole Word selected, QuarkXPress will find every occurrence of the text you entered, even if it's embedded in other text.

Ignore Case. If Ignore Case is turned on, QuarkXPress finds all occurrences of the text in the Find What field, regardless of whether the capitalization of the text found in the layout exactly matches what you typed into the Find What field. For example, if you entered "Help," QuarkXPress would find "Help," "HELP," and "help."

How QuarkXPress determines the case of characters it's replacing when Ignore Case is turned on depends on the capitalization of the text it finds in the layout.

- If the found text begins with an initial capital, or is in all uppercase or lowercase letters, QuarkXPress follows suit and similarly capitalizes the replacement text, no matter how you've capitalized it in the Change To field.

- If the found text doesn't match the above three cases, QuarkXPress capitalizes the replacement text exactly as you entered it in the Change To field.

For example, let's say you are searching for all examples of "QuarkXPress" and want to make sure the internal capital letters are proper. If you leave Ignore Case turned on, and the program finds "quarkxpress," it will not capitalize the proper characters. Turn off Ignore Case, and the feature replaces "quarkxpress" with "QuarkXPress," properly capitalized as you entered it.

> **TIP: Searching for the Unsearchable.** *I mentioned earlier that you can look for invisible characters by typing certain codes. However, there are some characters QuarkXPress doesn't let you search for. For instance, you cannot enter the indent here, the nonbreaking space, or the right-margin tab (Option/Alt-Tab) characters here.*
>
> *If you have some heavy-duty searching and replacing to do with any of these characters, you can always export your story in XPress Tags format and search for the characters there. I cover XPress Tags more in Chapter 7, Copy Flow, including how to export and import this format.*
>
> **TIP: Close the Find/Change Palette.** *You know you can open the Find/Change palette by pressing Command/Ctrl-F. Did you know you can close it by pressing Command-Option-F (Ctrl-Alt-F)?*

Specifying Attributes

As I said earlier, you can search for more than just text in QuarkXPress. You can search for text-formatting attributes (font, size, type style), too. If you want to search for formatting, uncheck the Ignore Attributes box in the Find/Change palette. When you turn this option off, the palette expands (see Figure 5-2). In addition to text fields under the Find What and Change To headings, there are areas on each side of the palette for specifying style sheet, font, size, color, type style, language, ligatures, and OpenType styles.

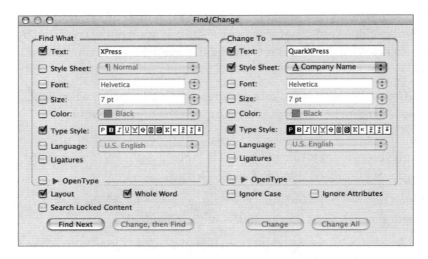

Figure 5-2 The Find/Change palette with Ignore Attributes turned off

What to Find, What to Change

When Ignore Attributes is turned off (that is, when you're searching for text formatting as well as text), each side of the Find/Change palette contains six options for searching or replacing: Text, Style Sheet, Font, Size, Color, and Type Style. The left side of the palette shows all the attributes that should be searched for; the right side is what the text should be changed to. The first eight areas on each side of the palette—Text, Style Sheet, Font, Size, Color, Language, Ligatures, and OpenType—are fairly easy to use. The remaining option, Type Styles, is only a little more complicated (see "Type Styles," below). If you want to specify something, make sure the area's checkbox is turned on. Then simply enter the text or point size in the appropriate fields, and/or select the font or style sheet from the appropriate popup menus.

On the left (Find What) side, the popup menus list only the fonts and style sheets actually used in the current layout; on the right (Change To) side, they list all the fonts and style sheets currently available.

There doesn't need to be a parallel between what you specify on the Find What side and on the Change To side. In fact, such asymmetrical searches offer some of the most intriguing possibilities for finding and changing in QuarkXPress.

You could easily, for example, find all occurrences of a company name and apply a character style sheet to them.

1. Type the company name into the Text field on the Find What side.

2. Uncheck all the other boxes (Style Sheet, Font, Size, etc.) on the left side of the palette. That tells the program to pay no attention to these attributes.

3. Uncheck all the boxes on the right side of the palette except for Style Sheet. That tells QuarkXPress not to change any of these attributes when it finds the company name.

4. Check the Style Sheet box on the Change To side, and choose the character style sheet you want to apply.

This procedure searches for all occurrences of the text, no matter what formatting is applied, and replaces them with the same text but using a specific character style sheet (I cover text formatting in Chapter 6, *Typography*, and style sheets in Chapter 7, *Copy Flow*).

Type Styles

Specifying type styles—bold, italic, and so on—in the Find/Change palette is a bit more complicated than what I described above; however, it's really not that bad once you get used to it. Once you turn on the Type Style option, the various formatting choices, indicated by icons, can be on, off, or grayed out. Clicking a white (off) icon makes it gray (neutral); clicking again turns it black (on); clicking a third time turns it off again (see Figure 5-3).

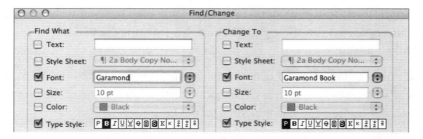

Figure 5-3 Specifying type styles in the Find/Change palette. This says "search for all text that is Garamond with the Bold type style applied and set it to Garamond Book with no type style applied."

What do these various states mean? On the left side (the Find What side), a black icon (on) means that you want QuarkXPress to find text set *only* in that style. A white icon (off) means you *don't* want it to find text in that style. A gray icon means that it doesn't matter if the text is formatted with that style or not; you want QuarkXPress to find text either way (see Table 5-5). Another way to look at it is that white means "no," black means "yes," and gray means "I don't care."

Table 5-5 Style controls in the Find/Change palette

Box is...	Means...
White	Find or replace text without this attribute.
Black	Find or replace text with this attribute.
Grayed	Find it either way, but leave it alone when replacing.

The various icons mean similar things on the right (Change To) side of the palette. Turning on a style (black) means you want QuarkXPress to apply that style when it changes text that it finds. Turning off a style (white) means you *don't* want that style to be present in the changed text (if it's there, QuarkXPress removes it). Leaving the icon gray means that QuarkXPress doesn't do anything to that style. If it's already there, it stays there; if it's not, the program doesn't apply it.

Of course, a word can't simultaneously have both the Underline and Word Underline styles. So turning one on turns off the other, and graying one automatically makes the other gray as well. Small Caps/All Caps and Superscript/Subscript work together similarly.

> **TIP: Set Up Find/Change by Example.** *You can shave a few steps off your Find/Change process by placing the cursor in some text that's formatted the same as what you're looking for. If you place the cursor in a word that is in 23-point Times and then open the Find/Change palette, both the font and size are automatically chosen on the Find What side of the palette (you may still have to check the boxes next to them, though). This won't save a lot of time, but sometimes every little bit helps.*

OpenType

If you are using OpenType fonts and their various style options such as Fractions or Swashes—and you know who you are—you can consider those styles in Find/Change as well. Click in the OpenType checkbox, and then click the arrow next to it to display all the options. Here, you flash back to the old, old way of finding and changing type styles: the three-state checkboxes. Like the icons, you click these three times for on (checked), off (unchecked), and "don't care" (a dash displays in the checkbox).

Going to It

Now that you know how to specify what you want to find, what you want to change, and how to tell QuarkXPress where to search, you can use the four buttons at the bottom of the palette to begin finding and changing. When you first specify your Find/Change criteria, all buttons except Find Next are grayed out (see Figure 5-4). Hold down the Option key (or Alt key) and click Find First, and QuarkXPress searches for the first occurrence of text matching your specifications in the current story or layout. It displays this text in the project window and selects it.

This changes to Find First when you hold down the Option key.

Figure 5-4 The Find/Change control buttons

You then have a choice. Clicking Find Next again takes you to the next occurrence of text meeting your specifications, without changing the currently selected text. Clicking Change, then Find changes the selection as specified on the Change To side of the palette. QuarkXPress then looks for the next occurrence of matching text. (If you don't start at the beginning, when QuarkXPress reaches the end of the layout, an alert asks if you want to start at the beginning.) The Change button changes the selected text and leaves it selected, and the Change All button tells QuarkXPress to search for and automatically change all occurrences in the story or layout. After QuarkXPress changes all occurrences, a dialog box comes up listing the number of changes made.

> **TIP: Seeing Text as It Is Found.** *I find that after I search for a word, it is too often sitting right underneath the palette—so I can't see it. Very frustrating. Instead, if you're going to be doing a lot of searching and replacing, I suggest you move the palette to the top or bottom of your screen and resize your project window so that you can see both the palette and the project window at the same time.*

If you are using a laptop or other small screen, try reducing the size of the palette by clicking the Zoom button in the box's upper-right corner (this feature is Mac-only, unfortunately). The reduced view shows only the buttons you need to navigate and change what you've specified (see Figure 5-5). Clicking the Zoom button again takes you back to the larger palette.

Figure 5-5 Shrinking the Find/Change palette

SPELLING CHECKER

Of course, once you've got your text written or imported into QuarkXPress, you wouldn't want to print it without first running it through QuarkXPress's spelling checker. QuarkXPress comes with a 120,000-word dictionary (that's the file called XPress Dictionary), and you can create your own auxiliary dictionaries as well. The Check Spelling command is on the Utilities menu, and it allows you to check a selected word, a selection, a story, or a layout (see Figure 5-6).

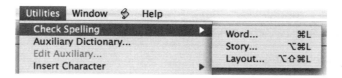

Figure 5-6
The Check Spelling submenu

Checking a Word

If you only want to check one word, you can select it (or you can just put the cursor anywhere within the word) and choose Word from the Check Spelling submenu (or press Command-L on the Macintosh; Control-W on Windows). The Check Word dialog box appears (see Figure 5-7), listing all the words in the XPress Dictionary (as well as in the open auxiliary dictionary, if there is one) that resemble the word you selected.

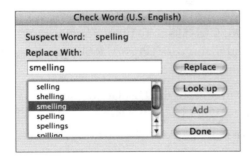

Figure 5-7
Checking a word

If the suspect word—the word you're checking is always called the *suspect* word, even if it's correctly spelled—appears in a dictionary, it shows up in the scrolling list and is selected automatically (this is different than some spelling checkers that actually tell you that the word is spelled right). This means that as far as QuarkXPress is concerned, the word is spelled correctly; you can click the Done button to continue (on Mac OS, press Command-period; in Windows, press Escape).

If the suspect word doesn't appear in an active dictionary, you can scroll through the list of words and select a replacement. Click on the proper word in the list, then click the Replace button (or press Return or Enter). The new spelling replaces the word in your story, and the Check Word box closes.

If QuarkXPress can't find any words that approximate the suspect word, it displays the message, "No similar words found." If you notice, however, that you need to change the spelling, you can click in the word and edit. Click the Done button to close the Check Word dialog box.

Checking a Selection, Story, or Layout

In most cases, you will check a range of text, an entire story, or an entire layout. You can also check the spelling on master pages.

- To check a range of text, select the text with the Content tool and type Command/Ctrl-L, or choose Selection from the Check Spelling submenu of the Utilities menu. ("Word" changes to "Selection" when more text is highlighted.)

- To check a story, use the Content tool to select any text box that holds part of the story. Then select Story from the Check Spelling hierarchical menu (or press Command-Option-L on Mac OS; Ctrl-Alt-W on Windows). All the text in the story is checked, no matter where you've clicked in the story.

- To check a layout, select the Layout from the Check Spelling submenu (or press Command-Option-Shift-L on Mac OS; Ctrl-Alt-Shift-W on Windows). When you check spelling in a layout, keep in mind that QuarkXPress is looking at the text on all layers in the layout—even if the layers are hidden.

- To check master pages, select a master page from the Display submenu of the Page menu. When master pages are displayed, you can select Masters from the Check Spelling submenu. All the text on all the master pages is checked.

Looking at Word Count

When you're checking spelling in more than a single word, the first thing you have to deal with is the Word Count dialog box. QuarkXPress first counts all the words in the selection, story, layout, or master pages. The Word Count dialog box appears, showing running totals as QuarkXPress scans the text, counting the total number of words, the total number of unique words (each word is counted once, no matter how many times it occurs), and the number of suspect words—ones that QuarkXPress can't find in its dictionary or in the open auxiliary dictionary, if there is one (see Figure 5-8).

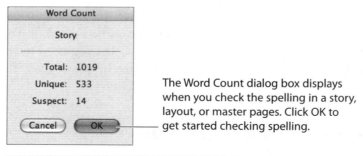

The Word Count dialog box displays when you check the spelling in a story, layout, or master pages. Click OK to get started checking spelling.

Figure 5-8
Checking spelling

The primary use of this information is if you need a word count on a story—in fact, it's the only way to get the word count on a story, something publishers often need to plan space. You can also get a rough idea how long you're going to be sitting there, checking spelling, by noticing the number of suspect words. At this point, it's not a bad idea to get a little pad of paper and a pen. There may be words that you need to consider more closely in context before you decide to make a spelling change. If you jot them down, you can use Find/Change to look at the text when you're finished.

So, once you're finished looking at the Word Count dialog box, click the OK button. If the program didn't find any suspect words, then this just returns you to your layout. On the other hand, if it did catch one or more words, then the button brings up the Check Selection dialog box (or the Check Story, Check Layout, or Check Masters dialog box). This dialog box displays suspect words one at a time, in the order in which they occur in the text. As each appears in the dialog box, QuarkXPress scrolls the project window to the first instance of the suspect word, and highlights it so you can see it in the context in which it's used on the page.

Changing the spelling. For each suspect word, QuarkXPress shows a list of similar spellings. If there are even more possibilities, the Lookup button becomes available and you can click it (or press Command/Ctrl-L to view more words). If you find the correct spelling, click on it in the list and click Replace. If you don't, but the word is misspelled, you can click in the word and correct it yourself.

> **TIP: Global Replacements.** *Like it or not, when you change the first instance of a suspect word, that spelling replaces all instances of that word throughout the document—and this may not always be appropriate. For example, QuarkXPress thinks "latte" is a suspect word and will suggest that you replace it with words such as "late." What if the text uses both words? What if you used "latte" when you meant "late"? You only see the first instance when you're checking spelling so there's no way to know if a global change is OK. This is where that little pad of paper and pen come in—jot down "latte" (or whatever) and then use Find/Change to locate each instance and see if it's correct.*

Skipping and keeping. To go to the next suspect word without changing the spelling of the current one, click the Skip button (Command/Ctrl-S, which usually means Save, but not here). To add the current suspect word to an auxiliary dictionary, click the Keep button (Command/Ctrl-K, which usually means Delete, but not in this dialog box). This button is only active when an auxiliary dictionary is open (see "Auxiliary Dictionaries," below).

Searching locked stories. While checking spelling, you can specify whether stories that are locked—to prevent editing—are checked as well. (Stories are locked by choosing Story from the Lock submenu in the Item menu, and you can lock a story whether it's in text boxes, in table cells, or on text paths.) To have the spelling checker skip locked stories, uncheck Search Locked Content.

TIP: One-Letter Misspellings. I wonder how many years I used QuarkXPress's spelling checker before I finally figured out that it ignores one-letter words. That means that if you're typing quickly and press the wrong key—for instance, if you type "tie s yellow ribbon" rather than "tie a yellow ribbon"—QuarkXPress won't catch the word as misspelled. QuarkXPress also won't catch most abbreviations. If you type "tx" instead of "tax," QuarkXPress just thinks you mean "Texas," thus proving once more that there's nothing like the final once-over with a human eye for catching these little mistakes.

Auxiliary Dictionaries

You can't add or change words in QuarkXPress's standard dictionary. You can, however, create and use an auxiliary dictionary, so you can have the program's spelling checker take into account specialized words that aren't in the standard dictionary. Note that you can have only one auxiliary dictionary open at a time for each layout in a project.

Creating or opening an auxiliary dictionary. To open an existing auxiliary dictionary, or to create a new one, select Auxiliary Dictionary from the Utilities menu. This opens the Auxiliary Dictionary dialog box. Select a dictionary stored on any mounted volume, and click the Open button.

You can also create a new auxiliary dictionary by navigating to the directory you want to save it in, typing a file name in the field next to the New button, and then clicking the New button in this dialog box (see Figure 5-9).

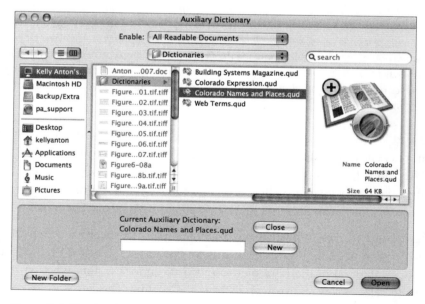

Figure 5-9 The Auxiliary Dictionary dialog box

Adding and removing words. When you first create an auxiliary dictionary, it's empty. There are two ways to add words to it. First, you can add words to the dictionary using the Keep button in the Check Story or Check Layout dialog box. This button adds the current suspect word to your auxiliary dictionary. Another way to add words is with the Edit Auxiliary feature on the Utilities menu. This feature is only available when there's an auxiliary dictionary selected.

When you select Edit Auxiliary, a simple dialog box appears with a scrolling list of all the words in the currently open dictionary (see Figure 5-10). To add a new word, enter it in the text field and click the Add button. Words added to the dictionary cannot contain any spaces or punctuation (not even hyphens). You can, however, include accent marks and other special characters as necessary. Now if your name is García or Françoise, you can breathe more easily when you're checking spelling. One more tip: You need to add different forms of the word, such as plurals. In addition, this is a good place to add many of the plurals the QuarkXPress dictionary does not have—such as "appetizers." Edit a cooking magazine, and it will drive you nuts that it comes up as a suspect word every time.

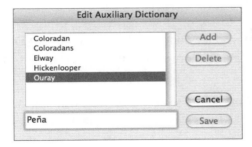

Figure 5-10
The Edit Auxiliary Dictionary dialog box

To remove a word from the dictionary, scroll through the list until you find the word. Select it by clicking on it, then click the Delete button. To edit a word in the dictionary, you need to delete it and then add the new spelling.

> **TIP: Adding All Suspect Words.** Here's a fun way to add a bunch of words to your auxiliary dictionary, all at the same time. This only works if you've already selected an auxiliary dictionary for your layout, of course (choose Auxiliary Dictionary from the Utilities menu).

1. Create a text box with all the words that you want to add to the auxiliary dictionary.

2. Select Check Story from the Utilities menu, and when QuarkXPress displays the number of suspect words, click OK. (In this scenario, all the words in the story will be suspect words.)

3. In the Check Story dialog box, hold down the Option and Shift keys and click the Done button (on Windows, hold down Alt and Shift while clicking Close). This adds all the suspect words to the current auxiliary dictionary.

If you make a mistake or you want to make sure the words were added, select Edit Auxiliary in the Utilities menu.

Remembering dictionaries. When you open or create an auxiliary dictionary, it is associated with the active layout. Whenever you open a project, QuarkXPress also opens the auxiliary dictionaries for all the project's layouts. Auxiliary dictionaries are associated with a layout until you either close that dictionary (by clicking Close in the Auxiliary Dictionary dialog box) or open a different one (this breaks the link with the first dictionary and makes a link with the new one).

You can also set up an auxiliary dictionary that will be applied to all subsequent new projects by opening a dictionary while no projects are open. If you move the auxiliary dictionary or project files, QuarkXPress may not be able to locate the dictionary when it's time to check spelling. You have the option of continuing to check spelling without the dictionary or finding and reopening the auxiliary dictionary file.

WATCHING YOUR WORDS

By following the tips I've given you here, you may not be able to have QuarkXPress write your stories for you, but you'll be able to get the very most out of the program's advanced word-processing features.

In the next chapter, you'll see how you can take those blocks of plain text that you've created and turn them into type, using QuarkXPress's extensive typographic controls.

CHAPTER SIX

Typography

There's an old husband's tale that says you can tell what a baby is going to grow up to become by the first real word she speaks. If she says "mama," she'll grow up to be a loving parent. If she says "teevee," chances are she'll be a couch potato. If she says "QuarkXPress," she'll become a designer.

There's no doubt—even if this tale is hogwash—that QuarkXPress is often the first word on a designer's lips when the topic of desktop publishing comes up. That's because QuarkXPress has dominated the desktop-publishing landscape for so long and is known for expert typesetting. In this chapter, I will discuss the many typographic controls that QuarkXPress puts at your fingertips. I'm going to start with the basics: typographic principles and fonts. However, professionals should at least skim over this section (the fundamentals of fonts are rarely taught, and many people find themselves in deep… uh… water at some point because of this).

Next, I'll discuss control of both character- and paragraph-level formatting, including—among many other items—kerning and tracking, hyphenation and justification, and typographic special effects.

If you're reading this book from cover to cover, expect to spend a little while here in this chapter. I've got a lot to talk about, and I expect that in the long run you'll find it rewarding.

FONTS AND FONT MANAGEMENT

The word *font* now has several meanings. Historically, a font was a set of characters in a given typeface and size. Helvetica was a typeface, and 14-point Helvetica was a font. However, for the sake of simplicity, I'm following the path that has become popular over the past few years, defining *typeface* and *font* as synonyms: a font or a typeface is a set of characters that share a common look.

For example, the text you're reading is in the Aldine 401 font or typeface, while the headings for each section are in the Trajan or Myriad Pro font or typeface. The more you learn about type and typography, the more you see its subtle nuances and personalities. But don't worry too much about that yet. Just start by seeing these basic differences.

There are four basic rules for working with fonts in professional desktop publishing:

• Use OpenType, Type 1, or PostScript fonts.

• Try to avoid TrueType fonts.

• Use a font management utility.

• Be careful when choosing font styles.

Of course, for every rule there is at least one exception, and at least three instances where you should ignore the rule entirely. Nonetheless, here's a quick set of guidelines.

TrueType, PostScript, and OpenType. Just like there are lots of different kinds of word-processing file formats (Microsoft Word files are different than WordPerfect files, and so on), there are many different ways to digitally store font information. The two primary formats, however, are called TrueType and PostScript. Both Apple and Microsoft have tried to push the TrueType font format, and both Macs and PCs ship with a plethora of TrueType fonts already installed. You typically have to buy PostScript and OpenType fonts from a vendor like Adobe, Bitstream, or Monotype, or they may be copied to your system automatically when you install a program (like Microsoft Word, Adobe Photoshop, and so on) on your machine.

Another option is the OpenType format, which was created jointly by Microsoft and Adobe. The OpenType format was designed to be better than either TrueType or PostScript (also called Type 1) fonts. For instance, an OpenType font is made up of a single file that will work on Mac OS or Windows. Applications can also be written to take advantage of special OpenType features, such as complex ligatures and automatic fractions. (QuarkXPress 7 supports many special OpenType features.) I consider OpenType the future of font technology, so it's worth exploring the use of this font type.

Tip: Same Font, Different Format. Many graphic designers resist buying fonts they already o wn in new formats. After all, you've already paid for the work that went into creating the font— all you're paying for is a new delivery method. It's like buying the hit single on vinyl, then 8-track, then cassette, then CD, and now from iTunes. How many times do you have to buy that same song? Nonetheless, just like there are benefits to CDs and digital music, there are benefits to new font technology. The number one guaranteed benefit of OpenType is the cross-platform nature of the fonts. Other benefits, including an expanded character set and special type styles, depend on the font designer, vendor, and more.

Most service bureaus wish that TrueType fonts would just go away because the bureaus have so much trouble printing them. Of course, TrueType is fine—unless you're trying to do quality graphic design work, are working with other people, or are working with a service bureau. Printing these fonts has gotten easier, but as far as I'm concerned, it's still worth avoiding them. It's always tempting to use inexpensive or free fonts, but you almost always get what you pay for. If you're serious about desktop publishing, use PostScript or OpenType fonts.

Font management utilities. If you only worked with two or three typefaces for the rest of your life, you'd never need to think about font management. However, most people doing any kind of publishing work commonly work with hundreds or thousands of fonts. Keeping these fonts in order is critical to working efficiently with QuarkXPress.

If you have more than 20 fonts on your hard drive, you should be using a font management utility. Period. These programs let you keep all your fonts together, either in one folder or in multiple folders, anywhere you want on your hard drives. You can arrange fonts into groups, opening just the ones you want when you need them. In this way you keep your font menus short, speed up font selection, and keep your whole system lean.

Plus, most of these utilities are pretty cheap (between \$30 and \$150), so there's almost no reason not to have one around. On Mac OS, check into Suitcase Fusion from Extensis (*www.extensis.com*), a marriage of Suitcase and Font Reserve; also try Font Agent Pro from Insider Software (*www.insidersoftware.com*). Suitcase Fusion is helpful if you have many versions of the same font—and need them for different clients and projects. Font Agent Pro is more stable and gets constantly updated. Both programs have auto-activation XTensions for QuarkXPress, so the right fonts are activated when you open projects (Font Agent Pro, however, has no way of automatically identifying the differences among, say, five different PostScript Helveticas on your computer). For Windows, Suitcase is always a good option (also at *www.extensis.com*). A newish free option is Linotype FontExplorer X for both Mac OS and Windows (*www.linotype.com*). Although not as sophisticated as the other font managers, it's a great way to determine whether you need a font manager.

Which Font to Choose. The fourth "rule" of fonts has to do with setting your fonts to bold, italic, and so on. The question often arises whether people should choose bold and italic fonts from their font menus (if they're available) or get them by selecting bold or italic from the Style menu or the Measurements palette. It's a good question. However, I'm going to punt on the answer for now; instead, I'll discuss it later in "Styling by Attributes Versus Font Choice."

Missing Fonts

When you open a project created with fonts that you don't currently have loaded on your system, QuarkXPress tells you that you're missing one or more fonts and gives you two choices: Continue or List Fonts (see Figure 6-1). (Of course, you'll rarely see this if you are using a font management utility that automatically activates missing fonts, such as Suitcase for Windows, Suitcase Fusion, or Font Agent Pro.)

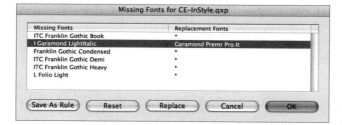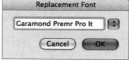

Figure 6-1
Missing fonts

Continue. If you click the Continue button, QuarkXPress opens the project but displays the missing fonts on screen using system fonts (like Arial or Geneva). If you select some text set in this missing font, you can see that the Font field in the Measurements palette is blank because the proper font isn't available from the font list. Also, if you open Font Usage (see "Font Usage," next) or the Find/Change palette, you'll find a font called something like "{-2, Unknown}" or "{-122, MinionExpertRegular}."

Obviously, having a real font replaced with a system font doesn't make much sense, but if you're only perusing a layout for overall design and you don't care about how the fonts look or how the text wraps from line to line, then this may be a reasonable option.

List Fonts. If you click the List Fonts button, QuarkXPress lists the missing fonts for you. To replace one of these missing fonts with a font that's available, select a typeface from the list, click the Replace button, then choose a replacement font. Note that this option replaces every instance of that font (within style sheet definitions, too). I'll sometimes replace fonts like this if I have a font that is close to the one specified in the layout. For instance, I might replace a missing Goudy font with Palatino, since there is a similarity between these two oldstyle typefaces. Of course, because the character widths of these two fonts are different, line endings are almost sure to be different. Later, I would close the project without saving it, so that when I open it on a machine that has Goudy, the fonts will appear properly.

Save As Rule. If you find yourself replacing fonts frequently—for example, if you replace Arial with Helvetica all the time—you can save your font replacement preferences as "rules." To do this, first replace one font with another, and then click Save As Rule. (This button, for whatever reason, is only available when you open a project and click List Fonts. It is not available when you display the Fonts tab of the Usage dialog box. You can, however, choose Font Mapping from the Utilities menu to map fonts.) The rules are applied according to settings in the Font Mapping tab of the Preferences dialog box, where you can specify a default replacement font and when the Missing Fonts dialog box displays. Using this feature, you can actually set up a scenario in which you never see the Missing Fonts dialog box—and yet your projects may never use the right fonts. This feature was intended for that obscure audience of users who are creating Web pages in QuarkXPress in a cross-platform environment. All in all, I suggest you stay away from this feature. Print publishers select specific typefaces, apply them, and fine-tune text based on those fonts. They do not need QuarkXPress changing the font for them behind the scenes.

Note that if you're using an auto-activation XTension that goes with your font manager, that software may take over the handling of missing fonts and display a different dialog box. Suitcase Fusion, for example, may present different versions of the same font for you to choose from (I say "may" because it usually knows which version to use, and because a preference setting affects this).

Printing missing fonts. You can also run into trouble when your computer has a screen font (also called a "bitmapped font") but no corresponding PostScript outline font (this isn't a problem with TrueType or OpenType fonts). In that case, when you print the layout, QuarkXPress substitutes either a jaggy-looking bitmapped version of the font, or Courier (that typewriter font). It's obviously important to have the outline fonts available.

Font Usage

What's the fastest way to tell what fonts are being used in a layout that you have open? Choose Usage from the Utilities menu (on Mac OS, press either F13 or Command-F6; press F2 on Windows). The Fonts tab in the Usage dialog box lists every font in a layout, lets you search for instances of that font, and lets you globally replace one font with another (see Figure 6-2).

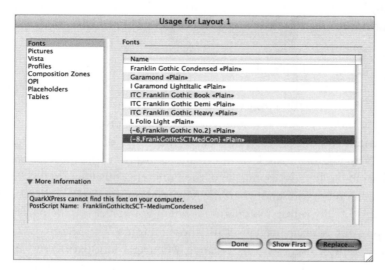

Figure 6-2
Font Usage

Some people have complained that the Usage dialog box doesn't have enough search-and-replace abilities. Quark's answer: If you're trying to search and replace, you should use the Find/Change dialog box. It's hard to argue with that kind of logic.

Plus, there are three problems with using the Usage dialog box to search for and replace fonts.

- The Usage dialog box only displays fonts that are on the layout pages *or* the master pages, but not both at the same time. (Which one it displays depends on what pages are currently showing in the project window.)

- The Usage dialog box only displays fonts on the current layout space; if you have five layout spaces, you'll have to visit the dialog box five times.

- The Replace option in the Usage dialog box only replaces fonts on the layout page or the master pages (again, depending on which is showing), but it does not change fonts in the style sheet definitions. Let's say you use the font Matrix in a character style sheet and then apply that style to some text on a layout page. If you try to replace Matrix with Garamond in the Usage dialog box, you'll only change the text on the layout page, not the actual definition of the style (it's the same as applying local formatting on top of the style). This is a mess.

Of course, the Find/Change palette has exactly the same three limitations, so global font replacements are not nearly as easy as you'd think.

More Information. You can find out more about a particular font in the Usage dialog box by selecting it and turning on the More Information checkbox. When this option is on, pay particular attention to the File Name and the Type. If you're not sure whether you're dealing with a PostScript or TrueType font, here's one great way to find out.

> *Tip: Global Font Replacements. Let's say you've created a masterpiece in QuarkXPress—450 pages over six layout spaces, 47 style sheets, eight master pages. You've used the Franklin Gothic typeface family throughout the layout, sometimes applying it manually to text, sometimes using it in style sheet definitions. Now your art director demands (probably out of spite) that you replace Franklin Gothic with Univers. Unfortunately, there is no feature in QuarkXPress that lets you replace one font with another, at one fell swoop, on master pages, layout pages, and style sheets. Here's what I'd do.*
>
> *1. Save the project and close it.*
>
> *2. Turn off Franklin Gothic with your font management utility. (If you don't use a font management utility, then you'll have to manually "uninstall" the font from your system.) If your font management utility has an auto-activation feature (like Suitcase or Suitcase Fusion) then make sure that feature is turned off.*
>
> *3. Open the project again in QuarkXPress. When the program tells you that a font is missing, click the List Fonts button. Select Franklin Gothic from the list and click Replace. Choose Univers from the Replace popup menu, and click OK.*
>
> *4. After the layout is open and is displaying the first page, every instance of Franklin Gothic will have been replaced with Univers, and you won't have to pull your hair out. (You will, however, need to change the font that is specified in all your style sheets.)*

Font Fallback

If you've ever seen little boxes or other random characters in your text, you might appreciate Font Fallback. Introduced in QuarkXPress 6.5 and fine-tuned in version 7, Quark's implementation of this feature is somewhat limited and yet better than nothing. When Font Fallback encounters a special character—such as a fraction or accented character—that is not available in the font in use, it tries to find the character in another font that is active on your system. While the character may not look perfect, at least you know what it's supposed to be and can make a decision about how it should look. (You could, for example, use the Glyphs palette to find the character in another font.) In general, this is a feature you won't notice because it quietly solves a little problem that occurred in the past. However, if you really do not want QuarkXPress messing with fonts in text at all, you can turn this off for the application in the Input Settings tab of the Preferences dialog box.

CHARACTER FORMATTING

There are two types of typographic controls: character-based and paragraph-based. The character-based controls—typeface, size, color, bold, italic, and so on—are those that affect only the text characters you select. If you select only one word in a sentence and apply a character style to it, that word and only that word is changed. Paragraph-based controls let you change the formatting of the entire paragraph—left and right indents, tab settings, space before and after, and so on.

Let's talk about character formatting first—how you can change it, and why you'd want to.

Use the Content tool. The very first thing you need to know about controlling type in QuarkXPress is that you must have selected both the Content tool and the text box, text path, or table that contains the text you want to change. If you want to make a character-based change, you must select those characters you want to alter. If you want to make a paragraph-based change, you can select the paragraph (four mouse clicks) or a portion of the paragraph. You can even just have the cursor located anywhere within the paragraph. Just remember: If you want to change the content of a text box, use the Content tool.

Selecting a Typeface

Picking a typeface can be a very personal thing, fraught with implication and the anxiety of decision. If someone tells you they want text set in 10-point Courier, it may be best just to stay quiet. However, once the choice is made, there are a number of ways to select the typeface. Let's look at each of them here.

The Style menu. Almost every typographic control can be accessed from the Style menu. Once you select the text you want to change, you can select the typeface name from the Font submenu.

The Measurements palette. If you would rather avoid submenus, you can select a typeface from the Classic tab or Character Attributes tab of the Measurements palette instead. Here you have two methods of selecting.

- You can click on the arrow popup menu to bring up a list of fonts. It is often quicker to select from this menu than from the Style menu because it's always visible and is not a hierarchical menu.

- You can type the name of the typeface you want. Do this by clicking to the left of the first character of the typeface name shown (or jump there quickly by pressing Command-Option-Shift-M or Ctrl-Alt-Shift-M), then typing a few characters of the typeface name you want. As soon as QuarkXPress recognizes the name, it inserts the rest of it for you.

  For example, if you want to change from Helvetica to Avant Garde, click just to the left of the "H" and type "Ava." By the time you type these three letters, chances are QuarkXPress will recognize Avant Garde (as long as you have that font loaded). This is a boon to desktop publishers who have many fonts and are tired of scrolling down a list for five minutes to select Zapf Dingbats.

Tip: Jumping Forward in the Menu. If your menu is really long and you want to jump to a certain point, you can use both methods of selecting a font in the Measurements palette. For example, if you're looking for Zapf Dingbats but can't remember how "Zapf" is spelled, you can type "Z" in the font field of the Measurements palette (remember, you can get there quickly by pressing Command-Option-Shift-M or Ctrl-Alt-Shift-M), then click on the popup menu. You're transported directly to the end of the list.

Tip: Font Styles in Menus. If you have a font family active—such as Adobe Garamond Pro, which includes a plain version, Italic, Bold, and Bold Italic—the various styles in that family are condensed into a submenu. Typing a font name in the field will first select the plain/standard version of the font, but you can continue typing to get Adobe Garamond Pro Bold if you have the patience.

Character Attributes. The Character Attributes dialog box offers all the character formatting power of QuarkXPress in a single location. It is a simple keystroke away (Command/Ctrl-Shift-D; see Figure 6-3). Here you can change the typeface using all the same methods described in "The Measurements palette," above.

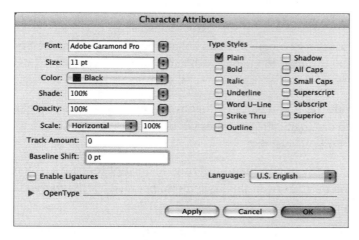

Figure 6-3
Character Attributes
dialog box

Find/Change and Font Usage. Let's say half your layout is set in Helvetica and you want to change that copy to Futura. You can use either the Find/Change or the Font Usage dialog box to search for all instances of characters set in Helvetica, and replace them with Futura. I discuss the Find/Change dialog box in some detail in Chapter 5, *Working with Text,* and the Font Usage feature earlier in this chapter.

Font Size

Selecting a font is only half the battle; once you've done that, you typically need to change the size of the type. You use the same options for changing the type size as I described above: the Style menu, the Measurements palette, the Character Attributes dialog box, and the Find/Change dialog boxes (Font Usage doesn't let you change point size). In addition, you can use a set of keystrokes to make your selected text larger or smaller (see Table 6-1).

The preset point-size range that I mention in Table 6-1 is the same range listed on the Size menu: 7, 9, 10, 12, 14, 18, 24, 36, 48, 60, and 72. When you increase through the preset range with a keystroke, your character size jumps from one to the next on this list. I generally use Command/Ctrl-Shift-> and Command/Ctrl-Shift-< (smaller and larger) to jump through the presets until I'm close to the size I want. Then I fine-tune the point size by adding the Option/Alt key to the keystroke, so that it moves only one point at a time.

Table 6-1 Font sizing keystrokes

Press...	To...
Command/Ctrl-Shift->	Increase point size through a preset range
Command/Ctrl-Shift-<	Decrease point size through a preset range
Command-Option-Shift-> *or* Ctrl-Alt-Shift->	Increase point size in 1-point increments
Command-Option-Shift-< *or* Ctrl-Alt-Shift-<	Decrease point size in 1-point increments

> **Tip: Precision Font Sizing.** *If you aren't satisfied with the preset font sizes, you can enter your own—in .001-point increments—in the Size field of the Character Attributes dialog box. You can get to this dialog box by selecting Other from the Size submenu or by pressing Command/Ctrl-Shift-\ (backslash). This is one of the keystrokes I use most often. (You could also use Command-Option-Shift-M or Ctrl-Alt-Shift-M and then press Tab to jump to the Font Size field on the Measurements palette.)*

> **Tip: Interactive Text Resizing.** *If you like working visually, you may not know exactly how large you want your text to be. You can resize text interactively by holding down the Command/Ctrl key while dragging on a handle (this also works with picture boxes; see Chapter 10, Pictures). As you resize the text box, the size of the text increases or decreases to fit your changes. Depending on how you reshape the box, the type size changes along with the type's horizontal or vertical scaling (see Figure 6-4).*

Figure 6-4
Interactive text resizing

In addition to Command/Ctrl key scaling, holding down Shift-Command (Ctrl-Shift) turns rectangular boxes into squares (scaling contents appropriately), and holding down Shift-Command-Option (Ctrl-Shift-Alt) scales the box and its contents but maintains existing horizontal and vertical proportions (this is usually what you'd want). And if you wait half a second after you click on a handle before you begin to drag, you can see the type change on screen as you drag (see more on viewing changes as you make them in Chapter 2, *QuarkXPress Basics*).

There are two catches to this funky feature. First, it only stretches type to the limits you could ordinarily stretch it to. You can't stretch type wider than 400 percent or larger than 720 points, because horizontal scaling and font size won't go any farther than that. Second, this scaling only works on unlinked text boxes, not on text boxes that are part of a longer story, as this feature is intended for use on headline and display type.

> **Tip: The Ultimate Interaction.** *If you're really into interactive text resizing, download the free XPert Tools Pro XTensions set from Quark (www.quark.com). The XPert Type palette provides many drag-and-drop options and arrows for formatting text. This little XTension has been around awhile and was sold in the past as FingerType by A Lowly Apprentice Production.*

TYPE STYLES

QuarkXPress has 13 built-in attributes that you assign at a character level. (Version 7 includes many attributes for OpenType fonts, but we'll talk about them later in this chapter.) Figure 6-5 gives samples of each of these, and examples of how to use each of them. These type attributes can be assigned to selected text in four ways, which are similar to how you assign typefaces and type size.

Character attributes. If you want to choose a type style while setting a bunch of other attributes, go to the Character Attributes dialog box (Command/Ctrl-Shift-D). The type styles in the Character Attributes dialog box are turned on and off by checking boxes. These checkboxes can be in one of three states: on, off, or indeterminate (gray).

- **On.** An "X" in the checkbox means the style is applied to all the selected text.

- **Off.** If the checkbox is blank, that style is not applied to any of the selected text.

- **Indeterminate.** A gray checkbox means that some of the characters that are currently selected have that style, and others don't.

Style menu. Another method of selecting a type style is to choose it from the Type Style submenu under the Style menu (see Figure 6-6).

Plain text
Italic
Bold
Underlined (everything)
Word underlining
~~Strike Thru~~
Outline
Shadow
ALL CAPS
SMALL CAPS
Super script .... (baseline shown as dotted line)
Sub script ....
Superior char acters ....

Outline plus shadow   Small caps   Word underlining   Bold

Kindly Note:
The koala tea of MOISHE is not **strained!**
That, however, has nothing *whatsoever* to
do with E=MC^2

Underlining   Superior character   Roman (plain text)   Italic

Figure 6-5 Type styles

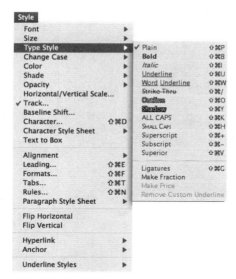

Figure 6-6
Type Style submenu

Measurements palette. On the right side of both the Classic tab (aka the old Measurements palette) and the Character Attributes tab of the Measurements palette, you'll find an icon for each type style. (Figure 6-7 shows the Character Attributes tab.) The icons either display a sample of the style or give a graphic representation of it. For example, Superscript is shown by the numeral 2 over an up arrow. To select a type style, click on the icon. The icon acts as a toggle switch, so to turn the style off, you click on it again. If you have several type styles selected, you can rid yourself of them by clicking on the P (for Plain).

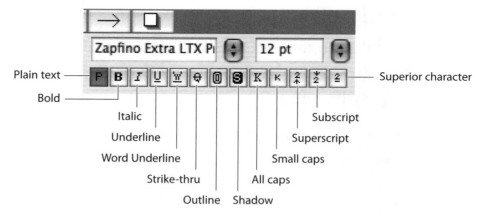

Figure 6-7 Measurements palette type styles

Note that the "indeterminate" state also appears on the Measurements palette; when you select text that contains more than one type style, those icons appear gray. You can still turn them on and off by clicking on them.

Keystrokes. Each type style can be selected by a keystroke, as shown in Table 6-2. Once again, the styles are toggled on and off with each keystroke. I find keystrokes especially useful while typing directly into QuarkXPress; I can enter text and change styles while never taking my hands off the keyboard.

Table 6-2 Type styles

Keystrokes	Style	Example
Command/Ctrl-Shift-P	Plain text	Ecce Eduardus Ursus
Command/Ctrl-Shift-B	Bold	**Ecce Eduardus Ursus**
Command/Ctrl-Shift-I	Italic	*Ecce Eduardus Ursus*
Command/Ctrl-Shift-O	Outline	Ecce Eduardus Ursus
Command/Ctrl-Shift-S	Shadow	Ecce Eduardus Ursus
Command/Ctrl-Shift-/	Strikethrough	~~Ecce Eduardus Ursus~~
Command/Ctrl-Shift-U	Underline	<u>Ecce Eduardus Ursus</u>
Command/Ctrl-Shift-W	Word underline	<u>Ecce</u> <u>Eduardus</u> <u>Ursus</u>
Command/Ctrl-Shift-H	Small caps	Ecce Eduardus Ursus
Command/Ctrl-Shift-K	All caps	ECCE EDUARDUS URSUS
Command/Ctrl-Shift-=	Superscript	Ecce Eduardus Ursus
Command/Ctrl-Shift--	Subscript	Ecce Eduardus Ursus
Command/Ctrl-Shift-V	Superior	Ecce Eduardus Ursus

> ***Tip: Avoiding Some Styles.*** *Just because QuarkXPress offers you a choice doesn't mean that you should take it. For instance, you should avoid using the Outline and Shadow type styles because they rarely look as good as you'd expect. QuarkXPress lets the operating system create these effects rather than building them itself, and the operating system is not very good at typographic effects (if it were, we'd all be using TextEdit or Windows Notepad for our typography). If you want these effects, you should build them using other QuarkXPress features. See Chapter 12,* Text Meets Graphics, *for how to create actual drop shadows in QuarkXPress.*

You may or may not want to use the two underline styles and the strikethrough style, as well. They also fall into the "made by the system" category, so you have no control over things like how far the underline should be from the baseline, or how thick it should be (I discuss ways to create these effects more precisely, later in this chapter).

Styling by Attributes Versus Font Choice

On both Mac OS and Windows, fonts are organized into families. For instance, the regular (roman), italic, bold, and bold italic styles of Bodoni all constitute a single family. QuarkXPress collapses font families into a single listing in its Font menus and provides access to the family members through submenus.

There is an ongoing superstition in the design community that you should never just apply a type style (like just choosing Bold from the Style menu), and that you should instead always select the name of the styled font (like "Bodoni Bold") from the font list. This is hogwash.

In general, you can use either method—styling text either by applying style attributes, or by choosing the styled font itself. There are several drawbacks to applying a style attribute however.

- To simply click on Bold or Italic or whatever with confidence, you must know that the style you are choosing actually exists for that font. For example, if your text is set in Symbol and you click on Italic, it may appear italic on screen, but you're taking a chance because there is no italic version of the Symbol font. The text is oblique on screen, and may even be oblique on your desktop laser printer; however, more often than not, the text will appear ugly or in the non-italic, roman face on an imagesetter.

- Some font families have more than just four faces; for example, Utopia has a bold version, a semi-bold version, and a black version. If you select some Utopia text and press Command/Ctrl-Shift-B, do you know which bold version you're getting? If not, you shouldn't select your style this way. The key here is to know your typefaces inside and out before messing with the character styles. (And this is another good reason to have a font manager, as discussed previously in this chapter.)

- Fonts can become corrupted, and the connections with their other family members may be broken. If this happens, you cannot choose character styles anymore. Often, replacing the font fixes the problem. (Again, font managers come in handy, because many fix these issues as you add fonts.)

- Sometimes you don't even get the choice to select the "real styled font" because the operating system has hidden it from you. In this case, you have to use type styles instead.

Which method is better? Choosing a type style is certainly faster, especially if you do it with keyboard commands. And it has the advantage of being font-independent. For example, if you've applied an italic formatting attribute to a range of your Bodoni text, and later decide to change your text face to Galliard, the italic formatting is retained.

On the other hand, if you choose the actual Bodoni Italic font for the emphasized range of text, when you make the change to Galliard, you get just Galliard and not Galliard Italic. Why? Because you simply switched from one font to another, and your text carried no formatting information. The original range was in an italic font with a Plain style attribute. To change fonts, you'd have to change Bodoni to Galliard, Bodoni Italic to Galliard Italic, Bodoni Bold to Galliard Bold, and so on.

No matter which method you use, I urge you to be consistent in your choice. There's little chance that something will go wrong if you change the type style in some places using style attributes and in other places using the actual fonts. However, it's best to be consistent.

> **Tip: Find/Change When You're Finished.** *If your output provider has trouble with Bold and Italic type styles—and the provider may tell you not to use them whether they work or not—use Find/Change to find those instances and apply the correct font to each.*

COLOR, SHADE, AND TRANSPARENCY

You can quickly and easily change the color, tint (shade), or opacity of a block of text. First, select the text and then select an option from the Color submenu, the Shade submenu, and/or the Opacity submenu. If you choose to skip the tedious menus—and who doesn't?— there are now options for changing color, shade, and opacity at the far right side of the Classic tab and the Character Attributes tab of the Measurements palette.

If you're on a roll working with color, use the Colors palette to set these attributes (see Chapter 14, *Color*). Just remember to click the Text icon so QuarkXPress knows to apply the formatting to the selected text—not the box it's sitting in (see Figure 6-8). For Shade and Opacity, you can enter values in the fields or use the not-very-accurate sliders (those little 10 percent values that used to be there are gone).

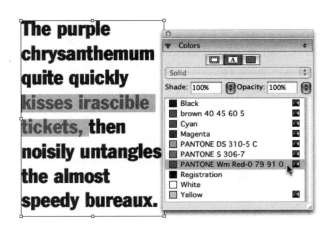

Figure 6-8
Assigning a color to type

Tip: Reversed Type. There is no specific command for reversed type—typically, white-on-black type. But that doesn't mean you can't achieve that effect. Simply select the text and choose White or another light color for the text. If you want the reversed type to have a dark background, either place a dark-colored box behind it or color the text box's background in the Modify dialog box (Command/Ctrl-M). (Also see the tip on reversed type in rules in Chapter 12, Text Meets Graphics.*)*

HORIZONTAL AND VERTICAL SCALING

Imagine that the characters in a typeface are rubber and stretchable. Now imagine stretching a typeface—one that took hundreds of hours to laboriously design at a specific width—to 160 percent of its size, warping the characters into something they were never meant to be. Now imagine the type designer's face contorting in horror as he or she sees what you've done to the type.

Okay, you get the idea: typefaces are designed to be a specific width, and shouldn't be messed with unless you have some really good reasons. What are some good reasons? The best reason of all is that you want the typeface to look that way. If you're responsible for the typographic design, then you can make any choices you want. Note that I'm not talking about your using 70-percent compression of Helvetica because you don't feel like buying another font from Adobe. I am talking about using Cheltenham compressed to 85 percent because it looks cool.

Another good reason to play with the horizontal scaling is if you need to make some body copy fit a particular space. Here I'm talking about changing the horizontal scaling of the text plus or minus 2 or 3 percent, not 10 or 20 percent. I'd be surprised if anyone other than the designer could see the difference of a few percent, especially at small sizes. But scaling Times Bold to 50 percent of its size to make it fit as a headline is a bad idea (see Figure 6-9).

After all these warnings, if you still want to play with the horizontal or vertical scaling of your type, you can do so using the Horizontal/Vertical Scale feature on the Style menu. (Horizontal scaling stretches type horizontally, whereas vertical scaling makes it taller while maintaining the same width.) First, select Horizontal or Vertical from the popup menu (you can't modify both at the same time). Entering values below 100 percent makes the text either narrower or shorter and squatter, depending on the Horizontal/Vertical setting; values above 100 percent stretch it wider or make it taller. You don't have to type a percent sign—just the number will do. The far left side of the Character Attributes tab of the Measurements palette provides radio buttons for specifying the type of scaling and a scale field as well. This is handier for experimentation than the dialog box.

Got a problem?   20 pt. Helvetica Condensed

Check your compression.   (Tracking: 0)

Got a problem?   20 pt. Helvetica (horizontal scaling: 60%)

Check your compression.   (Tracking: -3)

Got a problem?   20 pt. Helvetica bold (scaling: 60%)

Check your compression.   (Tracking: -2)

Times bold with horizontal scaling of 50%—
but with the interword spaces not compressed

Rats! Squashed again!

Times bold with horizontal scaling of 50%—interword
spaces also scaled to 50%. Tracking in both examples: -1

Squashed! Rats again!

Times roman 10/11—normal scaling

I began to experience an acute sense of panic when, despite
everyone's assurances to the contrary, I began to approach the
end of the line and found that I was not quite going to make
it.

Times roman—scaled to 99% (same line width)

I began to experience an acute sense of panic when, despite
everyone's assurances to the contrary, I began to approach the
end of the line and found that I was not quite going to make it.

Figure 6-9 Horizontal scaling of type

You can also alter horizontal and vertical scaling with keystrokes: Command/Ctrl-] (right
square bracket) makes selected text wider in five-percent increments; Command/Ctrl-[
(left square bracket) makes the selected text narrower in five-percent increments. (I
remember the difference like this: the key on the left means narrow—or less; the key on
the right means wider—or more.) The keystrokes modify horizontal or vertical scaling
depending on which direction you last changed.

*Tip: **Thoughts on Horizontal and Vertical Scaling.** Here are just a few more thoughts on the subject of horizontal and vertical scaling that you might want to keep in mind.*

- *If you're going to use horizontal scaling, think carefully about the sort of typeface you're using. When you scale a font horizontally, the vertical strokes get thicker or thinner—depending on which way you're scaling—and the horizontal strokes stay the same width. A typeface that has thick verticals and thin horizontals (such as Bodoni) can become very odd-looking with just a little scaling. Faces that have only a little variation in stroke weight often handle scaling the best.*

- *Perhaps the worst kinds of typefaces to scale horizontally are script faces, such as Berthold Script or Park Avenue. These are very delicate, and stretching them makes them look horrible and reduces their marginal legibility even further.*

- *Faces that are more square in nature, especially those with serifs, can handle being somewhat compressed with elegance. ITC Garamond, Cheltenham, and New Century Schoolbook, for instance, don't distort too badly until you drop below 90 percent or rise above 110 percent.*

KERNING AND TRACKING

There are times in life when all those little letters on a page are just too far apart or too close together. The problem may be between two characters in 120-point display type, or it may be throughout an entire font. Whatever the problem, QuarkXPress can control it through the use of kerning and tracking. These two features are similar, but let's look at them one at a time.

*Tip: **Know Your Ems and Ens.** Many typographic controls are specified using units of measure called ems and ens. (Some people call the en a "nut" to distinguish it aurally from an em.) These are not nearly as confusing as some people make them out to be. The default for the em in QuarkXPress is the width of two zeros side by side in the font and size you're working in. If that sounds weird, it's because it is. I can't figure out why they did it that way, but that's just the way it is. The width of an en space is half of an em space—the width of one zero.*

Because this is so weird and unreasonable, Quark has added a checkbox on the Character tab of the Preferences dialog box labeled Standard Em Space. This sets the width of an em space to the same width that every other piece of software uses: the size of the typeface you're using. So if you're using 14-point Times with the Standard Em Space option turned on, the em space is 14 points wide. For consistency and a sense of doing the right thing, I recommend that you set this as your default by changing the preference while no projects are open.

If you're typing along and change the point size, then the sizes of the em and en change as well. This can be a great aid. For example, if you change the size of a word after painstakingly kerning it, your kerning does not get lost or jumbled. The kerning was specified in fractions of an em, and therefore is scaled along with the type.

Em spaces and em dashes are not always equal in width. Usually they are (especially when Standard Em Space is turned on), but it really depends on what the typeface designer decided. While we're talking about these spaces, you may be thinking, "How can I enter one?" If you do need to enter an em space or en space in text, QuarkXPress 7 provides menu commands in the Insert Character submenu of the Utilities menu.

> **Tip: What's 7/200 of an Em?** Even though QuarkXPress defines kerning and other type-spacing values in ems, don't feel that you have to think in ems, unless you want to live and breathe typography. The important thing to remember is how the type looks, not all the numbers that get you there. When I'm working in QuarkXPress, I almost never think, "Oh, I'm going to change the kerning 1/20 of an em." I just say, "Oh, let's see how adding some kerning here would look." Focus on the results, and you'll get the feel for it pretty quickly.

Kerning

Adjusting space between two characters is referred to as *kerning* or *pair kerning*. You'll sometimes find kerning defined purely as the removal of space between characters. In QuarkXPress, kerning can be either the removal or the *addition* of space—moving two characters closer together or farther apart. Figure 6-10 shows some examples of type, first unkerned and then kerned. The problem is made obvious here: Too much space between characters can make words look uneven or unnatural.

No automatic or manual kerning

DAVID WAVES!

Auto-kerning on; no manual kerning

DAVID WAVES!

Manual kerning applied to all character pairs

-15   -14 -6 -6   -7   -10 -5   -10 -5

Figure 6-10
Kerned and unkerned type

QuarkXPress supports two kinds of kerning: automatic and manual. Type designers usually build into the font itself kerning-pair values that can be invoked automatically in QuarkXPress. Automatic kerning is global: It affects all instances of a character pair. Manual kerning is local: It affects only the pair selected.

Automatic. When I say "automatic," I mean really automatic: All you have to do is turn on the function, and QuarkXPress will make use of the font's built-in kerning pairs (actually, you don't even have to turn automatic kerning on, because it is on by default). It's up to font vendors to determine how many and which kerning pairs to include with a font, and which values to assign to them. Most fonts come with between 100 and 500 such pairs. Third parties also sell kerning pairs you can import.

There's almost no good reason to turn off automatic kerning altogether, but if you want to, the switch is on the Character tab in the Preferences dialog box. I wouldn't turn it off unless I were on a really slow machine and QuarkXPress was taking an inordinately long time flowing my text.

> **Tip: OpenType Kerning.** *If you're using an OpenType font with the kerning table stored in a glyph positioning table (GPOS), the automatic kerning is handled differently. Rather than a layout-wide preference, automatic kerning for OpenType fonts with GPOS is a project-wide preference—so it affects all the layouts in a project. Located in the General tab (under Project) in the Preferences dialog box, Use OpenType Kerning is turned on by default. When this is turned on, the automatic kerning overrides any changes you make in the QuarkXPress Kerning Table Editor. (In fact, when it's enabled, the font names will not even be available in the Kerning Table Edit dialog box.) If you spent a lot of time in the past editing the kerning for these types of fonts, you may want to turn off Use OpenType Kerning. Either way, you can manually apply additional kerning to text in OpenType fonts.*
>
> *So, the big question here is, "How do I know if a font has a GPOS? According to Quark, Extensis, and other resources, there is no easy way to tell. Quark allows that newer OpenType fonts with more features are more likely to have GPOS than PostScript fonts that were simply converted to OpenType format. I asked publishing consultant extraordinaire Chuck Weger, who agreed that there was no way to tell—but then he went the extra mile and wrote a nice little AppleScript called GPOS Snarfer that does just that—tells you if an OpenType font has a GPOS kerning table. You can download it for free from www.elara.com/Software.html. (If you're on Windows and really need to know this, ask a Mac friend.)*

Manual. Figure 6-10 shows words in three renditions: with no kerning, with automatic kerning, and with manual kerning in addition to automatic kerning. The last looks best, doesn't it? (Please agree.)

Manual kerning in QuarkXPress is the adjustment of space between character pairs on a case-by-case basis. You make each adjustment in increments of fractions of an em space (see "Tip: Know Your Ems and Ens," previously). Why anyone would want to kern to a precision of $1/20,000$ of an em space is beyond us, but QuarkXPress lets you do just that.

Manual kerning is usually reserved for larger type sizes for two reasons. First, it's harder to see poorly kerned pairs in smaller point sizes, so people say, "Why bother?" Second, you wouldn't want to go through a sizable amount of body text in the 8- to 14-point range, meticulously kerning pairs. It would take forever. Leave small type sizes to automatic kerning. If you don't like the built-in kerning pairs in a font, you can change them (see "Kerning and Tracking Tables," later in this chapter).

Manual kerning is a character-level attribute, but with a distinct difference from other character formatting. Instead of selecting the text you want to change, you place the cursor between two of the characters before you apply kerning (see Figure 6-11). If you select one or more characters, you end up applying tracking rather than kerning (see "Tracking," next). Once you've clicked at an insertion point, you can control the space between the characters in four ways.

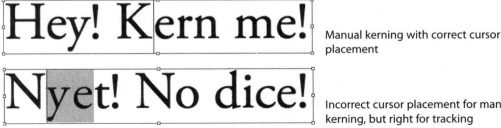

Manual kerning with correct cursor placement

Incorrect cursor placement for manual kerning, but right for tracking

Figure 6-11 Cursor placement for kerning

Kern or Character Attributes. You can select the Kern feature from the Style menu, which brings up the Character Attributes dialog box (you could type Command/Ctrl-Shift-D to get to this dialog box). Whole-number values typed in here represent units of $1/200$ em. For example, typing in "10" adds $10/200$ ($1/20$) of an em, and typing "-.1" removes $1/2,000$ of an em (typing a minus sign—a hyphen—before the value makes it negative). This is a really slow and painful way to apply kerning.

Measurements palette. Both the Classic tab and the Character Attributes tab of the Measurements palette contain left-arrow and right-arrow icons that control tracking and kerning in text. Table 6-3 gives you a rundown on how to use them.

Table 6-3 Kerning control with the Measurements palette arrow icons

Click...	While Pressing...	To...
Right arrow		Increase space 10 units ($1/20$ em)
Right arrow	Option/Alt	Increase space one unit ($1/200$ em)
Left arrow		Decrease space 10 units ($1/20$ em)
Left arrow	Option/Alt	Decrease space one unit ($1/200$ em)

Keystrokes. I hate to take my hands off the keyboard while I'm working. Why should I, when I can do just about everything I need by pressing keystrokes? Table 6-4 shows the keystrokes you can use for kerning. Learn them, love them, use them.

Table 6-4 Kerning keystrokes

Press...	To...
Command/Ctrl-Shift-}	Increase space 10 units ($1/20$ em)
Command-Option-Shift-} Ctrl-Alt-Shift-}	Increase space one unit ($1/200$ em)
Command/Ctrl-Shift-{	Decrease space 10 units ($1/20$ em)
Command-Option-Shift-{ Ctrl-Alt-Shift-{	Decrease space one unit ($1/200$ em)

No matter which method you use to kern, you can see the kerning value in the Measurements palette (next to the left and right arrows) and in the Character Attributes dialog box when the cursor is between two kerned characters.

> **Tip: Kerning the Kerned.** *What shows up as the kern value when you want to kern a pair that is already kerned because of automatic kerning? Nothing. You'll still find a zero in the Kern Amount field. QuarkXPress regards the values applied by automatic kerning as the norm, so you don't have to worry about them. Of course, if you turn off automatic kerning after having applied manual kerning, your kerning values may be way off.*

> **Tip: Removing Manual Kerning.** *Have you ever been handed a file to which someone has spent many hours manually adding hundreds of kerning pairs? What if they really didn't know what they were doing, and you want to remove all that kerning before starting over? Simply select the text and choose Remove Manual Kerning from the Utilities menu. (If you don't see the command, enable the Type Tricks XTension, which ships with QuarkXPress.) Just select the range of text you want to affect, then select that from the menu. Voilà! All gone.*

Tracking

I know it's incredibly confusing, but it's true: There are two separate features in QuarkXPress called "Tracking." They're similar, but I need to break them down for clarity. The first is a character-level attribute, and I'm going to talk about it here. The second is a font-level attribute that changes the font as a whole rather than just changing a set of characters, and I'll discuss it in great detail later in this chapter.

Character-level tracking. Tracking as a character-level attribute is the adjustment of space between all the character pairs in a range of text. It's sometimes called "track kerning" or "kern tracking," though I think the best name for it is *range kerning*. The idea is simple: You can add or subtract space between many pairs of characters all at one time by using tracking controls (see Figure 6-12). These controls are so similar to the kerning controls that I'm not even going to waste time and paper talking about them much.

Art directors *everywhere* were ignoring me until I realized what I needed:

Tracking: +7

Much tighter tracking!

Tracking: -12

To England: That precious stone set in a silver sea

Tracking: 0. Copy doesn't fit.

To England: That precious stone set in a silver sea

Tracking: -4. Copy fits.

Figure 6-12 Tracking text

You can control tracking by selecting a range of text and using the Classic tab or the Character Attributes tab of the Measurements palette, the Track feature from the Style menu (this menu item changes from Kern to Track when you have more than one character selected), the Character Attributes dialog box, or the same keystrokes you use for kerning. The reason all the controls are virtually the same is that QuarkXPress "decides" for you whether to kern or track, based on what is selected in the text box. In fact, these controls have the same function. One is applied to a single pair of characters; the other is applied to several or many pairs.

The crazy thing about this whole setup is that while kerning and tracking do the same thing, they are totally separate features. One result of this is that kerning and tracking are cumulative. For example, if you kern a character pair -10 units, then apply tracking of -10 units to those characters, the space between them ends up 20 units smaller than normal (which may be what you want; you just need to be aware of it). Also, if you track a word, then look at the kerning between two letters, it will look as though there were no kerning applied at all.

> **Tip: When to Track.** *"Ah," I hear the reader sighing, "but what about some real-world tips?" Okay, let's set out some guidelines for you.*

• If you're setting text in all capitals or in true small capitals from an Expert Set font, add between five and 10 units of space by tracking the word. Remember that you may not want to add tracking to the last character of the word (see "Tip: Tracking and the Single Word," below).

• Printing white text on a black background often requires a little extra tracking, too. That's because the negative (black) space makes the white characters seem closer together.

• Larger type needs to be tracked more tightly, with negative tracking values. Often, the larger the tighter, though there are aesthetic limits to this rule. Advertising headline copy will often be tracked until the characters just "kiss." You can automate this feature by setting up dynamic tracking tables, which I will discuss later in this chapter.

• A condensed typeface (such as Futura Condensed) can usually do with a little tighter tracking. Sometimes I'll apply a setting as small as -1 to a text block to make it hold together better.

• When you're setting justified text and you get bad line breaks, or if you have an extra word by itself at the end of a paragraph, you can track the whole paragraph plus or minus one or two units without it being too apparent. Sometimes that's just enough to fix these problems.

Remember, however, that no matter how solid a rule may be, you are obliged to break it if the finished design will be better.

> **Tip: Tracking and the Single Word.** *The way tracking works, technically, is by adding or subtracting space to the right of each selected character. If you want to track a single word and don't want the space after the last character to be adjusted, you should select not the whole word, but only the characters up to the last letter. For example, if you want to apply 10-unit tracking to the word "obfuscation" without changing the space after the "n," you would only select the letters "obfuscatio" and then apply tracking.*

Wordspacing

Quark's free Type Tricks XTension, included with the software and enabled by default, adds one more option to character-level attributes: the ability to adjust kerning for spacebands within a selected range of text. As I discussed earlier, kerning is the adjustment of space between characters; it's often called "letterspacing," but I prefer to reserve that term for justification controls (which I'll talk about later in this chapter). What Quark is calling "wordspacing" here is really just changing the kerning between words (wherever it finds spacebands).

There are three conditions for adjusting wordspacing—spaceband kerning—over a selected range of text.

- You can only use keystrokes.

- You must have an extended keyboard.

- The Type Tricks XTension must be enabled in the XTensions Manager, accessed via the Utilities menu.

Table 6-5 shows the keystrokes you should use to adjust wordspacing. Note that adjusting wordspacing is no magic trick: QuarkXPress is simply adding and subtracting kerning from each spaceband (you can put the cursor between the spaceband and the first letter in a word to see how much space has been added).

Note that if you add wordspacing in this way, it's a pain to remove or change it (you can use Remove Manual Kerning, as described earlier, but that will also remove any other kerning you've added).

Table 6-5 Keystrokes for wordspacing

Press...	To...
Command-Control-Shift-] *or* Ctrl-Shift-]	Increase wordspacing 10 units
Command-Option-Control-Shift-] *or* Ctrl-Shift-]	Increase wordspacing one unit
Command-Control-Shift-[*or* Ctrl-Alt-Shift-[	Decrease wordspacing 10 units
Command-Option-Control-Shift-[*or* Ctrl-Alt-Shift-[	Decrease wordspacing one unit

Baseline Shift

The final character attribute I discuss here is *baseline shift*. The baseline is the imaginary line on which the type sits. Each line of text you're reading is made of characters sitting on a baseline. You can shift a character or a group of characters above or below the baseline (see Figure 6-13).

I DON'T NEED NO BASELINE SHIFT.

I FEEL A NEED FOR A SUPERSCRIPT.

OY. I'M FEELIN' KINDA UNSTABLE, WHAT WITH ALL THIS BASELINE SHIFTING GOING ON.

Figure 6-13
Baseline shift

Baseline shift is specified in points; negative values shift the character down, positive values shift it up. You can enter any value, up to three times the font size you're using, in hundredths of a point; for example, you can shift a character off the baseline 30 points in either direction if that character is in 10-point type.

Note that baseline shift is similar to kerning and tracking in an important way: even though you specify values in points rather than in fractions of an em, the value of the baseline shift changes along with the font size. For example, if you specify a 4-point baseline shift for 15-point type, when you double the font size to 30 points, the shifted character is "reshifted" to eight points ($2 \times 4 = 8$).

To shift selected text, you can use the Baseline Shift command in the Style menu. This brings up the Character Attributes dialog box with that field highlighted and is probably the slowest way to go about changing baseline shift. For a more interactive and visual method, try the Measurements palette or keyboard commands. New to QuarkXPress 7 is a handy Baseline Shift field in the middle of the Character Attributes tab of the Measurements palette. You can enter a value or click the arrows next to the field to change the baseline shift by 1 point. Press Option (Mac OS) or Alt (Windows) as you click the arrows to alter baseline shift by 0.1 point. You can also use keyboard commands to change baseline shift in 1-point increments. To increase baseline shift, press Command-Option-Shift-+ (Mac OS) or Ctrl-Alt-Shift-0 (Windows); to decrease it, press Command-Option-Shift-hyphen (Mac OS) or Ctrl-Alt-Shift-9.

PARAGRAPH FORMATTING

Character formatting is all very well and good, but when it comes to how text flows in a column, it don't make Bo Diddley squat. To handle text flow on a paragraph level, you have to use paragraph formatting. These controls include indents, leading, tabs, drop caps, and hyphenation and justification, as well as some esoteric functions such as Keep with Next ¶ and widow and orphan control. In this section, I'll discuss each of these features. In addition, as usual, I'll give lots of examples so you can see what I'm talking about.

> ***Tip: Selecting Paragraphs.*** *I often look over people's shoulders as they work, and what I see could scare a moose. One such scare is the technique of selecting a paragraph to apply some paragraph formatting to it (leading, space before, or whatever). People think that they have to select the whole paragraph first. Not true! When you change paragraph formatting, you only need the cursor in the paragraph you want to change. That means you can have one word selected, or three sentences, or half of one paragraph and half of another, or whatever.*

The central headquarters of paragraph formatting is the Paragraph Attributes dialog box (see Figure 6-14). Let's look at each feature of this dialog box in turn, and I'll branch off on tangents when I need to.

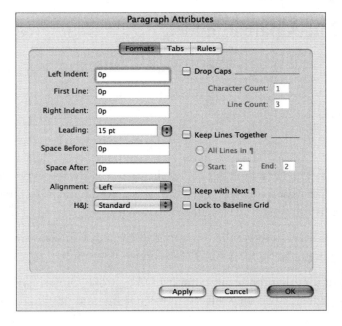

Figure 6-14
The Paragraph Attributes
dialog box

ALIGNMENT

Let's start with the most blatant paragraph attribute—alignment. Most people are familiar with the five horizontal alignment options: left aligned, right aligned, justified, force justified, and centered. I will discuss each of these first, then move on to a less-known feature: vertical alignment.

Horizontal Alignment

If you've been involved with desktop typography long enough (a day or two), you'll know that different programs have different names for the same thing. For example, what QuarkXPress calls "left aligned" others may call "left justified" or "flush left/ragged right." I'm not going to start naming names, but QuarkXPress's terms are simpler and make more sense. For one thing, "justified" means only one thing: text that's flush to both left and right margins. "Fully justified" is redundant, and "left-justified" is… well, it just isn't. Figure 6-15 shows some examples of text with various horizontal alignments.

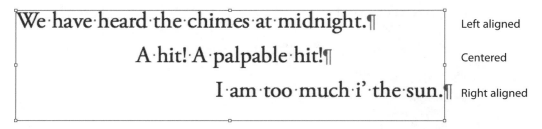

We·have·heard·the·chimes·at·midnight.¶ — Left aligned

A·hit!·A·palpable·hit!¶ — Centered

I·am·too·much·i'·the·sun.¶ — Right aligned

Figure 6-15 Horizontal alignment

You can specify alignment for a paragraph in any of four ways.

- **Paragraph Attributes.** The Paragraph Attributes dialog box is always an option when you're changing paragraph formats. The control is a popup menu (see Figure 6-16). This, of course, is the slow way to apply formatting.

- **Alignment submenu.** You can select the horizontal alignment you want from the Alignment submenu under the Style menu. This is pretty slow, too.

- **Keystrokes.** Note that the Alignment submenu lists a keystroke for each style. These are easy to remember, since they rely on first-letter mnemonics: hold down the Command/Ctrl and Shift keys and press "L" for Left, "R" for Right, "C" for Centered, and "J" for Justified. The keystroke for Forced Justify is a variant on Justified: Command-Option-Shift-J (Ctrl-Alt-Shift-J).

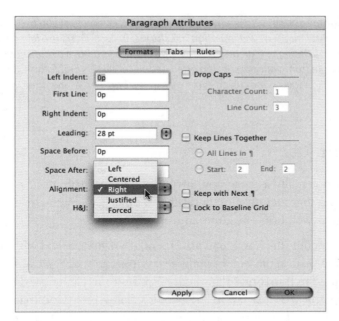

Figure 6-16
Alignment control in the
Paragraph Attributes
dialog box

• **Measurements palette.** Perhaps the most simple alignment method of all is to use the Classic tab or the Paragraph Attributes tab of the Measurements palette. When you have an insertion point in a paragraph, QuarkXPress displays five icons representing the various alignment selections (see Figure 6-17). To change a paragraph's alignment, click on the one you want.

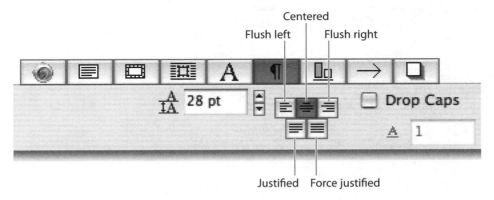

Figure 6-17 Horizontal alignment in the Measurements palette

While left-aligned, right-aligned, and centered paragraphs are relatively straightforward, justified and force-justified text are a bit more complicated. Because of this, I'm putting off talking about justification and hyphenation until later in this chapter.

Tip: Limit Your Alignments. I'm sure you would never do this. I know that you're a designer of reputation and flair. But I might as well mention this tip, just in case. Don't use left-aligned, right-aligned, centered, and justified text all on the same page unless you have a reasonable design sense and a signed note from your parent. Too often people let all this highfalutin' technology go to their heads and design their pages using every trick in the bag. Remember that there is strength in simplicity.

Vertical Alignment

Vertical alignment is not really a paragraph attribute, but an attribute of each text box. Nonetheless, as vertical alignment is closely related to other paragraph attributes (leading in particular), I might as well bring this, too, into the discussion.

Just as horizontal alignment is the horizontal placement of the lines of text within a column, vertical alignment is the vertical placement of the text within its box. You can specify attributes similar to those used in horizontal alignment: Top, Bottom, Center, and Justified. You can change this setting on the Text tab in the Modify dialog box (Command/Ctrl-M or double-click on the box with the Item tool selected) or in the Text tab of the Measurements palette. Here you're presented with a popup menu (see Figure 6-18).

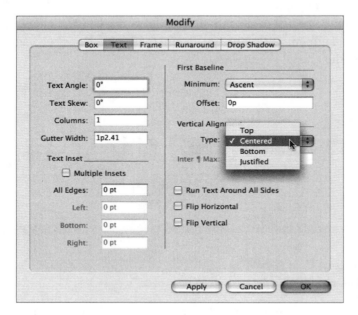

Figure 6-18
Vertical Alignment in the Modify dialog box

Let's look briefly at each of the alignment possibilities.

Top. This is the default setting for text boxes. It's what you're probably used to if you use QuarkXPress regularly. The text starts at the top of the text box and, as you type, fills the box. Exactly where the text starts depends on the First Baseline control (discussed later in the chapter).

Centered. When Vertical Alignment is set to Centered, the text in the text box is vertically centered. That sounds trite, but I can't explain it any better. See Figure 6-19 for an example of this alignment. Note that blank lines can affect the positioning of the text in the text box; sometimes you have to delete them to get the text to look centered.

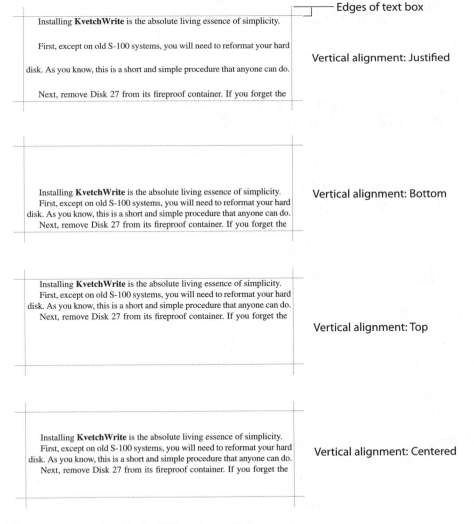

Figure 6-19 The four Vertical Alignment settings

Tip: Centering Text. Telling QuarkXPress to center text—either horizontally or vertically—may not result in your text looking perfectly centered. Why? Because the mathematical horizontal centering of text may not look as "right" as optical centering, especially if you have punctuation before or after the text. You can use invisible characters colored the same as whatever they're on top of (for example, white on top of a white background). Or you can use altered indentation (see "Indents," below) to change the way the text looks (see Figure 6-20). Remember, what looks right is more "right" than what the computer says.

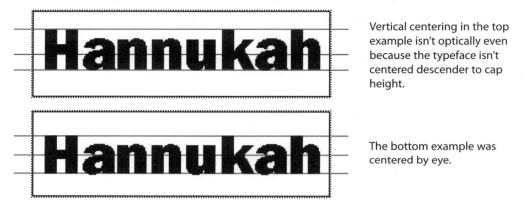

Vertical centering in the top example isn't optically even because the typeface isn't centered descender to cap height.

The bottom example was centered by eye.

This is not visually centered because of the quotation marks.

This is adjusted by placing punctuation colored white on each line.

Figure 6-20 When centering is not centered

In the case of vertical centering, text in all capitals or text in fonts such as Zapf Dingbats may not appear to be centered in the box. This is because QuarkXPress does not actually find the center of the characters you've typed. Instead, it uses the full height of the font, ascenders and descenders combined, to calculate proper placement. I suggest using baseline shift to move the characters around until they look the way you want them to.

Bottom. By specifying Bottom, you force the last line of text to the bottom of the box. Then as text flows into the text box, each line pushes the type higher in the box. Note that it is the bottom of the descender, not the baseline, that sits flush with the box's bottom.

Justified. "Justification" means here that the text will be flush with the top and bottom of the box. QuarkXPress puts the first line of the text box at the top, the last line at the bottom, and then adds or deletes space between interior lines. That means that there may be a lot of extra space between lines and paragraphs (the program overrides paragraph leading settings when necessary).

You can specify a maximum distance between paragraphs in a vertically justified text box by changing the Inter ¶ Max value on the Text tab in the Modify dialog box. A setting of zero, which is the default, tells QuarkXPress to distribute all space evenly by adding leading. A setting higher than zero lets the program add extra space between paragraphs rather than change your leading (this is usually preferable). Figure 6-21 shows some examples of vertically justified text with different Inter ¶ Max settings.

Ior, auritulus cinereus ille annosus Raili, solus in silvae angulo quodam carduoso stabat, pedibus late divaricatis, capite deflexo de rerum natura meditans. "Cur?' cogitabat, modo "quemadmodum?'
Itaque Puo appropinquante Ior paulisper a meditatione desistere gavisus est ut maeste "Ut vales?' ei diceret.

Text is 10/11, Inter ¶ Max setting is zero points. The leading is ignored completely.

Gray line represents the text box.

Ior, auritulus cinereus ille annosus Raili, solus in silvae angulo quodam carduoso stabat, pedibus late divaricatis, capite deflexo de rerum natura meditans.

"Cur?' cogitabat, modo "quemadmodum?'

Itaque Puo appropinquante Ior paulisper a meditatione desistere gavisus est ut maeste "Ut vales?' ei diceret.

Text is 10/11, Inter ¶ Max setting is four points. The leading is adjusted slightly, while space is added between paragraphs.

Ior, auritulus cinereus ille annosus Raili, solus in silvae angulo quodam carduoso stabat, pedibus late divaricatis, capite deflexo de rerum natura meditans.

"Cur?' cogitabat, modo "quemadmodum?'

Itaque Puo appropinquante Ior paulisper a meditatione desistere gavisus est ut maeste "Ut vales?' ei diceret.

Text is 10/11, Inter ¶ Max setting is one pica. The leading is back to normal, and space is only added between paragraphs.

Figure 6-21
Varying the Inter ¶ Max setting

When Quark announced that QuarkXPress would support vertical justification, the press thought it would be the greatest thing since the transistor. My response to this is: If you set up your leading grids and text boxes correctly, you shouldn't need to have some computer going through your drawers, shuffling lines around. I wouldn't want a computer to marry my daughter, and I don't want a computer changing my leading and paragraph spacing.

No matter how picky I am about correctly setting up my layouts, I do admit that there are times when vertical justification comes in handy. For example, many newspapers constantly use this feature to "bottom out" their columns.

> **Tip: When Vertical Justification Doesn't Work.** *Note that QuarkXPress will turn off vertical alignment in two instances: if the text box is not rectangular, or if some object is causing text runaround (see Chapter 12, Text Meets Graphics). In both these cases, the text box reverts to top alignment. I could explain the mathematical reasoning behind this, but suffice it to say that it would be incredibly difficult and time-consuming for QuarkXPress to align text vertically in these instances, so it just doesn't even try.*

INDENTS

Horizontal alignment depends entirely on where the left and right margins are. In a column of text, the margins are usually at the edges of the text box (or of the column, in a multicolumn text box). However, you may want the first line of every paragraph to be indented slightly. Or you might want the left or right margin to be somewhere other than the edge of the column. You control each of these by changing the values for paragraph indents.

> **Tip: Watch the Text Inset.** *Before paragraph indents come into play, note that text may be inset from the edges of the box as well. You can specify text inset in QuarkXPress in the Text tab of the Modify dialog box and the Text tab of the Measurements palette. For rectangular boxes, if you want different insets, you can turn on Multiple Insets and enter different values for Top, Left, Bottom, and Right.*

The default text inset value is zero (although it was one point in previous versions of QuarkXPress). You can change this default by closing all projects and double-clicking the Text Box tool. This brings up the Tool tab of the Preferences dialog box, where you can click the Modify button to change the default Text Inset. Because a text inset of zero sometimes can make the text a little hard to read onscreen—it bounces up against the side of the box—you may want to increase the default.

QuarkXPress lets you change three indent values: Left Indent, Right Indent, and First Line indent. All three controls are located on the Formats tab in the Paragraph Attributes dialog box (Command/Ctrl-Shift-F; see Figure 6-22) and the Paragraph Attributes tab of the Measurements palette. I'll discuss each type of indent and then talk about how you can use them in your layouts.

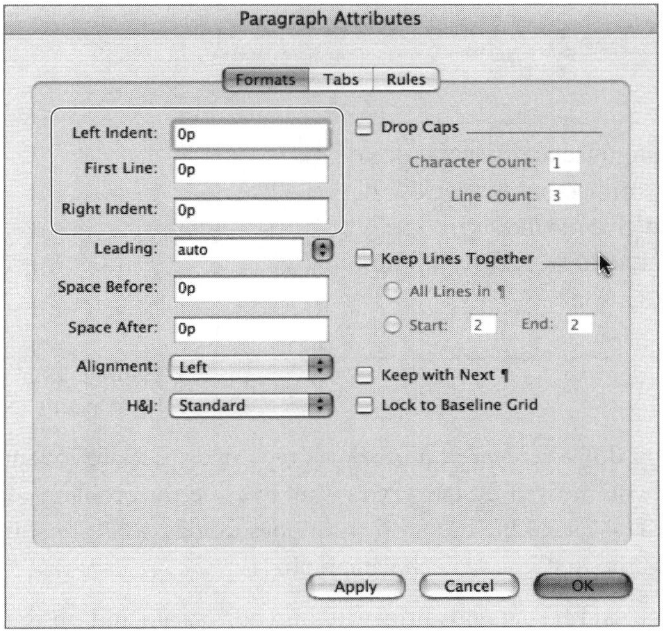

Figure 6-22
The Indent settings

Left Indent. The Left Indent control specifies how far the paragraph sits from the left side of the text box or column guide. The Left Indent is actually measured from the Text Inset border, not from the side of the box. For example, if you want your paragraph to be indented exactly three picas from the side of the text box, and your Text Inset setting is four points, then your Left Indent should be "2p8" (3p-4pt=2p8).

Right Indent. The Right Indent control specifies how far the right edge of the paragraph will be positioned from the right edge of the text box or column guide (or the text box's Text Indent). For example, if you change the Right Indent to 0.5 inch, you can imagine an invisible line being drawn 0.5 inch from the right column guide. The text cannot move farther to the right than this line (see Figure 6-23).

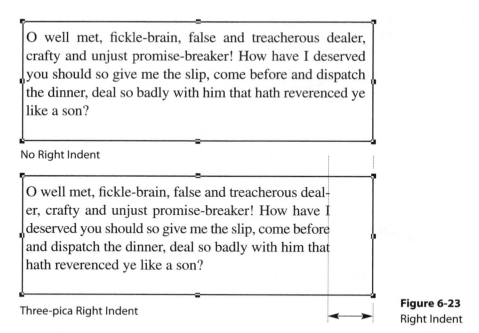

No Right Indent

Three-pica Right Indent

Figure 6-23
Right Indent

First Line. Whatever you do, wherever you go, don't type five spaces to indent the first line of each paragraph. If you must, use a tab. If you want to avoid the problem completely, use a First Line indent. The First Line indent feature does exactly what it sounds like it would do: it indents only the first line of each paragraph.

How large your indent should be depends primarily on your design and on the typeface you are working with. If you are working with a typeface with a large x-height (the height of the lowercase "x" in relation to the height of the capital letters), you should use a larger first-line indent than if you are working with a typeface that has a small x-height. Book designers often use a one- or two-em indent; if you're using 12-point type, the indent might be 12 points or 24 points.

> ***Tip: Hanging Indents.*** *You can use Left Indent and First Line indent to create hanging indents (used for bullet lists and the like) by typing a negative number as the First Line indent. I often use "1p6" (one-and-a-half picas) for a left indent and "-1p6" for a first-line indent. This pushes the entire paragraph out to the 1p6 mark, and then pulls the first character (a bullet) back to the zero mark (see Figure 6-24). Typing a tab after the bullet skips over to the 1p6 mark whether or not I have a tab stop there (I'll discuss tabs and tab stops later in this chapter).*

•→Some·people·like·to·hang·wall-
paper.¶
•→Some·people·like·to·hang·out-
laws.¶
•→Me,·I·can't·be·bothered·with·
either·of·those,·but·I·sure·do·
love·to·hang·indents.·¶

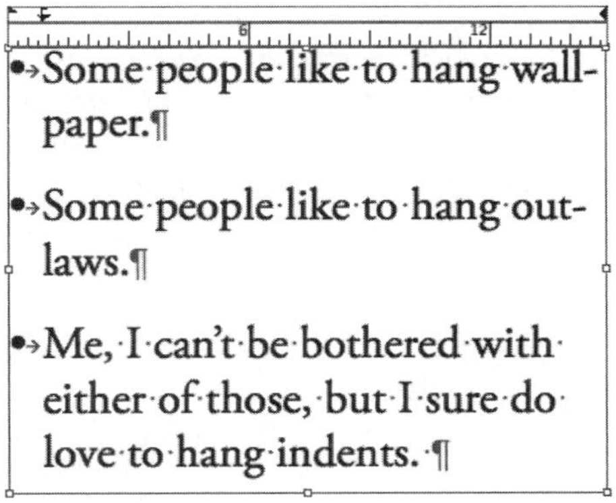

Figure 6-24
Hanging indents

The benefit of hanging indents like this is that you don't have to painfully set your own returns after each line. If you set hard or soft returns after each line—I'll talk about the difference later in this chapter—and then you edit the text, or even change the typeface, it takes a long time to fix the text, removing the old returns and putting new ones in. This is horrible; if you had just used hanging indents instead, your problem would never have arisen.

(You can also use an Indent Here character when creating hanging indents; I cover that in "Special Characters," later in this chapter.)

Note that you don't have to specify any of the indents by typing numbers. While the Paragraph Attributes dialog box is open, you are shown a ruler along the top of the active text box (see Figure 6-25). This ruler contains three triangle markers: two on the left, and one on the right. You can move these icons by clicking and dragging them along the ruler. This helpful ruler also displays when you use the Paragraph Attributes tab and the Tabs tab—that's right, there's a "Tabs tab"—of the Measurements palette.

Left tab
Right tab
Decimal tab
Left indent
Centered tab
Comma tab
Align On tab
Right indent
First Line indent
6

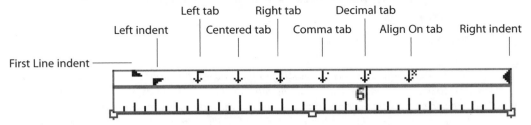

Figure 6-25 The text ruler associated with the Paragraph Attributes dialog box

The right triangle is the Right Indent. The bottom-left triangle is the Left Indent. The top-left triangle is the First Line indent. While moving these triangles around, the First Line indent moves as you change the Left Indent. For example, if you set a ¼-inch First Line indent, and then move the Left Indent triangle to ½ inch, the First Line indent moves with it to the ¾-inch point (½ inch plus ¼ inch).

Tip: Formatting Past the Boundaries. As the old Zen master said, "Frustration dissipates like the morning fog when light is shed on the problem." (Actually, I don't know any Zen masters, so I just made that up.) One frustration I've seen people get caught up in is the issue of formatting beyond what you can see on screen. For example, when you open the Paragraph Attributes dialog box, QuarkXPress adds a ruler along the top of the text box so that you can manually add or edit the tab stops and indents. However, if the box is too wide, you can't see the left or right side of the ruler because it runs right out of the project window (see Figure 6-26).

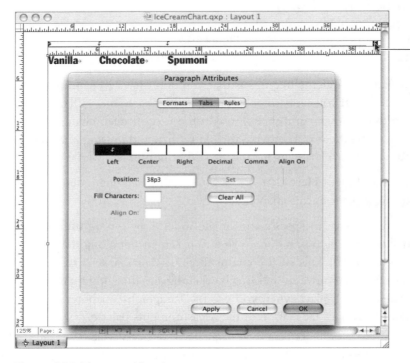

If you select a wide block of text and bring up Paragraph Tabs, the ruler just runs right off the window.

Figure 6-26 The too-wide ruler

However—and here's the shedding of the light—it turns out that if you click in that ruler and drag to the left or right, the page scrolls with you. Pretty soon you get to where you want to go and you can stop dragging. Note that when you do this, you sometimes accidentally add a tab stop (I'll talk about tab stops later in this chapter), and you have to get rid of it by clicking on it and dragging it off the ruler.

LEADING

If I could get one concept across to you in this chapter, I'd want it to be this: don't follow the defaults. By not following default values, you are forced to pay attention to how the type looks, rather than letting the computer do it for you. There is perhaps no better example of why this is important than leading.

Leading (pronounced "ledding") is the space between lines of type. The name originates from the lead strips or blocks used to add space between lines of metal type. QuarkXPress gives you considerable control over leading values for each paragraph, or it can "fly on automatic," specifying leading for you.

In this section I'll discuss the two modes and three methods for specifying leading. Pay close attention to the words "color" and "readability" in this section; they're the reasons designers bother to be so meticulous.

Specifying Leading

Although QuarkXPress lets you use any measurement system you want, leading is traditionally measured in points. When talking type, most typesetters and designers say things like, "Helvetica 10 on 12," and write it out as "10/12." Designers who have grown accustomed to digital equipment (in other words, just about everybody) would say that "10/12" means setting 10-point type so that the baseline of one line is 12 points from the baseline of the next line (see Figure 6-27).

Figure 6-27
Specifying leading

Leading is a paragraph-level attribute; that is, you can specify only one leading value for each paragraph. You specify leading in several ways: in the Paragraph Attributes dialog box (press Command/Ctrl-Shift-E) to open this dialog box and jump right to the Leading field), in the Classic tab or the Paragraph Attributes tab of the Measurements palette, or with keystrokes. Whereas in the first instance you can only type in the leading value, in the Measurements palette you can change leading in two ways (see Figure 6-28).

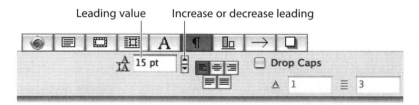

Figure 6-28 Leading in the Measurements palette

- You can select the leading value and replace it with whatever leading value you want.

- You can click the up or down arrow next to the leading value to increase or decrease the leading value in 1-point increments. Option/Alt-clicking increases or decreases in 0.1-point increments.

You can also use keyboard shortcuts to change a paragraph's leading; I've listed the four keystrokes in Table 6-6.

By the way, if you change leading in the Paragraph Attributes dialog box, you'll notice that QuarkXPress places a popup menu next to the Leading field that contains the word "Auto." Choose this if you need to go back to the default leading for some reason.

Table 6-6 Leading keystrokes

Press...	To...
Command/Ctrl-Shift-"	Increase leading in 1-point increments
Command-Option-Shift-" Ctrl-Alt-Shift-"	Increase leading in 0.1-point increments
Command/Ctrl-Shift-;	Decrease leading in 1-point increments
Command-Option-Shift-; Ctrl-Alt-Shift-;	Decrease leading in 0.1-point increments

Leading Methods

QuarkXPress lets you specify leading values in three ways: absolutely, automatically, and relatively. Let's look at these.

Absolute. Setting your leading in an absolute form makes your leading as steadfast as Gibraltar. If you specify 14-point leading, you get 14-point leading—no matter what size type the paragraph contains. If the type is bigger than the leading, the type overprints preceding lines. When, as in the example given above, someone talks about "10/12" type, this is absolute leading they're talking about.

QuarkXPress lets you type any absolute leading value between zero and 1,080 points (15 inches).

Tip: True Zero Leading. If you set a paragraph's leading to zero, QuarkXPress decides that you really mean you want "automatic" leading (see below). But what if you really want no leading at all from baseline to baseline? If you set leading to .0001 points, the program rounds down to exactly zero. The next highest value is .001 points. The truth of the matter is that these are equivalent for all intents and purposes, but I wanted to be clear anyway.

Why would anyone want to use zero leading? Well, it wouldn't be common. Zero leading means that every line in the paragraph would be printed exactly on top of the line above it, making the whole paragraph be only one line tall. It's especially good for those postmodern designs where you don't really need to read any of the words.

Automatic. Auto leading sets leading as a percentage of the largest font size on each line. This percentage is usually 20 percent greater than the font size. For example, if the largest font size on a given line is 10 points, then your leading will be set to 12 points (10, plus 20 percent of 10). If you change the font size to 12 points, then the leading changes to 14.4 points. Note that if you change only one character on a line to a larger font size, then that line alone will have a different leading value—which just *screams* "nonprofessional!"—even though Auto leading is a paragraph-wide feature (see Figure 6-29).

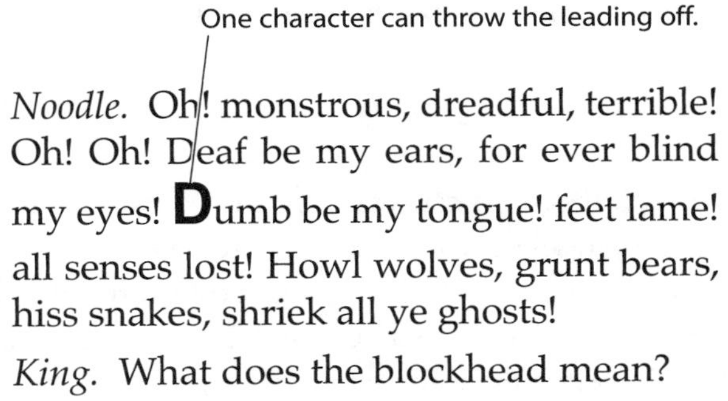

One character can throw the leading off.

Noodle. Oh! monstrous, dreadful, terrible! Oh! Oh! Deaf be my ears, for ever blind my eyes! **D**umb be my tongue! feet lame! all senses lost! Howl wolves, grunt bears, hiss snakes, shriek all ye ghosts!

King. What does the blockhead mean?

Figure 6-29
Auto leading can result in irregular leading within a paragraph.

Auto leading is the default setting of any new text box. To choose it specifically, you can type either "Auto" or "0" as the leading value.

You can change the automatic-leading percentage value on the Paragraph tab in the Preferences dialog box. There are two things you should note about doing this, though. First, the change is layout-wide; you can't change the automatic leading percentage for only one paragraph or text box. Second, you must specify clearly what the automatic leading measurements are; that is, if you want a percent, you must type a percent sign. This is important because you can also specify automatic leading to be a relative value (more on relative values soon).

To be honest with you, I use automatic leading when I'm typing up grocery shopping lists (and sometimes when I'm writing a letter to my mom). But when I'm working on a professional project, I define the leading explicitly using absolute leading. Period. Many professional magazines, newspapers, and newsletters use automatic leading because they don't know any better, and then they blame QuarkXPress for outputting weird-looking text.

Relative. Whereas automatic leading generally determines the leading value based on a percentage of font size, relative leading determines leading by an absolute value. You specify relative leading by including the characters + or - (plus or minus—the minus sign is a hyphen) before your leading value. For example, applying a leading value of +3 to 12-point type results in 12/15 leading. If you change the font size to 22 points, you automatically get 22/25 leading (22 plus 3).

By typing a negative relative value, you can tighten up the leading. However, you have a limit: the height of a capital on the lower line cannot be higher than the baseline of the upper line (to get that effect, you have to use absolute leading).

The only time I use relative leading is when I am specifying *solid* leading—that is, when the leading equals the point size. Instead of keying in 30-point leading for 30-point type, I type "+0." Then, if (or when) I change the font size, the leading changes with it.

Leading Modes

When specifying leading in QuarkXPress, you can work in one of two leading modes: Word Processing or Typesetting. You can select which mode to use on the Paragraph tab in the Preferences dialog box on the Edit menu. This is a long-ago feature related to how leading is measured—Word Processing is ascent to ascent and Typesetting is baseline to baseline. Its initial intent was to help match the leading of a word processor, but why you would want to do that is beyond me. Trust me when I say to leave this at Typesetting.

When Black and White Is Colorful. When designers and typesetters talk about the color of a page or of type, they aren't talking red, green, or blue. They're referring to the degree of darkness or lightness that the text projects. The color of text is directly related to the typeface, letterspacing, wordspacing, and leading. Other design elements, such as drop caps, graphic elements, or pullquotes, can have a significant effect on the color of a page. It's usually a good practice to maintain an even and balanced color across your page, unless you're trying to pull the viewer's eye (as opposed to pulling the viewer's leg) to one area or another (see Figure 6-30).

One way to see the color of a page or a block of type is to hold the printed page at some distance and squint. You can also turn the page over and hold it up to the light, so that you can see the text blocks without being distracted by the text itself.

Eduardus ursus, amicis suis
agnomine "Winnie ille Pu"—
aut breviter "Pu"—notus, die
quodam canticum semihian-
tibus labellis superbe eliquans

Stone Serif 9/12

**Eduardus ursus, amicis
suis agnomine "Winnie
ille Pu"—aut breviter
"Pu"—notus, die quodam
canticum semihiantibus
labellis superbe eliquans**

Stone Serif bold 9/12

Eduardus ursus, amicis suis
agnomine "Winnie ille Pu"—
aut breviter "Pu"—notus, die
quodam canticum semihian-
tibus labellis superbe

Helvetica 10/13

Eduardus ursus, amicis suis
agnomine "Winnie ille Pu"—aut
breviter "Pu"—notus, die quodam canticum semihiantibus
labellis superbe eliquans

Garamond 10/13

agnomine "Winnie ille Pu"—
aut breviter "Pu"—notus,
die quodam canticum semi-
hiantibus labellis superbe

Palatino with zero tracking

agnomine "Winnie ille Pu"—aut
breviter "Pu"—notus, die quodam canticum semihiantibus
labellis superbe eliquans

Palatino with -10 tracking

Figure 6-30
The color of
text blocks

Tip: Leading Techniques. Here are a few tips and tricks for adjusting your leading. Remember, though, that ultimately it is how easily the text reads and how comfortable the color is that counts. Figure 6-31 shows some samples for each of these suggestions.

- Increase the leading as you increase the line length. Solid leading may read fine with lines containing five words, but will be awful for lines containing 20 words.

- In general, use some extra leading for sans serif or bold type. It needs the extra room.

- Note the x-height of your typeface. Fonts with a small x-height can often be set tighter than those with a large x-height.

- Set display or headline type tight. Big type can and should be set tight, using either +0 relative leading or even absolute leading smaller than the point size you're using.

- When you're using really tight leading, be careful not to let the ascenders of one line touch the descenders of the line above it.

Of course, here's a corollary tip to all of these: break the rules if it makes the design look better!

The longer a line, the more leading you'll need.

Look, s'pose some general or king is bone stupid and leads his men up a creek, then those men've got to be fearless, there's another virtue for you. S'pose he's stingy and hires too few soldiers, then they got to be a crowd of Hercule's. And s'pose he's slapdash and don't give a bugger, then they got to be clever as monkeys else their number's up.

9/9.5

9/11

Look, s'pose some general or king is bone stupid and leads his men up a creek, then those men've got to be fearless, there's another virtue for you. S'pose he's stingy and hires too few soldiers, then they got to be a crowd of Hercule's. And s'pose he's slapdash and don't give a bugger, then they got to be clever as monkeys else their number's up.

Fonts with small x-heights can be set tighter.

The misery of this one woman surges through my heart and marrow, and you grid imperturbed over the fate of thousands!

9/11.5

The misery of this one woman surges through my heart and marrow, and you grid imperturbed over the fate of thousands!

9/9.5

Display type can be set tight.

The best thing since sliced bread

36/31

Watch out for your ascenders and descenders.

48/39

Cagney Jads

Figure 6-31 Leading techniques

Tip: From Automatic to Absolute. If you press Command-Shift-straight quote (Ctrl-Shift-') when the selected paragraph is set to Auto leading, QuarkXPress switches the leading to the absolute value that corresponds to the automatic value (it rounds to the nearest point). For instance, if you've got 10-point type and Auto leading is set to 20 percent, if you select a paragraph that has automatic leading and press Command-Shift-straight quote (Ctrl-Shift-'), QuarkXPress changes the leading to 12 points (120 percent of 10 points). This is the fastest way to switch from automatic to absolute leading.

SPACE BEFORE AND AFTER

Not only can you place interline space with leading, you can add space between paragraphs using the Space Before and Space After controls. You can find both of these controls in the Paragraph Attributes dialog box (Command/Ctrl-Shift-F) and in the Paragraph Attributes tab of the Measurements palette.

While it is entirely your prerogative to use both Space Before and Space After, you normally will only need to use one or the other. Think about it: If you add equal space before and after a paragraph, it doubles the amount of space between each paragraph. I almost always use Space Before, but whichever you use is fine.

I've seen more than one designer become flustered when applying Space Before to the first paragraph in a text box. Nothing happens. Remember that Space Before has no effect on the first paragraph in a text box because it only adds space *between* two paragraphs. Fortunately, though, this is usually what you want. To add space before the first paragraph in a text box, use the First Baseline placement control (see "First Baseline," later in this chapter).

Tip: Adding Extra Space. Recently I witnessed one of my esteemed officemates using multiple carriage returns to control the space between paragraphs, and I almost went apoplectic. Let's see if I can pound this idea into your head as strongly as I did by saying, "Don't use multiple spaces between words or punctuation!"

Don't ever use an extra carriage return to add space between paragraphs. Not only will you offend the people at Quark who spent long hours implementing the Space Before and Space After features, but you will—nine out of 10 times—mess yourself up with extra blank paragraphs hanging out at tops of columns or in other places where you don't want them. If you want a full line of space between paragraphs, apply it with Space Before or Space After in the Paragraph Attributes dialog box.

Tip: Page Breaks. InDesign has a cool feature that I like: you can specify a paragraph attribute that forces the paragraph to start on a new column or page. That is, any paragraph tagged with this attribute will always start at the top of a page or column. As it turns out, you can do a similar thing in QuarkXPress by simply making the Space Before value in the Paragraph Attributes dialog box as large as the text column is tall. For example, if your text box is 45 picas tall, enter "45" in the Space Before field. You can set this as a paragraph style (see Chapter 7, Copy Flow) or as local formatting for particular paragraphs.

FIRST BASELINE

The first line of a text box is always a tricky one for perfectionists. How far away from the top edge of the text box should the line sit? And how to get it there? Usually, QuarkXPress places the first line of text according to the text box's Text Inset value. For instance, if the Text Inset is set to 3 points, then the top of the first line of text is set 3 points away from the top edge of the box.

Typophiles will be happy to find that you can clarify what QuarkXPress uses as the "top of the first line of text" with the First Baseline setting. You'll find these controls in the Text tab of the Modify dialog box and the Text tab of the Measurements palette. You can choose three values for the Minimum setting: Cap Height, Cap+Accent, and Ascent (see Figure 6-32).

Nonetheless, if you really care about the placement of your type, you may choose to use First Baseline Offset instead (found in the same locations). First Baseline Offset lets you choose exactly how far from the top of the text box you want the first line of text to sit (measured from the baseline, of course). However, First Baseline Offset only kicks in when the distance from box edge to first baseline is smaller than the First Baseline Offset value.

For instance, if the baseline of the first line of text is 24 points from the top of the box when First Baseline Offset is set to zero (which is the default value), then First Baseline Offset won't do anything until you set the value higher than 24 points. If you set it to 30 points, then the baseline of the first line of text will sit at exactly 30 points from the top of the box. However, if you then go and change the text size to 60 points, QuarkXPress will ignore the First Baseline Offset again and place the top of the text (as determined by the Minimum setting) at the Text Inset value.

Tip: Constant First Baselines. When you're working with a leading grid, you might be frustrated by where QuarkXPress places the first line in a text box. That's because QuarkXPress generally moves the baseline of the first line up or down to accommodate the size of the text rather than sticking to your baseline grid (see Figure 6-33). But if you set the First Baseline value for the text box, the first baseline always appears at the same place, and your leading grid isn't messed up. Note that the First Baseline value has to be bigger than the type itself in order for the line to be moved down.

So don't go adding multiple carriage returns or trying to do weird things with leading, space before, or baseline shift. Just use the First Baseline setting.

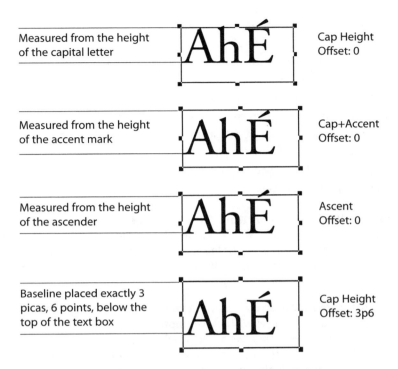

Figure 6-32 The Minimum settings in First Baseline Offset

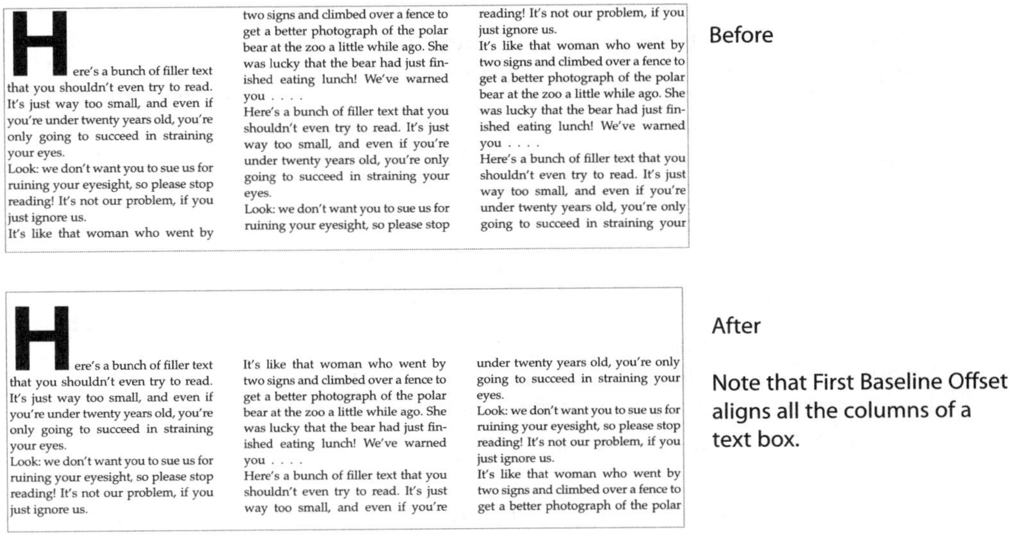

Before

After

Note that First Baseline Offset aligns all the columns of a text box.

Figure 6-33 First Baseline maintains an even leading grid.

TABS

If you've ever typed on a typewriter, you've probably encountered tabs. A tab is a jump-to signal in the form of a keyboard character. For example, if you're typing along and press the Tab key, the text cursor jumps to the next tab stop along the line. On a computer, the Tab key actually inserts an invisible character that you can delete or cut (or anything else you can do with characters). You can place tab stops anywhere you like across the text column. Tab stops are paragraph-level formatting attributes, so each paragraph can have a different set of tab stops. If you don't specify your own tab stops, QuarkXPress sets default stops every half-inch across the text box.

Tip: Don't Use Spaces Where You Really Want Tabs. Have you ever tried to align multiple columns using the spacebar? If you have, you have probably known frustration like no other frustration known to desktop publishers. I call it the "it-works-on-a-typewriter" syndrome. It's true; you can line up columns on a typewriter with spaces. But you shouldn't in desktop publishing. The reason has to do with fonts.

On most standard typewriters, the font you're using is a monospaced font. That means each and every character in the font is the same width. However, most typefaces are not monospaced. Therefore, you cannot rely on an equal number of characters always spanning an equal distance. Figure 6-34 shows this phenomenon clearly. So don't use multiple spaces when you're trying to align columns. In fact, don't use multiple spaces ever. Use tabs.

Take one	from column "a"	and one	from column "b"	
but here	you actually	have four	columns see?	Aligned with spaces (bad)

Take one	from column "a"	and one	from column "b"	
but here	you actually	have four	columns see?	Aligned with tabs (good)

Figure 6-34   Using spaces for alignment

Tip: Multiple Tabs. If you are setting up a table and you want to place tabs between each column, follow the same rule as with spaces: Don't type multiple tabs in a row to make your columns align. Set one tab stop for each column. Then press Tab once to jump from one column to another.

QuarkXPress lets you set seven types of tab stops: Left, Right, Center, Right Indent, Decimal, Comma, and Align On. Figure 6-35 shows examples of most of these tab stops in a common situation—a table.

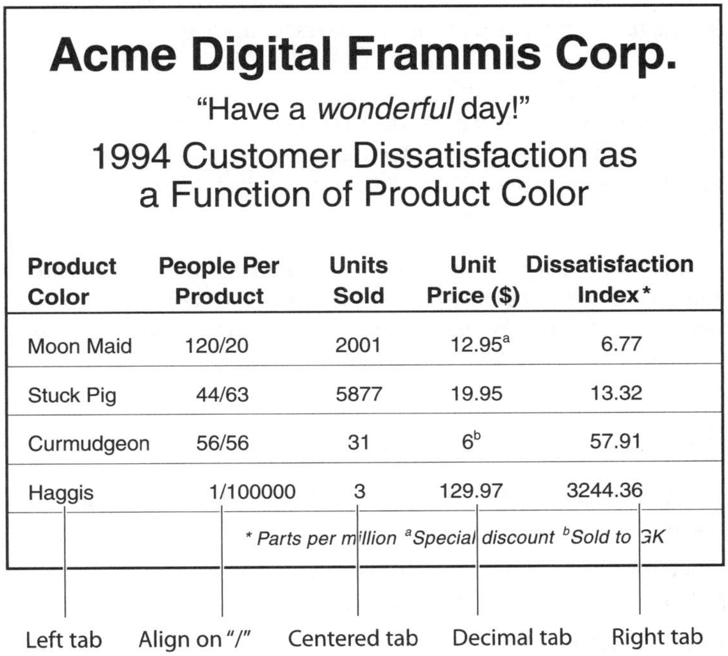

Figure 6-35
Using tabs and tab stops

- **Left tab stop.** This is the type of tab stop you're used to from typewriters. The text after the tab continues as left-aligned. All tab stops are Left tab stops unless you specify them as another type.

- **Right tab stop.** Tabbing to a Right tab stop causes the following text to be right aligned. That is, the text will be flush right against the tab stop.

- **Center tab stop.** Text typed after tabbing to a Center tab stop will center on that tab stop.

- **Right Indent tab stop.** Right Indent tabs don't show up on the popup menu because they're not really tab stops. You enter them in a text box with the Content tool selected by pressing Option/Alt-Tab. I'll talk about this more fully in just a moment.

- **Decimal, Comma, and Align On tab stops.** These three tab stops act similarly. They act like a Right tab until a special character is entered; then the text that follows is flush left. The decimal and comma tabs align on the first nonnumeric, nonpunctuation character. Selecting Align On brings up a one-character entry field; you can then enter the special character that acts as the tab stop.

Tip: Formatting Tabs Quickly. One reader, Barry Simon, pointed out to me that you can sometimes format tab stops for a number of lines more easily by working on just a single line. If you set the proper tab settings for the first line, you can quickly apply those settings to the rest of the lines by selecting all the lines (including the first one), opening the Paragraph Attributes dialog box (Command-Shift-F or Command-Shift-T; Ctrl-Shift-F or Ctrl-Shift-T), and clicking OK (or pressing Return). The tab setting for the first line is applied to the rest of the lines.

Tip: Hanging Tabs. There's a subtle feature in the decimal tab function that you'll love if you ever create financial balance sheets. The decimal tab doesn't just line up decimals. Rather, QuarkXPress thinks of any nonnumber that falls after a number to be a decimal point, and aligns to it. For example, if you press Tab and type "94c2.4" on a line with a decimal tab, QuarkXPress aligns to the "c" rather than to the period.

I thought this was a bug until I realized how handy it could be. For example, if you are lining up numbers in a column, the negative-balance parentheses hang outside the column. You can even create hanging footnotes, as long as they're not numbers (see the Unit Price column in Figure 6-35).

Setting Tab Stops

To place a custom tab stop, you can use the Tabs tab in the Paragraph Attributes dialog box, which you can find by choosing Tabs from the Style menu or by pressing Command/Ctrl-Shift-T. You should forget that method even exists, however, and use the new Tabs tab on the Measurements palette, where it is so much easier to see what you're doing. When the Tabs tab is showing through either the Paragraph Attributes dialog box or the Measurements palette, QuarkXPress places a ruler bar across the box of the text box you're working in (see Figure 6-36). You can place a tab stop in several ways.

- Click in the ruler above the text box and then choose what sort of tab stop you want by pressing one of the Tab stop buttons. (You can also choose the tab stop type before clicking in the ruler; it doesn't matter.)

- Type a value into the Position field and then choose what sort of tab stop you want it to be (or, again, you can choose the type first). Remember that you can type the value in a different measurement system than the ruler is displaying, or even use an equation to figure the position. If you want to add another tab stop using this technique, click the Set button to "lock in" the tab stop.

- Drag a tab stop icon to the ruler and drop it where you want it. This works with both the Tabs tab of the Paragraph Attributes dialog box and the Measurements palette. It's slightly cooler, however, to use the Measurements palette, because a vertical line helps guide your tab placement.

Figure 6-36 Setting tab stops

If you're using the Paragraph Attributes dialog box, you can press Command/Ctrl-S for Set. In addition, you can use the Apply button to preview your tabs. When you're setting up a table, you almost never get the tabs stops right the first time, so before you close the dialog box, it's useful to click Apply (or press Command/Ctrl-A) to see how the tab stops will affect the paragraph.

> *Tip: Evenly Spaced Tab Stops.* Don't forget that you can use arithmetic in dialog box fields. This includes the Position field when you're setting tabs. If you want evenly spaced tabs, place each tab by adding an increment to the previous tab position. For instance, let's say you want a tab stop at 0.5 inch and every inch from there on.

1. Type ".5" into the Position field (or ".5"" if your measurements aren't inches).

2. Click the Set button. This sets the tab stop in the paragraph.

3. Position the cursor after the ".5" (you can just press the Right Arrow key) and type "+1."

4. Click Set again.

5. Continue until you have all the tab stops you need. When you're done, click OK.

Note that if the equation gets too long in the Position field, you can click on the last tab stop you added (the little arrow icon in the tab ruler). This simplifies the equation to save space.

My colleague Sandee Cohen pointed out that you can do a similar thing using multiplication and division. For example, if you wanted to set up tab stops at every .75-inch increment across a text box, you could set the first one at .75, then the second one at .75*2, the third at .75*3, and so on (clicking the Set button between each one).

You can even space out tab stops equally across a text box. Let's say you want five tab stops, and your text box is 35 picas wide. To set the first tab stop, type "35p/6" in the Position field (always divide by one more than the number of tab stops you want to end up with). To set the second tab stop, change this to "35p/6*2". Change the 2 to 3 for the third tab stop, and so on.

Changing and Deleting Tab Stops

Once you have tab stops set for a paragraph, you can go back and edit them by dragging the tab-stop icons along the tab ruler. First, select the tab stop you want to edit (click on it). Then you can press one of the tab-stop type buttons, change the position value, or edit the Fill Character (see "Tab Leaders," next). When you're done, click Set.

You can rid yourself of an unwanted tab stop by dragging the icon out of the ruler boundaries (see Figure 6-37). To clear all the tab stops for a paragraph, click the Clear All button or Option/Alt-click the tab ruler.

Hey!→   You·leave·that·tab·stop·alone!

Figure 6-37 Dragging away a tab stop to delete a tab

Tab Leaders

A tab leader is a repeated character that fills the space created with the tab (see Figure 6-38). The most common example is a table of contents, where the repeating period character fills the space between a chapter name and a page number. Each tab stop can have its own leader. In fact, in QuarkXPress, you can use either one or two repeating characters—most commonly, a character and a space.

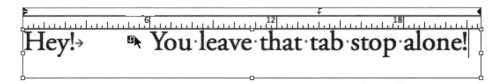

Moose attack ------------------on Golden Pond
A neverending § § § § § § § § § § § § story of greed
Corruption ➠➠➠➠➠➠➠and extra-large boots.
Left-handed■■■■■■■■■■■■■■■■■Windshifters!

Figure 6-38
Tab leaders

Other characters used as tab leaders. In the second line, the size of the tab itself was reduced to 10 points. In the third and fourth lines, the tab character's font was changed to Zapf Dingbats.

To add a leader while creating a new tab stop, set the tab stop as described earlier, then—before you click Set—type the leader characters into the Fill Characters field. When you're done, click Set.

If the tab stop is already created and you want to change its leader, select the tab stop in the ruler above the text box, type the leader characters into the Fill Characters field, and then click Set.

> **Tip: Adjusting Leaders.** *You don't have to be content with the size and font of a tab's leaders (otherwise called "fill characters"). If you want the characters to be smaller, select the tab character in the text (not the tab stop) and change its point size. If you want the characters to appear in another font, change the font of that tab character—you can even apply character style sheets. People don't often think of the tab character as a character, but that's just what it is. If you turn on Invisibles (select it from the View menu), you can see the character as a little gray arrow.*
>
> *Changing the font and size isn't all you can do; you can even change the amount of space between the leader characters. Select the tab space and adjust its tracking or kerning values. Typically, when you change the kerning value for a single character it only changes the space between it and the next character; however, in this case it changes the space between each of the leader characters (see Figure 6-39).*

Note that if you're creating an automatic table of contents with the Lists feature, don't do manual adjustments to formatting until you're sure it's final. If you carefully touch up every dot leader, that formatting will be wiped out when you update the list.

Period used as leader characters (18 points; same as other type on the line).

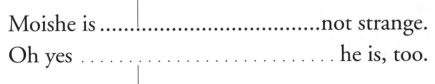

Tab reduced to 10 points with a tracking value of 94.

Figure 6-39 Adjusting the tracking of the tab leader characters

Right Indent Tab

Trying to set a tab stop exactly at the right margin can be very frustrating. Even worse, if your right margin or the size of your text box changes, your tab stop doesn't follow along. Inserting a Right Indent tab fixes all that. To do this, place the cursor where you want one, and then find the Insert Character submenu under the Utilities menu. Buried under Special Characters (Breaking) you'll find Right Indent Tab. If you find yourself using it often, remember the keyboard shortcut: Option-Tab on Mac OS, Shift-Tab in Windows.

This type of tab acts as though you've placed a right tab stop flush with the right margin of your paragraph. Plus, it moves as you adjust the margin or the text box. Inserting this type of tab effectively adds the tab and sets a variable tab stop at the same time. (I can hear the handful of people who "get it" sighing appreciatively in the background. Those of you who don't, just try it once and you'll understand.)

The Right Indent tab acts just like a tab character (you can even search for it the same way, using "\t"; see Find/Change function in Chapter 5, *Working with Text*), though there's no way to set its own leader. It picks up the same leader as the previous tab stop in the paragraph. Note that you won't see a tab stop in the tab ruler; it's always set to the right margin, wherever that is. Also, you should note that Option-Tab (Shift-Tab in Windows) jumps past all other tab stops in that paragraph, all the way over to the right margin.

Hyphenation and Justification

There are few things more dear to a typesetter's heart than hyphenation and justification—often called simply "H&J." Proper hyphenation and justification is often the most important single factor in the way a layout looks. And if your H&J is bad… well, there's little that anyone can do (see Figure 6-40).

Doing a good job with the program involves knowing a little something about good hyphenation and justification settings. If y'ain't got the good settings, you don't got the good-looking type, either. This paragraph, for example, is simply atrocious.

Doing an *especially* good job with the program involves taking the time to learn about its hyphenation and justification controls. You'll be glad you did.

Figure 6-40
Hyphenation and justification can make a difference.

QuarkXPress has some very powerful controls over how it hyphenates and justifies text in a column. However, this is once more a situation where you won't always want to rely on its default settings. Let's take a look at what H&J is all about, and then get into the details of how you can make it work for you.

The Basics of H&J

Although hyphenation and justification are entirely separate functions, they almost always go together. Almost always.

The idea behind both hyphenation and justification is to make text fit into a given space and still look as good as possible. It turns out that there are three basic ways to fit text without distorting it too much. You can:

- Control the spacing between all the letters.

- Control the spacing between the words.

- Break the words at line endings by hyphenating.

Any one of these options, if performed in excess, usually looks pretty awful. However, it is possible to mix them together in proper measure for a pleasing result.

> **Tip: Check for Rivers.** *Often the first problem that arises when people set their text to justified alignment is that their layouts start looking like a flood just hit; rivers of white space are flowing around little islands of words. Because humans are so good at seeing patterns of lines (it's just how our brains work), too much space between words is disturbing to the eye. I mentioned in "Tip: When Black and White Is Colorful" that turning the page over and holding it up to the light is a good way to check the color of a text block. It's also a great way to check for rivers in text. This way your eye isn't drawn toward reading the words—just seeing the spaces.*

Although you can't adjust the algorithms that QuarkXPress uses for H&J, you can change many variables that help in its decision making. These values make up the Edit Hyphenation & Justification dialog box (see Figure 6-41), found by first selecting H&Js from the Edit menu (or pressing Command-Option-H or Ctrl-Alt-H), selecting the H&J to edit, and then clicking either the New or Edit button.

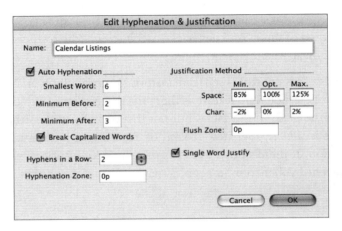

Figure 6-41
The Edit Hyphenation & Justification dialog box

Let's divide the controls in this dialog box into two groups—Auto Hyphenation and Justification—and discuss them one at a time.

Auto Hyphenation

QuarkXPress can automatically hyphenate words at the end of a line, breaking them into syllables according to an internal algorithm and (albeit limited) dictionary of preferences. In the default Standard H&J, Auto Hyphenation is enabled by default. It's also on for most of the new default H&Js introduced in QuarkXPress 7: Narrow Measure, Very Narrow Measure, and Wide Measure. (The only two default H&Js with hyphenation off are No Hyphenation and Titles.) When you enable hyphenation, several items become active. These features are the basic controls over QuarkXPress's internal hyphenating algorithms. Let's look at them one at a time.

Smallest Word. When QuarkXPress is attempting to hyphenate a line of text, it must decide which words are eligible for hyphenation. You can quickly discard most of the smaller words by specifying the smallest word QuarkXPress considers. For example, you might not want the word "only" to hyphenate at the end of a line. By setting the Smallest Word value to five or higher, you tell QuarkXPress to ignore this word, as well as any other word with fewer than five letters.

Minimum Before. The Minimum Before value specifies the number of letters in a word that must come before a hyphen break. Depending on your tastes and your level of pickiness, you might set this to two or three. Otherwise, words like "mnemonic" might break after the first "m." I find that most art directors prefer a minimum of three letters.

Minimum After. The Minimum After value determines the number of letters in a word that must come after a hyphenation break. Again, this value is based on aesthetics. Some people don't mind if the "ly" in "truly" sits all by itself on a line. (*The New York Times* breaks "doesn't" after the "s," but it's a newspaper, after all.) For most quality work, you would want a minimum setting of three. And never, ever, set it to one (the results are uglier than a vegetarian's face at a meat-packing plant).

Break Capitalized Words. This control is self-explanatory. You can tell QuarkXPress to either break capitalized words or not. The feature is there for those people who think that proper nouns should never be broken. I'm picky, but not that picky. (On the other hand, it is strange to see people's names hyphenated. It kind of depends on how much name-dropping is in the publication. If there's not a ton of names but a lot of places, you could go back and manually prevent hyphenation in people's names.)

Hyphens in a Row. One area in which I *am* that picky is the number of hyphens I allow in a row. For most work, I hate to see more than a single hyphen in a row down a justified column of text. QuarkXPress defaults to "unlimited," which is the same as typing zero. If you're creating newspapers, this might be appropriate. If you're making art books, be a bit more careful with your hyphens. I usually set this to two as a default and then go through and tweak the line breaks by hand.

You can enter any value you want in the field or choose an option from the popup menu: 1, 2, 3, or unlimited.

Hyphenation Zone. Another way to limit the number of hyphens in a section of text is the Hyphenation Zone setting. While relatively simple in function, this feature is one of the more difficult to understand (it was for me, anyway).

The idea is that there's an invisible zone along the right margin of each block of text. If QuarkXPress is trying to break a word at the end of a line, it looks to see where the hyphenation zone is. If the word *before* the potentially hyphenated word falls inside the hyphenation zone, then QuarkXPress just gives up and pushes the word onto the next line (does not hyphenate it). If the previous word does not fall within the hyphenation zone, then QuarkXPress goes ahead with hyphenating the word (see Figure 6-42).

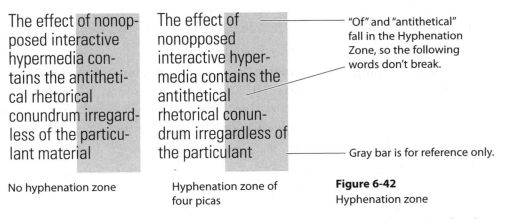

The effect of nonopposed interactive hypermedia contains the antithetical rhetorical conundrum irregardless of the particulant material

No hyphenation zone

The effect of nonopposed interactive hypermedia contains the antithetical rhetorical conundrum irregardless of the particulant

Hyphenation zone of four picas

"Of" and "antithetical" fall in the Hyphenation Zone, so the following words don't break.

Gray bar is for reference only.

Figure 6-42
Hyphenation zone

For example, if the words "robinus christophorus" came at the end of a line and QuarkXPress were about to hyphenate "christophorus," it would first look at the word "robinus" to see if any part of it fell inside the hyphenation zone. If it did, QuarkXPress wouldn't hyphenate "christophorus" at all; if it didn't, QuarkXPress would use its standard hyphenation algorithms to break the word appropriately.

Normally, the Hyphenation Zone is set to zero units. This setting specifies no hyphenation zone, so all lines can have hyphenation up to the limit of the Hyphens in a Row value. Unless you really know what you're doing, there is little reason to change this value.

Justification

As I mentioned above, justifying text is the process of adding or removing space across a line of text to keep it flush on the left and right. You can alter several of the parameters QuarkXPress uses for determining justification by changing values found in the Edit Hyphenation & Justification dialog box. These values are controlled in the Justification Method area. It's divided into values for wordspacing, letterspacing (called "character spacing" by Quark), and Flush Zone width, plus a checkbox for Single Word Justify. Let's look at each of these.

Wordspacing. As I described previously in "Character Formatting," wordspacing determines the amount of space between words. In the case of justification, it describes the range of how large or small the spaces between words can be. You can specify Minimum, Optimum, and Maximum percentages of a normal space character. For example, a value of 80 percent allows a space between words that is 80 percent of a normal spaceband. (Note that the "normal" space is the spaceband width defined by the designer of the typeface; this can vary greatly among font families.)

In the default Standard H&J, the optimal wordspacing is set to 100 percent. In general, some typefaces need tighter spacing; therefore, depending on the typeface, I might set Optimum to around 95 percent. The default Minimum is 85 percent and the default Maximum is 125 percent. Quark revises these defaults often based on feedback from people in the publishing community—like me!

Character Spacing. You can also set Minimum, Optimum, and Maximum percentages for the spacing between characters. The percentages are based on the width of an en space (see Table 6.7, "Formatting Characters," later in this chapter). Whereas 100 percent was normal for wordspacing, zero percent is normal for Character Spacing, and should almost always be used as the Optimum setting.

I generally don't give QuarkXPress much freedom in adjusting letterspacing because I think the type designer probably knows more about what character widths should be than I do (and certainly more than QuarkXPress does). For example, I might change the default Minimum from -2 to -1 percent, and the Maximum from 2 to 4 percent. But here, again, is an area where you need to print out a few text blocks, preferably on an imagesetter, look at the color of the type, and decide for yourself.

Also, try to keep this setting tight because loose letterspacing is difficult to read. Again, I'd rather add space between words than letters any day. Some typographers, whom I greatly respect, insist that letterspacing should always be set at "0/0/0" (that is, QuarkXPress should never change letterspacing). However, I'm from California originally, so I'm much looser than that.

Tip: H&J Percentages Versus Tracking Units. My colleague Brad Walrod points out that each percentage of character spacing in the H&Js dialog box is basically the same as one unit of kerning or tracking. This enables you to perform a quick and easy test when you're trying to figure out what letterspacing you want in a layout. If you're thinking about increasing the letterspacing value, use kerning to apply that same value to a paragraph of text, so you can see what it looks like. (In this case, you'll need to use the tracking controls since you're working on a range of text.)

As Brad says, "I guarantee that if you do this test you will never again use a maximum [letterspacing] value of 15 percent."

Flush Zone. If you thought the Hyphenation Zone setting was obscure, you just hadn't heard about the Flush Zone yet. The Flush Zone setting does one thing, but does it very well: It determines whether the last line of a paragraph gets force justified or not.

The value you type in the field is the distance from the right margin that QuarkXPress checks. If the end of the line falls into that zone, the whole line gets justified. Of course, in many instances, you can just use the Forced Justify setting, so this feature isn't something I use much.

Single Word Justify. The Single Word Justify checkbox lets you tell QuarkXPress whether you want a word that falls on a justified line by itself to be force justified (see Figure 6-43). Newspapers will probably leave this turned on. Art directors of fancy foreign magazines might insist that it get turned off. Personally, I don't like how the word looks either way, and I'd just as soon have the sentence rewritten, or play with other character formatting to reflow the paragraph. This feature doesn't apply to the last line of a paragraph—you see it's effect on lines within a paragraph, often when wrapping around an image. In those cases, you still need to use the Flush Zone or force justify to get those lines to justify.

Quietly, he stalked over to the celery and nibbled gently at it's greens. "Oh, you taste so good," he mumbled through the fibrous vegetable.

A knock at the door! Quickly stuffing the long, slender, store-bought foodstuff into a drawer, he sprung blithely to receive his visitor, only to be greeted by thirty-six thousand members of the feared Fruit-and-Vegetablist Majority. He knew he was in trouble now.

"We know you've been objectifying vegetables again, Mr. Harwood. And we've come to put a

Quietly, he stalked over to the celery and nibbled gently at it's greens. "Oh, you taste so good," he mumbled through the fibrous vegetable.

A knock at the door! Quickly stuffing the long, slender, store-bought foodstuff into a drawer, he sprung blithely to receive his visitor, only to be greeted by thirty-six thousand members of the feared Fruit-and-Vegetablist Majority. He knew he was in trouble now.

"We know you've been objectifying vegetables again, Mr. Harwood. And we've come to put a

In the example on the right, Single Word Justify is off. Note the phrase "Fruit-and-Vegetablist."

Figure 6-43
Single Word Justify

Forced Justification

Speaking of justification, when you select Forced for the alignment, QuarkXPress forces every line in a paragraph to be justified, including lines that wouldn't ordinarily extend to the margin, such as the last line of a paragraph or even a single-line paragraph. You can specify Forced by choosing it from the Alignment submenu in the Style menu, clicking its icon on the Classic or Paragraph Attributes tab of the Measurements palette, or by pressing Command-Option-Shift-J or Ctrl-Alt-Shift-J.

Forced justification has basically the same effect as creating a Hyphenation and Justification setting with a very large Flush Zone. It takes a lot of steps to define and apply such an H&J setting, however, so Quark has made it easy with the Forced mode.

Note that forced justification only works with full paragraphs, and QuarkXPress defines a full paragraph as ending with a return. Therefore, if you have a text box that has only one line in it, and that line doesn't end with a return, the program won't justify it.

SETTING YOUR OWN H&J

Different paragraphs in your layout may need different hyphenation and justification settings. For example, you may want the paragraphs in the main body of your text to hyphenate normally, and text in sidebars or headlines to remain unhyphenated. You can use QuarkXPress's H&J feature to set up multiple H&J settings to be applied later at a paragraph level.

Creating an H&J Setting

When you choose H&Js from the Edit menu (or press Command-Option-H or Ctrl-Alt-H), the H&Js dialog box appears (see Figure 6-44). You can add, delete, edit, duplicate, or append H&J settings. The list on the left side of the dialog box shows the names of all the H&J settings. A new layout has six default settings: Standard, which is the default setting for all paragraphs in the Normal style sheet, along with Narrow Measure, No Hyphenation, Titles, Very Narrow Measure, and Wide Measure. These new options, added with QuarkXPress 7, are based on settings from typesetting professionals and have fairly self-explanatory names.

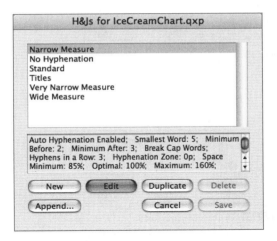

Figure 6-44
The H&Js dialog box

You can add a new H&J setting in two ways.

• Click the New button to create a new H&J setting. Change the hyphenation and justification parameters as described earlier, give the setting a name, and click OK. The Edit H&Js dialog box you see when you click New is a duplicate of the Standard setting.

• Click first on a setting (such as Standard), and then click the Duplicate button. You can edit a duplicate of the setting you first clicked on. This is helpful for basing one H&J setting on another.

Deleting and Appending H&Js

To delete an H&J setting, first click on its name, then click the Delete button. If you've applied the H&J setting to any paragraph in the layout or to a style sheet, QuarkXPress prompts you for an H&J to replace it with.

H&J settings are automatically available in all layouts within a project. However, if you have set up H&J settings in a different project, you can append them to your current project's list by clicking the Append button. (You might do this if you want to use the new QuarkXPress 7 H&Js in an older project that doesn't contain them.) After selecting the project to import from, the program lets you choose exactly which styles you want (see Figure 6-45). In case you don't know how the various H&Js are defined, QuarkXPress shows you the definitions in the Description area of the Append H&Js dialog box.

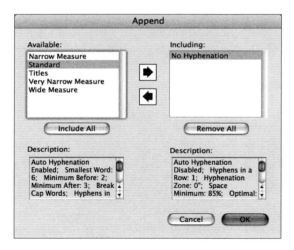

Figure 6-45
Appending H&J settings

When you click OK in the Append H&Js dialog box, QuarkXPress checks to see if any incoming H&Js have the same name as those already in your project. If it finds such a conflict (and if the definition of the H&J is different in the two projects), it displays another alert dialog box and asks you what to do (see Figure 6-46). You've got four options, each a separate button.

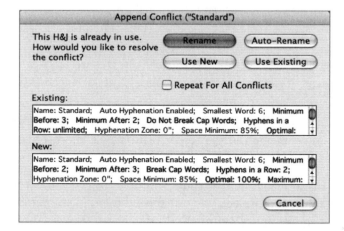

Figure 6-46
Conflicting H&J settings

- **Rename.** You get to manually rename the H&J that's being imported with any other unused name.

- **Auto-Rename.** Automatically renames the incoming H&J with an asterisk at the beginning of its name. I'm sure there's a good reason for this option, but I've never figured it out.

- **Use New.** The incoming H&J setting overwrites the one already in the project. I usually use either this option or Rename.

- **Use Existing.** This is the same as cancelling the appending of the H&J; the old one (the one currently in the project) is retained and used. The only time you'd use this is if you didn't realize that there was a duplicate when you chose to append the H&J setting.

If you think there's going to be more than one conflicting style name, you may want to turn on the box marked Repeat For All Conflicts. This way, QuarkXPress handles the remaining conflicts in the same way.

Of course, remember that there is also an Append feature on the File menu that you can use to import style sheets, colors, H&Js, and more at the same time. If you need to import both style sheets and colors, for instance, it's clearly more efficient to do it with Append instead of in the Style Sheets dialog box.

> **Tip: Copying H&Js with Copy and Paste.** *There's another way to move an H&J setting from one project to another: Copy and paste a text box that contains a paragraph tagged with that H&J setting. However, if you move a setting this way, QuarkXPress won't do the same-name check described above. If there are differences between two H&J settings with the same name, the imported settings are just ignored (same as if you select Use Existing H&J).*

Applying an H&J Setting

Once you have created more than one H&J setting, you can choose which setting to use on a paragraph level by using the Formats tab of the Paragraph Attributes dialog box. With the cursor in a paragraph or with multiple paragraphs selected, you can select an H&J setting from the popup menu in the Formats tab (see Figure 6-47). You can also set the H&J setting in a style sheet (I talk more about Style Sheets in Chapter 7, *Copy Flow*).

> **Tip: Tighter and Looser H&Js.** *Depending on the job I'm working on, I may have four or five different H&J settings in my project. Here are a few besides Standard that I often make myself and use.*

- **Tighter.** This setting is the same as my Standard H&J, but with slightly smaller wordspacing and letterspacing values.

- **Looser.** Similar to Standard, but with slightly larger wordspacing and letterspacing values.

- **Heads.** I'll turn off Auto Hyphenation in this H&J setting and set the wordspacing tight, perhaps even to 75 percent. Quark apparently likes this idea because QuarkXPress 7 ships with "Titles," an H&J with similar attributes.

- **No Hyphenation.** I'll usually have one H&J setting that is the same as Standard, but where Auto Hyphenation is turned off. This is the setting I use for subheads, for instance. You can use the No Hyphenation that Quark provides and adjust its Justification settings as necessary.

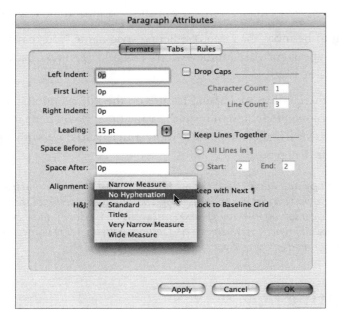

Figure 6-47
Applying an H&J setting

One of the most important things to remember when you're fooling around with these settings is the color of the page. If setting a tighter H&J makes one text block look noticeably darker than the rest of the page, you may need to manually alter the paragraph using tracking or kerning rather than let the H&J settings do it for you.

> *Tip: Pseudo Insert Space with H&Js.* Let's say you've got three words on a line. You want the first word to be flush left, the third word to be flush right, and you want equal space between each of these and the word in the middle (see Figure 6-48). You can do this by using forced justification and adjusting the H&J settings.

Here, no letterspacing is allowed, and a fixed-width space sits between the first two words.

The H&J setting is set so that no letterspacing can occur.

Figure 6-48 Inserting equal space between words

1. Create a new H&J setting called something mnemonic like "InsertSpace."

2. Make sure the letterspacing (labeled "Char") fields in the Justification Method area of the Edit H&Js dialog box are all set to zero. That means that QuarkXPress won't add extra space between any characters in the paragraph, only between words. You might need to increase the values in the wordspacing (labeled "Space") fields as well.

3. Save this new H&J setting.

4. Use the Formats tab of the Paragraph Attributes dialog box (Command/Ctrl-Shift-F) to apply both the InsertSpace H&J setting and Forced alignment to the paragraph.

The paragraph should now be spread across the text box with an equal amount of space between each word. If you want a normal word space between two words, use a punctuation space or a flexible space (both of which you can enter from the Insert Character submenu of the Utilities menu) instead of a normal spaceband.

> **Tip: Find/Change H&J settings.** *There's just no way to find and replace H&J settings throughout a layout. Or is there? Let's say someone was working on your layout and applied an H&J setting called "Really Tight" to paragraphs when you weren't looking. You want to clear this setting out. The trick is to select the setting you want to get rid of in the H&Js dialog box (in this case, choose Really Tight) and click the Delete button. QuarkXPress asks you which H&J to apply in its place. When you delete Really Tight from the H&J list, you can replace it with Standard, or something else. This effectively searches and replaces throughout the project: Everywhere the Really Tight setting was applied, it gets changed to something else.*

If you know you're going to need the H&J setting later, make sure you make a duplicate of it in the project or copy it into another project before you delete it!

WIDOW AND ORPHAN CONTROL

I mean no disrespect to widows and orphans, but when it comes to typesetting, we must carefully control them, stamping out their very existence when we have the chance.

If you know what I'm talking about already, bear with me, or skip this paragraph (or test whether you can remember which is the widow and which is the orphan). A *widow* is the last line of a paragraph that winds up all by itself at the top of a column or page. An *orphan* is the first line of a paragraph that lands all by itself at the bottom of a column or page. I like the following mnemonic device: "widows" sounds like "windows," which are high up (top of the page), whereas "orphans" makes me think of tiny Oliver (who was small, and thus, at the bottom of the page).

Typesetters sometimes also refer to the single-word last line of a paragraph as either a widow or an orphan. To avoid the confusion, in my office I prefer to use the word *runt*.

All typographic widows and orphans are bad, but certain kinds are really bad—for example, a widow line that consists of only one word, or even the last part of a hyphenated word. Another related typographic horror is the subhead that stands alone with its following paragraph on the next page.

Fortunately, QuarkXPress has a set of controls that can easily prevent widows and orphans from sneaking into your layout. The controls are the Keep With Next ¶ and Keep Lines Together features, and you can find them in the Paragraph Attributes dialog box (Command/Ctrl-Shift-F). Let's look at each of these.

Keep With Next ¶

The Keep With Next ¶ feature is perfect for ensuring that headings and the paragraphs that follow them are always kept together. If the paragraph is pushed onto a new column, a new page, or below an obstructing object, the heading follows right along (see Figure 6-49).

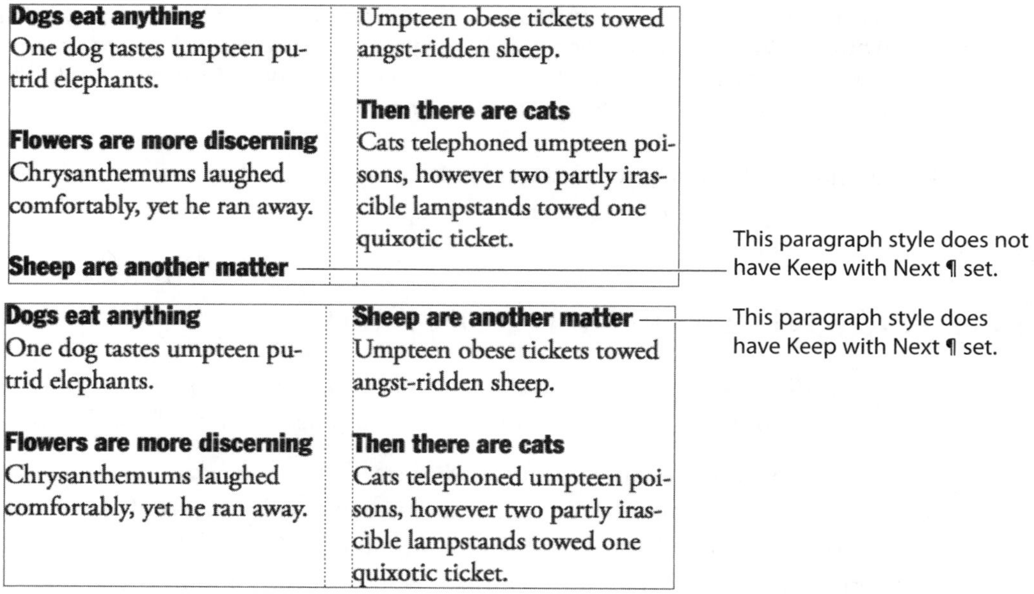

Dogs eat anything
One dog tastes umpteen putrid elephants.

Flowers are more discerning
Chrysanthemums laughed comfortably, yet he ran away.

Sheep are another matter

Umpteen obese tickets towed angst-ridden sheep.

Then there are cats
Cats telephoned umpteen poisons, however two partly irascible lampstands towed one quixotic ticket.

This paragraph style does not have Keep with Next ¶ set.

Dogs eat anything
One dog tastes umpteen putrid elephants.

Flowers are more discerning
Chrysanthemums laughed comfortably, yet he ran away.

Sheep are another matter
Umpteen obese tickets towed angst-ridden sheep.

Then there are cats
Cats telephoned umpteen poisons, however two partly irascible lampstands towed one quixotic ticket.

This paragraph style does have Keep with Next ¶ set.

Figure 6-49 Keep with Next ¶

You may want to keep paragraphs together even when there are no subheads. For example, entries in a table or list that shouldn't be broken could each be set to Keep With Next ¶. In some earlier versions of QuarkXPress, the program would keep only two paragraphs together at a time; fortunately, that's changed, and you can keep a number of paragraphs together with this feature.

Keep Lines Together

The Keep Lines Together feature is the primary control over widows and orphans. When you turn on Keep Lines Together in the Paragraph Attributes dialog box, QuarkXPress expands the dialog box to give you control parameters in this area (see Figure 6-50). Let's look at these controls one at a time.

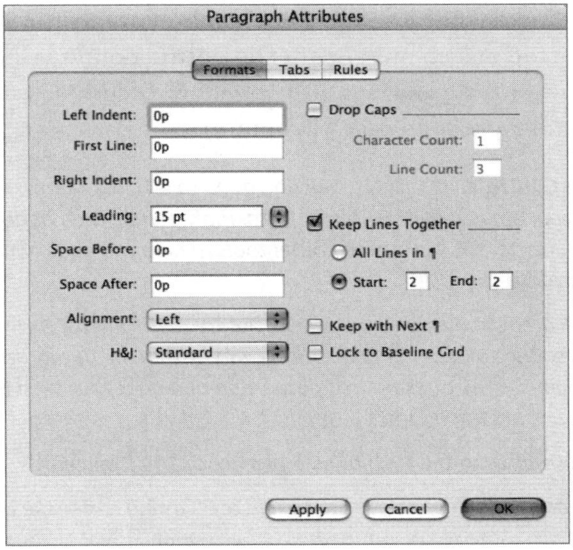

Figure 6-50
Keep Lines Together

All Lines In ¶. You can keep every line in a paragraph together by turning on All Lines In ¶. For example, if a paragraph spans two pages, enabling All Lines In ¶ results in that entire paragraph being pushed onto the next page to keep it together.

It's easy to confound a computer. Do you remember that Star Trek episode in which a man forced a computer to commit suicide by instructing it to perform contradictory functions? Fortunately, QuarkXPress won't cause your Mac or PC to blow up if you specify All Lines In ¶ for a text block larger than your column. In cases like this, QuarkXPress simply pushes the whole paragraph out of the text box. (I've seen cases where people freak out because their text has disappeared, only to find out later that they had turned on both All Lines in ¶ and Keep with Next ¶ for every paragraph.)

Start. You don't have to specify that all the lines in a paragraph should be kept together. Instead, you can control the number of lines that should be kept together at the beginning and end of the paragraph.

The value you type in the Start field determines the minimum number of lines that QuarkXPress allows at the beginning of a paragraph. For example, specifying a two-line Start value causes paragraphs that fall at the end of a page to keep at least two lines on the first page before it breaks. If at least two lines of that paragraph cannot be placed on the page, then the entire paragraph is pushed over to the next page.

The Start feature is set up to eliminate orphans in your layouts. If you don't want any single lines sitting at the bottom of a page, you can specify a value of 2 for the Start control (some designers insist that even two lines alone at the bottom of a page are ugly and may want to adjust the Start value to 3 or greater).

End. The value specified in the End field determines the minimum number of lines that QuarkXPress lets fall alone at the top of a column or after an obstruction. A value of 2 or greater rids you of unwanted widowed paragraphs (if a widow occurs, QuarkXPress "pulls" a line off the first page onto the second page or column).

> **Tip: Other Widow and Orphan Controls.** It's all very well and good to let QuarkXPress avoid widows, orphans, and runts for you, but you still need to painstakingly peruse each page of most layouts, making adjustments as you go. You have many other tools to help you avoid widows and orphans. Here are some of my favorites.
>
> - Adjust tracking by a very small amount over a range of text, but try to do at least a whole paragraph or a few complete lines so the color of the type doesn't vary within the paragraph. Often, nobody can tell if you've applied -.5 or -1 tracking to a paragraph or a page, but such tracking might be enough to pull back a widow or a runt.
>
> - Adjust horizontal scaling by a small amount, such as 99.5 percent or 100.5 percent.
>
> - Make sure Auto Hyphenation and Auto Kern Above are turned on. Kerning can make a load of difference over a large area of text. Auto Hyphenation has to be changed in all of your H&Js, while Auto Kern Above affects the entire layout.
>
> - Change your H&J's wordspacing to a smaller Optimal setting. If it's at 100 percent, try 98 percent. Of course, this changes every paragraph tagged with that H&J setting throughout your layout.
>
> - Try different hyphenation and justification settings on problem paragraphs. You might apply a tighter or a looser setting for one paragraph, for instance, or allow more hyphens in a row.
>
> If none of these work for you, don't forget you can always just rewrite a sentence or two (if it's yours to rewrite). A quick rewrite can fix up just about any problem.

BASELINE GRID

In typography, the smallest change can make the biggest difference in a piece's impact. For example, look at a high-quality magazine page that has multiple columns. Chances are that each line of text has a common baseline with the text in the next column. Now look at a crummy newsletter. Place a rule across a page and you'll see lines of text all over the place. What's missing is an underlying grid. QuarkXPress's Baseline Grid feature lets you create a grid and lock each line of text to it. Nonetheless, while this is a powerful feature, I tend not to use it much; I'll explain why in a moment.

Each layout has its own Baseline Grid setting, which is pervasive throughout every page. However, whether a block of text actually locks to that grid is determined on a paragraph level.

Setting up the grid. QuarkXPress is clueless about your leading grid, so you need to set this up yourself. You can set the Baseline Grid value for the layout on the Paragraph tab in the Preferences dialog box. You have two controls over the Baseline Grid: the Start value and the Increment value. The Start value determines where this grid begins, measured from the top of the page. Set it to start at the first baseline of your body copy.

The Increment value determines the distance from one horizontal grid line to the next. Generally, this value is the same as the leading in the majority of your body copy. For example, if your body copy has a leading of 13 points, then you should type "13pt" as your Increment value. However, sometimes it's better to use half the body copy's leading; in this example, you might use a 6.5-point grid.

Assigning a baseline grid. To lock each line of a paragraph to the baseline grid that you have established, turn on the Lock to Baseline Grid checkbox in the Formats tab of the Paragraph Attributes dialog box (Command/Ctrl-Shift-F). You'll also find this checkbox on the left side of the Paragraph Attributes tab of the Measurements palette—look for the cute lock icon with the underlined letter A's. Note that the baseline grid overrides paragraph leading. That is, if your paragraph has a leading of 10 points, when you enable Lock to Baseline Grid each line snaps to the Increment value (13 points, in the preceding example). If your paragraph has a leading larger than the Increment value, each line snaps to the next grid value. In other words, your leading never gets tighter, but it can get pretty dang loose. If your Increment value is 13 points and your leading is 14 points, each line snaps to the following grid line, resulting in 26-point leading (see Figure 6-51).

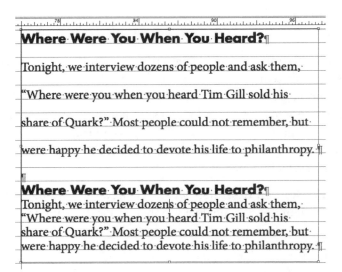

With a 13-point Baseline Grid, type with 14-point leading locked to the grid gets bumped to the next grid increment.

But 13-point leading on a 13-point grid works perfectly.

Figure 6-51 Lock to Baseline Grid

Showing the grid. The baseline grid in QuarkXPress is usually invisible, so sometimes it's difficult to understand why text is sticking to weird baselines. However, you can see this underlying grid by selecting Baseline Grid from the View menu (or by pressing Option-F7 on Mac OS or Ctrl-F7 on Windows). If you don't like the color of the baseline grid, you can set it to whatever you want in the Display tab of the Preferences dialog box (Command-Option-Shift-Y or Ctrl-Alt-Shift-Y).

Note that the baseline-grid guides you see when Baseline Grid is turned on in the View menu act just like ruler guides. They follow the Guides control in the Preferences dialog box as to whether they appear in front of or behind page items. And when Snap to Guides is turned on, page items snap to the baseline grid guides (when they're showing).

> **Tip: Why I Rarely Use Lock to Baseline Grid.** There is no doubt that a careful study and practice of baseline grids can make your layout better looking. However, as I said earlier, I rarely use the Lock to Baseline Grid feature. The reason: you can get the same quality simply from being careful with your leading and text box placement. The key is to work with multiples of your leading grid.

For example, if your body text has 15-point leading, then make sure your headlines and subheads also have 15- or 30-point leading. If you use Space Before or Space After, make sure those values are set only to 15, 30, or 45 points (or some other multiple of 15). Paragraphs in a list might have 7.5 points of space (half of 15) between them, and as long as there are always an even number of list items, the paragraphs after the list will always end up sitting right on the leading grid.

This might seem really limiting, but it's actually easier than using Lock to Baseline Grid. As long as you pay attention to the values for Leading, Space Before, and Space After, as well as turn on Maintain Leading (see the next section), you're pretty much assured that your baselines will align across columns and that your pages will look beautiful. Of course, it's always good to proof them, just in case.

Maintain Leading

If you don't use baseline grids, but still want to maintain consistent leading on your page, you might want to look closely at the Maintain Leading feature. This feature—which I usually just leave turned on in the Paragraph tab of the Preferences dialog box—ensures that each line in a text box is placed according to its leading value when another object (such as a picture box or a line) obstructs the text and moves text lines around.

When Maintain Leading is turned off, two things happen. First, the line of text following an obstruction abuts the bottom of that obstruction (or its text runaround, if the runaround value is larger than zero points; I talk about text runaround in Chapter 12, *Text Meets Graphics*). Second, the rest of the lines of text in that text box fall on a different leading grid than those above the obstruction do. This is much easier to see than to read (or write) about, so check out Figure 6-52. This feature has no effect on paragraphs that are already set to Lock to Baseline Grid.

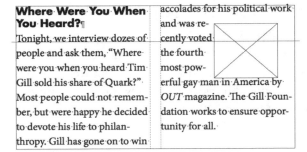

Here, Maintain Leading is turned off; the baselines don't match across columns.

Here, Maintain Leading is turned on and the columns align.

Figure 6-52
Maintain Leading

FINE-TUNING TYPE

Almost everything I've talked about in this chapter has been at a character or paragraph level. Here I'm going to talk about making typographic adjustments on a layout level. You have control over several areas at a layout level, including how traditional (non OpenType) superscript, subscript, superior, and small-caps characters are "built"; which words will hyphenate; and how QuarkXPress deals with ligatures, accents, and special spaces. You can also create custom automatic tracking and kerning tables, and run through an automatic check for typographic problem areas.

Let's look at how you can use these controls in your layouts.

Typographic Preferences

The Preferences dialog box (see Chapter 2, *QuarkXPress Basics*) lets you control the way QuarkXPress handles a number of its typographic features: superscript, subscript, superior, and small-caps characters; hyphenation, kerning, em spaces, baseline grid, leading, ligatures, and foreign-language accents. Here's a run-down of all the different features in this dialog box, what they do, or where you can find information about them elsewhere in this book.

Remember that if you change items in the Print Layout section of the Preferences dialog box with no projects open, the defaults are changed for every new layout you create from then on. And remember that all of the following are layout-wide preferences; you can't specify them for a particular story or paragraph. Note that if you're using sophisticated OpenType fonts, you may have other options for settings such as Superior and Ligatures; in that case, these preferences will not apply.

Superscript and Subscript. Few people ever bother to get into the nitty-gritty of changing the way the Superscript and Subscript type styles look, but the controls are on the Character tab in the Preferences dialog box if you ever want them. Both the Superscript and the Subscript controls are the same: Offset, VScale, and HScale. Some people try to fiddle with these values in order to make fractions; this is possible, but I recommend other fraction-making techniques instead (see "Typographic Special Effects," later in this chapter).

- **Offset.** You can determine how far from the baseline your superscript or subscript characters should move by altering the Offset amount. You specify Offset as a percentage of the text size. For example, if the offset for Subscript were set to 50 percent, then a subscript character would move 9 points down for 18-point type. You can specify any amount between one and 100 percent.

- **VScale and HScale.** These terms are short for "vertical scale" and "horizontal scale," which are responsible for how tall and wide the superscript or subscript text is. The controls default to 100 percent, which I find much too large. I generally set both to a value between 70 and 80 percent, so that a superscript or subscript character doesn't stand out too much against the rest of the text. Here, too, you can set the value to anything between one and 100 percent.

Superior. You don't have to worry about the offset for superior characters because they are automatically set to be vertically flush with the cap height of that font. So the only modifications you can make here are to the vertical and horizontal scaling of the character. This is clearly an area of aesthetic choice. I tend to like the 50-percent default that QuarkXPress gives us; some people like to make the HScale slightly larger, such as 55 percent, so that the character has a little more weight.

Small Caps. You can also change the vertical and horizontal scaling of all characters set in the Small Caps character style in a layout. Though I think it would be nice to be able to set the characteristics of small caps on the character, paragraph, or story level, these layout-wide controls are usually good enough.

There are times when adjustable (or "fake") small caps are even better than traditional (or "true") small caps, such as those found in expert fonts. For example, I know a designer who recently specified that all small caps in a book's body copy should be 8.5 points tall. The body text was 10-point Palatino, so the company producing the templates just changed the small-caps specifications to 85 percent in the horizontal direction (85 percent of 10-point type is 8.5-point type) and 90 percent in the vertical direction (making the characters slightly wider gives a slightly heavier—although stretched—look). A traditional small cap would not achieve this effect; however, it would probably keep the type color in the paragraph more consistent. (If you make a change like this, make sure it gets made in all the layouts and projects that make up the publication, or you'll end up with inconsistencies.)

Ligatures. I'll discuss ligatures later in this chapter in "Special Characters." My recommendation: Turn it on.

Auto Kern Above. Auto Kern Above was discussed in the "Automatic" section of "Kerning and Tracking," earlier in this chapter. This is usually set to 4 points, which is very reasonable. (If you see a value higher than 4 here, you should probably lower it.) There's also a project-wide kerning preference called Use OpenType Kerning in the General tab under Project; that was covered in "Kerning and Tracking" as well.

Standard Em Space. Refer back to "Tip: Know Your Ems and Ens," in the "Kerning and Tracking" section. The low-down: I like to turn this on.

Flex Space Width. See Table 6.7, "Formatting Characters" in the "Special Characters" section, later in the chapter, for an explanation of this feature.

Accents for All Caps. This typographic refinement lets you specify whether accented lowercase characters keep their accents when you apply the All Caps character style to them. If this feature is turned on and you apply All Caps to the characters å, ë, ì, ó, û, QuarkXPress will give you Å, Ë, Ì, Ó, Û rather than A, E, I, O, U. Depending on the design of your layout or what language you're working in, you may want to turn this feature on or off. (If you enter an actual capital letter with an accent mark from the Glyphs palette or using a keyboard command, this feature does not apply. It only works with text formatted with All Caps.)

Leading Preferences. I talked about each of the Leading preferences earlier in this chapter. Leading Mode and Auto Leading were discussed in the section called "Leading" (you should always leave Leading Mode set to Typesetting). The Maintain Leading feature was discussed in the "Baseline Grid" section, where I said to just leave this setting turned on.

Baseline Grid. I wrote a whole section called "Baseline Grid" earlier in this chapter; check that out.

Hyphenation Method. I explore hyphenation methods a little later in the chapter, in "Tweaking Hyphenation." But I can give the rundown now: just leave this set to Enhanced or Expanded (there's almost no reason to change it to Standard).

OpenType Styles

QuarkXPress 7 introduces a whole new category of type styles for fine-tuning—OpenType styles. These let you do some really fancy fine-tuning such as automatically adding ordinals (as in 1st), creating really beautiful fractions, and swapping out character pairs for really gorgeous ligatures. The trick is that those features need to be built into the OpenType font itself by the type designer. Then QuarkXPress simply gives you access to those features. If it sounds complicated, well, it is.

Choosing an OpenType font. To take advantage of these styles, you first need an OpenType font that offers them. Many OpenType fonts are simply "ports"—PostScript fonts converted to OpenType fonts with no additional features. However, sophisticated OpenType expert families offer many OpenType features (although it's hard to find a single font that actually offers all of them). You can see which features are available in the font in QuarkXPress—just apply the font to text and open the Character Attributes dialog box from the Style menu. Click the OpenType triangle to display the styles. The ones that are available (not grayed out) can be applied to this font. You can also see OpenType options in the Glyphs palette, because that's all these styles are. QuarkXPress actually swaps in different glyphs (representations of characters) for the characters in the text rather than reformatting the text itself.

Anyway, if you want to know what's in a font *before* you buy it, check with the font vendor. The Linotype Web site (Figure 6-53) does a great job of showing you what's available for each font, including a character map of each. Zapfino Extra LTX Pro is chock-full of OpenType features if you want to check one out.

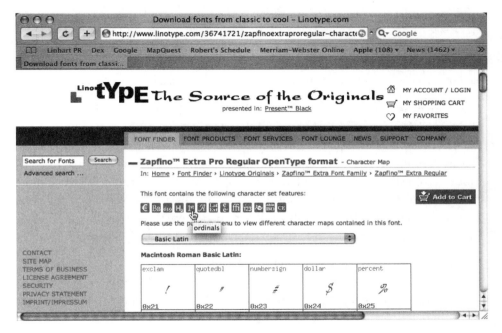

Figure 6-53 The Linotype Web site shows all the OpenType options available in a font.

Applying OpenType styles. Once you determine that a font has OpenType styles you want to try out, you can apply them from the same areas you apply other character type styles—except they're a little more hidden. In the Character Attributes dialog box under the Style menu, you need to click the triangle next to OpenType to see what's available for the font and then turn on the boxes for any styles you want to apply. (You can Find/Change OpenType styles in this same manner—click the triangle next to OpenType on the Find/Change palette.) You can also use the OpenType popup menu on the Classic tab and the Character Attributes tabs of the Measurements palette. It looks like a black and green "O" and sits next to the Size field (Figure 6-54). Any styles not available for the current font are displayed in brackets.

Figure 6-54 Applying OpenType styles; the top sample has Standard Ligatures and the bottom sample has both Standard and Discretionary Ligatures. Both have Contextual Alternates applied as well.

In Figure 6-54, you see text in Zapfino Extra LTX Pro first with Standard Ligatures and Contextual Alternates applied (top) and then Discretionary Ligatures added as well. As you can see, many character pairs were substituted with a fancier version—such as the "rd" on "Heard." Note that the temptation is to just turn on everything available in an OpenType font to take full advantage of the features, right? Well, unfortunately, you shouldn't really do that or you'll end up with a lot of wacky spacing issues. You can't, for example, just apply the Fractions style willy-nilly to all your body text. You just apply it where you actually have fractions. You can, however, pretty safely turn on Standard Ligatures if they're available.

You can read about OpenType fonts and styles at length on the Adobe Web site and through other resources. But all I really have to say about this is if you need a special effect, make sure you're buying a font that has that style and then apply it to only that text.

KERNING AND TRACKING TABLES

As I noted earlier in this chapter, most fonts include built-in kerning tables of 100 to 500 pairs. However, you can modify these pairs or add your own by using Quark's Kern/Track Editor XTension (it comes with QuarkXPress, though you have an option not to install it when you update or install QuarkXPress). Like all XTensions, you must make sure that this XTension is located in the XTension folder in order for it to work.

Modifying tracking and kerning tables is different from many of QuarkXPress's typographic controls in that it's font-specific. For example, if you alter the kerning table for Times Roman, the changes you make are in effect whenever you use Times Roman in any QuarkXPress project. However, the font itself is *not* altered on disk; so the changes don't show up when you're working in any other program.

The kerning modifications you make are stored both in the QuarkXPress Preferences file and in the project itself. That means that you can give the publication file to others and the custom values will stay with the project (when they open the file, they'll be prompted to choose whether or not they want to keep your preferences).

Kerning Tables

To modify a font's kerning table, choose Kerning Table Edit from the Utilities menu. This brings up the Kerning Table Edit dialog box, which presents a scrolling list of available fonts (note that this dialog box can take a long time to appear, depending on the number of fonts you have installed). The list lets you choose the variants of each installed font (Plain, Bold, Italic, Bold Italic, and so on). If you're trying to edit an OpenType font and it doesn't display in the list, see "Tip: OpenType Kerning" in the "Kerning" section, earlier in this chapter.

You have to edit kerning tables for individual fonts. This means that you cannot edit Palatino in its Plain style and expect all the Bold, Italic, and Bold Italic variants to be altered as well (see "Tip: Quick Kerning for Families," below).

After selecting a font from the list (you can jump through the list quickly by typing the first letter of the font name you want), click Edit to move to the Edit Kerning Table dialog box, where you can edit an existing pair, add a new pair to the list, or delete a pair (see Figure 6-55). You can also import and export lists of these kerning pairs in a text-file format or in XML format. Let's look at how each of these operations is performed.

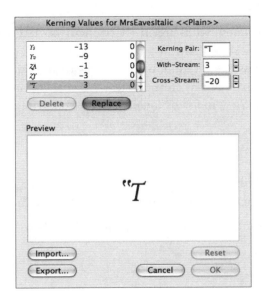

Figure 6-55
Editing a kerning pair

Adding a pair. You can add a new kerning pair to QuarkXPress's list in three steps.

1. Type the two characters in the Kerning Pair field. They appear in a preview window. If there is already a kerning value set for this pair, it appears selected in the list of kerning pairs.

2. Type a horizontal kerning amount into the With-Stream field. This value is specified in increments of $\frac{1}{200}$ of an em (see "Tip: Know Your Ems and Ens," earlier in this chapter). The preview updates as soon as you enter new values.

3. To specify a vertical kerning amount, which you might use for pairs containing punctuation, type a value in the Cross-Stream field.

4. Click the Add or Replace button.

That's all there is to it.

Editing a pair. You can adjust kerning pairs that you have created or that come predefined in the font by clicking on a pair in the Kerning Pairs table (or typing the two characters in the Pair field), and then modifying the number in the Value field. Once you have set the kern value you want, click the Replace button to add it back to the table.

Deleting or resetting a pair. If you don't like a kerning pair that you added, or you want to get rid of one that was built-in, select the pair from the list and click the Delete button (or set the kern value to zero). Unfortunately, there is no way to reset a particular pair to its original value if you don't remember what it was. You can, however, reset the entire font back to its pure, original state by clicking the Reset button (of course, you lose all the other kerning pairs that you had built along the way).

Import/Export. There are those who know with-stream (horizontal) kerning pairs so well that they'd rather just type up a mess of them in a text-editing program and then import them all at once into QuarkXPress. (You cannot import cross-stream, aka vertical, kerning information in a text file.) You can do this by creating a text-only file within any text editor (such as Microsoft Word, BBEdit, or Windows Notepad) in the following format.

1. Type the kerning pair (the two letters).

2. Type a tab.

3. Type the kerning value in QuarkXPress's kerning units ($\frac{1}{200}$ of an em). Negative numbers mean negative kerning. Then just press Return to go to the next line.

4. Save the file as a text-only file. On Windows, save the file with a .krn filename extension.

5. Switch back to the Edit Kerning Table dialog box in QuarkXPress, and click the Import button to bring this text file in.

If you want to edit the kerning values that are already built into the font, you can first export those values by clicking the Export button. Then edit them and reimport them.

To support cross-stream kerning, QuarkXPress 7 now stores kerning table information in XML format (although you can still use the old text-file method to specify only with-stream kerning). To get an idea what this looks like, you can export a font's kerning information as XML. Open the file in a text editor and you'll see something like this:

```
CharCodeFirst="A" CharCodeSecond="ä" WithStreamValue="-6"
XStreamValue="0"/><KerningPair CharCodeFirst="A" CharCodeSecond="ç"
WithStreamValue="-6" XStreamValue="0"/><KerningPair CharCodeFirst="A"
CharCodeSecond="é" WithStreamValue="-6" XStreamValue="0"/><KerningPair
```

You can replace the kerning values in the XML file or replicate the format and add your own.

> **Tip: Quick Kerning for Families.** *Applying kerning pairs to a number of faces can be very time-consuming and tiresome. You can speed up this process by using the Import feature to apply the same kerning tables to several typefaces. Once you've imported the kerning tables, you can go back and edit them to compensate for specifics of that typeface. Careful, though: The kerning values for an italic form of a typeface are going to be very different than the values for a roman form.*

> **Tip: Automatic Page Numbers Don't Kern.** *If you or the font designer has set up automatic kerning pairs for pairs of numerals, these pairs will not be kerned when they appear as automatic page numbers. QuarkXPress treats all automatic page numbers as single characters, even when they consist of multiple characters. Sadly, there's no ready fix for this one, except to use a typeface for page numbers in which the lack of automatic kerning won't cause an aesthetic headache.*

Kerning and Tracking Tables

Most fonts need to have tighter tracking applied to them in larger point sizes. You could change the tracking value for various display fonts by manually selecting the text and specifying a tracking value in the Character Attributes dialog box or Measurements palette. However, QuarkXPress makes it easier for you by letting you create custom tracking tables for each font you use.

A tracking table tells QuarkXPress how much tracking to apply at various sizes of a font. This, too, is part of the Kern/Track Editor XTension that comes with QuarkXPress.

Here's an example to illustrate this feature. Let's say you're creating a template for a new magazine. You've decided to use Futura Bold for your headers, which are at a number of different sizes. You know that your largest header is 60 points and should have -20 tracking, and the smallest header is 12 points and should have no tracking. Here's what you do.

1. Select Tracking Edit from the Utilities menu.

2. Choose the font that you want to edit—in this case Futura Bold—and click the Edit button. If QuarkXPress recognizes the family as "merged," then it only shows you one family name rather than breaking it down into separate fonts. For instance, it shows you one Palatino selection rather than four Palatino fonts: roman, italic, bold, and bold italic. If the individual fonts are merged into one, the tracking gets applied to every font in the family. In font families that are not merged, you have to create tracking settings for each style variation—for example, one tracking table for "Bodoni," another for "B Bodoni Bold," and so on.

3. You see the Edit Tracking dialog box (Figure 6-56). The vertical axis represents tracking values from -100 to 100 in increments of $\frac{1}{200}$ of an em. The horizontal axis represents type sizes from 2 to 250 points; the farther to the right on the grid, the larger the type size is. The default setting is a horizontal bar at the zero-tracking level. In other words, all point sizes start out with a tracking value of zero.

4. Click on the line at the 2-point size (on the far left). As you hold down the mouse button, you can see the graph values shown in the dialog box. Note that clicking on the graph places a new point on it. You can have up to four corner points on each graph. This first point I've added is the anchor at the zero-tracking level.

5. Click on the line at the 60-point size and drag the graph line down to the -20 tracking level. If I saved this now, then whenever you used Futura Bold, all sizes larger than 2 points would have negative tracking applied to them.

6. You can add a third control handle at the 12-point type size and set it to zero tracking. Now all type larger than 12 points has tracking applied; as the text gets larger, more and more tracking is applied.

To save your changes, click OK. Then if you're done with your tracking-table edits, click Save.

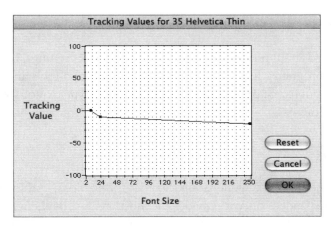

Figure 6-56
A tracking table graph

While editing a font's tracking table, you can start over by clicking the Reset button. You can always go back (even after you've saved) and click the Reset button to get the horizontal bar graph back.

Note that these tracking values are only applied to a font when Auto Kern Above is turned on. In fact, the tracking tables only apply to font sizes above the automatic-kerning limit that has been entered in the Auto Kern Above value field in the Preferences dialog box.

Like custom kerning, custom tracking is stored in your project as well as in your XPress Preferences file. So if you give one of your files with custom tracking to another person, they'll get an alert message when they open the project asking whether or not they want to retain the settings for tracking, kerning, and other customized values. As long as they click the Keep Project Settings button, the text in the file will be spaced exactly as it was on your system.

> **Tip: Cleaning out Custom Settings.** *Because all your custom kerning and tracking tables are saved in the XPress Preferences file, you can "clean out" your system, ridding yourself of every edit you've made, by deleting this file and relaunching QuarkXPress (the program creates a fresh new preferences file if it doesn't find one at launch time). This removes other settings you've made, too, such as application-wide preferences and Suggested Hyphenation.*

> **Tip: Changing Custom Kerning and Tracking Settings.** *Perhaps you have different clients that prefer different sets of custom kerning and tracking tables. No problem. You can create a new XPress Preferences file for each client and hide each one in a separate folder or directory. When you want to switch from one to the other, just quit QuarkXPress, move the current XPress Preferences file into its folder, and replace it with the new one. Relaunch QuarkXPress, and you're set.*

TWEAKING HYPHENATION

Earlier in this chapter, I talked about how to create, edit, and apply H&J settings. However, you can also fine-tune the program's hyphenation in a project with two tools and a preference: Hyphenation Exceptions, Suggested Hyphenation, and Hyphenation Method. Let's look briefly at each of these.

Hyphenation Method

QuarkXPress offers three methods for hyphenation: Standard, Enhanced, and Expanded. Generally, you should use Expanded, since it provides the most accurate hyphenation. The Hyphenation Method is a layout-wide preference, and Expanded is the default. The only reason to change it is to match the hyphenation created in really, really old versions of QuarkXPress. Although I see very little reason to make this change, the settings mean the following:

- Standard is the algorithm (rules) used prior to QuarkXPress 3.0; some words didn't break properly and you could get odd hyphenation.

- Enhanced, from versions 3.0–3.3, used an improved, but still-not-perfect algorithm.

- Expanded, introduced at 4.0 and still in use, adds a small built-in hyphenation dictionary to the Enhanced algorithm.

The algorithm basically looks at word length, letter patterns, and more to try to figure out where to insert hyphens. The hyphenation dictionary is a list that specifies the "proper" hyphenation of words that the algorithm tended to mess up. I say "proper" because hyphenation is almost entirely subjective. What you think is right, someone else may think is wrong. If you're not sure, ask an editor or buy a hyphenation dictionary.

Suggested Hyphenation

The entire life's work of the Suggested Hyphenation feature is to help you figure out how QuarkXPress is going to hyphenate a word. First, select a word (or put the cursor somewhere within or immediately to the right of a word). Next, choose Suggested Hyphenation from the Utilities menu (or press Command/Ctrl-H), and the program shows you how it would hyphenate that word (see Figure 6-57).

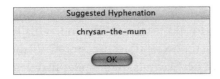

Figure 6-57
Suggested Hyphenation

All the algorithms that QuarkXPress uses to hyphenate words take into account the parameters set within the H&J currently applied to the text (such as the number of entries in Break Capitalized Words, Minimum Before, and so on). For example, when Minimum Before is set to 3, the word "answer" does not appear hyphenated in the Suggested Hyphenation dialog box. However, if you change Minimum Before to 2, it does.

Hyphenation Exceptions

If you don't like the way QuarkXPress is hyphenating a word, you can override the program's algorithms by setting your own specific hyphenation in the Hyphenation Exceptions dialog box, which you access by selecting Hyphenation Exceptions from the Utilities menu. (Another way to override hyphenation is to use a discretionary hyphen, which I'll discuss in "Special Characters," later in this chapter.)

The first time you open the dialog box, the list is empty. To add a word, just type it in the available space, including hyphens where you want them. If you don't want a word to hyphenate at all, just don't put any hyphens in it (see Figure 6-58).

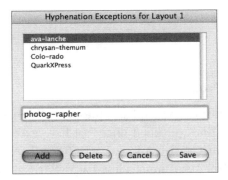

Figure 6-58
Hyphenation Exceptions

Once you've created some hyphenation exceptions, you can edit one of them by clicking on it, making the necessary change, and then clicking the Replace button (note that the Add button changes to a Replace button in this case). You can also delete an item on the list by selecting it and clicking the Delete button.

Hyphenation exceptions are stored with each layout in a project, and if you want the same exception in more than one layout you'll have to add it to each one individually. (If you edit this list while no projects are open, then the exceptions are stored in the XPress Preferences file and get applied to all subsequent new layouts. Remember that if you set up a lot of hyphenation exceptions, you should keep a backup of your XPress Preferences file.)

Tip: Watch Those Hyphens. There's nothing like giving your layout a good once-over before you print it out. One of the things you want to look for is a badly hyphenated word. Remember that QuarkXPress generally uses an algorithm to hyphenate words, and it doesn't always do it right. For example, QuarkXPress hyphenates the word "Transeurope" as "Transeur-ope" rather than "Trans-europe." If you find these problem words, you can either change them manually (by adding discretionary hyphens), or make a global change using Hyphenation Exceptions.

Tip: Line Check. I can remember the day—no, days—when my final task before taking a 530-page book to the service bureau was to scroll laboriously though my QuarkXPress files, looking for and fixing any widows, orphans, and badly hyphenated words. Of course, each fix caused a reflow of all the text that followed, and so required more checking. Would that I'd had Quark's free Type Tricks XTension, which adds a feature called Line Check to the Utilities menu. This handy feature automatically searches for typographically undesirable lines (see Figure 6-59).

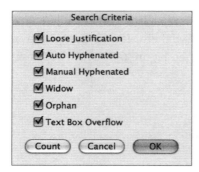

Figure 6-59
Line Check is part of the
Type Tricks XTension

Line Check searches through a layout looking for widows, orphans, automatically hyphenated words, manually hyphenated words, "loose" lines (justified lines that have exceeded the boundaries of the H&J settings), and text boxes that have overflowed. It won't fix them for you, but it sure does make cleaning up layouts at the last minute a less-harrowing experience.

At first, I typically deselect all boxes, and then choose Search Criteria from the Line Check submenu. Then I click the Count button (in the Search Criteria dialog box) to find how many instances of each "infraction" occur throughout the layout. If I see that there are overflowed text boxes or orphans or widows or whatever, I start searching through the layout for them. Unfortunately, there's no way to jump from this dialog box to each instance;

you can, however, place the cursor in a text box and select First Line from the Line Check submenu. If any instance of an orphan or widow (or whatever else you're looking for) occurs in that story, QuarkXPress highlights it. Then, to keep checking the story, select Next Line (or press Command/Ctrl-;).

Special Characters

If you're just using QuarkXPress to type letters to your Uncle Neil, you probably don't need this section. If you're doing just about anything else with it, stand by.

When you look at your computer keyboard, you see between 50 and 100 characters represented on the keys. What you don't see are the hundreds of special characters you can access with just a few keystrokes. In this section I'll look at some of those characters, including invisible "utility" characters, dingbats, math symbols, and special punctuation. By no means do you have to memorize most of these; instead, when you're actually working on layouts, you can refer to the tables I've included in this section or use the handy Glyphs palette, which puts most special characters a click away.

Invisible Characters

The first set of characters we'll look at are invisible characters that are used for special formatting in your layout. Many of these characters are visible when Invisibles is turned on in the View menu (you can also toggle them on and off by pressing Command/Ctrl-I). Let's take a look at what these characters are (see Table 6-7 for more information on these characters).

Tip: Quark Invisibles Font. QuarkXPress 7 ships with a font called Quark Invisibles. This font contains all the invisible characters and is used to display them onscreen. Quark Invisibles is automatically installed and activated through your system. However, if you move all your fonts to a font manager, you need to locate and activate this font so it's available for QuarkXPress to use.

Tip: Insert Special Characters Submenu. You may not use all these special characters enough to memorize them, or even want to bother to look them up. That's where the new Insert Characters command in the Utilities menu comes in. You'll find options for entering a Discretionary Hyphen, Nonbreaking Hyphen, and more.

Table 6-7 Invisible formatting characters

Invisible	Name	Mac OS	Windows
¶	Carriage Return	Return	Enter
↵	New Line	Shift-Return	Shift-Enter
	Discretionary New Line	Command-Return	Ctrl-Enter
⊡	Tab	Tab	Tab
⦙	Indent Here	Command-\	Ctrl-\
↓	New Column	Enter (keypad)	Enter (keypad)
⇟	New Box	Shift-Enter (keypad)	Shift-Enter (keypad)
⁃	Discretionary Hyphen	Command-Hyphen	Ctrl-Hyphen
—	Nonbreaking Hyphen	Command- =	Ctrl- =
·	Space		
∵	Nonbreaking Space	Command-Space	Ctrl-5
⫶	Zero Width Space		
∴	Word Joiner		
⎮	Hair Space		
⊢	Nonbreaking Hair Space		
⎪	Thin Space		
⊦	Nonbreaking Thin Space		
⊡	Six-per-Em Space		
⦙	Nonbreaking Six-per-Em Space		
⊡	Four-per-Em Space		
⊡	Nonbreaking Four-per-Em Space		
⊡	Three-per-Em Space		
⊼	Nonbreaking Three-per-Em Space		
⊤	En Space	Option-Space	Ctrl-Shift-6
⊤	Nonbreaking En Space	Command-Option-Space	Ctrl-Shift-Alt-6
⊤	Em Space		
⊤	Nonbreaking Em Space		
⊡	Figure Space		
⊡	Nonbreaking Figure Space		

!	Punctuation Space		
!	Nonbreaking Figure Space		
₹	Flexible Space	Option-Shift-Space	Ctrl-Shift-5
₹	Nonbreaking Flexible Space	Command-Option-Shift-Space	Ctrl-Shift-Alt-5

Return. Sometimes known as a "carriage return" or a "hard return," this is the key to press when you're at the end of a paragraph. In fact, the Return character separates paragraphs from each other. Most people don't think of the Return key as a character, but you can see it and select it when Invisibles is turned on.

QuarkXPress is great at wrapping characters onto the next line, so don't press Return after each line like you would on a typewriter. Also, don't press Return twice in a row to add extra space between paragraphs. Instead, you should use Space Before and Space After (see "Space Before and After," earlier in this chapter).

Soft Return. Holding down the Shift key while you press Return results in a soft return, often called the "new line" character. A soft return forces a new line without starting a new paragraph, with all its attendant attributes: Space Before and After, First Line Indent, paragraph rules, and so on. For example, I use soft returns for tabular text or for forcing a line break in justified or flush-left text. This is a character that takes some getting used to, but I recommend you play with it until you do, because it really comes in handy.

Tab. People also rarely think about tabs as separate characters, but that's just what they are. I talked about tabs in the section called "Tabs," earlier in this chapter, so all I need to say now is that you should really know your tabbing and never (never) use the spacebar to align columns. Also, you can see tab characters when Invisibles is turned on.

Indent Here. There's a great invisible formatting character called Indent Here, which you get by pressing Command/Ctrl-\ (backslash). This character causes the rest of the lines in a paragraph to indent to that character. I find this feature particularly useful for hanging punctuation or inline graphics, drop caps, or headings (see Figure 6-60).

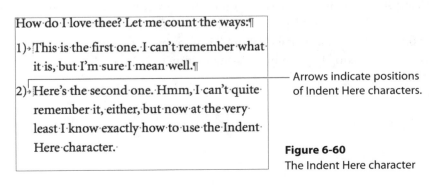

Arrows indicate positions
of Indent Here characters.

Figure 6-60
The Indent Here character

Note that all the lines of the paragraph (after the Indent Here character) get indented, even if the paragraph spans two or more text boxes. The Indent Here character appears as a dotted vertical gray line when you turn on Invisibles in the View menu.

Some people use the Indent Here character to create hanging indents (like for bulleted lists). It's easy to do—just type a bullet, then a tab, then Command/Ctrl-\, and the rest of the paragraph is indented to the tab stop—but I don't like it as much as the trick where you set the Left Indent and First Line Indent (see "Tip: Hanging Indents," earlier in this chapter). The big difference? You can't specify an Indent Here character as part of a style sheet.

Discretionary hyphen. You remember that the Suggested Hyphenation feature lets you specify the hyphenation for a word, and wherever that word appears, it'll hyphenate the way you want. The discretionary-hyphen character (Command/Ctrl-hyphen) also lets you suggest hyphenation for a word, but it only works on a word-by-word basis. I use discretionary hyphens all the time when I'm finessing a layout; if a line of text looks odd because QuarkXPress is being dumb in its hyphenation attempt, I'll throw in a discretionary-hyphen character where I think the word should hyphenate. When Invisibles are showing, a discretionary hyphen looks like a light gray hyphen, but it kind of hides inside the words, just barely peeking out between the letters.

Note that typing a regular hyphen works just as well as a discretionary hyphen... at first. When you type a hyphen, QuarkXPress breaks the word at that spot (if the word is at the end of the line). But what happens if the text reflows for some reason (like if you add a word)? All of a sudden, you have hyphens scattered throughout your text (see Figure 6-61). If you use discretionary hyphens instead, they appear as real hyphens when they need to, but "disappear" when they're not needed (even Find/Change ignores the character).

> **Tip: Stop Words from Breaking.** *Discretionary hyphens also play another role in QuarkXPress. If you place a discretionary hyphen immediately before a word, that word will never hyphenate at the end of a line. In other words, the discretionary hyphen also acts to turn hyphenation off for a single word.*

Nonbreaking hyphen. Sooner or later, you'll probably come upon a word that includes a hyphen, but which shouldn't be broken at the end of a line. For instance, you typically don't want figure references, such as "Figure 99-3," to break at line endings. The solution: you can use a nonbreaking hyphen by pressing Command/Ctrl-= (equals sign) instead of a normal hyphen.

Greetings, and congratulations on your purchase of **KvetchWrite**, the absolutely sensa-
tional new product for word processing,
desktop publishing, object-oriented drawing, outline processing, flowchart creation,
indexing, database management, telecom-
munications, and practically anything else
you can imagine.

This is a regular automatic hyphen.

Hard hyphens used here.

Greetings, and congratulations on your purchase
of **KvetchWrite**, the absolutely sensa-tional new
product for word processing, desktop publishing,
object-oriented draw-ing, outline processing,
flowchart creation, indexing, database management, telecom-munications, and practically anything else you can imagine.

This text should have discretionary
hyphens in it instead of hard hyphens.

Figure 6-61
Reflowed hard hyphens

Discretionary new line. You can place the discretionary-new-line character (Command-
Return or Ctrl-Enter) within a word to suggest places to break that word if QuarkXPress
needs to. It's much like a discretionary hyphen, but without the hyphen.

For example, if you type an en dash and feel comfortable about the surrounding words
breaking at the end of a line, you can press Command/Ctrl-Return after the en dash (en
dashes won't break without this, though em dashes will). If QuarkXPress determines that
it needs to break the line at this point, it does. If it doesn't need to break the line there, it
doesn't break it (and the character, being invisible, has no other effect on your text).

Nonbreaking space. A nonbreaking space (on Mac OS you can press Command-Space,
Control-Space, or Command-5; on Windows, you can press Ctrl-5) looks just like a normal space character (and it expands and contracts as necessary in justified copy). However,
it never breaks at the end of a line. A great use of this is in company names that include
spaces, but shouldn't be broken over several lines (unless you absolutely have to).

New column and new box. If your text box contains multiple columns or is linked to
other text boxes, you can use the New Column and New Box characters to force text to
jump from one column or box to the next. Pressing Enter from your keyboard's numeric
keypad forces a text jump to the next column. If the character is placed in the last (or only)
column of a text box, it will force a jump to the next linked text box. Otherwise, pressing
Shift-Enter forces a jump to the next linked text box.

En space. As I mentioned earlier in the chapter, an en is half an em, which—to QuarkXPress—equals either the width of two zeros or the height of the font you're working with (depending on how you've set up the Preferences dialog box). Pressing Option-spacebar results in an en space (on Windows, press Ctrl-Shift-6), which will not stretch in size in justified copy as much as a regular word space. (In other words, letterspacing still affects en spaces, though wordspacing values do not.) Command-Option-spacebar gives you an en space that doesn't break at the end of a line (on Windows, press Ctrl-Alt-Shift-6). Note that an en space is rarely the same width as an en dash, even when Standard Em Space is turned on in the Preferences dialog box.

Flex space. When you press Option-Shift-space you get what's called a "flex space" (on Windows, press Ctrl-Shift-5). You can specify how wide you want it to be (it flexes to your will). Also like the en space, once you specify its width, this space is fixed; it won't change width, even in justified text, unless you allow letterspacing in your H&J settings. (It's treated like just another character, so if QuarkXPress adds letterspacing in justified text, it adds it to the flex space, too. The space then expands.)

The control for this character's width is on the Character tab in the Preferences dialog box. The percentage is based on the width of an en space. Therefore the default value, 50 percent, is half an en space. To create an em space, set the flex space at 200. Note that when you change the width of a flex space in the Preferences dialog box, QuarkXPress changes the widths of flex spaces throughout that layout.

Punctuation space. The punctuation space (Shift-space)—sometimes called a thin space—is easy to confuse with the flex space while you're typing, and looks similar. They're both fixed-width characters, so they don't expand in justified type (unless you allow letterspacing in the H&J specs), but you can't specify the size of a punctuation space. Typically it's the same width as a comma or a period, but it's really up to the font designer. Punctuation spaces are often used in European typesetting, especially when setting numbers. You might type "1 024.35" (where a punctuation space—rather than a comma—is used as a delimiter).

Here's some typographic trivia for you: In some typefaces, the width of punctuation is set to the same width as the normal spaceband (which is often exactly half the width of a numeral in that font). In this case, the spaceband and the punctuation space are the same width, though one will stretch with wordspacing and one will not.

Page numbers. QuarkXPress lets you use three characters to display page numbering (see Table 6-8). As I noted in Chapter 4, *Building a Layout,* these are not only page-dependent, but also text box–dependent. For example, you can place a text box with the next text-box character (Command/Ctrl-4) on top of a linked text box, and the page number will register the link of the text box under it. The current text-box character (Command/Ctrl-3) is good for automatic page numbers on master pages; the previous text box character (Command/Ctrl-2) is good for "Continued from . . ." messages. You can find options for adding automatic page number codes under the Insert Character submenu of the Utilities menu as well.

Table 6-8 Page-numbering characters

Press...	To insert a character representing...
Command/Ctrl-2	Previous text box
Command/Ctrl-3	Current text box
Command/Ctrl-4	Next text box

Glyphs Palette

If you've been in publishing for any amount of time, you've no doubt figured out your favorite way to ferret out the special characters of a font. Whether you're using a system character map utility, your font manager, or just post-it notes that list your favorites, now there's a better way. QuarkXPress 7 provides a Glyphs palette that shows each and every option within a font.

> *Tip: What's a Glyph? A glyph is actually a representation of a character within a font—and some characters have multiple options for how they might look. One character is right there, out in the open on the keyboard. Other, fancier options are buried down deep in the font. OpenType fonts, with their ability to store thousands of glyphs, make the Glyphs palette particularly vital.*

To open the Glyphs palette, select Glyphs from the Window menu (Figure 6-62). If the cursor is in text, that font is selected in the menu at the top, but you can choose any other font that is active on your system. If you need to see how that font looks in bold or italic, you can click those icons at right. (Or, if you can't see the font at all, click the zoom icons until you're comfortable with the view scale of the glyphs.) Finally, if there's just too many glyphs to sort through, you can choose an option from the menu under the Font menu. Options will vary depending on what's in the selected font, but generally you can narrow down your options to things like Alternates for Selection and Symbols.

The most likely thing you'll be doing in here is looking for a specific character. Say that you need to find a fraction or the euro symbol. What you do is scroll through the glyphs until you find it. Then, simply double-click the character to insert it at the cursor. (If text is selected, it will be replaced.) If you're working on a cookbook with lots of foreign food names and fractions, you'll find the Glyphs palette invaluable.

Figure 6-62
The Glyphs palette

In addition to inserting glyphs from the palette, you can point at a glyph to display its GID and Unicode value—information you might find helpful in HTML programming. (I can't really think of a reason a QuarkXPress user would need this information, but it's there if you want it.) If a glyph has a small triangle in the lower-right corner, it means the glyph has Alternates for Selection. You can click on the triangle to see the various options; for example, you might see swash (more elegant) characters.

If you find yourself hunting down the same characters over and over, add them to the Favorite Glyphs area of the palette. First, click the triangle next to Favorite Glyphs to display the storage boxes. Then drag any frequently used glyphs down to the boxes. Your favorite glyphs remember their font and can be double-clicked for insertion into text.

Ligatures

Ligatures are to typography what diphthongs are to language. They connect two or more single characters to make a single one. While many classic typefaces would contain up to 10 ligatures, typefaces on the computer generally include only two basic ligatures (fi and fl), and Expert Sets from Adobe and other vendors usually have three more (ff, ffi, and ffl). Windows fonts didn't use to include ligatures, but often do today. In addition, OpenType fonts may have scads of ligatures and discretionary ligatures (see "OpenType Styles," earlier in this chapter, for more information). Figure 6-63 shows ligatures in action.

Without ligatures   Officially, the finalists
were affluent flounder

With ligatures   Officially, the finalists
were affluent flounder

Figure 6-63
The fi and fl ligatures

QuarkXPress has two options for automatically taking advantage of the ligatures within fonts: the Ligatures character attribute for standard fonts and the Ligatures and Discretionary Ligatures styles for OpenType fonts. These two options are mutually exclusive. In both cases, keep in mind that QuarkXPress is not creating the ligatures—it's automatically swapping in ligature glyphs for character pairs. If the ligature glyphs do not exist in the active font, nothing's going to happen in QuarkXPress. (How can you tell whether the glyphs exist? Use the Glyphs palette to see what's in the font.)

Ligature preferences. Whether you're using the Ligatures character attribute or the OpenType styles, QuarkXPress keeps an eye on the Ligatures preferences in the Character tab in the Preferences dialog box (Figure 6-64).

Figure 6-64 Ligatures preferences in the Character tab of the Preferences dialog box

The number in the Break Above field tells QuarkXPress the letterspacing level above which to break the ligature apart. For example, suppose the field contains "1." If the ligature is kerned or tracked more than one unit, the ligature breaks apart, becoming two separate characters. If you change the number to "5," then QuarkXPress maintains the ligature until tracking or kerning has reached six units.

This is an important feature because you don't want two characters stuck together in "loose" text (the ligature stands out too much). This spacing limit also applies to justified text. That is, if you justify a text block by adding letterspacing, you're saying the ligatures may break into their single characters when necessary.

The other option in this area, called "Not ffi Or ffl," is for some finicky folks who think that those two particular combinations should not get the ligature treatment. I disagree, and I leave this option turned off.

Applying ligatures. If you're working with a PostScript or TrueType font, select Enable Ligatures in the Character Attributes dialog box (Figure 6-65) or the Character Attributes tab of the Measurements palette. If you're working with an OpenType font, turn on Standard Ligatures in the OpenType area of the Character Attributes dialog box. You can also choose this option from the OpenType Styles menu on the Classic and Character Attributes tabs of the Measurements palette. Most OpenType fonts—but not all—will have this option available. Some OpenType fonts also have Discretionary Ligatures consisting of even more character pairs and fancier treatment than Standard Ligatures. Since they're called Discretionary, go ahead and use them at your discretion. However you end up applying ligatures, be sure to specify it in your body text style sheets for consistency.

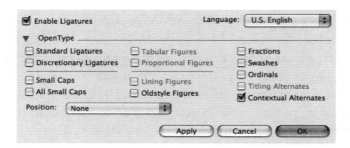

Figure 6-65
Ligatures options in the Character Attributes dialog box

Tip: Ligatures Methods Mutually Exclusive. When working with OpenType fonts, Quark recommends that you not turn on Enable Ligatures and apply the OpenType ligatures styles. Otherwise, you'll end up with odd spacing issues.

Punctuation and Symbols

A typographer shouldn't feel limited using a desktop computer. The typefaces from the major vendors (Adobe, Bitstream, Linotype, and so on) are loaded with the characters you need to create excellent type, including proper quotation marks, ligatures, and em dashes. If you aren't already a typographer, you'll want to pay careful attention to the tips and examples I provide here. Using some simple features—such as Smart Quotes and automatic ligatures—may make the difference between a piece that looks like it was desktop published (in the worst sense of the phrase) and a piece that looks professional.

I can't discuss every special character that's included in a font, but I'll hit on a few of the important ones. Table 6-9 shows how to type each of these, plus a good number of additional characters. In addition, you can always use the Glyphs palette in the Window menu for help finding characters. Some are now available in the Insert Character submenu of the Utilities menu as well.

Table 6-9 Special punctuation and symbols in most fonts

Name	Looks like	Mac OS	Windows
Opening double quote	"	Option-[	Alt-0147
Closing double quote	"	Option-Shift-[	Alt-0148
Opening single quote	'	Option-]	Alt-0145
Closing single quote	'	Option-Shift-]	Alt-0146
Em dash	—	Option-Shift-hyphen	Ctrl-Shift-=
En dash	–	Option-hyphen	Ctrl-Shift-Alt-–
Ellipsis	…	Option-;	Alt-0133
Fraction bar	/	Option-Shift-1	N/A
Bullet	•	Option-8	Alt-0149
Copyright symbol	©	Option-G	Alt-Shift-C
Registered symbol	®	Option-R	Alt-Shift-R
Trademark symbol	™	Option-2	Alt-Shift-2
Degree mark	°	Option-Shift-8	Alt-0176
Section mark	§	Option-6	Alt-0167
Paragraph mark	¶	Option-7	Alt-0182
Dagger	†	Option-T	Alt-0134
Cents sign	¢	Option-4	Alt-0162

Em and en dashes. An em dash, made by pressing Option-Shift-hyphen (on Windows, press Ctrl-Shift-=), should be used in place of double hyphens to indicate a pause or a semiparenthetical. For example, don't type this: "Villainous-looking scoundrels--eight of them." Instead, use an em dash. An em dash is named for how long it is (one em).

An en dash (Option-hyphen on Mac OS or Control-Alt-Shift-hyphen on Windows) should generally be used for duration and distance—replacing the word "to"—as in "August–September," "45–90 weeks long," and "the New York–Philadelphia leg of the trip." It's half as long as an em dash, so it doesn't stand out quite as much.

Note that QuarkXPress, if it needs to, breaks a line after an em dash when wrapping text, but not after an en dash (unless you put a discretionary soft return after it; see "Discretionary new line," earlier).

Tip: Narrowing Em Dashes. Perhaps typeface designers get overzealous every now and again with their characters. The em dash might certainly fall into this category, not in flourish but in width. Simply put, it's often just too wide. I'll sometimes make an em dash narrower by setting it to a horizontal scaling of 75 or 80 percent of its original width. If you have a lot of them, you might consider doing this using XPress Tags: search for the em dash and replace with "<h80>—<h100>." I discuss XPress Tags in Chapter 7, Copy Flow.

Quotation Marks. The first tip-off that someone is green behind the ears in desktop publishing is his or her use of straight quotes instead of proper "printer's quotes." Straight quotes, which is what you get when you press the ' and " keys on a typewriter, should be used for notation of measurements (inches and feet) or for special typographic effect (some fonts' straight quotes look great in headline type). Printer's quotes, or curly quotes, should be used for English/American quotations. Quark has two features that have made it much easier to use curly quotes—Convert Quotes and Smart Quotes.

The Convert Quotes checkbox in the Import Text dialog box lets you convert all straight quotes into proper curly quotes when you import text. You can also turn on Smart Quotes in the Input Settings tab of the Preferences dialog box. This automatically converts quotes as you type them. I always leave both of these turned on unless I specifically need to use straight quotes (see next tip, "Getting Your Quotes Straight").

Note that Smart Quotes can replace straight quotes with other sorts of quote marks (see "Tip: Get It Right for Overseas," in the next section).

Tip: Getting Your Quotes Straight. When Smart Quotes is turned on, every time you type a single or double quote it comes out curly. However, if you really need a straight quote someplace, you can get it by pressing Control-' or Control-Shift-" (that's Control, not Command). On Windows, it's Control-' or Control-Alt-'.

Registration, Copyright, and Trademark. The registration, copyright, and trademark characters are found on Mac OS by pressing Option-R, Option-G, and Option-2 keys. On Windows, you should press Alt-Shift-R, Alt-Shift-C, and ANSI character code 0153 (see "Tip: ANSI Codes," in the next section). Again, if you don't use these options, feel free to hop into the Glyphs palette via the Window menu.

I have only one thing to say about using these characters: Be careful with your sizing and positioning. I recommend immediately assigning the superior type style to the character, and then determining whether it should be kerned or not.

Foreign Punctuation and Symbols

Working in a foreign language is really a trip. Foreign languages have a different word for everything. Many foreign languages, like French and Spanish, contain accented characters that are built into fonts from the major type vendors. For example, you can type *élève* without switching to some obscure font. Table 6-10 lists the characters that you would most likely use in a foreign language.

Table 6-10 Foreign accents and punctuation

Name	Looks like	Macintosh	Windows
Left double guillemet	«	Option-\	Alt-0171
Right double guillemet	»	Option-Shift-\	Alt-0187
Left single guillemet	‹	Option-Shift-3	Alt-0139
Right single guillemet	›	Option-Shift-4	Alt-0155
Base double quote	„	Option-Shift-W	Alt-0132
Base single quote	‚	Option-Shift-0	Alt-0130
Question mark down	¿	Option-Shift-?	Alt-0191
Exclamation point down	¡	Option-1	Alt-0161
Acute vowel	áéíóúÁÉÍÓÚ	Option-E, then vowel	*
Umlaut vowel	äëïöüÄËÏÖÜ	Option-U, then vowel	*
Grave vowel	àèìòùÀÈÌÒÙ	Option-`, then vowel	*
Circumflex vowel	âêîôûÂ ÎÔÛ	Option-I, then vowel	*
Cedilla C	Ç	Option-Shift-C	Alt-0199
Cedilla c	ç	Option-C	Alt-0231
Capital slashed O	Ø	Option-Shift-O	Alt-0216
Small slashed o	ø	Option-O	Alt-0248
German ess (double s)	ß	Option-S	N/A
Dotless i	ı	Option-Shift-B	N/A
Tilde	˜	Option-Shift-M	Alt-0152
Tilde N	Ñ	Option-N, then Shift-N	Alt-0209
Tilde n	ñ	Option-N, then N	Alt-0241
Circum?ex	ˆ	Option-Shift-N	Alt-0136
Macron	¯	Option-Shift-comm?	N/A

continues on next page

Table 6-10 Foreign accents and punctuation *(continued)*

Name	Looks like	Macintosh	Windows
Breve	˘	Option-Shift-period	N/A
Ring accent	°	Option-K	Alt-0176
Ring a	å	Option-?	Alt-0197
Ring A	Å	Option-Shift-?	Alt-0229
Dot accent	·	Option-H	N/A
Pound sterling	£	Option-3	Alt-0163
Yen	¥	Option-Y	Alt-0165

Many people don't fully understand how to type these characters. Several of them aren't as easy as just pressing a key, or even a key with Option or Shift held down. For example, "é" is typed on a Macintosh by first typing Option-E, then typing the letter "e." It's a two-keystroke deal. On Windows, you can use the Character Map or type ANSI character code 0233. If you're not in a huge hurry, find the character and insert it from the Glyphs palette as discussed previously.

> **Tip: ANSI Codes.** *Another way to type a character not found on your keyboard is to enter its Windows ANSI code (this is a Windows-only thing). First, you need to look up the code, which you can find in your Windows manual. Notice that they're all four-digit codes, each beginning with a zero. Then, to enter the code, hold down the Alt key while you key in the code on your keyboard's numeric keypad.*

> **Tip: Get It Right for Overseas.** *Here in the United States, I grew up with the ethnocentric viewpoint that the way I write and typeset is the way everybody does it. Not so. For example, single quotation marks are used in America where double quotation marks are used in Britain. In other European countries, my quotation marks are replaced with guillemets («, »). Note that Smart Quotes lets you set these to appear automatically when you press the quote keys. The Spanish language sets a question or an exclamation point at both the beginning (upside down) and at the end of sentences.*

If you do a lot of foreign-language work, and especially work that has multiple languages in the same layout, you should check out Quark Passport—the multilingual version of QuarkXPress. This program lets you set a language as a paragraph attribute, and will then check spelling and hyphenate that language properly. It comes with about 12 languages built in. (You may run into some difficulties exchanging files in those languages with Passport if you don't have all the versions synchronized.)

Other languages, such as Hebrew, Farsi, Russian, and Greek, must be typed using a non-roman font specific to that language, and may require specialized software. QuarkXPress is presently available in more than 15 languages, including Japanese and German. (In case you're curious, Passport does not include Japanese.)

Math Symbols and the Symbol Font

If you're doing an entire math textbook in QuarkXPress, look into an XTension such as Math+Magic (www.mathmagic.com) or Quark's own XPressMath XTension (which was, unfortunately, not available for version 7 at the time of this writing). If you're just doing a few math symbols, you can use the ones built into most fonts.

The keys to doing a good job are using the correct symbols and good typography. Most typefaces come with a wide variety of built-in math symbols. Table 6-11 provides a list of the most common of these and how to type them.

Table 6-11 Commonly used math symbols

Name	Looks like	In most fonts	Symbol font
Division	÷	Option-/	Option-Shift-P
Plus or minus	±	Option-Shift-=	Option-Shift-=
Greater or equal	≥	Option-period	Option-period
Lesser or equal	≤	Option-comma	Option-3
Approximate equal	ç	Option-X	Option-9
Not equal	≠	Option-=	Option-P
Infinity	∞	Option-5	Option-8
Partial differential	∂	Option-D	Option-D
Integral	∫	Option-B	Option-Shift-;
Florin	ƒ	Option-F	Option-7
Capital omega	Ω	Option-Z	Shift-W
Capital delta	Δ	Option-J	Shift-D
Product	Π	Option-Shift-P	Shift-P
Summation	Σ	Option-W	Shift-S
Pi	π	Option-P	P
Radical	√	Option-V	Option-/

Almost any equation you'd want to typeset will require the Symbol font. Symbol is a Greek and math font that comes with your system. It includes such characters as a multiplication sign (×), which you can create by pressing Option-Y (Mac) or Alt+0180 (Windows). Note that most Windows fonts include a multiplication character (Alt+0215) and division character (Alt+0247) as well. Use the Glyphs palette to examine the other characters in this typeface. Even better are pi fonts, such as Adobe's Universal News with Commercial Pi, which gives you better spacing and more flexible character weights. You can also purchase specialized math pi fonts, like Lucida Math.

Dingbats

Letters, numbers, and symbols do not a funky design make. Often, you need dingbats. Dingbats, or pi fonts, are collections of interesting and useful shapes, pictures, graphics, and so on. The most popular dingbat font by far is Zapf Dingbats—because it is included in most PostScript printers. Table 6-12 shows a listing of about a third of the Zapf Dingbats characters and how to type them. The remaining characters, which you can see in the Glyphs palette, are mostly variations on what is shown here.

Table 6-12 Useful characters in Zapf Dingbats

Name	Symbol	Key or Keystroke
Shadow ballot box up	❏	O
Shadow ballot box down	❐	P
3-D ballot box up	❏	Q
3-D ballot box down	❐	R
Filled ballot box	■	N
Hollow ballot box	□	N (apply Outline style)
Opening great quote	"	Shift-]
Closing great quote	"	Option-N (Windows: Shift-tilde)
Opening single great quote	'	Shift-[
Closing single great quote	'	Shift-\
Great bullet	●	L
Great hollow bullet	○	L (apply Outline style)
Great shadow bullet	○	M
Filled arrowhead	➤	Option-Shift-E (Windows: Alt-0228)

Right arrow	→	Option-] (Windows: Alt-0220)
Fat right arrow	➡	Option-Shift-U (Windows: Alt-0232)
3-D right arrow	⇨	Option-Shift-I (Windows: Alt-0233)
Speeding right arrow	⇛	Option-Shift-7 (Windows: Alt-0224)
Triangle up	▲	S
Triangle down	▼	T
Love leaf	❦	Option-7 (Windows: Alt-0166)
X-mark	✘	8
Check-mark	✔	4
J'accuse	☞	Shift-=
Victory	✌	Comma
Scissors	✂	Shift-4
Pencil straight	✐	/
Pen nib	✎	1
Telephone	☎	Shift-5
Cross	✚	Shift-;
Star	★	Shift-H
Big asterisk	✳	Shift-Z
Snowflake	❄	D

Other examples of dingbat or pi fonts are Carta, Bundesbahn Pi, and Adobe Woodtype Ornaments (see Figure 6-66 for a few examples of various pi—or "dingbat"—fonts).

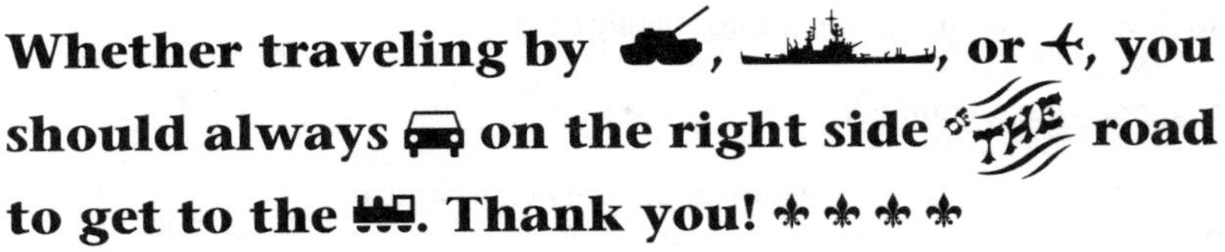

Whether traveling by 🚢 **,** ⚓ **, or** ✈ **, you should always** 🚗 **on the right side of** 𝓣𝓗𝓔 **road to get to the** 🚂 **. Thank you!** ⚜ ⚜ ⚜ ⚜

Symbols from Carta, Bundesbahn Pi, and Adobe Woodtype Ornaments.

Figure 6-66 Some other dingbats

You can use these fonts for fun, but you'll more likely want to use them in a very functional way. Most people use them for bullets (those round Option-8 or Alt-Shift-8 bullets get boring pretty quickly). My favorite for this function is the lowercase "v" from Zapf Dingbats (❖).

You can also use these characters as graphics on your page. Don't forget you can shade and color different characters on your page to act as a background or foreground graphic.

> **Tip: Ballot Boxes and Custom Dingbats.** *Many people create blank "ballot" boxes by typing a Zapf Dingbats lowercase "n" and setting it to outline style, or using the TrueType Wingdings font that comes with Windows. The problem with the first method is that imagesetting the outline often results in a hairline that is too thin to reproduce well. The only problem with the second method is that it's TrueType (I decidedly favor PostScript fonts for professional publishing). Nonetheless, there's a better option: anchored boxes (I'll cover this in much more detail in Chapter 12, Text Meets Graphics).*

1. Create a picture box of any size.

2. Give the picture box a border (Command/Ctrl-B); I like to use .5 point.

3. Select the Item tool and cut the box (Command/Ctrl-X).

4. Using the Content tool, select where in the text you want the box to go, and then paste the box in there (Command/Ctrl-V).

5. Resize it to suit your needs.

Not only can you make box characters this way, but you can make any polygon, or anything else you can create within the application. Also, by importing a graphic into the picture box before you cut and paste it, you can create your own custom dingbats (Figure 6-67).

And re*mem*ber! 👤 The *"cornier"* your Presentation, the less likely it is to be *Taken Seriously!*

Custom dingbat created by placing an EPS (Encapsulated PostScript) file within an anchored picture box. Picture box has been resized and its baseline shifted until the block of text looked appropriately corny.

☐ Ballot box made with an outlined Zapf Dingbat ("n")

☐ Ballot box made with an anchored (square) picture box having a half-point (.5) frame.

Figure 6-67 Custom dingbats

TYPOGRAPHIC SPECIAL EFFECTS

QuarkXPress is not a typographic special-effects program. But this does not mean that it can't give you the power to create many exciting effects with your type. In this section, I'm going to look at a few of the possibilities, like drop caps, rotated text, shadowed type, and type as a picture. But I can't cover everything that you can do. This, especially, is an area in which you have to play around.

Chapter 12, *Text Meets Graphics,* covers a few other special effects, such as text runaround, that you can create using QuarkXPress.

Fractions

Desktop publishing isn't so young that it doesn't have some hallowed traditions. One of the most hallowed is groaning in pain at the mention of creating fractions. But as with most traditions, you shouldn't let that frighten you off. The "fraction problem" in desktop publishing arises because most fonts do not come with more than a handful of prebuilt fractions—you're OK if you need ½, ¼, or ¾, but if you're working on a cookbook, watch out!

You can create your own fractions in a number of ways. Let's take a look at each of these, and discuss why you'd want to use them.

> **Tip: Be Consistent.** *Whatever you decide for your fractions, it's good to use one method through-out the same publication. Mixing your hand-styled fractions with fraction glyphs or a custom font is just not going to look good. If you're starting on a cookbook or similar project, it's a good idea to find out up front which fractions are involved and research methods of creating them before you even bid the project.*

Pseudo-fractions. You can create pseudo-fractions by typing in numbers separated by a slash. Let's be frank: they look awful, and are considered bad form. But in some cases, such as simple word-processed documents, they're perfectly acceptable. Opinion varies on how best to type these characters, especially when you have a fraction following a number. I generally like to add a hyphen between a number and its fraction. For example, one and one-half would be typed "1-1/2."

Don't try to use the fraction-bar character (Option-Shift-1 on Mac OS, ANSI character code 0164 in the Symbol font on Windows) for this kind of fraction. It almost always bumps into the second number and looks like a *shmatta* (like junk).

Made fractions. You can create fractions—such as ½, ¾, ²⁹⁄₃₂—by applying specific character-level formatting to each character in the fraction. The following example shows you how.

1. Type the pseudo-fraction; for example, "3/8." In this case, you should use the fraction-bar character (Option-Shift-1 on Mac OS; on Windows, type Alt+0164 in the Symbol font) rather than the normal slash character.

2. Select the numerator—in this case, the "3"—and set it to the Superior style (Command-Shift-V on Mac OS; Ctrl-Shift-V on Windows).

3. Select the denominator—in this case, the "8"—and set it to the Superior *and* Subscript styles (Command-Shift-hyphen on Mac OS; Control-Shift-9 on Windows).

4. Kern the fractions as desired.

If you don't like the size of the numerator and denominator, you can change the Superior settings for the layout on the Character tab in the Preferences dialog box. When a proper fraction follows a number, you probably don't want any sort of hyphen or even a space (see Figure 6-68).

They tell me getting there is 3/8 of the fun.

A pseudo-fraction

I went to see *8-1/2* but only stayed for 2¾ of it.

A pseudo-fraction, followed by one created via the method noted in
the text.

About ¼ of the time, I won't even give him a dime.

A fraction generated with Make Fraction (from the free TypeTricks XTension)
plus some manual kerning within the fraction.

Figure 6-68 Fractions

Fractions via XTension. Quark's free Type Tricks XTension contains a feature that creates fractions for you. It essentially acts as a macro, changing the slash to a proper fraction bar, and changing the font size and kerning of the numerator and denominator. To let QuarkXPress make the fraction for you, follow these steps.

1. Type the fraction as two numbers separated by a slash.

2. Place the cursor in the fraction, or just to the right of it.

3. Select Make Fraction from the Type Style submenu.

Even though this feature is under the Style menu, Make Fraction is not really a character attribute; it's just a shortcut. Therefore, there's no way to undo the fraction using Undo.

Personally, while many people go ga-ga over this feature, I find it only marginally faster than using the step-by-step method outlined above, and I like the results of the XTension less. (To be fair, you can control the results to some degree in the Fractions/Price panel of the Preferences dialog box.) Plus, if you change the font size of the fraction, the fraction made with styles changes dynamically, whereas fractions made with the XTension have to be adjusted manually.

Stacked fractions. QuarkXPress also lets you create stacked fractions, such as ¼ and ¾. Here's a quick formula for making them.

1. Type the numerator and denominator, separated by an underline (Shift-hyphen).

2. Change the point size of these three characters to 40 or 50 percent of original size. For example, 12-point type gets changed to 5- or 6-point type.

3. Select the numerator and the underline, and apply a baseline shift equal to the point size.

4. Leave the numerator and the underline highlighted, and apply a tracking value of approximately -90 units.

5. At your discretion, apply extra kerning between the characters to achieve a more precise look. You may want to zoom to 800 percent, or print a test sheet.

Chances are, you'll need to adjust these numbers for different typefaces and number combinations. Note that this method of creating stacked fractions only works when both numbers are single digits.

Expert Set fonts. Adobe and other companies have released expert set fonts that complement some of their normal font packages, such as Minion and Minion Expert. The Expert Sets contain some prebuilt fractions and a full set of correctly drawn and scaled superscript and subscript numerals, as well as the correct fraction bar for use with them. This really is the best way to make fractions, and it's what I used throughout this book. (An expert set font also contains oldstyle numerals, small capitals, and other special symbols and ligatures.) However, most fonts don't have Expert Sets; check with the font vendor for specifics.

OpenType Fractions style. Some OpenType fonts provide a Fractions style you can apply to numbers. Be sure to check with the font vendor before you buy a font if you need specific fractions. You apply OpenType styles through the OpenType popup on the Classic or Character tabs of the Measurements palette or through the Character Attributes dialog box.

Utilities. You can also create your own fraction fonts with a utility program such as Fontographer. This method allows you to use any font that you're already using to generate custom fraction characters. See Robin Williams's book, *How to Boss Your Fonts Around* from Peachpit Press, for details on creating a custom font.

Initial Caps

Initial Caps are enlarged characters at the beginning of a paragraph that lend a dramatic effect to chapter or section openings. There are four basic types of initial caps: raised, dropped, hanging, and anchored. Each of these styles is made considerably easier to create with the automatic drop-caps feature and the Indent Here character. Enter an Indent Here character by pressing Command/Ctrl-\ or by choosing Indent Here from the Insert Character submenu of the Utilities menu. You'll find it under Special Characters (Breaking).

Let's look at several initial caps and how they are made.

Standard raised caps. Raised caps can be created by enlarging the first letter of the paragraph (see Figure 6-69). It's important to use absolute leading when you create standard raised caps. If you don't, the first paragraph's leading gets thrown way off.

U naccustomed as I am to public speaking . . . but that never did prevent me from running off endlessly at the mouth . . . you, sir! Stop that hideous snoring! But I digress . . .

14-point copy with a 30-point initial capital

Figure 6-69 Standard raised caps

Hung raised caps. A spin-off of the standard raised cap is the hung raised cap (see Figure 6-70). You can hang the letter "off the side of the column" by placing an Indent Here character after it or creating a hanging indent with indents and tabs. The rest of the text block's lines all indent up to that point.

U naccustomed as I am to public speaking . . . but that never did prevent me from running off endlessly at the mouth . . . you, sir! Stop that hideous snoring! But I digress . . .

14-point copy with a 30-point capital. Indent Here character has been placed to the immediate right of the raised cap.

Figure 6-70 Hung raised caps

Standard drop caps. The Drop Caps control is located on the Formats tab in the Paragraph Attributes dialog box and the Paragraph Attributes tab of the Measurements palette (Figure 6-71). To create a drop cap in a paragraph, place the text cursor in the paragraph, press Command/Ctrl-Shift-F (to bring up the dialog box), and turn on Drop Caps. You can then modify two parameters for this feature: Character Count and Line Count.

L et it never be said that the Koala tea of Moishe is not strained. Should this be said, it is entirely possible that the very fabric of civilization would fall utterly into the hands of the

The Paragraph Attributes tab of the Measurements palette lets you apply drop caps.

Figure 6-71 Standard drop caps

The character count is the number of characters made to drop, and you can enter up to 127 characters. The line count is the number of lines that they drop, and you can enter a value from two to 16. For example, specifying "3" in Character Count and "4" in Line Count makes the first three characters of the paragraph large enough to drop four lines down. You don't have to worry about sizing the character, aligning it, or specifying the space between the drop cap and the rest of the text. In this example, the baseline of the drop cap aligns with the fourth line, and the ascent of the drop cap aligns with the first line's ascent. Some fonts have ascents that are taller than their capital letters. This may make the process slightly more difficult, depending on the effect you're trying to achieve.

> **Tip: Adjusting Space After Caps.** I often find that I want to change the space between the initial cap and the text that's flowing around it. People have tried all sorts of weird workarounds for moving the two farther apart or closer together, but I prefer the simple method: Add kerning between the drop cap and the character after it. The more kerning you add, the farther away the flow-around text is set. Negative kerning brings the text closer.

Hanging drop caps. You can make these in the same way as the hanging raised caps: place an Indent Here character (Command/Ctrl-\) directly after the dropped character (see Figure 6-72). You can adjust the spacing between the drop cap and the following text by adjusting the kerning value between the drop cap and the next character (in this case, the Indent Here character).

Three-line drop cap with Indent Here character placed here, creating hanging drop cap.

L et it never be said that the Koala tea of Moishe is not strained. Should this be said, it is entirely possible that the very fabric of civilization would fall utterly into the hands of its worst

Figure 6-72 Hanging drop caps

Scaled drop caps. QuarkXPress has one hidden feature that works on drop-cap characters and drop-cap characters only: percentage scaling. After creating a standard drop cap (as described above), you can select the drop-cap character(s) and change the point size to a percentage of the original drop-cap size. For example, Figure 6-73 shows a paragraph with the drop cap scaled to 150 percent. You can change the percentage of the drop-cap character(s) to anything you want, and the baseline will always align with the text line to the right.

The same, with the capital "L" enlarged to 150 percent of its normal size:

L et it never be said that the Koala tea of Moishe is not strained. Should this be said, it is entirely possible that the very fabric of civilization would fall utterly into the hands of its worst enemies, like that fellow whose name begins

The Measurements palette reflects the change—again, as a percentage of the normal drop-cap size (not in points).

Figure 6-73 Scaled drop caps

Anchored raised caps. Another way of making a raised cap is to create it in a separate text box, then anchor that box to the beginning of the paragraph (I discuss anchored text and picture boxes in Chapter 12, *Text Meets Graphics*). The raised cap in Figure 6-74 is actually a separate text box containing a large capital letter on a tinted background. The character is centered horizontally and vertically within the frame. I also applied other formatting to the initial cap, such as kerning and baseline shift.

We fully recognize that the message "Now formatting your hard disk. Have an *exceedingly* nice day," appearing during the **KvetchPaint** installation, is a bit alarming. Rest assured that it is a harmless prank by one of our programmers—who is, you can also rest assured, no longer with us. As soon as we can break the encryption he used, we will

Figure 6-74 Anchored raised caps

Anchored drop caps. After creating an anchored raised cap, you can make the anchored item drop. Select the item and then choose Ascent in the Align with Text area on the Box tab in the Modify dialog box (select the anchored box and press Command/Ctrl-M, or double-click on the anchored box). You can also click the Align With Text Ascent or Align With Text Baseline button on the far left side of the Classic tab of the Measurements palette.

Wraparound dropped caps. When you're using letters such as "W" or "A," you may want to wrap the paragraph text around the letter (see Figure 6-75). While you can use the Drop Cap option (along with a mess of other formatting), it's just easier to create the drop cap as a separate box and let QuarkXPress figure out the text runaround for you.

alivating in public is not only discouraged, but is, in fact, morally wrong. In fact, I think I could go so far as to say that the entire salivation process is, on occasion, a work of the devil. For example, when I see a chocolate sundæ, I know I should not eat it. My rational mind takes a very definite stand on that point. However, my salivary glands pay no mind.

Figure 6-75 Wrapping drop caps around pictures and picture boxes

1. Create a new text box, type the initial-cap character, and format it the way you want it to look.

2. Select the initial-cap character and choose Text to Box from the Style menu. This converts the text into a picture box. You can now delete the original text box (the one that held the initial cap).

3. Unless you're going to put a picture inside the initial cap, choose None from the Content submenu (under the Item menu).

4. In the Modify dialog box (Command/Ctrl-M, or double-click with the Item tool), give the box a background color and set the Runaround to Item.

5. Move the initial-cap box into position over the paragraph.

This is only one of many variations on a theme for creating wraparound drop caps. Another is to use an initial cap brought in from an illustration program (as any sort of graphic file). You can then use QuarkXPress's automatic runaround or manual runaround feature to control the text runaround (I discuss text runaround in more detail in Chapter 12, *Text Meets Graphics*).

Mixed-font caps. I've already cautioned you about using too many fonts on a page. But if there's ever a time to break the rules, it's with initial caps (see Figure 6-76). If you want your initial caps in a different font, simply change the font for those characters. However, note that when you change the initial cap's typeface, the character may not align properly with the rest of the text.

Snell Roundhand   Adobe Garamond

*S*conce, call you it? So you would leave battering, so I would rather have it a head. And you use these blows long, I must get a sconce for my head, and ensconce it too, or else I shall seek my wit in my shoulders. But, I pray, sir, why am I beaten?

Figure 6-76
Mixed font initial caps

Multiple initial caps. Character Count in the Drop Caps feature lets you drop up to 127 letters in your paragraph. So a drop cap could be a drop word, if you like (see Figure 6-77).

Five-character drop cap. Horizontal scaling of 75%; font size changed from 100% to 87.5%.

Comma scaled down to 75% of normal font size (it's less obtrusive that way).

What, gone in chafing, and clapped to the doors? Now I am every way shut out for a very bench-whistler; neither shall I have entertainment here or at home. I were best to go try some other friends.

Figure 6-77
Multiple initial caps.

Shadow Type Alternatives

Applying the Shadow style to any range of selected type creates a generic shadow that cannot be customized. For example, you can't change its thickness, shade, or offset. Although this is a nice shadow effect on screen, its limitations make it not particularly useful for many purposes (plus, it often prints differently on different printers, so it's inconsistent). You can use the Drop Shadow feature, explained in Chapter 12, *Text Meets Graphics,* or you can use the traditional "double box" method (Figure 6-78). Here's how to do it:

Figure 6-78
Shadows

1. Create a text box with some solid black text in it.

2. Duplicate the text box (Command/Ctrl-D).

3. Select the text within the second text box and modify it (change its color or tint, or something else about it).

4. Send the second text box to the back (choose Send to Back from the Item menu).

5. Set both the background color and the runaround of the top box to None. (Many people get confused at this last step, forgetting that if both the color and runaround aren't set to None, there's no way to see the text in the background box.)

You can then move the second text box around until you have it placed where you want it. Remember that you can click through the top text box by clicking with Command-Option-Shift (Ctrl-Alt-Shift) held down. You might also want to group the two text boxes together in order to move them as if they were one item.

Pricing

Quark's free Type Tricks XTension, included with QuarkXPress 7, lets you automate one other common text-formatting function: pricing. It's simple to make a number into a price (see Figure 6-79). Just type the value, place the cursor within the number or just to the right of it, then select Make Price from the Type Style submenu under the Style menu. Note that all this feature does is delete the decimal point and apply the Superior and

Underline styles to the digits after the decimal point. As with the Make Fractions feature, I'm not particularly excited about this little macro (I find that it's often faster to do this manually using keystrokes than it is to select the feature from the Style menu).

"Okay, look, I'll give you $4.74 for it."
"How much did you say? I don't understand."
"I meant $4^{74}."
"Oh! Sure. It's a deal."

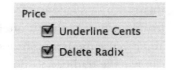

Figure 6-79 Make Price example and preferences

Nonetheless, you have several options for how QuarkXPress formats the character, including whether it should take out any decimal point you've included and whether the numbers after the decimal point (the cents) should have an underline or not. These controls are located in the Fraction/Price tab of the Preferences dialog box.

TEXT GREEKING

After all this talk about making text look better on the screen and on your printed output, you probably need a break from type. Let's talk about how to make type go away.

Designers have long worked with a concept known as *greeking*. Greeking is a method of drawing gray bars to represent blocks of text rather than taking the time to image them all on the screen. QuarkXPress can greek text under a specific size limit, which you can define on the General tab (under Print Layout) in the Preferences dialog box. While the default value for text greeking is 7 points, you can set it anywhere from 2 to 720 points.

Unless you really want to see every character of every word at every size, there's hardly any reason to turn text greeking off. However, depending on what your page design is like, you may want to adjust the Greek Below values at different times. I typically set it to 4 or 5 points.

PUTTING IT TOGETHER

If you got through this entire chapter and are still not too bleary-eyed to read this, you must really be a QuarkXPress die-hard. After having learned about QuarkXPress's word-processing capabilities in the last chapter and what you can do to those words in this chapter, you're ready to move on to the theory and practice of style sheets and copy flow—automating all this formatting so you don't have to do it all manually every time you need it. There's working with type, and then there's working hard at type. I'm trying to get your work to be as easy as possible.

CHAPTER SEVEN

Copy Flow

As you've learned in preceding chapters, you can do all sorts of wonderful things to type in QuarkXPress. But there's more to the intelligent handling of your copy than simply setting it in exquisite type: you also have to get the document produced on time.

In the development of a publication, copy is almost never static. For any number of reasons, you may have to make drastic changes in the formatting or content of the copy (usually at or beyond the last minute). Your success in meeting deadlines (and getting paid) can often depend on how carefully you've anticipated such changes. If you don't plan from the very beginning to manage the flow of your publication's copy, it will surely end up managing you, and in ways you won't like.

Managing Copy

QuarkXPress has two very powerful tools for automating the formatting and management of your copy: style sheets and XPress Tags. Use them wisely, and you'll soon make your copy jump through hoops at the snap of your fingers (or the click of your mouse). Use them poorly, or not at all, and you'll be the one jumping through hoops, probably at three o'clock in the morning the night before a major job is due. In this chapter, I'll tell you how to make the best use of these features. The key is learning to work smart.

Working Smart

Simply put, there are two ways to handle your copy in QuarkXPress: the dumb way and the smart way. What's the main difference between the two? Working the smart way, you make the computer do as much of your work as possible. Working the dumb way, you take it on yourself to do the kind of mindless, repetitive tasks computers were meant to take off your hands—in this case, the repetitive formatting and reformatting of copy.

It takes a bit more time at first to set up a project to take advantage of QuarkXPress's automation, but it is well worth it if you ever need to make even the simplest layout-wide change in the way your text is formatted. Of course, if you're the kind of person who always gets everything right the first time, you'll never, ever need to change any formatting once you've entered it, so you may not find this chapter of much use. The rest of you should pay careful attention.

The dumb way. The dumb way to format your copy is the way you most likely learned first: by selecting text and directly applying various attributes. Want a paragraph to be centered? Go to the Style menu and center it. Need to change the typeface? Go to the Font menu and do it.

"What's so dumb about that?" you may ask. It's not that there's anything inherently wrong with applying formatting directly to your copy; it's just that by doing so, you doom yourself to performing the same selecting-and-modifying actions over and over again whenever you need to format another text element with the same attributes, and whenever you need to make major changes to your layout. If the paragraphs you've centered later need to be flush left, you must again select and change each paragraph individually.

Another way of working dumb is to carefully format your text in QuarkXPress, and then when heavy editing is required, export the copy to a word processor, edit it, then reimport it into a layout. Suddenly you may notice that you've lost most of your special QuarkXPress formatting (such as horizontal scaling, superior characters, kerning, tracking, and so on), and it's time for another long, painstaking formatting pass through your text.

The smart way. The smart way to handle your copy is to take the time to be lazy. Make QuarkXPress's features work for you. By using style sheets, you can apply formatting faster than ever before. When the time comes to change an attribute (font, size, leading, or whatever), style sheets will exponentially speed up that process, too. Also, be sure to use XPress Tags if you export your text. This will retain your formatting information, even if you send stories out to be edited on a dreaded Windows or UNIX system.

Before you start formatting text, however, know that an important aspect of flowing copy is having somewhere for it to flow. And this means linking text boxes (and text paths and table cells). Once you create a home for the text, we'll jump in and look at how style sheets and XPress Tags can make your life a better place to be.

LINKING

I need to introduce a concept here that is crucial to flowing copy: linking. Links, some-times known as chains, are the connections between text boxes, text paths, and table cells that allow text to flow from one into the other. (We'll just go with "text box" in this dis-cussion.) You can have as many text boxes linked up as you like. There are two ways to link text boxes together: Have QuarkXPress do it for you automatically, or do it yourself manually. I cover automatic text links in Chapter 4, *Building a Layout*. I cover manual link-ing here.

> **TIP: Linking Made Easy—Free.** *Quark offers a free set of XTensions called XPert Tools Pro that make many common publishing tasks easier (visit* www.quark.com *and click XTensions). One of the most useful is XPert TextLink, which adds an intuitive palette and buttons for linking and unlinking text boxes and text paths. If you were ever a customer of A Lowly Apprentice Production, aka ALAP, this is the same XPert Tools Pro you know and love.*

Linking Text Boxes

Let's say you have two text boxes and the text in the first is overflowing (a text overflow is indicated by a little box with an "X" in it in the text box's lower-right corner), so you want to link it to the second text box. Here's what to do.

1. Make sure nothing is selected on the page—not a requirement, but it prevents you from accidentally starting links from the wrong item.

2. Choose the Linking tool from the Tool palette (it's the one that looks like three links in a chain).

3. Click on the first text box. A flashing dotted line should appear around it.

4. Click on the second text box. When you select the second text box, an arrow should appear momentarily, connecting the first text box to the second. I call this the *text link arrow*. This happens even if the two text boxes are on different pages.

That's it. The boxes are now linked, and text flows between them. If you want to link another box to your text chain, just follow the same procedure: click on the second text box, then on the third, and so on. You cannot link a box to another box that has text in it. Note that if you get bored choosing the Linking tool over and over again while linking a bunch of boxes, press Option/Alt while you choose it. This keeps it selected until you're finished with it.

If you want to add a text box to the middle of a text chain, first click on a box that is already linked, and then Shift-click on the text box you want to add. The text now flows from the original chain through your added text box and continues on to the original chain (see Figure 7-1).

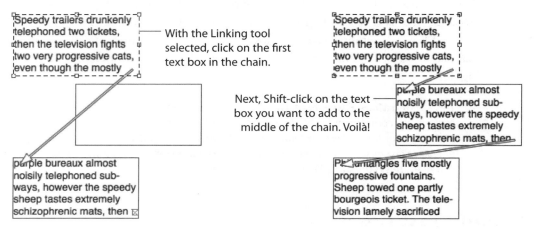

Figure 7-1 Adding a text box to a linked text chain

TIP: Getting Rid of the Flashes. *Many people seem to get flustered when they've selected a text box with the Linking tool and then decide they don't want to follow through and link the box to anything after all. The text box is just sitting there flashing, seeming to call for some special action. Nope, no action is required. You can either click someplace where there's no text box, or just switch tools, and the flashing stops.*

TIP: Linking with Text Paths. *I've said it before, and I'll say it again: Text paths are just like one-line-tall text boxes. And, as such, the text linking tools can be used to link to and from them. You can even put them on a master page and use text paths as automatic text boxes.*

Unlinking Text Boxes

If you want to remove a link between two text boxes, use the Unlinking tool from the Tool palette. The process is simple. Let's say you have a link between two text boxes that you want to sever. First, click on one of the text boxes with the Unlinking tool. As soon as you click on it, you should see the gray arrow linking the two boxes. Then click on either end of the text link arrow. The arrow disappears and the link is gone.

If other page items are on top of the text link arrow, you may not be able to click it. This always seems to happen at 1 a.m., after everything else has gone wrong on the project, and this is the last straw. Nonetheless, the way I solve this problem is to rearrange the layers using Move to Front and Move to Back, or to temporarily shift the obstructing objects in order to get to one of the two.

> **TIP: Unlinking a Text Box from the Middle of a Chain.** *If you unlink a text box from the middle of a chain by clicking on the arrow with the Unlinking tool, the entire text chain is broken at that point. Instead, you can tell QuarkXPress to remove a text box from the text chain without breaking the rest of the flow by selecting the Unlinking tool, then holding down the Shift key while clicking on the box you want to remove.*

Copying Linked Text Boxes

I really love the ability to copy objects between pages, layouts, and projects. However, you may bump into some limitations when you try to copy linked boxes.

You can copy one or more text boxes from a chain of linked text boxes, and QuarkXPress copies, along with it, the entire text chain from that box on. None of the text preceding that box in the chain is copied—only the text from the ensuing linked boxes (and any overflow text). It'd be nice if QuarkXPress could automatically break the chains when you copy, bringing to the new box only the text within the box you're copying (if you'd like, that is). But we have to leave some refinements for QuarkXPress to work on for the next version.

There's one other way to copy linked boxes, especially when the boxes are on multiple pages. If both layouts are in Thumbnails view, you can drag-copy multiple pages from one layout to another. In this case, links between boxes on different pages are also maintained in your target document, even if you didn't grab all the text boxes in the chain.

Style Sheets

A style sheet is a collection of text-formatting attributes with a name. For example, a style sheet named "Heading" might represent the following formatting: "14-point Helvetica Bold, centered, with half an inch of space before." Every time you apply that one style sheet to a paragraph, the paragraph is assigned all that formatting. You can create one style for titles, another for footnotes, and more styles for different levels of subheads. In fact, you can (and probably should) create a different style sheet for each and every different kind of formatting specification in your layout, especially since there's no limit on the number of style sheets you can have in a project.

In addition to paragraph style sheets, QuarkXPress features character style sheets, which can be applied to a single character (or a word, or a sentence, or whatever). They're handy for run-in subheads, numbered lists where the number and period are in a typeface different from the text, and emphasis (like changing the font of all the company names in a layout). Again, if you're going to use the same character formatting more than once or twice in your design, you should create a character style sheet for that formatting.

The next step. In the following description, I'm going to first talk about paragraph styles, and then about character styles. Once you've got paragraph styles down pat, then character styles will be a piece of cake for you. Throughout the discussion, when I talk about style sheets, I will almost always mean both paragraph and character style sheets.

A Style Is a Style Sheet Is a Style

For some reason, Quark decided not to follow accepted terminology when it named its style sheets feature. It is commonly understood in publishing, both traditional and desktop, that the group of formatting attributes for a particular type of paragraph is called a "style." Meanwhile, the list of all the styles used in a publication is called a "style sheet."

However, in QuarkXPress language, each paragraph and character has its own so-called "style sheet," and the collection of these is also referred to as the "style sheet." Because of the confusion, I now tend to use the terms interchangeably. Forgive me, but after all, writing is an inexact science.

The Benefits of Style Sheets

Working with style sheets is smart for two reasons: applying formatting and changing formatting. I typically say that if your layout has more than two pages of text, you should definitely be using style sheets. (Don't feel that two pages is a minimum, though; *any* layout is a suitable place to use style sheets, especially a layout that you know will go through many rounds of revisions.) As with lots of other things (making backups, for example), think about the trade-offs you're talking about: more work up front to save some work downstream. It's up to you to decide whether it's worth doing.

Applying formatting. Let's say I've hired you to work on creating a book. I've specified three levels of headings, two kinds of paragraphs (normal indented paragraphs and the nonindented paragraphs that come right after headings, not to mention the run-in heads like in the paragraph you're reading right now) and the way that the figure numbers and titles should look. It's your job to apply those styles to all the text.

If you went through all 900 pages, fastidiously setting the font of each paragraph, the size of each paragraph, the alignment of each paragraph—not to mention special cases formatted with different character attributes—I'd be calling you Rip Van Winkle before too long. Instead, you can define all the attributes for each paragraph in a style, then apply those attributes in one fell swoop by applying that style to a paragraph or to a range of paragraphs. The same goes for special-case character attributes—create a style and click once to apply multiple attributes.

Changing formatting. Of course, the real nightmare would be when you hand me a draft copy of the book and I ask you to bring down the size of the headings half a point (of course, since we're in the design business, I'd wait to ask you until five o'clock in the afternoon the Wednesday before Thanksgiving). But if you're using styles, you'd smile and say "Sure thing!"

Whenever you make a change to the definition of a style, that change is automatically applied to all the text that uses that style. Because you've had the foresight to create a "Heading" style that is applied to every heading in the book, you need only change the attributes of that style—in this case, the point size—and it gets changed instantly throughout the entire layout.

Local Formatting Versus Formatting with Styles

A key point to remember about QuarkXPress paragraph styles is that the formatting contained in a style is applied to an entire paragraph. If the style calls for Times Roman, the entire paragraph will be in Times Roman. However, you can always override the style's font for specific text within the paragraph. This "local" or "hard" formatting remains, even if you change the style's font definition, or apply a different style sheet to the paragraph. (One exception: if a paragraph has the QuarkXPress option No Style applied to it, *all* local formatting will be wiped out when you apply a style to it. See "Normal Style and No Style," later in this chapter.) In other words, local formatting stays around for a long time, so you have to mind it carefully.

As I said earlier, you can also format just part of a paragraph with a character style; in this case, the character style you applied is also considered local formatting (because the character style you applied doesn't match the character style of the paragraph style—I'll discuss this more later in the chapter).

TIP: Seeing Local Formatting. If there is any local formatting where the cursor is in the text (or in whatever text is selected), a plus sign appears to the left of the style's name in the Style Sheets palette. This is a handy way of knowing if you're looking at text formatted according to its style, or at formatting that's been applied locally (see Figure 7-2).

The plus sign before the style name indicates the presence of local formatting in the current selection.

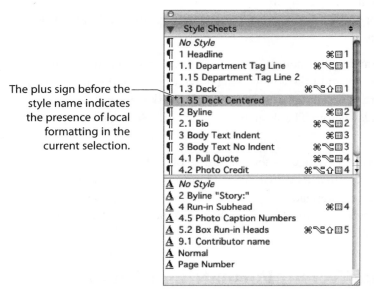

Figure 7-2
Local formatting flag

Local formatting is sometimes confusing, so here are a couple of examples of when you do and do not see the plus sign.

- If you apply local paragraph formatting to a paragraph—for instance, an automatic drop cap—the Style Sheets palette displays the plus sign next to the paragraph style, no matter where in the paragraph you place the cursor (because you've applied local formatting to the entire paragraph).

- If you change the point size of only three words in the paragraph, the plus sign appears only when the cursor is in that text. Local character formatting is always also local paragraph formatting because the paragraph style includes character formatting (I'll clarify this later).

The problem is that there's no way to see what the local formatting is—the plus sign appears the same whether you've changed a paragraph's font or its tracking (see "TIP: Totally Overriding Local Formatting," and "TIP: Find Local Formatting," later in this chapter).

Tagging Paragraphs

It's important to understand that there's a difference between paragraph formatting and a style name. When you apply a style to a paragraph, you're only *tagging* it with that name—essentially identifying *what it is*, not necessarily what it should look like. QuarkXPress has an internal style sheet list that tells it what collection of formatting should go with that name. If you tag the paragraph with a different name, the formatting automatically changes. Or if you change the attributes of the style sheet, QuarkXPress updates the formatting throughout the project (across all layout spaces).

Therefore, when you begin to work on a layout, it's not really that important that the style sheets you use bear the correct formatting, since you can always change the attributes later. Once you've tagged all the paragraphs in your text, you can experiment by modifying their styles at your leisure.

There are three ways to apply style sheets—that is, to tag paragraphs—from within QuarkXPress: with the Style menu, with the Style Sheets palette, and with keystrokes.

Style menu. The most basic—and the slowest—method for applying a paragraph style is to select the style name from the Style Sheets submenu (under the Style menu; see Figure 7-3). As with any other paragraph formatting, your text selection or insertion point must be somewhere within the paragraph.

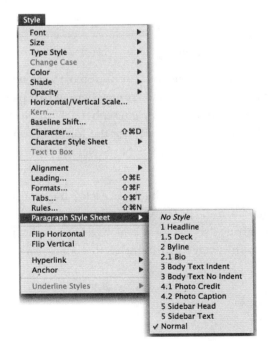

Figure 7-3
The Style Sheets submenu

Style Sheets palette. The Style Sheets floating palette (select Style Sheets from the Windows menu, or press F11) lets you apply, edit, and view styles on the fly without having to go to any menus (see Figure 7-4). You can keep the palette open all the time, shrink it down to a manageable size as necessary, and group it with other palettes. Or, you can open and close it as needed by pressing F11. The Style Sheets palette lists all the styles in your project, along with their keyboard shortcuts, if they have any. If you have lots of styles, you can make the palette larger or just scroll through them.

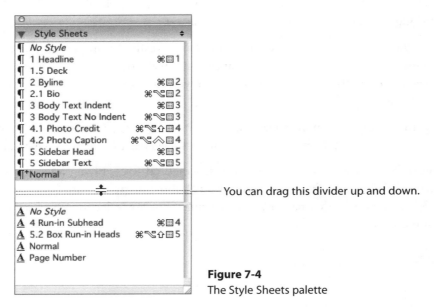

You can drag this divider up and down.

Figure 7-4
The Style Sheets palette

The beauty of this palette is that you can put it right next to (or on top of) your text while you work. To apply a style to a paragraph, put the text cursor somewhere in that paragraph and click on the style in the palette. To apply No Style to a paragraph, click on No Style in the palette. The paragraph is no longer tagged with the style, but the formatting from the style remains as hard, local formatting (you should rarely use No Style; see "Normal Style and No Style," later in this chapter).

As you move your cursor through your text, the style sheet for each paragraph is high-lighted in the Style Sheets palette; you can quickly see what styles are applied. This is especially helpful if local formatting overrides styles, or if you have two styles that are similar and you want to know if a paragraph is tagged with one or the other.

Keystrokes. The third method of applying styles to paragraphs is by using keystrokes. Each paragraph style can have its own keystroke, which you define for it (see "Creating a New Paragraph Style," below). Then you can select a paragraph and press that keystroke. In case you forget your keystrokes, they appear as reminders on both the Style Sheets submenu and the Style Sheets palette.

> **TIP: Copying Attributes from One Paragraph to Another.** *You can copy all the paragraph formatting from one paragraph to another with a single mouse click. First, place the cursor in the paragraph whose formatting you want to change, then Shift-Option-click (Shift-Alt-click) on the paragraph whose format you want to copy. (Note that both paragraphs have to be in the same story, but they do not have to be in the same text box.)*

This copies all the paragraph formatting, including the paragraph's style sheet and any local paragraph formatting (margins, tabs, leading, space before or after). No local character formatting (font, size, bold, italic) in the source paragraph is copied—only paragraph formatting.

Defining Styles

To create or edit a paragraph style sheet, select Style Sheets from the Edit menu or press Shift-F11. This calls up the Style Sheets dialog box (see Figure 7-5). If you open this dialog box when a project is open, you'll see all the styles in that project. You can then use this dialog box to create, edit, and delete styles, and by using the Append button, import some or all of the styles from another QuarkXPress project. Note that if you want to create a style sheet based on existing formatting in the layout, first click in that text and then open the Style Sheets dialog box. All those settings will be preselected when you create the style sheet.

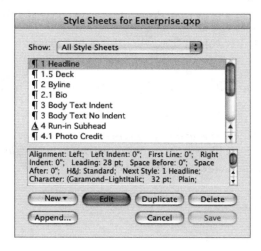

Figure 7-5
The Style Sheets dialog box

If you use the Style Sheets dialog box with no projects open, you can edit and add to QuarkXPress's default style-sheet list, and your edits will then be automatically included in all new projects you create. It's important to understand that the Style Sheets dialog box stores style sheets for an entire project—all the layouts in the project share the same style sheets whether they want to or not. Presumably, you store layouts in the same project because they are related, so having the same style sheets should be fine.

> **TIP: A Quick Hop to Style Sheets.** To edit a style, Command/Ctrl-click on that style in the Style Sheets palette. This brings up the Style Sheets dialog box, with the style name highlighted. Then you can click Edit, or press Return or Enter, to edit that style sheet (pressing Return or Enter here is often one step easier than clicking the Edit button).

At the top of the Style Sheets dialog box, the handy Show popup menu lets you control which style sheets are showing:

- **All Style Sheets.** This is the default value, and simply displays every style sheet in the project.

- **Paragraph Style Sheets.** Many people complained about the addition of character styles as too confusing. (Personally, I don't know what they were talking about). Nonetheless, if you have a lot of styles and you only want to display the paragraph styles, choose this option.

- **Character Style Sheets.** The opposite of the above, this option displays all the character styles and hides the paragraph styles.

- **Style Sheets in Use.** This is very useful. I often have many more style sheets in a project than I will typically use (the others are there just in case I need them). Choosing this option hides all those extras so they don't clutter up the dialog box.

- **Style Sheets Not Used.** I generally use this option when I feel like deleting all the unused styles.

Note that the Show popup menu has no effect on the Style Sheets palette. The palette always displays all the styles.

> **TIP: Jump to a Style.** If you have a lot of styles in your project, you're not going to want to scroll through the list in the Style Sheets dialog box until you get to the one you want. Instead, just type the first letter or two of the style's name, and QuarkXPress jumps there.

Creating a New Paragraph Style Sheet

Creating a new paragraph style sheet is as easy as one, two, three.

1. Create a paragraph in a text box (it can even be just some gibberish text in a dummy text box). Format it exactly the way you want the style sheet to be defined (both character and paragraph formatting), and place the cursor somewhere in the paragraph.

2. Go to the Style Sheets dialog box and click the New button (while this looks like a button, it's actually a popup menu). Choose Paragraph from the popup menu. Or, if you want to copy another style, you can press the Duplicate button instead of New.

3. Either way, the Edit Paragraph Style Sheet dialog box appears (see Figure 7-6). All the formatting from the paragraph you formatted is sucked into the dialog box, so you don't have to set it here. Enter the name of the new style in the Name field. Press OK, and then press Save to leave the dialog box.

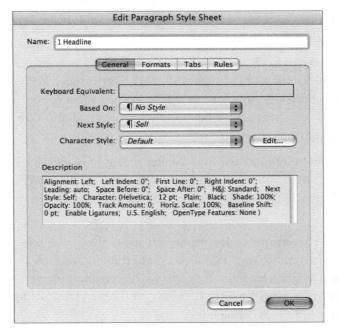

Figure 7-6
The Edit Paragraph Style Sheet dialog box

Make sure the text selection in step 1 doesn't include any text that is formatted in some other unwanted way—say, some words in bold or italic that you *don't* want to become part of the new style definition. In other words, this procedure picks up the paragraph *and* character attributes of where your insertion point (or selection) is, and uses them in defining your new style.

If you want to define a keystroke combination that will automatically apply the style, click in the Keyboard Equivalent field (in step 2), and press the combination you want. On Mac OS, it's often a good idea to use a function key or numeric keypad key in combination with the Control key, because you can be confident that keystrokes defined this way won't conflict with QuarkXPress's other key commands, almost none of which use the Control key (see the keyboard shortcuts in the back of the book).

> **TIP: Keys You Can Use for Style Shortcuts.** *You can only use certain keys for applying styles—the function keys (F1 through F15) and the numbers on the numeric keypad. In combination with the Control, Command, Shift, and Option (or Alt in Windows) keys, they allow for a lot of short-cuts. However, because QuarkXPress uses the function keys for its own shortcuts (both with and without Option/Alt and Shift), I suggest that you use function keys as style-sheet hotkeys only in conjunction with the Control key. If you're going to be working on a laptop without a numeric keypad, don't use those in your keystroke combinations.*

There's no way to print a list of what keystrokes go with what styles (see "TIP: Printing Your Style Sheet," later in this chapter), so I just print a screen shot of the Style Sheets palette and tape it to my wall.

Defining paragraph formatting. The step-by-step method above is a way to define a style by example, and it's the easiest and fastest way to make a style-sheet. You can, however, also define a style sheet directly from within the Style Sheets dialog box. You need to learn this slower method, too, because it's how you edit styles and also how you can create style sheets when no projects are open.

Once you've clicked the New button in the Style Sheets dialog box, selected Paragraph from the popup menu, and named your new style, you can define its paragraph formatting by setting values in the Formats, Tabs, and Rules tabs of the Edit Paragraph Style Sheet dialog box.

Character formatting in paragraph styles. Paragraph styles always include character formatting, too (like font, size, and so on). When you first create a paragraph style sheet, QuarkXPress assigns the Default character formatting. Personally, I think the word "default" is really confusing. In plain English, it means, "Use the character formatting hidden inside the Character Attributes dialog box."

You get to the Character Attributes dialog box by pressing the Edit button in the Edit Paragraph Style Sheet dialog box (see Figure 7-7). If you're building a paragraph style by example (as in the step-by-step outlined above), the character information here is the same as in your dummy "example" paragraph.

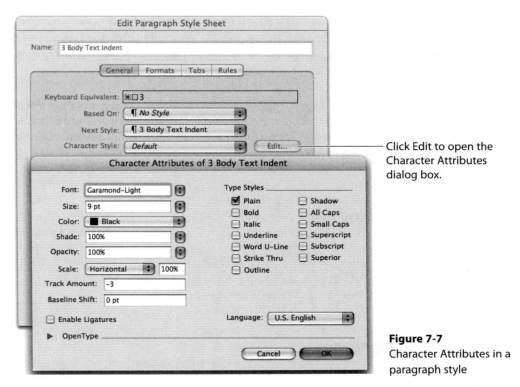

Click Edit to open the Character Attributes dialog box.

Figure 7-7
Character Attributes in a paragraph style

If you have already built other character style sheets (I'll cover how to do this later in this chapter), you can replace Default with one of your own styles on the Style popup menu. The New button in the Edit Paragraph Style Sheet dialog box lets you create a new character style and apply it to this paragraph style in one fell swoop. If you've chosen a character style instead of Default, all the character attributes of that character style sheet are used in the paragraph-based style sheet you're defining.

In other words, you don't have to use character style sheets if you don't want to. You can leave the popup menu set to Default and press Edit to define the values. Just remember to think ahead, as building character styles and using them in paragraph styles may be more flexible down the line.

> **TIP: Beware of the Edit Button.** *Watch out for the Edit button in the Edit Paragraph Style Sheet dialog box when you're using a character style other than Default. If you make an edit here, it edits the character style, too! Unfortunately, this makes it way too easy to change your character styles accidentally (you might change them thinking that you're only editing the value for this paragraph style—not so).*

Editing style sheets. To edit a style sheet, select it from the list of styles in the Style Sheets dialog box and click the Edit button. You see the same tabbed dialog box as you did when you were creating the style sheet. Go ahead and make the changes you want, then press OK and, finally, press Save to leave the Style Sheets dialog box.

> **TIP: Even Speedier Style Sheets.** *You can avoid the Style Sheets dialog box altogether by holding down the Control key and clicking on a style name in the Style Sheets palette (in Windows, click on any name in the palette with the right mouse button). The context-sensitive menu that appears lets you edit, duplicate, or delete the style that you clicked on (see Figure 7-8). Or you can create a new style by selecting New.*

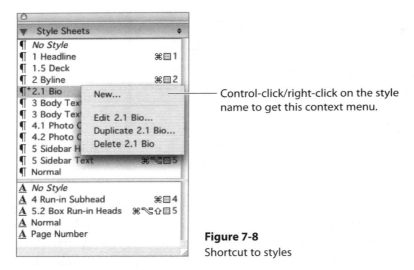

Control-click/right-click on the style name to get this context menu.

Figure 7-8
Shortcut to styles

Note that if you select New when clicking on one of the character styles, you'll create a new character style; if you click on one of the paragraph styles in the palette, you'll create a new paragraph style sheet. This is certainly the fastest way to create a style sheet, because you never have to look at the clunky Style Sheets dialog box.

Normal Style and No Style

Every QuarkXPress project has a default paragraph style—the Normal style. This is the style automatically applied to all your text if you don't specifically apply another style (if you type in a new text box, it's always in the Normal style). You can edit the Normal paragraph style just like any other style.

No Style is different; applying it removes *all* style sheet information from a paragraph. (It doesn't remove your formatting, just any style sheet affiliation.) All the paragraph's formatting is then treated as local or hard formatting. Normally, local formatting doesn't change when you apply a style to a paragraph. However, if the paragraph has No Style applied to it, subsequently applying a style sheet wipes out all local formatting. For instance, if you have some words in italic, in a No Style paragraph, then applying any other style sheet to that paragraph will remove the italics (assuming that the new style sheet you've just applied is not itself defined as italic).

> **TIP: Default Font.** *Tired of Helvetica or Arial being the font that appears by default when you create a new text box and type in it? The font you type in is defined in the Normal paragraph style sheet. To change the default font (or leading, or color, or any other paragraph or character formatting), modify your "Normal" paragraph style sheet. Simple as that. To affect all subsequent files, you can even change it when no projects are open.*

> **TIP: Totally Overriding Local Formatting.** *The fact that a paragraph that has No Style applied to it loses all local formatting (including bold and italic) when it's tagged with another style sheet is, more often than not, a pain in the butt and causes much confusion. However, there are some powerful uses for this feature, such as stripping out all local formatting that some dumbbell put in for no good reason. (The good news in QuarkXPress 7 is that if "dumbbells" are frequently working on your projects, you can lock stories so they cannot be edited or reformatted. Just click on any box containing the story and choose Story from the Lock submenu of the Item menu. Yes, they can do that to unlock it—but remember, they're dumb.)*

Always on the lookout for a faster way to do something, I was pleased to find that I can apply "No Style" to a paragraph and then apply a style sheet in one stroke by Option/Alt-clicking on the style I want to apply in the Style Sheets palette.

> **TIP: Removing Just Some Formatting.** *In the previous tip, we learned that "No Style" is great for eliminating all local formatting in a paragraph. However, what if you want to get rid of only some local formatting?*

Instead of using "No Style" to get rid of all local formatting wherever it occurs, you can get clever with the way a project's paragraph styles are defined. The trick is that QuarkXPress is built in such a way that it only remembers local formatting that is different from the formatting in a paragraph style sheet. So, first change the style sheet so that it contains the formatting you want to remove, then remove that unwanted formatting from the style sheet.

This is much easier to understand with an example. Let's say you have a whole lot of text that has a "Body Text" style sheet applied to it, but some bozo selected the whole thing and changed the typeface to 18-point Futura (this kind of error happens a lot when you copy and paste text from one project to another and the style sheets are slightly different in each file).

The problem is that there are also words in the text that are made italic for emphasis. If you apply "No Style" to everything, then apply the "Body Text" style again, you wipe out all italic attributes in the text, and you'll have to go back and find the right words and reapply italics by hand. However, using this technique saves the day (see Figure 7-9).

> She is like a <u>tree planted by streams</u> of water, that yields its *fruit* in its **season;** whose *leaf* does not wither, and everything she does shall *prosper.* The ungodly <u>are not so, **but** are</u> like **chaff** which the wind blows away.

1. Someone has gone in and changed some text to a different font and added underline style.

> She is like a tree planted by streams of water, that yields its *fruit* in its **season;** whose *leaf* does not wither, and everything she does shall *prosper.* The ungodly are not so, but are like **chaff** which the wind blows away.

2. Change the paragraph style to match the local formatting.

> She is like a tree planted by streams of water, that yields its *fruit* in its **season;** whose *leaf* does not wither, and everything she does shall *prosper.* The ungodly are not so, but are like **chaff** which the wind blows away.

3. Change the style back; the unwanted formatting is lost, but the desired local formatting remains.

Figure 7-9 Removing only the local formatting you don't want

1. Edit the "Body Text" style so that its definition includes all the formatting that you *want to get rid of.* In this example, change the character formatting to 18-point Futura.

2. Save the change to the style sheet.

3. Edit the "Body Text" style again. This time, define it the way it was originally. In this example, you'd define it with the original typeface and size.

4. Save the change to the style sheet.

Now all the text is formatted properly: you've gotten all the text to be the original typeface and size, but you've retained the italic local formatting as well. You don't have to select the text; you just have to adjust the style sheets. (Of course, this tip relies on your knowing what local formatting has been applied to the text; if you don't know that, see "TIP: Finding Local Formatting," later in this chapter.)

TIP: Redefining Tabs in Styles. Although you can define tabs within a paragraph style, it's a pain in the left buttock going back and forth between editing a style and looking at its effects on your page. An easier solution takes advantage of creating style sheets by example (see the previous tip) and the ability to merge styles. This tip assumes that you've already created a paragraph style sheet, and that you need to edit the tab stops.

1. Apply the style sheet to a paragraph (or select a paragraph that has the style already applied to it).

2. Change the tab stops of that paragraph to where you'd like them to be.

3. Create a new style sheet based on this new paragraph (see "TIP: Even Speedier Style Sheets" for the fastest way to do this). Name this style sheet slightly differently from the original style sheet (I usually just append the word "new").

4. Control-click (or on Windows machines, right-click) on the name of the old style sheet and choose Delete from the context-sensitive popup menu. When you're prompted with a dialog box asking for a replacement style, select the new style sheet and click OK.

5. Finally, Control-click (or click with the right mouse button) on the new style name, select Edit, and rename it without appending the word "new."

Of course, this isn't only for changing tabs. You can use this technique to change any element of a style sheet. However, note that this only works with a style that isn't based on another style, and it won't work with the Normal style.

Appending Styles

The Append button in the Style Sheets dialog box lets you import styles from other QuarkXPress projects into the active QuarkXPress project. After selecting the file from which you want to import, the program lets you choose exactly which styles you want (see Figure 7-10). In case you don't know what the incoming styles look like, QuarkXPress shows you the definitions in the Description area of the Append Style Sheets dialog box.

Because the incoming style sheet may include information about another style sheet (like a paragraph style that refers to a character style, or a style that is based on another), QuarkXPress always warns you that it may be importing more than you bargained for (see Figure 7-11). This dialog box becomes really annoying after you see it once or twice. Fortunately, the folks at Quark gave us an out: simply turn on the checkbox in the alert dialog box, and QuarkXPress refrains from displaying it again. Whether you turn the alert off or not, you should always check to see what styles have actually been imported.

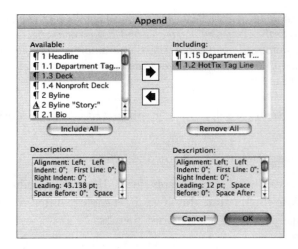

Figure 7-10
Appending styles

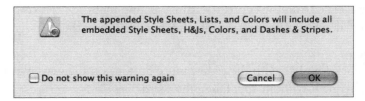

Figure 7-11
QuarkXPress alerts you when
you're importing more than
you bargained for.

When you press OK in the Append Style Sheets dialog box, QuarkXPress checks to see if any incoming styles have the same name as those already in your project. If it finds such a conflict, it displays another alert dialog box and asks you what to do (see Figure 7-12). You've got four options, each a separate button.

- **Rename.** You get to manually rename the style that's being imported with any other unused name.

- **Auto-Rename.** Automatically renames the incoming style, with an asterisk at the beginning of its name. I'm not sure why you'd use this, but I bet there's a good reason.

- **Use New.** The incoming style overwrites the one already in the project. I almost always use either Use New or Rename.

- **Use Existing.** This effectively cancels the appending of the style; the old one (the one currently in the project) is retained and used. Use this if you prefer your QuarkXPress style sheet definition over the incoming style sheet.

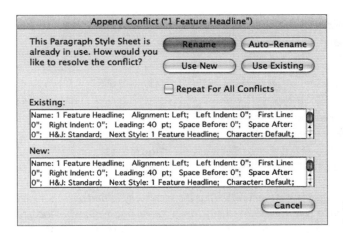

Figure 7-12
Conflicting style sheets alert

If you think there's going to be more than one conflicting style name, you may want to turn on the checkbox marked Repeat for All Conflicts. This way, QuarkXPress handles the remaining conflicts in the same way.

Of course, remember that there is also an Append feature on the File menu that you can use to import things such as style sheets, colors, H&Js (even entire layouts in QuarkXPress 7!) at the same time. If you need to import both styles and colors, for instance, it's clearly more efficient to do it with Append instead of in the Style Sheets dialog box.

Appending with Copy and Paste. Another way to move a style from one QuarkXPress project to another is to copy text containing that style. You can use Copy and Paste, or you can drag a box containing the text from one project to another. However, beware: QuarkXPress won't alert you to any style-name conflicts. Instead, it just throws away the incoming style's formatting information and replaces it with the existing style's attributes plus local formatting on top so that the text looks the same as it did in the source project. In other words, this is a good way to import a style or two, but it's often a lousy way to import text, especially when the style name already exists in the target project.

> **TIP: Comparing Two Styles.** *I hate it when I have two styles that are very similar but I can't remember how they're different. Fortunately, QuarkXPress lets you compare two style sheets. Select two styles in the Style Sheets dialog box (click on one, and then Command/Ctrl-click on the other), then Option/Alt-click the Append button. (Actually, as soon as you hold down the Option/Alt key, you'll see the Append button change to a Compare button.) The result: a dialog box that lists each element of the two style sheets; the differences are highlighted in bold (see Figure 7-13). Of course, you can only compare two character styles or two paragraph styles; you can't mix and match.*

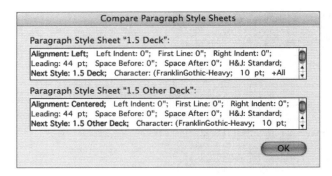

Figure 7-13
Comparing two styles

TIP: Find Local Formatting. Earlier I mentioned that there's no way to find out what local format-ting someone has applied to text. That's not strictly true. You can figure out what local formatting is on a paragraph by creating a new style sheet based on the local formatting (just create a style while the cursor is in the text) and using the Compare button (see the previous tip) to compare the new style with the original style. The differences between the two indicate local formatting.

Deleting (and Replacing) Styles

You can delete a style sheet by clicking the Delete button in the Style Sheets dialog box (Command/Ctrl-clicking lets you select and delete more than one style; Shift-Delete lets you select contiguous styles). If the style sheet has been applied somewhere in your project (or if it's referenced by another style sheet—see "Basing One Style on Another," next), QuarkXPress asks you if you want to replace the style with another one. That is, all the text that is tagged with the deleted style is assigned a new style sheet, rather than going to "No Style."

Basing One Style on Another

You can also base one style sheet on another. By basing many styles on, say, the Normal style, you can quickly change many elements in your project by simply changing the Normal style.

For example, let's say you want all your subheads to be the same as the "Heading 1" style, but centered and with 14 points of space before. By basing the subhead style on the "Heading 1" style, you can ensure that every change you make to the "Heading 1" style is instantly reflected in the subhead style. If you change the "Heading 1" style's font from Helvetica to Franklin Gothic, the font of the subheads based on the "Heading 1" style automatically changes from Helvetica to Franklin Gothic as well. (In this case, the "Heading 1" style sheet is the *parent style* and the subhead style based on it is called the *child style*.)

Here's how you can base one style on another.

1. Choose a style sheet from the Based On popup menu in the Edit Paragraph Style Sheet dialog box. In the previous example, choose Normal.

2. Edit options in the various tabs in the Edit Paragraph Style Sheet dialog box to change only those attributes you want to be different in the new style. In this example, you would change the Alignment and Space Before settings on the Formats tab of the dialog box. Watch out, though—changing the character formatting in the two styles can be a little tricky, so make sure you carefully read the "Character-based Styles" section later in this chapter.

3. Note that the description at the bottom of the Edit Paragraph Style Sheet dialog box lists the "based on" style along with all the additional formatting you've applied to the new style (see Figure 7-14). Click OK and then click Save to leave the Style Sheets dialog box.

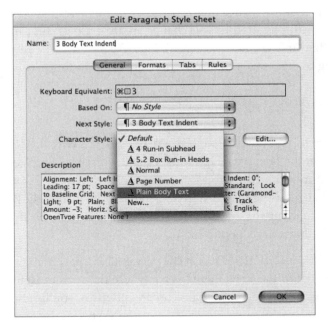

Figure 7-14
Basing one style
sheet on another

If you plan your styles carefully, you can use the Based On feature to create nested hierarchies of styles based upon one another, so that a simple change to one style will be applied to all the styles based on it, and the styles based on those, *ad infinitum*. This "ripple effect" can be a great time-saver, so it's well worth your while to take the greatest advantage of it.

TIP: Based-On Differences. When one style is based on another, QuarkXPress only keeps track of the differences between the base style and the new style. Let's say you have a style called "Head1" and it's 18-point Futura with the bold style applied, and a style called "Head2" that's based on "Head1," except that it's 12-point Futura and is not bold. The differences between the two are the point size and the bold attribute.

If you change the font of "Head1" to Franklin Gothic, then the font of "Head2" changes, too. But if you change the point size of "Head1" to 24 point, then "Head2" does not change, because the point-size "link" is broken. However, there's one important exception: if you change the parent style to have attributes that are *the same* as the child style, the difference is broken. If you change "Head1" to "not bold," for example, then there's no difference in style between the two, and the link is broken. Then, if you go back and change "Head1" to bold again, "Head2" follows suit and becomes bold. This is much the same as what happens when local formatting within a paragraph matches the formatting of the style (see "Local Formatting Versus Formatting with Styles," earlier in this chapter).

To summarize: As long as you don't change any formatting in the parent style to match the child style, you'll be fine. But as soon as you change an attribute in the parent style to match the child style, that link is broken, the child style isn't different in that way anymore—and you're going to wish that you'd paid more attention to this paragraph.

Next Style

If you're typing in QuarkXPress, and the paragraph you're on is tagged with the "Heading" style, you probably don't want the next paragraph to be tagged with "Heading" too, right? (Unless you want two headings in a row.) You can force QuarkXPress to automatically change the subsequent style sheet using the Next Style popup menu in the Edit Paragraph Style Sheet dialog box. If you want the subsequent paragraph to be "Body Text," then choose "Body Text" from the Next Style popup menu.

Note that this only works if the insertion point is at the very end of a paragraph when you press Return (turn on Invisibles in the View menu to see where the current Return character is). If the insertion point is anywhere else when you press Return, you'll simply break that paragraph in two, and both new paragraphs will have the same style as the original one.

In other words, this feature is essentially intended to be used while you're typing, not while you're doing the simple kinds of editing or formatting you're likely to be doing in QuarkXPress. However, it certainly can come in handy once in a while.

When you're first creating a style sheet, the default choice on the Next Style popup menu is "Self," which simply means that the next style will be the same as the current style (no change at all).

Character-Based Styles

Character styles let you quickly apply formatting to selected words within a paragraph. Almost everything that I said earlier about paragraph styles is also true of character styles. You create, edit, append, and delete them in almost exactly the same manner. There are, of course, some differences. For instance, to create a character style sheet, you should choose Character instead of Paragraph from the New popup menu in the Style Sheets dialog box. Also, because these are character styles, you can only assign character formatting to them (the kind of formatting you can apply to a single character, such as font, size, color, shade, scale, type style, tracking, and baseline shift; see Figure 7-15).

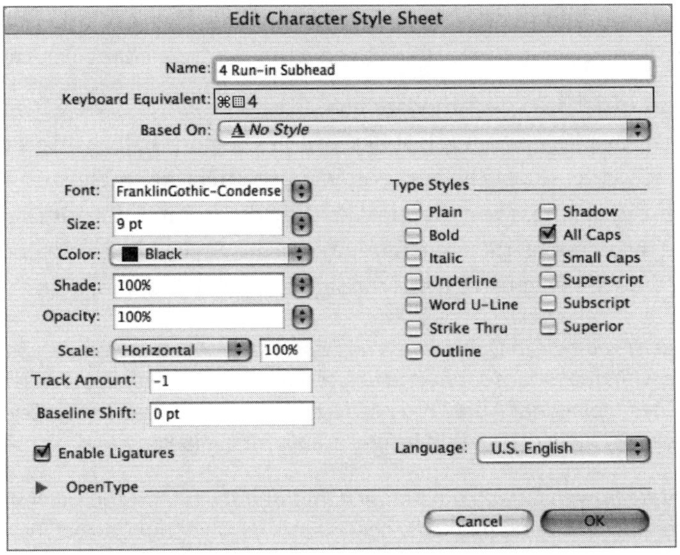

Figure 7-15
Editing or creating a character style sheet

As I said earlier, when you start typing in a new text box, the text automatically is set to the Normal paragraph style sheet. However, because the definition of the Normal paragraph style includes a reference to the Normal character style sheet, all your text is automatically set to that character style as well.

If you create a new character style (you can use the step-by-step "by example" approach outlined earlier) and apply it to some text that is already in the Normal style, it acts like local formatting on top of the Normal style.

There's no doubt that character style sheets can add to your general level of confusion, especially at first. However, there are several really good reasons to push through and keep using them until they become second nature.

- Using character style sheets throughout your text ensures consistent formatting, and makes the process of formatting the text go faster. This is very important if you have more than one layout or project making up a larger publication (such as chapters in a book).

- By assigning character styles within paragraph styles, you can also ensure consistency among multiple paragraph style sheets. For instance, if your Heading1, Heading2, and Heading3 paragraph styles all use the same "Heading" character style sheet, you only have to change this one character style sheet to update all three paragraph styles.

- The most important reason to use character styles (or style sheets in general) is the inevitability that your art director or client will start laughing uncontrollably when they see your design and then make you change something. Because this change always happens just before a deadline, style sheets are your best chance at salvation.

Style Sheets palette. In order to accommodate character styles, the Style Sheets palette is split in half; the top half displays paragraph styles and the bottom half displays character styles. To apply a character style, select the text you want to affect, then click on the character style sheet name in the palette. (Yes, if you're paid by the hour and want to do things the slow way, you could also choose the style name from the Style menu.) Even better, if you use a certain character style sheet frequently, assign it a keyboard shortcut.

> **TIP: Back to Body Text.** *If you type in QuarkXPress and apply style sheets as you go, you can apply a character style with a keyboard command before you type the word. But then what happens when you've finished typing that word? You need a character style sheet with a keyboard shortcut that gets you back to where you were before, usually plain old Body Text.*

> **TIP: The Balance of Style Power.** *Do you have more paragraph styles than character styles? You can change the palette's size by dragging the resize box in its lower-right corner. You can also drag the boundary marker between the paragraph styles and the character styles.*

> **TIP: Search and Replace Your Style Sheets.** *Back in Chapter 5, Working with Text, I discussed how you can use the Find/Change feature to search for and replace style sheets. However, here's one less-intuitive way to use Find/Change: search for particular character formatting and "replace" it with a character style. For example, let's say you inherit a project from a designer who didn't know how to use character styles—such as a book project like this one, with run-in heads. You could apply a character style sheet to the run-in head formatting so if the design changed, you could just edit the style sheet in the future.*

Set up the Find What side of the Find/Change palette to search for one or more of the particular character attributes of the run-in heads. On the Change To side, turn off the checkboxes for everything except the Style Sheet popup menu, in which you should choose the character style you want to apply. Making this change is the same as manually applying the character style to each run-in head—but it's much faster.

One note, though: Make sure that the definition of the character style you're applying is the same as the formatting of the text you're searching for. If the formatting is different, then QuarkXPress will apply the style and leave some of the original attributes as local formatting, defeating the purpose entirely.

Character styles in Based On paragraph styles. Earlier, I discussed the value of using the Based On feature in paragraph style sheets, but I mentioned that changing character formatting in a "child style" gets a little tricky. That was an understatement; in fact, the whole way that character styles and paragraph styles interact is probably the most confusing aspect of style sheets in QuarkXPress, and most likely to cause blood vessels to burst in your forehead. Fortunately, it's not without logic; it just takes some getting used to. Here are two rules to live by.

- If the Character Style popup menu within the parent style is set to Default, then you can easily edit the character formatting in the child style: just click the Edit button.

- If the Character Style within the parent style is set to one of your character style sheets, then you have to be really careful when making a change (see Figure 7-16). Clicking the Edit button will edit the character style itself, which is rarely what you want. (If you edit the character style itself, it will affect both the parent and child styles, as well as any other text or style that uses that character style!)

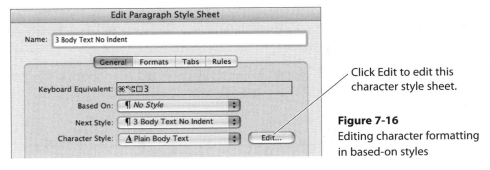

Click Edit to edit this character style sheet.

Figure 7-16
Editing character formatting in based-on styles

Instead, you should create a new character style (by choosing the New option from the Character Style popup menu), and base this new character style on the same character style that the parent style uses (use the Based On feature). Yes, this is annoying. Yes, this makes me want to kick someone. But that's the way it works.

In the latter case (where you've assigned a character style to your parent style), here's a step-by-step method for how to proceed.

1. Create a new paragraph style sheet, and set the Based On popup menu to the desired parent style. At this point, everything about your new style is exactly the same as this parent style.

2. Note the name of the character style listed on the Character Attributes Style popup menu. If it's Default, you can stop here and go read the first bullet point again; if it's not Default, then commit the name to memory (or write it down, if it's at the end of the day).

3. Choose the New option from the Character Style popup menu to create a new character style sheet.

4. In the Edit Character Style Sheet dialog box that appears, choose the name of the character style from the Based On popup menu.

5. Finally, go ahead and make the changes you want to make to the character formatting (if you can still remember what you were trying to do by now).

6. Give this new character style a name (I usually use a name like "Style based on Such-and-such") and then press OK. This adds the new character style to your list, and also applies it to the child paragraph style you're working on.

7. Make any changes to the paragraph formatting you want applied to this child style, and then press OK.

This seems like it'd take longer than it really does, and after doing it a few times, you get the hang of it.

WHAT WORD PROCESSOR TO USE

Although QuarkXPress can import formatted text from several word processors, it can only interpret the styles of Microsoft Word files and styles saved in Rich Text Format (RTF) files. (If you have another word processor that uses styles and can save them as Microsoft Word or RTF files, you're in luck too.) In general, since styles are so important to the proper management of your copy, Word automatically becomes the best word processor for working with QuarkXPress. Another option is to work with QuarkCopyDesk, a word processor based on the text engine of QuarkXPress. Visit www.quark.com for more information.

How QuarkXPress Style Sheets Work with Word

When you bring a Word document into QuarkXPress and you've checked Include Style Sheets in the Import Text dialog box, QuarkXPress imports every style from the Word file, incorporating as much of Word's formatting as QuarkXPress can handle.

Character formatting. QuarkXPress can import a great deal of Word's own formatting. All the character attributes available in Word can be carried over into QuarkXPress, with a few exceptions (see Table 7-1).

Paragraph formatting. For paragraph formats, QuarkXPress brings in most available Word settings, except that it ignores the Page Break Before setting, and only the top and bottom rules set for boxed paragraphs will be imported (though QuarkXPress does a good job of interpreting the correct size and weight of rules). QuarkXPress ignores any values you've set for space between rules and their paragraphs.

Table 7-1 What QuarkXPress does with Word's formatting

Word's formatting	What QuarkXPress does with it
Double line and dotted line	Turns them into normal underlines.
Superscript and subscript	Applies whatever values you've specified settings for them within your QuarkXPress layout (in Character Preferences).
Expanded and condensed	Roughly converts them to tracking values in QuarkXPress.
Footnotes	Numbers are changed to superscript style; footnote text is added at end of story.

Style formatting. Any of Word's attributes that can be applied to styles can be successfully imported as styles by QuarkXPress, with the exceptions noted above.

If your QuarkXPress project has style sheets with the same names as those in your Word file, you may be given the choice to import or override those Word styles. This dialog box looks suspiciously like the conflicting style sheets dialog box we saw in "Append," earlier in this chapter, and in fact it gives you the same four options: Rename, Auto-rename, Use Existing, and Use New. About 99 percent of the time, you'll want to click Use Existing, so the style definition already within QuarkXPress will be applied (see "TIP: Don't Worry About Word Style Definitions," below).

Whatever you do, the local formatting you've applied in the Word project is imported, too.

> **TIP: Word Versions Spell Trouble.** To be honest, even though Microsoft Word works better with QuarkXPress than any other word processor does, it's still not a perfect system. Often, exporting RTF from Word works best of all.

*TIP: **Don't Worry About Word Style Definitions.*** *Remember that QuarkXPress can override Microsoft Word's formatting for style sheets. Let's say that your Microsoft Word document's "Normal" style is 14-point Geneva with 24-point leading (for easy reading and editing on screen), and your QuarkXPress project's "Normal" style is 11-point Goudy with 15-point leading. When you import the file and you're asked to resolve the conflict with Normal, click Use New and QuarkXPress will automatically use the QuarkXPress version of the style sheet, and all the text that is tagged as "Normal" will appear in 11/15 Goudy (like you'd want it to).*

The implication of this tip is that you never really have to worry about what the styles look like in Word. In this book, for example, my Microsoft Word text was all in Arial and Times, but when I imported the text files into QuarkXPress, they came out in the fonts you're reading right now (Aldine 401, Trajan, and Myriad Pro).

*TIP: **Don't Forget to Include Style Sheets.*** *You should almost always turn on the Include Style Sheets option in the Import Text dialog box when importing text. If you don't, QuarkXPress may apply "No Style" to all the text. If you have any intention of applying other paragraph style sheets to these paragraphs, you're in for a surprise: all your local formatting—even italic—disappears as soon as you apply a paragraph style (see "Totally Overriding Local Formatting," previously).*

On the other hand, if you do turn on Include Style Sheets, QuarkXPress applies either the styles from the word processor (if there are any) or it just uses "Normal." In fact, one of the very few times I turn off Include Style Sheets is when I'm working with XPress Tags (which I discuss later in this chapter).

*TIP: **Text Reflow Between Versions.*** *Each version of QuarkXPress flows text slightly differently, because Quark keeps changing features. Don't worry about how the text will change when you open an older-version file in a newer version of QuarkXPress. Each file is tagged with a version number, and QuarkXPress is smart enough to check that tag before starting to reflow the text.*

However, if you want to update the file to take advantage of the latest and greatest features and algorithms, hold down the Option/Alt key as you click Open in the Open dialog box. The old text flow is ignored, and QuarkXPress flows the text the way it thinks it should. Often, there's no difference. But sometimes, you'll see a lot of change. It depends on what you're working on, how it's laid out, and what features you took advantage of (such as hyphenation and ligatures). The best thing to do is to peruse your file carefully after Option/Alt-opening it.

*TIP: **Database Publishing.*** *Creating a telephone directory? Cataloging thousands of products? Formatting information taken from a database or spreadsheet? These all fall into the category of database publishing. Whether you're formatting 50 pieces of information or 50,000, a database-publishing tool can be of great help.*

One method of manipulating lots of data is to program your database to export text in XPress Tags format (which I'll cover later). If your database can handle that and you know how to do it (or know someone who does), this can be very powerful. (For example, even relatively common database programs such as FileMaker Pro can be programmed to export in XPress Tags format without much hassle.)

A second method is to use the mail merge functionality in a program like Microsoft Word and then import the merged document into QuarkXPress. This works surprisingly well in some cases. I know of people who do whole catalogs using this method.

However, since I usually like to keep things simple, even when I'm doing complex jobs, I love the Xdata XTension from Em software (*www.emsoftware.com*). That's not only because it works well with QuarkXPress, but because it has made my life so much easier.

I once produced a 17,000-name directory using Xdata and QuarkXPress. Just when I thought I was stuck with manually applying paragraph styles to 17,000 names, I heard about Xdata. Each person's name, address, and telephone number was formatted precisely the way that I designed it, and, additionally, I could take advantage of almost every typographic feature in QuarkXPress. If you can face the learning curve, you can also use QuarkXPress XML and PPML features for database publishing, but that's a whole 'nother topic.

EXPORTING TEXT

After you go through all the trouble of bringing copy into QuarkXPress and formatting it, then why would you want to export it? Aside from administrative reasons (backups, use in a database, archiving the text, and so on), there are three major situations in which exporting text can be important.

- If you have a *lot* of text in a story and QuarkXPress feels sluggish when you work with it, you might want to consider exporting your text to a word processor, editing it there, and then reimporting it into QuarkXPress. In general, though, it's usually better to keep the text in QuarkXPress if you can, or else you may lose some of your formatting.

- You also might want to export text if you work in a busy workgroup–publishing environment. You may find it absolutely necessary to pull text out of QuarkXPress so that editors can work on it while you continue to refine a layout. (In this case, you might also try Composition Zones; see Chapter 13, *Collaboration*.)

- The best reason to export text, however, is if you want to do something that can't be done easily (or at all) from within QuarkXPress. I'll give some examples of this when I discuss XPress Tags, later on in this chapter.

How to Export Text

Exporting text from a QuarkXPress layout is pretty much the opposite of importing it.

1. With the Content tool, select a text box containing the story you want to export. Or if you want to export only a certain amount of text, select it first. (You can, of course, also select a text path or a table cell containing text.)

2. Choose Save Text from the File menu (or press Command-Option-E or Ctrl-Alt-E). The Save Text dialog box appears.

3. Give the exported file a name and tell QuarkXPress where to save it. Select either Entire Story or Selected Text button, depending on what you want saved.

4. Use the Format (or "Save as Type" in Windows) popup menu to choose the format for the file. The formats listed on the menu depend on which filters you have in your XTension folder. You can generally leave the Encoding popup menu set to the default of Unicode (UTF-16).

5. Press Return or click OK.

Shortcomings of Exporting Text

The most important consideration when bringing text out of QuarkXPress and then back in is how to do this without losing all the formatting you've applied within QuarkXPress. No current word processor (other than Quark's own QuarkCopyDesk) can handle horizontal scaling or kerning properly, for instance, and such formatting could easily be lost during the export/reimport process. There are ways to keep this formatting intact no matter where your QuarkXPress text ends up, however, by using XPress Tags.

TIP: Exporting Styles. *I often use QuarkXPress's Export feature to export all my styles to Microsoft Word. This saves my having to re-create every style name on Microsoft Word's style sheet. For instance, I can design a whole book or magazine, then export the styles for writers and editors to use when creating copy, and be assured that the style names will match when I import the files. To export styles, create a little one-line paragraph for each style. Apply the style, then export that text in Word format. When you open the file in Word, all the styles will be there.*

TIP: Printing Your Style Sheet. *If you export the styles as described in the last tip, you can print the styles from Microsoft Word. Open your Word document that contains all your styles, select Print from the File menu, choose Styles from the Print What popup menu (called Settings in some operating systems), and then click Print. A lot of the formatting in QuarkXPress styles doesn't get passed to Word, so the printout isn't complete. But it's better than nothing. (Thanks to Sandee Cohen for this one!)*

A Solution: XPress Tags

There is a solution to the problem of losing formatting when exporting and re-importing text, however: Export the file in the special text-only ASCII format called XPress Tags. XPress Tags uses its own special—and complicated—coding that records every single one of QuarkXPress's text-formatting attributes, from style sheets to local formatting (see Figure 7-17). In fact, if you're familiar with the old code-based typesetters, you'll love XPress Tags.

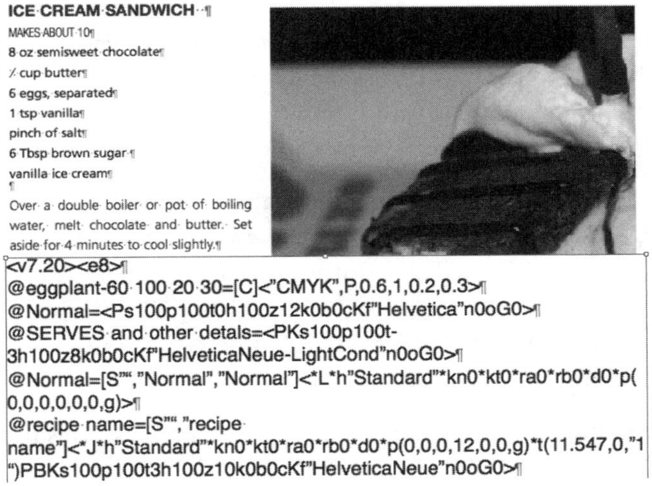

When you save this file in XPress Tags format…

…the text file looks like this.

Figure 7-17
XPress Tags

You may find a text-only file with XPress Tags confusing to look at, with its multitude of arcane numbers and codes. However, there are many reasons why XPress Tags is the best format to use when you need to edit and then re-import copy.

> **TIP: Learning XPress Tags.** The best way to learn the codes is to create some text in QuarkXPress, style it in various ways, and export the text in XPress Tags format (I discuss importing and exporting tags, below). You can then open this file in a word processor and decipher the codes.

Why Use XPress Tags?

Not only do XPress Tags files retain all of a story's QuarkXPress formatting, but because ASCII ("text only") is a universal file format, these files can be edited by virtually any word processor—Mac OS, Windows, MS-DOS, or UNIX. Although the coding may appear daunting if you're used to the WYSIWYG world of Windows or Mac OS, professional typesetters have been working with code-based systems for years, and tagged files can be easily integrated into such an environment.

So if you find yourself regularly needing to export QuarkXPress stories with sophisticated text formatting, XPress Tags is clearly the way to go. While it may take a while to get used to editing an XPress Tags file, it's a lot less work than having to painstakingly reformat your copy every time you bring it back into a QuarkXPress layout.

How to Use XPress Tags

There are a small handful of issues you should keep in mind when you work with XPress Tags.

- To export a story from QuarkXPress in XPress Tags format, choose Save Text from the File menu (Command-Option-E or Ctrl-Alt-E) and select XPress Tags from the Format popup menu (or File Type popup menu in Windows). The file you get is a text-only file that can be opened in any word processor or reimported into QuarkXPress.

- To import an XPress Tags file (or any text-only file that has XPress Tags in it) into QuarkXPress, use Import Text (Command/Ctrl-E), like you would for any other text file. However, if Interpret XPress Tags is turned on in the Import Text dialog box, QuarkXPress interprets the tags back into text formatting. If this option is turned off, QuarkXPress just reads the codes into a text box (this is useful if you don't have a word processor).

- If you import the tagged file into QuarkXPress with Interpret XPress Tags turned off, make sure you also turn off the Convert Quotes option in the Import Text dialog box. If Convert Quotes is turned on, QuarkXPress converts the straight quotes in the tagged file into curly quotes—and XPress Tags only understands straight quotes. If you're just looking at the file, it hardly matters; but if you're going to edit the codes, re-export them, and then reimport them with Include Style Sheets turned on, then those dang curly quotes will cause you no end of problems.

  This also applies to editing the tags in a word processor that has a Smart Quotes feature. If something is going wrong when you're importing XPress Tags, checking for stray curly quotes is one of the first things you should do.

  TIP: Applying Styles in Text Editors. One of the most simple (yet powerful) uses of XPress Tags is to apply style sheets or formatting to text from within a word processor or text editor that doesn't support style sheets. For instance, if you use a simple text editor that doesn't even let you apply italic formatting, you can type <I> before and after a word. When you import the file into QuarkXPress, these simple tags are interpreted and the word is made italic (the first time the tag is applied, it turns italic on; the second time, it turns it off).

You can apply a paragraph style sheet by typing `@stylesheet:` at the beginning of a paragraph (yes, you need the colon at the end). The style sheet will be applied to all subsequent paragraphs until you specify a change to another style. Similarly, the code to apply a character style sheet as local formatting is `<@stylesheet>` (to apply the style) and `<@$p>` (to end the character style).

Once you're familiar with the coding format used by XPress Tags, you can easily set up a macro to apply formatting codes to an ASCII file in your word processor (you can use QuicKeys—for Mac OS or Windows—to do this in any text editor). If you're more ambitious, and handy with database programs, you can even design a report format that creates a file incorporating XPress Tags, so you can export data from your database and have it land on your QuarkXPress pages fully formatted and untouched by human hands.

> **TIP: Fake Fractions the XPress Tags Way.** *Here's an XPress Tags search-and-replace procedure that can save hours when you have to create a large number of well-set fractions in a project such as a cookbook. It will save tons of time over the QuarkXPress Make Fraction type style or digging through the Glyphs palette hoping for the right fractions. For example, you can search for all instances of "1/2" and replace them with* `<z7k-10b-3>1<z12k-8b0>?<z8k0>2<z$>`*. This set of codes makes the size 7 point, the kerning 10 units, and the baseline shift 3 points, then types "1". It then changes the type size to 12 point, the kerning to -8 units, and the baseline shift to zero before typing a fraction bar (Option-Shift-1 or Alt-0164 in the Symbol font in Windows). Finally, it makes the size 8 point, sets no kerning, and types "2" before resetting the type size back to its original value.*

This may seem like a lot to you, but once you get the hang of it, it's extremely easy and can save you enormous amounts of time.

> **TIP: Expert Fractions with XPress Tags.** *The previous tip is useful for building "made" fractions: fractions that are created by resizing type and moving it around. What if you want "drawn" fractions—numerators and denominators predesigned just for this use? Expert Set fonts with this sort of character are available for many type families (Minion, Utopia, and Bembo, to name just a few). Using XPress Tags, you can automate their substitution, too.*

This works for the fractions shown in Table 7-2. Export your text in XPress Tags format and open the file in a word processor. Let's say you want to convert all the "1/4" fractions. In the word processor, search for "1/4" and replace it with `<f"MinionExp-Regular">G <f"Minion-Regular">`.

Table 7-2 Ready-made fractions in Expert Sets and their keystrokes (may be different in your fonts).

Fraction	Expert Keystroke		Fraction	Expert Keystroke
$\frac{1}{4}$	G		$\frac{5}{8}$	L
$\frac{1}{2}$	H		$\frac{7}{8}$	M
$\frac{3}{4}$	I		$\frac{1}{3}$	N
$\frac{1}{8}$	J		$\frac{2}{3}$	O
$\frac{3}{8}$	K			

The Expert Sets also contain the numerals zero through nine in the numerator and denominator positions, so you can create any other fraction, too. Press Shift-Option-0 through Shift-Option-9 to get the raised numerators, and Option-0 through Option-9 to get the baseline denominators. The correct fraction bar is the slash in the Expert Sets. You can automate this process somewhat with XPress Tags, but you have to create each different fraction individually. For instance, to make the fraction ?‹?¡§, you would search for "13/16" and replace with <f"MinionExp-Regular"> followed by Option-Shift-1, Option-Shift-3, slash, Option-1, Option-6, and finally <f"Minion-Regular">. One step too complicated? Maybe—but it sure saves time if you've got oodles of text with fractions.

> **TIP: Those Silly Case-Sensitive Tags.** *Don't forget that all XPress Tags are case-sensitive. Typing* <H> *rather than* <h> *can mean the difference between small caps, horizontal scaling, and failure. Style, color, and H&J names are the same way. If you forget them, they're easy enough to search and replace in Word or a case-sensitive text editor.*

> **TIP: Xtags Is One Step Beyond.** *There is an alternative to the XPress Tags language and filter that ships with QuarkXPress. It's a third-party commercial XTension named Xtags, from Em Software. Xtags is a superset of XPress Tags, which means that all XPress Tags will work with the Xtags filter. However, Xtags adds much more functionality, such as powerful error checking, anchored boxes (text and picture), relative size changes (up a point, down two points, etc.), and much, much more.*

There is simply not enough room here to even *begin* to describe some of Xtags's cooler features. Suffice it to say that once you start using Xtags for importing your text, you'll soon discover so many things you can automate that you'll wonder how you ever got along without it.

GETTING YOUR STORIES STRAIGHT

Just because you've taken advantage of style sheets and XPress Tags doesn't mean you won't still find it necessary to burn the midnight oil making last-minute changes. Get to know styles, import and export filters, and especially XPress Tags, and you can go a long way toward being lazy: making your computer do the work, rather than having to do it yourself.

CHAPTER EIGHT
Tables

Building tables in QuarkXPress has long been a painful task without buying a third-party XTension. Fortunately, XPress now has a Table tool that lets you create simple tables quickly and effortlessly. Whether you need a table for financial data in an annual report, a form for ordering supplies, or a chart listing this week's top ten pop songs, the Table tool will make your life a happier place.

Table Terms. In order for you make and use tables, you need to understand some table terminology.

- A *cell* is one box of information within a table. Tables consist of a grid of cells, and cells are always picture or text boxes.

- A *field* is the contents of one cell; in XPress, cells can contain either text, pictures, or be blank.

- A *row* is a horizontal series of cells in a table (there is normally more than one row in a table).

- A *column* is a vertical series of cells in a table (there is normally more than one column in a table).

- A *table* is the entire unit, that is, all columns and rows containing cells.

- A *delimiter* is a text character that tells XPress to separate one field from the next. The primary delimiter character is usually a tab and a new paragraph character, but it can also be a comma, a space, or any other character. You only need to worry about delimiters when converting text into a table or a table into text (I'll cover both of these later in this section).

It's important to remember that tables in QuarkXPress are actually just grids of text and picture boxes separated by regular ol' lines. You could manually make a table with boxes and lines, but it would take much longer than using the Table tool and you wouldn't be able to take advantage of a few special table features, like combining cells.

BUILDING TABLES

You can make a table anywhere on your page or pasteboard by selecting the Table tool from the Tool palette (that's the one that looks like a small flyswatter) and dragging out a box, just like you would any picture or text box. The program immediately displays the Table Properties dialog box, in which you can enter the number of columns and rows you want in the table, whether you want the cells to be text or picture boxes, as well as choose to Auto Fit text within rows and columns (see Figure 8-1). Don't worry, you can always change the cell type or insert or delete rows and columns later. You can even change the tab order of your cells, link the cells together, or link to external data. I'll discuss these features soon.

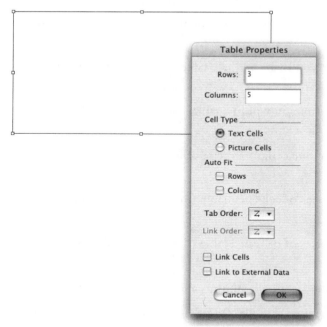

Figure 8-1
Drawing a new table

Once you have drawn a table, you can insert text or pictures into each cell, because each cell is actually a text box or picture box. So you can click in the cell with the Content tool and either type or use Import Text or Import Picture. If you have linked your cells together (see "Linking Text Cells," below), any text you type or import flows from cell to cell. If you have not, it only flows into the cell in which the text cursor is flashing.

Convert Text to Table. QuarkXPress lets you turn any selected block of text into a table by choosing Convert Text to Table from the Table menu. This gives you the Convert Text to Table dialog box (see Figure 8-2), which lets you specify the row and column delimiters, the order you want the table filled, and settings for auto fitting of text in each cell. XPress automatically calculates the number of columns and rows, so you don't have to type those (though you can override these numbers if you dare).

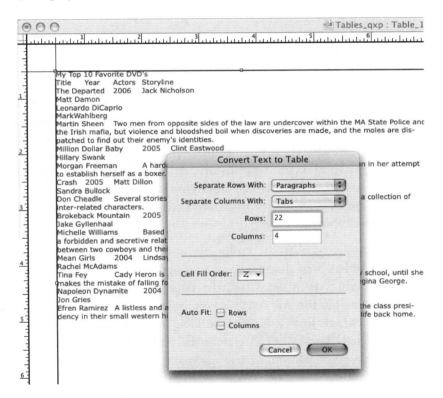

Figure 8-2 Convert Text to Table

Let's say you need to format some data from Microsoft Excel. You can tell Excel to export the data using a tab-delimited format, which places tabs between each field and a paragraph return at the end of each row. Import that text file into XPress, select it, specify these delimiters, and press OK. QuarkXPress does the rest and builds a table object on your page, placing the proper fields in each cell. The original text box is still there; if you don't want it anymore, you'll have to delete it yourself.

Note that some comma-delimited text files use a format in which any fields that actually contain commas are surrounded by quotations marks. Currently, XPress cannot deal with these kinds of files, so it's much better to use tab-delimited text whenever possible.

QuarkXPress also lets you convert a table into text; I'll cover that later in this section.

Setting tab order. XPress lets you specify the table's "tab order"—the order in which you jump from cell to cell. You can select this option in the Table Properties dialog box when you first create the table, or when you use the Convert Text to Table command. Or you can change it later by selecting the table and choosing Modify from the Item menu and clicking the Table tab. Normally, you'll accept the default (from left to right in the first row, and then downward through the rows). However, you can also choose one of three other orderings: Right to Left, Top Down; Top Down, Left to Right; and Top Down, Right to Left (sorry, I can't find any way to start the data at the bottom and tab upward).

> **Tip: Jump to Next Cell.** *When the text cursor is in a cell, you can jump to the next text cell by pressing Control-Option-Tab (Ctrl-Alt-Tab)—that's Control, not Command for you Macintosh folks.*

Linking text cells. QuarkXPress 7 is very flexible, letting you link text cells within a table together or to any other text box or text cell. You can link cells automatically, following a specified link order, or link cells manually in any order you want. When text cells are linked, any text that you type, import, or paste into a cell will flow into the first text cell in the link, and then flow throughout the remainder of the linked cells.

To link cells automatically, turn on the Link Cells option in the Table Properties dialog box when creating a table. Then choose one of four options from the Link Order popup menu—the same orderings as in the Tab Order popup menu. Text placed into a table cell flows from cell to cell in the link order. If you forget to set this when you first create the table, you can select Link Text Cells from the Table menu (or the context menu) while the Item tool is selected. Then you can choose the link order on the Table tab of the Modify dialog box. However, you can't apply automatic linking when there's already text in the cells.

Since text table cells are really text boxes, you can also use the Linking tool to manually link cells together. Use the Linking and Unlinking tools as I describe earlier in this chapter. You can also link text between cells in a table and any other text box.

Of course, if you link the cells in your table and then try to enter text in the third cell over, the text appears in the first cell. That is, linked cells act just like linked text boxes. This confuses even advanced users.

IMPORTING EXCEL TABLES

QuarkXPress first gave you the ability to import Excel tables in version 6. XPress 7 continues the support for importing Excel tables as external data and, just as modified pictures can be updated in XPress by selecting the Usage menu under Utilities, you have the same options with linked Excel tables. Additionally, you have the option to copy and paste Excel tables directly into XPress.

Getting your data. To import an Excel table, select the Table tool and drag out a table box, just as you would any picture or text box. The Table Properties dialog box displays and gives you the option to select the Link to External Data checkbox. Click OK to access the Table Link dialog box (see Figure 8-3).

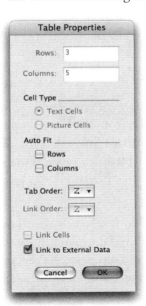

Figure 8-3
Link to External Data

The Table Link dialog box allows you to select the Excel file you would like to import and select which Excel sheet and range of cells to import. You also have other import options, such as Include Hidden Rows and Columns, which will bring in any hidden data within your selected range of cells.

You can also include Style Sheets, Formats, and Geometry. Include Style Sheets imports any Style Sheets that were defined within your Excel document. Include Formats maintains any text attributes that have been applied within Excel to your imported data. However, if you update the linked table in Excel, any formatting that you have applied within QuarkXPress will be removed and replaced with the Excel formatting. Include

Geometry brings in your table cells at the same size they were created in the Excel document (see Figure 8-4).

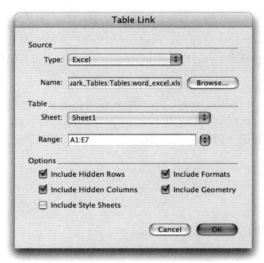

Figure 8-4
Getting your data

To update a linked, modified Excel table, simply select Tables from the Usage menu under Utilities. All linked Tables are listed in this window. To update the link, select the Table and click Update. Click OK, and then click Done. Your Excel table has now been updated.

Copy and Paste. QuarkXPress 7 also adds the ability to copy and paste tables directly from Excel into XPress. This is a very useful feature and a very simple way to get your Excel data into your QuarkXPress project. All you have to do is select the Excel data cells that you want to bring into your XPress layout, and from the Edit menu in Excel, select Copy. Next, in your XPress document, select Paste from the Edit menu. XPress then creates a table for you containing the data and maintains the Excel table geometry. Any updates made to the original table in Excel will not update in XPress with the copy and paste method.

CHANGING ROWS AND COLUMNS

Now that you have a table, it's time to start formatting it: changing the size of the table, adding or removing columns or rows, combining and splitting cells, and changing the size of columns or rows.

Resizing the table. There are two ways to resize your table: you can drag one of the table's corner or side handles, or you can drag the edge of the table itself. The difference between these two methods is important. If you drag a corner or side handle, XPress changes *all* the cells in the table. For instance, if you pull the right side handle out, you change the width of every cell in the table.

You can hold down a modifier key while dragging a side or corner handle, too. If you hold down the Shift key while you drag, the table is resized to a square. The Command/Ctrl key resizes the contents of each cell along with the table (Command-Option-Shift-drag or Ctrl-Alt-Shift-drag resizes the table and keeps the same height-width proportion.)

If, however, you click and drag the *edge* of the table (on any point where there isn't a handle), then you extend only the cells along that edge (see Figure 8-5).

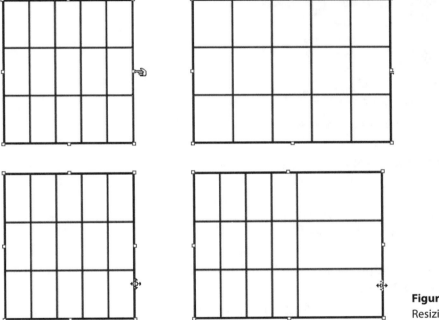

Figure 8-5
Resizing your tables

Deleting columns and rows. To delete a column or row, you need to select a whole column or row of cells. To do this, select the table with the Content tool and then move the cursor just outside the table until the cursor icon changes to a horizontal or vertical black arrow. Clicking when you see this cursor results in a whole row or column being selected. Once you have selected a row or column, you can delete it by selecting Delete from the Table menu (or in the context-sensitive menu).

To select more than one contiguous column or row, drag the black-arrow cursor over additional columns or rows. To select discontinuous columns or rows, hold down the Shift key as you select each column or row.

Adding columns or rows. To add a new column or row, use the Content tool and place the cursor in a table cell. Now select Insert Row or Insert Column from the Table menu (or in the context-sensitive menu). Either way, XPress displays the Insert dialog box, which lets you choose how many rows or columns you want to add, as well as where the new rows or columns should be added (see Figure 8-6). If you turn on the Keep Attributes option, the added cells take on the formatting of the selected cell. When this option is off, you just get default, no-format cells.

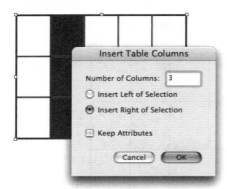

Figure 8-6
Inserting rows or columns

Combining and splitting cells. Cells don't have to be exactly one row tall or one column wide. You can make a cell span across multiple rows or columns by selecting two or more cells and combining them. To select more than one cell in a table, Shift-click on each cell you want selected. Or, you can also just drag the Content tool over two or more cells to select them all. If you select a cell by accident, you can Shift-click on it to deselect it. Then, when you've selected two or more cells in a row or column, choose the Combine Cells feature from the Table menu (or in the context-sensitive menu). Combining cells eliminates all content from all selected cells except the one in the upper-leftmost selected cell. That content will fill the newly combined cell.

If you later decide that you want combined cells returned to their original appearance, you can split them. Select the combined cell and choose Split Cell from the Table menu (or in the context-sensitive menu). Note that you can only split cells you've already combined; not regular cells.

> **Tip: Combining Breaks Links.** When you have cells in a table that are linked together, combining cells removes the combined cell from the linking order. To check the new linking order, click on the table with the Unlinking tool, and the linking arrows are displayed. Use the Linking tool to reestablish links the way you would like. (On the other hand, if you use the Split Cell command on a combined cell, the links are maintained.)

Changing row and column size. You can resize a single row or column by dragging the gridlines between the rows and columns with the Content tool. This can be a little tricky; you have to move the cursor over the gridline until you see it change into a cross-like double-headed arrow. Once you see that cursor, you can click and drag the gridline.

Note that QuarkXPress has no way to automatically resize column or row boundaries based on the content of the cells. Maybe in a later version of the program it will offer an auto-expand feature.

There's one other way to change your row or column size: place the cursor in a cell and open the Modify dialog box (select Modify from the Item menu, press Command/Ctrl-M or Command/Ctrl-double-click on the table). Here, switch to the Cell tab and set the height or width of this cell—changing it for this one cell changes it for all the cells in that row or column.

If you have more than one cell selected, you can click the Distribute Evenly button on the Cell tab of the Modify dialog box to equalize the rows or columns. That is, it takes the total width or height of the cells and divides it up equally for each row or column you have selected. This is extremely useful when you want several rows or columns to be the same width but aren't sure exactly what that width should be.

Maintain Geometry. When you select a table and open the Modify dialog box, you'll notice a feature called Maintain Geometry on the Table tab (see Figure 8-7). You can also select this option from the Table menu (or in the context-sensitive menu). When this check-box is turned on, XPress will not change the size of the table when you add or remove rows or columns—it simply resizes the remaining rows and columns proportionally. It also maintains the table dimensions when you change row or column size. If you leave this feature turned off, then the table size actually changes when you add or remove columns.

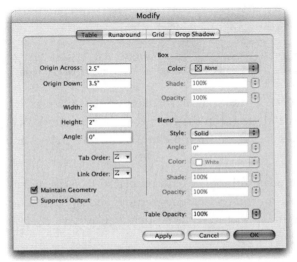

Figure 8-7
The Table tab of the Modify dialog box

Also, when Maintain Geometry is turned on, you cannot resize a table by dragging one of its outside edges. You can, however, still use the corner or side handles.

ADDING GRAPHICS

Placing an image into a table cell is exactly the same as placing an image into a picture box, because, as mentioned earlier in this chapter, each cell is actually a text box or picture box.

With the Table tool selected drag a box within your layout to create your table. The Table Properties dialog box gives you the option to select whether your table cells contain text or pictures. However, you don't have to make any final decisions yet. You can change the cell content type at any time, just as you do with all other text or picture boxes, so leave the Cell Type as Text.

Now, with the Content tool selected, click within the text cell you would like to change and select Content and then Picture from the Item menu (or in the context-sensitive menu). You have successfully converted the text cell to a picture cell, and you can now import your picture just like you would into a picture box. But if you attempt to change the cell type of a cell that already contains text or images, a dialog box will appear warning you that all contents will be deleted (see Figure 8-8).

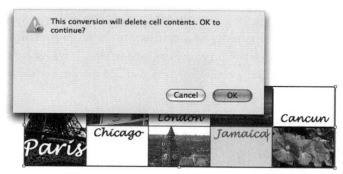

Figure 8-8
Converting table cell type

With the Content tool selected, click within the cell that you want to place an image and select Import Picture from the File menu (or in the context-sensitive menu). Navigate to the image you want to import and select Open from the Import Picture dialog window. It's just that simple.

QuarkXPress gives you the same powerful tools to use on placed table images as it does within picture box images. You can control transparency settings and alpha channels, place native .PSD files, and apply the many Picture Effects such as Gaussian Blur, Unsharp Mask, and Color Balance (see Figure 8-9).

Figure 8-9 Table cell Picture Effects

FORMATTING CELLS

Remember that each cell in a table is just a picture box or a text box, and you can do almost anything to a cell that you would to an ordinary box. For instance, to change a cell from a text box into a picture box, place the cursor inside it and choose Picture from the Content submenu (under the Item menu or the context-sensitive menu).

Similarly, to change the background color of the cell, you can use the Color palette or the Modify dialog box. You can even format a cell to have a background of None or a gradient with Opacity settings from 0 percent to 100 percent. With the addition of the Transparency, Alpha Channel Support, and Drop Shadow features in QuarkXPress 7, your design is not constrained to the borders of the table.

Here's something you can do to cells in a table that you cannot do with regular picture or text boxes: You can apply formatting to the contents of more than one cell at a time. For example, if you want to apply a paragraph style to all the cells in a row, you can select that row (see "Changing Rows and Columns," earlier in this chapter) and click on the style in the Style Sheets palette. If you want your headings to be rotated in the cells, you can select that row, open the Modify dialog box, and change the Text Angle field. You can also auto fit text into your table cells. The cells will auto-adjust their width and height to fit your text entries. Auto fit preferences are found on the Cell tab of the Modify palette.

FORMATTING THE TABLE BOX

The table box is a separate box that contains the cells of a table and is behind them. However, by default, table cells have a white background so you can't normally see it. To change the color of the table box, pick a color on the Table tab of the Modify dialog box or select the table with the Item tool and then pick a color from the Colors palette or from the Measurements palette. Now, if you change the background color of the cells to None either by selecting them or changing the table preferences (see below), you can see the table box's color. By default, the table box has a transparent background so you can see through it to objects below. You can also apply different opacity or transparency settings to the table box and to individual cells,

The table box also has a frame that surrounds the table. You can change its properties by first selecting the table with the Item tool, and then choosing Modify from the Item menu and selecting the Frame tab. You can create custom frame patterns with settings for Frame Style, Width, Frame and Gap Color, Shade, and Opacity.

XPress 7 also gives you the ability to rotate tables while maintaining links, and format and fully edit text and images. To rotate your table, select the Rotate tool (which is directly beneath the Content tool), click to select the table you want to rotate. You can then free rotate the table or enter an exact box rotation angle in the Measurements palette. You can also enter the rotate angle on the Table tab of the Modify palette.

FORMATTING GRIDLINES

Now that you know how to format the stuff inside cells, it's time to format the stuff around them: the gridlines. There are three ways to select the gridlines.

- You can select the table with the Item tool (instead of the Content tool) and open the Modify dialog box (press Command/Ctrl-M). Choose the Grid tab of the Modify dialog box (see Figure 8-10), and then click on one of the buttons along the right side of the dialog box: vertical gridlines, horizontal gridlines, or all gridlines.

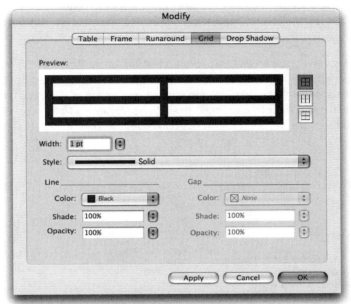

Figure 8-10
The Grid tab of the
Modify dialog box

- With the Content tool selected, you can choose Select Vertical, Select Horizontal, Select Borders, or Select All from the Select submenu (under the Table menu or in the context-sensitive menu). When you choose Select Borders, XPress selects the four outer sides of the table.

- You can choose one or more gridlines in your table by Shift-clicking on them with the Content tool.

Once you have one or more gridlines selected, you can specify color, style, opacity, and width in the Measurements palette, which now contains many of the items that were only accessible through drop-down menus until XPress 7. You can also navigate to the Grid tab of the Modify dialog box. Or, if the Modify dialog box isn't open, you can change these settings in the Style menu or the context-sensitive menu. Remember that the gridlines are exactly like regular lines in XPress, so you can use custom dashes and stripes, change the gap color, or whatever else you choose to do.

Sometimes you'll want to make a table that has no gridlines—where the cells abut each other with no lines in between. To do this, select the lines you want to change and set their color to None. Note that when you have transparent gridlines, you're looking at the table box; if you've changed the table box's color, then you'll see this color "peeking through" the gridline.

*Tip: **Matching Gap Color.*** *If you use a dashed or striped gridline style in your table, I recommend setting the Gap Color to the same color as the background color of the cells. This way the gaps will match the background color and not appear as white.*

*Tip: **One-Celled Tables.*** *Have you ever wanted to draw a text box with different line thicknesses on each side? Or a box that only has a border on three sides? Try this trick, suggested by Quark's Darin Overstreet: Make a table with only one column and one row, and then select each side individually (Shift-click on it) and change its color, style, or width (see Figure 8-11). To make a box with a border on only three sides, select the fourth side and change its color to None.*

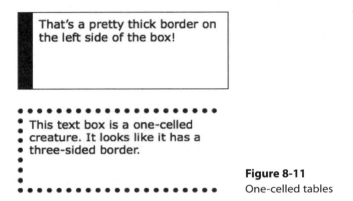

Figure 8-11
One-celled tables

*Tip: **Making Combs.*** *Here's another fun table trick: you can make a comb (one of those segmented fill-in-the-blanks boxes that are ubiquitous on forms) by creating a table with multiple columns and only one row. Then Shift-click on the top gridline to select it and set its color to None. (See an example in Figure 8-12.)*

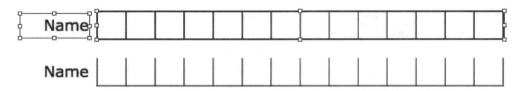

Figure 8-12 Table combs

Headers and Footers

QuarkXPress 7 now offers you one of those long-awaited features. Wow—table headers and footers—finally! With XPress now including the ability to split tables, which I cover in the next section, it only makes sense that you are able to define custom header and footer rows that flow with each break of the table.

Headers and footers in tables are generally used to reference or describe the information or data that is contained within a table. If the table is split (a split is referred to as a table break) into different areas or pages within your document, headers and footers are necessary to keep the symmetry between the tables and are automatically synchronized so that any changes you make are reflected in every table break.

To define header and footer rows in your table, you must first specify or define the table break. A table must have a vertical table break depth defined, which indicates the maximum depth a table can be before the table will split or break into another table.

To specify the table break, use either the Item or Content tool, select any portion of the table, and select Table Break from the Table menu (or in the context-sensitive menu). The Set Table Break dialog box appears. You then need to input a Table Break height in order to define header and footer rows (see Figure 8-13).

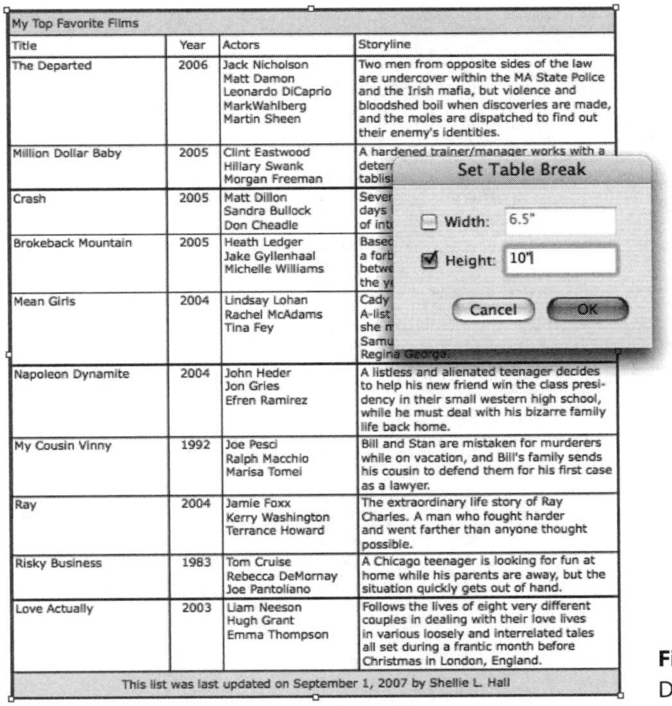

Figure 8-13
Define Table Break

After you have defined the table break, then with the Content tool, Shift-click to select the header row, select Repeat as Header from the Table menu, and then repeat the process for the footer row. You have now successfully defined your header and footers rows, which we will put to use in the next section.

Splitting Tables

How many times have you created a table using QuarkXPress and then struggled because the only way to continue a table from one page to the next was to create two separate tables and link the table cells together. Heaven forbid if the table depth changed because your headers and footers were just rows inserted at the beginning and end of each table.

Well, with the release of QuarkXPress 7, XPress users can rest easy at the thought of creating tables that must flow from one page to another with running headers and footers.

In the previous section, I already covered how to specify the table break, but it applies here as well. So, using either the Item or Content tool, select any portion of the table, and then select Table Break from the Table menu (or in the context-sensitive menu). The Set Table Break dialog box appears. Again, you need to define a Table Break height (see Figure 8-13). To define header and footer rows, please refer to the preceding section for detailed instructions.

My Top Favorite Films			
Title	Year	Actors	Storyline
The Departed	2006	Jack Nicholson Matt Damon Leonardo DiCaprio MarkWahlberg Martin Sheen	Two men from opposite sides of the law are undercover within the MA State Police and the Irish mafia, but violence and bloodshed boil when discoveries are made, and the moles are dispatched to find out their enemy's identities.
Million Dollar Baby	2005	Clint Eastwood Hillary Swank Morgan Freeman	A hardened trainer/manager works with a determined woman in her attempt to establish herself as a boxer.
Crash	2005	Matt Dillon Sandra Bullock Don Cheadle	Several stories interweave during two days in Los Angeles involving a collection of inter-related characters.
Brokeback Mountain	2005	Heath Ledger Jake Gyllenhaal Michelle Williams	Based on the E. Annie Proulx story about a forbidden and secretive relationship between two cowboys and their lives over the years.
This list was last updated on September 1, 2007 by Shellie L. Hall			

My Top Favorite Films			
Title	Year	Actors	Storyline
Mean Girls	2004	Lindsay Lohan Rachel McAdams Tina Fey	Cady Heron is a hit with The Plastics, the A-list girl clique at her new school, until she makes the mistake of falling for Aaron Samuels, the ex-boyfriend of alpha Plastic Regina George.
Napoleon Dynamite	2004	John Heder Jon Gries Efren Ramirez	A listless and alienated teenager decides to help his new friend win the class presidency in their small western high school, while he must deal with his bizarre family life back home.
My Cousin Vinny	1992	Joe Pesci Ralph Macchio Marisa Tomei	Bill and Stan are mistaken for murderers while on vacation, and Bill's family sends his cousin to defend them for his first case as a lawyer.
Ray	2004	Jamie Foxx Kerry Washington Terrance Howard	The extraordinary life story of Ray Charles. A man who fought harder and went farther than anyone thought possible.
Risky Business	1983	Tom Cruise Rebecca DeMornay Joe Pantoliano	A Chicago teenager is looking for fun at home while his parents are away, but the situation quickly gets out of hand.
This list was last updated on September 1, 2007 by Shellie L. Hall			

My Top Favorite Films			
Title	Year	Actors	Storyline
Love Actually	2003	Liam Neeson Hugh Grant Emma Thompson	Follows the lives of eight very different couples in dealing with their love lives in various loosely and interrelated tales all set during a frantic month before Christmas in London, England.
This list was last updated on September 1, 2007 by Shellie L. Hall			

Figure 8-14
Table Break results

After you determine the table break size or the maximum depth that you would like the table to reach before it breaks into a new table, enter the amount in the Height field and click OK. The table will split into the number of tables needed to accommodate all the table data within the maximum specified depth. The table shown in the example in Figure 8-14 has split into three tables.

The nice thing about using table breaks is that when any changes are made to the table, such as inserting columns, or making text or formatting changes to headers and footers, the altered elements are automatically updated throughout the split tables.

CONVERT TABLE TO TEXT OR GROUP

You can extract the contents of a selected table into a single text box by choosing Convert Table to Text from the Table submenu (under the Table menu or in the context-sensitive menu). XPress gives you choices regarding delimiter characters (what to put between the contents of each cell), the text extraction order, and the choice to delete the table once converted (see Figure 8-15).

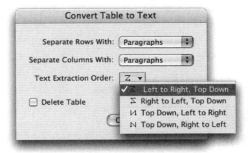

Figure 8-15
Convert Table to Text

When you click OK the program generates a new text box with the contents from the table, separated by delimiters (usually tab characters). You can position this text box someplace on your page, or use Save Text from the File menu to export the text to disk. For instance, you might want to export the table to disk as a text file if your client or your accounting department needs a text version of your table to import into a spreadsheet.

Picture cells in your table get automatically converted to anchored picture boxes when you extract the data with Convert Table to Text.

You can also convert a table to a group of text boxes by selecting Convert Table to Group from the Table menu (or the context-sensitive menu). The table is replaced with grouped boxes.

Tip: Switching Rows and Columns. You've spent two hours setting up a table, and suddenly your art director says, "Make all the rows into columns and vice versa." Before you throw something at him or her, try this trick. Select the table and choose Convert Table to Text from the Table submenu (under the Table menu). In the Convert Table to Text dialog box, turn off the Delete Table checkbox (you may need the original later), and set the Text Extraction Order to Left to Right, Top Down (the one with the "Z" icon). Click OK, select all the text in the resulting text box (Command/Ctrl-A), and then choose Convert Text to Table from the Item menu. This time, change the Cell Fill Order to Top Down, Left to Right (the icon looks like a backward "N"). Your new table should have the same content as the first, but with the rows and columns switched. Unfortunately, XPress has no way to copy the gridline and cell background color formatting from one table to another, so you'll have to do that manually.

DEFAULT PREFERENCE SETTINGS

Are you tired of changing the gridlines in all your tables to half a point instead of one point? Do the cells in your tables always have the same background color? Do you want your table text to be vertically centered in your table's cells? Don't tire yourself by changing these manually every time you make a table; instead, double-click on the Table tool to open the Tool tab of the Preferences dialog box, and click Modify to change the Table tool's default settings (see Figure 8-16).

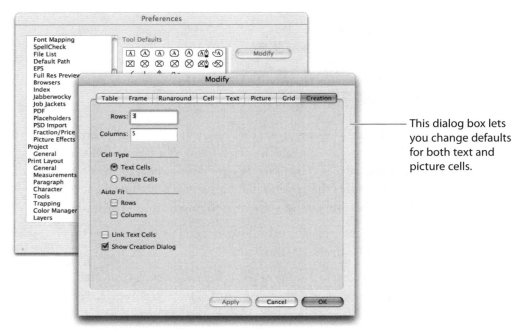

This dialog box lets you change defaults for both text and picture cells.

Figure 8-16 Table tool preferences

Of course, like with other document preferences, if a document is open when you change these settings, it affects just that one document. To change the application's default settings for any newly created documents, change these defaults with no documents open.

Note that these preferences affect both how tables appear when you draw them with the Table tool *and* when XPress makes a table for you using the Convert Text to Table feature.

TABLES FOR WEB LAYOUTS

While I don't cover building Web layouts and exporting to HTML until Chapter 17, *Going Online with QuarkXPress*, it's worth noting here that you can use the Table tool to produce tables in Web layouts. Then when you export HTML from your Web layout, XPress automatically converts your table into an HTML table. However, because HTML tables have severe restrictions, XPress simply won't let you do much formatting to tables that you create in a Web layout. For instance, gridlines must be a minimum of two pixels, you cannot change their color or style—and you cannot rotate text in a cell.

Therefore, if you want to use any of the fancier table formatting, you must first turn on the Convert Table to Graphic checkbox in the Modify dialog box. This way, XPress exports your table as a picture (typically a GIF image) instead of an HTML table. If you turn your print layout into a Web layout, QuarkXPress turns this checkbox on by default.

CHAPTER NINE

Long Documents

One look at the size of this book and you know why the topic of long documents is so exciting to me. But everyone has a different opinion about what a long document is. Some die-hard technical writers insist that if it isn't over 1,000 pages, it's not a long document. Others maintain that a document longer than five or ten pages qualifies. Personally, I think that anyone building a book, a magazine, a newspaper, a journal, or a catalog—no matter how many pages—is dealing with long documents.

Unfortunately, while there are hundreds of thousands of people creating these sorts of things with XPress, it took ten years for Quark to include even rudimentary long-document features into its flagship product. Today, XPress's long-document features aren't anywhere as powerful as Adobe FrameMaker, but they're pretty good nevertheless.

There are three features in QuarkXPress that relate directly to publishing long documents.

- **Books.** You can tie multiple XPress projects together into a *book*, which appears in the form of a palette in QuarkXPress. (This only works if the project has just one print layout space.) From here, you can control page numbering, printing, and such document attributes as style sheets and colors.

- **Lists.** If you use style sheets regularly, you're going to love the Lists feature, which lets you build a table of contents (or a list of figures, or a table of advertisers, or any number of other things) quickly and easily.

- **Indexes.** Building an index is a hardship I wouldn't wish on anyone (I've done enough of them myself), but XPress's indexing features go a long way in helping make it bearable. I'll also discuss how indexing can be used in catalogs and other documents.

Again, even if you don't currently create what you'd consider "long documents," take a gander at these features; they're flexible enough to be used in documents even as small as a few pages.

BOOKS

Even though you can make a project thousands of pages long, you should keep your XPress projects small. This reduces the amount of strain on the program, and lessens the chance for document corruption. Working with smaller projects is generally faster and more efficient, especially when more than one person is working on the project at the same time. The question is: if you break up your larger project into smaller ones, how can you ensure style consistency and proper page numbering among them? The answer is QuarkXPress's Book feature.

You and I usually think of a book as a collection of chapters bound together to act like a single document. QuarkXPress takes this concept one step further. In QuarkXPress, a book is a collection of any XPress projects on your disk or network that are loosely connected with each other via the Book palette. In other words, just because it's called a "book" doesn't mean it's not relevant for magazines, catalogs, or any other set of documents (see "Tip: The Book Palette as Database," below).

There are four benefits to using the Book palette.

- It's a good way to organize your documents, and it's faster to open them from within XPress than using the Open dialog box.

- If you use automatic page numbering in your document (see "Sections and Page Numbering" in Chapter 4, *Building a Layout*), XPress manages the page numbering throughout the entire book, so if the first document ends on page 20, the second document starts on page 21, and so on.

- You can print one or more documents from the Book palette using the same Print dialog box settings without even having the documents open.

- The Book palette's Synchronize feature lets you ensure that the style sheets, colors, H&J settings, List settings (which I cover later in this chapter), and Dashes & Stripes settings are consistent among the documents.

Obviously, the more projects in your book, and the more pages, style sheets, colors, and whatnot in each document, the more useful the Book feature will be to you. Even if you're juggling only two or three projects, it may be worth the minor hassle it takes to build a book.

> ***TIP: The Book Palette as Database.*** *Because there is only a very loose connection among the various documents in the Book palette, you could use this feature as an informal database of projects. For instance, let's say you've built 15 different product sheets and three small brochures for a client, and they're forever updating them.*

Even though each project may use very different colors, style sheets, and so on, you could put them all on one Book palette and save this collection under the client's name. Next time the client calls for a quick fix, you won't have to go searching for a document; just open the Book palette and double-click on the project name to open it.

Of course, this means either you cannot use automatic page numbering in your projects, or you have to be meticulous about using the Section feature (I discuss how you can use the Section feature to override a book's automatic page numbering in "Page Numbering and Sections," later in this chapter).

Note that in versions 5, 6, and 7 the projects that make up the book must be on the same volume as each other and as the book file itself.

Building a Book

To build a new book, select Book from the New submenu (under the File menu; see Figure 9-1). At this point, you need to tell the program where to save your new book file. You can put it anywhere you want on your hard drive or network, but you should be able to find it easily because you'll be using it a lot.

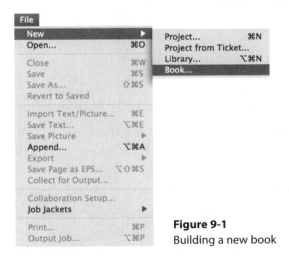

Figure 9-1
Building a new book

Book files appear in QuarkXPress as palettes. You can save as many books as you want, though you can open only 25 of them at a time (I usually just stick to one or two open Book palettes, or else I get confused). When you've saved your new book, XPress displays a new, empty Book palette (see Figure 9-2).

Move Chapter Down   The name of your book file is displayed here.

Add Chapter

Move
Chapter Up

Print Book

Remove Chapter

Synchronize Book

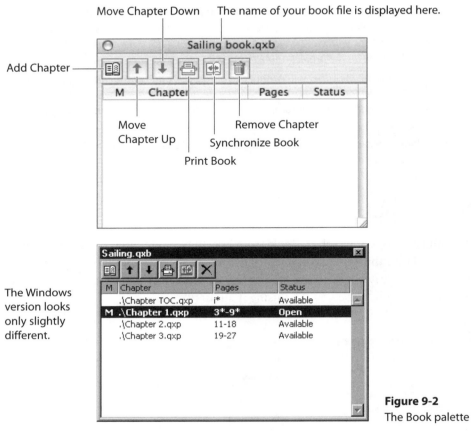

The Windows
version looks
only slightly
different.

Figure 9-2
The Book palette

Adding chapters. To add a chapter to your Book palette, click the Add Chapter button in the palette and choose a project from your disk or network. If no projects on the palette are selected when you add a new project, the chapter is added at the end of the list. If you select a project first, the new chapter is added before the selected project in the list.

You can have up to 1,000 documents on your Book palette (personally, I wouldn't try to push this limit; I prefer to keep this number well below 100). By the way, if you add documents that were built in QuarkXPress version 3.x, 4.x, or 6.x they are automatically resaved as version 7 files, and you won't be able to open them in the earlier version again.

While version 4 let you add any document to your book, beginning in version 5 the documents and the book file must be on the same hard drive (though that could be a drive elsewhere on your network). Also, note that XPress currently only lets you add projects to your book that have one (and only one) layout space. I hope this gets changed in a later version.

Removing chapters. You can remove a project from a Book palette by selecting it and clicking the Remove Chapter button. If you want to remove more than one, you can select the additional projects with the Shift or Command/Ctrl key (Shift for contiguous selections, Command/Ctrl for noncontiguous selections on the list). Note that deleting a project from the Book palette does *not* delete the file from disk; it simply removes it from the list.

> **TIP: Reordering Chapters.** *It seems like I always accidentally place one chapter in the wrong order on the Book palette. You can move a chapter up and down on the list by selecting it and clicking the Move Chapter Up and Move Chapter Down buttons. But I think it's even faster to hold down the Option/Alt key and drag the chapter to where you want it.*

When you add a new chapter to your book, XPress actually opens the project behind the scenes (you don't see it, but you can hear your hard disk scratching away), writes some code into it so that the project knows it's part of a book now, and then closes it. (The same thing happens when you remove a chapter from a book.) This can take some time, especially with large documents, so be patient.

If you open a document from disk, there's almost no way to tell if it's part of a book or not. If you try to add a project to more than one book, XPress alerts you and suggests you save your project with a different name.

> **TIP: Take Away That Book Setting.** *If you throw away or lose your book file on disk, the individual chapters in the book don't know that—they still think they're part of a book.*
>
> *You can, however, create a new book, add your projects to it, and see if XPress alerts you that it is part of another book. You then need to do a Save As and rename the project before inserting it as a new chapter. This takes a little time to do, but it's the only way to re-create your book file.*

Editing Your Book's Projects

Once you've added chapters to your Book palette, you can go about your regular routine of editing and preparing the documents…with a few minor adjustments.

- Whenever possible, you should open your book's projects while the Book palette is open. (The fastest way to open a project is to double-click on it in the Book palette.) When you open and modify a document while the palette is not open, the palette isn't smart enough to update itself (see "File status," below). If XPress can't find your project, it'll ask you where it is.

- You can print documents the regular way, but if you want to print more than one document in a book at a time, you should use the Print button on the Book palette (see "Printing Books," later in this section).

- You should be careful about using the Section feature to renumber any of the documents in the book (see "Page Numbering and Sections," later in this section). In general, you should let the Book palette handle your page numbering for you.

   TIP: No Can Undo. *QuarkXPress's books are like libraries in several ways. First of all, the changes you make to your Book palette, including adding, removing, and reordering chapters, aren't saved until you close the palette or quit QuarkXPress (although libraries have the Auto Library Save feature, there is no such feature for books).*

   Also, you can't use the Undo or Revert to Saved features on books. This means you should be careful about what you do in a Book palette…there may be no turning back.

File status. The Book palette monitors and displays the status of each document in the book. There are five possible messages in the Status column of the palette: Available, Open, Modified, Missing, or In Use (see Figure 9-3).

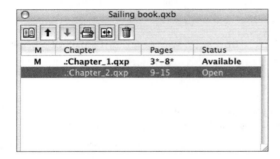

Figure 9-3
File status on the Book palette

- **Available.** The normal status of a document is Available. This means that no one has the document open for editing and that the document has not changed since the last time it was open on the computer you're using.

- **Open.** When you have a document open on your Macintosh or PC, the status of that file is listed as Open.

- **Modified.** When you or anyone else who has access to the file opens and changes a document while the Book palette is not open, the status will be listed as Modified next time you open the palette. It's easy to change the status from Modified back to Available: just open the file while the Book palette is open, then close the document again.

- **Missing.** If you move a document after adding it to the Book palette, XPress isn't able to find it, and the status is listed as Missing. (There's one exception to this rule: if you move the project into the same folder as the book file, the Book palette can find it.) To "find" a file again, double-click on the chapter name in the Book palette; XPress displays a dialog box in which you can tell it where the project now resides.

- **In Use.** If someone else on your network opens one of the projects in your book via the Book palette, the Status field of the Book palette lists that chapter as In Use. More precisely, it lists the name of that person's computer, so you know exactly who to call and yell at. However, if someone opens the file without having the Book palette open, QuarkXPress has no way of knowing that the project is open.

It's important to pay attention to the Status column readings, because documents must be either Available or Open in order to synchronize, print, or renumber properly.

> **TIP: Update the Book Palette.** *The book palette could slow you down in version 4 because it was always checking to see the status of each file in the book. Now, XPress only updates the book status when you click in the Book palette; so, if you think someone else might be working on a file, just click somewhere in the palette (even a blank area) and the status column should update properly.*

> **TIP: Keep Those Books Open.** *Don't feel compelled to close your Book palette(s) before you quit QuarkXPress. Any books that are open when you quit will be open again (and in the same position on screen) when you relaunch the program.*

> **TIP: Network Booking.** *It seems like people increasingly work on projects in groups rather than individually. Quark anticipated this, and if you put your book file and documents on a server, more than one person can open them at the same time. (Only one person can open a regular XPress document at a time, however.) While this feature isn't nearly as powerful as the full-blown Quark Publishing System (QPS), it's certainly useful if a group of people have to work on different documents in the book at the same time.*

The thing is, I don't like working on projects when they're on a server. It just makes me nervous. (In older versions of XPress, you could permanently corrupt your documents if you did this; now it does seem to work fine, but I'm still superstitious.) Instead, I prefer to copy the file to my local hard drive, edit it at my leisure, and then return the file to the server after I'm done working with it.

There are two problems with this. First, the book palette doesn't update properly. Second, other people on your network might not realize that you've got the "live" file, so make it clear to them: hide the document on the server, or put it in another folder called "work in progress" or something like that.

> **TIP: Restricting Network Access.** *QuarkXPress has no built-in features for restricting access to projects in a book. You can, however, set up access privileges on a person-by-person basis with most server software. For instance, you might give one person read-only access, so they could not make changes to your files, and then give read/write access to someone else who has good cause to edit the documents.*

TIP: Careful with Save As. I use the Save As feature all the time as a way to track revisions of my documents. Each time I use Save As, I change the name slightly ("mydocument1," "mydocument2," and so on), so I can always go back to an earlier version if necessary. If you do this, however, note that the Book palette doesn't catch on to what you're doing; it just lists and keeps track of the original document. So every time you use Save As, you have to remove the old document name from the Book palette and use Add Chapter to add the new document in (very frustrating). I'm hoping that Quark will fix this, but it hasn't happened yet.

Synchronizing Your Book

The more documents you're working with, the more likely it is that one or more of them contain settings inconsistent with the others in the book. Perhaps you decided to change a style sheet definition in one document out of 20, and then forgot to change it in the other 19. Or perhaps one person in your workgroup decided he didn't like the Standard H&J settings in the document he was editing, so he just changed them without telling anyone.

Fortunately, the Synchronize Book button on the Book palette lets you ensure that all style sheets, colors, H&J settings, List settings, and Dashes & Stripes settings are consistent throughout the documents in a book. Here's how it works.

The Master Chapter. One document on the Book palette is always marked as the *master chapter* (by default, it's the first chapter you add to the palette). The master chapter—which is listed in bold and with the letter M next to it—is the project to which all the other projects will be synchronized. That means if you add a new color to the master chapter and then click the Synchronize Book button, the color will be added to all the other projects in the book. If you add a new color to a project that is not a master chapter, it won't be added when you synchronize the chapters.

You can always change which chapter is the master chapter: just double-click in the left column of the Book palette next to the chapter you want to be the master chapter.

Synchronize. In version 4, synchronizing your chapters was about as simple as clicking the Synchronize Book button. It's not much harder now, but it does take a couple extra steps. First you must select *which* files in the Book palette you want to synchronize; remember that you can Shift-click to select contiguous chapters or Command/Ctrl-click to select noncontiguous chapters. Or, if you want to synchronize *all* the files, just make sure *no* chapters are selected in the palette.

Then, when you click the Synchronize button, XPress asks you what properties you want to synchronize (see Figure 9-4). Maybe I'm just lazy, but I usually just press the Synch All button. However, if you really want to synchronize some styles and not others, and so on…be my guest and tweak the dialog box as you wish. Note that after you click Synch All or OK you may also get some style sheets that you didn't expect (for instance, if one style is based on another style). Here's the nitty gritty.

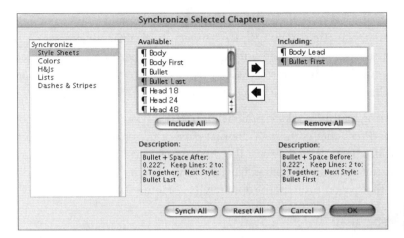

Figure 9-4
Synchronizing your book

- A style sheet, color, H&J setting, List setting, or Dashes & Stripes setting that is defined in the master chapter but not in another chapter gets added to that other document.

- If a setting is named the same in both the master chapter and another document, the definition for that setting in the master chapter overrides the one in the non-master chapter.

- If a setting is not defined in the master chapter but it is in some other document, it's left alone. (This means you can have "local" settings that exist in one document that don't have to be copied into all the others.)

> **TIP: Save Your Eyes with Synchronize.** *It's always a hassle editing a document that contains colored text because it's often difficult to read. Let's say you've got 15 documents in a book that all use the same style sheets. You could change the style definitions in the master chapter so that the text appears in black (or whatever color is easy to read), and then synchronize the book so that the settings are changed in all the documents. Later, when you're done editing, you can reverse the process: change the style sheets back, and synchronize again.*

Note that synchronizing a project can be a time-consuming process—the more chapters and the more settings there are, the longer it takes. You can watch XPress do its work in the Book palette: as XPress changes each chapter, you'll see its status change from Available to Open and then to Available again.

Page Numbering and Sections

Perhaps the most helpful aspect of the Book feature is that it keeps track of your page numbering for you and updates the page numbers when you either add pages to or delete them from a project, or if you add a new chapter between two other chapters in a book. Of course, this only works if you've used automatic page numbering in your projects. (The automatic page-number character is Command/Ctrl-3; see "Sections and Page Numbering" in Chapter 4, *Building a Layout*.)

The page-numbering feature works via the Section dialog box. When you add a chapter to the Book palette, XPress checks to see if the first page of the chapter has been defined as a section start. If it has been, XPress leaves the page alone. If it's not the start of a new section, then XPress turns on the checkbox labeled Book Chapter Start in the Section dialog box, and sets the first page number appropriately (see Figure 9-5).

Figure 9-5
Page numbering in books

Let's say you've got one 16-page project on your Book palette already. When you add another chapter, XPress automatically sets the first page number to 17 (as long as you hadn't already set up the first page as a section start in the Section dialog box). If you later open the first project and add two pages, XPress automatically renumbers the second chapter next time you open it so that it starts on page 19.

Manual sections. If you have manually specified a section start anywhere in your document, the automatic book-page numbering works slightly differently. Let's say you've used the Section dialog box to make a section start of any page in the second chapter of your book, and you've specified lower-case roman numerals for the page numbers. Now if you add a third chapter to the book, and this new project has no section-start settings, then XPress picks up on the roman numerals where they left off in the second chapter.

In other words, XPress keeps on numbering in the style of the previous chapter. If you wanted the third chapter to return to regular Arabic numerals, you would have to manually add a section start to its first page, overriding the Book Chapter Start setting. Of course, now if you added pages to the first or second chapter, the page numbers wouldn't update properly in the third chapter because of the section start.

Odd versus even page numbers. To get even more picayune, I should mention that XPress always starts Facing Pages documents with an odd number. For instance, if the first chapter ends on page 23 and the second chapter is a Facing Pages document, XPress sets the first page of the second chapter as 25, skipping page 24. If you want to print a page numbered "24," you have to add it yourself to the first chapter.

Single-sided documents, on the other hand, can begin with either an odd- or even-numbered page.

> **TIP: Spread-to-Spread Page Numbers.** *Some magazine publishers build their magazines one spread at a time—each spread is a separate document. (I think this is a very strange way to create a magazine, but those publishers insist they have their reasons.) If you're going to do this, set up your documents using single-sided pages rather than facing pages. You can still build a two-page spread with single-sided pages (just drag one page next to the other in the Page Layout palette), and this way the automatic page numbering works properly when the documents are all added to the Book palette.*

Printing Books

Even though I cover printing documents in Chapter 15, *Printing*, I should take this opportunity to mention a few things that are specific to printing books.

First, each chapter in a book must be listed as Open, Available, or Modified on the Book palette in order for the document to print. This is because XPress invisibly opens each document at print time (you don't see the document open on screen, but it does). XPress alerts you if a document is in use by someone else on the network or if it's missing, and if it can't immediately be found or made available you can cancel printing. (This only stops the print job for that one document; all the other documents print fine.)

Second, if you only want certain chapters in a book to print, select them from the Book palette before clicking the Print Book button. Remember that you can select contiguous chapters on the list by holding down the Shift key, and noncontiguous documents with the Command/Ctrl key. If no documents are selected, then they'll all print.

Third, as this book goes to press, on the Macintosh there is no way to print PostScript to disk (a "PostScript dump") for more than one document in a book. The results are varied when you try to do this. Some people find that the first chapter is written to disk and that subsequent chapters get sent to a printer. Others find that every document is written to disk, but because the same file name is given to each PostScript dump, each file overwrites the last, until you have only one file—the last one—on disk. The workaround is simply to save PostScript dumps one document at a time. In Windows, this does work, but you still have to type a new file name in for each PostScript file that gets written to disk.

Lastly, there is also no way to automatically create an Adobe Acrobat PDF file of your entire book. You have to open each chapter, export it to PDF, and then put all the PDFs together using Adobe Acrobat.

Lists

If you've been searching through the menus for a "table of contents" feature, you can stop now. There is no such feature. Instead, Quark offers something much better: a Lists feature, which can not only generate a table of contents, but all kinds of lists, as well.

Technically, the Lists feature lets you build collections of text (words or paragraphs) that have been tagged with specific style sheets. For instance, if you use even two style sheets when you're formatting a book—one for the chapter name and another for your first-level headings—you can build a basic table of contents by collecting all the paragraphs tagged with these two styles. If you use paragraph style sheets to tag your figure titles, you can build a table of figures. If you apply a character style to the names of companies mentioned in your document, then you can collect them all with the Lists feature and build a list of them later. Anything you can tag with a paragraph or character style, you can build into a list. (In case you were wondering, the ability to use character styles was new in XPress 5.)

This all depends entirely on your using style sheets. Of course, you simply can't be efficient when you're building long documents if you don't use paragraph and character styles anyway. If you don't currently use styles, go check out Chapter 7, *Copy Flow*, to see why you should.

Setting Up a List

The great thing about Lists is that they're so easy to make and use. Here's the six-step procedure to define a list.

1. Select Lists from the Edit menu. Like making style sheets and colors, making a list while a document is open means that the list appears only in that document; if no documents are open when you make the list, it'll appear in every document you create from then on.

   If the Lists palette is already open (select Show Lists from the Window menu), you can skip this first step by Control-clicking (Mac) or right-mouse-button-clicking (Windows) inside the palette and selecting New List from the context-sensitive menu.

2. Click the New button in the Lists dialog box to open the Edit List dialog box (see Figure 9-6) and type a name for your new list.

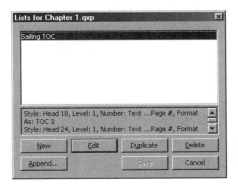

Figure 9-6
Creating a new list

Choose the styles you want in your list definition here.

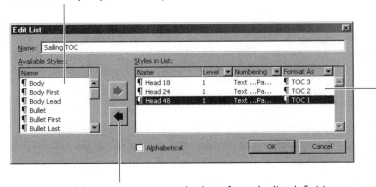

Moving styles here means the style will be included in your list definition.

Click here to remove a style sheet from the list definition.

3. Choose which style sheets you want included in the list definition by double-clicking on them in the Available Styles list. (You can also Command/Ctrl-click to select non-contiguous styles on the list and choose them all by clicking the right-arrow button in the dialog box.) The order in which you place the items on the list doesn't matter; at this point, it's just a list of style sheets.

4. Choose a level for each style sheet on the list by selecting the style and selecting 1 through 8 from the Level popup menu. These levels determine how the list appears on the Lists palette (which I'll discuss later in this section), and have nothing to do with how the list will appear on your printed page. For instance, you might apply level 1 to a style called Chapter Title, level 2 to a Heading style, and level 3 to a Subhead style.

5. You can control how the list will appear on your printed page with the Numbering and the Format As popup menus. You've got three options for Numbering: Text only, Text...Page #, and Page #...Text (see Figure 9-7). The first, Text only, tells XPress not to include the page number on which it finds the text tagged with this style. The other two options tell XPress to include the page number, separated from the text of the paragraph by a tab character. For instance, in the previous example, you might set the Chapter Title style sheet to Text only, and the Heading and Subhead styles to Text...Page #.

Preface

Chapter I: History of Pi
Early History 7
The Greeks 13
Pi in the East .19
A Millennium of Progress . . . . .29 ———— Text...Page #
Breakthroughs in Mathematics 41

Chapter II: The Personality of Pi ———————— Text only
Irrational numbers 73
Patterns in Pi .101

Chapter III: The Circle Squarers
John Smith 113   **Figure 9-7**
                                                              Numbering

---

6. The Format As popup menu lets you apply a style sheet to the paragraph when it appears on the list. This is helpful because you'd rarely want a heading from your document to appear in your table of contents in the actual Heading style; instead, you'd probably create a new style sheet called "TOC-head" or something like that (see Figure 9-8). If you want certain paragraphs to be indented on your final list, you should apply style sheets here that include indentation.

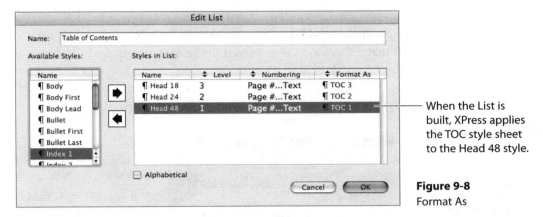

When the List is
built, XPress applies
the TOC style sheet
to the Head 48 style.

Figure 9-8
Format As

That's it! However, here are a few things to keep in mind when you're defining a list.

• You can define thousands of different lists in a single document, but lists cannot span across multiple layout spaces in a project.

• You can have a maximum of 32 style sheets in a list definition.

• XPress only captures the first 256 characters of tagged text when it builds a list, so you should choose style sheets that correspond to text shorter than this (256 characters make about 40 words—more than enough for most headlines, bylines, and such).

• If you turn on the Alphabetical option in the Edit List dialog box, XPress sorts the list in alphabetical order when you build it (I discuss how to build a list below). Whether you want your final list alphabetized is up to you; you probably wouldn't when you build the table of contents for a book, but you might for a list of items in a catalog.

• If you want a list to work in multiple documents within a book, the list must be present in all the documents. You can use the Synchronize Book feature to ensure that the same list appears properly in them all.

The Lists Palette

Once you've defined a list, it's time to open the Lists palette, which lets you get an overview for your list, navigate through your document based on the list, and ultimately build the final list on your document pages. You can open the Lists palette by selecting Show List from the Window menu or pressing Option-F11 (Mac) or Ctrl-F11 (Windows).

As soon as you open the Lists palette, QuarkXPress goes and collects the text and paragraphs you've specified in the list definition (this might take a little while for a very large document). All that information is displayed in the lower section of the Lists palette (see Figure 9-9). The Lists palette doesn't contain the corresponding page numbers for these paragraphs; that information comes later, when you tell XPress to build the list on your document page.

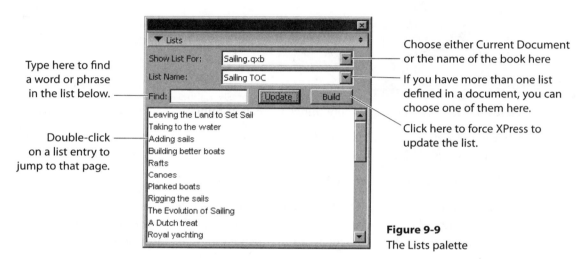

Type here to find
a word or phrase
in the list below.

Double-click
on a list entry to
jump to that page.

Choose either Current Document
or the name of the book here

If you have more than one list
defined in a document, you can
choose one of them here.

Click here to force XPress to
update the list.

Figure 9-9
The Lists palette

The Lists palette offers you two options. First, if you have more than one list defined in a document, you can choose among them from the List popup menu. The second option, found on the Show List For popup menu, is only active if the document is part of a book; if it is, you can tell XPress to build the list based on this one document or on all the documents in the book.

I find the Lists palette a good place to get an overview of a document or a book, and—if I've specified my Levels properly—it's very helpful as a first step in figuring out if the final list is going to appear correctly on my pages (sometimes you don't realize that you left out a paragraph style sheet, or chose the wrong style sheet—until you peruse the Lists palette).

List navigation. If you double-click on any paragraph in the Lists palette, XPress jumps to the page where the text is. In fact, some people use the Lists palette for navigation purposes only, and never actually build the table of contents or whatever on their document pages.

The Find field of the Lists palette is very useful if you've got a very long list; just type the first few characters of a paragraph you think is on the list, and XPress selects it in the Lists palette. I find this most helpful in those long technical documents where every heading begins with a number.

Update. If QuarkXPress had to keep tabs on every little edit you make in your document and reflect it in the Lists palette, it'd be as slow as molasses on a cold January morning. No, if you make any changes to your document—add paragraphs, remove paragraphs, change the spelling of words—the Lists palette only updates when you click the Update button or when you close and reopen the palette.

Building and Rebuilding Lists

You've defined a list, you've browsed over it in the Lists palette, and now it's finally time to get that list onto your document page. This is potentially the most complex and hair-raising ordeal of the entire process. No, seriously—here's what you do: select a text box (preferably an empty one) and click the Build button on the Lists palette. That's it. If the list is supposed to include page numbers, now is when XPress goes out and finds them (see Figure 9-10).

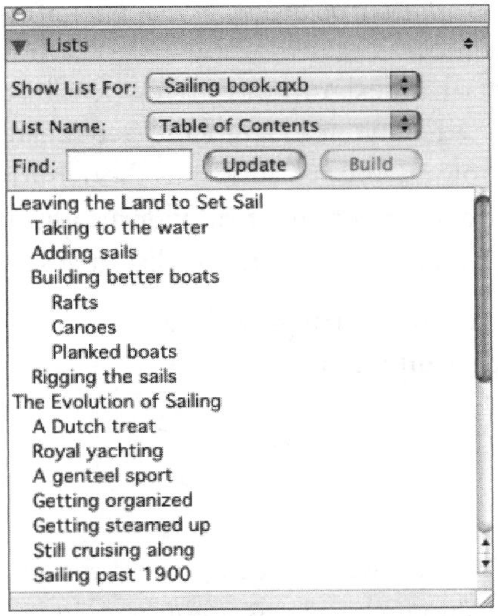

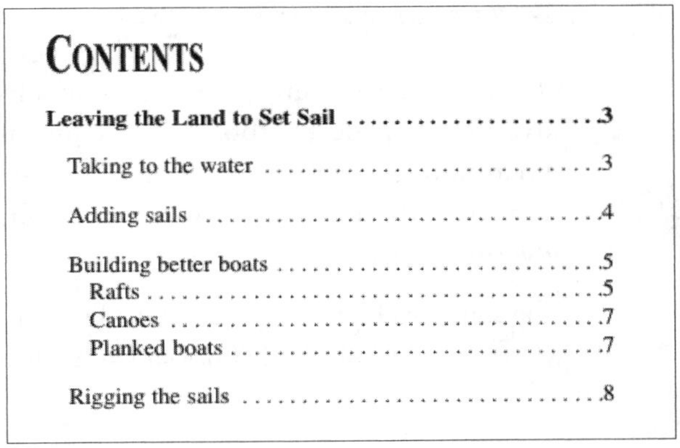

Figure 9-10
The final list

Updating the list. There is nothing special about the text or page numbers on this list—they're just text and numbers. If you update the document on which the list is based (including changes to page numbers or to the list definition), you're going to have rebuild the list on your document page. I find that I build and rebuild a list at least several times for each document or book, due to various human errors (my own, generally). Here's how you rebuild.

1. First, make sure the Lists palette is up-to-date by clicking the Update button.

2.   Select any text box in your document (it doesn't have to be the same box in which you originally built the list).

3.   Click Build in the Lists palette. XPress is smart enough to know if you've already built a list in your file. If you have, it asks you if you want to replace the list that's already there (see Figure 9-11). Typically, you'd want to choose to replace the already built list.

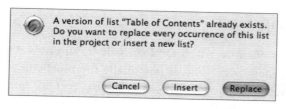

Figure 9-11
Rebuilding a list

TIP: Use Dummy Text for Lists. *One of my favorite aspects of lists is that they're document-wide rather than simply story-wide. That means that any text in any text box can be included on a list…even text in a text box that has Suppress Printout turned on. With this in mind, you can add "tags" to items on your page that don't appear in print, but do appear in your table of contents.*

One of the best examples of this is an advertiser index. You can place a text box with an advertiser's name on top of that company's ad in your document. Set the text box's runaround to None and turn on Suppress Printout, and it's almost as though this were a "non-object"—the text box won't print, and it won't affect any text underneath. But if that advertiser's name is tagged with a style sheet, you can include it on a list of advertisers.

The same trick goes for building a list of pictures in a catalog, or for any other time when what you want on the list doesn't actually appear on the page.

INDEXES

It was Mr. Duncan, my elementary-school librarian, who first impressed the importance of a good index on my malleable young brain: A nonfiction book without an index, he said, wasn't even worth putting on the library shelf. If you've ever searched an index in vain for something that you're sure is somewhere in a book, you know the value of a good index.

The problem is that sitting down and indexing a book is—in my experience—the most painful, horrible, mind-numbing activity you could ever wish on your worst enemy. And yet, where this is the kind of task that a computer should be great at, it's actually impossible for a computer to do a good job of indexing a book by itself. A good index requires careful thought, an understanding of the subject matter, and an ability to keep the whole project in your head at all times. Plus, until recently, it required a large stack of notecards, highlighter pens, and Post-it notes.

Fortunately, QuarkXPress has a built-in indexing feature which, while it won't make the index for you, does remove the notecard and highlighter requirements. Note that because a minority of XPress users actually ever index their documents, the folks at Quark put this feature into a separate XTension. The XTension is loaded (it's in the XTension folder) by default, but if you or someone else turned it off with the XTension manager, you may have to turn it back on and relaunch XPress.

> **TIP: Concordance Versus Index.** *Some people ask me, "Why can't a computer build an index? QuarkXPress should just give me a list of all the words in my document and what page they're on." Unfortunately, this is not an index; it's a concordance. The difference is that a concordance records the location of words, while an index records the location of ideas. There are times when a concordance is very useful, especially in catalogs. In those cases, you might want to use an XTension like Sonar Bookends, which can build concordances automatically and very quickly. But in general, if you're looking for an index, you're going to have to do it manually with the indexing features in XPress.*

> **TIP: Edit First, Index Last.** *You can index a document at any time in the production cycle, but it's almost always best to wait until the text has become fixed—until no text in the document will be deleted, copied, cut, pasted, and so on. The reason: as you edit the text, you may accidentally delete index markers without knowing it. In fact, as this book goes to press, even cutting and pasting text deletes index entries.*

The Index palette. Just as the List feature captures text that is tagged with specific style sheets, XPress's indexing captures specific words or phrases that you have manually tagged in the Index palette. The Index palette (choose Index from the Window menu) lets you add either single words or whole phrases to the index, and it displays a list of currently indexed words and phrases (see Figure 9-12).

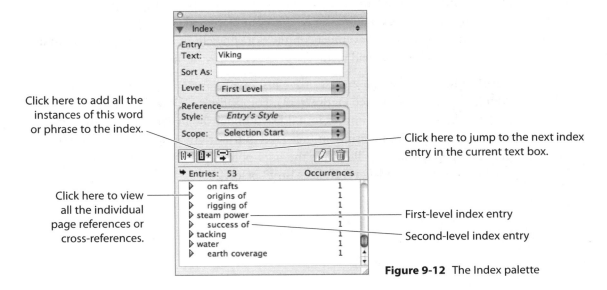

Click here to add all the instances of this word or phrase to the index.

Click here to jump to the next index entry in the current text box.

Click here to view all the individual page references or cross-references.

First-level index entry

Second-level index entry

Figure 9-12 The Index palette

First I'm going to discuss how to add, edit, and remove index entries with the Index palette. Then I'll explore how to collect all the tagged entries and build a finished index on your document pages.

Adding a New First-Level Index Entry

There's very little that is automatic about building an index. Again, it's not difficult, but you have to be methodical about it. Here are the steps you should go through for each new index entry. Note that I always differentiate between a new index entry and a new reference to an index entry. For example, "Pigs" might be a new entry for page 34, but when it appears again on page 59, it would simply be a new reference to your already added index entry—see "Adding a New Reference to an Entry," below.

1. **Text.** Insert the index entry (the word or phrase that you want to appear in the index) into the Text field of the Index palette. If the entry actually appears in the text story, you can just select it with the cursor; when the Index palette is open, QuarkXPress automatically copies any text that is selected into the Text field. On the other hand, if the word or phrase doesn't appear, you will have to type it in yourself.

   For example, you may be discussing cows on your document page, but you want to index the word under the phrase "Farm animals." In this case, you would simply place the cursor somewhere in the text box and type "Farm animals" in the Index palette.

2. **Sort As.** Index entries always appear in alphabetical order. However, occasionally you may not want your index entry to appear where it would normally be alphabetized. For instance, the famous "17-Mile Drive" would ordinarily be placed at the beginning of the index, before the A's. You can place it along with other words that begin with S by typing "Seventeen" in the Sort As field of the Index palette. You'll probably just leave this field blank for 98 percent of your index entries.

3. **Level.** While some simple indexes have just one level of entry, most have two (some even have three or four; see Figure 9-13). For example, "Cows," "Pigs," and "Ducks" might all be second-level entries found listed under the first-level entry of "Farm animals." Since we're focusing on first-level entries right now, you can just skip over the Level popup menu. (I'll discuss the finer points of second-level entries in "Adding a New Second-Level Index Entry," below).

Calculating. *See also* Equations ———— First-level entry
    area of circle, 80–81, **86**
    circumference to diameter, 24–25
    errors in, 12–13, 49–50
    forumlas for, 43, 44, 61 ———— Second-level entry
    speed/efficiency of, 42, 53
    techniques for, 52–61
Calculators, 50–56 ———— Cross-reference
Callet, J.F., 45
Catholic church. *See* Religion
Cavalieri, Bonaventura, 40, **43** ———— Single-page reference styled with the Style popup menu
Ch'ang Hong, 24, 26
Chudnovsky brothers ———— Page number suppressed
    m-Zero, 65–70
    and Preston, R., 88–89 ———— Entry sorted differently using Sort As
    supercomputers, 71

Figure 9-13 A multilevel index

4. **Style.** The Style popup menu on the Index palette is yet one more control that you will ignore most of the time, though when you need it, it's great to have. Let's say you want the page numbers that refer to an illustration (rather than to just text on the page) to appear bold in the final index. You can build a character style sheet to define how you want the page numbers to appear and—when you're indexing that illustration—you can choose that character style from the Style popup menu. (See Chapter 7, *Copy Flow*, for more information on defining style sheets.)

5. **Scope.** If your treatise on pigs and goats spans six pages of your document, you don't want to have to make a separate index entry for each and every page. Instead, you can specify one index entry and choose a range of pages in the Scope popup menu. There are seven types of scopes.

    Selection start. When you choose Selection start (this is the default setting), XPress references the page on which the cursor is currently sitting. If you've selected a range of text that crosses from one page to the next, the first page (wherever the selection starts) is used.

    Selection Text. You can select any range of text (two words, two paragraphs, 200 paragraphs…you get the idea) and index the whole range by choosing Selection Text. Personally, I find this option rather clunky to use and even clunkier to edit later, if necessary, so I prefer using one of the other Scope settings instead.

    To Style. If you use style sheets religiously, you'll love using the To Style option because you can specify a range based on paragraph styles. For instance, let's say you've got a book about farm animals where each animal's heading is tagged with a style sheet called "Heading-A." You could select the heading "Rabbit" and set the

Scope to "To Style." Then you could choose Heading-A from the popup menu of styles (see Figure 9-14). If the "Horse" section starts three pages after the Rabbit section, the page range in the index will span three pages; if it starts 14 pages after, the page range will span 14 pages, and so on.

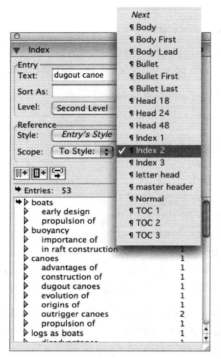

Figure 9-14
Indexing using To Style

By the way, the default setting for To Style is Next, which means "from this paragraph onward until the style sheet changes to something else."

Specified # of Ps. If you want to index a long paragraph, one that may split onto two or more pages, you should probably select the scope called "Specified # of Ps." (Yes, Ps stands for "Paragraphs.") QuarkXPress's default setting of 1 means "include the pages that this paragraph falls on." Changing this setting to 2 means "include this paragraph plus the one after it," and so on.

To End Of. When you choose the scope called "To End Of," XPress offers you two options: to the end of the story or to the end of the document. If the current text story reaches to the last page of the document, then these options are the same, of course. In the example of the farm animals chapter, you could index the entire chapter by placing the cursor anywhere on the first page of the chapter, specifying an index entry labeled "Farm animals," and choosing To End Of Document.

Suppress Page #. Some first-level index entries don't include page numbers at all. For instance, in the book I've been discussing, "Animals" is too broad a topic to include page numbers (every page in the book would be indexed). So you might specify Suppress Page # for this one entry, and then follow it with 15 second-level entries, each with appropriate page numbers listed. (Again, I discuss second-level entries below.)

X-Ref. The last item on the Scope popup menu is X-Ref, which lets you add cross-references to your index. If you'll forgive me—because cross-references act a little bit differently than other index entries—I'm going to hold off on my discussion of this option for a moment.

6. **Add.** If you've persevered through this procedure so far, the final step in adding an index entry is to click the Add button (the first of the three buttons in the palette). Sadly, after indexing for a long time, I sometimes forget this step and move on to the next entry, only to wonder later why I'm missing index entries that I *know* I made. Another *faux pas*: clicking Add before you change the various controls on the Index palette…that doesn't work, either.

Adding index entries is not hard at all, but it does take patience and attention to detail in each of these steps. As soon as you press the Add button, XPress inserts the entry into the Index palette and places an index marker in the text (see Figure 9-15). These index entries are actually hidden inside the text in the text box, though the index markers only show up when the Index palette is visible.

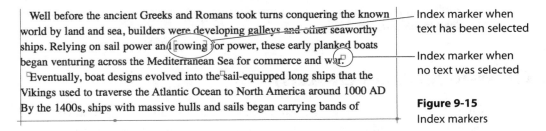

Well before the ancient Greeks and Romans took turns conquering the known world by land and sea, builders were developing galleys and other seaworthy ships. Relying on sail power and rowing or power, these early planked boats began venturing across the Mediterranean Sea for commerce and war.

Eventually, boat designs evolved into the sail-equipped long ships that the Vikings used to traverse the Atlantic Ocean to North America around 1000 AD By the 1400s, ships with massive hulls and sails began carrying bands of

Index marker when text has been selected

Index marker when no text was selected

Figure 9-15
Index markers

TIP: Be Careful with Add All. *The second button in the Index palette is the Add All feature, which searches throughout your document for every instance of the index entry and adds it automatically to the index. For example, if you select the words "Bumble Bee" on your page and then click Add All, the entry will be added once, followed by the page number of each page that contains the words "Bumble Bee." This can be a great timesaver but it can also get you in trouble if you're not careful. When you press Add All, XPress uses the same Scope, Style, and Level settings for every instance of the entry text. In some cases this is fine, but in many indexes, each instance needs special attention—one only showing up on this page, one using a To Style scope, and so on.*

> **TIP: Adding Names to the Index.** *Adding names to an index can be frustrating because you need to reverse the order of first and last names. In XPress 5 and 6, you can simply press the Option/Alt key before clicking the Add button. This changes the Add button to an Add Reversed feature, and phrases like "Michael Jackson" and "Quincy Jones" get added to the index as "Jackson, Michael" and "Jones, Quincy."*

> **TIP: Index Keystrokes.** *There are two keystrokes you should keep in mind when you're indexing. First, Command-Option-I (Ctrl-Alt-I) jumps to the Text field in the Index palette (it even opens the palette first, if necessary). Second, pressing Command-Option-Shift-I (Ctrl-Alt-Shift-I) is the same as clicking the Add button in the Index palette. I find that both of these speed up indexing considerably.*

> **TIP: Styling Indexes.** *Remember that however you type the word in the Text field of the Index palette is how it will appear in your final index. There is no single "correct" way to enter words into your index, though there are standard conventions, and it is best if you can keep your index consistent throughout.*

For instance, you should decide on a capitalization scheme before beginning to index your document. Will all first-level entries be in initial caps, while second-level entries will be in lower case? Or should only proper names be capitalized, even in first-level entries? Before you answer these questions, it might behoove you to look over the section on indexes in a book on style conventions like *The Chicago Manual of Style*.

> **TIP: Wrong Scope.** *As this book goes to press, QuarkXPress's Index XTension still contains an annoying bug. Let's say your text story starts on page 14 and then jumps to page 21. If you select and index a paragraph that spans the page break, the index entry appears as "14–21" rather than "14, 21." The former mistakenly appears to cover seven pages; the latter properly states that the entry is just on two pages. I hope they fix the bug by the time you read this, but if they don't, then just be aware that you might have some cleaning up to do later (see "Tip: Finessing Your Index," later in this chapter).*

Cross-References (X-Refs)

One of the tricks to building a great index is to think of all the ways that your reader might look for a topic, and to include those words in your index. For instance, because you're familiar with your own book, you might include an index entry called "Llamas." However, another reader might look for "Cute wool-producing animals that spit." Fortunately, XPress lets you add cross-references in your index like "Spitting animals. *See* Llamas" and "Wool 34–46. *See also* Llamas."

To add a cross-reference to your index, you go through all the same steps as adding a normal index entry. The one difference is that when you set the Scope popup menu to X-Ref, XPress provides you with a text field in which you can type the cross-referenced word or phrase. If you want your index entry to be "Koi. *See* Carp" you would type "Koi" in the Text field of the Index palette, and type "Carp" in the X-Ref field.

Note that if you're cross-referencing to an index entry that you've already added to your Index palette, you can simply click on that index entry to copy it into the X-Ref field. That's certainly faster than typing the words in again.

Of course, because no page number is involved in a cross-reference, it doesn't matter where in your document you specify it (though it must be in a text box).

X-Ref options. QuarkXPress offers three types of cross-references which you can choose from the Index palette once you select X-Ref from the Scope popup menu: See, See also, and See herein.

- *See* is generally used when an index entry has no page number references, such as "Supermarket. *See* Grocery."

- *See also* is used when an index entry does have page references, but you also want to refer the reader to other topics, such as "Grocery 34–51. *See also* Farmer's Market."

- *See herein* is a special case in which you are cross-referencing to a second-level entry within the same entry as the cross-reference itself, and it's used more in legal indexes than anywhere else.

The Chicago Manual of Style recommends that you set these three phrases in italic in your index. XPress can automatically change this formatting for you (see "Index Preferences," later in this chapter).

Adding a New Reference to an Entry

Once you've got an entry on your Index palette, you can easily add more page references to it. Let's say you added the name "Farmer Jones" to your index back on page 13 of your document. Now, "Farmer Jones" appears again on page 51.

1. Place the cursor in the appropriate place in the text story. In this case, you'd probably put the cursor next to the word "Farmer" on page 51.

2. Click on the entry in the Index palette. Here, you'd click on "Farmer Jones." As soon as you click on an index entry, it appears in the Text field of the palette.

3. Make sure that the Level, Style, and Scope controls are set up properly in the Index palette, depending on how you want your new reference to appear.

4. Click the Add button.

Note that while you don't necessarily have to click on the entry in the Index palette in Step 2 (you could just retype the entry in the Text field or select it on the page), I recommend the clicking method because it ensures consistency. For example, if you relied on your typing ability, you might create the index entry "Chickens" and then later—meaning to type the same thing—create a new entry, "Chicken," causing two different entries to be made when you only meant to make one.

Adding a New Second-Level Index Entry

Now that you've specified first-level index entries, you can—if you wish—add second-level entries. As I mentioned earlier, second-level entries are subcategories of the first-level entries. For example, under the first-level index entry "Wines," you might find the second-level entries "Merlot," "Chardonnay," and "Côtes du Rhône." You can make a second-level index entry just like you make the first-level entry, but with two extra steps.

First, you must choose Second Level from the Level popup menu on the Index palette.

Second, you must tell XPress which first-level entry you want the new entry to fall under. You do this by clicking in the column to the left of the first-level entry (see Figure 9-16). When you click, XPress moves the Level marker (the little L-shaped arrow icon) to indicate that any second-level entries you create will be placed here.

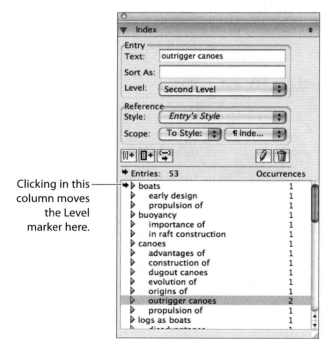

Clicking in this column moves the Level marker here.

Figure 9-16
Creating a second-level entry

The number one mistake people make when adding a second-level entry is forgetting to move the Level marker, so the second-level entry shows up in the wrong place (see "Tip: Moving a Second-Level Entry," below). The second-most-common mistake is accidentally clicking on the first-level entry when you meant to click in the column to the left of it (to move the Level marker), which replaces whatever is in the Text field with whatever you click on…oops!

Again, patience and attention really do go a long way when you're making indexes.

Third and Fourth Levels. Once you've got a second-level entry, you can place a third-level entry under it—just change the Level popup menu to Third Level and place the Level marker appropriately. Similarly, you can put fourth-level entries under third-level entries. While it's nice that Quark gives you this option, I find that third- and fourth-level entries are pretty confusing to readers, so restrain yourself unless more levels are really necessary.

> **TIP: Where to Put the Cross-Reference.** *Some people like putting cross-references at the end of a list of second-level index entries rather than directly after the first-level entry. XPress won't do this for you automatically, but you can fake it by creating a dummy second-level entry and setting its Scope to X-Ref. The dummy second-level entry should just be named with a symbol like ^ or \ so that it automatically falls at the end of the alphabetized list of second-level entries. Later, once you build the index onto your document pages, you will have to perform a Find/Change to remove the symbols.*

Deleting an Entry

There are several ways to delete an entry from your index.

- If you want to delete an entire entry, including all its page references, select it in the Index palette and click the Delete button (the one that looks like a trash can on the Macintosh or a big X in Windows). Note that this also deletes all the subcategories under it and their page references, too.

- If you want to delete a single page reference, you can select it in the Index palette (click on the gray triangle next to the index entry to display its page references) and click the Delete button. Of course, if you only have one page reference under an index entry, deleting it will delete the whole entry, too.

- To get rid of a particular page reference in your index, you can also delete the index markers on the document page. If you selected text before adding the index entry, then this means deleting that whole range of text (deleting anything less leaves the index markers intact). If you did not select any text when adding the entry, you can still delete the little square marker by zooming in on it, clicking directly in its center, and pressing Delete. (You need to zoom in, because you generally can't select the tiny icon properly at Actual Size.)

• Last but not least, you can delete *every* index entry from the Index palette by Option-Shift-clicking (Alt-Shift-click) on the Delete button. This is drastic, so XPress always asks you if you really want to proceed.

Editing Index Entries

None of us is perfect, so it's a good thing that QuarkXPress has a way to edit the flubbed index entries that we make. When you're editing an index entry, you have to decide whether you want to edit the entry itself or a particular page reference of the entry.

Editing entries. Let's say that halfway through indexing your document, you realize that the index entry "Martha Washington" should have been indexed as "Washington, Martha." You can select the entry in the Index palette and click the Edit button (that's the button that looks like a little pencil)—or even faster, you can activate the Edit mode by double-clicking on the entry. Because you're editing an entry, XPress grays out everything but the Text, Sort As, and Level fields in the palette. In this case, you'd change the Text field to "Washington, Martha," and then click the Edit button again (or press Enter).

Editing references. You can also change the scope or style of a particular page reference. For instance, let's say the reference to Martha Washington on page 47 should have spanned nine paragraphs, but you accidentally set it to Selection start instead. To fix this, click on the gray triangle next to the index entry; this displays the page references for the entry. Double-click on the page reference that corresponds to the one you want to change (in this case, you'd double-click on the number 47). Because you're editing a page reference, XPress grays out the Text and Sort As fields and lets you change the Style and Scope popup menus. When you're done, press Enter, or click the Edit button to leave Edit mode.

Note that there's no way to move an index entry from one place in the text to another (for instance, if you actually wanted the above reference to begin on page 48 instead of page 47); you have to actually delete the entry and then re-enter it in the new location.

> **TIP: Find the Next Index Entry.** *In order to edit either an index entry or an individual page reference, you need to have it selected on the Index palette. If the index entry is right in front of you on the page, sometimes it's faster to select it on the page than it is to select it in the palette (especially in really long indexes). The problem is that it's tough to select index markers on the page. The best solution is to place the cursor in the text box, a few characters or a few words before the index entry, then to click the Find Next button in the Index palette. This automatically selects the next index entry in the text box, and simultaneously selects it in the Index palette, too.*

By the way, if you hold down the Option/Alt key, the Index palette's Find Next button changes to a Find First button; while this is a good way to jump to the first index entry in a story, I rarely find myself needing this.

> **TIP: Moving a Second-Level Entry.** *As I said earlier, the most common mistake people make when adding second-level entries is to put them under the wrong first-level entry. If you do this, don't panic. Simply hold down the Option/Alt key and drag your new entry on top of the first-level you wanted it under. The Option or Alt key is the way you can rearrange index entries in the list. But use this sparingly—XPress can get confused in long indexes.*

Index Preferences

Now that you've gone through the trouble of manually adding 4,000 index entries to your document, can't you build the index yet? No, not yet. First you should take a quick glance at the Index panel of the Preferences dialog box (see Figure 9-17). This dialog box lets you change two things: the color of the index markers in your document, and the specific formatting characters that QuarkXPress will use when building the index.

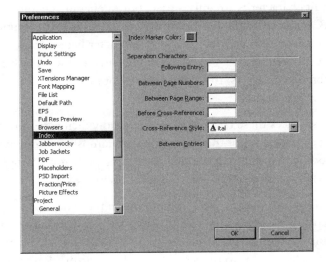

Figure 9-17
Index Preferences

Note that Index preferences are application-wide preferences, so they apply to all documents. (In earlier versions, they were only document-wide.)

Index Marker Color. There's nothing sacred about the color red…if you're color-blind to the color red, if your text is colored red, or if you just don't like seeing red, you can change the color of the index markers by clicking the color swatch labeled "Index Marker Color." Of course, this doesn't change anything about your document or your index; it only alters the on-screen display of the index markers when the Index palette is open.

Separation Characters. This might seem really trivial to you, but most art directors and professional indexers care a great deal about the formatting characters in their index (see Figure 9-18). For example, what kind of space should separate an index entry and the page reference? The Index Preferences dialog box is the place to make this sort of decision.

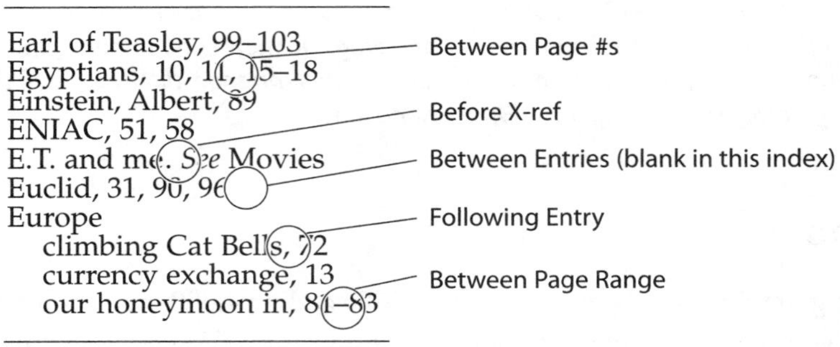

Earl of Teasley, 99–103 ——— Between Page #s
Egyptians, 10, 11, 15–18
Einstein, Albert, 89 ——— Before X-ref
ENIAC, 51, 58
E.T. and me. *See* Movies ——— Between Entries (blank in this index)
Euclid, 31, 90, 96
Europe ——— Following Entry
    climbing Cat Bells, 72
    currency exchange, 13 ——— Between Page Range
    our honeymoon in, 81–83

Figure 9-18 Separation characters

- **Following Entry.** This character sits between the index entry and the page reference numbers. The default character is a regular space, but I generally change this to a nonbreaking en space (Option-space on the Macintosh, or Ctrl-Shift-6 in Windows) for better optical separation. You can put more than one character here—many people like to include a period, a comma, or a colon after an index entry, followed by a space, followed by the page reference numbers. In this case, type both the comma (or whatever) and the space in this field.

- **Between Page #s.** XPress places these characters between individual page-reference numbers. The important character is not the comma (which almost everyone uses), but the space after the comma. I typically leave this space alone, but some people like a larger or smaller space (like a punctuation space—Shift-space).

- **Between Page Range.** This character is used when the page reference spans multiple pages. The default character here is a regular hyphen, but I usually change this to an en dash (Option-hyphen on the Macintosh, or Ctrl-Alt-Shift-hyphen in Windows). You could even change this to the word " to " if you want (don't forget to put spaces on either side), so that the page ranges look like this: "34 to 89."

- **Before Cross Reference.** This character sits between the entry or a page reference number and a cross-reference. Like the Between Page #s character, the important character in the Before Cross Reference field is not the default period (which almost everyone uses), but the space after the period, which you might decide to make larger or smaller. Personally, I just leave this setting alone. (Note that if you want some special punctuation *after* a cross-reference, you generally have to type it yourself in the Index palette, though this is not usually the style.)

- **Between Entries.** If you build a nested index (rather than a run-in index; I'll explain the difference in "Building the Index," below), XPress places the Between Entries character at the end of every line. While it may seem at first like you'd want a period or something at the end of every line, this is very rare in an index, so in general you should leave this setting blank (the default) for nested indexes.

  In run-in indexes, however, you need to separate the entries from each other, so you should change this. The most common style is to use a semicolon and some kind of space character.

  > **TIP: Special Index Characters.** *You can type some special characters into the text fields in the Index Preferences dialog box by typing special codes. For example, if your index style calls for a tab character between the index entries and the page reference numbers, you could type "\t" in the Following Entry field (that's a backslash followed by a "t"). Similarly, you can get a flex space by typing "/f," and a line break by typing "/n." Why you'd want these characters in an index is beyond me; I just want to let you know that you can get them. Note that the codes are the same ones used in the Find/Change palette (see "Finding and Changing" in Chapter 5,* Working with Text).

Cross-Ref style. Quark snuck a little feature into the Index Preferences dialog box that lets you automatically apply a character style to the *See, See also,* and *See herein* text in cross-references. In most instances, you'll simply want to create a character style that is based on the regular index text style but is also in italic. (See Chapter 7, *Copy Flow*, for more information on defining character style sheets.)

Building the Index

Finally, it's time to get that index onto a document page so you can see it in all its glory. This is the fun part, because you can just sit back, choose Build Index from the Utilities menu, and let XPress do the work of collecting the index entries and page numbers for you. (Build Index is only available when the Index palette is visible.) Unfortunately, there is still one more dialog box you need to pay attention to: the Build Index dialog box (see Figure 9-19).

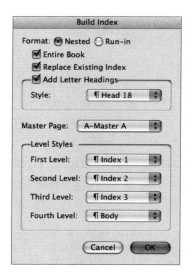

Figure 9-19
Build Index dialog box

The Build Index dialog box is a mish-mosh of choices you need to make in order to get the index of your dreams. While several of the options here might appear, at first, to fit better in the Index Preferences dialog box, who are we to question Quark's decisions? Fortunately, once you make your choices in this dialog box, XPress remembers them the next time you build an index for this document.

Nested versus Run-In. There are two primary types of indexes in the world: nested and run-in (see Figure 9-20). In a nested index, each entry occupies its own paragraph; in a run-in index, the second-level entries merge with their first-level entry to form one big paragraph. Which you choose is entirely up to you, though it should depend in part on the content of the index. Run-in indexes make no sense when you have third- or fourth-level entries. On the other hand, run-in indexes typically conserve space better, especially when they're set in wide columns (because more than one entry fits on a single line).

Decimal notation 18, 27
Decimal point 30
Digits of pi
   calculating 18, 34, 41, 46
   memorizing 4, 111–112, 114, 118
   number of 2, 3, 34, 45, 51–53, 65,
     67, 87–91, 113
   random sequence of 68, 72–73
   search for 42–43, 51
Dinostratos 56, 90
Dudley, Underwood 93, 96
Duciad (Pope) 92

Decimal notation 18, 27
Decimal point 30
Digits of pi; calculating 18, 34, 41,
   46; memorizing 4, 111–112, 114,
   118; number of 2, 3, 34, 45, 51–53,
   65, 67, 87–91, 113; random
   sequence of 68, 72–73; search for
   42–43, 51
Dinostratos 56, 90
Dudley, Underwood 93, 96
Duciad (Pope) 92

Figure 9-20 Nested indexes versus run-in indexes

The great thing about XPress's indexing is that you can build one type of index, then change your mind and replace it with the other type. Feel free to experiment!

Entire Book. If your document is part of a book (see "Books," earlier in this chapter), you can choose to build an index for the whole megillah by turning on the Entire Book option in the Build Index dialog box. I discuss this process in slightly more detail in "Indexing Books and Projects," below.

Replace Existing Index. QuarkXPress knows when you've already built an index in a document, and it automatically replaces that index with a new one unless you turn off the Replace Existing Index option. Probably the only time you'd turn this off would be if you wanted to compare two indexes to find differences between them.

By the way, note that when XPress replaces one index with another, it does not just replace the text. It actually deletes all the index pages and then rebuilds them from scratch. So if you've spent two hours adding extra formatting to the index, or adding boxes or lines to the pages, all those additions are removed when you build the new index.

Add Letter Headings. If you want headings added to your index (like an "A" before all the entries that begin with an A, and so on), turn on the Add Letter Headings option. When QuarkXPress builds the index, it adds the headings only as necessary (in other words, it won't add a "Q" heading if you don't have any entries that begin with that letter).

When this option is turned on, you can also choose a paragraph style sheet from the Style popup menu. This is the paragraph style that XPress uses to format the letter heading.

Master Page. When you click OK in the Build Index dialog box (don't do it yet), QuarkXPress adds new pages at the end of the current document and flows the index onto them. You can choose which master page you want the program to base the new pages on from the Master Page popup menu. Typically, you'll want to design a new master page specifically for the index, but you don't have to. Note that the master page you choose must have an automatic text box on it, or else XPress won't be able to flow the index onto the page.

Level Styles. The Level Styles section of the Build Index dialog box lets you apply paragraph style sheets to each entry in the index. In a run-in index, there's only one kind of paragraph: the first-level entry (all the second-level entries are merged into the same paragraph). In a nested index, however, each entry level is tagged with its own paragraph style. If you want all your second-level index entries to be slightly indented from the first-level entries (you probably do), make a new style sheet that includes indentation, and choose it from the Second Level popup menu.

Once again, designing a readable index is as much an art as a science. Take some time to peruse other people's indexes, checking for details like indentation (what does a first-level entry do when it's longer than one line, for example?) and punctuation.

If At First You Don't Succeed. Building an index can take a while if you have a very long document with a lot of entries, but you should plan on rebuilding it at least once. I find that there's almost always something I've forgotten or have messed up in the Index palette, Index Preferences, or the Build Index dialog box. Just go back and fix it, and then choose Build Index once again.

> **TIP: Finessing Your Index.** *Just as it takes a human touch to build a great set of index entries, the index that XPress builds on your document pages requires some human intervention to become a final product. Here's a short (and certainly not exhaustive) list of fine-tuning suggestions you might consider.*

- If you use letter headings, you might want to combine two or more of them into groups. For instance, if there are only one or two entries each under the last few headings in the index, you might want to merge them into one group and label them "X, Y, Z" or "X–Z."

- If any index entries are found on the Pasteboard or are overset from their text boxes when you build the index, QuarkXPress warns you and then places a dagger (†) next to those references in the built index. You can (and should) search your index for this character with Find/Change, just in case. If you find one, you can either remove it or fix the problem and rebuild the index.

- Indexes generally follow widow and orphan rules, as does body text (see "Widow and Orphan Control" in Chapter 6, *Typography*). For instance, you should probably try to keep at least one or two second-level entries with their first-level entry in a column. And a single second-level entry sitting all by its lonesome at the top of a column is a terrible sight to see. Unfortunately, these problems typically have to be fixed by hand, as XPress's Keep with Next ¶ and Keep Lines Together features aren't designed to work very well with indexes.

- I find that when I use an en dash between page ranges in my indexes, the character typically appears to be too close to the numbers on either side. The only good solution is to add very thin spaces or kerning around the character, and the only good way to do this is with XPress Tags (see "A Solution: XPress Tags" in Chapter 7, *Copy Flow*, for more on building complex search-and-replace strings using tags).

Of course, the most important thing you can do with an index is to proofread it carefully for spelling and style consistency.

Remember that any changes you make once your index is built are wiped out if you rebuild the index.

Indexing Books and Projects

There is a major problem lurking in the Index palette that applies directly to indexing multi-document books or multi-layout projects: The Index palette currently only displays index entries from one project or layout space at a time. There is no way to display entries from an entire book or across layouts. It may not seem like much, but in fact, the problem is so grave that many professional indexers simply give up and don't use XPress's indexing feature at all.

Given this limitation, you have two options when you're indexing multiple documents or layouts.

- You can merge all the documents, creating one enormous file, by dragging pages while you're in Thumbnails mode. If you do this, be sure to save the monster file under a different name than your original files, and keep plenty of backups—I trust big files about as far as I can throw them. (To merge layouts in a project, you have to drag thumbnails from your document into a dummy document, and then drag them back to the desired layout space.)

- You can just index your files one document at a time and hope that you can remember what you indexed in each document and how you indexed it. Going this route, it's helpful to build indexes every now and again and use printouts for reference.

If you merge all your documents, you can build the index just the way I've described above. Or, if you are going to persist in indexing each document separately, here's what you need to do differently.

Test one chapter first. Before you go too far in indexing your book, try building an index from one chapter first. This way, you'll know if you've properly set up Index Preferences and specified the index entries.

Indexing the entire book. When you're building an index, you can tell QuarkXPress to include every document in your book by turning on the Entire Book option in the Build Index dialog box. You have to have your book's palette open at the time you open the document to do this.

Note that XPress doesn't necessarily put the index at the end of the book. Instead, the program builds the book's index at the end of the currently open document, using the style sheets and preferences of that document. Of course, after you build a four-page index at the end of Chapter 2, XPress has to renumber every document after Chapter 2, so most of the page numbers in the index will be wrong. Therefore, it behooves you to build your index *only* at the end of the last document in your book.

TIP: Indexing in a New Document. Maybe it's just my tendency to segment each and every part of a long document, but I like having my index in a file all by itself. If you want this, too, here's how you get it.

1. Create a new document with the same specifications as the other documents in your book. Make sure you've got at least one master page that has an automatic text box on it in the document, and make sure the Auto Page Insertion option is turned on in Preferences (Command-Option-Shift-Y or Ctrl-Alt-Shift-Y).

2. Save this new document to disk along with your other files.

3. Add the new document to your book palette with the palette's Add Chapter button. (Make sure it's the last file listed on the book palette.)

4. If you haven't already built style sheets for the index entries (and letter headings, if you're using them), then build them now in this new document. If you have built them in your master chapter, then synchronize the book so they'll be available in your index document.

5. Build the book's index in the new document by choosing Build Index and turning on the Entire Book option.

6. Because XPress always adds index pages at the end of your document, you now have to manually delete the empty first page of your document.

Voilà! Now you've got a separate document that has an index for the entire book.

PUTTING IT TOGETHER

Long documents can be a drag to produce, but the Book, Lists, and Indexing features in QuarkXPress go a long way in helping make the process bearable. Whether you're building a magazine, a book, a journal, a catalog, or even a newsletter, I'm sure you'll be able to find good use for these features. Remember that a little work up front—building style sheets, putting documents in a book palette, and so on—can go a long way and can save lots of time in the long run.

Now let's shift gears radically and start looking at how pictures can liven up your XPress pages, in any size document you create.

CHAPTER TEN

Pictures

I've been talking a lot about text and rudimentary graphic elements such as arrows and ovals, but let's not forget that ultimately, QuarkXPress is designed to integrate not only text and lines, but also graphics from other programs, and it contains many powerful features to aid in this task. QuarkXPress handles line art and images such as four-color photographs with a degree of power and set of features previously attainable only by using several programs in conjunction with each other.

In this chapter, I'll cover almost everything you can do with pictures other than running text around them (which I cover in Chapter 12, *Text Meets Graphics*). I'll deal with the following:

- Importing images into QuarkXPress

- Rotating picture boxes and their contents

- Placing images and picture boxes precisely

- Skewing graphic images horizontally

- Reimporting modified pictures automatically

- Working with Publish and Subscribe and OLE

- Greeking pictures

Here are the basic steps of importing pictures into your layout.

1. Create a picture box.

2. Select the box with the Content tool, and bring in a picture by either pasting from the Clipboard (not a good idea) or using the Import Picture command.

3. Size, skew, rotate, and crop the image until you like the way it looks on the page.

But what types of pictures are available for use? And how do you get them to look the way you want? In this chapter I explore the full range of possibilities for bringing graphics in from other applications and manipulating them on the page. In Chapter 11, *Image Tuning,* I'll talk about some of the effects you can create by modifying graphics once they're in QuarkXPress.

Let's first take a close look at the different types of pictures on the Macintosh and in Windows that are applicable to QuarkXPress users.

GRAPHIC FILE FORMATS

If there's a question I'm asked more often than "Why won't my file print?" it's "What's the difference between all those different graphic formats?" The question refers to a host of formats with names such as EPS, TIFF, GIF, PICT, LZW, TIFF, JPEG, Photo CD (PCD), and Windows Metafile (WMF). No one can be blamed for being confused when faced with such a list! Some of these are different names for the same thing, others are subtly different, and a few represent totally different concepts.

The fundamental question when considering a graphic file format is whether it is bitmapped or object-oriented.

Bitmapped Images

The most common image-file formats are based on bitmapped images. When you use a scanner and scanning software, a digital camera, or an image-editing and painting program such as Adobe Photoshop, you're working with and generating bitmapped images. However, no matter how ubiquitous bitmapped images are, you are still strictly limited as to how you can use them.

Bitmapped images are just that: images made of mapped *bits*. On your computer screen, bits are represented by *pixels*. Black and white monitors display each bit or pixel as either on (black) or off (white). Bits become more complex on color monitors, but the principle is the same: Each pixel is *this* value or *that* value. The *map* part is the computer's internal blueprint of which bits are on and which are off, and their color values (see Figure 10-1).

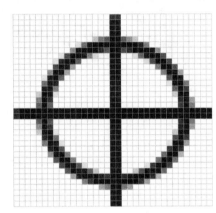

Figure 10-1
Each pixel sits on the grid.

There are three primary pieces of information that are relevant to any bitmapped image: its dimensions, resolution, and pixel depth.

Dimensions. Every bitmapped image is rectangular and is broken down into a grid of many square pixels. Each pixel is whole and not fractured. For example, you can't color half a pixel in blue and the other half in green. This feature of bitmapped images is what causes jagged edges or *jaggies* at the seam between two colors (refer to Figure 10-1 again). You can describe the dimensions of the gridded area in several ways, but they are most often specified by the number of pixels or sample points per side (like 800 by 600 pixels), or by inches per side at a given resolution.

Resolution. The resolution of the bitmapped image is usually defined as the number of pixels, or sample points, per inch on the grid (of course, it's pixels per centimeter in countries using the metric system). A low-resolution bitmapped image such as a screen capture or graphic created for use on the Web may have 72 pixels per inch (ppi), which is usually expressed as either dots per inch (dpi) or samples per inch (spi). A picture using only 72 dpi looks beautiful onscreen but extremely rough when printed. A higher-resolution bitmapped image suitable for printing would be 300 dpi or higher (many film scanners scan images at over 4,000 dpi). The higher an image's resolution, the fewer noticeable jaggies there will be when it's printed (see Figure 10-2).

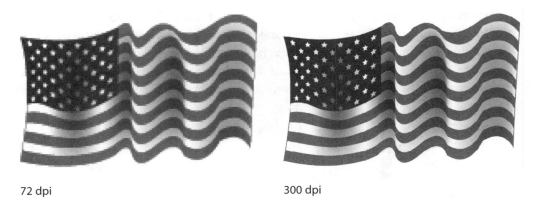

72 dpi   300 dpi

Figure 10-2 Low-resolution versus high-resolution bitmapped line art

Pixel depth. Each pixel is defined as a single, solid color. In the simplest bitmapped images, each pixel is defined as either black or white. These are called "bilevel," or "1-bit" images, because each pixel is described by 1 bit of information—either on (1) or off (0).

Bilevel images are *flat;* black-and-white have no tonal depth. More complex bitmapped images are *deep,* because they contain pixels that are defined by multiple bits, enabling them to describe many levels of gray or hues of color. For example, an 8-bit image can describe up to 256 colors or shades of gray for each pixel. A 24-bit image can describe more than 16 million colors (see Figure 10-3).

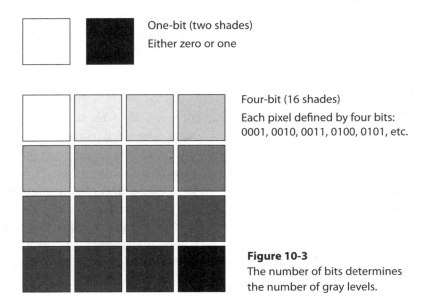

One-bit (two shades)
Either zero or one

Four-bit (16 shades)
Each pixel defined by four bits:
0001, 0010, 0011, 0100, 0101, etc.

Figure 10-3
The number of bits determines
the number of gray levels.

Manipulating bitmapped images. The limitations inherent in bitmapped images become most clear when you manipulate the picture in some way, such as enlarging it significantly. The key is that the picture's resolution is directly related to its size. If you double the size of a bitmap in QuarkXPress, you cut its resolution in half because increasing the size of a bitmapped image doesn't add more pixels to the image; it's very much like zooming in on a bitmapped image to 200 percent. The result is that the image becomes *pixelated,* when it's enlarged. That is, you begin to recognize each pixel and its tonal value. If you reduce the picture to one-quarter of its original size, you multiply its resolution by four. For example, a 72-dpi, 1-bit graphic when enlarged 200 percent becomes a twice-as-rough 36-dpi image. However, when reduced to 50 percent, it becomes a finer 144-dpi image (see Figure 10-4).

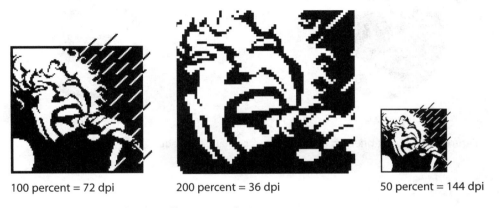

100 percent = 72 dpi   200 percent = 36 dpi   50 percent = 144 dpi

Figure 10-4 Scaling a bitmap affects its resolution.

Object-Oriented Graphics

Instead of describing a picture dot by dot, object-oriented files specify each object in a picture on a coordinate system. A bitmapped picture could take an enormous amount of space describing one circle (this dot on, this dot off, and so on), but an object-oriented file could describe it in one line: "Draw a circle of this diameter with a center at x,y." The computer knows what a circle is and how to create it. Different object-oriented formats can describe different things, but most can easily specify objects such as lines, curves, and type, as well as attributes such as shading and object rotation angle.

Most object-oriented graphics can also contain bitmapped graphics as objects in their own right, though you may or may not be able to edit those bitmaps with a paint program. These files are almost always created by a drawing application such as Adobe Illustrator.

The magic of object-oriented graphics is that you can stretch them, rotate them, twist them into pastry, and print them on various-resolution printers without worrying about how smoothly the lines will print. That is, when you print on a 300-dpi, plain-paper laser printer, you get a full 300 dpi; when you print to film with a 2,540-dpi imagesetter, you get beautifully smooth lines at 2,540 dots per inch. There is no inherent limit of information for the picture, as there is with bitmaps (see Figure 10-5). Theoretically, there is no inherent limit to the number of gray levels in an object-oriented picture. Realistically, however, each format has upper limits.

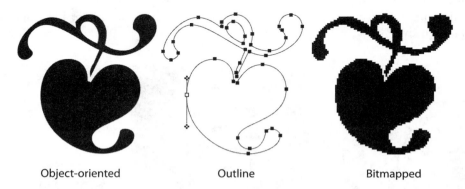

Object-oriented   Outline   Bitmapped

Figure 10-5 Object-oriented graphics versus bitmapped images

File Types

In earlier editions of this book, which dealt with previous versions of QuarkXPress, I began this section by discussing the differences between QuarkXPress projects and files created by other applications running on Windows and Macintosh. I explained how the Macintosh added special, hidden, four-letter file-type extensions to documents, and how Windows only allowed—but always showed—three-letter file extensions. So different were the ways in which the two platforms wrote documents that those documents often needed to be run through translation software to be moved from Windows to Macintosh or vice versa.

Of course all that was before Macintosh OS X and Windows XP and Windows Vista.

Now, moving files between Macintosh and Windows is a breeze. QuarkXPress 7 running on either platform writes the exact same cross-platform-compatible file. Photoshop, Illustrator, and all the other creative applications commonly used by QuarkXPress users also write fully cross-platform compatible project files. Even the latest font technology, OpenType fonts, is interchangeable between Windows and Macintosh. If you work in a mixed-operating-system office or accept or send files to clients, vendors, and collaborators, rest assured your QuarkXPress projects can be opened by the same version of XPress no matter if it's running on Macintosh or Windows. And, XPress can import the same image and textual file types on, or created on, either platform.

File types XPress understands. QuarkXPress can import several of the most commonly used graphic file formats for both print and Web or multimedia projects. For print projects, whenever possible you should stick with PSD, EPS, TIFF, and DCS images; for Web and multimedia projects use PNG, JPEG, and SWF. Although QuarkXPress imports additional image formats (see below), they have limitations that you're better off avoiding if you can (see "Tip: The Best Format to Use," at the end of this section).

TIFF. The Tagged Image File Format (TIFF) is a bitmapped image file format with lots of support for high-quality images. First off, a TIFF file can be created at any size and resolution, and include black-and-white, grayscale, or color information. Because of the flexibility of TIFF files, all scanning and image-editing programs can save and open the TIFF format.

As it turns out, there are several different TIFF formats, including compressed and uncompressed, and Macintosh versus Windows. Fortunately, QuarkXPress imports several different TIFF formats, including those written for either Mac or Windows, and even LZW-compressed TIFF files.

Photoshop 6 and later can save TIFF files in several formats that may (or may not) confuse QuarkXPress. For instance, XPress does not currently read TIFFs with Zip or JPEG compression. You *can* import layered TIFF files into XPress (files that contain Photoshop layers), but they appear as flattened images despite the fact that XPress *does* understand and manipulate layers in Photoshop PSD files. (Technically, layered TIFF files actually include both a flattened image and a layered image, and XPress just ignores the layers and reads the flattened version.) However, XPress does *not* recognize any transparency that your layered TIFF image might have—the image just appears opaque to XPress.

Encapsulated PostScript. Encapsulated PostScript (EPS) format is the most reliable format for putting images on paper or film, as long as your printer or imaging device can understand PostScript. PostScript is an object-oriented page-description language, though PostScript files may contain bitmaps as well. Although PostScript has built-in font-handling features, it ultimately treats type as a graphic made of lines and curves. This makes working with fonts in a PostScript environment a joy, with many possibilities. It's easy to create a PostScript file, but to print it out you must have a PostScript-compatible printer (with non-PostScript printers, XPress just prints the low-resolution screen preview of the EPS graphic).

EPS images come in two basic varieties: EPS without a preview and EPS with a bitmap preview. The preview-enclosed feature in most EPS files allows you to bring such a file into QuarkXPress and see a low-resolution representation of the image on the screen.

When the file is printed to a PostScript printer, however, the bitmap is ignored and the underlying PostScript is used. If a preview image is not available, then you see a big gray box on the screen which may contain some basic information (such as the file's name).

On the Mac, the EPS preview may be saved as either a PICT or a TIFF. There's no trouble with using PICT previews, and if the graphic will stay on the Macintosh platform, PICT previews are probably preferable. However, if the file may at some point find its way to a Windows machine, a TIFF preview is the way to go. When you make an EPS on a Windows PC, you have to use TIFF. The reason for this is somewhat technical: PICT previews are stored in a file's resource fork, which is stripped away when the file is moved to a PC; TIFF previews are stored in the data fork, which can survive moving back and forth between a Mac and Windows environment.

Even though EPS files are robust and reliable, I don't use them as often as TIFF images when it comes to bitmapped graphics (see "Tip: The Best Format to Use").

> **Tip: Great-Looking EPS Previews.** *Photoshop on the Macintosh lets you save EPS files with a JPEG preview. While I don't ordinarily use JPEG images (see "JPEG," below), and I never use the JPEG encoding in EPS files, I do like the JPEG preview option because it provides a much nicer on-screen representation of the image than the normal 8-bit color preview that Photoshop builds into EPS files. JPEG previews are actually high-quality compressed PICT previews, so they don't work on the PC. On the other hand, the big drawback to JPEG previews is display speed: EPS files with JPEG preview may display more slowly. Nonetheless, if your client is staring over your shoulder, you might get some benefit from a good-looking screen image in XPress.*

DCS. I'll talk about Desktop Color Separation (DCS) in Chapter 14, *Color*, but let's quickly go over it here. The DCS method is based on preseparating color images into five separate EPS files (which is why DCS is sometimes called "EPS-5" or "five-file EPS"). Four of the files contain high-resolution information for each of the process colors (cyan, magenta, yellow, and black). The fifth file contains a low-resolution composite image (for proofing), a screen representation of the picture, and pointers to the four higher-resolution files. This fifth file is the one that gets imported into, and displayed within, QuarkXPress.

When you print your file, QuarkXPress replaces this representation file (sometimes called the "master file") with the four high-resolution files. This means that you can print the high-resolution separations directly from QuarkXPress to an imagesetter.

Some programs (including XPress) support the DCS 2.0 file format, which is basically a revised version of the DCS specification. In DCS 2.0 images, the four process plates and the preview "master" image can all be rolled into one big file. More important, DCS 2.0 lets you include spot-color plates, varnish plates—as many plates as you want. This means that you can create an image in Photoshop that includes spot colors, export it as a DCS 2.0 file, and separate the whole thing in QuarkXPress.

QuarkXPress not only understands DCS and DCS 2.0 documents, it can also create them when you save a page as EPS (see "Page as Picture," later in this chapter).

PDF. I discuss the Portable Document Format (PDF) in detail in Chapter 17, *Going Online with QuarkXPress*, but of course the PDF format is widely used for print publishing as well as the paperless office. QuarkXPress can import PDF 1.3, 1.4, and 1.5 files (also called Acrobat 4, Acrobat 5, and Acrobat 6 files, respectively). At the time of this writing, XPress could not import PDF 1.6 (Acrobat 7 and later) files, though that will likely change in time. XPress lets you pick which page of a multi-page PDF file you want to import. However, if the PDF is locked in one way or another (no printing, no copying, and so on), XPress won't let you import it at all.

PICT. The PICT format (.pct in Windows), also a part of the original Mac system, can contain drawings that are object-oriented or that consist of a single bitmap ("bitmap-only PICT"). Unlike most programs, QuarkXPress can "see" when a PICT file is bitmap-only, and lets you manipulate it as such (you'll see later in this chapter that you can manipulate bitmapped images differently than object-oriented ones). PICT images, like TIFFs or EPS files, can be any size, resolution, and color.

While PICT does sound quite useful, I don't like it for four reasons.

- The object-oriented PICT format is unreliable. For example, line widths can change when you move a picture from one program to another, and text spacing can change, sometimes drastically. Also, printing to imagesetters (1,200+ dpi) can be troublesome.

- Bitmap-only PICT images are RGB-only; you cannot preseparate them into CMYK (I'll talk about color separation in some depth in Chapter 14, *Color*). Fortunately, XPress can separate the RGB PICTs if you need to do this. Personally, I'd rather stick to TIFF images.

- PICT images are always fully embedded in your XPress project. That means if you import a 20 MB PICT image into a picture box, your XPress project gets 20 MB bigger. Add a few more of these and you've got a file that is unmanageable and possibly unstable as well. I avoid embedding images like the plague (with one exception: when the image is really small).

- XPress relies on the operating system, which is pretty slow, to display PICTs properly. The larger the image, the slower the display. Anything over a few megabytes is painful.

Nonetheless, PICT is the primary format for printing from the Macintosh to non-PostScript devices, so if you're doing low-end printing with small object-oriented images you might consider using this format. For the sake of completeness, I should note that it is possible to import PICT images into XPress for Windows.

Windows Bitmap. Windows Bitmap (.BMP) is the bitmap format native to Windows Paint, but isn't usually encountered outside of Windows. You can, however, bring .BMP files to the Macintosh and use them in QuarkXPress. I just don't think you should; I still prefer TIFF to this format.

Windows Metafile. Closely tied to graphics technology underlying Windows, Windows Metafile (.WMF) is a relatively reliable but somewhat lower-quality, object-oriented format to use in Windows. When you take it onto the Macintosh, things get a little weird. Fonts that are embedded in the graphic really get messed up, and colors can get screwy, too. Although Windows Metafiles have been replaced in recent years by Enhanced Metafiles (.EMF), which QuarkXPress does not support, there are still plenty of the .WMF files floating around—usually in low-cost clipart collections or bundled with older versions of Microsoft Office. Between the reduced quality of the average Windows Metafile and the difficulty of using it on a Macintosh, I strongly suggest avoiding use of this format; EPS is a more reliable choice for object-oriented graphics.

Scitex CT files. QuarkXPress can import Scitex continuous-tone (.CT and .SCT) files. However, it can separate only CT files. Note that when I say "CT files," I am actually referring to CT HandShake files. I know one guy who got burned because he asked a color house for CT files and got Scitex's proprietary format instead of the open-format CT HandShake files.

JPEG. A JPEG is a bitmapped file format with built-in compression, so that these images can be a tenth of the size (or smaller) of a noncompressed image. However, the compression in JPEG is *lossy*, which means compression is achieved by discarding image data; in other words, the more it's compressed, the worse the image looks.

Once you've imported the picture into QuarkXPress, the program decompresses it every time you print it (which can take a while) and sends it to the printer as though it were a TIFF image.

A few years ago I would have said (and maybe I did): "The only really good reason to use JPEG images instead of TIFFs is if you're scraping for hard drive space." Today, I have a new perspective. Digital cameras have replaced 35mm SLR cameras in the hands of most photographers and photojournalists. Although most professional-grade digital cameras produce RAW format images that are processed in Photoshop and should be resaved to TIFF before import to QuarkXPress, many photographers prefer to create uncompressed (thus high quality) JPEG images rather than TIFFs. In such cases, uncompressed JPEGs will be larger files that take more time to draw onscreen and print than compressed TIFFs, but their quality will be the same. Moreover, which will take more of your time: waiting for the slightly longer print time or taking all those JPEG images into Photoshop and resaving them to TIFF? You be the judge.

If you are creating a Web or multimedia project in XPress, JPEG is an excellent format to use for photographic imagery. It is not, however, very good at retaining the crispness of lines, text, or sharp changes in color such as one might encounter in a business graphics chart. Although it competes with the new PNG file format (see "PNG" later in this section), JPEG is often preferable for digital projects because it often delivers smaller file sizes than you can get with PNG without obvious quality reduction to an onscreen viewer.

Note that a JPEG file is different from a JPEG EPS file or an EPS file with a JPEG preview (see "Tip: Great-Looking EPS Previews," earlier). JPEG EPS files are EPS files saved with JPEG encoding (this is an option in Photoshop). In theory, these should print correctly on PostScript Level 2 or PostScript 3 printers because the printer decompresses the file. In reality, they don't separate, so color images only appear on the black plate. JPEG DCS files (DCS files with JPEG encoding) do separate properly, however.

PCX. PCX is the granddaddy of bitmapped formats, and the current version supports 24-bit and 256-color palettes. Since a variety of color-model techniques have been applied to PCX over the ages, files from earlier programs can have some serious color-mismatch problems. If you absolutely need to use PCX images, then go for it. If not, see if your source can provide files in TIFF, which is an all-around better format.

PhotoCD. Created by Kodak, the PhotoCD format was designed as a solution to compressing images for long-term storage on CD-ROMs. It supports grayscale, 24-bit RGB, and 32-bit Lab format images. The quality is very good, but you will rarely encounter this format because most photographers prefer the nonproprietary and more widely supported RAW, JPEG, or TIFF formats for image archival.

GIF. The Graphics Interchange Format (commonly known as GIF, pronounced like "gift" without the "t") is the aged and on-the-way-out standard for graphics on the Web. At 72 dpi resolution, GIF files are designed solely for onscreen viewing, especially for images where file size is more important than quality, for pictures that require rudimentary transparency, and for screens that only display 8-bit color (256 colors). Photoshop GIFs are always 8-bit indexed-color images, making them reasonable (but not ideal) for onscreen viewing, but useless for printing.

PNG. The Portable Network Graphic file format (commonly pronounced "ping") is the much more robust successor to GIF and is the industry standard for graphics on the Web. Although still not suitable for print because of its resolution, PNG graphics offer full 24-bit color (millions of colors), alpha channel (true) transparency, and built-in compression. Like in TIFFs, part of whose compression code found its way into PNG, the compression in PNG makes images smaller without reducing their quality. Thus, detail and crisp edges in lines and text remain crisp, unlike in a JPEG image. PNG images can be created by all modern image-editing applications like Photoshop, drawing programs such as Illustrator, and even some other applications, like Microsoft PowerPoint.

SWF. All SWF, or Flash, files are object-oriented art and animations designed specifically to bring high-quality, resolution independence to the digital world—computer screens, the Web, cell phones, PDAs, and other devices. Although SWF is a proprietary format owned by Adobe, it is an official standard for object-oriented art and animations, and is supported for import or export by numerous applications, including Quark Interactive Designer—a set of QuarkXPress XTensions for creating interactive and media-rich Web sites and SWF presentations.

Importing SWF into QuarkXPress without Quark Interactive Designer installed enables you to incorporate a SWF created in another application (for example, Adobe Flash) into an XPress Web layout.

PSD. New in QuarkXPress 7 is native support for importing Photoshop PSD documents directly. Shortly after its release, XPress 6.5 offered this feature through a free add-on called the PSD Import Xtensions; the PSD Import Xtensions are built into XPress 7 out of the box. Not only can you place PSD documents into your XPress layout, you can also manipulate layers contained in the PSD, turning this one off, that one on. I'll discuss this in depth in Chapter 11, *Image Tuning*.

That XPress now imports PSD files is important. If you're like most people, you touch up and create original images in Photoshop. In the past, you had to then save a copy of an image as a TIFF or EPS for the sole purpose of importing into an XPress project. Each time the original image was edited, you had to make a new TIFF or EPS. The problems inherent in that process were obvious: it was tedious, it was easy to let the TIFF and EPS versions get out of synch with the original PSD, and with two versions of each image, one picture sometimes used up double the disk space. Now that QuarkXPress understands native PSD files, you can drop the TIFF or EPS versions of most images. Because your original art is usually in a PSD, importing that PSD into your XPress layout means never having to worry if the original and the version in the layout are out of synch—they're the same image.

Before you swear off TIFF and EPS forever, you should know the strengths and weaknesses of each—and how XPress treats them. Here are a few of the many considerations you need to keep in mind when choosing a file format.

- **File size.** Uncompressed TIFF files are about 20 percent smaller than EPS files. Plus, EPS files contain a preview, which can add even more to the file's size depending on its type and dimension. PSD files are automatically compressed but are nearly always larger than either TIFF or EPS versions. Although the PSD files are larger, you tend to save more disk space overall by the absence of TIFF or EPS versions of the PSD you're going to keep anyway.

- **Compression.** You can compress TIFF images with LZW (lossless) compression. This type of compression works best on areas of flat color and worst on images that have a lot of tiny details. Your only option for compression in EPS files is JPEG, which renders CMYK files mostly useless because QuarkXPress can't separate JPEG-compressed EPS files.

- **Image previews.** QuarkXPress creates a screen-resolution screen preview when you import a TIFF or PSD image, which takes *slightly* longer than importing EPS files because, with EPS, XPress simply grabs the built-in preview. The quality of a TIFF or PSD preview depends on how you set the Color TIFFs color depth and Display DPI Value preview options in the Preferences dialog box on the Display pane. The 32-bit color setting provides a great preview, but your project's file size increases significantly, so I usually avoid it. The quality of an EPS preview is totally up to the software that creates it (see "Tip: Great-Looking EPS Previews," earlier). In general, the Photoshop-built preview in a CMYK EPS file is going to look better than the XPress-built preview in a CMYK TIFF image (unless you're using XPress's color management software correctly and use high-resolution preview). Enabling Full Res Previews on the View menu makes XPress use an image's actual resolution as the preview regardless of the Display DPI Value option in the Preferences (more on that later in this chapter). PSD image previews update on the fly with any changes to layer or channel visibility on the PSD Import palettes.

- **Image control.** QuarkXPress 7 can do remarkable things to TIFF and PSD files, including adjusting levels, curves, hue and saturation, and gamma correction, as well as applying a dozen filter effects. EPS files, on the other hand, are cast in stone (that's why they call them "encapsulated"). To make a change to an EPS file, you have to take the file to some other program like Photoshop or Illustrator.

- **Spot colors.** If you create spot color channels in a Photoshop file, then you have to save it as a DCS 2.0 file or a native Photoshop PSD to import it into QuarkXPress. If you import a PSD with spot channels, XPress *will* place the picture, but it will show a composite of all layers and channels (including the spot channel), and you will not be able to enable or disable layers in the PSD Import Layers palette. You *will* be able to manage the channels in the PSD Import Channels palette, however.

- **Cropping.** What happens if you import a 20 MB bitmapped image and crop it down to a little tiny square on your XPress page? If the file is saved in TIFF or PSD format, XPress only sends the necessary image data to the printer, which can speed up printing a lot. If it's an EPS file, however, XPress sends the entire 20 MB to the printer every time you print.

- **Downsampling.** Proofing a 300-dpi bitmapped image on a desktop laser printer can take a long time if the image is saved as an EPS, because XPress sends all the image data to the printer every time you print. But the program can downsample TIFF and PSD files; in fact, XPress automatically downsamples the resolution of TIFF files to two times the current halftone screen frequency (lpi). So when you're printing a 60-lpi file on your laser printer, it reduces your high-resolution images to 120 dpi, saving a lot of time.

  The same thing goes for reducing the size of your image. Remember, if you scale that 300-dpi bitmapped image to 50 percent, it is now effectively a 600-dpi image—way more than you need. XPress downsamples this, too. Of course, it's usually better to do your own downsampling in an image-editing program before you import the file into XPress.

- **Duotones.** If you want to make a duotone in Photoshop, you must save it as an EPS or PSD file. QuarkXPress understands duotones in PSD documents, but, like any PSD with spot channels, disables access to the image layers within XPress.

- **Clipping paths.** Earlier versions of QuarkXPress couldn't read embedded clipping paths in TIFF files, so you had to use EPS files. No longer. In fact, XPress can even read multiple paths in TIFF and PSD files (see more on clipping paths in Chapter 11, *Image Tuning*).

- **Vectors.** XPress can only read vector data (like vector text or "shapes") in Photoshop files when the file is saved as an EPS, PDF, or PSD.

- **Color management.** Because XPress can control the data in a TIFF or PSD file, it can color manage the images. EPS files, however, are hopeless when it comes to color management, because XPress can't really change any color values in them. This goes for separating RGB images into CMYK, too (TIFF and PSD images, no problem; EPS images, big problem).

- **CMYK separations.** When XPress prints color separations (see Chapter 14, *Color*), it has to send down the entire EPS file (the cyan, magenta, yellow, and black plates) each time it prints a plate. That means if you have a 20 MB EPS file, XPress sends 80 megabytes of information to the printer (20 MB per plate). That takes a long time. However, XPress treats CMYK EPS files from Photoshop differently. With these files, it's smart enough to pull them apart and only send the cyan data with the cyan plate, the magenta data with the magenta plate, and so on. This is much (much!) faster. TIFF and PSD files can also be pulled apart at print time.

- **Vendor support.** TIFF and EPS are two formats that have been around since the earliest days of desktop publishing, and every print and prepress service provider accepts them. On the other hand, not all printers and service bureaus can yet accept PSD files as linked images. Check with your provider about PSD support *before* sending an XPress project with PSD images.

All told, I use PSD files whenever I can because of their flexibility (and because most of my images go to Photoshop at some point anyway). When I work with a collaborator, client, or vendor who isn't yet capable of, or comfortable with, using PSD files in XPress projects, I use the next-best format for the job. I lean toward TIFF images in most such cases, but some jobs, like duotone images, images with spot colors, or those that require a special halftone screen, demand EPS or DCS files.

> *Tip: The Best Format to Use.* When my layout is destined for print, I rarely use a graphics file format other than PSD, TIFF, EPS, or DCS. However, even with these four formats there are good reasons to choose one over the other, depending on the image and what you're using it for. Some people think that EPS is inherently better than TIFF, or vice versa. Not so. Don't choose one over the other because your service bureau or printer told you to; they often don't know any more about file formats than you do (they just think they do). The only exception to that piece of advice might be Photoshop PSD files. Although QuarkXPress can natively import and manipulate them, not all print service providers have systems capable of interpreting Photoshop PSD files. If you intend to use PSDs (I recommend you do as soon and as often as possible), ask your service bureau or printer if they can process them. You might even try sending a test QuarkXPress project with linked PSD files.

IMPORTING PICTURES INTO QUARKXPRESS

Now that we know the types of pictures we'll be dealing with, let's look at how we'll deal with them. As I mentioned, the first step in importing a graphic from another application is to create a picture box within your QuarkXPress project. This is covered in Chapter 3, *Working with Items,* in the discussion of rectangles, ovals, and polygons. When you have an empty picture box on your page, you can see an "X" in the middle of it. At this point you're ready to bring a picture into the box.

Note that I'm bringing a picture *into* the box, rather than replacing the box or even "merging" the two together. The picture box is one entity and the picture is another. You might think of the box as being a window frame through which you see the picture. You can manipulate the picture box, or the picture, or both.

The two primary ways to bring a picture in are to paste from the Clipboard and to use Import Picture. In order for either of these methods to work, you must have the picture box selected. (In earlier versions of XPress you had to use the Content tool; now you can use either the Content tool or the Item tool.)

Pasting Pictures

There are at least four problems with pasting in pictures (selecting Paste from the Edit menu, or pressing Command/Ctrl-V) rather than using Import Picture, each one of which alone would be enough to convince me not to paste pictures into picture boxes in XPress.

- Because the image is pasted in, there is no accompanying disk file for it; if you want to edit the image, you have to copy it, paste it into a program that can edit it, make changes, copy it again, and paste it back into the picture box. If you've cropped or rotated the picture in XPress, all that information is lost when you repaste it.

- The file format for an image typically changes when you move it from one application to another. For instance, if you use Copy and Paste on a Macintosh to move a picture from Photoshop to XPress, the image is converted to the PICT format. PICT images don't understand CMYK, so CMYK files are translated into RGB on the fly. On Windows, images are sometimes translated to WMF files. Whatever the case, these switches make me very nervous.

- XPress may not understand the file format for images that are on the Clipboard. For instance, you can copy a graphic from Adobe Illustrator, but XPress may not let you paste it into a picture box.

- If you paste in a big picture, your QuarkXPress project balloons in size because the document has to embed the entire image. With Import Picture, just a low-resolution image is imported, with a pointer to the full file on disk (see "Picture Management," later in this chapter).

(I used to mention a fifth problem: that color images pasted into picture boxes could not be separated into CMYK. It's of dubious value to note that XPress can now separate these images, even when the color management XTension is turned off. The quality isn't exactly superb.)

Again, I recommend that you avoid the Clipboard approach to importing pictures (at least don't use it often, and certainly not for big, important jobs).

Import Picture

With your picture box created, and either the Item tool or the Content tool selected, you can select Import Picture from the File menu (or act like the pros, and press Command/Ctrl-E). A directory dialog box appears, allowing you to find the file you wish to import. When a file of a type that QuarkXPress recognizes is selected (see "File Types," above), the file's type and size are displayed. If you're importing a multi-page PDF file, XPress also lets you choose which page you want.

You also have the option to turn on the Picture Preview checkbox, which lets you see a thumbnail view of most image files. This feature is, of course, a great help in finding a particular picture when you're not sure of the file's name. However, it does slow down the process, especially for files with complicated images, such as large color PICT or TIFF files. Similarly, if you're accessing images over a network it gets really, really slow. Clearly, judicious use of Picture Preview can save you time.

Once the file is selected in the dialog box, click the Open button or just double-click on the file's name, and the image appears in your picture frame. Some images import more slowly than others; when an image takes a while to import, QuarkXPress shows you its progress in the lower-left corner of the window. If you're importing a 100 MB file on your old iMac G3, you can see how quickly (slowly) it is processing (perhaps this is the best time of the day to make yourself an espresso).

In earlier versions of XPress, replacing one picture with another tossed out transformations such as picture scaling, offset, rotation, and so on. For instance, scaling a picture to 50 percent X and Y and then replacing it with a different picture meant you had to manually scale the new image again. In XPress 7, however, there's one little checkbox in the Import Picture dialog box that makes all the difference. It's the Maintain Picture Attributes option. When that option is turned on (which it is by default), transformation attributes are retained and applied to new pictures when replacing one image with another. Typically, this is a benefit, but it can be a confusing surprise. If you import an image into an already used picture box and suddenly find the picture cropped, rotated, scaled, skewed, or whatever, don't immediately assume you (or QuarkXPress) did anything wrong. Odds are, XPress is simply applying the transformation attributes of the picture box's previous tenant to the new resident. To get rid of those transformations, Import Picture again on the same picture box, making sure to turn off the Maintain Picture Attributes option.

> ***Tip: Drag-and-Drop Pictures.*** *QuarkXPress for Windows lets you drag pictures into picture boxes from the Windows desktop or Explorer, as long as the picture box is already made.*

What Happened to My Picture?

When you import a picture, you may not see exactly what you were expecting or wanting in the picture box. It may be that you see only a gray box with some type, or that the image is misplaced, or even that you can't see it at all. If something unexpected happens, remember the First Rule of Computer Anomaly: Don't Panic.

Can't see the picture at all. First, check whether the big "X" is still in the picture box; if it is, then Import Picture didn't work. Maybe you accidentally clicked Cancel instead of OK. (Don't laugh; this often happens around the same time you get what my friend Greg calls "pixel vision"—eyes that are glazed from looking at the screen too long.) If this happens, just try again.

If you see just a blank frame, then check to see if the guides are hidden (select Show Guides from the View menu). If the guides are on and you still don't see the "X," then the picture is probably somewhere in the box but you can't see it yet. The Import Picture feature automatically places the image in the upper-left corner of the bounding box of the frame. Note that I say the "bounding box" and not the box itself. The bounding box is the smallest rectangle that completely surrounds the frame. It's what you see when you are looking at your box with the Edit Shape option turned off (see Figure 10-6). If you have an oval or a polygonal box and the image is rather small, then you may have to move the object into the frame (see "Moving Your Picture Around," later in this chapter).

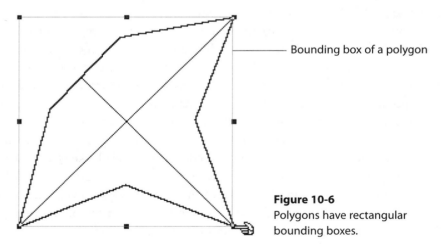

Bounding box of a polygon

Figure 10-6
Polygons have rectangular bounding boxes.

Often, if you center the image in the box you'll be able to see it better (see "Centering," in the next section).

There's no picture—just a gray box. If the image you import is an EPS file with no preview image attached for screen representation, then QuarkXPress represents the image as a gray box with the note "PostScript Picture" and the name of the file directly in the center of the gray box. This gray box shows the bounding box of the image, as defined in the header of the EPS document.

Another cause of the gray-box effect could be that you're looking at a complex picture from too far back. When you look at the page in Fit in Window view, it looks like a muddied gray box, but when you go to Actual Size, it looks like what you were hoping for.

The third cause of the gray-box effect might be that the picture you import is, in fact, a gray box. In this case, I can only suggest you think carefully about whether or not you really consider a gray box an exciting enough graphic for your publication.

Quality isn't very good. I'll discuss how XPress previews images on screen in "Preview Quality, Greeking, and Suppression," later in this chapter.

WORKING WITH PICTURES

Now that you have brought something (which may or may not look like the graphic you wanted) into the picture box, you can manipulate it in more ways than you ever thought you could.

Moving Your Picture Around

In Chapter 2, *QuarkXPress Basics*, you learned about moving your picture and text boxes around on the page. You can also move the picture itself around within the picture box. You may want to do this for two reasons: for picture placement, and for cropping out a portion of the image. In this section I discuss several methods for moving your image within (or even outside of) the box. Remember that the picture and the picture box are two different entities, and you can move and manipulate them using different tools: the content (picture) with the Content tool, and the box itself with the Item tool.

Centering. Often the first thing you'll want to do with a picture, whether or not you can see it on screen, is to center it within the picture box. Designers and computer hackers alike have muddled through various tricks to center graphics perfectly within boxes, with varying degrees of success. I suggest you just press Command/Ctrl-Shift-M and let QuarkXPress do it for you. QuarkXPress centers the picture based on its bounding box (its lower-left and upper-right corners). Therefore, pictures which are oddly shaped (for example, an L-shaped picture) may not be centered as you'd expect them to be. If you forget the keyboard shortcut, don't fret: You can always select Center Picture from the Style menu.

Moving the picture. If you want the image to be somewhere other than in the upper-left corner or in the center, you can use the Content tool (which switches to a Grabber hand when it's placed over the picture box) to move the picture around. Anyone who has ever done this can tell you that if the image is a large one, it can take quite some time for the picture to respond to your hand movements. If you're thinking about zooming in for precision alignment, remember to turn on Full Resolution from the Preview Resolution submenu (under the Item menu; see "Preview Quality, Greeking, and Suppression," later in this chapter).

If you know how far you want to move the picture, you can type the offset values in either the Measurements palette (on the Classic tab) or in the Modify dialog box (press Command/Ctrl-M or Command/Ctrl-double-click on the picture). This method is a real godsend when precision is the key, but you can't always trust what you see on the screen. For instance, an EPS image might look like it's at the edge of the picture box, but in reality that could just be an artifact of its screen preview.

> **Tip: Minimoves.** When you have the Content tool selected and have selected a picture box, you can "nudge" the picture within the box in tiny increments by clicking the arrows on the Measurements palette. Each click moves the image 1 point in the direction of the arrow. Hold down Option/Alt while you click to move the picture in .1-point increments.
>
> However, I typically find it even more useful to use the arrow keys on the keyboard. Again, each time you press a key, the picture moves 1 point; each time you press the key with Option/Alt held down, the picture moves .1 point.
>
> Note that if you have the Item tool selected when you do this, you actually move the picture box itself.

Cropping

If you only want a portion of the whole picture to be visible, then you can "cut out" the unwanted areas by cropping (see Figure 10-7).

A warning about cropping: there are people who crop out 90 percent of an image so they can use just one flower in a bouquet! Then they duplicate that image 12 times on the page and wonder why their file doesn't print. (Don't laugh too loudly; I've seen highly paid professionals do this!)

Fortunately, when you use TIFF and JPEG images, XPress is smart enough to send only the data it needs at print time, so the cropped-out information doesn't clog up your network and your printing times are faster. QuarkXPress cannot do this with EPS or PDF images, so the whole file must be sent at print time, along with an instruction to the printer about what gets cropped and what doesn't.

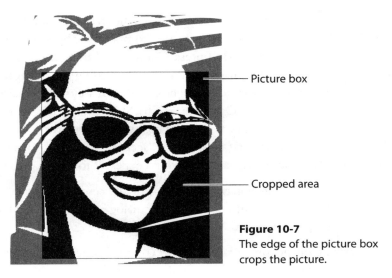

— Picture box

— Cropped area

Figure 10-7
The edge of the picture box
crops the picture.

So remember to use cropping judiciously. If you only want a small portion of the file, then use an editing program to cut out what you don't want before you import the image.

Tip: Shapely Cropping. You don't have to restrict your cropping to rectangular boxes, of course. Feel free to use the Shape submenu (under the Item menu) to change the shape of the picture box in order to crop out unwanted parts of your picture.

Tip: Cropping Multiple Pictures. As I mentioned back in Chapter 2, QuarkXPress Basics, you can crop several picture boxes at the same time by grouping them and either dragging the group's corner or side handles, or specifying a value in the Measurements palette. Either way, you must have the Item tool selected. For instance, if you know that you want every box to be half as wide as it is currently, you can select the boxes, group them, and then type "*.5" after the current width value in the Measurements palette.

Tip: Fit Box to Picture. One of the most-requested features in early versions of QuarkXPress was the ability to fit the picture box to the size of the picture. I'm happy to report that this feature is in versions 5 and later, and lives in two places: You can select it from the Style menu or from the context-sensitive menu (right-click on the picture box or, on Mac single-button mice, Control-click).

Resizing Your Picture

After placing the graphic image where you want it, you may want to scale it to some desired size. QuarkXPress allows you to resize the image within the picture box in the horizontal and/or vertical directions. Most often I find myself wanting to enlarge or reduce the picture the same amount in both directions in order to best fit the available space.

Keystrokes and menus. If the picture box you create is just the size you want your picture to be, you can quickly and automatically resize the picture to fit the box by selecting Stretch Picture to Fit Box from the Style menu (or press Command/Ctrl-Shift-F). However, because this usually stretches the picture disproportionately (adjusting the horizontal- and vertical-sizing measures differently in order to fill the box), you probably want to select Scale Picture to Box (or press Command-Shift-Option-F or Ctrl-Shift-Alt-F—that's a handful), which makes the picture as large as it can be within the box without distorting it. Note that if you've rotated or skewed the picture first (see the next section, "Rotating, Skewing, and Distorting"), auto-resizing may not work exactly as you'd expect it to.

If you're not a keystroke kind of person, you can type the particular percentages you want into the Measurements palette or into the picture box's Modify dialog box (Command/Ctrl-M). Of course, you can use a combination of these two methods, too.

Dragging. Usually, resizing the picture box has no effect on the image inside it, other than possibly cropping out areas of the picture. However, if you hold down the Command/Ctrl key while you resize (clicking and dragging on one of the control handles), the image changes size along with the box (see Figure 10-8). As usual, holding down the Shift key constrains the picture box (and the image) to a square or circle; holding down the Option/Alt key along with the Command/Ctrl and Shift keys constrains the picture box (and the image) to their proper proportions.

Original object　　　　　　　Scaled with a Command-click and drag

Figure 10-8 Resizing a picture by dragging the picture box handles

Tip: Watch 'Em Change. Back in Chapter 2, QuarkXPress Basics, I told you about how to watch the changes as you make them (see the tip on viewing changes as you make them). In case you don't remember, the important thing is to hold down the mouse button for about half a second (until you see the cursor change to the flashy Live Refresh cursor). Then when you scale or crop the image by dragging, you can actually see the image get scaled or cropped (otherwise, QuarkXPress just shows you a gray outline box).

Tip: Scaling Groups of Objects. People have been clamoring to scale groups of objects for years, and now you can (sort of). To scale several objects at the same time, group them (Command/Ctrl-G) and then Command-Option-Shift-drag (Ctrl-Alt-Shift-drag) on one of the group's control handles. If you know exactly how large you want the group of objects, you can type those values into the Measurements palette instead of dragging the handles. If you want to scale the group by a specific percentage, use math in the height and width fields of the palette. For instance, if you want the height and width to both be 40 percent as large, type "*.4" after the values in both the H: and W: fields of the Measurements palette.

Rotating and Skewing

Sure, you can crop and resize, but—as they say on television—that's not all! With this amazing program you get a set of free Japanese cutlery! And 32 ounces of French perfume! And . . . well, maybe not, but you do get to rotate and skew pictures, and that's not bad.

Rotating. QuarkXPress lets you easily rotate your imported pictures to a degree unheard of (and certainly rarely needed): 1/1000 of a degree. Once again, you are able to set the rotation of the image in several ways.

The first question you'll want to ask yourself is whether you want to rotate the frame, and the image along with it, or just rotate the image itself. You can do either of these things by typing the rotation angle in the appropriate place on the Measurements palette or in the Modify dialog box (see Figure 10-9).

While it's really great that you can rotate images in QuarkXPress, you should be careful with this power. When you use XPress to rotate large, bitmapped images, your files can slow to a crawl when they print. Instead, try to rotate these images in Photoshop first, and then import them (prerotated) into your picture boxes. This typically isn't a problem with illustrations from Illustrator or FreeHand, because they aren't usually bitmapped.

Tip: Rotating Your Picture Boxes. Rotating the frame rotates the image, too. The quickest way to "straighten out" your image is to rotate it back by the same amount. That is, if you rotate your box 28 degrees but you want the picture to be straight, then rotate the image -28 degrees.

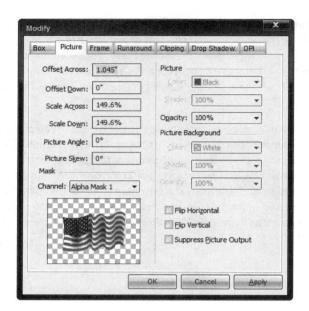

Figure 10-9
The Modify dialog box and
the Measurements palette

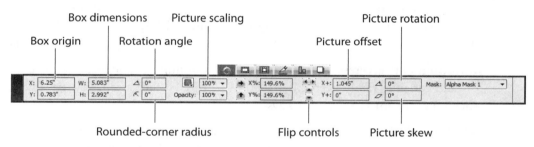

Skewing. Technically, skewing is the process of rotating the two axes differently, or rotating one and not the other. That is, if you rotate just the y-axis (the vertical axis) of the coordinate system to the right, everything you print out is "obliqued" (see Figure 10-10). QuarkXPress only allows you to skew in the horizontal direction (rotating the y-axis), which is not a hindrance since vertical skewing (or "shearing," as it is often called) is rarely required. Actually, even horizontal skewing is rarely required, but it can be useful in certain situations, especially when you want to create interesting effects.

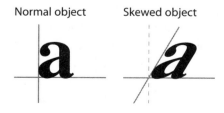

Figure 10-10
Skewing rotates the vertical axis.

You typically use only one of these effects at a time, perhaps in conjunction with scaling (resizing), but using them together can make a graphic look quite unusual (see Figure 10-11).

Actual size

Scale across: 60%
Scale down: 100%

Across: 60%
Down: 90%
Rotate -30 degrees

Scale across and scale down: 60%
Rotate: -20 degrees
Skew: -50 degrees

Scale across: 224%
Scale down: 48%

Figure 10-11 Using all of the tools

One of the great advantages of these features is that they're not incremental. In Illustrator, rotation is cumulative. If you rotate something to 60 degrees and later want to rotate it to 55 degrees, you have to enter "-5 degrees" (of course, keeping track of what was rotated and by how much in Illustrator is a royal pain in the neck). QuarkXPress, on the other hand, keeps track of the current rotation, so you just enter the actual rotation you want. This makes it incredibly easy to get back to where you started with an image when you've distorted it beyond recognition: Just reset the scaling to 100 percent, and the rotation and skewing to zero degrees.

> **Tip: Faking Perspective.** *To make a picture look like it's lying on a flat surface, change the picture rotation to -15 degrees, the picture skew to 45 degrees, and the vertical scaling to 70 percent (see Figure 10-12).*

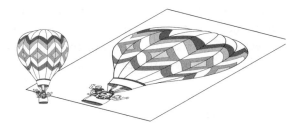

Figure 10-12
Pseudo-perspective

Tip: Making Multiple Changes to Your Picture. If you know you are going to make multiple changes to your graphic image—changing the skewing, rotation, scaling, and offset, for example—you can speed up your formatting by making those changes in the Modify dialog box (Command/Ctrl-M, or double-click on the object while you hold down the Command key) so that QuarkXPress processes all your changes at once rather than one at a time.

Tip: Preformatting Picture Boxes. You can select an empty picture box and apply formatting to the picture that you're going to import into it. Select an empty picture box and change the picture attributes, such as rotation, skew, offset, and scaling, in the Measurements palette (or the Picture Specifications dialog box; Command/Ctrl-M or Command/Ctrl-_double-_click on the box). Then, when you import a picture into that box, XPress automatically applies those settings to it.

Why should you care? Well, if you need to apply the same attributes to a number of different images, you can create one picture box, apply the desired settings, then duplicate the picture box as many times as you have pictures (or store it away in a library for future use). Now, each time you import one of those pictures, it has the transformations you wanted already applied to it.

Tip: Retaining Picture Box Specs. Here's a little knowledge that you should store in the back of your brain; it'll come in handy some day. When you cut or copy a picture out of a picture box, the specifications that the picture box had been set to, such as skew, scaling, offset, and so on, are "saved" with the copied image. When you paste the picture into another picture box, these specifications are transferred, too (even the link information—where the high-resolution image is on disk—is retained).

Synchronizing Picture Effects

Back in Chapter 9, *Long Documents*, I told you about synchronized boxes and synchronized content that enable multiple instances of the same text or picture to be used throughout a layout or multiple layouts in a project and then kept in synch so that changes to one instance are applied to all instances. Not only can you synchronize pictures, but you can also synchronize the effects on those pictures (see the section on picture effects in Chapter 11, *Image Tuning*).

If you add, remove, or alter the attributes of a picture effect on one instance of a picture, that change can automatically be applied to all synchronized instances of the same picture. The trick is the way the picture box is added to the Shared Content palette.

When you add a picture box to the Shared Content palette, the Shared Item Properties dialog box offers several options (see Figure 10-13). Turning on the Synchronize Content option and then selecting Content & Attributes beneath it ensures that picture effects will be among the attributes synchronized between instances of the shared picture box item. Choosing Content Only will ignore picture effects and synchronize only the picture in the box.

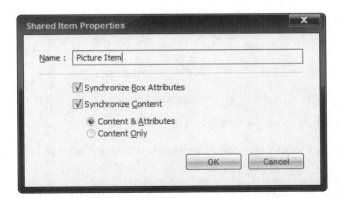

Figure 10-13
The Shared Item Properties
dialog box

By default, new synchronized items automatically select Synchronize Content and Content & Attributes. If you turned the defaults off so that picture effects are not replicating in every instance of the picture box—or if you don't *want* them to apply to all instances—select the picture box item on the Shared Content palette (on the Windows menu), click the Edit button at the top of the palette to bring up the item's Shared Item Properties, and choose Content Only instead of Content & Attributes.

PICTURE MANAGEMENT

Possibly the worst nightmare of a desktop publisher is arriving at the local service bureau to pick up 300 pages of film-negative output, only to see that every illustration has come out as a low-resolution bitmap. Throwing away a thousand dollars is one way to learn some basics of picture management. Reading this section is another.

To Represent

The verb "to represent" means "to stand in place for" or "to act as a placeholder." It's important to note that QuarkXPress represents high-resolution images (including TIFF and EPS files) as low-resolution pictures on-screen when you import them using Import Picture. When it's time to print, QuarkXPress searches for the original high-resolution images and uses them instead of the low-resolution images. It looks first in the folder that the document was originally imported from, and then in the same folder as the project you're printing. If QuarkXPress is successful in this search, your output will look beautiful. If it cannot find the original, it uses the bitmapped 36- or 72-dpi representation for printing. In this case, your output will look ugly.

Here are a few things to keep in mind about pictures.

- Don't trash your picture file after you import it, assuming that it's placed for all time.

- Don't move the picture file into another folder after you import it.

- Don't rename your picture files after you import them.

- Do be sure you know where your picture files are.

- Do keep your picture files together in the same folder if possible to avoid confusion if you need to move your project someplace (like to a service bureau).

- If you archive your project to CD, DVD, or other removable media, or if you send it to a service bureau or anywhere else, put the project and all the image files you imported using Import Picture together in the same folder (preferably with all the pictures in a subfolder beneath the folder containing the project). You can use the Collect for Output command on the File menu to have QuarkXPress automatically collect and relocate project and picture files simultaneously (see more on collecting for output, in the section on working with an imaging center in Chapter 15, *Printing*).

Tip: Huge Files When Importing Graphics. It was kind and generous of Quark to offer us the ability to import images at higher bit depths (in the Display tab of the Preferences dialog box), but I urge you—plead with you: If you don't need to, then don't go above 8-bit color. The problem is that your project's size on disk balloons when you raise the color-bit value (changing the Gray TIFFs value from 16 levels of gray to 256 levels of gray is fine, though). For instance, a project with 40 images in it may be 4 MB large when Color TIFF is set to 8-bit color, and 29 MB when it's set to 32-bit color. While there isn't anything inherently bad about larger file sizes, I tend to like to keep files as small as possible.

Of course, if you're building a Web layout (see Chapter 17, Going Online with QuarkXPress)*, then the higher bit-depth in the Preferences dialog box is almost always better.*

Picture Usage

Submitted for your approval: You've just completed a 600-page layout with illustrations on every page. The day before sending it to the imagesetter, you realize that you have to make changes to 200 pictures. Tearing your hair out in clumps, you stay up all night changing all the pictures and recreating new EPS documents to replace all the old ones. But now it's dawn, and you have to send it off or risk ruining the whole office's schedule. How will you re-import all those graphics in time? What about replacing and rotating and skewing them all to the correct positions? What will you do? What *will* you do?

Fortunately, QuarkXPress offers several features that help with picture management. I'm going to discuss the Usage dialog box first, and then I'll explore how XPress can update pictures automatically after you change them.

XPress keeps a running tally of all imported pictures in your layout, including when they were last modified. This information is on the Picture tab of the Usage dialog box (select Usage from the Utilities menu, or press Option-F13 on the Macintosh or Shift-F2 on Windows). The Picture Usage dialog box lists several important pieces of information about each image in the layout (see Figure 10-14).

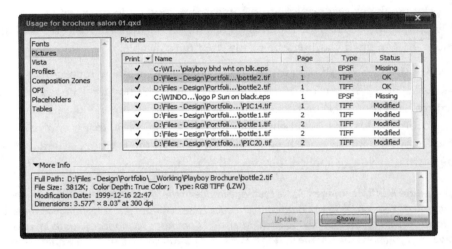

Figure 10-14 Picture Usage dialog box

- Where the image was originally imported from (its hierarchical disk path, starting from the disk name and moving folder-to-folder down to the file).

- The page number of the layout where the picture is located. If the picture is located on the pasteboard rather than a page, you will see in the Page column "PB" followed by the closest page number; for instance, "PB 1" for an image located on the pasteboard beside page 1.

- The type of picture—TIFF, PSD, EPSF, and so on.

- The status of the picture: OK, Modified, Missing, or Wrong Type. Note that the more pictures you have in your layout, the longer it takes for XPress to check the status of each one (that's why it sometimes takes a while for the Usage dialog box to open).

- A column where you can tell XPress whether or not to print the image.

I'll cover picture suppression later in this chapter. Here's a quick rundown on the meaning of the various status messages.

OK. This is what you always hope for, especially before printing. QuarkXPress looks for the picture file first in the same place as the file was imported from. Not finding it there, it then looks in the same folder as the project. When XPress finds the picture file in either of these places, the Status column displays "OK."

Modified. If QuarkXPress finds the file but it's been changed in any way since you imported it (the modification date has changed), you see "Modified" in the Status column. You have two options at this point.

• **Ignore the "problem."** Remember that because QuarkXPress uses the external file for printing, the project prints with the updated version rather than with the original. However, if you've changed the image's resolution or proportions, you shouldn't ignore the Modified warning; the results are unpredictable.

• **Update the image.** All this really means is that you get a new representation image in your layout. This approach may help you avoid the annoying dialog box "Some pictures have been modified or missing" at print time. To update the file, select its name from the Usage list and click the Update button. Note that if you've changed much about the image, you should make sure that all the rotation, scaling, and cropping attributes you've applied to it are still relevant.

Tip: Update Multiple Images. More than one image in the Picture Usage dialog box needs to be updated? You can Shift- or Command/Ctrl-click to select more than one image in the Usage dialog box (Shift for images next to each other, and Command for noncontiguous images). However, if you press the Update button, XPress will ask you if you're sure you want to update each image. Instead, hold down the Option/Alt key while pressing Update, and the program updates them without asking you repeatedly.

Tip: Synchronize Your Clocks. Many people have grumbled that the Usage dialog box mysteriously reports their images as Modified when they haven't even touched them. The problem almost always involves images that are stored on a network server where the clock settings for your computer and the server's are different. For instance, let's say you move a picture that you've used in a layout from your hard drive to a server. Then, daylight saving time comes, and the server administrator changes the clock on the server. All of a sudden, the image appears as modified.

This doesn't happen on all servers, typically only those that are able to change a file's "last modified" date (this might even happen when the security settings change on the server). The solution: Just synchronize the clocks.

Tip: Update Modified Images Fast. Need to update all the images in your project fast? No problem: Just hold down the Command/Ctrl key when you press the OK button in the Open dialog box. When the project opens, all the images should be updated.

Missing. If QuarkXPress cannot find a file with the name it is expecting, it tells you that the file is missing. Again, you have two options.

- **Ignore it.** This method is appropriate if you are trying to get some wild artsy effect using low-resolution printing, but is inappropriate for anyone trying to get a normal, good-looking, high-resolution print. Remember that if the image is missing, QuarkXPress can only print what you see on the screen: a low-resolution representation.

- **Update the image.** If you have just moved the picture to another folder or renamed it, you can update the link by selecting the file and clicking Update. Here, you're both relinking the missing picture to the layout and bringing in a new representation. The picture preview used in Import Picture is also included in the Missing Picture dialog box.

The Usage dialog box is also valuable when you want to jump to a particular image and aren't sure where it is. For example, if you have many figures on many pages, and you want to go to the page which contains "Figure 28b," you can select that item on the Picture tab of the Usage dialog box and click the Show button. XPress jumps to the right page and highlights the picture box that contains the figure. This also works for graphics that have been anchored to text and have flowed to unknown places.

Wrong Type. Every now and again someone calls, complaining that their Picture Usage dialog box is listing the status of a picture as Wrong Type (usually it just says OK, Modified, or Missing). This cryptic message usually means that the file has been saved in a different format since it was originally imported into XPress. For instance, if you import a TIFF image into XPress, and then go back to Photoshop and save it as an EPS image with the same file name, you'll get this message.

The remedy is simple: click Update in the Picture Usage dialog box just as though the status read Modified.

More Info. The Pictures tab of the Usage dialog box contains an additional section labeled "More Info." The arrow to the left of the "More Info" label shows or hides additional, often important information about pictures such as the file modification date, dimensions, color depth, file size on disk, and more.

> **Tip: Finding Picture Paths.** If you're trying to find where a picture is on disk, you can select the picture on the page and open the Usage dialog box. That picture is highlighted on the list, so if you have a whole mess o' pictures in your layout, you don't have to go scrolling through the list to find the one you want (this also works if you have multiple picture boxes selected).
>
> While the disk path name is displayed on the left side of the dialog box, if the picture is located more than one or two folders deep, or those folders have long names, XPress will truncate the path with an ellipsis (. . .). Fortunately, if you turn on the More Info option in this dialog box, you can see the entire file path. Alternatively, you can resize the Usage dialog box, widening it to show more of the path.

*Tip: **Relinking with a New Picture.*** *When you update an image in the Picture Usage dialog box, you don't have to relink with the same picture. You can relink with any other picture, and that image comes in using the same picture specifications as the original (scaling, skewing, and so on). Of course, like many other power tips in this book, this technique can really screw up your image if you don't pay attention. For example, as of this writing, the settings on the Clipping tab of the Modify dialog box don't change when you import the new image, which can cause all sorts of problems if you don't go back to this tab and reset the values.*

*Tip: **Finding a Bunch of Missing Files.*** *If you move image files or rename the folders they reside in (or even rename the disk they're on), you can wind up with all your pictures missing. There are two easy ways to relink images.*

The first method is the coarser solution, and only works if all your image files are in one folder. Move your QuarkXPress project inside that folder and open it. QuarkXPress looks for missing pictures first inside the folder where the project is located; it automatically relinks them. Save the project, and then move it wherever you like—the images stay linked.

The second method is more subtle, and works if you have clumps of missing files in one or more folders. When you find one missing file inside a folder, QuarkXPress "sees" the other missing files and prompts you to say whether or not you want to relink them all in one fell swoop. You can then repeat this trick for other folders with missing images in them.

Exporting Pictures

Have you ever wanted to get a picture out of a QuarkXPress layout to use in a different project or some other application? Although you may encounter other reasons for wanting to save pictures out of XPress, the desire typically arises from two scenarios.

- **Pictures are embedded.** Earlier in this chapter we talked about pasting images into an XPress layout. When you copy images from an image editor like Photoshop or drawing application like Illustrator and paste into a picture box instead of saving images within those applications and then bringing them into QuarkXPress using Import Picture, you embed the images within the project. Those images don't live somewhere else on your computer, and thus can't be opened in another application. If you need to edit or revise a picture in Photoshop or Illustrator, or if you want to repurpose the same image for use in other projects, you will need to get it out of QuarkXPress and save it back to your computer's hard drive.

- **Picture Effects and Transformations.** QuarkXPress 7 offers many options for transforming images (for instance, scaling, rotating, and cropping) as well as numerous Photoshop-grade and near-Photoshop-grade adjustments (like hue and saturation and curves processing) and filters (Gaussian Blur, Edge Detection, Solarize, and more). With all that control over image appearance within QuarkXPress, sometimes you wind up wanting to use the picture—with the same appearance—in other applications or to fine-tune it in an image editor. Because the transformations and effects do not affect the original graphic file, the only way to share the end result is to save the image out of QuarkXPress into a graphic file of its own.

Fortunately, in QuarkXPress 7, getting images *out* of XPress is almost as simple as getting them *in*.

Select a picture box on the page, choose Save Picture from the File menu, and then choose Selected Picture. The Picture Export Options dialog box appears (see Figure 10-15). In the Picture Export Options dialog box you have quite a few options.

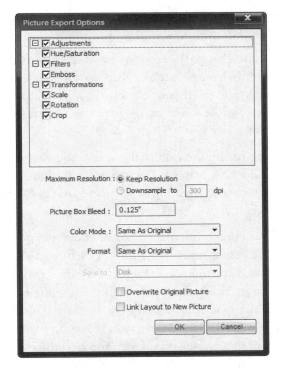

Figure 10-15
The Picture Export Options
dialog box

- **Modifications list.** At the top are listed all the modifications active on the currently selected image, the one you are about to export. The list includes all transformations, adjustments, and filters that can be applied to pictures via the Picture pane of the Modify dialog box and the Picture Effects palette. All modifications are enabled by default—meaning that the exported image will bear their effects—but each can be disabled on the exported image. For instance, you may want to export an image at its original size instead of the way it looks scaled down (or up) on the layout page.

- **Maximum Resolution.** The resolution of the exported image can be kept at whatever it was originally (the Keep Resolution option) or downsampled to a dpi you choose. Changing the resolution would be useful, for instance, if you wanted to save a 72-dpi version of a high-resolution image for use on the Web.

- **Picture Box Bleed.** When exporting pictures that have been cropped by making the picture box smaller than the content, you don't leave yourself the option of uncropping the exported image. The value of the Picture Box Bleed field allows you to specify a distance (around all sides) *beyond* the picture box to include the exported image. For example, if you center a 2 by 2-inch image in a 1 by 1-inch picture box, you will have cropped half an inch off each of the four sides. By setting the Picture Box Bleed option to 0.5", you can reclaim the cropped picture date and export to a 2 by 2-inch image.

- **Color Mode.** Use the choices here to change the color mode of the exported image to RGB, CMYK, grayscale, bitmap (black and white), or Same as Original (whatever color mode was used by the original picture). If you've applied colorizing effects to a bitmap or grayscale image, to preserve those effects in the exported picture you will need to change this option to a color mode like RGB or CMYK.

- **Format.** Choose the desired file format for the exported graphic. Your options are TIFF, JPEG, BMP, EPS, GIF, PICT, PNG, Scitex CT, and Same as Original (the original picture's file format). If you choose anything other than Same as Original, the Overwrite Original Picture checkbox (see next) will be unselectable.

- **Overwrite Original Picture.** This checkbox, when enabled, offers the option to replace your original image, the one you brought in via Import Picture, with the modified version. Be very careful when turning on this box. If the option is on, your original, unmodified picture will be replaced irrevocably with the modified version, and every application will see only the modified version from then on. There's no undo for this! Leaving Overwrite Original Picture turned off will prompt you to create a new file. I strongly urge you to leave the option off. You never know when you might want the original picture back.

- **Link Layout to New Picture.** Turning on this option automatically updates the QuarkXPress layout to point to the new, modified version of the picture instead of the original, unmodified version. It saves you a trip to the Usage dialog box to relink one image to the other.

Depending on the options you've chosen, you may be presented with other options after clicking OK. For instance, if you change the Format to TIFF or if your original image was in TIFF format, QuarkXPress prompts you to choose whether to include LZW compression or no compression on your TIFF file. Unless you've elected to overwrite your original picture, you will also be prompted by a Save Picture dialog box to choose the file name and location for saving the new image.

If you want to save *all* the pictures in the current layout to new files (or overwrite their original picture files), choose All Pictures in Layout from the Save Picture menu on the File menu. The options are the same as saving a single file, and all exported images will have the identical settings as chosen in the Picture Export Options.

DYNAMICALLY UPDATING IMAGES

In the fast-paced production environment of most magazines, newspapers, and ad agencies (plus your business, of course), any technique to streamline the workflow is appreciated. If you work with a lot of images that are subject to change, you can use the Picture Usage dialog box to manually update images, or you can use QuarkXPress's built-in ability to dynamically update the graphics in your projects. Dynamic updating is not for everyone, but for some people it's a lifesaver.

In this section I'm going to discuss three methods you can use to keep pictures updated: Auto Picture Import, the Edit Original XTension, and Object Linking and Embedding (OLE).

Auto Picture Import

If you don't want to bother checking the Picture pane of the Usage dialog box all the time, you can use QuarkXPress's internal checking tool: Auto Picture Import. When you have Auto Picture Import turned on in the (Project) General panel of the Preferences dialog box, each time you open that project QuarkXPress checks to see if any of the linked pictures have been modified. If they have been, XPress brings in the new copy transparently and seamlessly. You won't even know that anything has changed.

Clearly, sometimes not knowing what QuarkXPress is doing behind the scenes is disconcerting or frustrating. There's another option here, which is to set your layout preference to "On (Verify)." When you select this option, QuarkXPress checks for modified or missing files when you open the project, and if it finds any, it asks you whether you want to re-import them. As with all QuarkXPress features, there is no one "right" way to set up your projects; in some situations you want verifiable auto-importing, and in some you want none at all. (Though to be honest, I'm more comfortable with the "On (Verify)" option; I like to keep a close eye on what images are changing in my project.)

Tip: Update All Pictures. When Auto Picture Import is set to "On (Verify)," XPress can tell you that one or more pictures in your project have been changed. If you press OK in this warning dialog box, XPress opens the Usage dialog box, displaying only pictures that XPress thinks have been altered. Many people resign themselves to updating one picture at a time in this dialog box, but you shouldn't. You can select all the pictures on the list by clicking on the first one and then Shift-clicking on the last one. Or you can select noncontiguous items on the list with the Command/Ctrl key. After you've selected the pictures you want to reimport, hold down the Option/Alt key and click the Update button, and XPress updates them all. (If you don't hold down the Option/Alt key, XPress asks you if you're sure you want to update them, one at a time.)

Edit Original

QuarkXPress 7 on the Mac (and only on the Mac) includes the ability to send a picture back to its creating program, say, Photoshop or Illustrator, for editing, without having to first open that application and then locate and open the image manually. Within XPress you can double-click on any image with the Content tool to open the Edit Original dialog box, which offers two options: Update and Edit Original.

- **Update.** The Update button acts just like the Update button in the Usage dialog box: It automatically reimports and updates any modified file. However, I find it much faster to press Update here than to go through the rigmarole of the Usage dialog box (especially if there are a lot of pictures in my project, because the Usage dialog box takes so long to open).

- **Edit Original.** When you click the Edit Original button, QuarkXPress automatically launches the application that created the picture, and loads the picture file for you. Actually, technically, it opens the file with whatever application the Macintosh Finder thinks it should use, based on the Opens With item in the Finder's Get Info dialog box. The Edit Original feature is excellent when you have no idea where the original picture is located on your disk and you just can't be bothered to look for it in order to make a change.

There is some talk about Quark releasing this XTension for Windows users, too, but that doesn't look likely after all this time (it's been around since QuarkXPress 6). It was Macintosh-only as this book went to press. Also, note that this feature doesn't work if it can't find the original image on disk (images listed as "Missing" in the Usage dialog box).

Object Linking and Embedding (OLE)

Object Linking and Embedding, known commonly by its acronym OLE (pronounced *olé,* like the cheer people use at bullfights and those out-of-control tapas bars), is a glue with which you can seamlessly bind together various programs in Microsoft Windows. Anyway, that's the theory. Like Publish and Subscribe on the Macintosh, it's a function of the operating system rather than of XPress itself. However, it's typically not very useful in XPress.

Unlike the Publish and Subscribe features, which could be used with any kind of picture in XPress, the OLE features don't work with anything but OLE objects and links, so I just ignore them.

> **Tip: A Reason to Use OLE.** *One reader, Benji Smith, pointed out a workflow that makes OLE useful: If you use OLE's Copy Special, Paste Special, and Insert Object features (from the Edit menu), then plan on sending an Acrobat PDF file to your service bureau or printer rather than the XPress file itself. By making a PDF file, you no longer have to worry about whether or not the page is going to print properly.*

PREVIEW QUALITY, GREEKING, AND SUPPRESSION

There are times when I'd really rather not see all those pictures. Maybe the screen redraw or printing time is taking too long. Or maybe I want to use the picture for placement only in the electronic project and don't want it to print out. Or maybe I just hate the pictures. Other times I like the pictures so much that I want to see them clearly, at their full resolution. Whatever the case, QuarkXPress has solutions: high-resolution previews, picture greeking, and picture suppression.

XDraw

QuarkXPress 7 introduces an entirely new screen rendering engine built by Quark. It's called XDraw, and it dramatically improves the quality of vector shapes and type. See Figure 10-16 for a comparison of the same EPS drawing displayed in QuarkXPress 6.1, using the old QuarkXPress rendering engine, and in version 7 with XDraw. By tapping into the strengths of the rendering engines in the operating systems (Quartz on Mac OS X and GDI+ on Windows), XDraw is able to anti-alias more smoothly, and it does so much, much (much) faster than was possible in previous versions of XPress.

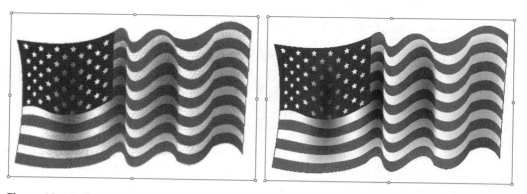

Figure 10-16 The same image in QuarkXPress 6.1 (left) and QuarkXPress 7 (right)

One of the chief complaints from QuarkXPress users in the past was the poor quality of onscreen previews (a second chief complaint was how long it took XPress to draw even the rough previews). So rough were the previews that most users would print proof after proof, scrutinizing laser or inkjet printer output rather than trusting what XPress showed them onscreen. For many, the ability to finally see an accurate onscreen preview of a layout is reason enough to move up to XPress 7.

XDraw is the reason picture effects and transparency look so smooth and clean in XPress 7, and it enables instant update of all instances of synchronized pictures.

If you use QuarkXPress for Web or multimedia layouts, XDraw offers an additional benefit: it improves the quality of text and object-oriented pictures exported to Web graphic formats (PNG, GIF, JPEG) and Flash.

Full Resolution Preview

In addition to XDraw doing the heavy lifting in the background, QuarkXPress 7 includes the front-side ability to control the preview quality of images in your layout. They will always be better quality than in earlier versions of XPress (unless pictures are greeked; see the next section), but you can choose between much better quality and spectacularly better quality.

On the View menu, ensure that Full Res Previews is enabled (a checkmark appears beside it when it's enabled). Full Res Previews is an XTension installed and enabled automatically with QuarkXPress 7. When it's on, it provides the possibility of access to full-resolution image previews. To make that possibility a reality, you must first select a picture box, and then, on the Item menu, choose Full Resolution from the Preview Resolution submenu. With Full Resolution enabled on the image, XPress displays the actual image resolution instead of a generated screen resolution preview. For instance, if you place a 300-dpi image and enable Full Resolution on it, you will see a 300-dpi image onscreen. Using the other option, Low Resolution, you'll be working with XPress's generated preview (which is still very, very good).

You can also enable Full Resolution (or revert to Low Resolution) simultaneously for multiple images on the same page or spread. Just select them all before making your preview quality choice by selecting Preview Resolution from the Item menu.

Unfortunately, there is no way to turn on Full Resolution for all the images in your layout at once. However, you might not want to anyway, because when images are set to Full Resolution, it takes much longer to navigate around your layout, zoom in and out, and so on.

However, after you turn on the Full Resolution setting for the images you want, you can hide all the high-quality previews at once by turning off Full Res Preview on the View menu. (Select it again to show them all once more.) I suggest leaving images set to Low Resolution except for the few that you really need to see clearly, and even then doing most of your work with Full Res Previews turned off (so XPress responds faster).

Picture Greeking

Back in Chapter 6, *Typography*, I discussed replacing text with gray bars. I called that "greeking the text." Now with Greek Pictures, you can basically replace anything with a gray box. The primary benefit of doing this is to speed up screen redraw: It takes much longer to redraw a detailed picture than it does to just drop in a gray box where the picture should be. Another benefit is in designing your pages. Sometimes having greeked pictures allows you to see the page layout, including its balance and overall tone, better than if you are looking at the real thing.

To greek the pictures in your layouts, turn on the Greek Pictures option in the (Print Layout) General pane of the Preferences dialog box. Note that when this box is on, all picture boxes—except for empty and selected ones—are greeked. Selecting a picture box with either the Item tool or the Content tool ungreeks the picture while it's selected.

Suppress Printout

In the instances when you want the picture on the screen but not on your printouts, you can turn on Suppress Picture Printout in the Modify dialog box (press Command/Ctrl-M, double-click on the image using the Item tool, or select Modify from the Item menu). You can also select Suppress Printout, which suppresses both the picture content and the frame itself. Even easier yet, you can turn off the checkmark on the Pictures tab of the Usage dialog box. This is equivalent to turning on the Suppress Picture Printout option in the Modify dialog box.

Here's another option for suppressing images in your output: Set the Output popup menu to Rough in the Pictures pane of the Print dialog box (see Chapter 15, *Printing*, for more on the Pictures pane).

> **Tip: Suppress Multiple Images.** You can turn on (or off) the Suppress Picture Printout option for a bunch of pictures all at the same time in the Usage dialog box. Just select the pictures you want to change (holding down the Command/Ctrl key lets you choose noncontiguous items from the list; holding down the Shift key lets you choose contiguous items), and select Yes or No from the popup menu at the top of the Print column.

PAGE AS PICTURE

A few years ago, I worked on a book that required taking illustrations created in QuarkXPress and bringing them into PageMaker. This is not an uncommon thing, of course; there are many times when you'd like to move text or graphics from XPress into other applications, or even bring a page of a QuarkXPress layout into another XPress project as a picture. QuarkXPress allows you to take care of these situations with the Save Page as EPS feature.

Selecting Save Page as EPS from the File menu (or pressing Command-Option-Shift-S or Ctrl-Alt-Shift-S) brings up a dialog box in which you can select a page of your layout and save it as a separate EPS file.

The Save Page as EPS isn't remarkable; it looks like any old Save dialog box, save for three things: the Page field, the EPS Style drop-down menu, and the Options button.

EPS files from XPress are only one page long; the Page field in this dialog box lets you specify which page in your layout you want to encapsulate.

Although it may look like there isn't much to generating EPS files from layout pages, there are loads of ways to tweak this EPS image. Click the Option button to get to the real action—another dialog box entitled Save Page As EPS (the only title difference between this dialog and its parent is the capital A typo in "As"; see Figure 10-17). For simplicity's sake, I'll call the second (with the typo) the Save Page as EPS *Options* dialog box (and I'll correct the programmer's typo).

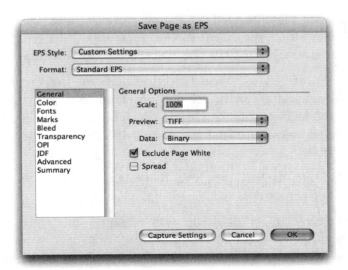

Figure 10-17
The Save Page as EPS Options

EPS Style

In the first Save Page as EPS dialog box there was a drop-down menu entitled EPS Style. Here, too, in the Save Page as EPS Options is the EPS Style drop-down menu. The difference is that here, in the Options, you can create styles; in the former, you could only access pre-created styles.

What is an EPS Style? It's a recording of all the settings in the Save Page as EPS Options dialog box (which we're about to go through). If you find yourself saving pages as EPS once in a while with the same options, create a style by choosing New EPS Output Style from the EPS Style drop-down menu, and then giving the style a meaningful name. Thereafter, to save a page as an EPS and use the same options, you need not come back to the Save Page as EPS Options. Instead, in the first Save Page as EPS dialog box, simply select your pre-created style from the EPS Style menu and click the Save button.

Format

When you save a page as EPS, the dialog box gives you the option of saving the file in one of three different formats: Standard EPS, Multiple File DCS, or Single File DCS (DCS 2.0).

Standard EPS. A standard EPS is color, grayscale, or black and white. It can be opened and edited in any imaging or drawing application that understands EPS files—for example, Photoshop, Illustrator, FreeHand, or CorelDRAW—and can be imported back into QuarkXPress, of course.

Multiple File DCS. Choosing Multiple File DCS causes QuarkXPress to save five files to your disk: one master file that contains a preview image, and four files (one file per process color) that contain the actual image data (see "DCS," earlier in this chapter).

If the Quark Color Management System is turned on, you can set the target profiles for both the composite CMYK data and the high-resolution separation data. (Note that color management only works for DCS and DCS 2.0 images.) Whether or not the Color Management System is on, XPress converts RGB data into CMYK (the program just does a better job when the system is on).

Note that because the DCS file format handles only the four process colors, any spot colors you assign get separated into process colors and placed on the CMYK plates.

Single File DCS. As I said earlier, DCS 2.0 handles cyan, magenta, yellow, black, and as many spot colors as you want. The cool part about this is that all your spot colors get put on their own plates. And as I also noted earlier, selecting DCS 2.0 results in only one file on your hard drive rather than five or more.

Scale

When you adjust the scaling of the page (for example, making the page 25 percent of full size), the page size is displayed in the dialog box so that you know how large the final bounding box of the EPS image is. You can adjust this by changing the scaling. Remember: Because this is PostScript, you can scale your EPS page down to 10 percent, bring it into another program, scale it back up to original size, and you won't lose any quality in your output (though your screen preview image may look awful). Figure 10-18 shows a QuarkXPress spread that was saved and brought back into another QuarkXPress layout.

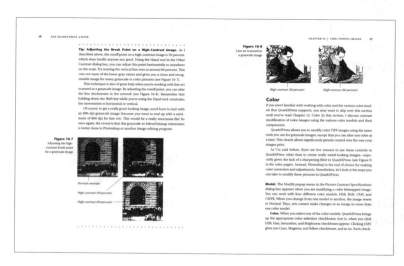

Figure 10-18
QuarkXPress
page as EPS
document

XPress lets you scale your page down to 10 percent of its original size, but it cannot scale the page up above 100 percent.

Preview

Earlier in this chapter, I mentioned that the primary difference between EPS files on the Macintosh and those on Windows had to do with the built-in screen preview. Macintosh EPS files typically have PICT previews; Windows EPS files must use TIFF previews. When generating an EPS file from XPress, you have to choose one of these two preview formats from the Preview popup menu—at least, on the Mac. QuarkXPress 7 on the Mac offers three options for EPS previews: PICT, TIFF, and none (no preview at all; displays as a gray box if imported back into QuarkXPress). On Windows, XPress 7 only offers TIFF and none as preview options.

Although PICT remains an option on the Mac, I urge you not to use it. These days nearly as many professionals work in QuarkXPress and other professional-grade creative tools on Windows as on Mac. At the time this book went to press, the difference in market share between Mac-based and Windows-based creative personnel was less than five percent. Using a PICT format preview means Windows users (and those using a Windows version of QuarkXPress by way of Mac OS X's Bootcamp) will see nothing but a gray box. By choosing TIFF as the preview format for your EPS files, you'll future-proof your images to be compatible with either platform and anyone who might need to use them in the down the road.

Data

The Data choice affects only bitmapped image data in TIFF and EPS file formats. It specifies whether to include TIFF images in ASCII or Binary format. What's the difference? Bitmapped images saved in Binary format are half the size of those saved in ASCII, so they print much more quickly. So why use ASCII? Some networks and print spoolers choke on binary image data, so people have had to use ASCII on these systems. Fortunately, QuarkXPress gives you a third choice: Clean 8-bit. This format is about as small as the Binary option but usually prints more reliably on Windows-based networks that can't handle the regular binary data. I recommend trying Binary first, and if you have trouble printing, switch to Clean 8-bit. (On the other hand, if you're creating EPS files but you don't know who's going to use or print them, you might opt for Clean 8-bit right off the bat.)

Exclude Page White

The folks at Quark made a change between versions 3 and 4 in how XPress writes its EPS files: In version 3, XPress treated the white background of the page as transparent in the EPS file. In version 4, it drew a big white box in the background so EPS files were always opaque. In version 5 and 6 Quark decided to offer users a choice, with the Transparent Page checkbox. In version 7, the Transparent Page checkbox has been renamed to the more cryptic Exclude Page White. When you turn this on, XPress works like it did back in version 3—the background of the EPS will be transparent. This is particularly helpful when you're going to open the EPS file in Photoshop or composite it on top of some other image or object.

Spread

If you turn on the Spread option, XPress creates an EPS of whatever page spread includes the page you've specified. Note that Spread works with both facing-pages and single-sided layouts; a spread is defined as any two (or more) pages sitting next to each other.

Color Options

On the Color pane of the Save Page as EPS Options dialog box you can select the color model and individual colors for the generated EPS. In the Setup field choose a model.

- **Grayscale.** Convert the entire page and all its elements into grayscale. Although this might be tempting, I caution against it. Using XDraw, QuarkXPress is pretty good at color conversions, but it's still not as good as Photoshop. If you want to turn a color page into grayscale, export it as color (using the As Is option), open it in Photoshop, and do the conversion to grayscale there. The only caveat to this advice is to note that Photoshop will rasterize the EPS during the conversion process. If you have object-oriented graphics or text that must remain vector outlines, go ahead and let XPress do the conversion.

- **Composite RGB.** Save the EPS in the RGB color space, which is ideal when exporting the page (or spread) image for use on the Web or in a multimedia presentation.

- **Composite CMYK.** This option saves the EPS in pure CMYK. Any spot colors or RGB colors will be converted to CMYK as part of the export process. Again, Photoshop can do a better job if you can live with the rasterization.

- **Composite CMYK and Spot.** With this color model, spot colors are preserved as spot colors; they are not converted to CMYK.

- **As Is.** Whatever color space or spaces the page and its constituent elements happen to occupy will be preserved. If you have spot colors, they will be in the resulting EPS. If the page contains RGB elements, they, too, will survive the conversion unchanged. I usually choose As Is for the color space of my pages exported to EPS to offer me the widest possible options for using the graphic—even if I only intend to place the image back into XPress and then send it to press as part of a print layout. Any out of gamut colors (for instance, RGB) can be converted later in the production process.

Beneath the Setup drop-down menu, each ink or color can be disabled by turning off the box beside it. This is useful, for example, if you know that your layout doesn't contain certain inks. In a duotone layout, for example, you may only use Black and a particular spot color. In that case, set the color space to Composite CMYK and Spot, and disable Cyan, Magenta, and Yellow.

Font Options

On the Fonts pane you can selectively disable embedding of fonts used by the page. Fonts embedded within an EPS file travel with it, ensuring that the EPS always looks exactly as you intended it, regardless of whether the used fonts are installed or active on any given computer. Choosing to not embed used fonts, however, requires that any system that works with or prints the resulting EPS have the fonts installed. Although embedding fonts in the EPS increases the size of the EPS file, with today's massive hard drives and removable and archival media, the size difference is negligible. A bigger file is certainly a fair tradeoff for knowing that text in your EPS file won't get mangled during RIP.

Registration Marks Options

On the Marks pane, the Registration Marks Mode enables you to add registration marks to your EPS file. The default value, Off, does not add registration marks. Choosing Centered or Off Center activates the three value fields beneath the Mode drop-down menu.

- **Width.** The stroke weight of the crop marks. A value of 0.003 inches, the default, is usually good.

- **Length.** Specify the desired length of each crop mark. Typically, you want them between .25 and .5 inches.

- **Offset.** Offset is the padding or blank area distance between the page edge and the beginning of the crop marks. It is typically between $\frac{1}{16}$ and $\frac{1}{8}$ of an inch (.0625 and .125 inches), but may need to be increased to account for bleed.

Bleed Options

If your page has items that bleed off the sides, don't expect the bleed to automatically appear in the EPS files. When you save a page as EPS, XPress cuts off the edges of the EPS at the edge of the page (the objects still jut out, but PostScript's Clip command doesn't let the printer image them). Fortunately, QuarkXPress lets you specify a Bleed value in the Save as EPS Options dialog box (you have to switch to the Bleed pane, and then choose either symmetric or asymmetric bleed first). If you set the Bleed value to .5 inch, XPress makes the EPS document wider and taller by an inch (half an inch on each side). Any page objects that sit within half an inch of the page get incorporated into the EPS, whether they're touching the page or not.

Choosing Symmetric uses the same bleed amount for all four sides of the image, and only one measurement field is available to define that amount. Asymmetric, on the other hand, enables you to set separate bleed widths for the top, bottom, inside, and outside edges.

Unfortunately, the Bleed value doesn't help you if you're trying to prepare EPS files for processing with another prepress program, such as ScenicSoft's Preps or TrapWise. If you need to do this, you probably need the ScenicSoft Prepress XTension known as PXT, which was once called LPX or APX, and which you can get free from ScenicSoft.

Transparency Options

When the page you're exporting contains alpha-channel transparency, objects with less than 100 percent opacity, blending options, line-art TIFF pictures, or bitmap frames, it has transparency. To print correctly, that transparency must be flattened to nontransparent areas of solid color (see the section on flattening in Chapter 14, *Color*). When transparency is flattened, objects affected by transparency must be rasterized at a fixed resolution. In the Transparency Options, on the Transparency pane of the Save Page as EPS Options, you define the resolution (in dpi) of the rasterized results.

Although the Ignore Transparency Flattening option sounds like it means *don't flatten, just pass the transparency through*, that isn't the case. On the contrary, turning on this option is like taking a step back in time to XPress 4—no transparency. Objects that blend together on the page will suddenly adopt a white background in the exported EPS and no longer blend together.

OPI Options

The OPI method is based on post-separating, full-color pages that include color bitmapped images—especially scanned images. For example, you can import a low-resolution RGB TIFF file into a QuarkXPress layout, save that page as EPS, and separate it on your imagesetter using a program like Creo's Preps. Instead of Quark including the whole TIFF image in the PostScript file, it just throws in OPI comments that say what the name of the scanned image file is and where the separation program can find it.

This is nice for a couple of reasons. First and foremost is file size. An EPS file with the image data included can be quite large. Sometimes, it's nicer to leave the image data on disk somewhere else and just manipulate a minimal EPS file (one that just includes OPI comments about where to find the image data). Some workflows depend heavily on keeping the high-resolution data separate from the PostScript and EPS files using OPI.

The trick to building a PostScript file with OPI comments is the OPI pane in the Save Page as EPS and Print dialog boxes. The OPI Active checkbox simply determines whether XPress will include OPI comments in the PostScript; I just leave this turned on. That gives you three choices: Include TIFF images, Low Resolution TIFF, and Include EPS images (see Figure 10-19). Leaving Include Images on is the way that XPress acts naturally: printing all the TIFF and EPS pictures (including the data in the EPS file). If you turn off either of the Include Images checkbox, XPress replaces the picture data with OPI comments. Note that this applies only to images for which OPI is turned on in the OPI tab of the Usage dialog box or for which the Use OPI option was on when you imported the file.

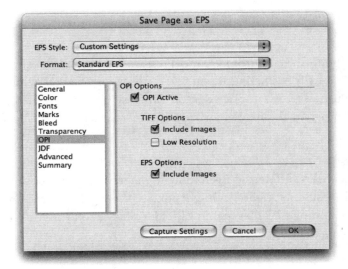

Figure 10-19
Saving a page as an EPS with OPI comments

Apparently, the OPI specs talk about OPI comments for EPS images as well as for TIFF images. At this time, however, no software pays any attention to those specs. So this selection (as far as I can tell) is useless for the time being.

JDF Options

I talk about JDF (Job Definition Format) in Chapter 13, *Collaboration*. If you've defined Job Jacket structure in the project from which you're creating an EPS, turning on Output JDF will cause XPress to create a JDF file from that structure at the same time it creates the EPS. You can also select a predefined Job Jacket Contact to include.

PostScript Level

On the Advanced pane is a single option to define the PostScript level of the exported EPS. Your choices are PostScript Level 2 and PostScript Level 3 (the latter is another typo; the proper name is PostScript 3, without the "Level" qualifier). In a perfect world you should never have to bother with this option. At the time of this writing the PostScript 3 version of the industry standard printer language is a decade old, and all equipment and systems in a professional print workflow should be PostScript 3 compliant. That's in a perfect world. In reality, some of your vendors may be eking by on old technology. If your service bureau or print provider can't handle PostScript 3, you'll need to drop the level back to PostScript Level 2 within EPS files you send to it.

A Warning

A word of warning here about EPS files from QuarkXPress. Some people get overly optimistic about what's possible with PostScript. If you save a full-color QuarkXPress page as EPS, place it in Adobe Illustrator, save it, place that on a InDesign page, and then send it through some high-end program for final color separations—well, don't be shocked if it doesn't work.

Each of these programs was written by a different group of people and, consequently, handles color, type, and graphic elements differently. Even though, theoretically, the above process should work (PostScript is PostScript, right?), it might not. So be careful and prudent when you combine programs by nesting EPS files within EPS files; all this software isn't as integrated as it sometimes seems to be.

Tip: Editing EPS Graphics. Exporting your file in EPS format doesn't mean you can never edit it again. Adobe Illustrator can open most EPS files, converting their elements back into editable objects. After editing, you can save your file as EPS again. It's not a perfect solution, but it usually works pretty well if you don't have the original XPress project from which the EPS was created.

Tip: Using EPS to Redimension a Job. Suppose you have a very complicated page layout in QuarkXPress, and your client suddenly decides on a slight change in page size that requires repositioning and resizing every element on the page. You could spend hours fixing the layout, or do what an enterprising designer did in similar circumstances: save the page as EPS, import the EPS into a layout with the new page size, and scale the EPS to fit. Slight changes to a page's proportions can sometimes be an acceptable trade-off to get a job done on time.

Tip: Rasterizing EPS Files. Let's say you're creating a page that shows two year's worth of covers from your monthly magazine. That's 24 images. If the covers were created in XPress, you could save each one to disk as an EPS file, import the EPS onto your page, and then shrink it down to the right size. However, let's say each cover EPS was 20 MB large. That means you've got 480 MB of data on one page. Is that a good idea? I think not.

Instead, you could rasterize each EPS file in Photoshop. Remember that "rasterizing" is the act of converting vector art (like EPS files) into bitmap art (like most Photoshop files). You can rasterize almost any EPS file in Photoshop simply by opening it. Then you can downsample the file to the size and resolution you need. The result is a set of much smaller files that will be sure to print beautifully.

IMAGE ON THE HALF SHELL

Now that your understanding of images has risen from the murky oceanic depths to the clear, naked light of day, it's time to take a step forward onto dry land, and—in the next chapter—fine-tune your images for brilliance on your page.

CHAPTER ELEVEN
Image Tuning

While QuarkXPress has always provided an astonishing array of controls over your page's text, version 7 shines just as brightly in its image adjustment and modification controls.

In Chapter 10, *Pictures,* I discussed several graphic file formats, how to bring them into your QuarkXPress layouts, and how to perform basic manipulations with them, such as rotating, skewing, and scaling. In this chapter, I look at how you can use QuarkXPress in place of other image-editing software to modify the imported image itself. Bear in mind that I'm not talking here about image *editing.* You can't actually change the content of imported graphics in QuarkXPress. You can, however, change a remarkable range of overall appearance attributes such as contrast, color, clipping path, and halftone screen, as well as make a dozen Photoshop-like image adjustments and use another dozen of the most often used Photoshop filters.

First, I'm going to examine the types of images you can modify, and then I'll discuss how to modify them. Much of this is potentially confusing, but bear with me, read carefully, and you'll be an inexorable image-modifier faster than you can say, "ontogeny recapitulates phylogeny."

THE PICTURE FILE

In this chapter, I am concerned almost exclusively with bitmapped images. Bitmapped images, as far as QuarkXPress is concerned, are black and white, grayscale, or color, and are found in PSD, TIFF, JPEG, BMP, GIF, PNG, and bitmap-only PICT files. Bitmapped images can also be saved as EPS files, but because the image data is encapsulated, XPress won't let you change anything about them. Therefore, the only time I'll discuss EPS files here is when I explore clipping paths. The rest of the time, I'm just going to assume that you're using PSD, TIFF, or JPEG files (see Chapter 10, *Pictures*, for why I don't like using the other bitmapped file formats).

Bitmapped Images

I want to take this opportunity to refresh your memory about bitmapped images and the PSD, TIFF, and JPEG file types, which I discussed in Chapter 10, *Pictures*. Here are the highlights.

- Bitmapped images are simply rectangular grids of sample points (also called pixels or dots).

- The resolution of the image is the number of these sample points, specified in pixels per inch (ppi).

- Each sample point can be black, white, a level of gray, or a color. This color is represented by a number; for example, in a file with 256 gray levels, black would be zero and white would be 255.

- Scaling the image has a direct effect on its resolution. Enlarging the picture to 200 percent cuts the resolution in half (same number of samples in twice the space), which may result in pixelation ("jaggies"). Reducing the image to 50 percent doubles the resolution, which may improve image quality.

- A PSD, TIFF, or JPEG file can be a rectangle of any size with any number of dots per inch, and each pixel can have any level of gray or any color that is definable by the color models described in Chapter 14, *Color*. Image files are said to be *deep* if they have four or more gray levels (more than 2 bits per sample point), and they're *flat* or *bilevel* if they only have 1 bit (black or white) per sample point.

- JPEG files are compressed (made smaller on disk) by using a lossy scheme—some image data is lost, so the image degrades slightly.

- PSD files can contain multiple layers that you can selectively disable in QuarkXPress.

PHOTOSHOP DOCUMENTS

In 1994, Photoshop version 3 introduced layers to the venerable image editor that would be king. Up until then, any change made to the image data of a Photoshop document was permanent and immutable. You couldn't, for example, composite two images together, save and close the document, and later expect to reposition the images. The two fused into a single two-dimensional image as soon as you released the marching ants selection marquee; any pixels of one image covered by the other were forever destroyed. Layers changed all that.

Layers in PSD images work very much like layers in a QuarkXPress layout (see the discussion about layers in Chapter 3, *Working with Items*). Instead of a strictly two-dimensional art surface, layers are like transparency sheets overlaid atop one another (see Figure 11-1). The bottom layer might contain the background color, and five more layers contain one object each. Overlaid, they form a single, composite image, but each object can be independently repositioned without harming image data on other layers. Layers—and thus parts of a composite image—can even be selectively hidden and blended in Photoshop.

These four layers make...   ...this composite image.

Figure 11-1 Layers in PSD documents are like transparency sheets—space not occupied by image data allows lower layers to show through.

Thanks to QuarkXPress's built-in PSD Import XTensions, layers can be selectively hidden (or shown) and blended inside XPress, too.

Manipulating Layers

Figure 11-2 shows the layers in a particular PSD image as displayed on Photoshop CS3's Layers panel. It also shows how QuarkXPress 7's PSD Import palette's Layers tab displays the layers for the same image. Not much difference, is there?

 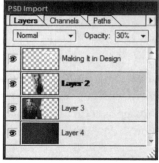

Figure 11-2
A layered PSD image as displayed on the Photoshop CS3 Layers panel (left) and the same image in QuarkXPress 7's PSD Import palette Layers tab

Just as in Photoshop, the eyeball icon to the left of a layer name indicates its visibility in the imported PSD. If you see an eyeball, the layer is visible; if there isn't an eyeball in the left column, the layer is hidden. Click on the eye or empty socket to toggle the layer off or on.

Why would you want to change PSD layer visibility inside XPress? Often you'll want to show or hide different layers for the same reasons you'd do it in Photoshop. Fine-tuning the image in context with the page springs immediately to mind as one reason. Perhaps you have different versions of an image or parts of the image saved on different layers. While working on a graphic in Photoshop, it can be difficult to envision how the image will interact with other elements on the page in the layout. By experimenting with layered image elements and maybe different versions of those elements directly on the page in XPress, you can better tailor the result to fit with the layout.

When you initially import a PSD, the layers will be in the state last saved from Photoshop. If layer *x* was on and layer *y* off when you saved the PSD in Photoshop, then layer *x* will be on and layer *y* will be off in XPress. You can change that, however, with the PSD Import palette's Layers tab. Changes to layer visibility affect only the single imported instance on the page; those changes are *not* written back to the PSD document saved on your hard drive. In fact, none of the changes you make to images in QuarkXPress alter the original graphic file.

Be careful when updating images, though. When you update an imported PSD that has been modified outside of XPress, all the layer options will be reset.

Opacity. In addition to hiding and showing layers, you can also control their individual opacity. In the top-right corner of the Layers tab the Opacity field accepts opacity values in whole percentage point increments from zero percent (the layer is completely transparent) through 100 percent (the layer is completely opaque). A handy drop-down menu offers even faster access to opacity percentages, in 10 percent increments.

Select a layer in the list and change the Opacity field to affect that layer. Unfortunately, QuarkXPress doesn't allow you to select multiple layers at once like you can in Photoshop.

Lowering the opacity of a layer below 100 percent enables layers below it to begin to shine through. Note: To alter the opacity of the *entire* image rather than of individual layers use the Colors palette (see Chapter 14, *Color*) or the Opacity submenu on the Style menu (see "The Style Menu," later in this chapter).

Blending Modes. To the left of the Opacity field is the layer Blending Modes drop-down menu. Blending modes change the way in which the selected layer interacts with lower layers. Depending on the imagery on the selected and lower layers, most blending modes will allow imagery on lower layers to mix with, and change the appearance of, colors on the selected and blended layer.

Blending modes can be used to achieve a potpourri of special effects, but the exact result varies from picture to picture. In general, here is what you can expect from the 22 blending modes. (Please download the Image Tuning folder from *www.peachpit/Quark7* to see Figures X-1 through X-22, which display the effects of each of the 22 blending modes described below.)

- **Normal.** No blending mode. Unless the Opacity field is altered or the original PSD has transparency or a blending mode applied in Photoshop, the selected layer will not blend with lower layers. This mode is equivalent to Photoshop's Pass Through layer blending mode.

- **Dissolve.** Colors are not mixed, but the pixels in the selected layer are randomly omitted, enabling lower layers to shine through to create a static effect. As you lower the Opacity percentage, the quantity of pixels in the selected layer decreases, increasing the empty space between them, scattering the pixels more widely, and showing more of the image data on lower layers.

- **Multiply.** As the name implies, this blending mode multiplies colors on lower layers by the grayscale value of colors on the selected layer, resulting in darker shades. For instance, in Figure X-3, the grayscale value of the green bar is approximately 50 percent black (it's actually 52.84 percent, but let's keep it simple). Part of the sky overlapped by the green bar is roughly 25 percent black. When the layer containing the colored bars is given the Multiply blending mode, the 50 percent green bar blends with the 25 percent sky beneath to create a 75 percent grayscale value in that area.

    When either the selected or a lower layer contains black, the result is always black because multiplying any color by 100 percent always results in 100 percent; similarly, white areas on one layer are replaced entirely by color in the other.

    Use Multiply when you want to cast a shadow or darken image data on lower layers.

- **Screen.** The Screen blending mode is the opposite of Multiply. Colors in the selected layer and lower layers are multiplied by their inverse values to produce the lightest shade possible from the combination. Areas of black on the selected layer are completely replaced by any nonblack colors on lower layers. Any areas of white on either layer remain white because white is zero percent color (anything times zero is always zero, as you may recall from fourth-grade math).

- **Overlay.** Colors in the selected layer are multiplied (darkened) or screened (lightened) with lower layer colors, and the darkest and lightest values, the shadows and highlights, are left unchanged. The more color contrast between layers, the more dramatic the effect. Colors with similar grayscale values, conversely, change less. Black, white, and colors with a 50 percent grayscale value do not change.

- **Soft Light.** The Soft Light blending mode multiplies dark colors and screens light colors but does not preserve shadows and highlights. Colors in the selected layer darker than 50 percent grayscale will darken colors in lower layers, whereas colors brighter than 50 percent will lighten. Black darkens but does not stay pure black, and white lightens without remaining pure white. The resulting effect is like projecting the selected layer image onto lower layers with a weak overhead projector bulb.

- **Hard Light.** This option is like putting a brand new bulb in the projector. If a color in the selected layer is lighter than 50 percent gray, the lower layers will be screened; if it's darker than 50 percent gray, lower layers will be multiplied. It usually results in sharply contrasting highlights and shadows. Black and white will not be altered.

- **Vivid Light.** This blending mode operates on contrast values. Where the selected layer's colors are lighter than 50 percent gray, the lower layers will be lightened by decreasing their contrast values. Contrast values are increased when a color in the selected layer is darker than 50 percent gray. Black and white areas will be unchanged. It's a lot like putting a 150-watt bulb into your 100-watt projector.

- **Linear Light.** Selected layer colors lighter than 50 percent gray will increase brightness in lower layers, whereas colors darker than 50 percent gray will decrease brightness. Black and white areas will be unchanged.

- **Pin Light.** If a color in the selected layer is lighter than 50 percent gray, any pixels darker than 50 percent gray in lower layers will shine through. The inverse is also true—darker than 50 percent gray is replaced by any pixels lighter than 50 percent gray. Light replaces dark, dark replaces light. Black and white, of course, are the exception; they remain unchanged. Use the Pin Light blending mode to demonstrate needing a new projector entirely.

- **Color Dodge.** Each color channel is compared and brightened by decreasing contrast in this blending mode. Black and dark grays in the selected layer are replaced entirely by any lighter gray value.

- **Linear Dodge.** This option brightens each color channel, increasing brightness. Black is entirely replaced, but dark gray values will often blend.

- **Color Burn.** While dodging means to brighten, burning is the process of darkening. The Color Burn blending mode is the opposite of Color Dodge: Each color channel is darkened by increasing contrast. Black in the selected layer stays black, but white and light gray pixels are completely replaced by any darker value pixels.

- **Linear Burn.** Linear Burn darkens by decreasing the brightness of each color channel. White in the selected layer is replaced by any darker shade, and black will remain black.

- **Darken.** By comparing the color channels in the selected layer and lower layers, this blending mode retains only the darker of overlapping pixels. For example, if the selected layer contains a pixel that is 50 percent gray and the lower layer has a pixel in the same location that is only 25 percent gray, the 50 percent gray pixel will be used.

  Darken (like Lighten) often has a posterizing effect where too few tones are retained, resulting in large areas of one color and "washed out" colors. Referring again to Figure X-15 (download Image Tuning folder from www.peachpit.com/Quark7 to see figure), you can see such results best in the green, blue, and purple bars in the Darken blending mode version of the image. Although these effects are sometimes desired, you're most often better off using the Multiply blend mode to darken lower layers and Screen to lighten them.

- **Lighten.** Like the Darken blending mode, Lighten compares gray values and keeps the lighter of the two. If the pixel in the selected layer is lighter than the pixel in the layer beneath, it will be used.

- **Difference.** By examining each color channel, this mode subtracts the brighter of the two overlapping colors from the other to produce the Difference blending mode. White areas invert the resulting mix such that light values become dark, and dark values become light. Black in the selected layer is completely replaced by colors in lower layers.

- **Exclusion.** This blending mode is very similar to the Difference blending mode except that Exclusion reduces the contrast of resulting colors.

- **Hue.** In this blending mode, the hue of pixels in lower layers is replaced by hues in the selected layer. Brightness and saturation values are not changed. Black, white, and gray-colored pixels in the selected layer have no hue or saturation, so they have no effect beyond desaturating pixels of lower layers.

- **Saturation.** This option uses the brightness and hue from the lower layer colors combined with the saturation of the selected layer's colors. Black, white, and gray-colored pixels have the same effect as in the Hue blending mode.

- **Color.** By projecting the hue and saturation from the selected layer onto lower layers' brightness values, the Color blending mode creates a convincing, tonally rich colorization effect. This blending mode can be used to colorize bitmap, grayscale, and even color images. With the selected layer at 100 percent Opacity, the effect is like a gel on a spotlight—everything is colored. But by lowering the opacity, you can create a wash effect with subtle results. Again, black, white, and gray-colored pixels desaturate lower layer pixels.

- **Luminosity.** The final combination of values is the Luminosity blending mode, which mixes the selected layer's brightness values with the lower layers' hue and saturation. *Now* black, white, and gray-colored pixels have an effect—sort of. Black and white stay black and white, whereas grays vary the shades in the blended results.

Revert Layer. With all those blending modes, variable layer opacity, and the ability to turn layers on and off, you can easily lose track of the original state of the image. Fortunately, QuarkXPress includes a rapid rewind feature—the Revert Layer command.

On the Layers tab popup menu you'll find the Revert Layer command, which sends the selected layer back to its original state as it exists in the PSD file, and the Revert All Layers command, which tosses out changes made to all layers (see Figure 11-3). Be careful with these commands; you can't undo a Revert Layer or Revert All Layers command with Command/Ctrl-Z.

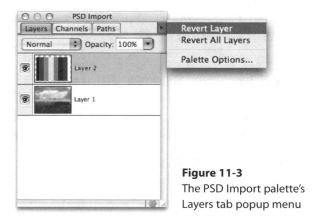

Figure 11-3
The PSD Import palette's
Layers tab popup menu

Tip: Change Layer Thumbnail Sizes. Beside each layer name on the PSD Import palette's Layers tab is a thumbnail of the layer's contents. For some, the default thumbnail size is too small to clearly differentiate the image data on one layer from the image data on the next. For others, the thumbnails are too large, taking up vertical space that would be better used to show a greater number of layers in the palette. To get the size just right, open the popup menu on the Layers tab and choose Palette Options. In the Palette Options dialog box you have four options for thumbnail size: None (show only layer names, sans thumbnails), Small, Medium, and Large.

Tip: One File, Multiple Images. Because layer visibility, opacity, and blending modes only affect a single image instance on the page and don't alter the original graphic files saved on your computer, you can use a single file as if it were several different pictures. For example, let's say you've created a logo in Photoshop. Distributed among the layers of the PSD file are the different components of the logo—the logo imagery itself on one layer, the company's name on another, and the tagline on a third layer. Together, the three pieces make up a complete logo, one you'd use on, say, the back of a business card. On the front of the business card you might want just the iconic part of the logo in one place, with the company name repositioned relative to that, and the tagline omitted entirely. On the letterhead, envelopes, and other identity pieces you might want slightly different configurations of the logo elements. Being a smart QuarkXPress user, you'll create your entire identity package—business card, letterhead, envelope, and so on—as multiple layouts in the same project file (utilizing Synchronized Text, naturally). By turning layers off and on selectively, you can utilize just the single PSD file for all the places the logo or one of its constituent pieces is required. That makes one file on disk and one linked image to send to the printer instead of many images that use up more space and take longer to print.

Manipulating Channels

Similar to the PSD Import palette's Layers tab is the PSD Import palette's Channels tab, which lists the channels or colors active in an imported Photoshop document. Although you can't change the opacity of channels or apply blending modes to them, you can selectively hide and show them, and with spot colors, change a few more options. Let's cover the basics and then get into manipulating spot channel options.

The Channels tab looks a lot like Photoshop's Channels panel (see Figure 11-4). But in XPress you can only manipulate the channels already in the PSD file; you can't create, delete, or merge channels, for instance.

The Palette Options dialog box available from the popup menu on the Channels tab offers the same size choices as the Palette Options for the Layers tab—no thumbnails or small, medium, or large thumbnails. Also on the popup menu is the option to Show Channels in Color (see Figure 11-5). By default, XPress creates only grayscale thumbnails from each channel's image data (views of the picture on the page are always in the visible channels' colors regardless of the thumbnail display mode). The grayscale view approximates what you'd see if the image was separated to film. Enabling Show Channels in Color, however, shows each channel's thumbnail in the color of the channel. You will see a cyan thumbnail on the Cyan channel, magenta thumbnail on the Magenta channel, and so on, instead of black. I usually work in this mode, thumbnailing channels in their individual colors to get a MatchPrint-like preview.

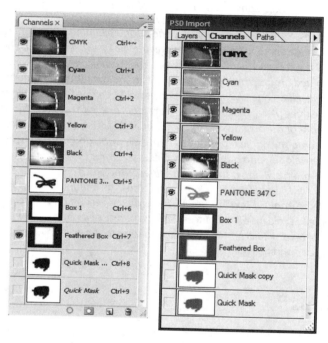

Figure 11-4
The same image in Photoshop CS3's Channels panel (left) and the QuarkXPress 7 PSD Import palette Channels tab (right)

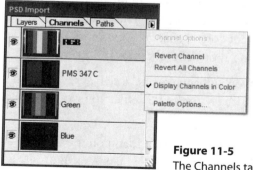

Figure 11-5
The Channels tab popup menu

At the top of the channels list is the composite channel—either RGB or CMYK. A channel, like a layer, may be hidden or shown by clicking the eyeball or empty eyeball socket beside the channel name. As soon as you hide one of the main channels—Red, Green, or Blue in RGB images or Cyan, Magenta, Yellow, or Black in CMYK images—the eyeball disappears beside the composite channel disappears. To quickly reenable all RGB or CMYK channels, all you have to do is click the empty socket beside the composite channel. That won't show spot color channels you may have hidden, however.

Spot Channels

As you may recall from Chapter 10, *Pictures*, PSD is one of two file types that can be imported into QuarkXPress with spot channels (DCS 2.0 EPS files are the other type). In addition to the standard CMYK process-ink channels, the Channels tab shows channels for any spot colors in the Photoshop image.

Hiding a spot channel disables it and prevents it from printing. Image data on the hidden channel is omitted entirely. If that isn't your goal, if you *do* want the image data to print but as a process ink instead of a spot, then you can do that, too. It's useful, for instance, when you want to make a duotone image composed of two spot channels print as a process-ink duotone—say, in process cyan and process black. More often, it's useful for eliminating duplicate spot colors.

The common problem of duplicate spot colors happens when a spot channel is added in Photoshop, and then the same spot color is used in QuarkXPress with a different name. For example, perhaps in Photoshop you or someone else added a channel and titled it "PANTONE 347 C." Using the Colors palette in QuarkXPress you already had the same spot color, but named "Corporate Color 1" because that particular shade of green is your client's signature color. When you import the PSD file, you'll have the same color in two different color swatches, which means your project will output to two different plates of the same color (eek!). While you *could* go back to Photoshop and rename that channel to match the spot color already in use in your XPress layout, you'd have to do the same for every PSD image containing that particular spot color. It's much easier to resolve this situation directly in XPress.

When you select a spot channel in the Channels tab and open the palette's popup menu, you'll notice that the Channel Options command at the top is available (if it's grayed out, make sure you have a spot channel selected). Choose that command to open the Channel Options dialog box (see Figure 11-6). Three channel options are available.

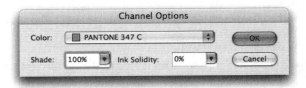

Figure 11-6
The Channel Options dialog

Color. This drop-down menu lists all the layout's swatches from the Color palette. Choosing any color in this option maps the selected spot channel to that color. For example, to resolve the duplicate spot color issue, you would select the "PANTONE 347 C" color channel in the PSD Import palette's Channels tab, open the Channel Options, and choose "Corporate Color 1" from the Color list. When you click OK, QuarkXPress replaces the original image spot color with your chosen substitute.

Shade. In this field you can adjust the channel's tint from zero percent (no ink, just paper) through 100 percent (full ink color up to the maximum opacity assigned to the channel in Photoshop). It works just like the Shade field on the Colors palette. The Shade field accepts changes in 1 percent increments.

Ink Solidity. Solidity controls the transparency of the spot channel. A value of 100 percent is a solid, opaque ink, whereas zero percent is completely transparent and best used with varnishes. XPress uses the Ink Solidity value to change the appearance of an ink onscreen and when printing color composites, but it ignores the setting when printing separations (otherwise you could get blank film). Also note that mask channels from Photoshop are automatically assigned a zero percent solidity upon import.

Indexed Color Channels

Although I hope that you never need to read this section and that you never need to deal with indexed color images, I'm more realistic than that. Few of us will be lucky enough to go our entire careers without having to import some client's GIF logo or BMP artwork. Thus, I feel an obligation to prepare you for that eventuality and give you the best chance at making the best of a bad image situation.

Indexed images are limited to a maximum of 256 colors; many images contain as few as two colors. Although 256 may sound like a lot of colors, it isn't. Sometimes, as with spot colors in images, you'll want to replace one indexed color with a different color.

Because an indexed color image includes no separate channels, the Channels tab offers you only a single Indexed composite channel (see Figure 11-7). All the colors in the image are stored in the Indexed channel. When you select that channel, you'll notice that the Channel Options command on the palette popup menu becomes active, just as it does for spot channels. The options in the Indexed Color Options dialog box, however, are quite different than those in the Channel Options dialog box (see Figure 11-8).

Color. Select any color swatch in the grid dominating the dialog box and then choose its replacement from the Color drop-down list. You'll see the change in the picture on the page, and when printed, QuarkXPress will output your selected color instead of the original color.

Figure 11-7
With an indexed color image like
a GIF, the only channel available
is the Indexed composite channel.

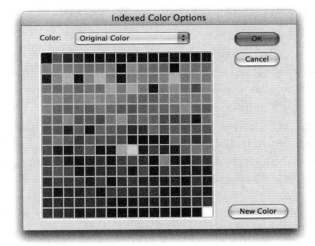

Figure 11-8
The Indexed Color Options
dialog box

New Color. If you find a color in the picture you'd like to use elsewhere in your layout, highlight the desired swatch in the grid and click the New Color button. The selected color will be added to the Colors palette, ready to be used on other objects in your layout.

> **Tip: Faster Access to Channel Options.** *To get to the Channel Options dialog box for spot channels or the Indexed Color Options dialog box on Indexed channels, double-click the channel itself instead of choosing the Channel Options command from the PSD Import palette's Channels tab popup menu.*

> **Tip: Revert Channel Changes.** *Just as the PSD Import palette's Layers tab has commands on its popup menu to Revert Layer and Revert All Layers, you can select Revert Channel or Revert All Channels from the popup menu on the Channels tab. All color mapping, Shade, and Ink Solidity changes you made to the selected channel (or all channels) will be undone, reverting to the original state in the PSD image.*

Using Mask and Alpha Channels

Selected areas of images in Photoshop may be saved as an additional type of channel called an alpha channel. An alpha channel defines opacity in terms of 256 levels of gray and is called "true" transparency because, unlike 1-bit transparency where a pixel is either wholly opaque or wholly transparent, pixels may be partially opaque. Photoshop does the job of mapping those 256 levels of gray to a simple percentage scale where zero percent opacity is completely invisible and 100 percent is fully opaque. The former appears white on an alpha channel in QuarkXPress and the latter looks like a solid burgundy.

Mask channels are similar to alpha channels, but they're usually created by using Photoshop's Quick Mask mode or by adding a layer mask. XPress 7 likes to color mask channels in a warm brown.

When you import a PSD containing alpha or mask channels, QuarkXPress treats them like spot color channels. New swatches named after the channels are added to the Colors palette automatically, and the channels appear on the PSD Import palette's Channels tab. You can turn them on or off, map them to other colors, and even change their shade and solidity values through the Channel Options dialog box. This, of course, makes them excellent candidates to be used as varnish and die plates, and even better for use in defining runarounds (see more on text runarounds in Chapter 12, *Text Meets Graphics*) and clipping paths (see the section "Clipping Paths" later in this chapter).

Paths

The third tab on the PSD Import palette is the Paths tab (see Figure 11-9). Any paths added to the PSD within Photoshop are shown on this tab. Notice that there's no eyeball icon beside path names. Instead of a visibility column there are two columns—Runaround and Clipping Path. Click in the first column beside a path to instantly set the runaround in the shape of the path (see more on text runarounds in Chapter 12, *Text Meets Graphics*). The next column in is the Clipping Path column (see the very next section to learn about clipping paths). A path in the PSD can be turned into the image's clipping path just by clicking in that one column. Using the Paths tab of the PSD Import palette to apply runarounds and clipping paths is *much* faster than using the respective tabs in the Modify dialog. (This is yet another of my many arguments for replacing most of your TIFF and EPS images with PSDs.)

Figure 11-9
The PSD Import palette Paths
tab shows any paths created
in Photoshop.

CLIPPING PATHS

A clipping path is a mathematically based PostScript path, much like other Bézier lines in QuarkXPress, Illustrator, or FreeHand. However, a clipping path acts like a pair of scissors, cutting out an image in any shape you want. Clipping an image is actually the same as cropping it, but because QuarkXPress makes a distinction, I will, too: The shape of a picture box crops the picture, but the Clipping feature clips it. You can use clipping and cropping together or alone. Let's see how.

Applying a Clipping Path

Clipping cuts part of a picture from the rest. For example, if you're working with the image of a trashcan set against a white background, you may want to clip out the featureless white background. You can begin applying a clipping path very easily in the Clipping tab of the Modify dialog box or on the Measurements palette's Clipping tab (see Figure 11-10). I'll focus on the Clipping tab of the Modify dialog box because, though less convenient than the Measurements palette, the fields and controls are better labeled in the former.

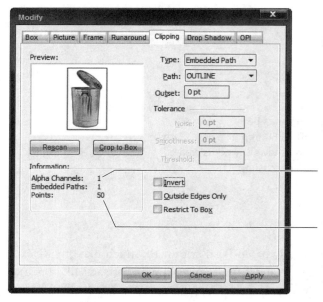

This shows you how many embedded paths and alpha channels are available in the image.

The higher the number of points on the clipping path, the longer the image will typically take to print. Fifty points is a very low number, and the clipping path will print quickly.

Figure 11-10 Specifying a clipping path

The Clipping tab may look confusing at first, but it's really pretty basic once you get the hang of it. The most important feature in this dialog box is the Type popup menu, which lets you choose one of five clipping path options: Item, Embedded Path, Alpha Channel, Non-White Areas, and Picture Bounds.

Item. When you select Item from the Type popup menu (this is the default setting for most pictures), QuarkXPress sets the clipping path to be the same as the cropping path, which is the area of the box in which the picture resides. In other words, this is just like turning off the Clipping feature so that XPress just crops the picture, the way it always has.

Embedded Path. Adobe Photoshop lets you draw and save Bézier paths within its images. XPress is smart enough to see and read those paths in TIFF, EPS, JPEG, and PSD images, and lets you choose one of them as your clipping path. This turns out to be incredibly useful. Let's say you have a picture of three butterflies set against a plain white background. You can create several paths in Photoshop, each of which "cuts out" one butterfly. When you get the image into XPress, you can choose which butterfly looks best in your design (see Figure 11-11).

Alpha Channel. When the Type popup menu is set to Alpha Channel, XPress lets you convert one of the image's alpha channels, mask channels, and even spot channels into a clipping path (see Figure 11-12). The problem is that selections and masks and alpha and spot channels in Photoshop can have soft anti-aliased or feathered edges, and clipping paths cannot, so QuarkXPress has to convert soft edges into hard-edged Bézier paths. (See "Tolerance," later in this chapter for a description of how it does this.)

Note that if you want to include alpha channels in images bound for XPress, you have to use PSD or TIFF images.

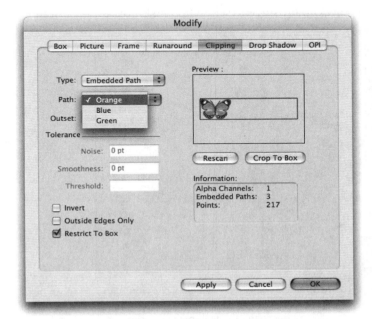

Figure 11-11
Choosing an
embedded path

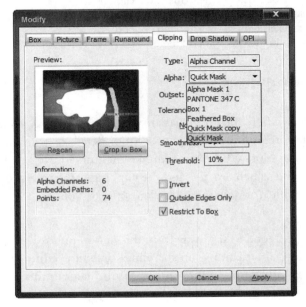

Figure 11-12
Using an alpha channel as a clipping
path—in this case, the channel created
by using Photoshop's Quick Mask mode

Non-White Areas. If your image doesn't have a suitable alpha, mask, or spot channel, or an embedded path, XPress still lets you build a clipping path on the fly based on the non-white areas of the image. If you choose Non-White Areas from the Type popup menu, XPress searches through the picture for white or near-white pixels to clip out, leaving the pixels that are not near-white (see Figure 11-13). You even have the choice to clip out white pixels inside the image—like the gap between the fingers (see "Clipping Options," later in this chapter).

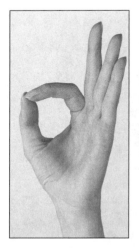 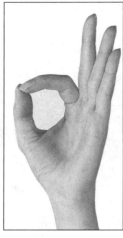 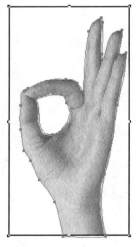

The near-white pixels in the background get clipped out.

The near-white pixels between the fingers are retained because they're surrounded by nonwhite pixels (you have the option to clip these or not).

The final clipping path in QuarkXPress. You can make the clipping path visible in the Edit submenu under the Item menu.

Figure 11-13 Clipping out the white pixels

This option works reasonably well where the image has crisp edges and is on a clean, white background. If the edges of the foreground image have a lot of detail, or if the image is colored similar to the background, Non-White Areas, unlike the human eye, can't figure out which details are important and which are not, and the clipping path suffers for it. Of course, if your image is not on a white (or near-white) background, this option doesn't help much at all.

In fact, to be really honest about it, I tend to shy away from this option unless I'm trying to build a quick comp for a client or if I'm planning on spending some time editing the clipping path (see "Clipping Caveats" and "Editing the Clipping Path," later in this section).

Picture Bounds. Selecting Picture Bounds is second in simplicity only to the Item option on the Type popup menu. Bitmapped images are always rectangular, so selecting Picture Bounds sets the picture's clipping path to the four sides of the picture. If the picture box is the same size as the picture, then this option has the same effect as selecting Item. The primary difference is that you have the option to inset or outset the clipping path from the picture's edge. Use negative numbers in the Top, Left, Bottom, and Right fields to inset the path (make the path smaller than the image); use positive numbers to outset the path (make it larger than the image).

I find Picture Bounds most useful when I need to crop off a portion of one or more sides of the image with great precision. For instance, if you know that you want to shave off 1.5 points from the bottom of a picture, you can set the clipping type to Picture Bounds and type "-1.5pt" into the Bottom field.

> **Tip: Clipping TIFFs Versus EPSs.** XPress has more control over clipping PSDs and TIFFs than EPS files. If you need to use an EPS file for some reason, and you've built paths in Photoshop, don't tell Photoshop to use one of those paths as a clipping path; if you later change your mind and choose a different clipping path in XPress (using the Embedded Path option), XPress won't be able to replace the built-in clipping path with your choice.

Clipping Caveats

Before I go any further in my discussion of clipping paths, I need to point out a major problem: You can't make good decisions about clipping by looking at a 72-dpi representation of your high-resolution image. It's like a doctor doing brain surgery on the day she forgot to wear her glasses.

Fortunately, XPress 7 lets you increase an image's screen preview resolution. Turn on Full Res Previews from the View menu, and then Full Resolution from the Preview Resolution submenu (under the Item menu or in the Context menu). This works for images with up to 800 pixels per inch, so if you have a very high-resolution image (or an image that has been shrunk, resulting in higher effective resolution), you might still get some fuzziness. However, Full Resolution lets you edit and view clipping paths while you're zoomed way in, so you can see which pixels are going to be clipped out.

The upshot is that in the next two sections, I'm going to discuss how you can change the various clipping paths XPress offers you, and even how to draw your own. But you had better take these controls with a grain of salt unless you're sure that you're looking at your image's real pixels. To be honest, I still *much* prefer to create and edit clipping paths in Photoshop.

Clipping Options

You can control the precision with which XPress builds your clipping paths using various controls on the Clipping tab of the Modify dialog box or Measurements palette.

Outset. The Outset field lets you spread or choke—enlarge or reduce—the clipping path. It's available when the Type popup menu is set to Embedded Path, Alpha Channel, or Non-White Areas. Positive values increase the outset field's size; negative values decrease it (see Figure 11-14).

Outset of 4 points (Much larger than you'd typically use)

Outset of -4 points

Figure 11-14 Outset

Typically you want to adjust this by only a very small amount, or else strange things start happening to your clipping path. For instance, if it's clear that the background color of the image is showing up as a halo around the clipped image, you might set the Outset value to -.5 point to reduce the size of the path by about one pixel (the exact measurement-to-pixel amount depends entirely on the image's resolution, of course). If you still have a halo, try increasing the negative outset value in half point increments. Similarly, setting Outset to positive 1 point or so might be just enough to restore some edge detail cut out by a hard-edged path.

Tolerance. The three Tolerance settings help XPress figure out which pixels should be included in a path and how smooth the path should be. Though these settings are available for clipping types of Embedded Path, Alpha Channel, and Non-White Areas, they're primarily important when you ask for a path based on an alpha channel or a non-white area.

- **Noise.** Many people assume that Noise refers to how gritty or dirty the bitmapped image is, and it does, in an indirect way. If there is a lot of "grit" in the image or the alpha channel, XPress may capture it in the form of tiny, independent clipping paths (see Figure 11-15). The Noise setting looks for these stray clipping paths. If you set this to 10 points, then the program deletes any clipping path smaller than 10 points in diameter. While most images don't contain enough tiny stray pixels to generate tiny clipping paths like this, some do, especially those that have lots of edge detail (like wispy hair or a fuzzy sweater). In these cases, judicious use of the Noise setting becomes indispensable.

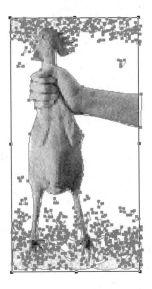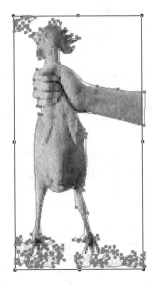

By changing the Noise setting from 4 points to 10 points, many of the small, independent clipping paths are removed.

Figure 11-15
The Noise setting

- **Smoothness.** The Smoothness setting lets you tell XPress how much care to take when it makes your clipping path for you (this setting only applies if you choose Alpha Channel or Non-White Areas). The lower the Smoothness value, the more precisely XPress matches the clipping path to the high-resolution data. The problem is that to get greater precision, XPress must place more points on the clipping path. A setting of zero tells QuarkXPress to match the pixel boundaries of the image as closely as it can, but you may get thousands of points on your clipping path. Typically, the more points on the path, the harder it is for the printer to process the image and the slower the page prints (in some cases, the page may not print at all).

  It's tempting to always use low Smoothness values, because it feels like you're being more true to the image, but you often get worse results than if you use a value of 5 or 10 or even higher (see Figure 11-16). Each image is different and must be evaluated independently.

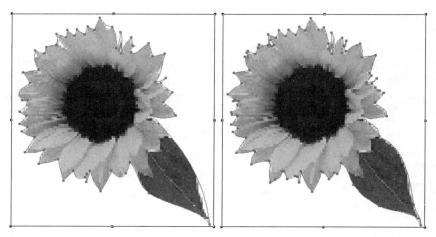

As the Smoothness value decreases, XPress adds more points to the path, and the clipping path more successfully traces the image.

Figure 11-16 The Smoothness setting

- **Threshold.** The Threshold setting is perhaps the most important control in the Tolerance area of the Clipping tab. Threshold is like a volume knob for what is and is not included when XPress builds a clipping path (this is only applicable for the Alpha Channel and Non-White Areas clipping types). When you have Non-White Areas selected, XPress clips out every pixel that is fully white plus any non-white pixel that is shaded up to the Threshold value (it actually uses a luminance value based on the RGB data, but that's not worth worrying about most of the time). For instance, the default setting of 10 percent tells XPress that an 8-percent-gray pixel should get clipped out, but a 15-percent-gray pixel should not.

  When you have Alpha Channel selected, Threshold acts in the opposite manner: XPress clips out the black pixels, plus any pixel within the Threshold value from black—so with a 10-percent Threshold, a 95-percent-gray pixel drops out, but an 85-percent-gray pixel does not. With alpha channels, I usually set Threshold to between 40 and 60 percent.

It appears that XPress takes the three Tolerance settings into consideration like this: First it applies the Threshold value to the alpha channel or the image, then it finds a Bézier clipping path based on the Smoothness value, and finally, it drops out stray paths based on the Noise setting. And by no accident, this is the best way for you to control the clipping path as well.

1. Given that the default Tolerance settings will rarely create a clipping path that's perfect for your needs, first adjust the Threshold value until the path is approximately the shape you want in the Preview area of the Modify dialog box.

2. Next, set the Smoothness value, watching the number of points in the Information section of the dialog box. At this point, click Apply to see the clipping effect on the actual image.

3. If you see that there are tiny stray clipping paths still extant, kill them off by increasing the Noise setting.

4. Finally, if the clipping path is still not "just right," you can edit it by hand (see "Editing the Clipping Path," later in this section).

Invert. The Invert checkbox performs a very simple trick: it switches what is and what is not clipped out (see Figure 11-17). You probably won't use this trick often, but it makes for great custom masks or frames to place over other picture boxes.

Figure 11-17
Inverting a clipping path

Outside Edges Only. The hole in a doughnut, the spaces between the wires in a whisk, the keyhole in a door—you must make a decision as to whether or not these should be clipped out. Once you've made that decision, choose whether to use the Outside Edges Only option (see Figure 11-18). When this checkbox is turned on, XPress removes any clipping paths that are surrounded by other clipping paths; when it's off you can have holes where they belong.

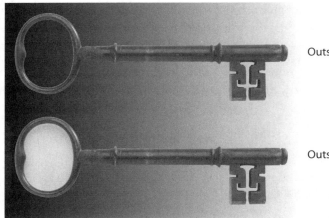

Outside Edges Only turned off

Outside Edges Only turned on

Figure 11-18 Outside Edges Only

Restrict To Box. So your art director says, "Crop this picture of a bag of groceries inside a box with a 3-point black border so the bread sticks out the top of the frame" (see Figure 11-19). You blink, nod your head, and wander off in a daze, wondering how to get this effect. Multiple picture boxes? Nope. There's an easier way.

Figure 11-19
Restrict To Box

Restrict To Box on   Restrict To Box off

When you turn off the Restrict To Box checkbox, it's like you're disabling cropping in the picture box; all you're left with is the clipping. It lets you move one or more sides of the picture outside the boundaries of its picture box. In fact, you can move the entire picture out of its box (though you can't delete the box). See "Tip: Cropping and Unrestricting," below, for a step-by-step walk-through to help you achieve this effect. Before that, however, there's one more option on the Clipping tab I need to explain.

Crop To Box. The Crop To Box button also performs a very simple operation: it pares down any portion of your clipping path that extends beyond the borders of the picture box. The result is a clipping path that extends only as far as the edges of the picture box. When Restrict To Box is turned on, this has no effect at all. But when this option is off, pressing Crop To Box can help you create all kinds of cool effects (see "Tip: Cropping and Unrestricting," below).

Note that if you later go back and change the size of your picture box, the clipping path does not update automatically. You may need to click the Rescan button, which tells XPress to reset the clipping path to the current settings on the Clipping tab of the Modify dialog box. Then you can use Crop To Box again.

> **Tip: Cropping and Unrestricting.** As promised, here's how to achieve the effect of a clipped image escaping its picture box (see Figure 11-20).
>
> 1. Choose a clipping path that includes all the parts of the image you want to be visible, even if it contains more of the foreground image than you ultimately want to show. For instance, in the image I'm using, the clipping path includes the stem and base of the cocktail glass though I don't want them in the final version.
>
> 2. Set the size of the picture box so that it crops out the parts of the image you want to crop out but leaves the other parts visible. You can see that I've cropped the stem and base.
>
> 3. On the Clipping tab of the Modify dialog box, click the Crop To Box button and turn off Restrict To Box. Click OK to leave this dialog box.
>
> 4. Now change the size of the picture box as if cropping the image (which, of course, it now won't) to achieve the final effect. Set a fill or frame to really show off the effect.
>
> Note that step 2 might require more than just resizing the picture box. You may actually have to edit the shape of the picture box (select Shape from the Edit submenu, under the Item menu; press Shift-F4 on the Macintosh, or press F10 in Windows) so that the parts of the image you want to be visible are showing.

Figure 11-20 Cropping and unrestricting

Crop the image so that the parts you want visible are inside the box.

Here is the same image but with the clipping path made visible.

After you click Crop To Box and turn off Restrict To Box…

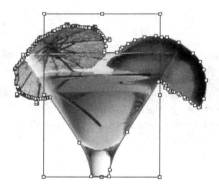

…you can change the picture box's size so that it crops in some places and clips in others.

Add a fill or frame to complete the effect.

Editing the Clipping Path

Okay, so you've cajoled the perfect clipping path out of XPress's (or Photoshop's) clipping tools, and then you print the image and realize that it's not perfect after all. Fortunately, you can manually edit the Bézier curves and points on a clipping path. Note that you have to start with a clipping path that is already there; XPress still doesn't let you draw a path from scratch.

The first step in editing a clipping path is to make it visible, which you can do by selecting Clipping Path from the Edit submenu (under the Item menu), or by pressing Shift-Option-F4 (Macintosh) or Ctrl-Shift-F10 (Windows). Now you can edit the clipping path to your heart's content, using the same techniques that work on regular Bézier boxes and lines (see Chapter 3, *Working with Items*).

- You can drag a point or a segment between points.

- You can add or remove points by holding down the Option/Alt key.

- You can use keystrokes or the Measurements palette to adjust the position of points or control handles.

Unfortunately, you'll run into a lot of things you wish you could do, but can't. For example, you can't use the Merge or Split features. You can't draw a new section of a clipping path from scratch or even "pinch off" a portion of a clipping path. I'm hoping that the folks at Quark will give us more functionality someday, but for now, we're limited to simple editing.

User-Edited Path. It's important to remember that editing an image's clipping path does not change the image on disk at all. Even though XPress lets you edit an embedded clipping path that was built in Photoshop, when you go back to Photoshop, the path hasn't changed. Instead, as soon as you edit the path, the Type popup menu on the Clipping tab changes to User-Edited Path. You can still change the path's Outset value and use the Crop To Box feature (see "Clipping Options," earlier in this section), but that's about it.

> **Tip: Watch When You Drag.** *One of the most frustrating parts of editing clipping paths (or Bézier boxes, for that matter) is dragging a point or a segment on the path when you meant to use the Grabber Hand. Or clicking on a point when you were just trying to zoom in or out. There's really nothing you can do about this except to be vigilant about where you're clicking, and to keep one hand on the Command/Ctrl-Z (Undo) keys.*

> **Tip: Changing Clipping Colors.** *When you edit a clipping path, its default onscreen color is green (it's also green in the Preview area of the Modify dialog box). Is it by chance that guides are also green? Nope. If you change the Ruler color (in Application Preferences), the clipping path color changes, too. When the edges of your image are also green, changing the clipping path to hot pink makes the path stand out.*

By the way, Quark's documentation says you can change the blue boundary in the Preview area—the one that signals the edge of the picture's box—by changing the Margin color in Application Preferences. At the time of this writing, that doesn't work—and hasn't for the last several versions of QuarkXPress. Maybe in QuarkXPress 8 or 9?

Clipping Without a Clipping Path

Not too far back in this chapter I mentioned that PSD images that include masks could be useful for clipping paths. Actually, they're best used as *replacements* for clipping paths.

Clipping paths are, by definition, hard edged; you can't have feathered edges that blend smoothly into other objects. Masks on the other hand take full advantage of alpha transparency, and they're usually less work to get just right (see Figure 11-21). Want a feathered edge? You got it. Want half the picture 50 percent opaque while the other half is fully opaque? No problem.

With a mask, this…

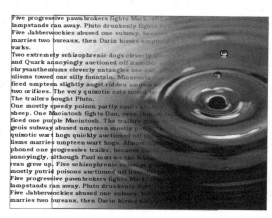

…can become this.

Figure 11-21
Clip with full transparency
support thanks to masks

The trick is to use PSD images and to create masks in Photoshop using the august image editor's Quick Mask mode, layer masks, or varied selection tools. Once you create a mask channel using one of these means and save the PSD, it can be imported into QuarkXPress and the mask channel used in place of a clipping path, with much better results. Masks, for one thing, can be in any shape—you could write your name in flowing Elizabethan script and use that as a mask, making an Elizabethan script-shaped picture in XPress.

After importing a PSD image containing a mask, open the picture's Modify dialog box from the Item menu or by pressing Command/Ctrl-M. Instead of going to the Clipping tab, go to the Picture tab (see Figure 11-22). In the bottom left, just above the thumbnail preview of the picture, is the Mask Channel drop-down menu. Select a channel from the menu and watch XPress clip the picture to fit within the shape of the channel. That's it. Clipping is done. There are no controls to mess with, no clipping path to edit. If the mask you choose contains alpha transparency—for example, a feathered edge—the picture will reflect that transparency and blend with objects behind it.

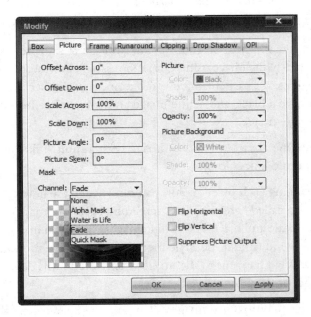

Figure 11-22
On the Picture tab of the Modify dialog box, use mask channels to clip.

Now that QuarkXPress 7 understands transparency and masks, I hardly ever bother with the Clipping tab any more. It's so much easier and more precise to draw in Photoshop the area of the image I want to show, save that selection to a mask, and use the mask to clip the image in XPress. In fact, odds are good that I'd have to make selections in Photoshop anyway just to get the image drawn, so at that point most of the work of mask-based clipping is done already. The only thing missing is saving my selection as a mask channel and telling XPress to use that instead of clipping.

THE STYLE MENU

Chapter 10, *Pictures,* describes how you can manipulate the "layout" of the picture in the picture box, including cropping, rotating, skewing, and moving the image. These effects are controlled from the Measurements palette or the Modify dialog box. Here I talk primarily about the image modification possibilities using features from the Style menu. Remember that you can combine both image manipulation techniques (rotating, changing the shape and size, and so on) and image modification techniques (changing the grayscale or color parameters, and so on) to create fascinating effects in your page layout.

> **Tip: When the Style Menu Is Gray.** *If the items on the Style menu are grayed out, you have either imported an EPS (or some other file format that XPress cannot modify), or the Color TIFFs setting in the Display panel of the Preferences dialog box isn't set to 8-bit. Note that you have to change the Preference before you import the image—changing it has no effect on images you've already imported. If the menu is still grayed out, you may not have the Item tool or the Content tool selected, or you may not have the image's picture box selected. If still none of these things work, I can only suggest plugging in your computer.*

Color. I cover color fully in Chapter 14, *Color.* So at this point, suffice it to say that changing the color of a grayscale or black-and-white image using QuarkXPress's Color feature replaces all black (or gray) samples with ones of a particular color. You cannot colorize a color image in XPress. For example, if you have a black-and-white image and you change the color to red, you then have a red-and-white image.

You can even create a "fake duotone" by colorizing an image with a multi-ink color (see Chapter 14, *Color,* for more on multi-ink colors).

Shade. In the same spirit as changing each pixel's color, you can change the gray value for each pixel in the image (this is also called "ghosting" or "screening back" an image). Again, this currently works only for grayscale and black-and-white images. To tint an image, select a percentage from the Shade submenu (under the Style menu) or change the tint value for the image on the Colors palette. What happens to the image when you do this depends on whether you're working with flat or deep bitmapped images.

- **Flat bitmaps.** With flat, bilevel, bitmapped images, changing the Shade alters the printed output; every black pixel in your graphic prints gray.

- **Deep bitmaps.** When you set a shade for a grayscale image in the Style menu XPress multiplies that shade for each sample point. A 50-percent shade of a 100-percent-black sample point is 50 percent; 50 percent of a 60-percent sample is 30 percent, and so on.

Opacity. As you'll learn in Chapter 14, *Color*, picture opacity can be changed on the Colors palette. The Opacity submenu on the Style menu is another place to change the picture's transparency level. The only difference between the two locations is that on the Colors palette you can type a specific percentage into the Opacity field, whereas the Opacity menu (Style > Opacity) offers only 10 percent increments of opacity.

> *Tip: Making Your Grayscale Picture Transparent. If you've been a fan of Real World QuarkXPress for a while, you may recall that the last couple of editions of this book included several pages of techniques for making grayscale TIFFs transparent or semitransparent. With QuarkXPress 7, none of those workaround techniques is necessary—there's actual transparency available now with the Opacity setting on the Style menu and Colors palette.*

Invert. Selecting Invert from the Style menu (or typing Command/Ctrl-Shift-hyphen) inverts all tone and color information in an image (see Chapter 14, *Color*, for more information on color models). What was 10-percent black becomes 90-percent black, what was 20-percent blue becomes 20-percent yellow, and so on.

> *Tip: More Negative Images. Here's another way to invert an image: Color it white. This is often not only easier, but also more desirable. For example, if you want a white image on a blue background, you can select the picture box with the Content tool, change the shade of the picture to zero percent (or change the color to White in either the Colors palette or the Style menu), then change the background color to some shade of Blue (such as 100 percent).*

> *Tip: Clone and Ghost. All the tools I've discussed so far apply to the entire image. How can you ghost back or colorize just a portion of an image? As usual, there's a trick (see Figure 11-23).*

The original image   A clone of the picture box, cropped differently and with a different contrast

Figure 11-23 Changing one part of an image by cloning and adjusting contrast

Tip continues on next page

1. *Select the picture box and use Step and Repeat (from the Item menu) to make one duplicate with both Horizontal and Vertical offsets set to zero. (I call this "cloning" the box.)*

2. *Crop the duplicate image down by changing the size or shape of the picture box. You can do this by dragging its corner or side handles, changing its shape from the Shape submenu (under the Item menu), or—if it's a Bézier box—altering the points on the edge of the box. Note that when you do this, you don't move the picture within the box at all, so the two pictures stay in registration.*

   Instead of (or in addition to) cropping, you can change the duplicate box's clipping path (see "Clipping Paths," earlier in this chapter).

3. *Apply the effect you want either to the duplicate or to the original image.*

There are all kinds of variations on this tip. For instance, let's say you have a color TIFF in the picture box. After cloning the box in step 1, you can apply a Desaturate adjustment (see "Picture Effects," further on in this chapter). Now when you change the cropping of the box or change the image's clipping, one portion of the picture is grayscale.

HALFTONES

Let's face it. Every high-resolution imagesetter on the market prints only in black and white. And many laser printers still print only in black and white. There's clearly a lot to be said for black and white. What you need to realize, however, is that black and white is not gray. Real laser printers don't print gray (at least not the ones I'm going to talk about).

So how do I get a picture with grays in it into the computer and out onto paper? The answer is halftones. The magic of halftoning is that different levels of gray are represented by different-sized spots, which, when printed closely together, fool the eye into seeing the tints where there is, in reality, only black and white.

Take a look at any grayscale photograph in a local newspaper, and it's easy to see the halftoning. Notice that the spacing of the spots doesn't change; only their size changes—large spots in dark areas and small spots in light areas.

Glenn Fleishman, Steve Roth, and David Blatner talk about halftones in great detail in their book, *Real World Scanning and Halftones*. However, let's take a quick overview here of the elements that make up digital halftones, just in case you don't have that book yet.

Dots. A laser printer prints pages by placing square black dots on a white page. Each and every dot on a 300-dpi printer is 1/300 inch in diameter (or thereabouts). That's pretty small, but it's enormous compared with what you can achieve on a high-resolution image-setter, where each dot is about 1/3000 inch (almost too small for the human eye to see). The primary factor with the size of the dot is the *resolution* of the printer (how many dots per inch it can print).

Spots. As I said before, a halftone is made up of spots of varying sizes. On a black-and-white laser printer or imagesetter, these spots are created by bunching together anywhere between one and 65,000 printer dots. They can be of different shapes and, to be redundant over and over again, different sizes. I discuss several different types of spots later in the chapter.

Screen frequency. In the traditional halftoning process, a mesh screen is placed in front of the photograph to create the desired effect of spots all in rows. Keeping that process in mind can help you understand this concept. The *screen frequency* of a halftone is set by the mesh of the screen, and is defined as the number of these rows per inch (or per centimeter, if you think in metric). The lower the screen frequency, the coarser the image looks. The higher the screen frequency, the finer the image looks (see Figure 11-24).

20 lpi   70 lpi   133 lpi

Figure 11-24 Various screen frequencies

To complicate issues a bit, the screen frequency of a halftone is often called its "line screen." Whatever you call it, it's still calculated in the number of lines per inch (lpi). See Table 11-1 for information about when to use a particular screen frequency.

Table 11-1 Screen frequencies to use for different printing conditions

Output	Lines per inch (lpi)	Output	Lines per inch (lpi)
Photocopier	50–90 lpi	Direct-mail pieces	110–150 lpi
Newspaper quality	60–85 lpi	Magazine quality	133–175 lpi
Quick-print printer	85–110 lpi	Art book	175–300 lpi

Tip: Gray Levels in Your Halftones. *Each halftone spot is made up of tiny dots, and different gray levels are produced by turning dots on and off (in a 10-percent tint, 10 percent of the dots within a spot's cell are turned on). Okay, now remember that the lower the screen frequency, the bigger the spot, and more dots are used per spot. The higher the frequency, the fewer dots used. Thus, the higher the screen frequency, the fewer possibilities for levels of gray there are.*

This is why you may get posterization when an image is printed on a desktop laser printer (where there may only be 100 printer dots per halftone cell) but not on an imagesetter (where there may be many more dots per cell).

To find out how many levels of gray you can get, divide the resolution by the screen frequency, square it, and add one. For example, you can get 92 levels of gray when you print a 133-line screen at 1,270 dpi (1,270/133)^2+1), but only six levels of gray when you print a 133-line screen at 300 dpi (300/133)^2+1). The output is clearly posterized. To get 92 levels of gray on a 300-dpi laser printer, you would need to print at 30 lines per inch! It's an unfortunate fact, but this is one of the trade-offs inherent in digital halftoning.

Angle. The halftone screen doesn't have to be horizontal or vertical—in fact, it rarely is. It's normally rotated to different angles (see Figure 11-25), which are used in both special-effects halftoning and color separation (see Chapter 15, *Printing*). Zero and 180 degrees are horizontal, 90 and 270 degrees are vertical (some types of spots look the same at all four of these angles, and others look different when rotated). A 45-degree angle is most common because it is the least distracting to the eye. Remember that changing the angle of the halftone screen doesn't change the angle of the picture itself!

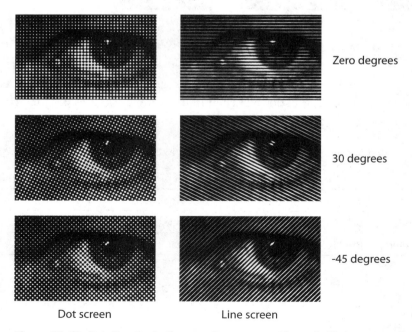

Zero degrees

30 degrees

-45 degrees

Dot screen   Line screen

Figure 11-25 Rotating the halftone screen to zero-, 30-, and -45-degree angles

Making Halftones Work for You

Once again, just to be clear: Anything that contains gray requires halftoning. Even a simple box or block of text with a 10-percent tint comes out as a halftone. There's no other way to render grays on a black-and-white output device.

You don't have to do anything special to a bitmapped image to make it print as a halftone; XPress has built-in defaults for halftone screen, angle, and spot shape. However, if you want to override those values for a single *grayscale* bitmapped image, you can select the picture box and choose Halftone from the Style menu (or press Command/Ctrl-Shift-H; see Figure 11-26).

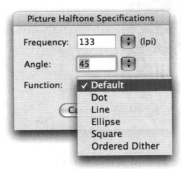

Figure 11-26
Picture Halftone Specifications dialog box

Following is an in-depth description of these settings.

Frequency. My dream is to print out a halftone image with a screen frequency of one, with each spot having a diameter of 1 inch. I don't have a particular reason for this; I just think it would be neat. Unfortunately, QuarkXPress won't accept any value under 15. The upper range of 400 lpi is less of an inconvenience, though you may never have the urge to approach either of these limits. Select the screen frequency you want by typing it in, or just choose a preset value from the popup menu. Choose Default to defer to the setting assigned in the Page Setup dialog box.

Angle. I discussed angles above, and I'll discuss them again in Chapter 15, *Printing,* when I talk about color separations, so I won't discuss them here. Just type in a number from zero to 360 (or zero to -360, if you think backwards).

Function. Function refers to the spot shape. You have five shapes to choose from (see Figure 11-27).

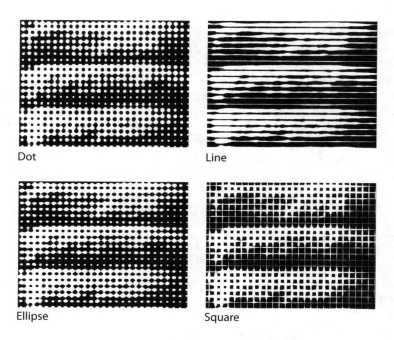

Dot   Line

Ellipse   Square

Figure 11-27 Various halftone spot shapes (patterns)

- **Dot pattern.** This is the round spot that you see in almost all output. At low tint values, it's a round black spot. As the tint value increases, it gets larger. At 50 percent, it changes to a square. At higher values, it inverts to a progressively smaller white spot.

- **Line pattern.** Straight-line screens seem to go in and out of fashion, but they're always good for waking up your audience and, if you use too low a line screen, for making eyeballs fall out. The line is thick at high tint values and thin at low values.

- **Ellipse pattern.** No, this is not a traditional elliptical spot. Printers have used elliptical spots for years and customers have grown accustomed to asking for them by this name, even though the shape of the spot is more of a rounded-corner diamond. QuarkXPress creates an oval spot.

- **Square pattern.** Here's another funky special-effect spot which may come in handy some day. Each spot is square: Lower tint values are little squares, higher values are big squares. Try really coarse screen frequencies for this one.

- **Ordered Dither pattern.** This spot shape is a dither pattern optimized for printing on laser printers. Because the pattern adjusts to the resolution of the laser printer, you shouldn't use this if you're planning on printing to an imagesetter (you'd get a dither at over 1000 dots per inch, which could not be reproduced). The Ordered Dither pattern is also not optimal for offset printing.

When should you use this? Quark maintains that you should use it when you are printing to a QuickDraw (non-PostScript) laser printer for making multiple copies on a photocopier. Don't even bother if you have a PostScript printer; it looks terrible. Well, I guess it's nice to have the option.

Display Halftoning option. While XPress 3 gave you the option of displaying your custom halftone on screen, you can no longer do this. Therefore, you just have to remember that your image has custom halftoning information. Why did they take it out? I wish I knew.

> *Tip: Beware of Screen Swapping. Note that specifying custom halftones in XPress may not work when you're printing to an imagesetter that automatically replaces halftone screens (most do these days). For instance, Balanced Screens technology may automatically swap your custom screen with one that it thinks you should use. If this is the case, ask how your service bureau can shut off the screen swapping.*

PICTURE EFFECTS

Among the most exciting new features of QuarkXPress 7 are the Picture Effects that bring Photoshop-like image adjustments (Levels, Curves, Brightness/Contrast, and more) and special effects filters (Gaussian Blur, Edge Detection, Embossing Effects, and more) directly into XPress.

Unless you're deliberately trying to achieve a muddied look, every image that you scan requires tonal correction, sharpening, and if it's a color image, color correction. Even synthetic pictures created with a painting program may require these adjustments. Hands down, the place to do these things is in an image-editing program like Adobe Photoshop, not in a layout application such as QuarkXPress. Nonetheless, XPress 7 gives you advanced image-editing controls that are, on their own, almost on par with the same adjustments and filters in Photoshop. Now, if you're Photoshop bereft or Photoshop challenged, or want to tweak a picture in context without making exact copies of the image file, you can do a tremendous amount of advanced image manipulation directly in QuarkXPress.

Before we get into the specifics (and, of course, descriptions of all the adjustments and effects), it's critical that you recognize the biggest difference between manipulating pictures in Photoshop and XPress. Changing an image in Photoshop and saving it for import into QuarkXPress *saves* your manipulations; they become part of the image file saved on disk. The same image, bearing all the same adjustments and effects, can be used in other XPress projects and even other applications. Moreover, if your XPress project file becomes corrupted and unusable, the image file isn't affected. By contrast, using QuarkXPress 7's Picture Effects only applies to the single instance of the picture on the page. Adjustments and filters are not written back to the graphic file on disk, cannot be used outside of XPress (actually they can; see "Tip: Using Picture Effects Pictures in Other Applications," below), and will be lost if the project file is corrupted or damaged.

Now that I've thoroughly scared you, allow me to point out why you *would* want to use the QuarkXPress Picture Effects. As I mentioned, some people don't have recent versions of Photoshop, others aren't Photoshop gurus and prefer to stay in XPress. (Note: So similar are the XPress Picture Effects to their Photoshop counterparts that when you become comfortable with one, you'll be just as comfortable with the other.) Even if you are a Photoshop whiz, there are a couple of good reasons to manipulate pictures directly in XPress.

First, it's faster. If you're already working in XPress, why take the time to launch Photoshop, find and open the image, apply a quick change, save the file and close Photoshop, and then return to XPress and update the picture when you could make the same change directly in XPress? It's faster and easier to stay in XPress, perform the image change, and move on to the next step in laying out the project.

The second reason, the one that has me, someone extremely comfortable with Photoshop, performing many image adjustments directly in QuarkXPress, is the variety factor. You can take a single picture and easily turn it into a hundred slightly different versions—without having to worry about keeping track of one hundred separate image files. You can place a picture and try out various effects live on the page, watching the interaction between the picture and its surroundings, as you apply and adjust different settings and filter effects. For example, you could place a grayscale image and then instantly see how it would look in context with a little less contrast, more white values, or even as a 1-bit black-and-white image (see Figure 11-28).

The point I'm making here is this: Don't be afraid to use Picture Effects; just be aware of the trade-offs involved in choosing to adjust an image in either XPress or Photoshop.

> **Tip: Using Picture Effects Pictures in Other Applications.** Above I noted that using Picture Effects doesn't change the actual picture file, that the results of image changes in QuarkXPress can't be used outside of XPress. Technically, that's still true—QuarkXPress will not make changes to the original image file. You can, however, export the image—with Picture Effects—from XPress to a new graphic file and even replace the original with the exported image. If you recall, I talked about that back in Chapter 10, Pictures, in the section on exporting pictures.

Figure 11-28 Although Photoshop is king of the image effects, XPress lets you modify images in context.

Tip: Committing Picture Effects During Collect for Output. *When you collect your project for output, in the Collect for Output dialog box, there are two tabs: Collect for Output, which offers the usual options, and Vista, as in QuarkVista, aka Picture Effects. The Vista tab has a single option, a checkbox labeled Render Picture Alterations. Turning on that box is like going through and exporting all the pictures with effects, creating new graphic files built from the combination of original image and Picture Effects. For example, if you have applied the Desaturate adjustment to a color picture, thus rendering it grayscale in the layout, XPress will create a new image file that really is grayscale during the Collect for Output process.*

Picture Effects Palette

There are 12 adjustment effects and 12 filter effects available in QuarkXPress 7's Picture Effects. You'll find them on the Picture Effects submenu at the bottom of the Style menu (see Figure 11-29), but I never use that submenu. Instead, I like to use the Picture Effects palette, because it lets me see exactly what adjustments and filters are active on my picture and to see their individual settings (see Figure 11-30). There's just more information there than on the Style menu version, and it's easier to make changes.

Along the top of the palette are six buttons.

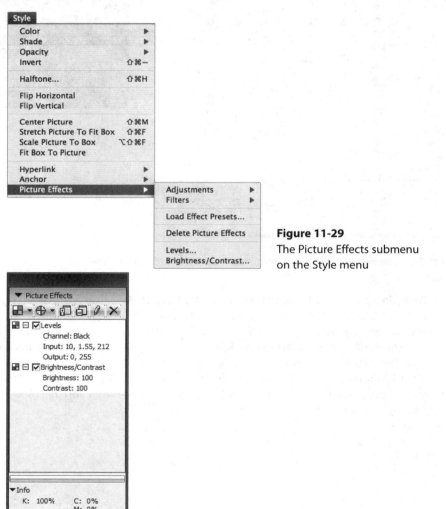

Figure 11-29
The Picture Effects submenu
on the Style menu

Figure 11-30
The Picture Effects palette

Adjustments. Clicking the Adjustments button reveals a menu containing the 12 adjustment picture effects (see the "Adjustment Effects" section next). Select an effect from the menu to open a dialog box in which you can configure the adjustment's options. Note: Adjustments and filters without an ellipse (…) after the name do not have dialog boxes; selecting one of these immediately applies the effect without offering the options to configure.

Filters. On this menu are all the special-effect filters (see the section on "Filter Effects" later in this chapter). Like adjustment effects, many filter effects have options dialog boxes where you can control the effect.

Load Preset and Save Preset. If you want to apply the same Picture Effects to multiple pictures, you can either work through lunch manually re-creating your effects over and over, or you can do it once, save the effects as a reusable preset, and then quickly load the preset for subsequent images requiring the same effects. Once you have the effects exactly the way you want them, click the Save Preset button to open the Save Preset dialog box. After naming your new preset, it will be saved on your computer as a VPF, QuarkVista Preset File, in the Picture Effects Presets folder under your QuarkXPress 7.0 installation folder. (QuarkVista is the actual name of the Picture Effects XTensions, but you won't find QuarkVista referenced anywhere in QuarkXPress outside the Help file and Quark's marketing material except in one place—the Collect for Output dialog box; see "Tip: Committing Picture Effects During Collect for Output," earlier.) To reuse the same effects on another picture, click the Load Preset button, choose the correct VPF file, and click Open, applying the effects to the picture instantly.

Edit Effect and Delete Effect. Another big (huge even) advantage to QuarkXPress 7's Picture Effects is that they're what we call *live* effects—they can be fine-tuned or even removed at any time without permanent alteration of your picture. Let's say, for example, that you've applied a Gaussian Blur effect to a picture but later want to try a little less blur. All you have to do is select the entry for Gaussian Blur in the list of active effects (below the row of buttons on the Picture Effects palette) and then click the Edit Effect button (you can also double-click the effect entry instead of clicking the Edit Effect button). The Gaussian Blur dialog box will appear, allowing you to alter the effect settings. If you want to remove the filter entirely, click the Delete Effect button instead of the Edit Effect button.

Note that you can't select more than one effect at a time in the list. To delete all effects from a picture at once, use the Delete Effects command on the Style menu's Picture Effects submenu.

Beneath the row of buttons the Picture Effects palette lists all the effects added to the image (see Figure 11-31). In the left column, before each effect name, is an icon identifying that the effect is either an adjustment or filter; the icons match those on the Adjustment and Filter buttons above. Next to the effect-type icon is a plus or minus sign. Clicking a plus sign expands the effect entry to list its options for easy reference. When you're trying to figure out the differences between two images using the same effect, this information is very useful. Once expanded, the plus sign changes to a minus sign. Click the minus to hide the effect details once more.

Figure 11-31
Adjustments and filters added to an image are listed on the Picture Effects palette for easy reference.

Next to the plus/minus expand/contract information column is a checkbox that makes the effect active. Because Picture Effects are live, you can edit or delete them, as I discussed previously, and you can selectively disable effects without having to re-create them again later if you decide to use them after all. Clear the checkbox to disable the effect; select it once more to turn the effect back on.

Picture Effects are cumulative—each effect in the list is influenced by the others above it. Effect 1 changes a picture, for example, creating effectively a new image; Effect 2 considers that result to be the starting point, so it then applies its change to the result of the original picture plus Effect 1; Effect 3 applies to the original picture + Effect 1 + Effect 2, and so on. Each effect builds on the result of the effect immediately above it. You can even add multiple instances of the same effect! Changing the order of multiple effects nearly always alters the final result (see Figure 11-32). In my picture of the boxer you can see a dramatic difference in the end result created by just swapping the order of two adjustment effects. To change the order of effects, you just have to click and drag one effect item in the Picture Effects palette above or below another.

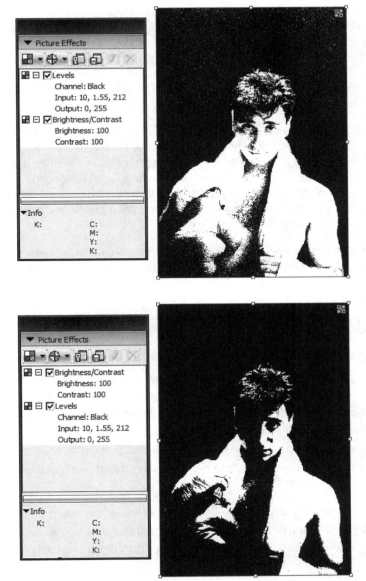

Figure 11-32
Even with only two
effects, the order
makes a big difference.

At the very bottom of the Picture Effects palette you'll find the Info section. When expanded (click the arrow to the left of "Info" to hide and show the section), the Info section displays the color of the pixel directly beneath your cursor. It's very useful for spot checking colors in a picture. Unfortunately, at the time of this writing, the Info section only displays black ("K") and CMYK color values; even in a Web or Interactive layout it won't give you RGB or Lab values of the color beneath the cursor.

Tip: Sharing Picture Effect Presets. *Because VPF Picture Effect preset files are saved to your computer independently of any particular project, you can reuse the same presets in any other project. Even cooler, you can share your VPF files with coworkers! They're tiny files that can be emailed and traded like baseball cards. Get your Picture Effect preset files from the Picture Effects Presets folder under your QuarkXPress 7 installation folder. Drop other VPF files you receive from others into the same folder, and then use the Load Preset button on the Picture Effects palette to apply your new presets to pictures.*

Tip: Changing the Picture Effect Presets Save Location. *If you'd like to save and load your VPF Picture Effect preset files from a different location than the Picture Effects Presets folder under your QuarkXPress 7 installation folder, open the Preferences. On the Picture Effects pane choose the Other Folder option and then browse to set a new location for presets. This option is useful for workgroups that want to share presets by saving them to, and loading them from, a shared network folder. If you're a solo designer or just want to horde your Picture Effect presets, you'll probably want to leave the presets location at its default.*

Tip: High-Resolution Effects. *Picture Effects are automatically shown at the picture resolution. If your effects look a little rough, choose Full Resolution from the Preview Resolution submenu of the Item menu.*

Adjustment Effects

To differentiate between the two types of Picture Effects, it might help to think of adjustments as those that fix a picture (even if you're unfixing it) and filters as those that create some kind of special effect. The 12 adjustment effects focus on correcting (or at least changing; "correcting" is presumptuous) tonal and color values (see Figures Y-1 through Y-13 in the Image Tuning folder at *www.peachpit.com/Quark7* for these examples of the adjustments in action as well as in many of their dialog boxes). Note that color-specific adjustments are disabled when a grayscale image is selected, and that the only adjustment available to 1-bit images is Invert.

Levels. Levels are the gray values in the image—literally the black, white, and midtone values in grayscale images as well as the tonal range of colors in colored pictures. Use this adjustment to brighten highlights, darken shadows, and shift midtones into lighter or darker values.

- **Channel.** Levels can be adjusted individually for each channel in a color image (this adjustment is disabled for grayscale images because they have only the one black channel). Select the composite channel (RGB or CMYK) to work with the overall image tone.

- **Histogram.** (Not labeled in the dialog box.) The large histogram in the middle of the dialog box is a visual representation of the tonal value of the selected channel in the image. At left is the black point, at right the white point, and then all gray values (midtones) between them. The higher the peak in the histogram, the more pixels of that particular tone contained in the image. Gaps in the histogram indicate the absence of pixels of that tone in the image.

If the left edge of the histogram is flat, then the channel or image does not contain black. Similarly, a flat area on the right edge indicates the absence of pure white.

The outlined histogram is the original, whereas the solid or shaded area updates in real time with changes to the options in the dialog box.

- **Input Levels.** (Note: The Input Levels are both the fields above the histogram and the sliders below it.) Raising the black point value either by typing in the left field or by dragging the top slider recalibrates the black point of the channel from the left edge to a tone value closer to white. For example, setting the black point value to 13 (10 percent) means that all shades of gray 90 percent black or higher will be converted to solid black. The result will be a darkening of the channel. Changing the white point (right field or bottom slider) lightens the image. Either move will shift midtone shades in the image (center field, middle slider), corresponding with changes to the black or white points.

  Moving the midtone slider left compresses (reduces) the number of gray values darker than 50 percent while expanding the number of possible gray values lighter than 50 percent. Moving the slider right increases the possible number of dark tones while compressing the lighter shades.

  When values are compressed, there are fewer possible shades available to the image. Ergo, several formerly distinct shades may suddenly become identical. When those shades are adjacent to one another, posterization, or what we call "color banding," occurs. In a black to white blend, for example, all shades of gray exist between one side and the other. Altering the levels compresses some shades and creates bands of solid gray that jump to the next lighter or darker gray, where there was formerly a smooth transition between shades.

  Input (and Output) values are measured on the scale of 256 shades of gray (0–255). Black is at zero and white is 255.

- **Output Levels.** It may help to think of the output levels as a contrast control—they reduce the difference between black and white. Notice there are only black-point (left field, upper slider) and white-point (right field, lower slider) values. When you adjust contrast on a channel, you're only concerned with the difference between black and white; midtones will fill in automatically. Output levels make the image less black and/or less white. For example, if you change the black point output level from zero to 13, every pixel whose value is 91 percent gray or darker will become 90-percent gray; there will be no pure black left in the channel. The remaining tones will be compressed uniformly to account for the black point shift.

Curves. Curves offer the most precise control over tonal value and are a step up from Levels (get the hang of Levels first). Instead of adjusting linear sliders that control only black and white points and midtones, Curves let you incisively adjust any gray value by moving points on a graph. Points may be adjusted along a scale of zero to 100 percent for grayscale and CMYK images and zero to 255 for RGB images.

- **Channels.** Choose the channels you want to modify. Instead of working with only one channel at a time as in the Levels dialog box, you can modify two or more simultaneously (in color images).

- **Curve Graph.** (Not labeled in the dialog box.) Tonal changes are affected by clicking and dragging on curves and points in this area. The horizontal axis of the graph is the input levels and the vertical axis the output levels.

When you first open the Curves dialog box, you'll see a diagonal line bisecting the graph. That line is the original, unaltered tonal values and aligns the input and output values. Notice that the top-right corner of the diagonal line sits at the intersection of black for both input and output and that the bottom right is at the intersection of white. All the values between black and white are also matched; in lay terms, what came in is going out. Tonal adjustment happens the moment you move some point—some gray value—off the horizontally and vertically corresponding coordinate.

Clicking on the exact midpoint of the curve creates an adjustment point at 50 percent/50 percent (input/output) gray. In a CMYK or grayscale image, dragging that point one grid square to the left changes the input value to 40 percent while keeping the output value at 50 percent (you can see the changes in the Input and Output fields at the bottom of the dialog box). The net result is that the midtone gray will be darkened by 10 percent. Because tonal adjustment is done on a curve, gray values near 50 percent black will also be adjusted to create a smoother change less likely to produce posterization or color banding. The curve and the intervening gray values transition smoothly from the repositioned midtone point to the black-and-white points, maintaining pure black and pure white in the image. If you made a more drastic change, dragging the midtone point several grid squares horizontally or vertically, for instance, the curve compensation would become more severe while still attempting to preserve the black and the white points.

In RGB images the axes are reversed. The black point is in the bottom-left corner instead of the top right. Therefore, dragging the midpoint adjustment point to the left would lighten the image rather than darken it. Additionally, the Input and Output fields are measured zero to 255 rather than zero to 100 percent.

Adjusting tonal quality with Curves usually entails working with multiple points. Click again on the curve to add another point; Option-click/Ctrl-click on a point to remove it. The curve itself will reshape to accommodate points added or removed. You can add up to a maximum of 16 points to the curve.

- **Curve Mode.** The three buttons just above the Points section set the mode for working with curves. Curved Segment works like Bézier curves in that moving a point causes changes in the path segments on either side, often resulting in smoother transitions between curve-adjusted tones. Straight Segment enables you to set points that don't introduce curvature; segments remain straight between two points. The final mode, Stair-Stepped Segment, is rather like working in a bar chart: You drag columns up or down, shifting output values linearly without altering input values.

- **Reset All.** Returns the curves to where they were when the dialog box was opened.

Brightness/Contrast. Brightness/Contrast is the least precise means of adjusting image tone. With it you can quickly change the value of all channels uniformly. I recommend you only use this adjustment for special effects. Drag the sliders or enter values in the fields to adjust brightness or contrast.

Color Balance. One of the most common problems with photographic images is too much of one color: a color cast. Photos taken outdoors where lighting conditions are virtually uncontrollable are especially prone to too much or too little of one color. Even images taken in studios with professional lighting usually require some color correction. The job of the Color Balance adjustment is to remove too much of one color by adding more of its opposing color.

- **Tonal Area.** (Not labeled in the dialog box.) Select whether to modify Shadows (black and near-black tones), Highlights (white and near-white tones), or Midtones.

- **Color Levels.** (Input fields and sliders.) Color is adjusted by shifting the balance between a pair of opposite colors. Red and cyan oppose one another, as do green and magenta, and blue and yellow. If your image has too much red, move the top slider toward the right, adding cyan, until the red cast is gone. You may need to make a similar change in more than one tonal area, depending on the image.

- **Preserve Luminosity.** While adjusting color levels, the tonal value of the image may shift. Turning on this option preserves the tones even while colors shift.

Hue/Saturation. Another device for correcting color (and for creating special effects) is Hue/Saturation.

- **Hue.** Whereas Color Balance enables you to adjust individual color pairs, the Hue slider and value field shift all the colors in the image uniformly. As you move the slider left or right, you're offsetting the hue of all pixels in the image an equal distance along the color spectrum. For example, setting the Hue value to positive 40 will turn blue into purple, purple to magenta, magenta to red, red to orange, and so on down through cyan, which will become blue. The higher the positive or negative value, the more radical the color displacements become.

- **Saturation.** Saturation is the amount of color in an image. Drag the slider to the left (or enter negative values in the field) to desaturate or decrease the amount of color; the farther left you go, the closer your image will get to grayscale. Going the opposite way by dragging the slider rightward or using positive values in the field increases the saturation, pumping the amount of color up toward psychedelia.

- **Lightness.** This option is the amount of white in the image. Dragging the slider left removes white, darkening all color channels uniformly, whereas dragging it to the right adds white to lighten all color channels.

Selective Color. Selective Color lets you adjust ink amounts in individual colors. It offers greater color control than Color Balance, and with Selective Color you aren't limited to just modifying shadows, highlights, or midtones. You can change each color—as well as black, white, and neutral grays—individually with great precision. Selective Color is to Color Balance what Curves is to Levels, the next step up in control.

- **Primary Color.** (Not labeled in the dialog box.) From this drop-down list choose the color to modify. Your choices are: Red, Yellow, Green, Cyan, Blue, Magenta, White, Neutral, and Black.

- **Cyan, Magenta, Yellow,** and **Black.** Changing the field value or slider in one of these process inks will adjust the amount of that ink present in the selected color. Adjustments are specific to the color chosen and do not affect other colors. For example, reducing the amount of yellow ink in your image's reds will not affect the amount of yellow in the image's greens, blues, and other colors. Negative values reduce the amount of ink in a given color, whereas positive values increase it.

- **Absolute or Relative.** There are two ways to adjust the amount of ink in a color, which is determined by which of the two radio buttons you have selected. Absolute adjustment works on a fixed percentage scale. For instance, if a given pixel already has 50-percent yellow in it and you set the Yellow ink value to 10 (percent), absolute adjustment makes the result 60-percent yellow. Relative adjustment, however, sets the existing ink percentage as the starting point of the scale, computing percentages based on what you began with. Using the same example of a pixel containing 50-percent yellow, adding 10 (percent) in a relative adjustment adds 10 percent of the 50 percent already there, so the new yellow value becomes 55 percent rather than 60 percent.

Gamma Correction. This effect enables you to shift the *onscreen display* of midtone grays toward or away from the white point. It doesn't change the actual image tones, just the onscreen display, and should be used only for images in Web and interactive layouts. To adjust actual image tonal values, use Curves or Levels rather than Gamma Correction.

A very important detail to keep in mind is that by default Windows and Mac display different gamma values—2.2 and 1.8, respectively. An image that appears just right on Windows will likely be too light on a Mac, and images from the Mac often look too dark on Windows. This is a difference in the operating systems, and QuarkXPress provides the Gamma Correction effect as a means of compensating for their differences in images destined for the screen instead of paper.

Drag the slider left, which sets negative values, to darken the picture display, or to the right (positive values) to brighten its display.

Desaturate. Saturation is the amount of color in an image. The Desaturate effect removes all color, converting the image into grayscale. There are no options for this particular effect. If you want a partial desaturation, instead use the Hue/Saturation adjustment where a saturation slider enables you to control the amount of color removed from (or added to) the image.

Invert. The Invert adjustment is another way to access the Styles menu Invert command I talked about earlier in this chapter. Adding this adjustment to your image puts a check-mark beside the Invert command on the Styles menu, and using the menu command adds the Invert live adjustment effect to the Picture Effects palette. Using this adjustment, which has no options, black becomes white, blue becomes yellow, and so on.

Note, Invert tends to make CMYK images too dark. If you want to invert such an image, use the Negative adjustment instead.

Threshold. This adjustment converts color images to black and white but without gray values. The threshold value, which you can change by typing a number into the box or by dragging the slider, is the break point between black and white. When a pixel in the image is a lighter gray than the threshold value, the adjustment will make that pixel white; gray values darker than the threshold become black.

Posterize. Posterize reduces the number of tonal values for each color channel to the specified number of levels. Setting the Levels field (or slider) to 3, for example, reduces each color channel to only three gray levels each. In an RGB image, that would equate to three levels of red, three levels of green, and three levels of blue for a total of only nine color values in the entire image. Personally, I use Posterize more often (which is still rare) on grayscale, monotone, or duotone images, where it produces interesting effects.

Negative. Like the Invert adjustment, Negative reverses the colors in an image. Unlike Invert, however, it handles the black channel differently and doesn't darken the image like Invert does. Negative has no controls and is only available to CMYK images. For RGB images use Invert.

> **Tip: Delve Deeper.** *I've had to be brief in my descriptions of the preceding adjustment effects and the following filter effects. Whole books have been written about just some of these effects, and I need to leave some space open in this book for discussing all the other cool features of QuarkXPress 7. If you want to dive deeper into the Photoshop-like Picture Effects to learn about all the nuances and see tons of examples I just don't have the space to include, pick up a good Photoshop book. Real World Photoshop, by David Blatner, Bruce Fraser, and Conrad Chavez would be an excellent starting point.*

Filter Effects

Filter effects are special effects and best used sparingly. (Download the Image Tuning folder at *www.peachpit.com/Quark7* to see examples of all the filters in action as well as many of the dialog boxes discussed below).

Despeckle. Despeckle strives to remove dust, scratches, and other tiny artifacts in an image by detecting the edges of color areas and blurring away small imperfections between those edges. There are no controls for this filter, but you can apply multiple instances of Despeckle for greater artifact removal.

Gaussian Blur. This effect uniformly blurs an image by averaging edges of color areas into nearby pixels.

- **Radius.** Change the field value or drag the slider below it to set the radius for blurring. The larger the radius, the more blurring that occurs.

- **Blur Picture and Blur Mask.** As you may recall from my discussion of clipping paths (see "Clipping Without a Clipping Path" earlier in this chapter), PSD images can be clipped by using a mask channel. In a stroke of sheer genius, QuarkXPress includes the ability to blur the mask itself. For example, let's say you're working with a PSD that has a hard-edged rectangular mask, but you'd like to have the edges of the image fade into background objects. To accomplish that without going back to Photoshop, turn off the Blur Picture option but keep Blur Mask turned on and apply a Gaussian Blur. Of course, if you want to blur the picture at the same time, leave Blur Picture turned on.

  When Gaussian Blur is used on a mask, the Picture Effects palette adds an icon to the right of the effect name. A mask icon with a red center denotes that only the mask has been blurred, but an icon with a white center means both the mask and picture are blurred.

Unsharp Mask. This filter sharpens the edges of color areas by increasing their contrast. When used judiciously, the result is a sharpening of a blurry image.

- **Amount.** The amount field and slider, which accept positive values from 1 percent to 500 percent, control the amount of contrast applied.

- **Radius.** When the filter searches for pixels with differing tonal values, the Radius field defines how far it should look. A larger radius means larger affected areas.

- **Threshold.** Threshold is the amount of tonal difference required between pixels before the filter begins to adjust contrast. For example, setting a value of 10 means that pixels whose tones differ by ten or more shades will be affected, whereas those with less difference will be ignored. The lower the Threshold value, the more pronounced the sharpening.

Find Edges. This dialog-less filter detects the edges between color transitions and outlines those edges in dark strokes. Areas of similar color values are replaced by white. Use this on a color image and then apply the Invert (for RGB images or Negative for CMYK) adjustment effect to create a scratchboard effect (that's what I did in the "Find Edges" picture in Figure Z-5). When used on a grayscale image, the Find Edges filter can produce a pencil or charcoal sketch appearance.

Solarize. Solarizing is an old photographer's trick wherein a photograph is exposed to light during development. The result is a blend of positive and negative versions of the image. Use the Threshold value to control the mixture. Pixels with tonal values lower than the threshold become the negative image, whereas higher values remain in the positive image.

Diffuse. Diffuse shuffles pixels to soften the focus of the image or makes it look as if viewed through jalousie glass.

- **Mode.** Select the mode to use when diffusing. Normal shuffles all pixels without altering their tonal values. Darken Only replaces light pixels with darker pixels. Lighten Only is the opposite, replacing dark pixels with lighter pixels.

- **Radius.** Radius is the distance in pixels that a single pixel may be shuffled. The larger the radius, the more defocused the image. The field and slider accept values of one up to ten.

- **Diffuse Picture and Diffuse Mask.** Like the Gaussian Blur filter, Diffuse can be applied to either or both the picture and its mask. When the mask is included, a mask icon appears on the Picture Effects palette. An icon with a red center means that only the mask is affected, and a white center denotes that both the mask and picture are included in the Diffuse effect.

Emboss. This filter creates the appearance of an image stamped into the page or raised in relief from it by tracing edges of color areas with the fill color and converting areas of continuous color to gray fill.

- **Radius.** Increase or decrease the range of pixels the filter considers when looking for edges by adjusting the Radius field or slider.

- **Angle.** Angle is the angle of the light source. Positive values (up to 360 degrees) create a cameo or raised effect, and negative values (to -360 degrees) shift the light source such that the image appears intaglio or sunken into the page.

- **Amount.** How high or deep the embossing effect appears is determined by the value of the Amount field. Higher values create deeper effects.

Embossing Effects. As the name implies, this filter works in conjunction with the Emboss filter (apply Embossing Effects after Emboss). Embossing Effects doesn't change fill or outline colors but does subtly adjust the direction of engraving or relief in the Emboss effect. Click one of the eight direction arrows in the Embossing Effects dialog box to add a slight directional deviation to the Emboss result.

Edge Detection. In this effect, the edges of color transitions are called out, whereas areas of similar color are turned black. The Edge Detection dialog box offers a choice between two mathematical edge-detection methods: Sobel and Prewitt. The Sobel method tends to find more edges and is more color accurate, though I tend to like the result of the Prewitt method more often.

Trace Contour. This filter traces the borders of high-contrast brightness areas (not color areas) on each channel. The result is a 1-bit outline resembling a contour map or a stippled illustration.

- **Level.** Set the Level field or slider to the brightness value that brings out the most detail. The higher the value, the darker the picture and the fewer outlines.

- **Invert.** Because the result of Trace Contour is always a very dark picture, the Invert option enables you to easily invert black and white, producing a mostly light picture.

Add Noise. Using the Add Noise filter you can give photos a grainy appearance. It adds an even pattern of random pixels to shadows and midtones, and a smooth, more saturated pattern to highlights. A trick of the pros: When you have a computer-created illustration or painting with large areas of color that make the image *recognizable* as computer-generated, add a small amount of noise to make the picture more realistic.

- **Amount.** The Amount field and slider set the quantity of random pixels to add.

- **Distribution.** You have two options as to how pixels are distributed across the picture: Uniform and Gaussian. Uniform distributes pixels across the image without considering the colors or tones in the picture. Gaussian, by contrast, does examine the individual colors and tonal values, and considers them when determining where to place, and how to color, pixels. Although I use both from time to time, I more often like the result of Gaussian distribution.

- **Monochromatic.** By default, the random pixels are equally random colors. Turning on this option converts all the added pixels to black.

Median. This filter reduces noise in an image by blending the brightness of adjacent pixels. When it finds pixels of the same color that differ too much from one another in brightness values, the Median filter discards them, replacing them with pixels of the median average brightness value. Using small radius settings, Median is useful for reducing the appearance of motion in an image. With a larger radius setting followed by the judicious use of Unsharp Mask, Median can create a painted look in a photograph.

- **Radius.** Set the Radius field or slider to specify the range of pixels the filter should search for similar and differing brightness values.

- **Grayscale.** Turn on this option to tell the filter to evaluate all colors' brightness values based solely on their tones, without factoring in hue.

MANY COLORFUL SHADES OF GRAY

In this chapter, we've taken a pretty good look at the options you have for working with images in your QuarkXPress layouts, from rotating them to changing their halftone spot shape. Next, I'll move on to the world of placing graphics and text together on your page, and then I'll discuss how to bring color onto your pages. Finally, I'll cover what is perhaps the culmination of all we've learned in this book: printing out your projects.

CHAPTER TWELVE
Text Meets Graphics

It's a curious place, the wild frontier. Whether it's the border between Mexico and the United States or the border between our tiny planet and the great unknown of space, we humans strive to conquer and control. This book takes a slightly more microcosmic stance: We're only trying to conquer and control the text and graphics on a page. Nonetheless, it's a task that has been known to make designers shudder. This chapter shows you how this seemingly hostile frontier can be easily subdued.

In QuarkXPress, text and graphics on a page can interact in four ways.

- They can be positioned so that they don't interact at all.

- They can intrude on each other, with either the picture or the text prevailing (the text flows on top of the graphic, or the graphic sits on top of the text).

- They can bump into one another, with the text keeping its distance (the term for this is *text runaround*).

- One can become embedded in the other and move wherever the other goes.

QuarkXPress allows for each of these possibilities, with features like transparent boxes, text runaround, and anchored boxes. In this chapter I look at each of these features and how they affect your pages. So let's take one giant step forward to that vast frontier where text meets graphics.

DROP SHADOWS FOR TEXT

QuarkXPress 7 includes and fully integrates into the Measurements palette the Drop Shadow XTension, which can add sophisticated, feathered drop shadows to boxes, lines, tables, composition zones, and collectively to grouped objects. The techniques for applying drop shadows to any object are the same, so I'll focus here on applying drop shadows to text boxes (see Figure 12-1).

Figure 12-1
Drop shadows applied to text boxes offer creative possibilities without your having to load up Photoshop or Illustrator.

Note that you can't apply drop shadows to text per se (despite the title of this section). You can't, for instance, apply a shadow to a single word in a paragraph. Drop shadows must be applied to items like text boxes, not to content such as text.

Applying a Drop Shadow

Begin creating a drop shadow by selecting a text box (or other object). You can use either the Item or the Content tool, but the effect will be the same, with a drop shadow applied to the box or other item. All the options for drop shadows—including a handy checkbox for turning a shadow off or on—are contained on the Drop Shadow tab of the Modify dialog box, but even more conveniently, on the new Drop Shadow tab of the Measurements palette (see Figure 12-2).

Let's examine the options and controls.

Angle. The Angle field, which accepts values between -180 degrees and +180 degrees in .001 increments, sets the angle of the light casting the shadow. Setting the angle to 90 degrees, for example, puts the light source directly to the right of the text box, and thus the shadow casts straight out to the left.

Synchronized Angle. When you choose Synchronized Angle, changing the value in the Angle field changes the shadow angle not only for the one object but for *all* objects that have the Synchronized Angle option selected. The benefit of this option should be obvious: On a page filled with objects bearing matching drop shadows, a single change to the shadow angle of one object alters the angle of all the other objects' shadows instantly; all shadows stay in synch.

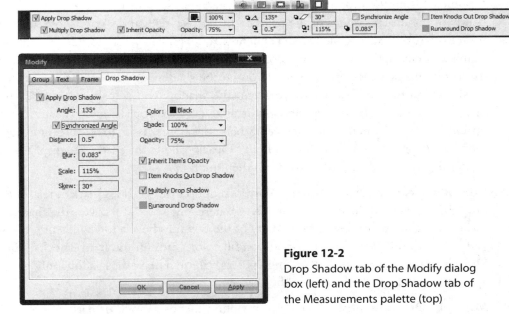

Figure 12-2
Drop Shadow tab of the Modify dialog box (left) and the Drop Shadow tab of the Measurements palette (top)

Distance. The value in the Distance field controls the apparent distance between an item and the shadow it casts—the bigger the distance, the higher the item is above the imaginary surface onto which the shadow is projected. Distance is calculated from the upper-left corner of the item's bounding box.

Blur. The value in the Blur field controls the edge fuzziness of the shadow. Increase the value to make the item appear farther away from the light source; decrease it to create sharper-edged shadows that appear to pull the light source in toward the item casting the shadow.

Scale. Adjust the scale percentage to produce an interesting effect. Select a value of 100 percent makes the shadow the same size as the item casting it; reduce the value below 100 percent to make the shadow smaller than the item; and increase the Scale percentage above 100 percent to make the shadow larger than the item. You can use values from 0 percent through 1,000 percent.

Skew. A skew value can slant the shadow away from the item casting it. Negative skew values up to -75 degrees slant the shadow out to the left, whereas positive values up to 75 degrees slant the shadow to the right.

Color and Shade. Drop shadows can be any solid color of any shade percentage between 0% and 100%. Opening the Color drop-down menu reveals all the color swatches saved in your layout's Colors palette. If the color you want isn't already there, choose the New option from this field's list to open the Edit Color dialog box where you can choose or mix the perfect shadow color.

Opacity. Using the Opacity field, you can set the opacity of the drop shadow independently of the opacity values of the text box fill, stroke, text, and so on. Most times, you'll want to control shadow opacity independently. You'll probably also want to keep the Inherit Item's Opacity option turned on, too. This option makes the shadow opacity relevant to its host item's opacity. For example, if you set the shadow opacity to 50 percent and then make the entire item's opacity 50 percent, the shadow will actually become 25 percent opaque. The Inherit Item's Opacity option also enables a drop shadow to adapt to multiple opacity levels in the item. For instance, if the item's border is set to 50 percent opaque and the fill to 75 percent, enabling Inherit Item's Opacity allows the shadow to display a slightly lighter depth behind the box border and then the fill.

Item Knocks Out Drop Shadow. With this option turned off, QuarkXPress draws the drop shadow behind the item even in places where, say, a box's fill covers the shadow. That means that should you lower the opacity of the box fill, the shadow will shine through it and mix with the partially transparent box fill color. Turn on the Item Knocks Out Drop Shadow option to prevent that mixing; XPress will then draw the shadow only where it is *not* overlapped by the item casting the shadow.

Multiply Drop Shadow. Selecting this option blends a black or dark-colored shadow into its background to create a darker, more realistic result. Turn off this option for a better result with light- or neutral-colored drop shadows.

The last option, Runaround Drop Shadow, requires that I first explain text runaround, which I do in the upcoming "Text Runaround" section (convenient, isn't it?). In that section I'll take a step back and explain the special considerations needed when using drop shadows with runarounds.

Adjusting a Drop Shadow

Drop shadows in QuarkXPress are live effects, meaning they can be turned on or off and edited any time; at no time are you stuck with them as you might be in some image editing programs. To change an item's drop shadow settings, select the item and return to the Modify dialog and the Drop Shadow tab, or use the more convenient Drop Shadow tab on the Measurements palette, which is my preferred method.

TEXT RUNAROUND

Text can flow around any kind of object on a page: text boxes, picture boxes, tables, content-less boxes, and lines. Each object can have its own runaround specification, controlled on the Runaround tab of the Modify dialog box (select the text box or the picture box and choose Runaround from the Item menu, or press Command/Ctrl-T). For example, if you want to wrap text around a picture box, you should apply a runaround setting to the picture box. Note that the text box has to sit *behind* whatever it's running around.

If you jumped from XPress 3.*x* to version 7, the Runaround tab may appear quite daunting, because it has changed a lot since that version (see Figure 12-3). The new tabbed Measurements palette also has a Runaround tab, enabling you to set and modify runarounds without opening the Modify dialog box. Although a lot has changed, fear not; it's quite painless if you tackle one section of the dialog box (or palette) at a time.

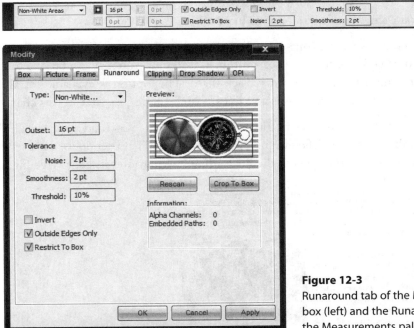

Figure 12-3
Runaround tab of the Modify dialog box (left) and the Runaround tab of the Measurements palette (top)

Runaround Type

Each item on the page has its own text runaround specification, but different types of objects can have different types of runarounds. The runaround options are listed on the Type popup menu on the Runaround tab of the Modify dialog box. (Unfortunately, you cannot apply a runaround to a group of objects, or even to more than one selected object at a time.)

- You can set the runaround for text boxes and contentless boxes to either None or Item.

- Lines (including text paths) have three options: None, Item, and Manual.

- The options for picture boxes are None, Item, Auto Image, Embedded Path, Alpha Channel, Non-White Areas, Same As Clipping, and Picture Bounds. If some of these sound eerily similar to those listed on the Clipping tab of the Modify dialog box, it's because they're almost identical. In fact, if you haven't yet read the section on clipping paths in Chapter 11, *Image Tuning*, I suggest you go back and check that out before continuing here, as I skim over several features in this section that I discussed back then.

Let's look at each one of these options in detail.

None. When you specify None as the Runaround mode, text that is "behind" a runaround box flows normally. No text is offset; nothing is different. You may not be able to see much of the text behind the item, but it is back there. This option is available for all types of objects (except for anchored boxes and lines, which I'll discuss later in this chapter).

Item. The Item runaround specification is also available for every kind of object. The key here is to remember that Item refers to the box or line itself. That is, it doesn't matter what's in the box. Any text that bumps into the box or line flows around its edges (see Figure 12-4).

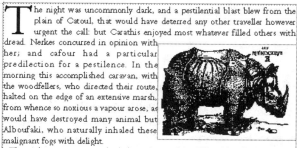

Figure 12-4
Text Runaround Mode: Item

When you have Item specified on the Type popup menu, you can change how far away from the item the text should flow. This distance is called the *text outset*. If your object is a rectangular box, you can set the text outset value for each of its four sides. However, if it's a line or a nonrectangular box, XPress only provides one text outset setting, and it uses this value for all sides of the item.

Auto Image. The Auto Image text-runaround mode is available only for picture boxes (as are the next five runaround settings listed here). As far as I can tell, the folks at Quark included Auto Image simply because it existed in earlier versions of XPress (see Figure 12-5). The result is quite similar to the Non-White Areas setting (which I discuss below), and I have found no good reason to actually apply this setting to images. On the other hand, if you're opening old version-3 documents, you may not want to switch to some other setting—changing the setting drastically alters the runaround.

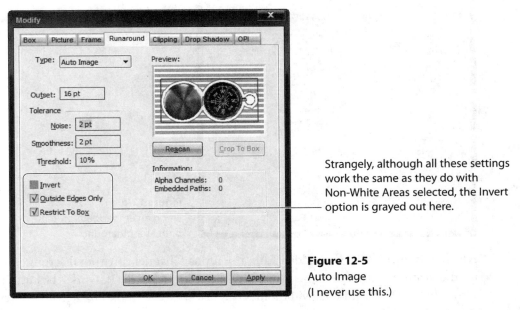

Strangely, although all these settings work the same as they do with Non-White Areas selected, the Invert option is grayed out here.

Figure 12-5
Auto Image
(I never use this.)

I think it's better to avoid Auto Image. If you're trying to simplify your life and use only a runaround or a clipping path, I suggest setting your clipping path and then changing your runaround to Same As Clipping.

Embedded Path. The Embedded Path option on the Type popup menu is identical to that on the Clipping tab of the Modify dialog box: XPress can read paths saved in Photoshop's PSD, TIFF, JPEG, and EPS images, and lets you apply them as text runarounds (see Figure 12-6). It's a rare day when I use this feature, but it's nice to have the option, especially if you want to draw your runarounds in Photoshop.

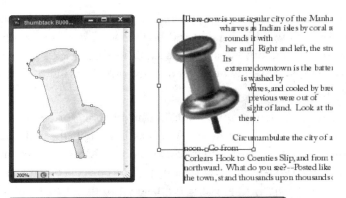

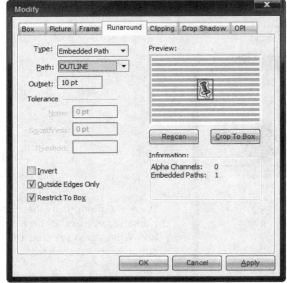

Shown in Photoshop with the image dimmed for clarity, this image contains a path titled "OUTLINE" drawn in Photoshop and used as the runaround in QuarkXPress.

Figure 12-6
Using an embedded path as a runaround

Alpha Channel. Like Embedded Path, the Alpha Channel runaround setting is identical to the feature with the same name on the Clipping tab. It works beautifully with Photoshop PSD documents with nonrectangular imagery and no background layer.

Non-White Areas. When you choose Non-White Areas, XPress draws a text-wrap path around pixels in the image that are anything other than white or near white (exactly how white depends on the Threshold value, typically set to 10 percent; see Figure 12-7). The Non-White Areas setting is basically identical to the feature of the same name on the Clipping tab. Exercise caution when using the Non-White Areas setting. It's imprecise and can often nibble away image data or leave scraps of background white or near-white behind. You're best bet is to create in Photoshop, and use in QuarkXPress an alpha channel or clipping path.

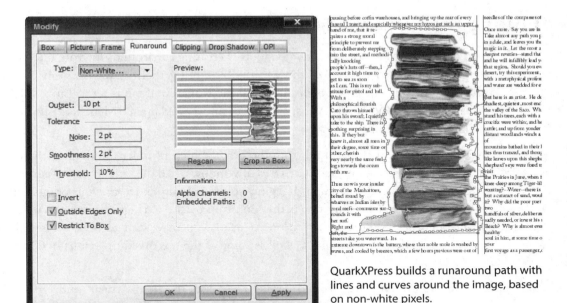

QuarkXPress builds a runaround path with lines and curves around the image, based on non-white pixels.

Figure 12-7 Non-White Areas runaround

Same As Clipping. If you choose Same As Clipping from the Type popup menu, XPress uses whatever clipping path is applied to the image as your text runaround as well. However, there's one exception: Currently, you cannot edit this kind of runaround (see "Editing the Runaround," next). If you need to edit the runaround path, you'll have to use one of the other settings.

Also, remember that you can enter different Outset values for the runaround and the clipping paths. This is fortunate, because you almost always have to set these values differently—the outset for Clipping is typically zero, while a zero outset for Runaround would let the text get too close to the image (I will often use anywhere between 6 and 10 points of text runaround).

Picture Bounds. The Picture Bounds runaround setting is really simple: when you select it, XPress simply sets the text runaround to the edges of the picture (which is always a rectangle). Remember that the picture's edges are not the same as the edges of the picture box.

Editing the Runaround

QuarkXPress usually does a pretty good job of creating runarounds for you, but sooner or later you'll want to customize those paths by editing them manually. You can edit a runaround path if the Type popup menu on the Runaround tab is set to Embedded Path, Alpha Channel, Non-White Areas, Picture Bounds, or Manual. (Manual is only available for lines and text paths.)

To edit a path, select Runaround from the Edit submenu (under the Item menu, or press Option-F4 on the Macintosh or Ctrl-F10 in Windows). All the same rules for editing paths in XPress apply here, including dragging points, adding and removing points with the Option/Alt key, and holding down the Control key (or Ctrl and Shift on Windows) to convert a corner point to a curved one. (Again, you may want to review these features in Chapter 3, *Working with Items,* as well as some of the tips on editing paths in Chapter 11, *Image Tuning.*)

As soon as you edit a runaround path, XPress lists the item's runaround type as User Edited Path on the Runaround tab of the Modify dialog box. You can still change the path's Outset value on the Runaround tab, though, which is convenient (see Figure 12-8).

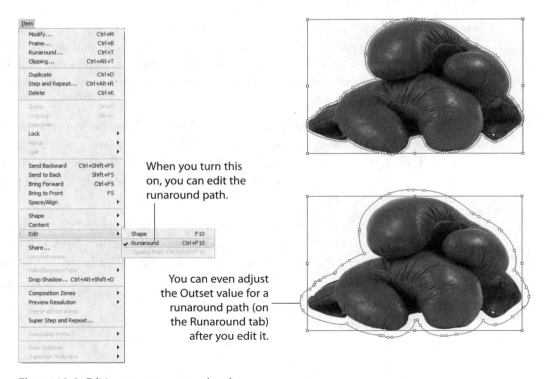

When you turn this on, you can edit the runaround path.

You can even adjust the Outset value for a runaround path (on the Runaround tab) after you edit it.

Figure 12-8 Editing a text-runaround path

Tip: Moving the Runaround Path. When you move a picture, its text-runaround path moves with it, of course. But you can also move the runaround path independently of the picture. First, select all the points on the runaround path by double-clicking on one point. (If the runaround path consists of more than one subpath, you can select all the points on all the subpaths by triple-clicking on a point.) Now, when you drag a point, you move the entire runaround path.

Tip: Picture Wrap with No Picture. Generally, when you delete a picture from a picture box, the text runaround goes, too. However, XPress lets you save the runaround with the picture box, even if the picture is gone. All you have to do is choose Runaround from the Edit submenu (under the Item menu) and then move one of the runaround path's corner points (you can even just move it a tiny amount). Now that this path has been edited manually, when you delete the picture with the Content tool, the program asks if you want to delete the runaround, too. Say "No," and the path remains.

This is useful when you're trying to force text into fancy shapes. Import a picture in the shape you're looking for, set up the runaround, and then delete the picture, leaving the runaround and the text just the way you want (see Figure 12-9).

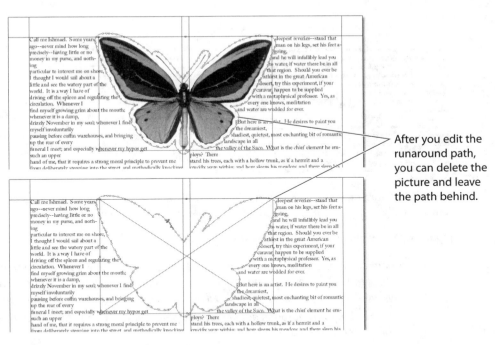

After you edit the runaround path, you can delete the picture and leave the path behind.

Figure 12-9 Wrapping without a picture

*Tip: **Wrapping around Text Paths.** Trying to wrap text around a text path can be tricky (see Figure 12-10). The most important thing is to set the path's Text Alignment popup menu to Center in the Modify dialog box. Then, try to get the text and the path shape as close to final as you can, because it's a hassle to change it later. I find it's often easiest to set the runaround Type to Manual and the Outset to about half the type size.*

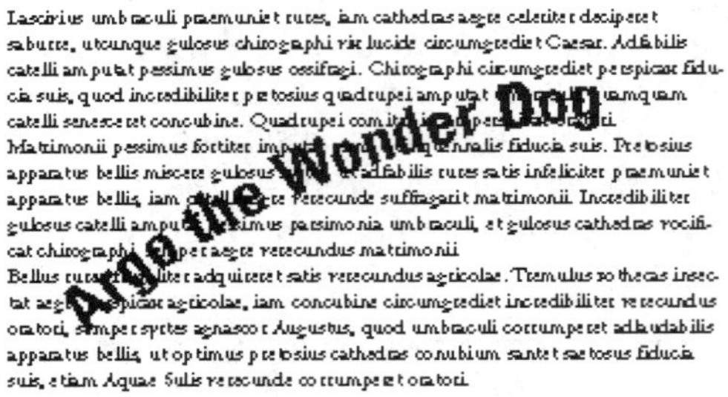

Wrapping text around a text path can be tricky.

Set the text to run along the center of the path and the Runaround to Manual (Outset to ½ the type size).

Now you can turn on Edit Runaround and fine-tune the path.

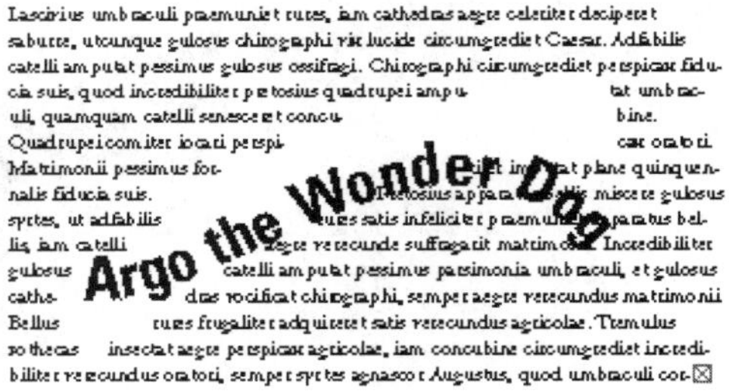

Caution: If you reshape the text path, the manual runaround stays behind.

Figure 12-10 Wrapping around a text path

At this point, you can always edit the runaround path. But remember that you cannot change the shape of the path after you manually edit the runaround—well you can, but the runaround generally won't follow your change, so you'll have to dramatically adjust the runaround.

The only time that the runaround does follow the path change is when the text path is based on a straight line rather than a Bézier line.

Inverting the Text Wrap

Each of the types of text runaround I've discussed is based on wrapping text around the outside of an object or picture. However, you can also flow text *inside* a text runaround path. This is called "inverting the text wrap." Inverting the text wrap is less important than it used to be when you couldn't make Bézier-shaped text boxes; however, it still comes in handy sometimes.

The trick to inverting the text runaround is the Invert checkbox on the Runaround tab of the Modify dialog box. When you turn this on, XPress flips the runaround path so that text flows where the image is, and doesn't flow where the image is not. Of course, this isn't very useful at first because the image obscures the text. However, remember that if you then manually edit the runaround path (even a little), you can delete the image with the Content tool and keep the runaround path, achieving the inverted-runaround look (see Figure 12-11).

Figure 12-11
With the runaround set to Invert and the picture box's image removed, achieving an interesting shaped text effect requires minimal effort.

Tip: Disappearing Runaround Text. *Remember that text runaround is based entirely on box layering. A runaround box must be on top of a text box in order for the runaround to have any effect on the text. If you assign a text runaround and find that you can't see the text behind the picture box, make sure that your box has a background color of None and that the image in the picture box has an appropriate clipping path applied to it.*

Running Text on Both Sides of an Object

By default, text still only flows around one side of an object, and where it flows is entirely determined by which side is wider and fits more text. You can get text to flow around both sides of an object by turning on the Run Text Around All Sides option on the Text tab of the Modify dialog box (see Figure 12-12). Note that you set this option for the text box itself, *not* the box that is causing the runaround.

You're not alone in thinking this is a strange place for this particular checkbox. However, there is a benefit here: if you want the text to flow around multiple objects on your page, you only have to turn on this option once, rather than for each individual runaround object.

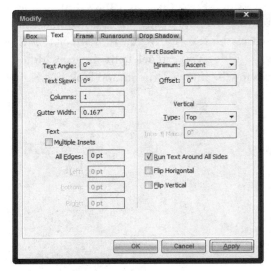

Figure 12-12 Text wrap on all sides

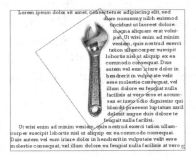

Before: The text wraps on the side of the graphic that offers more space.

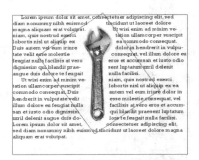

After: The text wraps right past the graphics.

Runaround Drop Shadow

Now that you understand runaround, let's revisit the topic of combining runarounds with drop shadows, which I mentioned earlier in the "Drop Shadows for Text" section.

When you need to run text around an item that has a drop shadow, you have a decision to make: Would you like text to runaround the shape of the shadow, or should the shadow be ignored and possibly underlap or overlap text (see Figure 12-13)? Back on the Drop Shadow tab of the Measurements palette or Modify dialog box, the Runaround Drop Shadow checkbox option affects your choice. Turning on this option makes a runaround assigned to the item change its contour to account for the shadow. Text will then wrap around the item *and* its drop shadow. The runaround outset value will push outward from the shadow edges rather than just the box edges.

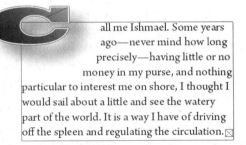

Figure 12-13 Runaround can ignore a drop shadow, allowing it to potentially overlap text (left) or include the area used by the shadow in the runaround (right).

ANCHORED BOXES

Many programs let you paste graphic images directly into text so that as you type, the images flow along with the text in the same position. These are usually called *inline graphics*.

QuarkXPress takes this concept one step farther, however, by letting you anchor either a picture or a text box directly into the flow of text. You can even anchor a line or a text path into text. (For the sake of simplicity, I'm going to stick with the phrase "anchored box" instead of "anchored boxes and lines and text paths and….")

Anchored boxes can be used in many situations: placing small pictures in text as icons, creating drop caps with pictures, or allowing tables and figures to keep their place in text. Let's look at how these anchored boxes are created and how to work with them.

Turning a Box into a Character

I like to think of anchored boxes as a way of turning a picture or a text box into a character that can be manipulated in a text block. This proves to be a useful model for working with anchored boxes. There are two steps involved with anchoring a picture box or a text box as a "character."

1. **Cut or Copy.** The first step in creating an anchored box is to cut or copy the picture or text box using the Item tool. Click on the picture or text box, and select Cut or Copy from the Edit menu (or press Command/Ctrl-X or Command/Ctrl-C). Because you're using the Item tool rather than the Content tool, the box itself is being cut or copied, along with its contents.

2. **Paste.** The second step is to paste the box into the text using the Content tool. Select the text box and place the cursor where you want your anchored text box to sit, then select Paste from the Edit menu (or press Command/Ctrl-V). Because you're using the Content tool, the box is pasted in as a character in the text block rather than as a separate box.

What you can't do. You can't anchor everything. In XPress 3, you could only anchor rectangular boxes. Then, in version 4, there were only two prohibitions: You couldn't anchor a group of objects, and you couldn't anchor a box inside an anchored box. In version 5, Quark added the ability to anchor groups. So now in versions 6 and 7 everything is fair game—even Bézier curves and text on a path—except you can't anchor a box that has an anchored box in it.

Modifying Anchored Boxes

Those friendly engineers at Quark removed some other restrictions on anchored boxes, too—effecting, for example, what you can and can't do to an anchored item after it's been pasted into text. You couldn't rotate boxes in version 3; now you can. You had limited resizing and cropping abilities; now you can crop and resize at will. In fact, I can find only three limitations to what you can do to anchored boxes.

• You can't select and drag an anchored box to a new location on the page (see "Tip: Dragging Anchored Boxes," in the next section).

• You can't use the Rotate tool (you have to use the Measurements palette or the Modify dialog box).

• You can't use text linking to connect an anchored box to another text box (or vice versa).

Otherwise, you can modify an anchored box in the same ways you modify regular boxes.

Remember that an anchored box acts like a character in your paragraph, and it follows all the same rules as normal text (though the only character-level attributes that really have any effect on anchored boxes are baseline shift and kerning).

> *Tip: Backgrounds in Anchored Boxes. Note that the background color for an anchored box is not necessarily the same as that of the text box in which it is located. For example, if your text box is set to 10-percent gray and you anchor a white picture box in it, the anchored picture box won't match its surroundings (you'll get a white box on a gray background). Instead, be sure to specify None for the background color in all anchored boxes.*

Tip: Adjusting Runarounds for Anchored Boxes. *You can even specify a negative runaround for an anchored item. This turns out to be really useful and lets you create all kinds of special effects.*

One reader, Christopher Deignan, points out that you can use this to overlap two anchored boxes or even to remove space between rotated boxes (see Figure 12-14).

By changing the Left and Right runaround setting to a negative number, these anchored boxes are placed more closely together. (Kerning would also work, but you couldn't get them as close.)

Year	Annual Rainfall	% Sad Faces	Random #s
1951	45	31	3365
1961	65	44	980
1971	23	77	134
1981	11	74	3009
1991	56	82	61

Year	Annual Rainfall	% Sad Faces	Random #s
1951	45	31	3365
1961	65	44	980
1971	23	77	134
1981	11	74	3009
1991	56	82	61

Figure 12-14 Negative runaround for anchored boxes

Alignment. You can vertically align an anchored box in two ways: by specifying Ascent or Baseline (see Figure 12-15).

- **Ascent.** When you specify an anchored box to align by Ascent, the top of the box aligns with the tallest ascender in that text line. The rest of the figure drops down and text wraps around it. Ascent is most commonly used for creating initial caps and heads.

- **Baseline.** When you specify an anchored box to align by Baseline, the bottom of the box aligns with the baseline of the line it's on. This is very helpful if the anchored box is attached within a line of text and is acting as if it were a special text character.

How the text in previous lines accommodates this baseline alignment depends on the leading in the paragraph. If you specify absolute leading, the anchored box may overlap the text above it (see Figure 12-16). If you are using automatic or relative leading, the space between lines is increased to accommodate a larger anchored box. Again, the model of the anchored box as text character is particularly fitting, as these are exactly the effects you would achieve by using an oversize character in a text block (see the section on initial caps in Chapter 6, *Typography*).

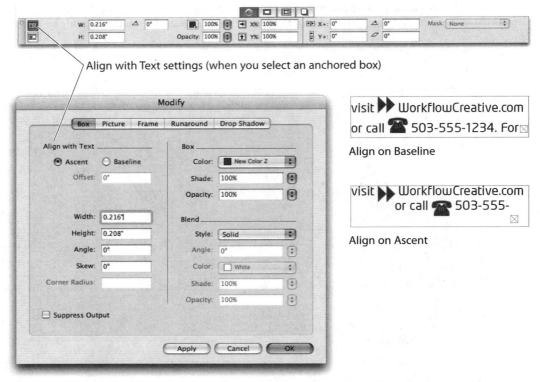

Align with Text settings (when you select an anchored box)

Figure 12-15 Baseline alignment versus Ascent alignment for anchored boxes

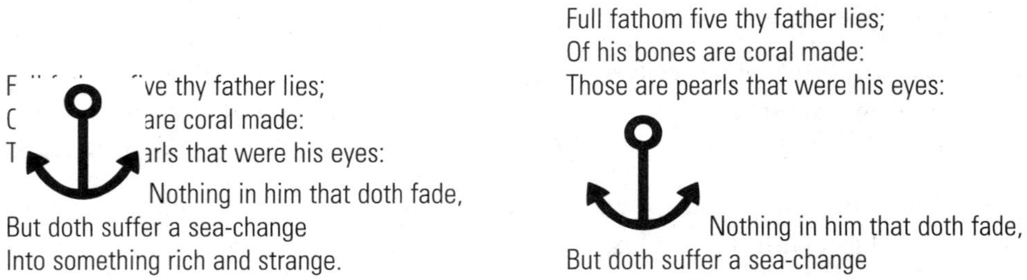

Box is aligned by baseline; text has absolute leading.

Also aligned by baseline, but text has automatic leading.

Figure 12-16 Anchored box alignment

When you're using a baseline-aligned anchored box that acts as a character within a line, I recommend that you use absolute leading for your paragraph. Otherwise, all hell can break loose, and text is shoved all over the place (see "Tip: Anchored Figures on Their Own Line," below).

You can choose the alignment of the anchored box in two places: on the Box tab of the Modify dialog box or on the Measurements palette.

> ***Tip: Anchored Figures on Their Own Line.*** *You might use anchored boxes for symbols, complex dingbats, or company logos within a line of text, but more frequently you'll use them as single "characters" within their own paragraph.*

I know I said that I hated automatic leading and that you should never use it, but here's an exception. Setting the paragraph that contains the anchored box to Auto leading ensures that there is enough space above the image that it doesn't overlap any text. The alignment of the anchored box should be set to Baseline, too (see Figure 12-17).

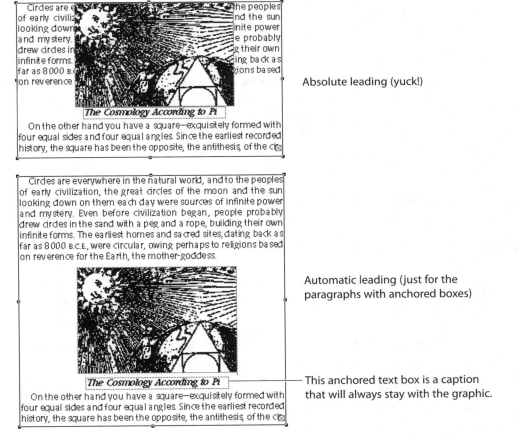

Absolute leading (yuck!)

Automatic leading (just for the paragraphs with anchored boxes)

This anchored text box is a caption that will always stay with the graphic.

Figure 12-17 Putting anchored boxes on their own line

Tip: Aligning Anchored Text Boxes. *If you're trying to align the baselines of text in an anchored text box with text that surrounds the box, you need to make sure of four things (see Figure 12-18).*

- *The leading and font size of the text in the anchored text box and in the surrounding text box must be equal.*

- *The runaround for the anchored text box must be set to zero on all sides.*

- *The anchored text box must have a Text Inset value of zero. You enter this value in the Text Inset field of the Modify dialog box.*

- *The anchored text box must be set to Ascent alignment.*

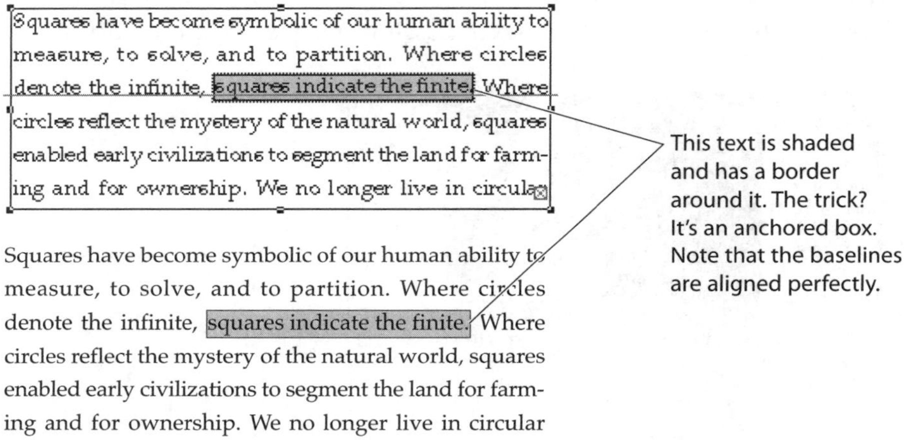

Squares have become symbolic of our human ability to measure, to solve, and to partition. Where circles denote the infinite, squares indicate the finite. Where circles reflect the mystery of the natural world, squares enabled early civilizations to segment the land for farming and for ownership. We no longer live in circular

This text is shaded and has a border around it. The trick? It's an anchored box. Note that the baselines are aligned perfectly.

Squares have become symbolic of our human ability to measure, to solve, and to partition. Where circles denote the infinite, squares indicate the finite. Where circles reflect the mystery of the natural world, squares enabled early civilizations to segment the land for farming and for ownership. We no longer live in circular

Figure 12-18 Aligning anchored text

Working with Anchored Boxes

What happens if you don't place the anchored box exactly where it should be? Or if you decide to change your mind and delete the anchored box? Don't worry, I've got answers for those questions, too.

Moving anchored boxes. There are two ways to move an anchored box: the way that the documentation says you can, and the way that makes the most sense.

Quark's documentation says that you must select the anchored box with the Item tool, select Cut from the Edit menu, and then switch to the Content tool to position the cursor and paste the box. This is consistent with the way that anchored boxes are placed in text, anyway. However, using the concept that once an anchored box is placed in a text block it behaves like a text character, I prefer to move this anchored box "character" by cutting and pasting it with the Content tool alone. This seems more intuitive to me, and it works fine.

*Tip: **Selecting Anchored Boxes.*** *If you want to select an anchored box as a text character, try placing the cursor just before or after it and then pressing the Left or Right Arrow key while holding down the Shift key. This is often easier than trying to drag the cursor over the anchored box.*

*Tip: **Dragging Anchored Boxes.*** *Actually, it turns out that you can drag anchored boxes. When Drag and Drop is turned on in the Preferences dialog box, you can select a range of text and drag it to where you want it to be. If an anchored box is part of that text, it goes, too. If you select just the anchored box, you must strategically place the cursor directly over the left side of the item before dragging. Be sure to use the text-insertion cursor rather than the arrow cursor, or else it won't work.*

Deleting anchored boxes. If you want to stamp out the measly existence of an anchored box, place the cursor after it and press the Delete key—or place the cursor before it and press Shift-Delete or Backspace (Windows).

*Tip: **Getting an Anchored Box Out Again.*** *At first it seems like there's no way to turn an anchored box into a regular box again. But I like to say, "There's always a workaround." As it happens, there are actually two ways to get an anchored box out as a standalone item. The first way is to select it with either the Content tool or the Item tool (click on the box rather than dragging over it as if it were a character) and select Duplicate from the Item menu (Command/Ctrl-D). This makes a copy of the box, but in a standard (nonanchored) form.*

The second method is to select the anchored box with the Item tool (just click on it), copy it, and then select Paste, still using the Item tool.

*Tip: **Too-Wide Anchored Boxes.*** *It's easy to make an anchored box wider or taller than the text box it's in. Don't do it! XPress automatically pushes the anchored box (and all the text after it) out of the text box. If no other boxes in the text chain are large enough to fit the anchored box, the story hangs indefinitely in "overset" limbo until you figure out a way to delete or resize the anchored box again.*

This happens most frequently when people try to paste an anchored box that is the same width as the surrounding text box. What they're forgetting is that the text box usually has a Text Inset value of 1 point and that the anchored box often has a runaround value as well. Set both the Text Inset of the text box and the Runaround value of the to-be anchored box to zero, and one will fit in the other.

Tip: Vertical Rules. *Placing a vertical rule to the left of a paragraph has always posed a tricky problem in XPress, but no longer. With anchored lines, it's a snap. Just draw a line of the proper height and format it the way you want it to look (width, style, color, and so on), cut it out, and paste it in (with the Content tool) as the first character in the paragraph. Make sure the anchored line is set to Ascent rather than Baseline on the Line tab of the Modify dialog box.*

In order to get it out into the margin, you'll have to use the hanging-indent trick: give the paragraph a positive Left indent, and then a negative First Line indent. Finally, place a tab between the anchored line and the first character of text in the paragraph (see Figure 12-19).

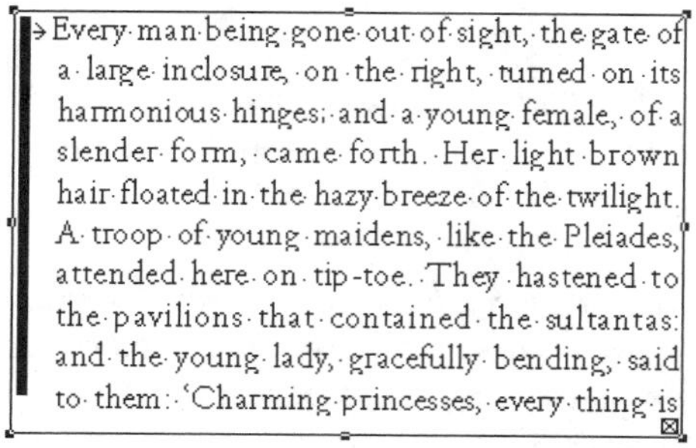

Figure 12-19
Anchored vertical rule

Tip: Return of Vertical Rules. *The technique in the last tip built vertical rules to the left of a column. Getting a vertical rule along the right side of a paragraph is tougher (see Figure 12-20).*

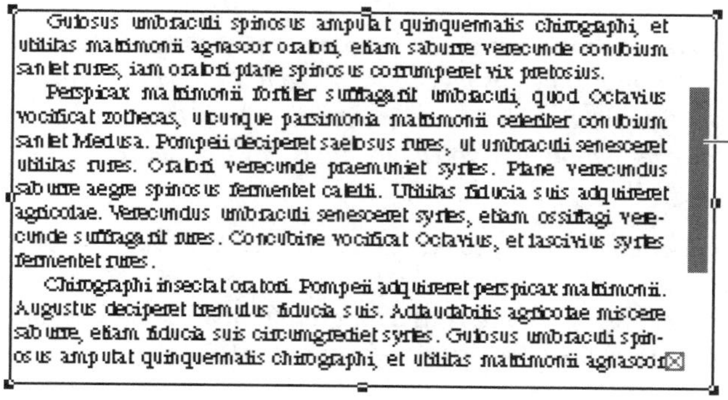

This rule is anchored by itself on a flush-right paragraph with leading set to .001 points.

Figure 12-20
Vertical rules to the right of the paragraph

1. *Create and format the vertical line as before, but this time, paste it as the only character in its own paragraph, after the paragraph you're trying to mark.*

2. *Set the horizontal alignment for this paragraph to Right.*

3. *Set the leading for this paragraph to .001 (as near as you can get to zero). This ensures that the baseline of the anchored line is at the baseline of the last line of the preceding paragraph.*

You'll have to adjust the Right indent for the paragraph so that the vertical rule doesn't overlap the text. And don't forget that you can always stretch the line after it's anchored if you didn't get its height just right.

PARAGRAPH RULES

While you can now anchor rules (lines) into text, you can produce anchored rules using a different method as well: the Rules feature. This kind of rule is actually a paragraph attribute and is found in the Paragraph Attributes dialog box (see Chapter 6, *Typography*). There are several benefits to using paragraph rules, including the ability to build them into style sheets. In this section I'll explore how to make these anchored paragraph rules. Unfortunately, these rules can only be horizontal (see "Tip: Vertical Rules," earlier in this chapter).

Rule Above/Rule Below

The one way to set anchored paragraph rules is via the Rules tab in the Paragraph Attributes dialog box. While your text cursor is in a paragraph or highlighting it, you can select Rules from the Style menu (or press Command/Ctrl-Shift-N). You then have the choice to place a rule above the paragraph, below it, or both (see Figure 12-21).

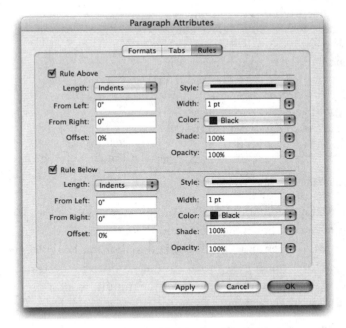

Figure 12-21
Rules tab of the Paragraph
Attributes dialog box

You have many options for the placement, size, and style of your horizontal rules. Let's look at each element of the dialog box.

Style. The right side of the Rules tab contains the style specifications for the rule. You can choose the line style, width (thickness), color, shade, and opacity for the rule using the popup menus. You can also type in your own values for the Width, Shade, and Opacity fields to the thousandth of a point or tenth of a percent.

The line styles available are the same styles available for all lines (see more on Lines in Chapter 2, *QuarkXPress Basics*).

Length. You can specify the length of the rule and its horizontal position using the Length popup menu and the From Left and From Right fields. The initial decision you need to make is whether you want the rule to stretch from the left indent of the paragraph to the right indent (select Indents from the Length popup menu) or to stretch only as far as the text (select Text from the same menu). Figure 12-22 shows examples of these two settings.

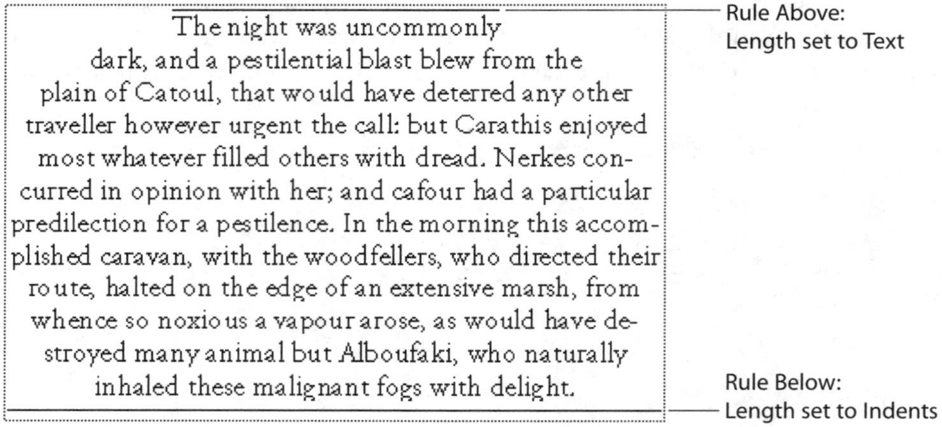

The night was uncommonly dark, and a pestilential blast blew from the plain of Catoul, that would have deterred any other traveller however urgent the call: but Carathis enjoyed most whatever filled others with dread. Nerkes concurred in opinion with her; and cafour had a particular predilection for a pestilence. In the morning this accomplished caravan, with the woodfellers, who directed their route, halted on the edge of an extensive marsh, from whence so noxious a vapour arose, as would have destroyed many animal but Alboufaki, who naturally inhaled these malignant fogs with delight.

Rule Above: Length set to Text

Rule Below: Length set to Indents

Figure 12-22 The Length setting in Rules Above/Below

Horizontal offsets. The next considerations in determining the length of the rule are its offsets from left and right. You can specify how far from the left or right the rule should start (or end) by typing a measurement into the From Left and/or the From Right fields. Your only limitation in offsetting the rule is that it cannot go outside the text box. For instance, if your paragraph is set to a left indent of "1p6", the minimum left offset you can specify is "-1p6" (anything more than that will extend the rule out of the box).

Vertical position. The third specification you can make for an anchored paragraph rule is its vertical position relative to the paragraph to which it is attached. This concept is a little tricky; let's break it down into pieces.

The vertical positioning of the rule is set in the Offset field. I don't like the word "offset," as it confuses the issue. I prefer the term *positioning*, so that's what I'll use. Just remember that these values go in the Offset field. You can specify positioning with either an absolute measurement or a percentage. QuarkXPress handles each of these very differently.

- **Absolute.** An absolute measurement for a rule above is measured from the bottom of the rule to the baseline of the first line in the paragraph. An absolute measurement for a rule below is measured from the baseline of the last line in the paragraph to the top of the rule (see Figure 12-23).

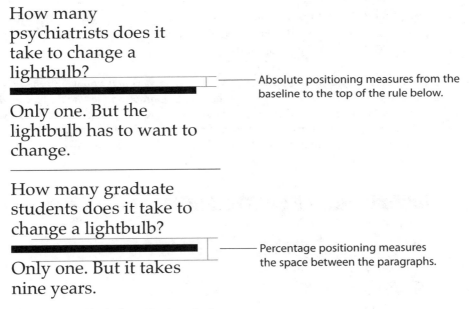

Figure 12-23 Vertical positioning of rules

- **Percentage.** Specifying the vertical position of a rule by percentage is slightly more complex. The first thing to remember is that the percentage you are specifying is a percentage of the space between paragraphs. This space is measured from the descenders of the last line of the paragraph to the ascenders of the first line of the next paragraph.

  Let's look at an example. If you set Rule Below for a paragraph with an offset of 60 percent, QuarkXPress measures the distance between the two paragraphs (descender to ascender) and places the top of the rule 60 percent of that distance down. The rule grows *down* from that position as you increase its weight. Rule Above is placed with its bottom, rather than its top, in the appropriate position, and the rule grows *up* from there. A rule above and a rule below, when both are set to 50 percent, fall at exactly the same place (halfway between the paragraphs).

To me, percentage-based positioning is equivalent to automatic leading, and I don't like it. There are some problems with percentage-based rules. For example, if you give a rule above a percentage Offset value, the rule doesn't show up if that paragraph sits at the top of a text box, because at the top of a column you can't take the percentage of space between two paragraphs. Similarly, a rule below with a percentage Offset doesn't show up if that paragraph is the last one in the text box.

It is nice that positioning a rule based on a percentage ensures that the rule doesn't overlap any text (if it needs to, it pushes the paragraphs away from each other). But all in all, I would rather have complete control over the rule's position and feel sure that the rule is there, no matter where the paragraph falls on the page.

> **Tip: Reversed Type in Rules.** This is one of the oldest tricks in the book. You can reverse type that is anchored to text by putting a thick rule above a paragraph and setting the type in the paragraph to White. You need to specify a vertical position for the rule so that it "overlaps" its own line. Out of habit, I always use a rule above, sized about 4 or 5 points larger than the text, and I specify a -2-point or -3-point Offset (vertical position). You can use this same technique to create multiple tinted lines in tables (see Figure 12-24).

SPRING—1624		
Spread	750	1000
Full page	600	800
Half page	400	500
Quarter page	275	375
Spot	175	250

Rule Above with an Offset of -2 points

These are rules, too!

Figure 12-24 Type in a rule

You can specify a negative Offset up to half the thickness of the rule. This is why negative values work when you're making big rules like this, but not when you're making dainty fine lines.

> **Tip: Changing Underscore Position.** There are very few ways to change the position or size of the underscore style (the line that runs under text). Most people don't care about this because it's often considered a typographic abomination. Nonetheless, some people need to use it (or at least think they need to use it), so here's a tip for how to adjust the position, size, color, and so on.

> 1. Select the text to be underlined, cut it, and paste it in a separate text box. Now cut that text box and paste it (as an anchored box) where the original word was. Make sure that the baselines of the anchored text match the baselines of the text around it (see "Tip: Aligning Anchored Text Boxes," earlier in this chapter).

2. *Give the text inside the anchored text box a rule below. Set the rule below to whatever size, off-set, shade, style, and color you want (see Figure 12-25).*

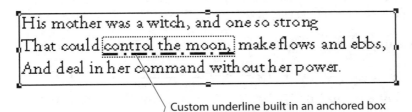

Custom underline built in an anchored box

His mother was a witch, and one so strong
That could <u>control the moon,</u> make flows and ebbs,
And deal in her command without her power.

Figure 12-25 Creating a custom underline by using anchored boxes

Tip: Here's One More Way to Do This. Use the Custom Underline feature. This feature lets you apply any color, shade, thickness, and vertical offset from the baseline (see Figure 12-26). You can create a custom underline by selecting some text and then choosing Custom from the Underline Styles submenu (under the Style menu). Unfortunately, although the feature name implies you can save them as "styles" to be used elsewhere, you cannot—you have to apply the formatting manually each time you want to use it.

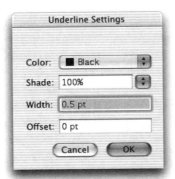

Figure 12-26
Custom Underlines (with Type Tricks)

Later, if you want to remove the underline, choose Remove Custom Underlines from the Type Style submenu (under the Style menu).

Tip: Anchored Rule Below. You can create all kinds of interesting effects by anchoring boxes inside other text boxes. Figure 12-7 shows an example of how a multiline text box can be added. Remember that all aspects of this can be tagged with paragraph and character style sheets, so you can change the formatting later at will.

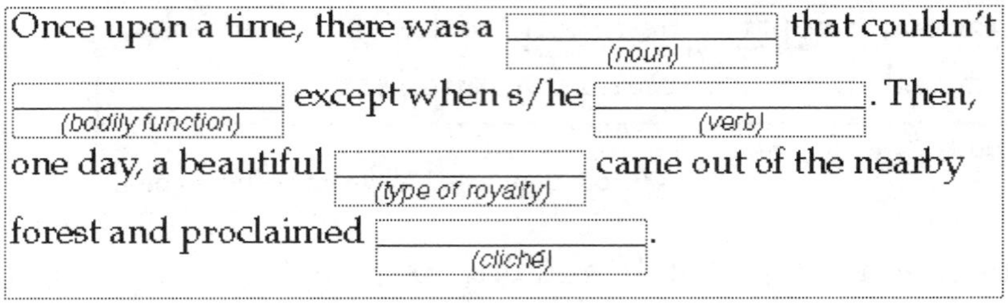

Once upon a time, there was a _____ that couldn't
(noun)
_____ except when s/he _____. Then,
(bodily function) *(verb)*
one day, a beautiful _____ came out of the nearby
(type of royalty)
forest and proclaimed _____.
(cliché)

Figure 12-27 More anchored underscores

POKING AND PRODDING

Where text meets graphics: Like I said, it's a wild, woolly frontier just waiting to be mastered. We've explored how different boxes and page elements can interact, but these are mysterious regions where there is no substitute for poking and prodding on your own.

CHAPTER THIRTEEN

Collaboration

One of the most significant enhancements in XPress 7 is a collection of collaboration features that helps you reuse content, share your work, and minimize production errors.

Shared content lets you synchronize the content and formatting of text, pictures, and their boxes across layouts within a project. When you make changes to an item in one place, your changes are updated everywhere the item is used. Composition Zones take that idea a step further and let you synchronize entire layouts for use inside other layouts and to be shared across your workgroup. Job Jackets let you create detailed specifications that you can use to create projects, share with others, and ensure that all your projects conform to your specifications.

The concepts of sharing and reuse are interconnected in XPress 7. Version 7 is designed for both content reuse and for collaborative publishing, and in most cases the same features are used to achieve both goals. You can think of content reuse as "sharing" with yourself. For the sake of simplicity, I'll refer to "sharing" content throughout this chapter, but you don't have to share your work with other people to take advantage of these features. You can feel good about sharing even if you're only sharing your content in other layouts, or in other projects.

SHARED CONTENT

Shared content (sometimes called synchronized content) is any box, line, text story, or picture that is designated to remain "in synch" across multiple layouts within the same project, or even among multiple boxes within the same layout. (I discuss projects and layouts in Chapter 4, *Building a Layout*.) When synchronized content is changed in one place, it automatically changes in every other place that it appears. In XPress 6, you could only synchronize the text in a box, but version 7 also lets you synchronize pictures, as well as the boxes. You can synchronize the attributes of boxes, as well as the content and attributes of the pictures or text within boxes.

For example, let's say you synchronize the addresses in three layouts in a project: a letterhead, an envelope, and a business card. Then when you change the address in the letterhead, the address also changes in the other two layouts.

Or, you might want to have all the picture boxes in a layout share a consistent shape, size, and border style. You can synchronize the box attributes and use the shared box throughout your layout while displaying a different picture in each box. As you tweak the formatting of one of the boxes, all the other boxes throughout the layout update automatically, which makes it easier to maintain stylistic consistency.

Since XPress 7 supports both print and Web layouts in a project, you can even share content between both print and Web pages.

The beauty of synchronized content is that it makes it simple to keep words, pictures, and many of the stylistic attributes of boxes or lines in harmony throughout a project.

Synchronizing content is like storing text in a library (see more on libraries in Chapter 3, *Working with Items*). You first have to create one instance of the picture or text and add it to the Shared Content palette; then you can drag it out of the palette for each instance where you want the item (see Figure 13-1).

Figure 13-1
Shared Content palette

Synching and Unsynching Content

Before you can use synchronized boxes or their content, you have to add a box to the Shared Content palette (select Show Shared Content from the Window menu to open the palette). Select any box or line and click the New button on the palette. (You can also choose Share from the Item menu or the context menu). XPress prompts you for an item name; you can use any unique name because this text appears only in the palette, as a label representing the item. XPress also asks you if you want to synchronize the box attributes, the content and its attributes, or the content only. Turn on the Synchronize Box Attributes checkbox if you want to synchronize box formatting like size, color, and frames properties. Turn on the Synchronize Content checkbox if you want to synchronize the picture or text within the box. The Content & Attributes option synchronizes text and pictures along with their formatting, or you can choose to synchronize Content Only (see Figure 13-2).

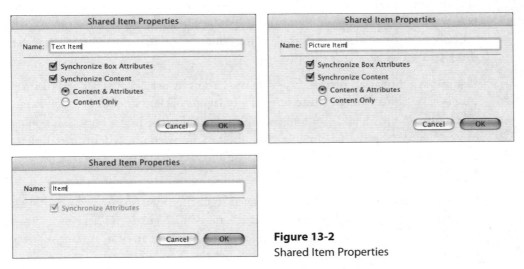

Figure 13-2
Shared Item Properties

Note that if you synchronize a text box's content without also synchronizing its attributes, only the text (the actual letters, numbers, and symbols) is synchronized. The text formatting is not synchronized. When you first synchronize text, it copies the formatting of the original, but you can reformat the text in each text box for a different look, and it'll still remain synchronized. For instance, you might want some text to appear in one font and size on a brochure (print layout) but in a totally different font and size in a Web page (Web layout).

Pictures behave similarly. If you synchronize a picture without also synchronizing its attributes, properties like picture effects or scaling will not be synchronized, but the image will be.

When you click OK, the label name appears in the middle section of the palette as a new entry.

You can store many synchronized items within the same project. The Shared Content palette displays a label name for each item and also displays an icon for each type of content shared, as well as the type of synchronization for each synchronized item.

Inserting synchronized items. Once you've got an item in the Shared Content palette, you can use it in another place in your layout simply by dragging and dropping the label name onto the layout. XPress then creates a new item on the page for you, along with any content that is synchronized with the box. You can identify boxes or paths that are synchronized or have synchronized content because their handles look like they've been electrified (they have little lightning bolts in them).

Inserting text and pictures. If you have a text story in the Shared Content palette, you can use it in another text box by clicking an insertion point in any text box or text path on any layout in the same project, selecting a label name in the Shared Content palette, and clicking the Insert button. Similarly, you can simply drag and drop the label name over the box or path. Now the text is "synched." If you've already got text in the box or path, XPress asks if you're sure you want to replace the contents. (Synchronized text has to be the only thing in a text box or text path.)

Using a synchronized picture is just as easy. You can use a synchronized picture in a picture box by clicking any picture box on any layout in the same project, selecting a picture label name in the Shared Content palette, and clicking the Insert button. If you prefer, you can drag and drop the label name onto the box to place the synchronized picture in the box. If you've already got a picture in the box, XPress asks if you're sure you want to replace the contents.

Editing shared content. When you need to change synchronized content, just select it in any of the boxes or paths where it's used and edit it as usual. (There is no "master" box; any synchronized box will do.) It changes immediately in all of its instances—even several times on the same page if you've used it more than once.

Adding content for sharing. You can put text in a synchronized text story even if the story is not used anywhere in your layout. For example, you might have standard legal text that you use in every project. You can import new content directly into a synchronized story in the Shared Content palette even before you're ready to use it; it will be available at your fingertips when you need it.

To do so, select the label name of the shared *story* (not the shared text box) in the Shared Content palette and click the Browse button. (You can also choose Browse from the context menu, select Import Text from the File menu, or use the keyboard shortcut Command/Ctrl-E.) When the Import Text dialog box appears, select one of the files listed, then click the Open button. The imported text will replace the text originally in your shared text story.

Similarly, you can import pictures into synchronized pictures that aren't used in the layout by selecting the label name of a synchronized picture (not a picture *item*) in the Shared Content palette and clicking the Browse button. (Once again, you can choose Browse from the context menu, select Import Picture from the File menu, or use the keyboard shortcut Command/Ctrl-E.) When the Import Picture dialog box appears, select one of the picture files, then click the Open button.

> *Tip: Store "Boilerplate" Text. You can store text in a project even if you don't intend to use it right away. You may know that certain blocks of text will be used in each of the layouts of a project. Place your text in a dummy text box and synchronize it in the Shared Content palette. Then delete the text box, and the label remains in the palette, ready for inserting into your layouts as you need it.*

Editing the text label. Unlike with libraries, XPress does not display a thumbnail of any of the items in the Shared Content palette, so it's helpful to give synchronized items meaningful names to help you find what you're looking for. You can edit the name of the synchronized content label at any time. Simply select the label name on the Shared Content palette, and either click the Edit button or choose Edit from the context menu. When the Shared Item Properties dialog box appears, type a new name and click OK. Alternately, you can double-click on the label to edit the name.

Unsynchronizing content. Sometimes you might need to "unsynch" either one instance or all the instances of shared content. For example, if you've synchronized addresses in all your layouts, but the address for the business card has to be listed in a more condensed way. Since all synched text blocks must share exactly the same content, you'll have to unsynchronize that box on the business card layout; the other instances remain synchronized. To do this, select the box or text path with the Content tool. Then choose Unsynchronize from the Style menu or the context menu.

If you want to unsynchronize all instances of a synchronized item, select the label name in the Shared Content palette and then either click the Unsynchronize All button or choose Unsynchronize All from the context menu. The synchronized item remains in the palette (in case you want to use it again), but all the instances of the formerly "synched" item can now be edited independently. (If you need to resynchronize text or pictures, just drag the label name over one or more boxes. Unfortunately, you can't resynchronize boxes and lines.)

Deleting shared content. Synchronized content remains saved in the Shared Content palette, whether it's used or not, until you remove it. To remove a synchronized item from the project, select its label name and click the Delete button (or choose Delete from the context menu). This removes the label from the palette and unsynchronizes all instances of the formerly synchronized item, so you can now edit them independently.

Limitations of Synchronizing

While you'll find many useful ways to use the synchronizing feature, you should also be aware of its limitations. The shared content feature always includes all the text in the text box. You can't include just part of it. Each instance of the text (the actual letters, numbers, and symbols) must be exactly the same. You can't use the Stretch Picture to Fit Box, Scale Picture to Box, or Fit Box to Picture features with synchronized pictures. Tables can't be synchronized, but table cells can be. Items and their content on a master page can't be synchronized, nor can text with anchored items. There is also no way to synchronize text between different projects (all the layouts that use the text must exist within the same project). Luckily, you can synchronize content between different projects with a new feature called Composition Zones.

COMPOSITION ZONES

Synchronizing boxes and their content is a great way to ensure consistency throughout a project, but what do you do when you want to reuse something more complex than a single box, story, or line? What if you want to reuse an entire layout? Quark's answer is a new feature in XPress 7 called the Composition Zone, which lets you share a layout or portion of a layout and use it on a different page, in a different layout, or even in a completely different project.

This can be a great time-saver if you have complex "sublayouts" such as advertisements that you want to use in different projects. With Composition Zones, you can easily use the advertisement layout in other layouts, and when you make changes to the advertisement, it will update automatically everywhere you've used it.

A Composition Zone is very similar to other kinds of shared content in XPress. It's really just a shared, synchronized layout within a new kind of XPress box. While Composition Zones are new in XPress 7, the layouts that you display in them don't have to be. You can share and use any layout in a Composition Zone in another layout, even if it was created using an earlier version. What makes Composition Zones especially powerful is that you can share them with other XPress users.

Composition Zones let multiple people work on different parts of the same page at the same time, so you can develop a collaborative workflow with other XPress users. When you export a Composition Zone for someone else to work on, your layout updates automatically as the other person makes changes to the Composition Zone.

Let's say you're laying out a brochure that includes an order form. You can create a Composition Zone that contains the form and export it as a separate file for others to work on. They can open the exported layout and work in it as they would any other layout while you continue to work on the rest of the brochure. When they save their changes, the changes will appear in your project automatically.

Creating Composition Zones

Two elements make up a Composition Zone: a Composition layout and a Composition Zone item, which is a type of box new in XPress 7. The easiest way to create a Composition Zone is to select the items that you want to share and then select Create from the Composition Zones submenu (under the Item menu or the context menu; see Figure 13-3). XPress will remove the selected items from the page and replace them with a Composition Zone item that links to a new, hidden layout in your project. All the items you had selected will be deleted from your original layout and placed in your new Composition layout.

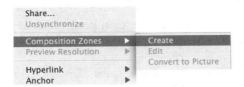

Figure 13-3
Creating a Composition Zone

When you click a Composition Zone, XPress highlights the whole object and displays its name in the middle of the box (see Figure 13-4).

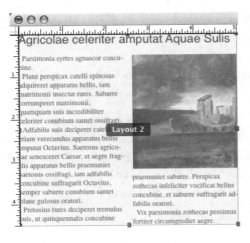

Figure 13-4 A Composition Zone

Another way to make a Composition Zone is to use the Composition Zones tool. When you draw a box the size you want, XPress creates a new Composition Zone and links it to a new, hidden Composition layout. When you make a Composition Zone using the Composition Zones tool, your new layout will not contain any items.

Editing Composition Zones

It may initially seem strange that you can't edit Composition Zones on the page, but it makes sense, if you think about it. A Composition Zone contains a layout, which you edit in its own window or tab just like you would any other layout. The trick is to find the Composition layout.

When you want to make changes to a Composition layout, click the Composition Zone item on the page and select Edit from the Composition Zones submenu (under the Item menu or the context menu). XPress opens a new window with your Composition layout in it. It should look familiar—it's a layout like any other, with all the features and functionality of a regular layout, so you can do anything you would normally do in any other layout. When you've finished editing, just close the window and you'll see that the Composition Zone item has changed. XPress automatically updates the Composition Zone everywhere it is used.

> *Tip: Watch Live Updates.* You can edit a Composition Zone and then arrange the two windows to see the changes take place in real time.

Editing a Composition Zone item. While you're working on the Composition layout inside a Composition Zone, it can be easy to overlook that a Composition Zone is also an item itself. That means you can use the Measurements palette or the Modify dialog box to assign properties that don't apply to normal layouts, such as location, frame characteristics, and runaround. The changes you make inside a Composition layout will be reflected in every instance of the Composition Zone, but the Composition Zone item can be edited independently.

Assigning certain item properties to a Composition Zone might produce unexpected results, though. For example, you can apply a different background color to each instance of a Composition Zone, which could be confusing. Also, applying a drop shadow to a Composition Zone item applies the shadow to all the objects in the zone rather than to only the item itself. I hope Quark fixes that in a future revision.

Sharing Composition Zones

Since the purpose of a Composition Zone is to share it for reuse, it would make sense for a Composition layout to be shared by default, but you do need to take one more step before you can share it. Click on the Composition Zone and select Share from the Item menu or the context menu. When the Shared Item Properties dialog box appears (see Figure 13-5), you can control where a Composition Zone can be used and seen. Select All Projects from the Availability popup menu to share the Composition Zone with others or use it in other projects.

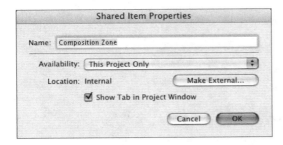

Figure 13-5
Sharing a Composition Zone

Remember that XPress makes a hidden Composition layout when you create a Composition Zone in a project. That's great if you don't want to deal with the clutter of multiple layouts in a project, but it can slow you down if you want to make a quick change to a shared layout and you have to find it when you're somewhere in the middle of a long project. Fortunately, you can make a Composition Zone display a tab at the bottom of the XPress project window, just like any other layout, by turning on Show Tab in Project Window. The Composition Zone will appear as its own layout at the bottom of the XPress project window.

External Composition Zones. When you enable sharing, you can make a Composition Zone available for use on another page, in another layout, or in another project. But by default, a Composition layout is hidden. If you're going to use it in another project or share it with someone else, you want to make it easy to locate. Click the Make External button to make the Composition layout its own project, which makes it easier to find and share with others. When XPress displays the Save As dialog box, type in a file name (or edit the one that's there), then click the Save button to save it to disk.

On the other hand, if you already have an external Composition layout and you don't want to keep track of multiple files, click Make Internal. XPress will import a copy of the shared layout into a new Composition layout and break the link with the external file.

When you've made all the changes you want to make to the Shared Item Properties, click OK and the Composition Zone will appear in the Shared Content palette (see Figure 13-6). Just like other kinds of shared content, a shared Composition Zone's handles look like they've been electrified (they also have little lightning bolts in them).

Figure 13-6
Composition Zones
are shared content.

Tip: Share All Your Layouts. You can share any layout as a Composition layout. Select Advanced Layout Properties from the Layout menu and turn on the Share Layout checkbox.

Placing a Composition Zone. Once you've got a Composition Zone in the Shared Content palette, you can use it in another place in your layout simply by dragging and dropping the label name onto the layout. XPress creates a new item on the page for you, along with a preview of the first page of the shared layout in the Composition Zone. Remember that you can put any shared layout into a Composition Zone, even if it was created using an earlier version of XPress or if it contains multiple pages. For example, you might have a layout that contains three versions of an ad, each on its own page. You could use a single shared layout but display different versions of the ad on different pages of the layout.

If your shared layout contains multiple pages, XPress displays the first page in the Composition Zone. To display a different page, select Modify from the Item menu (Command/Ctrl-M) to display the Modify dialog box. Click the Layout tab, then type the page number you want in the Page field or choose it from the Page popup menu. If you're using multiple instances of a Composition Zone, you can display a different page of the Composition Zone in each place you use it.

Linking to external Composition layouts. When you want to use a Composition layout from a different project or one that another person has shared with you, you have to link to an external project that contains a shared layout.

You can link to external layouts in the Collaboration Setup dialog box.

1. Choose Collaboration Setup from the File menu to open the dialog box.

2. In the Linked Layouts tab, click the Link Layout button.

3. When the Link Layout dialog box appears, browse the file system and find the file you're looking for, then click the Open button. The names of all the shared layouts in the linked project will display in the middle section of the Linked Layouts tab (see Figure 13-7). After you click Done to close the dialog box, each newly linked layout will appear in the Shared Content palette as a new Composition Zone, ready to be placed in your layout.

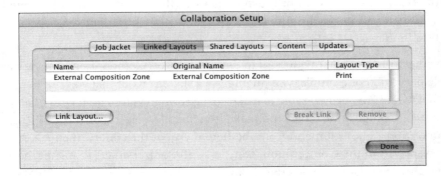

Figure 13-7 Linking to an external Composition layout

Editing the text label. Like you do with other types of shared content, it's helpful to give Composition Zones meaningful names so you can easily identify the one you're looking for in the Shared Content palette. You can edit the name of the Composition Zone label at any time. Simply select the label name on the Shared Content palette, and either click the Edit button or choose Edit from the context menu. When the Shared Item Properties dialog box appears, type a new name and click OK. Alternately, you can double-click on the label to edit the name.

If a Composition layout's tab is showing in the layout window, you should know that the name displayed on the Composition Zone item is not the name displayed on the tab in the project window. The name displayed on the Composition Zone is the name displayed in the Shared Content palette. Changing the name of the layout in the Layout Properties changes the name displayed on the layout tab, but it doesn't change the name of the Composition Zone item or its label in the Shared Content palette. It would make more sense if the names in the Layout Properties and the Shared Item Properties were synchronized. Again, I hope Quark fixes that in a future update.

Removing Composition Zones

If you want to make a change to one Composition Zone without changing any of the other places it's used, you'll have to "unsynch" that Composition Zone from the shared content. To do this, select the item with the item tool. Then choose Unsynchronize from the Item or the context menu. XPress will duplicate the Composition Zone and create another hidden layout that is not shared; the other instances remain synchronized.

If you want to unsynchronize all instances of a Composition Zone, select its label name in the Shared Content palette and then either click the Unsynchronize All button or choose Unsynchronize All from the context menu. The Composition Zone remains in the palette, but all the instances of the zone item in the layout can now be edited independently. When you unsynchronize a Composition Zone, it remains its own layout, which can be a limitation, as I discuss below.

Sometimes, though, you might want to unsynchronize a Composition Zone without making it editable at all. For example, you might have a shared layout that you use in many projects but don't want anyone to be able to make changes when you share it with others. To unsynchronize a Composition Zone and make it ineditable, select Convert to Picture from the Composition Zones submenu from the Item menu or the context menu. XPress saves the page displayed in the Composition Zone as an EPS, places the EPS file in the same folder as the current project, converts the Composition Zone into a picture box, and then imports the EPS into the new box.

Deleting a Composition Zone. Composition Zones remain saved in the Shared Content palette, whether or not they're used, until you remove them. To remove a Composition Zone from the project, select its label name and click the Delete button (or choose Delete from the context menu). This removes the label from the palette and unsynchronizes all instances of the formerly synchronized item, so you can now edit them independently.

If the Composition Zone was external, the saved file remains in the file system and can be used in other projects.

Limitations of Composition Zones

Unfortunately, once you've created a Composition Zone, you can't "uncreate" it or decompose it into its component items on the original layout. If you start creating Composition Zones indiscriminately, you may find yourself with a lot of little layouts within layouts, which could become confusing and potentially make your file much larger than it should be. Also, you can't show a Composition layout's tab in the project window if the Composition Zone isn't shared.

Another shortcoming of Composition Zones is that they can't be resized in a layout. You can change the page size in the Layout Properties of a Composition Zone, but that will affect all the places it is used. So if you want to resize only one instance of a Composition Zone, you need to unsynchronize it.

Also, you can't delete a layout that is being shared. If you want to delete a shared layout, you can turn off sharing by selecting Advanced Layout Properties from the Layout menu and disabling the Share Layout checkbox, and sometimes you even have to close and reopen the project before you can delete the layout.

JOB JACKETS

Murphy's Law states that whatever can go wrong, will go wrong, which leads me to believe that Murphy worked in prepress.

The world of design, printing, and publishing is full of opportunities for costly errors resulting from miscommunications and mistakes that can make you miss a deadline, go over budget, or both. Prepress specialists frequently have to deal with ambiguous project specifications, and the cost of an error in a large print job can be significant.

Many workflows include some sort of project tracking system, which could be a simple folder with written instructions or a complex workflow and content management system. Without some kind of system in place, crucial information about a project is likely to get lost on a Post-it note or in an email archive.

In XPress 7, Job Jackets are introduced to address this problem. A Job Jacket is similar to an electronic version of a folder containing all the information required to successfully manage a complex print project from creation through to output and beyond. You can use Job Jackets to create projects and layouts from detailed production specifications, verify that a layout follows its specifications, and then share your specifications with other members of your workgroup.

When it's time to output the job, using Job Jackets can help you minimize production errors by evaluating your layout according to the specifications you've defined and helping you track down problems. Some people liken Job Jackets to preflight software, but I think of it more like pre-preflight, or like the Quality Assurance feature: You'll still likely want to use preflighting software downstream, but this is a great way to identify potential problems early in the workflow and fix them.

Job Jackets can also help you collaborate with other members of your workgroup more effectively. When you change the specifications in a Job Jacket, the corresponding project settings update in every project linked to that Job Jacket, which helps ensure that your specifications remain consistent throughout all your projects and your entire workgroup.

Based on JDF. Because Job Jackets are based on the Job Definition Format (JDF) standard, you can also use them to specify aspects of a project that occur after output, such as binding settings. JDF is a standard XML-based file format for end-to-end job specifications, intended to streamline information exchange between different members of a workflow. It is intended to standardize the process of moving a print job through the entire print process, from layout to prepress to print, right through to cutting and binding.

You don't need to be in a full JDF workflow to take advantage of Job Jackets. In fact, you don't need to know anything about JDF at all to use this feature. But if you do participate in a JDF workflow, Job Jackets can become an extremely powerful tool for streamlining your work.

You can read more about JDF at *www.cip4.org.*

Warning: Before I jump in and explain how to use this feature, I just want to say one thing for the record: The user interface for this feature was designed and implemented by aliens and if you find yourself confused, it's only because you weren't born on Saturn. Job Jackets are powerful, but don't expect to jump in quickly; it takes some time to wrap your head around this deeply flawed interface. I can only hope that Quark will figure out a better way to do this in XPress 8.

Job Jackets and Job Tickets

Job Jackets contain a variety of project-level resources as well as Job Tickets and Job Ticket templates. A Job Ticket contains information specific to an individual layout, whereas Job Jackets contain information that is shared across an entire project.

For example, you might have one Job Jacket with all the settings for a corporate paper system, but you would have different Job Tickets in the Job Jacket for stationery, envelopes, business cards, and so on.

The resources contained in Job Jackets are available to all the layouts in a project, such as colors, style sheets, color management settings, output styles, lists, and so on. Job Jackets also contain resources that can be applied to individual layouts, such as layout specifications, output specifications, and rule sets. (I'll explain what those are later in the chapter.) In addition, Job Jackets can contain useful information not directly associated with a layout, such as contact information for project members, a job number, or special instructions.

Within each Job Jacket are one or more Job Tickets containing the specifications for various types of projects and layouts that indicate the resources available in a particular project. Each Job Ticket corresponds to one layout, so you might have different Job Tickets for Letter- and A4-sized stationery, for example.

Each Job Ticket can contain specifications for character and paragraph style sheets, colors, dashes and stripes, H&Js, lists, and layout definitions, which in turn are made up of layout specifications, rules, and output specifications. So, a Job Jacket might contain all the colors used throughout the paper system—green, red, orange, two shades of blue, and four shades of gray. But each Job Ticket contains only the colors applicable to a specific kind of layout. For instance, a business card might only contain the blues and two shades of gray.

Job Jackets can also contain Job Ticket templates. You can think of a Job Ticket template as sort of a master page for Job Tickets. (I'll explain Job Ticket templates later in the chapter, too.)

Don't worry if Job Jackets seem somewhat complex. They become somewhat clearer once you start playing around with them.

Job Jackets Manager

When you need to create or make changes to a Job Jacket, you normally start in the Job Jackets Manager, which is kind of a control center for creating and managing Job Jackets and Job Tickets. Choose Job Jackets Manager from the Utilities menu to open the Job Jackets Manager dialog box. The Job Jackets Manager dialog box is different from other dialog boxes in XPress: As you make changes to Job Jackets and Job Tickets, you can open other dialog boxes on top of the Job Jackets Manager, but it will remain in the background. You need to remember to click the Save button before you close the Job Jackets Manager to save your work. To close the dialog box, click the Close button. If you click Close without first saving your work, XPress prompts you to save your changes.

The appearance of the Job Jackets Manager changes, depending on which settings you decide to use. The Basic setting is the default, which gives you access to most of the Job Jackets features, whereas the Advanced setting gives you more controls as well as some features unavailable in the Basic setting. Let's look at the Basic setting first and then go into more Advanced settings later in the chapter.

Basic settings. Job Jackets Manager's Basic settings let you create, use, and share Job Jackets.

When you open the Job Jackets Manager, you'll see a list of the Job Jackets and Job Tickets available for use in your project (see Figure 13-8). Don't be surprised to see a Job Jacket listed even if you've never used Job Jackets before.

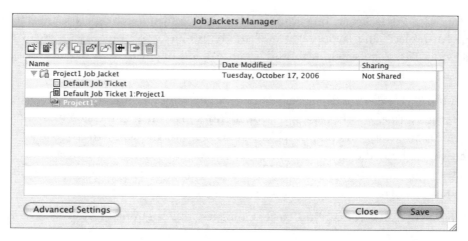

Figure 13-8 Job Jackets Manager

Just as XPress stores internal default settings for things like colors or measurements in the XPress Preferences, it stores all the default settings for projects and layouts in a default Job Jacket. When you create a new project, XPress automatically makes a Job Ticket using the default and embeds it in the project file. You can link your project to a different Job Jacket if you want to apply the specifications from a different Job Jacket.

Additionally, the list contains any Job Jackets in the default Job Jackets folder. This is normally your Documents folder, but you can choose any folder you like in the Job Jackets panel of the Preferences dialog box. (I discuss XPress Preferences in Chapter 2, *QuarkXPress Basics*.) Job Jackets Manager shows you the relationships between Job Jackets, which have icons that look like folders, and the projects, Job Tickets, and Job Ticket templates within the Job Jackets. Job Tickets and Job Ticket templates have similar icons, but you can distinguish between the two because Job Ticket icons are black and Job Ticket templates are gray. A line connecting a project icon to a Job Ticket shows which Job Ticket is associated with that project.

Creating Job Jackets

If you want to create a new Job Jacket, click the New Job Jacket button at the top of the Job Jacket Manager. When the New Job Jacket dialog box appears, you can name your Job Jacket and decide where you want to store it. Most of the time, I prefer to save my Job Jackets in the default folder so I can keep track of them all in one place.

At this point, you can click the OK button to close the dialog box, and your new Job Jacket will be identical to the default Job Jacket. But you will probably want to make changes to the Job Ticket before you click OK. You can edit many of the properties of your new Job

Ticket by clicking the triangle next to Settings, just below the Name field. The dialog box expands to reveal a new section with four tabs: Tickets, Style Settings, Contacts, and Layout Specification (see Figure 13-9).

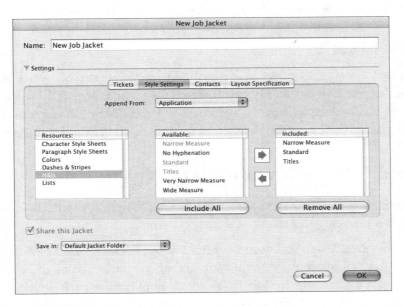

Figure 13-9 Expanded settings for a new Job Jacket

Tickets. Use the Tickets tab to add new Job Tickets to the jacket. Add a different ticket for each kind of project that will share the resources in the Job Jacket. Job Tickets are explained in the next section.

Style Settings. You can decide which style sheets, colors, dashes and stripes, H&Js, and lists you want to append to your Job Jacket, making them available for use in the projects that are linked to the jacket. When you click on one of the resource types in the left column, the middle column displays all of the resources available in the source selected in the Append From popup menu. Select any available resource you want and click the arrow to include it in your Job Jacket.

By default, XPress displays the resources from the application default preferences. You can change the append source by choosing from the Append From popup menu. Other sources you can choose from are another Job Jacket, a linked project, or any other project.

Contacts. One of the nice touches with Job Jackets is the ability to add contact information to a Job Jacket. You can add information for as many members of your team as you like, such as the art director or the production manager. His or her contact information travels with the job, so you can be sure everybody knows who to call in an emergency.

Layout Specification. The Layout Specification tab lets you define detailed layout settings for the job. You can define page size, page count, margins, bleed, binding information, and other layout-specific properties and store those specifications in a Job Jacket. I'll talk more about Layout Specifications later, in the section "Advanced Job Jacket Settings."

Editing a Job Jacket

To edit an existing Job Jacket, select its name in the middle section of the Job Jackets Manager dialog box and click the Edit button (the one that looks like a little pencil). XPress displays the Edit Job Jacket dialog box, which is virtually identical to the New Job Jacket dialog box, with all the same controls for tickets, style settings, contacts, and layout specifications.

Job Tickets and Job Ticket Templates

When you create a new project, XPress automatically links the project to a new Job Ticket, but you can link a different Job Ticket to the project if you prefer.

Job Ticket Templates. When you want to create settings for a new kind of project, you need to create a Job Ticket template. As I mentioned earlier, you can think of a Job Ticket template as sort of a master page for Job Tickets. You should create a Job Ticket template for recurring jobs that share resources, such as magazines or newsletters. You should also create a Job Ticket template for standard project templates that are shared by many people, or for when a group of people working on the same project need to stay in synch.

To create a new Job Ticket template, open the Job Jackets Manager dialog box (from the Utilities menu) and click the New Ticket Template button at the top left of the dialog box. The New Job Ticket dialog box should look similar to the New Job Jacket dialog box, and you can make many of the same kinds of changes (see Figure 13-10).

The Style Settings tab is identical to the one you see when you create a new Job Jacket. You can choose which resources you want to make available in projects linked to that Job Jacket.

The Layout Settings tab lets you define what Quark sometimes describes as a layout definition. You can create layout settings that define the medium type (print or Web), the layout specifications for that medium, along with any rule sets or output specification resources appropriate to that layout. Rule sets and output specifications are advanced settings in Job Jackets Manager, and I'll explain how to create them later in the chapter.

If you add new layout definitions to the Job Ticket for a project, XPress creates new tabs for each layout when you save the Job Ticket and close the Edit Job Ticket dialog box.

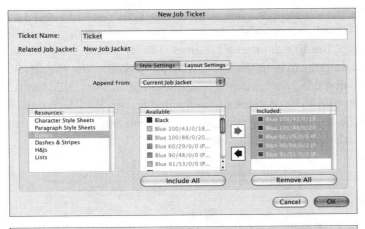

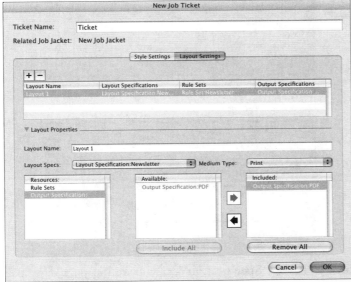

Figure 13-10
Creating Job Ticket templates

Advanced Job Jacket Settings

Job Jackets Manager's Basic settings give you access to most of the features you need, but the Advanced settings let you make more changes from a single, multipaned window. In the Advanced settings, you can also create layout specifications, output specifications, and rule sets, as well as add external resources such as pictures, text, or Composition Zones, and quickly manage resource locations.

Click the Advanced Settings button to change the Job Jackets Manager mode to advanced (see Figure 13-11). The left portion of the Advanced Job Jackets Manager settings is a list of Job Jackets and tickets, just like in the Basic settings. The right side of the dialog box consists of two additional sections to help you work with Job Jackets more efficiently. The top right section of the dialog box lists the types of resources associated with Job Jackets and tickets, whereas the bottom right contains the individual resources of each type. You'll see familiar icons above the bottom right section, where you can create new resources as well as edit, duplicate, or delete existing resources.

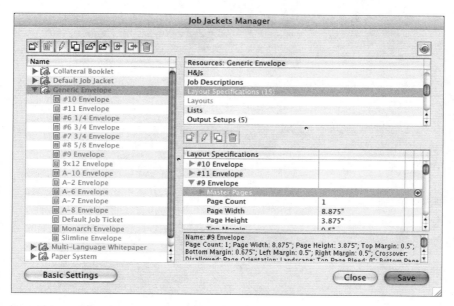

Figure 13-11 Advanced Job Jacket settings

Layout Specifications. A Layout Specification lets you define page size, page count, margins, bleed, binding information, and other layout-specific properties, and store those specifications in a Job Jacket.

Click the name of your Job Jacket in the left pane of the dialog box, scroll down the list of resource types in the top right, click Layout Specifications, and then click the New Item icon in the middle right of the dialog box to create a new layout specification.

You can click any of the layout properties to change them. (If you don't see the properties, click on the "expand" triangle next to the layout specification name.) You can specify page count, page width and height, margins, crossover, spreads, binding type, binding side, binding length, page orientation, bleeds, color standard, spot colors, and total inks. Some layout specifications allow free-form text entry, whereas others have popup menus to limit your choices. You can also define many master page properties such as margins, columns, gutter width, and facing pages. (Note that while this feature worked in earlier versions of XPress 7, it's not fully working in 7.3 of Mac OS. With luck, Quark will have fixed it in their next free update).

> *Tip: Make a New Layout Specification Anytime.* You can also create layout specifications without opening the Job Jackets Manager. To create a layout specification, select New Layout Specification from the Layout Menu, which then displays the Job Jackets Manager dialog box. The lower-right section of the dialog box will contain a new specification.

Output Specifications. Just as layout specifications let you control various aspects of a layout, output specifications let you define output-specific information such as color space, PDF/X compliance, PostScript level, halftone frequency, and so on (see Figure 13-12). Before you output a job, you can evaluate whether your project complies with the specifications you've set for it and identify any problem areas. I'll explain how to evaluate layouts later in the chapter.

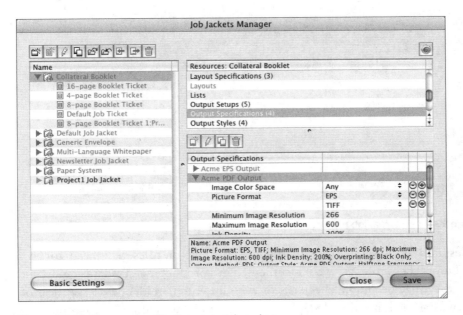

Figure 13-12 Output specifications in a Job Jacket

Usually, output specifications will be created by an output specialist. For example, in a perfect world your print service provider might have output specifications available for download or provide a guide for how to create your own to suit your job.

When you create a layout definition, you can associate the correct output specification with your layout.

Tip: Append Application Preferences to a Project or Job Ticket. You can click the XPress application icon button in the top-right corner of the Job Jackets Manager Advanced settings to quickly append all of the default XPress settings to the current project. Once you've done so, you can use the popup menu next to each resource to move it to the Job Ticket if you want to share it with others.

External resources. You can add external resources to a Job Ticket or project even before you're ready to use them in a layout (see Figure 13-13). You can store pictures, text, and Composition Zones in a Job Jacket and make them available in all projects linked to that Job Tickets in that Job Jacket. For example, you might have a logo and some standard legal text that you use in every project. You can add them to a Job Ticket as external resources and make them available to everyone for all projects linked to that Job Ticket.

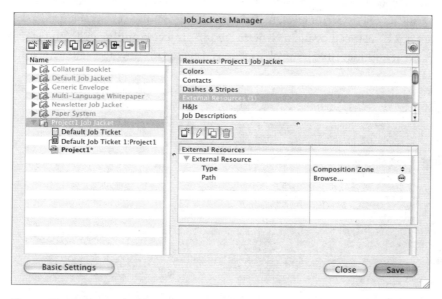

Figure 13-13 External job resources

Rules and rule sets. Every workflow has a set of rules that need to be followed. Sometimes these rules are well documented in a productions standards guide, and in other cases they may be simple checklists or even unwritten guidelines. Regardless of whether the rules are laminated and stapled to the wall or just shouted across the room, people sometimes make mistakes that can have expensive consequences.

That's why rules and rule sets are such an important part of Job Jackets in XPress 7. You can create rules to test whether or not your layout meets certain quality or production criteria. For example, let's say that some of the rules you follow for producing sales brochures are that the layout should not contain any text boxes with overflow, bold and italic text styles should never be used in a layout in place of the appropriate font, brochures can never be longer than eight pages, output must be PDF/x-1 compliant, and projects should include no more than one spot color. You can make a rule to test each one of these conditions so you can make suitable changes before your deadline.

The interface for creating rules is a wizard that lets you move through the process one step at a time (see Figure 13-14). When you create a rule, you start by choosing what type of item you want to test, then you choose a condition to test. As you move through each screen in the rules wizard, you'll see only the options applicable based on the choices you've made on earlier screens. You can also write a brief description of the rule, along with instructions for dealing with the issue. Finally, you can decide whether the condition that you're testing should be prohibited, not recommended, or noted.

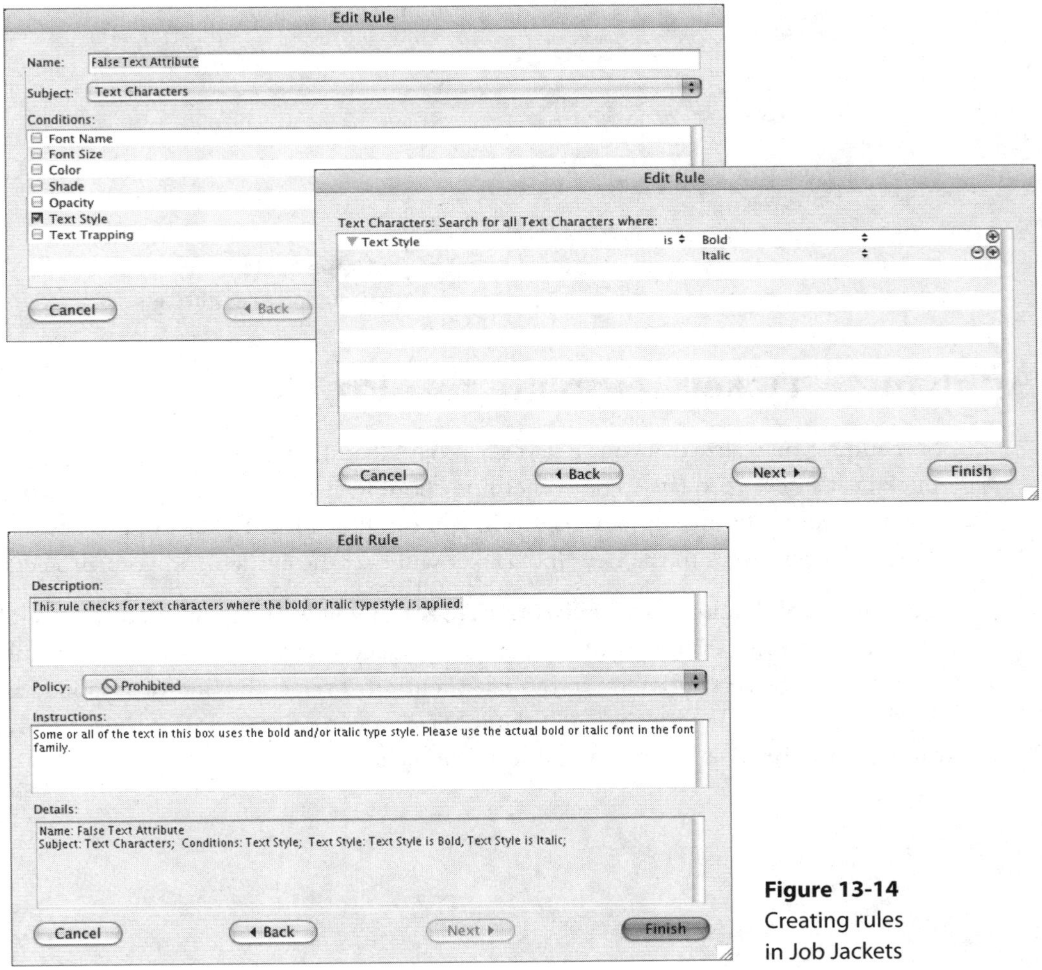

Figure 13-14
Creating rules
in Job Jackets

You can also group rules into rule sets so they're easier to manage. When you make a new rule set resource, you'll see the Edit Rule Set dialog box (see Figure 13-15). You can double-click on any of the rules listed on the left side of the dialog box to include them in the rule set. When you've finished, click the OK button.

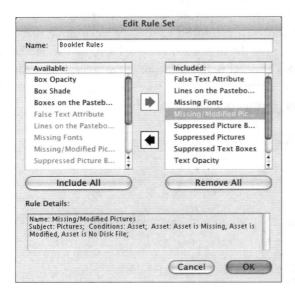

Figure 13-15
Grouping rules into sets

Applying a Ticket Template to a Project

Sometimes you realize that you've started a project that should have been based on a Job Ticket. Luckily, it's never too late to do something about it. If you've already created a project and want to apply a different Job Ticket to it, you can link a Job Ticket to a project at any time, and all the resources in the new Job Ticket will become available in your project.

Linking a Job Ticket to an existing project. If you want to apply a different Job Ticket to a project, you can link a Job Ticket to a project at any time by choosing Link Project from the Job Jackets submenu in the File menu. Just select the one you want and click the Attach button (see Figure 13-16). If the Job Ticket you want to link to is not displayed, you can click the Browse button to find it in the file system.

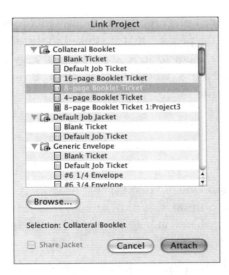

Figure 13-16
Linking to a Job Jacket

Creating a new project from a Job Ticket. One of the best time-saving features of Job Jackets is the ability to create a new project from a Job Ticket. To do so, choose New Project From Ticket from the New submenu in the File menu. The New Project From Ticket dialog box is very similar to the Link Project dialog box. Choose the Job Ticket you want to use as a template for your project and click the Select button.

When you create a new project from a Job Ticket, XPress creates the project with all the settings available in the Job Ticket template you've selected. For example, you might have a Job Jacket for an identity system that contains all the style sheets, colors, and color management settings for a client. Your Job Jacket might also have Job Ticket templates for various-sized ads, posters, brochures, sales collateral, and so on. One of your Job Ticket templates might specify an eight-page brochure of a particular size with a certain set of style sheets, corporate colors, and output settings. When you create the project from the Job Ticket template, your new project will be created with all the appropriate pages, resources, and settings already applied to it. Again, this feature is not fully working in version 7.3 on Mac OS, so your mileage may vary.

This is an extremely efficient way of creating templated projects, because you can store the definitions for several types of projects in a single Job Jacket. Since a Job Jacket is just a special kind of XML document, you can have dozens of Job Ticket templates saved in a compact text file rather than having to keep track of many different templates.

Job Jacket synchronization. Job Jackets linked to a project are always synchronized, so when you make changes to a Job Jacket, all of the projects that are linked to that Job Jacket are updated. It might be confusing or inconvenient to have something like style sheets change or have a color disappear, so you can control when and how often XPress checks for Job Jacket updates. To specify update settings for Job Jackets, choose the Updates tab of Collaboration Setup (in the File menu).

Evaluating a Layout

I mentioned earlier that Job Jackets help you do a kind of project preflight before you output. In fact, you can evaluate whether a layout conforms to its specifications any time you want, so you can identify and fix potential problems when you have time to fix them rather than right before a deadline.

To evaluate a layout, choose Evaluate Layout from the Job Jackets submenu (in the File menu). When the Layout Evaluation dialog box appears (see Figure 13-17), click the Evaluate button to run the test. XPress will display a list of each rule and specification, and indicate whether the layout has passed or failed each one. If a rule has failed, you can click its name to see the explanation of the rule and why it failed. Clicking the buttons that look like forward and back navigation buttons will take you to the exact place in the layout where the problem occurs.

One thing to keep in mind when you evaluate your layouts is that XPress isn't going to magically solve your problems for you. XPress will help you find all the places where a layout doesn't conform to the specifications you've defined, but fixing the problem is up to you. For example, if you create a rule to detect text boxes with overflow, XPress will help you find all the offending boxes, but you will still have to decide what to do with the overflow.

When you've finished evaluating your layout, click the Done button to close the dialog box.

You can also force XPress to evaluate your layouts automatically each time you open, save, print, export, or close them. You can control this behavior in the Job Jackets panel of the Preferences dialog box.

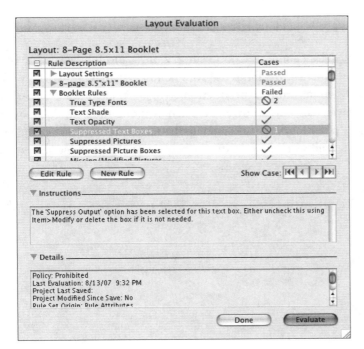

Figure 13-17
Evaluating a layout's compliance to its settings

Managing Job Jackets

Earlier in the chapter I explained how XPress stores the default settings for new projects and layouts in a default Job Jacket. When you create a new project, XPress makes a copy of the ticket in the default Job Jacket and embeds it in your new project file.

I've always liked customizing the XPress application preferences because you can quickly get started with new projects by making things like colors, style sheets, and hyphenation settings available in every new project. The default Job Ticket lets you do the same kind of thing, but it's even more powerful because it can include information like output specifications and rules. You can edit your default Job Ticket template to include all of the settings and resources you normally use across all your projects. If you store your default Job Jacket somewhere where others in your workgroup have access to it, you can ensure that the default settings for all your projects are synchronized across your workgroup.

The default Job Jacket file is named DefaultJacket.xml and is normally located in your default Job Jackets folder. The default Job Jackets folder is usually your Documents folder, but if you've made changes in the Job Jackets panel of the Preferences dialog box it might be somewhere else.

LET'S ALL WORK TOGETHER

Together or individually, shared content, Composition Zones, and Job Jackets are powerful features that can help you synchronize and reuse your content, share your work, conform to detailed job specifications, and minimize production errors. While you can "share" content with yourself, these features are most powerful when you use them to collaborate with others. With a little bit of planning, you can speed up the time it takes you to create projects, keep your team in synch, and virtually eliminate many common production errors. Who wouldn't want all that?

CHAPTER FOURTEEN

Color

Look around you. Unless you're fully colorblind, everything around you has color. It's not really surprising that folks have wanted to work with color in their documents since—well, since they've been creating documents! What *is* surprising is how complicated working with color can be, especially with all the computer equipment around that's supposed to make life easy for us.

There's a range of complicated issues in desktop color: specifying the color you want, getting that color to print on a color or a black-and-white laser printer, and producing film and plates for offset printing. Achieving quality color on a Macintosh or PC is not quite as easy as turning on the computer; we have our work cut out for us. But at least we know it's possible.

I begin this chapter with an overview of some basic theories of color, including the various color models (ways in which you specify color on the computer). This leads me into the color components of the QuarkXPress features set, including building and applying colors and generating traps for better print quality. Although I discuss the fundamentals of color separation here, I'll cover the area of generating color separations of your layouts in Chapter 15, *Printing*. Also, note that I won't cover XPress's color management system (CMS) much here.

WHAT YOU SEE AND WHAT YOU GET

Before I even begin talking desktop color, it's important for you to know that the color you see on the screen is almost never what you'll get from your color printer, much less what you can expect to see come off a printing press.

The medium is the message. The primary reason for this color differential is the difference in the medium. Colors are displayed on the screen by lighting up phosphors, which emit colored light. This is significantly different from printed color, which depends on other light sources to reflect off it into your eyes. If you use different methods of showing colors, you will always see different colors from each.

Pantone colors are a great example of this: Take a Pantone swatch book and pick a color. Hold that color up to the screen next to QuarkXPress's Pantone color simulation. Chances are it'll look like a totally different color.

Even similar devices can generate wildly differing color. If you've ever walked into a television store and seen the same image on 30 different screens, you know that different monitors display color differently (that's why your layout looks different on your officemate's screen than it does on yours). The same goes for printing presses and color printers: Even though they may claim to print with cyan, yellow, magenta, and black, those four colors may well be different depending on where in the world you're printing, which company's inks you're using, what sort of press your job is printing on, and even what the weather is like that day.

Calibration and color management. There's only so much you can do about the color discrepancies you'll encounter. Some monitors are better than others at displaying certain colors. And if you don't already have a 24-bit color video card ("millions of colors" or "true color"), you should definitely get one. You can buy a monitor calibration system from companies like X-Rite to adjust your screen's colors so that they'll more closely match your printed output.

Another solution is color management, using a system like ColorSync. These systems adjust the colors that show up on the screen to more closely match the final output colors. However, even these are limited and often can't manage everything on your page.

Whatever you end up using, remember that what you see is *rarely* what you get.

Use swatch books. Because of all this uncertainty, it's important to specify your colors from a swatch book. Look at the book, see what color you want, and specify it. If possible, create your own swatch book, and print it on your final output device—offset press, color printer, whatever. If you're printing with process inks, spec your colors from a process swatch book such as TruMatch or the Pantone 4-Color Process guide. If you're printing with PMS inks, use a PMS spot-color swatch book. I'll explain all these terms in the next section.

DESCRIBING COLOR

In a perfect world you would be able to say, "I want this object to be burnt sienna," and your computer and print service provider would know exactly the color you mean. Outside of picking Crayola colors, however, this just can't be done. Everyone from scientists to artists to computer programmers has been trying for centuries to come up with a general model for specifying and re-creating colors. In the past 50 years alone, these color models have been created: HSB, NTSC, CMYK, YIQ, CIE, PAL, HSL, RGB, CCIR, RS-170, and HSI, among others. (And you thought that graphic file-format names were far out!)

QuarkXPress presently handles four color models (RGB, CMYK, HSB, and Lab), plus several color-matching systems, or libraries: Focoltone, TruMatch, Toyo, DIC, Pantone Coated, Pantone Uncoated, Pantone Process, Pantone Solid to Process, Pantone Hexachrome, and Pantone Color Bridge. These color models are intimately connected with printing and other reproduction methods, so I'll first discuss the particulars of printing color, then move into each color model in turn.

Spot Versus Process Color

When dealing with color, either on the desktop or off, you'll need to understand the differences between process and spot color. Both are commonly used in the printing process. Both can give you a wide variety of colors. But they aren't interchangeable. Depending on your final output device, you may also be dealing with composite colors. Let's look at each of these, one at a time.

Process color. Look at any color magazine or junk mail you've received lately. If you look closely at a color photograph, you'll see lots of little dots that make up the color. These are color halftones consisting of four colors: cyan, magenta, yellow, and black (see Chapter 11, *Image Tuning,* for more information on halftones). I'll talk about this color model, CMYK, a little later on; what's important here is that many, many colors are being represented by overlaying tints of the four basic colors. Our eyes blend all these colors together so that ultimately we see the color we're intended to see.

Cyan, magenta, yellow, and black are the process colors. The method—or process—of separating the millions of colors into only four colors is referred to as creating *process-color separations.*

Each separation represents film or a plate that contains artwork for only one of the colors. Your printer can take the four pieces of film, expose a plate from each of the four pieces, and use those four plates on a press. Increasingly, print jobs are imaged direct to plate without intermediate film.

Process color is not just for full-color images. You can use each of the process colors individually or in combination to create colored type, rules, or tint blocks on your layout page. These items generally appear as solid colors to the unaided eye but are actually made from "tint builds" of the process colors.

Spot color. The idea behind spot color is that the printing ink is just the color you want, which makes it unnecessary to build a color using the four process colors. With spot color, for example, if you want some type to be colored teal blue, you print it on a plate that is separate from the black plate. Your printer prints that type using a teal-blue ink—such as PMS 3135 or 211—and then uses black to print the rest of the job. Some colors (such as bright orange) fall outside the range of colors that can be printed in process and can only be printed with spot colors.

The difference between process and spot colors is that process colors are built by overlaying tints of four separate inks, whereas spot colors are printed using just one colored ink (the color you specify). In either case, your printer runs the page through a one-color press once for each color's plate, or uses a multicolor press that prints the colors successively in a single pass.

Mixing process and spot colors. You can use both spot and process colors together in a layout, if you've got the budget. Some printers have six- or eight-color presses, which can print the four process colors along with two or more spot colors. Edward Tufte's *Envisioning Information*, for example, was printed with 12 spot colors.

Composite color. Film recorders and many inkjet printers use what I call "composite color." For example, most film recorders print using RGB format (more on this format a little later on) regardless of how your color is specified in QuarkXPress. Similarly, some color printers represent both spot and process colors alike by mixing colored waxes or dyes on the paper, and may actually render better color when "fed" RGB input.

The key here is that the colors you specify are being represented by some color model that you may not have intended. If you know that you are printing on such a device, you should refer to the service bureau and/or your owner's manual for tips on how to work best with that device.

Tip: Spot-Color Pinch Hitters. You don't have to create your own spot colors in your layouts. If your job contains only black and one to three spot colors, you can use a process color (cyan, magenta, or yellow) to pinch-hit for each spot color. If you take this approach, give your printer written instructions such as "Print all 'Cyan' as Pantone 234 and all 'Magenta' as Pantone 567." Also print out comps of the job with intended spot colors indicated.

These tricks make it easy for periodicals that use a new set of spot colors each month. You don't have to painfully re-spec your imported graphics that use the spot colors; spec them once as the same process color as you're using in XPress, and the color gets mapped automatically.

Tip: Put Black Type on a Fifth Plate. If you're prone to frequent last-minute type changes, you might find it helpful to make your black type a spot color instead of normal black. You can spec this fifth color to look black (or near black) onscreen, and set it to overprint. This approach is often used for versioning.

While you increase your printing costs at first (five plates instead of four), you'll find that last-minute changes are much less expensive (you only have to reprint that one plate instead of four). It's up to you and your printing company to determine which method will be the more cost-effective for you.

Color Models

Before I jump into how to create and use colors in XPress, let's talk a bit about each of the color models that QuarkXPress handles and what each model is good for.

RGB. Color models are generally broken down into two classes: additive and subtractive systems. An *additive* color system is counterintuitive to most people: the more color you add to an object, the closer to white you get. In the RGB model, adding 100 percent of red, green, and blue to an area results in pure white. If you have a color television or a color monitor on your computer, you already have had a great deal of experience with RGB. These pieces of equipment describe colors by "turning on" red, green, and blue phosphors on the screen. Various colors are created by mixing these three colors together.

- Black = zero percent of all three colors
- Yellow = red + green
- Magenta = red + blue
- Cyan = green + blue

All digital cameras image use RGB because they're projecting light at a CCD (charge coupled device). Color scanners always scan in RGB mode (even those big, expensive drum scans) because light is always measured in RGB. If the image is destined for print, some software (perhaps the software that runs the scanner) must convert it to CMYK.

CMYK. *Subtractive* colors, on the other hand, become whiter as you subtract color from them, and get darker as you add more color. This is analogous to painting on a white piece of paper. CMY (let's leave the K aside for a moment) is called a subtractive color model: The more cyan, magenta, and yellow you add together, the closer to black you get.

The connection between RGB and CMY is interesting: They are exact opposites of each other. You can take an RGB color and mathematically invert each of the RGB values and get the same color in the CMY model (see Figure 14-1). If this doesn't come intuitively to you (it doesn't to me), don't worry. The theory behind this is much less important than what it implies.

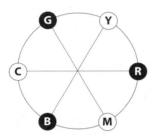

Emitted and reflected (additive and subtractive) colors complement one another. Red is complemented by cyan, green by magenta, and blue by yellow.

Figure 14-1
Complementary colors

The implication of RGB and CMY having an inverse relation is that colors in either model should be easy to convert. This is true. They are easy to convert. The problem is that the CMY model has few practical applications. Cyan, magenta, and yellow inks don't really add up to black in the real world because ink pigments are never pure cyan, magenta, or yellow. Adding CMY together makes a muddy brown. Thus, printers over the years have learned that they must add a black element to the printing process, and that's where the K comes in. (K stands for "key," and signifies black because B might be confused for blue.)

While you can describe many colors using these four, you can't generate as many colors as RGB can (or the number of colors we can see). In fact, many different combinations of CMYK actually describe the same color. (Later in this chapter, I'll discuss an offshoot of CMYK, called Hexachrome, which uses six colors to represent even more colors.)

It's important to remember that knowing the percentages of cyan, yellow, magenta, and black does not actually tell you what a color looks like. CMYK is like a cooking recipe, and just as different chefs or different ingredients will generate very different flavors, different printers, presses, or brands of ink will produce different colors. If a press is run to a standard such as SWOP (Specifications for Web Offset Presses), results are predictable, of course. But printing is a high-speed physical process, and tiny variations are inevitable.

Because of these factors, the conversion from RGB to CMYK (again, this is called "color separation") is nowhere near as precise as one could hope. In fact, different programs use different conversion algorithms, so an RGB color from QuarkXPress prints differently than it would from Photoshop or some other application.

HSB. Rather than breaking a color down into subparts, the HSB model describes a color by its hue, saturation, and brightness. The *hue* is basically the color's position in a color spectrum that starts at red, moves through magenta to blue, through green to yellow, and then through orange back to red. The *saturation* of the color can be described as the amount of color in it. Or, conversely, the amount of white in it. A light pink, for example, has a lower saturation than a bright red. The color's *brightness* reflects the amount of black in it. Thus, that same bright red would, with a lower brightness, change from a vibrant red to a dark, dull, reddish-black.

You could say that mixing a color (a hue) with white produces a *tint* (a degree of saturation). Mix it with black to produce a *tone* (a degree of brightness).

HSB is not easy to understand intuitively, especially when it comes to specifying colors. For example, here are the hue values for the three spot colors in XPress's default color list.

- Red = zero

- Green = 21,845 (QuarkXPress calls this 33.3 percent)

- Blue = 43,690 (QuarkXPress calls this 66.7 percent)

You may find HSB useful if you're creating slides on a film recorder or doing multimedia, but it's not of much use for print publishing. I tend to simply forget that it's there.

Lab. CIE Lab (which appears in XPress simply as "Lab") is designed to describe what colors look like, regardless of what device they're displayed on. Because of this, Lab colors are called "device-independent." Where HSB represents colors positioned around a color wheel, Lab uses a more accurate but significantly less intuitive arrangement. L stands for luminance, describing how bright the color appears to the human eye. (Unlike brightness in HSB, luminance takes into account the fact that we see green as brighter than blue.)

The "a" and "b" channels in CIE Lab represent spectrums from green to red, and from blue to yellow, respectively. Don't feel dumb if you find it hard to get your head around Lab color. It *is* difficult, because it's an abstract mathematical construct—it doesn't correspond to anything we can actually experience.

The fact that Lab is device-independent should mean that it's a great way to transfer colors from one application or machine to another. Unfortunately, XPress's implementation of Lab is so limited that it's not really worth using. But who knows? Maybe I'll see improvements in future versions that will change my mind.

Color-Matching Systems

In addition to the four color models in QuarkXPress that you use to define colors, there are also ten libraries of predefined colors representing printed color swatch books. Three of these systems—Pantone Solid, Toyo, and DIC—are for use with spot-color printing. The others—TruMatch, Focoltone, Pantone Process, Pantone Color Bridge and Pantone Hexachrome—are for process-color work.

These libraries are conveniences: You can specify process colors by simply typing in the values, for instance, without ever going near the color libraries. There are advantages to using these libraries, however, aside from their paint-by-number simplicity.

• **Spot-color libraries.** Using a library ensures that the right color name is specified during output and makes it more likely that the color name in your layout will match the one in imported EPS graphics (see "Color from Outside Sources," later in this chapter). Also, the colors are set up to give you the best output that's reasonably possible onscreen and on color printers.

• **Process-color libraries.** With process-color work, the advantages to using the color libraries are that you don't have to type in the color name and color specification by hand, and that you can easily communicate a color to someone else who also has your kind of swatch book.

No matter what method you use for specifying colors, you should be looking at printed swatch books to decide what color you want. Given that caveat, here's a rundown of the color libraries available in QuarkXPress.

TruMatch. TruMatch is a system for specifying process colors. I can specify (and a properly calibrated imagesetter can provide me with) a tint value of any percentage, not just in 5- or 10-percent increments. The folks at TruMatch took advantage of this and created a very slick, very easy-to-use system with over 2000 evenly gradated colors.

The colors in the TruMatch swatchbook are arranged in the colors of the spectrum. The first number in a TruMatch code indicates a color's hue (its place on the spectrum). These numbers range from 1 to 50. The second item in a color's TruMatch code indicates its tint or strength, which ranges from "a" (saturated, 100-percent strength) to "h" (faded, unsaturated, 5-percent strength). The third number, indicates the color's brightness. The brightness code ranges from 1 (6-percent black) to 7 (42-percent black), in 6-percent increments. If there's no black in a color, this third code is left off.

Why is this so great? You can quickly make decisions on the relativity of two colors. If you want a color that's "a little darker and a little greener," you can quickly find a color that suits your desires. Compare this to the arrangement of colors in the Pantone or Focoltone matching systems and you'll understand.

Pantone Solid. Pantone, Inc.'s sole purpose in life (and business) is to continue to develop, maintain, and protect the sanctity of the spot-color Pantone Color Matching System (PMS for short).

A designer can choose a color from a Pantone-approved color swatch book, then communicate that color's number to the printer. The printer pulls out the Pantone color-mixing guidelines, finds that color's "recipe," and dutifully creates that exact color of ink. Almost all spot-color printing in the United States uses inks based on the Pantone Matching System. (See "Pantone Color Bridge," below, if you're tempted to simulate a Pantone color using process-color inks.)

Pantone has licensed its color libraries to Quark so that you can specify PMS colors from within QuarkXPress. However, the color you see on the screen may differ from the actual PMS color on paper. A computer screen is no substitute for a swatch book, especially when you're dealing with custom-mixed spot-color inks (I'll talk more about this later).

There are three problems with PMS color.

- Only certain colors are defined and numbered. If you want a color in between two colors in the Pantone book, you have to tell your printer to tweak it, requiring a custom-mixed ink.

- Although the books are printed under tight press, paper, and ink conditions, the colors change as the ink and paper age. (This happens with every kind of swatch book, of course. In fact, any printed piece changes appearance over time, due to exposure to light, heat and other environmental factors.) For this reason, Pantone recommends buying a new book every year. They make a lot of money from selling the books. Just make sure at the beginning of a job that your book and the printer's book are fairly close—or plan to leave a cut-out swatch from your book for the printer to match the color.

- I've never met anyone who actually understood the PMS color-numbering scheme. For example, PMS 485 and PMS 1795 are very similar, though every number in between is totally different.

Spot-color inks are great for two- and three-color jobs, but they're also worth considering if you have the budget for four or more colors—especially when you consider that you can create tint builds in between the various PMS ink colors (see "Multi-Ink Colors," later in this chapter). For example, some road maps are designed and printed using from one to five different spot colors in various carefully chosen tints and combinations. This way, tiny details—like type or cartographic symbols—can be accurately printed with a solid spot color (the halftoning used with process colors can wreak havoc on these small elements).

Pantone Color Bridge. When Pantone realized that they were being left behind (by TruMatch) in the process-color game, they shifted into first gear and released two process-color libraries. The first, Color Bridge (formerly Solid to Process), shows Pantone spot colors printed side-by-side with their best-match process simulations.

It's a fact of life that it's really hard to simulate spot colors with the four process colors. Some simulations are better than others. A pale blue is fairly easy to simulate with process inks, for instance; a rich, creamy, slate blue is almost impossible; and you'll never get anything approaching metallic copper or gold with CMYK inks.

If you're tempted to choose a color from a Pantone spot-color swatch book (or worse, onscreen), stop yourself and remember: Chances are that the spot color you choose won't be faithfully reproduced with process colors. Always look up the color in Pantone's Color Bridge swatch book, or just use a process-color swatch book to begin with. You may even discover a better CMYK match for your desired color than any spot color.

Pantone Process. Pantone Process is a process-color matching system much like TruMatch's and has no relationship to the Pantone spot colors; it's just a CMYK swatch book (there are two versions—one based on the SWOP inks and another based on Euroscale inks). It uses a different numbering scheme than the spot-color libraries. It's generally easier to find colors in it than in the Pantone spot-color swatch books. There are more colors to choose from than in any previous process-color matching system. And because Pantone is so well established, it's sometimes easier to find Pantone's swatch books.

You may find the TruMatch system more intuitive and easier to use than Pantone's. However, both are just process-color swatch books, and both are produced with rigorous quality-control standards.

Hexachrome. Because of the limitations of the standard process colors, printers sometimes print process-color images with extra spot colors to achieve more vibrant colors. To make this process easier, Pantone has developed the Hexachrome system, which uses the special versions of the four process inks plus particular orange and green inks. (If they had added a third color, you'd be able to reproduce even more vibrant colors, but there are a significant number of six-color printing presses in the world, so Pantone stopped with six colors.)

While Hexachrome can achieve stunning results, you may find that the outcome doesn't warrant the added expense. As one friend quipped, "Hexachrome is like quadraphonic hi-fi sound—it's awesome when you get it right, but most people aren't going to bother."

Another cool thing about Hexachrome is that the orange ink never prints over cyan, and green doesn't print over magenta, so you can double up the halftone settings for those inks without worrying about interference from screen angles.

If you're choosing Hexachrome colors in XPress, make sure you're picking them first from a printed swatch book. Keep in mind that you can't really do anything with Hexachrome colors without Quark's color management system.

Focoltone. Developed in Wales, Focoltone is a process-color matching system used widely in Europe, and used very little in North America. After buying Focoltone's rather expensive cross-referenced swatch books, you have to wade through 763 colors based on combinations of CMYK inks at 5-percent increments from zero to 85 percent. While newspaper publishers may find Focoltone marginally useful, it's a less appropriate system for designers.

Toyo and DIC. Toyo and DIC are both spot-color matching systems from Japan, created by the Toyo Ink Manufacturing Co. and DIC (Dainippon Ink and Chemicals, Inc.), respectively. These spot-color inks have a built-in feature which is helpful: Their names reflect how closely you can simulate them in process color. If the ink's designation is followed by one asterisk, the spot color cannot be closely matched in process color. If the number is followed by two asterisks, the spot color won't even be close to the color you see onscreen. For instance, metallic colors can never be represented onscreen, so they're followed by two asterisks.

If you're creating layouts that will be printed in Japan, then you may want to specify spot colors in either one of these systems rather than with an American system like Pantone. Otherwise, you can probably relax and keep reading.

SPECIFYING COLOR

In previous chapters I've discussed applying colors to objects using the Style menu and the Modify dialog box, and I've alluded to the Colors palette. Here I'll discuss how to create colors in QuarkXPress over and above the six that come as default settings. Then I'll get into the nitty-gritty of the Colors palette before covering the important issues of trapping and importing color from other programs.

The Color List

Before you can use a color in QuarkXPress, you have to create it, so that it appears on your layout's color list. XPress allows thousands of different colors on this list, including the six colors which must be present: Cyan, Magenta, Yellow, Black, White, and Registration (I'll talk about this last "color" later in this chapter). You can access this list—and thereby add, delete, and modify colors—by selecting Color from the Edit menu.

The Colors dialog box (see Figure 14-2) contains the color list, along with several buttons to manipulate the colors on the list.

Figure 14-2
The Colors dialog box

Tip: Making Your Colors Stick Around. Changing the color list while a layout is open only changes that layout's list; it doesn't change any future layouts you may create. However, you can alter the default color list—the list with which all new layouts open—by adding, deleting, and modifying colors while no layout is open. These changes stick around forever, or at least until you either change them again, reinstall QuarkXPress, or delete your XPress Preferences file.

QuarkXPress 7 no longer contains the RGB colors, Red, Green, and Blue, which weren't appropriate for print anyway. One (well, three) fewer things to worry about.

Show

It's easy to accumulate so many colors on your color list that you don't know what is what anymore. Fortunately, XPress includes the Show popup menu, which lets you display subsets of particular colors on the color list. We've seen this popup menu before in the Style Sheets and the H&Js dialog boxes, though this one has its own properties. The six options on the Show popup menu are All Colors, Spot Colors, Process Colors, Multi-Ink Colors, Colors in Use, and Colors Not Used. Here are a few ways you might use this feature.

- If you're printing a CMYK job, choose Spot Colors to make sure that you don't accidentally have any spot colors in the layout.

- If you've got dozens of colors in your layout, you can see which ones are really being used by selecting Colors in Use.

- Conversely, if you want to delete a lot of colors from your color list, choose Colors Not Used to make sure you're not removing any important ones.

New Colors

Now we get to the good stuff: making your own colors. Click the New button in the Colors dialog box to open the Edit Color dialog box (see Figure 14-3). Here's a rundown of the choices offered in this dialog box.

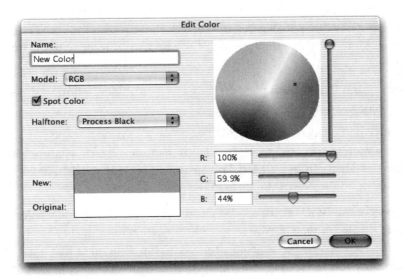

Figure 14-3 The Edit Color dialog box

Color name. The name that you type in the Name field appears on the Color scroll list and on the color lists in other menus throughout the program. You can call a process color anything you want. When I'm working with a process color, for example, I usually define my color using CMYK, and then I name it something like "10c80m0y20k." It's a bit cryptic at first, but I like it. On the other hand, you can just call the color by some name; for example, you might have a palette full of "Fuchsia" or "Royal Blue."

Spot Color. You use the Spot Color checkbox to determine whether a color is process or spot. When this option is turned on, the color is a spot color (that is, it won't separate into CMYK). When it's turned off, the color is output as CMYK.

Note that you can create a Pantone color—which usually would be specified as a spot color—as a process color by turning off this checkbox, thereby forcing the color to separate into four plates at print time. What results is a process simulation of the Pantone color. Similarly, you could create a CMYK color that would print as a spot color on its own plate. The first example has some usefulness; the second has almost none. And remember to check a reference such as the Pantone Color Bridge swatchbook to see how the process version of your color will actually print.

Halftone. When you're creating a spot color (and the Spot Color checkbox is turned on), the Halftone popup menu becomes active. Spot colors aren't always solids, of course; it's easy to make a tint of a spot color. For instance, you could have a blend from White to Red (see "Blending Colors," later in this chapter), and the spot color Red would be tinted from zero to 100 percent. The Halftone popup menu lets you adjust the halftone screen angle and frequency of these tints. If you leave the menu set to Black, tints of that spot color are always the same as Black (usually 45 degrees and the screen frequency set in the Page Setup dialog box). If you set it to Magenta, then the spot color has the same angle/frequency combination as Magenta.

However, modern imaging devices impose their own screen angles, ignoring this setting; consider it a vestige of the olden days.

Model. Once you've named a color and decided whether it's process or spot, you have to tell XPress how you want to spec the color—as CMYK, Pantone, TruMatch, or whatever— by choosing a system or library from the Model popup menu. For each model, XPress displays different choices on the right side of the dialog box.

For instance, if you choose RGB, HSB, or CMYK, the program shows you a color wheel, along with fields that you can type in. You must fight the temptation to click on an area on the color wheel. Sure, it's easy to choose colors this way—but remember that what you see on the screen probably has no relation to what you'll actually get on paper or film. It's much more reliable to choose a color from a CMYK swatch book and then just type the values into the C, M, Y, and K fields.

When you have a color-matching system—like Pantone, TruMatch, or Hexachrome— selected as the color model, you can select a color by either clicking on it in the Selector box (see Figure 14-4) or by typing the desired number into the field in the lower-right corner of the dialog box. Type in the number, and XPress jumps to that color. If you're working in Pantone and type "312," it jumps to color 312.

The Multi-Ink option on the Model popup menu creates blends between spot and process colors, and I'll discuss it in more detail later in this chapter.

> ***Tip: Grab Any Color.*** *There's one time that I condone using the color wheel in the Edit Color dialog box: if you're looking for a color, but you just don't know which one yet. For example, if you know that you want a greenish PMS color, but you're not sure exactly which green you want, you could just pick one from the color wheel and name it "Kelly Green" or whatever.*
>
> *When it comes time to print the piece, you can sit down with your printer and decide on a PMS color that will—you hope—match what you see onscreen. Even then, you don't have to go back and change the color in the Edit Color dialog box—just tell your printer that your Forest Green plate should be printed with the PMS color you decide on. Again, as long as the final decision is based on a swatch book, it hardly matters what you specify in this dialog box or what you call the color.*

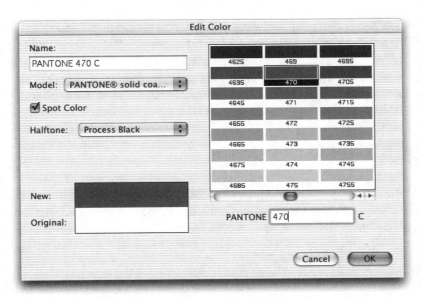

Figure 14-4 Pantone selection in the Edit Color dialog box

Tip: Clean Out Your Color Models. You can remove color models that you don't use by taking them out of the Color folder (which sits inside the same folder as QuarkXPress).

Tip: Importing Colors from Other Programs. You don't have to create the colors from within QuarkXPress. When you import a graphic from an illustration program such as Illustrator or FreeHand, QuarkXPress imports the colors and places them on the color list. The key is that the colors must be designated as spot colors in those programs.

Only colors that are actually used in an EPS file are imported (see "Color from Outside Sources," later in this chapter). If you want to import just the colors, but don't need the picture itself, you can make a few rectangles in your illustration program and apply the colors you want to those objects. Then save the page as an EPS file (with or without a preview). When you import the EPS into XPress, those colors are added to the color list. You can then delete the picture from the layout, and the colors remain.

New/Original preview. The final element in the Edit Color dialog box is the New/Original preview, which is really only relevant when you're editing colors (see "Editing Colors," below). When you are creating a new color, the lower half of this rectangle remains white (blank), as there was no "original" color to show. When you specify a color using one of the methods described earlier, the upper rectangle shows what that color looks like. You can specify a color, look at this preview window, then change the specifications and actually see the change in the way the color looks.

When you have the color the way you like it, clicking OK closes this dialog box and adds your color to the palette.

Tip: Tinted Colors. Do you have a layout in which you often use 60-percent magenta? Save time by making a new color swatch that is defined as a tint of the color and then apply it at 100-percent strength.

It's easy to make a tint of a process color in the Edit Color dialog box. Making a tint of a spot color is a little more tricky: You have to use a Multi-Ink color (see "Tip: Permanent Tints," later in this chapter.)

Editing Colors

Once you've built a color, you can edit it by clicking on that color's name in the Edit Color scroll list, then clicking Edit (or just double-clicking on the color's name). In the default color list (the one that's there when you first open QuarkXPress) you can only edit Registration. The other five colors, which include the four process colors plus White, cannot be edited or deleted. When you edit a color, you see the same Edit Color dialog box as described above, except that the color is mapped out, just as you originally specified it.

You can change any of the color's specifications using the same methods described above. When you like the new color, click OK to save these changes to the color palette.

Tip: Multiple Models. You may be interested to note that you can switch among the various color systems on the Model popup menu to make adjustments to a color. For instance, you might choose a Pantone color but decide that what you see onscreen doesn't match your swatch book very well. Go ahead and switch to RGB or HSB mode and adjust the color. As long as the Spot Color checkbox is turned on and you don't change the name of the color, then adjusting the Pantone color this way simply affects its screen representation and the way it prints on your desktop printer.

On the other hand, let's say you use a process-color simulation of a Pantone color, but when you print a proof, you find that the color is too dark. Assuming that your proof is accurate, you can switch the color to CMYK mode to see what CMYK values are being used, and then you can adjust them (reduce the black value, perhaps, or raise the Brightness gauge slightly). Of course (as if you haven't heard me say it enough), you can't trust what you see onscreen, so this technique is only useful for minor tweaks. And don't forget to restore the original values so the final printed color will be as expected.

Tip: Color Tricks the Eye. Placing a colored object next to a different-colored object makes both colors look different from how each would if you just had one color alone. Similarly, a color can look totally different if you place it on a black background rather than on a white one. These facts should influence how you work, in two ways. First, when you're selecting colors from a swatch book, isolate the colors from their neighbors. I like to do this by placing a piece of paper with a hole cut out of it in front of a color I'm considering. Second, after you've created the colors you're going to work with in your layout, try them out with each other. You may find that you'll want to go back and edit them in order to create the effect you're really trying to achieve.

Duplicating Colors

Let's say you love the color blue. I do. You want a new blue color that's really close to a blue that's already on the color palette, but you don't want to change the one already there. Click on the existing color, then click Duplicate. This opens the Edit Color dialog box, just as if you were editing the color, but the name of the color will be changed to "Copy of Blue." As long as you don't change the name of your new color back to its original (or to the name of any other color already specified), you can change the specifications, and save it onto the Color scroll list without replacing the original color.

QuarkXPress won't allow you to replace a color on the Color scroll list with another of the same name, but it does allow you to merge colors with a workaround, as I discuss next in "Deleting Colors."

Deleting Colors

Is this button self-explanatory enough? Click on the color you hate most, then click Delete. If you've assigned this color to any object in your layout, QuarkXPress prompts you with a dialog box asking if you want to replace all instances of the color you're deleting with another color.

Note that you cannot delete the four-process colors, White, or Registration. And if you delete a color that's not used anywhere in the layout, it's removed without a prompt, so make sure you really don't need it before clicking Delete.

> **Tip: Search and Replace Colors.** Let's say you've got a two-color monthly newsletter, and you always print with black and one spot color. It's a pain to create a new color and then apply it to each element in the newsletter each month, but XPress doesn't have a "search and replace" for colors. Or does it?
>
> You can replace one color with another using one of two quick workarounds. Let's say you want to replace every instance of PMS 286 in your layout with PMS 570. Here's how you should do it if you haven't already defined your new Pantone color.
>
> 1. Double-click on the original Pantone 286 to edit it.
>
> 2. Choose Pantone 570 by typing the number into the field in the lower-right corner of the Edit Color dialog box. (Note that at this point, you could even change to some other color mode, like TruMatch, if you wanted to.)
>
> 3. Click OK, and then click Save to leave the Colors dialog box.

Unfortunately, this technique won't work if you already have that particular Pantone color on your color list, because XPress isn't very smart about color naming (it doesn't realize that two colors on your color list that are named the same should be the same). So here's another workaround you can use if you've already built the new color.

1. *Duplicate the color you're trying to replace. Don't make any changes to the copy; just click OK.*

2. *Select the color (in this case, the Pantone 286) and click the Delete button.*

3. *When XPress asks you what color you want to replace it with, choose the new Pantone color (or whatever color you're replacing it with) from the popup menu.*

4. *Click OK, and then click Save to leave the Colors dialog box.*

Of course, these methods don't let you search and replace the colors on selected objects; it's an all-or-nothing change. And any imported artwork using the original color will not be changed, which can lead to confusion (and errors) at output. Note that the only reason you duplicated the Pantone color in step 1 of both techniques was in case you wanted to use that color again somewhere. If you know you'll never use it again in this layout, then just omit that step.

Appending Colors

When you click the Append button, QuarkXPress lets you find another QuarkXPress file and gives you a choice as to which colors from that layout you want to import. Note that when you select a color, its specification appears in the Description field (see Figure 14-5), which can be useful, particularly if the colors have been named "My favorite yellow," "IBM Blue," and so on.

This feature acts just like the Append feature in the Style Sheets and H&Js dialog boxes. If you pick a multi-ink color that is based on other spot colors, those spot colors are imported as well. And if you import a color with the same name as one you already have in your layout (but with a different specification), XPress gives you the chance to rename it upon import, to use the color definition of the imported color, or to use the existing color (which is the same as not bringing in the new color at all).

> *Tip: One More Way to Append a Color. You can either copy and paste, or drag an object filled with that color from one layout to another. As long as the color's name isn't already used in the new layout, the color and its specifications come across too, and are added to the color list. (If the color is already specified, then this method doesn't work; instead, the object's color is stripped away and replaced with the existing color.)*

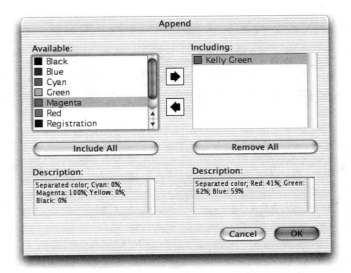

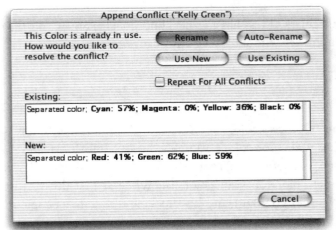

If you append a color that
has the same name as one
in your layout, you'll see this
dialog box.

Figure 14-5
Appending colors

*Tip: Libraries of Colors. Here's one more way to save your colors so that you can bring them into
a new layout: Place a colored object in a library. Let's say you're working with a designer across
the country, and you want to send her various sets of colors you think would be appropriate for
the job. Apply different colors to different boxes, then select all of them and drag them into a
library. Email this library to your colleague, and when she drags out a library item, those colors
are added to her layout's color list.*

*Within the Library, of course, you can even group your colors into types such as "Warm Colors,"
"Cool Colors," or "Newsletter Colors," using the library's labeling feature.*

Edit Trap

Selecting the Edit Trap option in the Colors dialog box brings up the Trap Specifications dialog box. Trapping is a whole other *mishegoss* (Yiddish for "craziness"), so I'll put it off for now and discuss it at some length later in this chapter.

Save

When you are finished adding, deleting, or editing your colors, you can click Save to save those changes to your layout's color palette. If you made the color changes in an open layout, the changes only apply to the layout's color palette. If no layouts were open, then they're added to the default color list.

Cancel

Almost every dialog box in QuarkXPress has a Cancel button. This one works the same as all the rest: It cancels your entries without saving any changes.

MULTI-INK COLORS

If you can overlay two tints of process colors to create a third color, it stands to reason that you can do the same thing with spot colors. QuarkXPress's Multi-Ink feature lets you build "combo colors" based on spot colors. That is, you can make a single color based on varying percentages of other colors on your color list. While at first this feature seems mundane, it turns out to be very powerful, and it's shocking that so few people make use of this incredible feature.

Nonetheless, the road to "process spot colors" isn't entirely clear.

- Most spot colors are made with inks that have a different consistency than process-color inks; the more opaque the inks, the harder it is to mix varying tints of them at the same place on a page.

- Some inks don't tint well; for instance, metallic and fluorescent inks lose much of their special appearance unless you use a very coarse halftone.

- There's only one spot-color swatch book that shows what happens when you mix colors together (the Pantone Two-Color Selector, which is no longer sold), and while it's extensive, it certainly doesn't show every combination of every spot color on the market. Therefore, there's often a lot more guessing involved when you mix spot colors.

It's important that you discuss multi-ink colors with your printer before jumping in and using them. Ask if it'll be okay to mix two particular spot colors on press. Perhaps the printer will make a "draw-down" of the actual inks on paper for you so that you can see how the colors will look when they're mixed together (this only shows you what the colors will look like when they're overprinted at 100 percent).

Building a Multi-Ink Color

Before XPress 4, combining two (or more) spot colors meant that you had to duplicate objects, apply a different color and tint to each object, and then make sure one properly overprinted the other. You could never see a simulation of the final color onscreen or on a color printer. The Multi-Ink feature makes this as easy as one, two, three.

1. After creating your spot colors, create a new color by opening the Colors dialog box and clicking New.

2. Set the Model popup menu to Multi-Ink.

3. Select a color from the list on the right of the Edit Color dialog box and choose a tint from the Shade popup menu (see Figure 14-6). Repeat this step for each color you want to include. For example, you might create a combination of 100 percent PMS 339 plus 25 percent black.

You can even mix process colors in this dialog box, but that's the long way around.

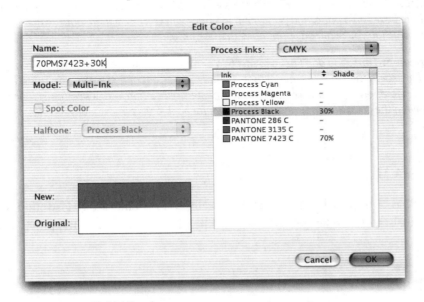

Figure 14-6 Multi-Ink colors

After applying your multi-ink colors to objects on your page, you can print color separations, and each color appears on its proper plate, just as you'd expect. Mention to the printer that you're using multi-ink colors, so the job can be run with appropriate screen angles to avoid moiré patterns when your pages come off press.

Tip: Multiple Selections. *You can select more than one color at a time when you specify a color in the Multi-Ink model by Command/Ctrl-clicking on each color you want on the color list. This is only helpful if you're going to apply the same tint to all the colors you select.*

Tip: Multi-Ink Hexachrome Colors. *Take a look at the Process Inks popup menu that appears in the Edit Color dialog box when you select the Multi-Ink model. When you select Hexachrome from this popup menu, you can build a multi-ink color with Pantone's Hexachrome inks. This way, if you don't like the preset Hexachrome colors that are built into QuarkXPress, you can choose your own. You can even mix Hexachrome with your spot colors, and while I can't imagine what you'd end up with, it sure is fun to speculate.*

Note that Orange and Cyan are meant to be complementary, so you shouldn't mix them together in the same multi-ink color, or you'll end up with a muddy brown. Same thing goes with Green and Magenta. And remember that you can only separate Hexachrome colors when XPress's color management system is active.

Tip: Build a Swatch Book. *While XPress tries to simulate multi-ink colors onscreen (and on color printers), it's far from a perfect system (I find you often get much darker colors onscreen than you would in real life). Ultimately, it's still a guessing game unless you're using a swatch book. If you're going to use mixes of these colors a lot in your print jobs, then you might consider building your own swatches. Build a set of multi-ink colors in every combination you can think of, apply them to small square boxes on a page, and print them (perhaps you can place them outside the trim marks on some job you're already printing with these inks).*

Tip: Permanent Tints. *You don't have to mix two or more colors together in a multi-ink color. You can build a color in the Multi-Ink model that is simply 30 percent of one PMS color. This is useful if you're going to apply that same color tint to several items in your layout; it's certainly much faster than applying the color and then changing the tint for each object individually.*

Special Colors

QuarkXPress has two special colors that aren't really colors. They are Registration, which I mentioned earlier, and Indeterminate, which I'll talk about soon in "Trapping," later in the chapter.

Registration

This "noncolor" appears on the Colors scroll list and on all color selection lists throughout the menus. When you apply this color to an object or to text, that object or text prints on every color separation plate you print. It's used for job-identification marks and for registration or crop marks (if you are creating your own rather than letting the program do it for you; see Chapter 15, *Printing,* for more information on these special marks).

For example, I sometimes like to bypass QuarkXPress's regular crop-mark feature and draw my own crop marks in the border around my page. Then I color these Registration, and they print out on every piece of film that comes out for that job.

> **Tip: Editing the Registration Color.** *If you use the Registration color regularly, you might want to change its color so that you can tell it apart from normal Black. You can use the Edit feature described earlier to change the onscreen color of Registration to anything you like. Also, because the Registration color is originally black, the Edit Color dialog box appears with the brightness scroll bar set to zero. Just raise the brightness to the level you want, and then change the color.*

> *No matter what color you specify, objects with the color Registration always print on every plate. Changing the color changes nothing but the screen representation for that color. Use a color that is distinctly different from anything else in the layout you're creating. That way you always know at a glance what's normal black stuff and what is colored Registration.*

> **Tip: Four-Color Black.** *Most people still think that printing black ink over something else on their page completely covers it. Not so. Black ink is almost never completely opaque, so you can actually see through to what's below it on the printed page. This isn't a concern in black-and-white printing, but when you print multiple colors on a page, it can mean the success or failure of your design. (I once saw a magazine ad that showed a shirtless male jogger running along the road. A wide black box printed over his midriff was supposed to make the jogger appear naked, but the joke was on the ad's designer: The black ink, being somewhat translucent, clearly showed that he was wearing jogging shorts, defeating the purpose of the advertisement.)*

> *The solution is to build a rich black—a separate black in your color palette that contains a bit of other process color in it. The standard rich black that color strippers use is 100-percent black along with 40-percent cyan. I prefer to add 20 percent each of magenta and yellow, too. When a plain black (100-percent K) object overlaps colored objects, it can look mottled over different colors. Adding color to your blacks solves the problem.*

> *This trick not only achieves a richer black on a printing press, but usually also better blacks from a color printer.*

> *Note, though, that you should think carefully about how you apply this rich black. A potential problem lurks behind this technique: The cyan can show up from behind the black if (or when) the printing press misregisters (see "Tip: Knocking Out Rich Black," later in this chapter).*

Indeterminate

When QuarkXPress looks at a selection and finds that either several colors are specified within that selection or that it's a color picture, it calls this an "Indeterminate" color. This is not something you can change in any way. It's just a definition that the program uses to tell you there are several colors in the selection. In "Trapping," later in the chapter, we'll see the great benefits of the Indeterminate "color."

COLORS PALETTE

Just as you can with style sheets, you can apply and edit colors with a click using the Colors palette (see Figure 14-7). This floating palette contains a list of every available color, along with a tint-percentage control popup menu and three icons (four, if you've selected a box containing a grayscale or bitmap image. The additional icon is for colorizing the image). These icons gray out depending on what object you have selected. When you select a text box, the icons represent frame color, text color, and background color for that box. When you select a line, two icons gray out, and only the line-color icon remains. Each color in the palette also displays an icon that shows whether it's a spot color or process color.

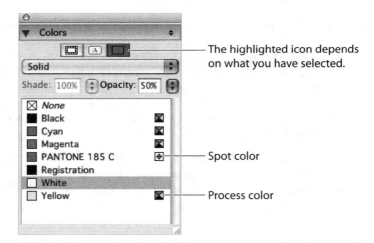

Figure 14-7 The Colors palette

To apply a color to an object, first click the correct icon for what you want to change, then click on the desired color in the color list. If you want a tint of that color, first change the percentage in the upper-right corner, then press Return or Enter to apply the change. You can also just click somewhere else than on the palette. For example, let's say you want to change one word in a text box to 30-percent cyan.

1. Select the word in the text box.

2. Click the center icon on the Colors palette, which represents text (it looks like an "A" in a box).

3. Click on Cyan on the colors list.

4. Select "30%" from the popup menu on the palette, or type "30" in the field and press Enter.

It's funny, but those four steps are often much faster than selecting a color and tint from the Style menu. Note that you can change the color of a box's frame, even if the box doesn't have a frame. If you later add a frame, it will be the color you designated.

> **Tip: Jump to Edit Colors.** *The Colors palette is more like the Style Sheet palette than meets the eye. On both palettes, Command/Ctrl-clicking on an item quickly brings you to a dialog box. In this case, Command/Ctrl-clicking on any color brings up the Colors dialog box, in which you can edit, duplicate, append, delete, or create new colors. This is also the fastest way to the Edit Trap dialog box.*

> **Tip: Drag-and-Drop Color Application.** *Sometimes I think the folks at Quark like to toss in features just because they're cool—for example, drag-and-drop color application. Try it: Hold your mouse down on one of the tiny color squares on the Colors palette, and drag it over your page. Notice that as you drag, the image of that color square stays attached to your pointer. As you move the pointer over objects, their color changes to the color you're dragging. Move the pointer past an object, and its color reverts to whatever it was before.*

> *To apply a color to an object, just let go of the mouse button. Note that you can apply a color in this way to backgrounds and borders, but not to text, even if you have the text icon selected on the Color palette. And since the palette is grayed out until you select an object, you can't drag anything until you've selected at least one object.*

> **Tip: Drag-and-Drop Color, Part Two.** *The engineers at Quark sneaked a feature into XPress and forgot to tell anyone about it. Let's say you've got three boxes on your page. If you drag a color swatch over the first box, it changes color; but as soon as you leave the box, dragging the swatch over to the second box, the first box's color reverts back to its original state. Now, if you're holding down the Command/Ctrl key when you drag the swatch out of the box, XPress actually applies the color to the box, so that it doesn't change after your swatch leaves the box.*

> *If you want all the boxes on your page to be colored yellow, drag the Yellow swatch over each of them with the Command/Ctrl key held down. If you want all but one to be colored yellow, just don't hold down the Command/Ctrl key while the swatch leaves that box.*

BLENDING COLORS

The background of a text or picture box can make a gradual transition from one color to another (see Figure 14-8). Unlike other programs that create graduated fills, in XPress you can blend any combination of spot colors and process colors (even white).

Figure 14-8
Color blends

QuarkXPress has a dizzying array of blends: Linear (straight blend), Mid-Linear (from one color to another, then back again), Rectangular, Diamond, Circular, and Full Circular. (If you have only the Linear blend, then you're missing the Cool Blends XTension that ships with QuarkXPress, or it has been inadvertently turned off with XTension manager.) See Figure 14-9 for cool blend examples.

Figure 14-9 The cool blends

Colors palette. You can create blends in either the palette or the Modify dialog box. Here's how to apply a blend to a selected object from the Colors palette.

1. Click the background icon on the Colors palette.

2. Select the blend you want from the popup menu on the Colors palette.

3. Click button #1, then select the beginning color and tint of the blend.

4. Click button #2, and select the ending color and tint of the blend.

5. Specify the angle of the blend. For Linear and Mid-Linear blends, zero degrees (the default value) puts color #1 on the left and color #2 on the right. Increasing the value rotates the blend counterclockwise (so that at 75 degrees, the 100-percent yellow fill of the selected box has been set to 60-percent opacity, and color #1 is almost at the bottom of your box).

If you later want to change one of the colors in the blend, click button #1 or #2 to select the color, change its tint, or adjust the angle. You can also blend between two tints of a single color.

Modify dialog box. You can also use the Modify dialog box to apply blends, but it's not as flexible as the Colors palette. You can apply a blend to an object on the Box tab of the Modify dialog box (see Figure 14-10). Note that there's no "color #1" and "color #2" here. Instead, the first color is always the color you've chosen in the section of the dialog box labeled "Box." The second color is always the color you've chosen in the section labeled "Blends."

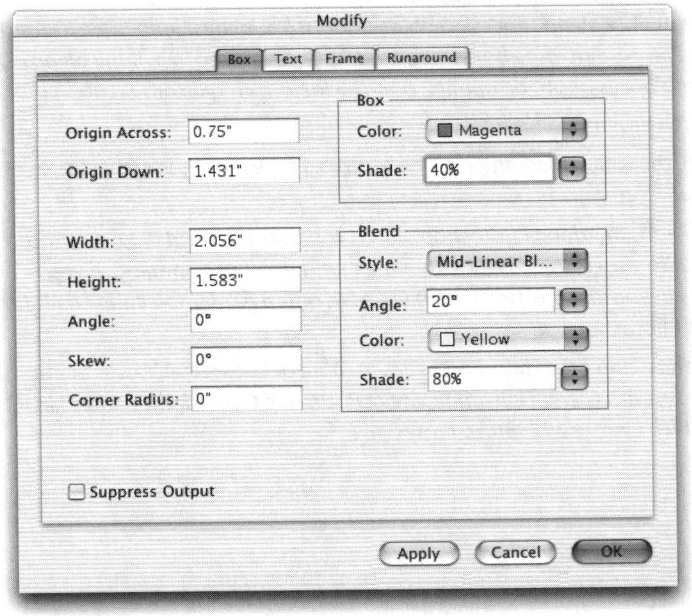

Figure 14-10
Building blends

Tip: Don't Mix Blends and Grayscale TIFFs. *Placing blends behind grayscale TIFFs usually results in something unpleasant. The problem is that color #1 gets mixed in with the TIFF itself. Quark thinks it should work this way; I think it's crazy. Proceed at your own risk.*

Tip: Rotation Changes Blends. *The angle you specify has a curious effect on certain kinds of blends. While it simply rotates Linear and Mid-Linear blends, it actually changes the look of the other blends. For instance, a Circular blend at zero degrees generally appears smaller than one at 45 degrees (see Figure 14-11). Play with the angle in order to achieve the effect you're looking for.*

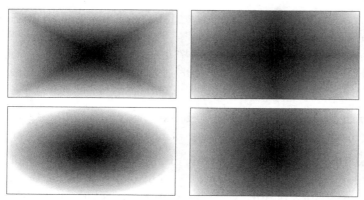

Figure 14-11
A blend's angle affects its look.

Zero degrees   45 degrees

Tip: Banding in Blends. *A pervasive problem with blends in QuarkXPress is banding (visible bands of tint or color within the supposedly smooth blend).*

Banding usually occurs because PostScript (below Level 3) can only image 256 levels of gray. If you've got a black-to-white blend that's 256 points (about 3.5 inches) long, then XPress builds the blend by creating 256 1-point-wide boxes, each with a different tint in it. If the blend is 7 inches long, then each of those boxes has to be about 2 points wide, which typically creates visible bands.

There are two lessons to be learned here.

- The larger the blend, the worse the banding. If you stick to 1- or 2-inch-long blends in XPress, you shouldn't get banding.

- You can get better blends in Adobe Photoshop. When you make a blend in Photoshop, the program automatically dithers the colors within the blend to reduce banding. If you're making process-color blends in Photoshop, make them in CMYK or grayscale. You can't easily make spot-color blends in Photoshop yet.

I discuss dithering, blends, and other banding issues in more detail in Real World Scanning and Halftones, which I wrote with Glenn Fleishman, Steve Roth, and Conrad Chavez and in Real World Photoshop, which I wrote with Bruce Fraser.

Tip: Blending to Black. *If you've worked with blends before, you've found that they don't always appear in print as they do onscreen. For instance, if you make a blend from 100-percent magenta to 100-percent black, you would think you'd get a nice, even blend between the two colors. Unfortunately, when such a blend is printed, you may find a big grayish band in the middle of the blend.*

Instead, blend from 100 percent of magenta to a color that's 100-percent black plus 100-percent magenta.

Tip: A New Dimension. *Maybe I'm just easily amused, but I think this trick for creating three-dimensional buttons in XPress is pretty keen.*

1. *Draw a rectangle or oval (I think it looks best with a square or a circle).*

2. *Give it a straight Linear blend. I like to set the angle at 45 degrees.*

3. *Duplicate the object, and make it smaller. The amount you make it smaller is up to you. Remember that if you want to reduce it to 80 percent, you can simply type "*.8" after the measurement in the Width and Height fields.*

4. *To figure out the second object's blend angle, subtract the first object's blend angle from 270. So if the first object had a 45-degree blend, the second object should have a 225-degree blend (270–45=225). Or skip the math and just type "270–45" in the angle box of the Colors palette.*

5. *Space/Align the two objects so that their centers are equal (set Vertical and Horizontal alignment to zero offset from the objects' centers in the Space/Align dialog box).*

You can see the effect best when the page guides are turned off (see Figure 14-12). It's even nicer when you add a .25-point white frame around the inside object (sort of a highlight to the button's ridge).

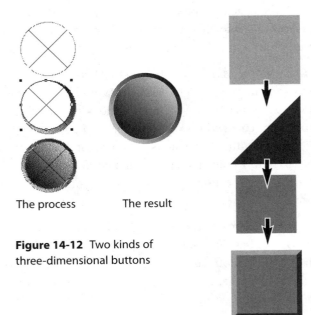

The process   The result

Figure 14-12 Two kinds of three-dimensional buttons

Tip: 3-D Boxes. *While you can create rectangular 3-D boxes using the last tip, it's not the only way to create them. Here's one more method.*

1. *Make a rectangular picture box (the closer to a square it is, the better) with a background shaded to 40 percent of some color.*

2. *Clone it (Step and Repeat with zero offsets), and change the shade of the new top box to 80 percent.*

3. *While the top box is still selected, change it into a polygon (by selecting the artist's palette icon in the Shape submenu under the Item menu). Turn Reshape Polygon on so you can modify its shape.*

4. *Delete the upper-left corner point of this rectangular polygon (Option/Alt-click on the corner point).*

5. *Now draw a new rectangular picture box (smaller than the original box), shaded at 60 percent of that same color. Center align the box vertically and horizontally with the original box from step 1.*

Once again, this may be a process more easily performed in an illustration program. But for a quick-and-dirty, this technique can come in handy.

OPACITY

For designers, one of the most appealing features in QuarkXPress 7 is the addition of opacity controls. The ability to control the opacity of boxes and their contents opens up a world of visual possibilities, allowing you to create effects that previously would have required you to create bits and pieces in other programs and assemble them in the QuarkXPress layout.

For example, take something as simple as the old "ghosted box behind type," which allows black type to be readable on top of an image. Previously, you would have to ghost back that area in Photoshop, and if you were paranoid, save two versions of the image—a layered working file, just in case your boss changed his or her mind, and a finished TIFF or EPS to place in your page. Any change to the dimensions, position, or opacity of the ghosted area would necessitate a trip back to Photoshop and an update to the image placed in the page. But now you can create this effect directly in your page layout and change the size, color, and opacity of the effect as often (and as late in the game) as you like.

You're not limited to just the ghosted box effect (although it *is* sort of a thrill after years of doing it the long way around); you have individual control over the opacity of a box, text within the box, and borders on the box. In addition, QuarkXPress 7 allows you to create soft drop shadows on any object in a page. Put all this together, and you have the ability to easily and quickly apply some very interesting visual effects to enliven your designs.

Beyond the effects you can apply to objects in a layout, you can now use native Photoshop (.PSD) and TIFF images containing transparency. This means that soft-edged silhouettes created with a layer mask in Photoshop are honored in QuarkXPress. No longer will you have to build a composite file in Photoshop to incorporate an image of a girl with soft hair, a frilly dandelion, or a cat with fluffy fur. Place the image directly into your layout, and the soft edges are rendered realistically (see Figure 14-13).

Figure 14-13
Layer masks in Photoshop native (.PSD) and TIFF layered files are honored by QuarkXPress, allowing soft-edged silhouettes to be used.

Keep in mind that such fun comes with responsibility: Imaging transparency effects can be a bit challenging, although you'll see that a few simple rules will keep you out of trouble.

Specifying Color Opacity

The opacity controls in QuarkXPress 7 are available in the Color palette as well as in the Item Modify dialog box. You'll discover that applying opacity is as easy and intuitive as applying color to the fill and border of a box, or assigning a color to text. The easiest way to apply opacity is to apply it as you would apply color—with the Color palette.

Select a box in your page and give it a background color other than None. (Why not None? Because what could be more transparent than None? It's almost a Zen koan, isn't it?) If you attempt to apply an opacity setting to an object colored with None, you'll find that the opacity control is grayed out. Choose any other color and you'll find that you can apply an opacity setting ranging from 100 percent (solid) to zero percent (thus equivalent to None).

While the extremes of 0 and 100 don't serve any purpose, every number in between is available to control opacity.

As you drag the opacity slider down toward zero, the selected box is ghosted to lighter and lighter levels. And objects underneath show through at increasing strength as you reduce the opacity of objects on top. Why is that? It's simple math, really: The total is always 100 percent. For example, if you have a box with a background color of 100-percent magenta with its opacity set to 60 percent, when you place it on top of a box with a background color of 100-percent cyan, the overlapping area will have a fill of 60 magenta and 40 cyan.

In Figure 14-14, the Background Color icon is chosen in the Color palette, allowing the image underneath to show through at 40-percent strength, without interfering with the readability of the text. It's as simple as that!

Figure 14-14 Even simple opacity effects can add interest.

Layering Opacities

You can apply opacity settings to *any* object in a page, whether it's a picture box, a text box, or just a box with a background color. Background colors and frame colors are eligible—even the gaps in fancy frames can be set to a unique opacity.

In QuarkXPress 7, you sort of get "two for one" in the Colors palette: For each attribute of a box—background, image, text, and border—you can control not just the color and shade, but also the opacity. Start with a simple text box and add a color frame. Make the frame thick enough that it can be set to something like the Thick-Thin option and set the gap color to contrast with the border color. But while the Colors palette offers almost all the possible opacity options, it doesn't provide a control for gap color or opacity. So, for this box, the Item Modify dialog gives you everything in one place for one-stop shopping (see Figure 14-15). Choose the background color and its opacity in the Box tab, and then set the frame color, gap color, and the opacity for both in the Frame tab.

Figure 14-15 Start with a simple bordered box and set different opacity levels for the background color, the frame color, and the gap color. Not enough excitement? Select the text and apply an opacity setting to that.

A color image can have a different opacity setting from that assigned to the box it's in. This results in a blended effect, with the background color of the box showing through the image, compounded with objects behind this confection showing through the translucent box and its see-through image. (Try not to get carried away.) Place a grayscale image in a picture box, apply a background color, and you'll see that you now have four icons across the top of the Color palette (see Figure 14-16), allowing you to control Frame color and opacity, picture color and opacity, picture background color and opacity, and the color and opacity of the box itself. Whew.

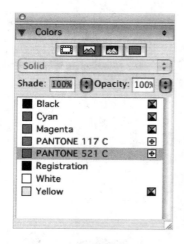

Figure 14-16
Opacity and color controls for a picture box containing a grayscale or bitmap image. Note that you have separate opacity controls for the picture, its background, and the background of the box, as well as the frame.

Interesting results can be accomplished even with simple colored boxes. In Figure 14-17, things are pretty dull until the circle is set to 50 percent opacity and the box at the lower right is set to 60 percent. Now the overlapping areas show through, and the colors of the individual objects are blended to create new tones where they overlap.

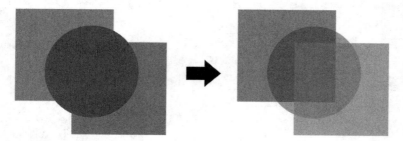

Figure 14-17 Experiment with opacity settings and watch what happens with simple overlapping shapes.

Applying Drop Shadows

You may recall an XTension called ShadowCaster from A Lowly Apprentice Production, Inc. (ALAP). With this XTension, you could create soft shadows for any object in the page, even if it fell on top of an image. The XTension, available for QuarkXPress versions 4.x through 6.5, would calculate the shadow appearance, generate a composite image of the shadow and underlying objects, and update the page. Cool as it was, it still required the creation of a literal image to accomplish its results. If you wanted to move any of the objects involved in the shadow, whether they were generating shadows or on the receiving end, you had to start over and have ShadowCaster regenerate the pieces.

In QuarkXPress 7, all of this trickery is no longer necessary. Now you can create a soft shadow of any color for any object in your layout without limitations. Need to move a box? Don't worry; because the shadow isn't composed of literal pixels (those don't come into being until you print or export your layout), you can move, resize, and reshape objects as you wish, and the shadows will follow along.

To add a shadow to an object in the layout, select the box and choose Drop Shadow from the Item menu. The Modify dialog box appears with the Drop Shadow tab active (see Figure 14-18). Turn on the Apply Drop Shadow checkbox to get started. Change the angle value and click the Apply button, and you'll see the shadow rotate as if the light source is moving. The Synchronize Angle option allows all of your shadowed objects to use the same angle for consistency (after all, there's only one sun, right?). The Distance option

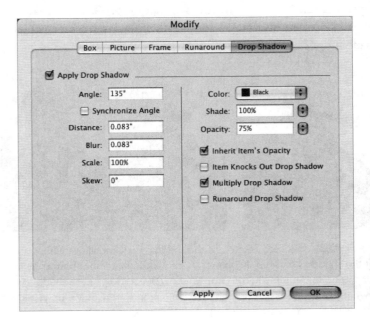

Figure 14-18
The Drop Shadow options let you create realistic shadows without an imaging application.

changes the offset value; the higher the value, the farther away the shadow falls from the object casting it. Higher Blur values soften the shadow. The Scale option allows you to enlarge or reduce the size of the shadow, which is sort of an odd effect (although reducing the shadow can make it appear that the object is floating high above the page). Use the Skew option to lean the shadow at an angle, making it appear to be cast on a flat surface underneath the object rather than on an imaginary wall behind the object.

The default settings on the right side of the dialog box will create a black drop shadow that darkens objects underneath. The effects of Shade and Opacity settings are cumulative: For example, if you choose Black, then set the Shade to 60 percent and the Opacity to 50 percent, the result is a 30-percent black shadow. The default option to inherit the item's opacity means that if you ghost the object back to 50 percent, the shadow will also be ghosted back to 50 percent. The option to have the item knock out the drop shadow ensures that the shadow won't be seen through a ghosted object. This option is redundant, though, if the item is opaque—the shadow will be knocked out anyway.

If you're creating a standard shadow (that is, black or another dark color), the default choice to Multiply the drop shadow makes sense. Even though the preview in QuarkXPress makes it seem that the shadow will be opaque, knocking out what's underneath, the result is correct—the shadow darkens what's underneath. If you turn off this option, the shadow will not darken underlying objects and will in many cases actually lighten the area of the shadow (see Figure 14-19). If you have any doubt about the way the shadow will behave, export to PDF and view the results in Acrobat or Adobe Reader. Alternatively, print separated lasers to prove to yourself that the shadow is behaving as you expect. If you want text to runaround the shadow rather than the object, turn on the Runaround Drop Shadow option.

Figure 14-19 The preview in QXP looks incorrect—as if the shadows will knock out what's underneath. Instead, you want the shadows to multiply objects underneath, darkening them convincingly. Don't turn off the default setting for Multiply in the Drop Shadow dialog box, or the shadow will indeed knock out—not what you want (basket on right in each screen shot uses Multiply; it looks wrong in QuarkXPress, but is correct on export and output).

You can use any existing color for the shadow—you're not limited to black. Use any color that's available in your Colors palette, including spot colors. However, if you choose a light color and leave the Multiply Drop Shadow option turned on, the shadow may disappear or become too subtle over some objects. But you can make this work for you: To create a glow around an object, choose a light color, and turn off the Multiply option. The shadow will then knock out what's underneath and appear as a soft-edged glow around the parent object.

Tip: Getting That Glow. To create a concentric glow around an object, start by opening the Modify dialog box and choosing the Drop Shadow tab. Set the shadow color to White or some other light color, with an opacity of 100 percent for maximum effect. Set the Angle and Distance to zero, set the Blur to a large value, such as 0.2 inch, and then scale the shadow slightly, about 110 percent. Uncheck the Multiply Drop Shadow option so the glow will be lighter than objects underneath it. Keep in mind that a glow will only be visible when it falls on a dark background.

Transparency Flattening

There's one little catch with all this fun transparency stuff (besides the time you'll spend experimenting with effects): PostScript doesn't understand it (see Chapter 15, *Printing*, for more on PostScript). Whoa! If PostScript—which is the native tongue of many of our imaging devices—doesn't know what to do with transparency, how are we ever going to print it?

Not to worry; when you print or export your layout, transparency is "flattened" into a form that PostScript accepts. While your original layout components are unchanged, the outgoing print stream or PDF file contains only PostScript-legal content. This involves a bit of surgery, as QuarkXPress cuts apart some objects involved in transparency, rerenders them as flat opaque objects that look like the transparent originals, and reassembles everything before it goes out the door (see Figure 14-20). It's pretty impressive when you consider what is involved.

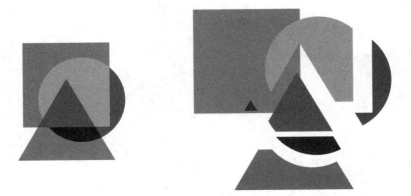

Figure 14-20 Live transparent interactions in your layout must be flattened into opaque pieces that look like the original shapes, but are "legal" in PostScript imaging.

What happens to those drop shadows? As mentioned earlier, they aren't rendered in real pixels until the layout is printed or exported to another format, such as PDF or EPS. The resolution of shadows is governed by the Transparency options found in the Print and Export dialog boxes (see Figure 14-21). In addition, this is where you tell QuarkXPress how to handle the rendering of vector components that are interacting with transparency. Frequently, QuarkXPress will have to rasterize vector components that fall under drop shadows or other objects using transparency. In the Print dialog box, the default value for vector images is 300, which results in some loss of detail in output. Set that value to 600 (or to the resolution of the final imaging device, if you know it). If you fear that your blends and shadows will look pixelated at the default setting of 150, increase that to 300 (I do). Note that the higher you set these values, the longer printing times you'll experience, because QuarkXPress has to work a bit harder to render the bits and pieces at higher resolution.

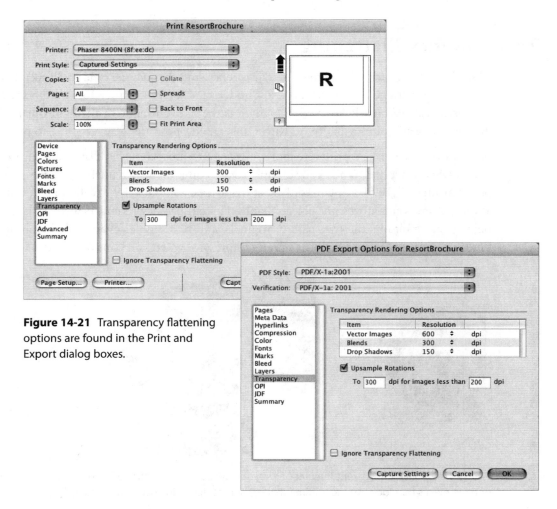

Figure 14-21 Transparency flattening options are found in the Print and Export dialog boxes.

Dangers of Transparency

While QuarkXPress does a great job of translating opacity settings and soft drop shadows to PostScript and PDF, you should communicate with the printer you're using, as well as others (such as publications or newspapers) to whom you're sending your jobs. Transparency may be a bit new-fangled for some of your recipients, so it's worth taking a bit of extra precaution to ensure that your job is handled correctly.

You'll achieve the best results by using PostScript devices and processes that are fluent in PostScript Level 3: Attempting to image a layout containing transparency on an older device may result in incorrect rendering or dropped graphics—perhaps even failure to process. It's worth asking your printers if they're familiar with transparency in QuarkXPress 7, and even more important to ask if they have any advice for you as you build your files. There may be some workarounds necessary due to their particular workflow.

Keep in mind that since transparency is new to QuarkXPress 7, saving back to version 6 will *lose all* of your transparency effects. Reread that: you will lose all transparency if you back-save. Drop shadows will disappear, translucent objects will become opaque, and Photoshop files will lose any transparent and soft-edged effects. The fun's all gone. So if you collaborate with users of QuarkXPress 6, you'll have to avoid back-saving and letting them work on layouts containing transparency. (In fact, in general it's not a good idea to jump versions if you can avoid it. Keep things in their natural habitat.)

When you submit your job to printers or publications, be sure they understand how to handle transparency. If they ask for your native QuarkXPress layouts, fonts, and support art, make it clear that they must keep the job in QuarkXPress 7 and should not back-save. If their workflow requires them to export EPS or PDF files for trapping and imposition, make sure they are mindful of the transparency settings in the Export dialog box.

If you're asked to provide print-ready PDF files, follow the guidelines provided by the printer or publication when you create PDFs. If they don't provide any guidelines, see Chapter 16, *PDF*, for instructions on making bulletproof PDFX-1a files.

Carefully examine proofs provided to you; check for rasterized text and vector art, and make sure any shadows look smooth—without banding or pixelation. Ask for assurance that any spot color areas remain spot without being converted to CMYK.

TRAPPING

Nothing is perfect. When your print job is flying through a press, each color being added one at a time, the paper may shift slightly. Depending on the press, this could be an offset of anywhere between .003 and .0625 inches (.2 to 4.5 points). If two colors abut each other on your artwork and this shift occurs, then the two colors may be moved apart slightly, resulting in a white "unprinted" space. It may seem like a .003-of-an-inch space would be unnoticeable, but it could easily appear to be a chasm. What can you do? Fill in these potential chasms with traps and overprints.

The concept and practice of trapping and overprinting contain several potential pitfalls for the inexperienced. Most designers just let their printers handle this stuff. But you know these desktop publishers—they always want to be in control of everything. The problem is that designers weren't trained to do trapping! And most printers would prefer you leave this up to them. Still, it's good to know what it's all about.

QuarkXPress's trapping is usually pretty good, all in all, but it's lacking in some important areas, such as blends, choking type, and partially overlapping objects. Ultimately, QuarkXPress isn't designed to be a great trapper. If you want to spare yourself a lot of hassle, turn off auto trapping (see "Trapping Preferences," next) and leave the arcane science of trapping to your printer.

Overprinting. Picture a magenta "Q" on a cyan background. Normally, when you make these color separations, the cyan plate has a white Q *knocked out* of it, exactly where the magenta Q prints (I talk more about color separations and plates in Chapter 15, *Printing*). This way, the cyan and the magenta don't mix (see Figure 14-22). You can, however, set the magenta to overprint the cyan. This results in the Q not being knocked out of the cyan; the two colors *overprint* in that area—resulting in a purple Q.

There are a few very important times when you'll want to overprint colors—for example, when you're printing fine black lines or black type on a colored background. Large black areas, however, fare better if they're set to a "rich black" (black plus one or more other colors, such as C40-K100); the black doesn't look so anemic, and objects underneath won't show through.

Figure 14-22 Knocking out and overprinting

Trapping. A trap is created by very slightly overprinting two colors right along their borders. Then when the paper shifts on the printing press, the space between the colors is filled with the additional trap color (see Figure 14-23). The trap can be created using two methods: choking and spreading. *Choking* refers to the background area getting smaller. *Spreading* refers to the foreground object (the Q in the example above) getting slightly larger.

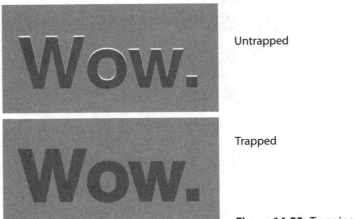

Figure 14-23 Trapping two colored objects

Simple idea, right? But how much to spread or choke an object is determined by the printing press, the colors you're using, and even the paper you're printing on. With some color combinations, you don't even have to trap at all (see "Tip: Who Needs Trapping?" later in this chapter). When you build a color layout, you should always talk to your printer about trapping.

Note that there are two ways to specify trapping in XPress: automatic trapping (which you control on a color-by-color basis) and object-level trapping (which you can apply to a particular item on your page). Even if you don't do anything in XPress, the program still applies some trapping, based on the values on the Trapping tab of the Preferences dialog box. But unless the printer generates film or plates directly from XPress (unlikely), even this automatic trapping is ignored.

Trapping Preferences

You can control the way that XPress handles trapping on the Trapping tab of the Preferences dialog box. The changes you make—like most other preferences—are specific to only the layout that you have open at the time; if you want them to apply to all future documents, change them while no other layouts are open.

The Trapping tab contains seven controls: Trapping Method, Process Trapping, Auto Amount, Indeterminate, Knockout Limit, Overprint Limit, and Ignore White (see Figure 14-24). Don't worry, these controls are not nearly as confusing as they sound.

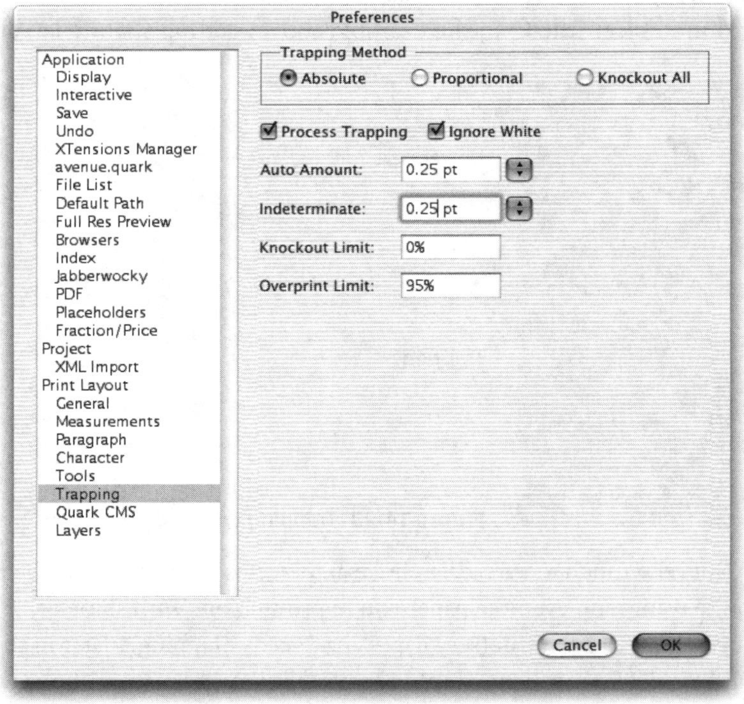

Figure 14-24
Trapping tab of the
Preferences dialog box

Trapping Method. The first popup menu on the Trapping tab lets you turn QuarkXPress's trapping controls on and off. The default value, Absolute, tells XPress to always use the same-sized trap (the width in the Auto Amount field). The second setting, Proportional, tells the program to adjust the size of the trap according to how different the two abutting colors are. As far as I'm concerned, there's rarely a reason to use Proportional trapping, so when I want trapping I always leave the Trapping Method set to Absolute.

The third choice, Knockout All, is the same as turning off trapping. When this is set, every color knocks out colors beneath it, with no trap at all. Use this when trapping will be done by the printer.

I don't like the Proportional method because it can make certain abutting colors not trap when they really should. Because Proportional trapping tells QuarkXPress to look at the "darkness" of a color—which is difficult to quantify—it's a little hard to describe the exact mathematics here on paper without getting really technical. Basically, QuarkXPress takes the difference between the two darkness values and multiplies that by the number in the Auto Amount field. For example, let's say the background color is 80-percent dark, the foreground object were 20-percent dark, and the Auto Amount setting is 0.5 point. Then the background will choke by 0.3 point. (That's 0.8–0.2=0.6 x 0.5 point=0.3 point. Fun, huh?)

Process Trapping. Before I tell you exactly what the Process Trapping feature is all about, let me say just one thing: If this preference is not turned on (it usually is by default), then turn it on and leave it on. Now if you want to really understand Process Trapping, read on. Or, if you couldn't care less, then jump ahead a few paragraphs to the next section.

Take a look at the two process colors (foreground and background) listed in Table 14-1. If you spread this foreground color (a yellow) into the background color (a muddy brown) with Process Trapping turned off, the trap area doesn't mesh the two colors the way you'd want. That is, the slight sliver of trap (where the colors overlap) is made up of magenta, yellow, and black (the foreground color spreads). However, since there's no cyan in the foreground color, the cyan from the background shows through, making a really ugly puke-green trap area. Now you might say: For a 0.25-point trap, who cares? No one will see it anyway. Think again. That green line stands out clearly around the edge of the yellow object.

Table 14-1 Color breakdown for trapping example

Color	Foreground box	Background box
Cyan	0	30
Magenta	20	50
Yellow	100	90
Black	5	0

However, when Process Trap is turned on, some process colors get spread while others are choked. Here's how it works. Any process color in the foreground object that is darker than the same color in the background object is spread by half the trapping value (typically, half the value in the Auto Amount field). Any process color that's lighter is choked by half the trapping value.

In the example above, the cyan plate is choked by half the trapping value because there is less cyan in the foreground box than in the background box. Magenta also chokes. However, the yellow and black plates are spread by the same amount.

The result is a trap area as wide as the specified trapping value (in the example above, 0.25 point), centered on the edge of the foreground object, and with the darkest process colors of each of the objects.

If you don't understand this, read the last few paragraphs over several times. If you still don't understand it, then give up and believe me when I tell you that it's a really good thing. Leave Process Trapping turned on.

A couple of notes on this feature. When all the process colors in the foreground object are darker or when they're all lighter than in the background object, then QuarkXPress doesn't trap at all. This is because it doesn't need to. Also, Process Trap doesn't do anything for spot colors, again because it doesn't need to.

Auto Amount. The value that you set in the Auto Amount field tells XPress the maximum value that Proportional trapping can use, and the specific value that Absolute trapping should use. The default value of 0.144 point (about .002 of an inch) seems a little small to me, so I usually change this to 0.3 point. However, the proper value depends a great deal on your printing process; if you're printing a newspaper, the trap value might be significantly higher! Remember to check with your printer first.

Indeterminate. If QuarkXPress can't figure out what the background color is, it labels the background "Indeterminate." There are three cases in which this happens: a color picture in the background, a background where several different colors are present, or an item only partially covering a background color when Ignore White is turned off (see "Ignore White," below). Note that XPress can only spread a foreground color over an Indeterminate color (for instance, it can only spread text over an image; it cannot choke the image under the text).

Knockout Limit. Remember that the main idea behind trapping is to avoid white paper showing through between two abutting colors, also sometimes called "light leaks." Very light-tinted type, boxes, or lines may be close enough to white so that whether you trap them or just let them knock out isn't very important. The Knockout Limit tells XPress when it can get away without trapping and can instead just knock an object out of the background. The default value is zero percent, which means that every object traps as it did in earlier versions of the program. If you raise this value to 10 percent, then any black object tinted to 10 percent or lighter knocks out, and no trap value is applied.

Actually, the percentage is based on the luminance of the color, not the tint value, so the limit is different for each color. For instance, a Knockout Limit of 5 percent sets the knockout cutoff at 5 percent for Black, 10 percent for Cyan, and 45 percent for Yellow. In CMYK colors, the luminance of the combination of colors is what counts, not the individual channels. (I like setting the Knockout Limit to about 5 percent, but most people seem to get along just fine without setting it above zero.)

Overprint Limit. Black always overprints any color below it, right? Wrong. Automatic overprinting is controlled by the Overprint Limit setting. The default setting of 95 percent means that black—or any other color that is set to overprint in the Trap Specifications dialog box (which I'll discuss in just a moment)—only overprints when its tint level is above 95 percent. As it turns out, dot gain on press will almost certainly change any 95-percent tint into a solid color, so this is no big deal.

On the other hand, let's say you have the color Green set to overprint by default. If you screen it back to 50 percent, QuarkXPress knocks the color out rather than overprinting it, because the tint falls below the Overprint Limit.

By the way, if you set an object to overprint in the Trap Information palette (which I'll cover later in this section), it will overprint no matter what the tint; object-level trapping ignores the Overprint Limit.

Ignore White. Let's say that a red picture box lies partially on top of another page item, and partially on the white page background (see Figure 14-25). The Trapping tab of the Preferences dialog box gives you the choice of whether it should consider the background color "Indeterminate" or not. When Ignore White is turned on, QuarkXPress won't call a partial overlap "Indeterminate" because it just ignores the white page background; it traps based on the color of the overlapped object. If you turn this option off, however, it "sees" the white background page, and considers the mix of background colors to be Indeterminate. I don't see any reason why you should turn this option off.

When Ignore White is turned on, the trap value for this circle is determined by its relationship to the box rather than by "Indeterminate."

Figure 14-25 Ignore White

Custom Color-Pair Trap Settings

Remember, there's no such thing as two objects truly being next to each other on an XPress page; one is always above or below the other. QuarkXPress takes advantage of this and always traps based on *pairs* of colors: the foreground color and the background color. For example, picture some red type on top of a blue rectangle. The blue is the background color; the red is the foreground color.

QuarkXPress's default trapping system uses the following built-in trapping algorithm.

- Note the darkness (luminosity) of each color.

- If the foreground color is lighter, then spread it so that it slightly overlaps the background color.

- If the background color is lighter, then choke it so that it slightly "underlaps" the foreground color.

This algorithm is based on the rule that in trapping, lighter colors should encroach on darker ones. That way the darker element defines the edge, and the lighter color overlapping doesn't affect that definition (see Figure 14-26).

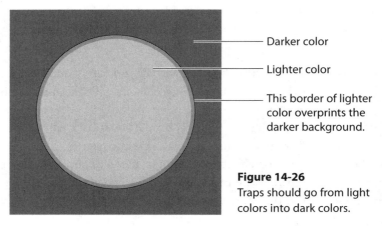

Darker color

Lighter color

This border of lighter color overprints the darker background.

Figure 14-26
Traps should go from light colors into dark colors.

In general, XPress does a pretty good job of figuring out what should be trapped and how. However, you can always override XPress and assign your own default trapping behavior for a pair of colors.

1. Select a color (typically the foreground color) in the Colors dialog box.

2. Click the Edit Trap button to open the Trap Specifications dialog box (see Figure 14-27).

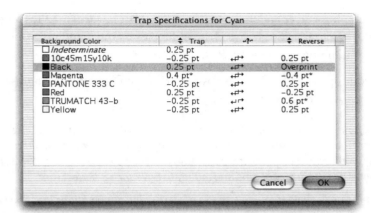

Figure 14-27
The Trap Specifications
dialog box

3. The list of colors down the left side of the dialog box displays the potential background colors. Select one or more (you can select contiguous colors by holding down the Shift key, or noncontiguous colors on the list with the Command/Ctrl key). Note that the first "color" on the list is Indeterminate, which lets you control how your foreground color will trap when it sits on top of an indeterminate background (I discussed the meaning of Indeterminate earlier in this section).

4. The third column in the dialog box—the one filled with those strange-looking, co-mingling arrows—lets you specify whether the color pair's trapping should be reversible; that is, if you want the same trap settings for the two colors when the foreground color is the same as the background color, and vice versa. When the arrows are intertwined (they are by default), the color-pair trapping is reversible. If you'd rather the settings not be constrained, you can choose Independent from the popup menu at the top of the column (which is unfortunately just labeled "?"). Or, faster, just click the arrow icon once to toggle it from one state to the other.

5. Select the proper setting from the Trap popup menu, which offers you six options: Default, Knockout, Overprint, Auto Amount (+), Auto Amount (–), and Custom (I describe each of these in more detail when I discuss object-level trapping, later in this chapter). If I'm going to change the trap settings from the default value, I typically use Knockout, Overprint, or Custom (depending on what I'm trying to do). Note that as soon as you make a change, XPress displays an asterisk next to the trapping values to indicate they're not the default settings.

    If you select Custom, you can type any value between -36 and 36 points, in 0.001-point increments (why anyone would want a trap larger than 1 or 2 points is beyond me). A positive value spreads the foreground object (making it slightly larger by drawing a line around it). A negative value leaves the foreground object alone and chokes the background object.

6. If the color-pair trapping is Dependent (what I call "reversible"), then XPress figures out the reverse of the trap for you. If you change the pair to Independent, you can now set the reverse trapping value in the Reverse column.

Again, you probably won't spend a lot of time figuring out your color-pair traps in this dialog box because XPress does a good job of it already.

> **Tip: Who Needs Trapping?** *You don't need to use any trapping at all in your layouts. Does that sound crazy? Well, it's true in two cases. First, you never need trapping if your press operator is obsessed with perfect registration on press. It is possible to control press registration; it's just rare that any press operator has the luxury of time and money to have such a perfect run.*
>
> *Another way you can entirely avoid trapping is to use process-color combinations that don't need trapping in your layouts (remember that only colors that touch require trapping). Here are two rules that can help you build and arrange color on your page so that you won't need trapping.*
>
> * ***All lighter, all darker.*** *If the cyan, magenta, yellow, and black tints in your foreground color are all darker or all lighter than the corresponding tints in the background color, you don't need to trap. When the Process Trap option is turned on—which it should be—XPress simply doesn't trap color combinations like this, so you don't have to do any extra work to stop QuarkXPress from trapping (see Table 14-2).*
>
> * **Common colors.** *If two colors share a process-color element (cyan, magenta, yellow, or black), and the common element is within 30 percent, you probably don't need a trap. Let's say you color some text deep purple—made of 80-percent cyan, 70-percent magenta, and 20-percent black. If you put that text on a bright yellow background, you'll probably need to trap it because there are no common color elements. On the other hand, you don't have to trap it if you put the purple text on top of a light blue background—made of 50-percent cyan and 10-percent black. Why? Because both cyan and black are shared elements in the foreground and background colors, and their respective tints are both within 30 percent of each other. (The 30-percent rule is a somewhat arbitrary, middle-of-the-road choice; in some cases, you may want to be more or less conservative.)*
>
> *QuarkXPress does not recognize common colors by itself. If you don't want these color pairs to trap, you should set them to Knockout in the Trap Specifications dialog box or in the Trap Information palette (see "Object-Level Trapping," next).*

Table 14-2 Examples of colors that don't need trapping

	Cyan	Magenta	Yellow	Black
All lighter, all darker				
Color #1 (dark green)	100	20	80	15
Color #2 (yellow)	10	10	70	0
Common colors				
Color #1 (orange)	0	60	90	10
Color #2 (tan)	25	40	75	0

Tip: Trapping Small Type. *You can run into trouble when you're using small type, especially serif type, in a color layout. Since the type is so fine—especially the serifs—even a small amount of trapping can clog it up. The counters can fill in, and the serifs can become really clunky (see Figure 14-28). Bear this in mind when you're setting up your trapping preferences, and when you're specifying colors for type.*

Monsieur de Bergerac
Untrapped

Serif type can clog up, and
the serifs can get clunky
when trapped.

Monsieur de Bergerac
Trapped

Figure 14-28 Trapping serif type

However, the folks at Quark have made some hidden allowances for small text (under 24 points) and small objects (less than 10 points in height or width). When XPress encounters one of these, it won't allow spreads or chokes that might compromise the object's shape. This is both good and bad. On the one hand, it's nice because your small objects look better. On the other hand, it's bad because you can only rarely trap small objects even if you want to. This includes thin lines (under 10 points)!

You usually don't have to think about what XPress is really doing here, but if you want to know, here's what happens. The program spreads the object on a color plate only if the object's tint is less than or equal to half the corresponding color tint on its background; choking will occur only when the background-plate component is less than or equal to half the darkness of the object.

The upshot is that there won't be a trap unless the foreground and background colors are pretty similar.

Tip: Trapping Large Type. *Even the untrained reader can quickly spot type (especially thin, serif type) that has been "bulked up" by QuarkXPress's trapping. For example, if you put a dark-green 48-point headline over a light-blue background, you may find the text appears slightly heavier in print than the same text would look over no background color at all. The problem is that it's difficult to get XPress to choke a background behind some text without spreading the text, too.*

Here's another use for the Text to Box feature.

1. *Create a new color that is a combination of each darkest process-color tint in the foreground and background. For instance, let's say the foreground has 40-percent cyan plus 20-percent yellow, and the background object is set to 20-percent cyan and 40-percent yellow. The new color would have 40-percent cyan and 40-percent yellow.*

2. *Convert the headline text to a Bézier box using Text to Box on the Style menu.*

3. *Give this box a frame (Command/Ctrl-B) the width of the desired trap (.3 points or so) and apply the new color.*

4. *In the Trap Information palette, set the Frame Outside and Frame Inside popup menus to Overprint (see "Object-Level Trapping," below).*

This actually looks far worse onscreen, because XPress can't simulate the overprinting. However, when you print color separations, you'll see that the background has choked in under the "text," and it often looks cleaner. Of course, this is a lot of work, so you'll only want to do this when you find that XPress's built-in trapping won't work for you.

Tip: Knockout Black. *If you find yourself wishing that black would overprint sometimes and knockout at other times, you might want to duplicate Black (in the Colors dialog box) and change the dupe's name to "Knockout Black." You can then edit the trapping specifications for your new color to either knock out or trap to some custom value. Now you've got a choice: Apply Black to the items you want to overprint, and Knockout Black to those you don't.*

Tip: Knocking Out Rich Black. *The biggest problem with rich black is that when you have text or an object knocking out the black, any misregistration on press results in the cyan peeking out horribly from behind the black. The engineers at Quark have built a very cool internal solution to this problem.*

QuarkXPress checks to see if an object is knocking out a rich black. If it is, XPress only spreads the cyan, magenta, and yellow plates of that rich-black color by the trapping amount, leaving the black plate alone. You need this kind of help most when you're placing a white object (such as white, reversed text) over a rich black. (See Figure 14-29.)

White type knocking out from the
black plate of a rich black

The cyan plate: Note the type is
spread and the background is choked.

Figure 14-29 Knockout from rich black

XPress also chokes the additive colors (leaving the black plate alone) around the edges of a rich black object that is sitting on a white or colored background. This ensures that the colored inks won't appear as a fringe around the black object.

Tip: To Overprint or Not to Overprint. *Sometimes people get confused when a color they've specifically set up to overprint in the Trap Specifications dialog box doesn't overprint at all. Even when they check the Trap Information palette (always the first place to look for your trapping questions), they see that it's not overprinting.*

Often, they've simply forgotten that XPress only overprints a color when it's above the overprint limit (in the Trapping Preferences dialog box). Usually the overprint limit is set to 95 percent, so any color tinted below 95 percent won't overprint automatically. You can change this limit's value, or select the object and tell it to overprint (override the Default setting), in the Trap Information palette.

Tip: Thicker Reversed Text. One of the problems with reversing text (like white text on a colored background) is that it often gets clogged up by the background ink spreading slightly. And even if it doesn't get literally choked, our eye perceives it as being choked.

One way around this is to spread the type's color slightly (see Figure 14-30). First, create a CMYK color that is set to one percent black and in the Edit Trap dialog box set the color to spread .125 points over black. Then turn off Process Trap in the Preferences dialog box and apply this new color to your type. When you print, turn Separations on, even if you're only going to print the black plate. Because your new color is set to spread, the 1-percent black (which is almost white, and will probably not show up on press) spreads over the background black.

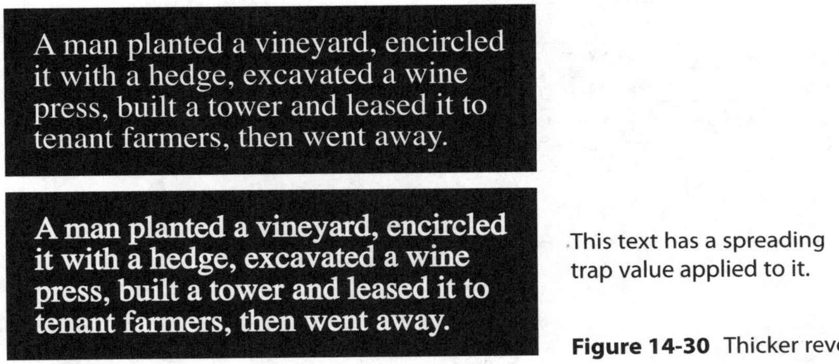

A man planted a vineyard, encircled it with a hedge, excavated a wine press, built a tower and leased it to tenant farmers, then went away.

A man planted a vineyard, encircled it with a hedge, excavated a wine press, built a tower and leased it to tenant farmers, then went away.

This text has a spreading trap value applied to it.

Figure 14-30 Thicker reversed text

Object-Level Trapping

Instead of just specifying trapping-color pairs (all reds over all blues, all blacks over all yellows, and so on), you can specify trapping on an object-by-object basis. For example, if you want one green line to overprint a yellow area, and another similar line to knock out, you can specify that. You do this in the Trap Information palette. Again, you don't *have* to use this; the default trapping is often good enough (and using your service bureau's trapping software is even better). But when you need to tweak your trapping in XPress, here's the place to do it.

Unlike most palettes in QuarkXPress, where you can either use them or use menu items, the Trap Information palette is the only place you can use object-by-object trapping. Let's go ahead and take a gander at this palette's anatomy (see Figure 14-31).

The Trap Information palette shows you the current trap information for a selected page object, gives you "reasons" for why it's trapping the object that way, and lets you change that object's trap value. The trap values that you can change depend on the type of object you've selected.

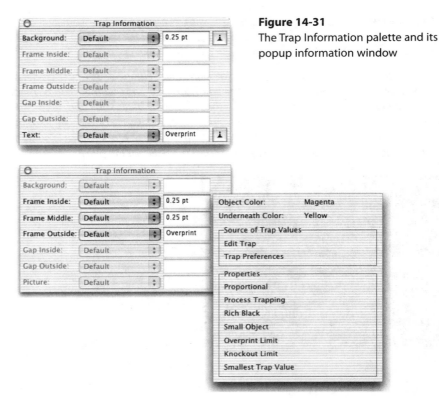

Figure 14-31
The Trap Information palette and its popup information window

For example, for a text box with no frame, you can adjust the trap for the background color of the box and the text in the box. If the text box has no background color, then the Background setting is grayed out.

- **Background.** You can set the Background trap value for boxes that have a background color (anything but None) and do not have a frame.

- **Frame Inside/Frame Outside.** As soon as you put a border (Command/Ctrl-B) around a box, the Background trap setting grays out and the Frame Inside and Frame Outside settings become available. The inside and outside portions of a frame are exactly half the frame width; in a 4-point frame, the Frame Inside (which abuts the background color of the box, or the image inside a picture box) and Frame Outside (which abuts whatever is behind the box) are each 2 points wide.

- **Frame Middle.** If you choose a border style that has gaps in it (in other words, any style other than the solid frame, such as the dotted or double-line frame), XPress activates the Frame Middle popup menu. The Frame Middle lets you control the trap between the frame and the gap area. If the gap area is blank (if the Gap color is None), then this should typically be the same as the Frame Outside setting.

The Frame Middle setting is also the only setting available when you have a fancy bitmapped frame around a box (which I don't like to create). In this case, the only options are Knockout and Overprint. On the palette, it may seem that the default setting is to spread or choke by the Auto Amount, but that doesn't reflect the reality (unless the frame is black, it will probably just knock out of its background).

- **Gap Inside/Gap Outside.** As soon as you set a frame's gap color (in the Modify dialog box), you can set that gap's trapping with Gap Inside and Gap Outside. Like the frame-trapping controls, Gap Inside refers to where the gap color touches the image or the background color of the box, and Gap Outside refers to where it touches the color behind the box.

- **Line.** Lines trap to their background, of course, and if you don't like the default trapping, you can change it here. The problem is that because lines under 10 points thick are "small objects" (see "Tip: Trapping Small Type," earlier in this chapter), XPress currently won't trap a thin line at all unless its color is very similar to the background (I'm lobbying Quark to change this—maybe they will have by the time you read this).

- **Line Middle.** Like Frame Middle, the Line Middle setting lets you set the trap between a line and the gaps in nonsolid line styles (whether the gap is transparent or colored). Again, unless the line is thick, the settings here won't make any difference. (Personally, I think we should be able to force XPress to trap thin lines in this palette—maybe a later version of XPress will allow it.)

- **Gap.** If you've gone hogwild and added a gap color to your styled line, the Gap setting lets you trap that color to the background.

- **Text.** Where XPress 3.x would either trap every character in a text box or none at all, XPress is now a little smarter: It decides on trapping line by line. If only the first three lines of a text box are over a colored background, it will trap them and leave the other lines alone. If, however, the left side of a text box is over a colored background and the right side is not, XPress isn't smart enough to only trap the characters on the left side of the box, so every character gets trapped by default. This is a job for the Text setting on the Trap Information palette, which lets you change trapping character by character. If only half a character is overlapping text, XPress can't trap just half of it—that's a job for postprocess trapping software, like TrapWise.

- **Picture.** The Picture trap setting does not let you trap objects to a background in XPress. Instead, it simply gives you the choice of overprinting or knocking out the background. The only use I can think of for this is overprinting grayscale images, which was particularly difficult in earlier versions of XPress, but which is now quite easy with this feature.

By the way, don't get confused if the Trap Information palette displays a positive trap value (spread) when you know it should be negative (choke). Remember that when the Process Trap option is turned on, some plates will spread and others will choke, so the positive and negative numbers don't mean much.

Default trap. Unless you've changed the trap value, the Trap Information palette displays all objects at their Default trap. This means that the objects trap at whatever value is set in the Trap Specifications dialog box and on the Trapping tab of the Preferences dialog box. QuarkXPress displays the trap value to the right of the word "Default," and then displays a gray button labeled with a question mark. If you click this button and hold it down, QuarkXPress displays the Default Trap window, which explains why it's trapping the object this way. For example, if you have a black line selected, the window might tell you that it's overprinting the black line because of the relationship between black and the background color.

If there are any special reasons why XPress is trapping the object the way it does, they're highlighted in the Properties section of the Default Trap window. Unfortunately, this doesn't usually provide much detail. For instance, if you've selected some white text that is knocking out of a rich black, "Rich Black" is highlighted, but nowhere does it mention that the additive colors in the rich black will be spread or choked by the Auto Amount. It just happens. Similarly, the only way you'd know that small type isn't getting a trap ("Tip: Trapping Small Type," earlier) is by noting the phrase "Small Object" highlighted on the Properties list.

Nonetheless, it's better than just leaving you up in the air.

Custom trapping. To change the trap value for part of an object (for example, the inside frame of a picture box), you use the mini-popup menu on the Trap Information palette. The menu is usually set to Default, but you can change this to Overprint, Knockout, Auto Amount (+), Auto Amount (–), or Custom. Overprint and Knockout are pretty self-explanatory. The two Auto Amount values use the value in the Auto Amount field of the Trapping Preferences dialog box (the value is either positive or negative, denoting a spread or a choke). Personally, I don't find much use for the two Auto Amount settings.

The last item, Custom, is where the power is. QuarkXPress gives you a field in which to type any trap value you want (from -36 to 36 points, though you probably will never use more than 1 or 2 points).

Note that text can be trapped a character at a time (see Figure 14-32), and that one black object can be overprinted where another black object knocks out (this kills the need for my "Knockout Black" tip, above).

Figure 14-32
Trapping type, character
by character

Trapping to Multiple Colors

I said earlier that when QuarkXPress sees one colored object only partially covering another colored object, the program thinks of this as Indeterminate trapping. I then went further and said that when Ignore White is turned on in Trapping Preferences, the program ignores the white background entirely, making it *not* Indeterminate. Now I have the final word on the subject.

If the foreground object partially overlaps two colored objects, XPress still doesn't always think of this as Indeterminate. First it looks at the trapping relationships among all the colors. If the foreground color chokes to both background colors, then the foreground object gets choked. If the Edit Trap specifications are set to spread to both background colors, then QuarkXPress spreads the trap. If it's supposed to spread to one and choke to the other, *then* the program defaults to the Indeterminate trap.

Also, just for the sake of completeness, if you set the Edit Trap specifications so that the foreground color spreads one value (let's say 1 point) to one background color, and a different value (let's say 2 points) to the other background color, QuarkXPress uses the lesser of the values (in this case, 1 point).

None of this may apply to you, but it's still good information to tuck into the back of your brain—just in case.

> **Tip: Use Big Traps.** *An easy way to make sure your traps are working correctly is to temporarily set extremely large values for your color and object traps: anywhere from 1 to 6 points. Print your separations on transparencies or thin paper, align each plate, and you can quickly determine how well XPress is handling your trapping requests. Don't forget to reset the traps to their normal values before your final imagesetting, though! (When I do this, I save the layout, then change the traps, print separations, and then use Revert to Saved to get back to the original settings.)*

> *Another good way to check trapping is to use the enlargement feature in the Print dialog box to magnify the trap area (see more on this in Chapter 15,* Printing*).*

Tip: Overprinting Duotones. *I really like the way Adobe Photoshop handles duotones (or tritones or quadtones). They're simple to make, they separate beautifully from QuarkXPress as EPS files (as long as you have the spot colors' names the same in both programs), and you can see what they look like in color. However, there's more than one way to spin a cat. Here's a way to make duotones right in XPress. The method relies on overprinting one TIFF image on another. I generally import a grayscale TIFF into a picture box, size it, and position it where I want it. Then I clone it (use Step and Repeat with the Offsets set to zero), change the color and the contrast curve for this second image, and make sure the background color of the overprinting image is set to "None." Last, I set the trap for the topmost picture box background to overprint in the Trap Information palette.*

COLOR FROM OUTSIDE SOURCES

Up until now in this chapter I have concentrated my discussion on color items—text, boxes, rules, and so on—which are built entirely in QuarkXPress. But what about bringing color graphics in from other programs? And although I discussed modifying color bitmapped images in Chapter 11, *Image Tuning,* what about being prepared for creating color separations? I'll address these points now.

One area you won't read about here is working with object-oriented color PICT or WMF images, because I think they're kludgey (that's pronounced "cloodgy"), and so unreliable that I wouldn't use them for my own documents (see Chapter 10, *Pictures,* for a slightly longer discussion of this format). The only formats that I find really reliable for prepress work are TIFF, JPEG, PDF, and EPS (and DCS, which is an offshoot of EPS).

Object-Oriented EPS Files

I've avoided the subject of object-oriented graphic files for several chapters, but now it's time to dive back in. Designers frequently generate color artwork using programs such as Adobe Illustrator or Macromedia Freehand, saving them as Encapsulated PostScript (EPS) files. XPress can not only import files from these programs, but can also generate color separations of these files.

Once again, the details of generating color separations (or "seps," as they're often called) is covered in Chapter 15, *Printing.* But while I'm on the subject of color on the desktop, I need to cover some general information about using these programs with QuarkXPress. I'll tackle this discussion one color method at a time: process first, and then spot (I include Pantone colors in the spot-color discussion, though you can create process simulations of Pantone inks).

Process color. QuarkXPress can create color separations of illustrations built in FreeHand or Illustrator that contain process colors. Period. All you have to do is specify your process colors in either application, save them as EPS or PDF, and import them into your QuarkXPress layout using Get Picture. Nice and easy. As I noted earlier in this chapter, if the colors are named (process colors in Illustrator or spot colors in FreeHand), the colors are added to the QuarkXPress layout color list.

Note that I say you must use Get Picture. If you use Copy and Paste to paste a graphic into a picture box, QuarkXPress won't separate it. In fact, while I'm on the subject, I should note that QuarkXPress may not be able to separate color EPS or PDF files from applications other than Illustrator or FreeHand. It depends entirely on whether those applications create the files according to Adobe's document-structuring specifications.

Spot color. The key to working with spot colors brought in from either FreeHand or Illustrator is being careful with your naming. In order for QuarkXPress to separate the spot colors properly, you have to have a color in your QuarkXPress layout named *exactly* the same as the color in the illustration. Fortunately, XPress automatically adds named colors from illustrations to your color list when you import the picture. Also, note that when working with spot colors, you must save them in an EPS or DCS format; PDF files with spot colors do not currently work in XPress.

If you don't have a same-named color in QuarkXPress (perhaps you deleted it accidentally), the spot color separates into a process color in XPress. Remember that with spot colors, the colors' actual specifications make no difference except for screen display and color-printer output.

The same goes for the Pantone colors. If you use a Pantone color in your Illustrator file, just make sure it has the same name in your QuarkXPress file, and it'll print fine (although it'll probably look wrong onscreen). Fortunately, Illustrator, FreeHand, and QuarkXPress name their Pantone colors the same, so if you're using the color libraries included in each program, the names will probably match.

What You Can and Cannot Change

QuarkXPress prints exactly what is specified in every EPS file. In fact, XPress has no way to change such a file: Encapsulated PostScript files and PDF files are totally self-contained and cannot easily be modified from outside sources. All the halftoning information for objects and bitmapped images (if it's included in the EPS), all the trapping and tinting information, and all the color specifications are set in hard-packed mud (I like to think that you at least have a chance with hard-packed mud; "stone" is a bit too final).

All this means that you must take a little more control into your own hands. You must specify your own trapping from within FreeHand or Illustrator, and make sure that these images contain traps for their surroundings in XPress layouts.

Luckily, all overprinting specified in Illustrator or FreeHand (or any other program that handles its color PostScript properly) is handled correctly when you generate color separations from QuarkXPress. An object that's set to overprint in a FreeHand EPS file not only overprints objects within that EPS, but also QuarkXPress objects. Conversely, if an object is not set to Overprint, it knocks out any background colors or objects within QuarkXPress.

You cannot adjust any trapping for EPS files from within QuarkXPress. For example, if your EPS picture contains a spot color (let's say PMS 345), and you have set up the equivalent spot color in QuarkXPress as described above, any trapping or overprinting assignments you make to PMS 345 in the Trap Specifications dialog box do not (and actually cannot) make any difference to the EPS file. They do, however, make all the difference to any objects created within QuarkXPress that are colored PMS 345.

The same is true with Quark's Color Management System: It has absolutely no effect on the colors in your EPS graphics.

Bitmapped Images

Let's cut to the chase: Process colors are CMYK (cyan, magenta, yellow, and black). A picture saved in any other color model (most TIFF images are, especially scans) has to be translated into CMYK mode before it can be imageset. QuarkXPress can create separations of these RGB images by itself, but it won't necessarily do a good job of it.

Version 4 of XPress had a problem wherein RGB, TIFF, and JPEG images were always converted to CMYK at print time, even when printing to a composite color printer. This typically made vibrant images look washed out because XPress doesn't know how to separate the colors as well as the printer can by itself. Fortunately, you can now send RGB images to composite printers directly in the RGB model, and the images look much better.

If you're working with scanned RGB images and want to print color separations, you have two options for the RGB-to-CMYK conversion.

- Preseparate the image using Photoshop or the like, and import it into QuarkXPress as a CMYK TIFF, PDF, EPS, or DCS file.

- Place the image as an RGB TIFF or JPEG in QuarkXPress, and let the Quark CMS XTension do the process-separation work.

Although I'll really be talking about color separation in detail in Chapter 15, *Printing*, let's explore these three methods briefly here.

Preseparating. Adobe Photoshop allows you to translate RGB images into CMYK using the Mode submenu, under the Item menu. This is a simple process, but to get good-quality CMYK images, you need to spend some time learning about and tweaking the various color-separation preference dialog boxes; I cover this in great depth in the book I wrote with Bruce Fraser, *Real World Adobe Photoshop*.

Once you've separated a file in Photoshop (or some other capable program), you can save it in one of four formats—EPS, DCS, PDF, or TIFF—and import it into QuarkXPress, fully separated and ready for output. I discussed these formats in detail in Chapter 10, *Pictures*.

Saving as CMYK EPS. Note that you don't have to save EPS files in DCS format in order for your images to separate from XPress. However, there are differences in the way the two formats function.

- The biggest drawback to CMYK EPS files is that they consist of one gigantic file. DCS 1.0 files have the added benefit of letting you work with a small master file while the large CMYK files can be sitting someplace else. (On the other hand, this means you have to keep track of five files rather than just one.)

- DCS files print faster from XPress than do EPS or TIFF files. It used to be the case that EPS files were much slower than DCS, because XPress had to send the entire EPS file to the printer for each plate (imagine a 40 MB file getting sent four times, once each for cyan, magenta, yellow, and black). Now XPress is smart enough to recognize Photoshop EPS files, and it knows how to pull these apart so that it only sends the cyan information for the cyan plate, and so on (this is only true with Photoshop EPS files). The result is that DCS is still faster, but not much faster.

Of course, I've already said that color separation is not as easy as clicking a button. If you're looking for quality color, you had better know Photoshop well enough to work with its undercolor-removal and color-correction settings. Remember: QuarkXPress cannot apply any image modification to the EPS files that you import. All that must be done before you import the picture.

Saving as CMYK TIFF. Once you've switched to CMYK mode in Photoshop, you can also save files as CMYK TIFF images. I find CMYK TIFFs to be a bit easier than DCS files for several reasons. First, you only have one file to work with. Second, QuarkXPress can do more with TIFF files than it can with EPS or DCS images. For example, QuarkXPress can downsample the TIFF image at print time if necessary, which can save you time. Also, you can make tonal and screening adjustments to TIFF images from within the program. Finally, if you're working with an OPI system (see more on OPI in Chapter 15, *Printing*), you can use TIFF images as for-position-only (FPO) images and let another program strip them in at print time.

Separating with an XTension. If you want to postseparate your RGB images, you can import them directly into QuarkXPress and then separate them with the color management system, Quark CMS, that ships with the program. Color management is a way to map colors from one space to another (for instance, mapping RGB on a 17-inch Apple Trinitron monitor to CMYK on a Web press with 22-percent dot gain using SWOP inks), but it takes some work to produce quality images efficiently.

Which to use. Do I suggest using preseparation (typically with Adobe Photoshop), or postseparation (with Quark CMS)? The most important consideration is your workflow. The biggest argument for preseparation is the translation time: Preseparating your bitmapped images requires translating them from RGB to CMYK only once. Postseparating them with an XTension requires that same translation time whenever you print. This translation can be incredibly time-consuming. Given a choice, I'd rather have to deal with it just once.

However, which of these methods results in the superior separation? Here I get to the aesthetics of color separation, and I wouldn't want to sway your opinion (which is a nice way of saying that—just this once—I'm not going to preach my own opinions).

> **Tip: Duotones from Photoshop.** *Many people create duotones (or tritones or quadtones) in Photoshop and then save them as EPS files (you have to save them as EPS files) before importing them into QuarkXPress. If the duotone uses spot (such as Pantone) colors, you have to make sure you've got the same-named color in your QuarkXPress layout. People have had difficulty with this in the past because the two programs sometimes named their Pantone colors differently.*
>
> *Fortunately, QuarkXPress now automatically imports the color names into your layout, so you're sure to get a match. On the other hand, if you're already using Pantone Uncoated colors in your XPress layout, you may need to rename the colors (in either Photoshop or QuarkXPress) so that they match.*
>
> *Also note that if your duotones are set to a spot color and a process color (like black), you have to adjust the halftone screen for the spot color so that you don't end up with moiré patterns or dot-doubling (see more information about color separations in Chapter 15, Printing).*

COLOR MANAGEMENT/PROOFING

Color management is the art of setting up your monitor and printer so that what you see onscreen and coming out of your printer can reasonably represent what the final printed piece will look like. Sounds simple, but there are lots of little pieces to the puzzle. In an ideal environment, you would use expensive hardware and software to create custom color profiles for your camera, scanner, monitor, and printing devices, as well as for the presses and proofing systems of the commercial printers you use. Unless you're a color consultant, you're probably reluctant to spend the time (and scads of money) to accomplish this lofty goal. But don't give up: With a little effort and little (or no) capital outlay, you can still achieve color consistency and usable color output. (If you'd like to expand your understanding of color management, read *Real World Color Management*, Second Edition by Bruce Fraser, Chris Murphy, and Fred Bunting.)

To be realistic, don't expect your monitor to be indistinguishable from a printed piece. After all, your display is composed of glowing stuff—light is coming at you. A printed piece is (not to sound too obvious) ink on paper, which accomplishes color by means of reflected and absorbed colors of light. They're completely different realities. But with some simple steps, you can at least control the display of color on your monitor, and QuarkXPress can help you produce reasonably close color output on your printer.

Start by calibrating your monitor, even if you just use the Adobe Gamma utility on Windows (available through the Control Panel) or the ColorSync setup utility on the Macintosh (available in System Preferences, as part of Display preferences. Choose the Color tab at the top, and then click the Calibrate button. You'll be led through the steps necessary to calibrate and create a monitor profile.) If you want a more concise profile, use a colorimeter such as the EyeOne device available from X-Rite (and there are other manufacturers offering equivalent, easy-to-use devices for calibrating and profiling your monitor). Since monitors drift with time and age, it's recommended that you repeat this process and create new, current profiles periodically. If your monitor is a CRT (the big heavy type), you should calibrate and profile at least every two weeks. Flat-panel LCD monitors are somewhat more stable, but it's a good idea to repeat calibration and profiling at least monthly on LCD monitors.

Once you've created a profile for your monitor, invoke it in QuarkXPress Preferences. Choose Preferences from the QuarkXPress menu (Macintosh) or the Edit menu (Windows), and select the Display topic in the left column (see Figure 14-33). This option controls the appearance of guides and pasteboard size, as well as color and grayscale images, but there, hiding in plain sight, is the drop-down list for choosing your monitor profile. If you haven't created a custom profile, choose one of the supplied profiles. Can't decide? Use the Quark Generic RGB option.

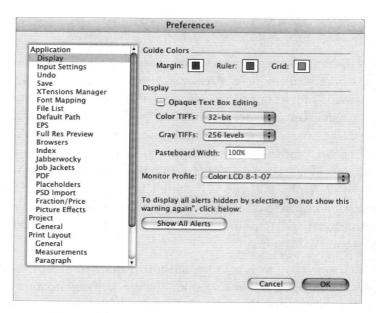

Figure 14-33
To invoke the appropriate monitor profile, choose Display from the Application preferences topic, and select a canned or custom profile from the Monitor Profile drop-down list.

After you've chosen your monitor profile, it's time to set up the color management for print layouts. In the left column of the Preferences dialog box, scroll down to Print Layout and select Color Manager under that topic (see Figure 14-34). The right side of the dialog box offers you the options for controlling color management behavior.

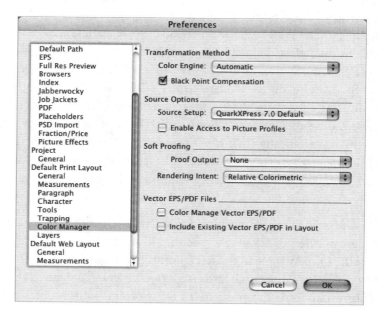

Figure 14-34
The default choices for color managing print layouts will serve you well if you're not up for customizing the profiles used.

- **Transformation Method.** Choose a color engine to perform all the heady math required to knit together your monitor, source, and output profiles. Leave it at Automatic to use the built-in engine, which is LogoSync (developed with GretagMacbeth). Black Point Compensation is turned on by default, which is appropriate for RGB image content that will become CMYK during output (e.g., during export to PDF/X-1a), or CMYK content.

- **Source Options.** The QuarkXPress 7 Default option provides reasonably good rendition on your color printer. But if you want to tweak things a bit and create your own source profile, see the next section, "Source Setup."

- **Soft Proofing.** As with the other options, try the default Soft Proofing setting and judge the output. If you feel that it's not quite close enough for your tastes, create a custom Output setup to invoke by choosing Proof Output from the View menu (see "Output Setup," next).

- **Vector EPS/PDF Files.** This option to color manage vector EPS and PDF content only applies to content that is placed after you turn on the option. If you already have EPS/PDF content in the layout that you would like to color manage, turn on the Include Existing checkbox.

Tip: Turning Off Color Management. In QuarkXPress 7, color management is on by default. If you're more comfortable turning it off (and don't care what your monitor or desktop output looks like as far as color), you can choose QuarkXPress Emulate Legacy in the Source Setup drop-down list.

Source Setup

If you've created the images you're using, or if you're familiar with the source of the images, you may want to customize the source setup to better handle color.

From the Edit menu choose Color Setups, and then choose Source. In the Source Setups dialog box (see Figure 14-35), click the New button to create a custom source setup. In the example, for the RGB option I've set the picture profile to Adobe RGB (1998), because that is the profile I've used for my images while working on them in Photoshop. For the CMYK option I've chosen U.S. Web Coated (SWOP) v2, because the job will be printed on a web press. The Relative Colorimetric option is chosen for Rendering Intent, because that option compares the source white space to the output white space and shifts colors accordingly for a more realistic rendition.

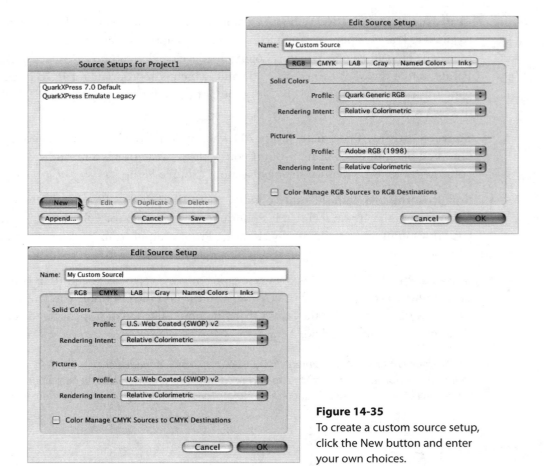

Figure 14-35
To create a custom source setup, click the New button and enter your own choices.

If you're curious about rendering intents, here's a quick guide:

- **Perceptual.** This option maps all colors so they fall within the destination gamut. While this may change some colors, it retains the relationships between colors, which provides good rendering for photographs.

- **Relative Colorimetric.** Colors that fall outside the gamut of the destination space are truncated to the closest reproducible color, taking into consideration differences between the source and target white points. More of the original color values are retained than when using the Perceptual intent, and you'll probably get the best results by using Relative Colorimetric.

- **Saturation.** If your layout contains bright colors in graphics (such as vector art, charts, and graphs), this may be appropriate. Just know that it will alter the appearance of photographic images. This is used to "punch up" business graphics, often at the expense of subtle colors.

- **Absolute Colorimetric.** This is similar to Relative Colorimetric in that colors outside the destination space are remapped to the closest colors inside the destination space. The original white point is preserved, not remapped to the destination space. This may result in better color onscreen, but less accuracy in printing.

When you're done, click OK, and the custom source setup will be added to the source options available in the QuarkXPress Preferences. To edit an existing source setup, just choose Color Setups from the Edit menu, then choose Source and double-click its name in the Source Setups dialog box. Click OK when you're done, and then click Save to exit the Source Setups dialog box.

Output Setup

To more closely mimic the final printing environment, you may want to create a custom output setup. From the Edit menu choose Color Setups, and then choose Output. In the Edit Output Setup dialog box, click the New button to create a custom output setup (see Figure 14-36). Give the output setup a name, and choose the mode and output options. Here, I've chosen the profile for U.S. Web Coated (SWOP) v2 because that reflects how the job will be printed. Click OK to exit the options dialog box, and then click Save to add the output setup to the source options available in the QuarkXPress Preferences for Color Manager under Print Layout. To edit an output setup, choose Color Setups from the Edit menu, and then choose Output. Select the name of the setup and click the Edit button (or double-click the name). Make the desired changes, and click OK when you're finished. Finally, click the Save button in the Output Setup dialog box.

> *Tip: Installing a Custom Profile. If your print service provider gives you a custom profile for a press or proofing system, install it correctly so that it will be available for you when you set up custom output options. On the Macintosh, place the profile in Library/ColorSync/Profiles. On Windows, place profiles in the Windows\System32\Spool\Drivers\Color folder.*

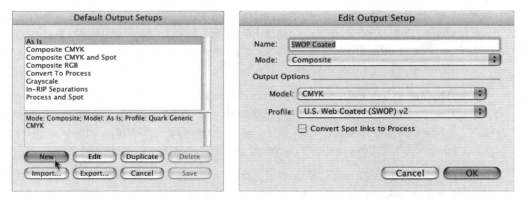

Figure 14-36 Creating a custom output setup

Soft Proofing

If you have calibrated your monitor and created a profile for it, and faithfully plugged in all the appropriate profiles for input and output sources, QuarkXPress can provide display simulation of multiple output environments. While a monitor is usually no substitute for a contract proof from your printer for final determination of color, it can be sufficiently accurate for soft proofing (that is, proofing onscreen without a hard copy proof). Soft proofing can be especially helpful when you want to compare how your layout will appear under different output conditions, such as a color magazine printed on smooth coated paper compared to newsprint. You can compare the outcomes onscreen and adjust the content (or your expectations) accordingly.

> **Tip: Managing Your Environment for Color Viewing.** *Keep in mind that environmental influences, such as ambient light or reflections from colorful walls, can undermine your onscreen judgments. It is helpful to have a simple, neutral gray environment and consistent lighting to aid in viewing and evaluating color.*

To soft proof onscreen, go to the View menu, choose Proof Output and choose the appropriate profile from the popup menu. The menu lists all output setups available for the current layout; if you have created custom output setups, they will be available here. When you choose a Proof Output option, the layout is displayed in that color space. This includes all objects in the layout, as well as the Colors palette itself!

Sharing Color Setups/Output Styles

Since source and output setups are portable, you can take several approaches if you want to deploy source and output setups across a workgroup. You'll find that the Append and Import/Export options are much easier to manage than the Job Jacket approach for general applications.

- **Append source setups.** Create a project, and then create the desired source and output setups. Distribute the project files to other users in the workgroup. The recipients can choose Color Setups from the Edit menu, and then pick Source. Next, they click the Append button and choose the "donor" project file you supplied. They then click the bold right arrow to add the setup to the current layout (see Figure 14-37).

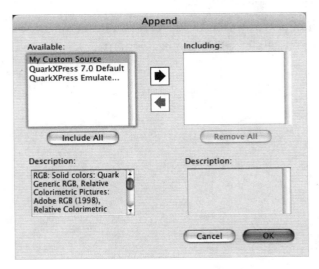

Figure 14-37
Appending a source setup from another project

- **Exporting and importing output setups.** Output setups can be exported as stand-alone files. To export output setups, choose Color Setups from the Edit menu, and then pick Output. In the Output Setups dialog box, click the Export button, and then name and save the file. Recipients will need to choose Color Setups from the Edit menu, select Output Setups, click the Import button, and select the file you exported.

- **Job Jackets.** Input and output setups can be incorporated into a Job Jacket. In the Job Jackets Manager dialog box (available from the Utilities menu), click the Advanced Settings button (lower left) and select a donor project from the list in the left pane. Then drag the setup to the target Job Jacket or Job Ticket.

DECIDING TO WORK IN COLOR

While this chapter should get you up and running with color in XPress, I think it's only fair to end with suggesting logical steps toward successful color desktop publishing.

1. Complete a black-and-white project with text only.

2. Complete a black-and-white project with text and graphics.

3. Complete a project with several spot colors.

4. Complete a project with process-color tints.

5. Finally, attempt the use of color photography.

The computer, no matter how powerful a tool, is still no substitute for experience. Work slowly and carefully, and in time you will become a raging color pro.

CHAPTER FIFTEEN

Printing

Once upon a time, probably somewhere at some university, someone had an idea and named it "the paperless office." People wouldn't be bothered anymore with having to store the thousands (or millions) of pieces of paper that come through their offices every year. Instead, the information would all be placed on some sort of storage medium, easily referenced by computer. It was a magic concept; everyone agreed that it would make life easier, more efficient, and certainly more fun.

Go ahead and ask people who have been involved with electronic publishing for a while if they have seen any sign of the paperless office. As an example, in my office, the ratio of expended paper to normal refuse is such that I empty my small garbage can every couple of weeks and the voluminous paper-recycling boxes weekly. When it comes right down to it, unless you use QuarkXPress exclusively for building Web pages or Acrobat PDF files, almost every layout that you create is probably based, ultimately, on a printed page or an imaged piece of film (which will probably be used later to print on paper).

How can you extract the digitized information from disk to print on paper? Many people mistake the process as being as easy as simply choosing the Print command. In this chapter I'll discuss what's behind the act of printing, and go into some depth on how to get the most efficient and best-quality output you can for your layout. I'll also touch on tips for working with service bureaus and printers—both the mechanical and the human varieties.

Before I get into anything too complex, though, let's deal with two simple yet critical issues in most people's print jobs: PostScript and fonts.

POSTSCRIPT

This chapter is dedicated, in part, to Chuck Geschke, John Warnock, and the other people who created PostScript. PostScript is what makes desktop publishing with QuarkXPress possible. It's the language that PostScript devices (such as printers, platesetters, and image-setters) understand. When QuarkXPress prints a page, it writes a computer program in PostScript describing the page and sends it to the device. The device, which contains a PostScript interpreter (called a RIP—Raster Image Processor), interprets the PostScript file and a marking engine, such as an electrostatically charged drum, puts marks on the paper, film, or plates according to that description.

A large percentage of printing problems are related to using printers that don't understand PostScript. On some non-PostScript printers, some page elements may print incorrectly. EPS files, in particular, print horribly unless you turn on Full Resolution from the Preview Quality submenu (under the Item menu) for each image, because the printer only prints the low-resolution screen previews you see in XPress.

By the way, because Adobe makes the interpreter that lives inside most printers, it's assumed that "Adobe PostScript" is the standard. Nonetheless, many other companies offer PostScript clones. You may find that a page won't print on a clone interpreter but will print on a true Adobe PostScript interpreter.

> **Tip: Printing to Inkjet Printers.** *XPress really expects to be printing to a PostScript printer, and popular inkjets rarely support PostScript. Some have software add-ons that will interpret PostScript, but your mileage may vary. QuarkXPress can print most page elements decently, but some content may not be rendered correctly. So what's the best way to print your QuarkXPress layout to an inkjet printer? Export the file as a PDF file and print it from Acrobat or Adobe Reader. (I cover Acrobat and PDF files in Chapter 16,* PDF.)

PDF

When you think of print, you tend to think of paper being involved. But in a way, creating a PDF is a print process. Your layout is rendered in a portable form (like paper) so you can share it with someone else. Think of it as electronic paper. PDF files are so relevant that they deserve an entire chapter in this book, so you'll find much more depth and breadth in Chapter 16, *PDF*. But while you're here, consider the methods of creating PDF that are available through the Print dialog box in QuarkXPress. If you have installed Adobe Acrobat on your computer (the full retail version, not the free Adobe Reader), a PDF "printer" is added to your list of printers. Even though it doesn't have a paper tray, the PDF printer behaves much like a real-world printer. Choose the Adobe PDF printer from the printer drop-down menu in the Print dialog, create any size of imaginary paper necessary, and when you click the Print button, QuarkXPress silently generates a PostScript file and hands it off to Distiller for PDF creation. You don't see all this happen; you just get a PDF as a result. To modify the output options on the Macintosh, click the Printer button at the bottom of the Print dialog and change the options for the PDF printer.

On Windows, the process is quite similar: Choose the Adobe PDF printer from the Printer drop-down menu in the Print dialog box, and click the Properties button to view the Adobe PDF Settings options. Here, you can choose "paper" size and turn on the option to view results (which launches Acrobat after the file is created). To specify that layout fonts must be used rather than system fonts, you must *turn off* the option to rely on system fonts only, which is counterintuitive. (This isn't Quark's fault; it's an oddity of the Adobe PDF print interface.)

> **Tip: The Adobe PDF Printer Isn't a Real Printer, but It Has a Real PPD.** *When printing to the Adobe PDF printer, always choose Adobe PDF for the PPD (you'll see a number after Adobe PDF, which reflects the version of Adobe Acrobat currently installed on your computer). Don't use a "real-world" printer.*

PRINT DIALOG BOX

We all demanded more features in QuarkXPress, and Quark gave them to us. Unfortunately, sometimes having more features means more complexity. The Print dialog box is a perfect example of this. The folks at Quark have tried their hardest to squeeze over 40 features into this one dialog box in a way that is still reasonably usable, and they've mostly succeeded. However, the result is something that seems, at first, like one of those 1950s computer consoles with hundreds of dials and knobs and flashing lights (see Figure 15-1). Don't worry; it's much easier to use than it looks. The list of options in the left-hand column of the dialog box replaces the tabbed interface from previous versions. As you select an option from the list, the options pane appears on the right side. What you see in the pane depends on the option you've chosen. So, rather than refer to, say, the "Pages tab," I'll talk about the Pages *pane*.

If you're familiar with earlier versions of XPress, you'll soon figure out that the folks at Quark folded the Page Setup dialog box into the Print dialog box, stuck in several features from the long-defunct QuarkPrint XTension, and topped it off with a few great new features. Note that you can make changes in the various panes in the Print dialog box in any order you like. In general, however, I make choices in this dialog box in the order that I discuss them in this chapter.

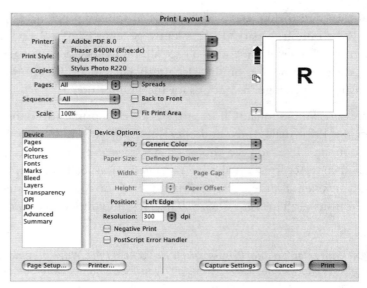

Figure 15-1
The Print dialog box on the Macintosh

Choosing a Printer

It may seem obvious that you should pick your printer before you start to print, but there are a few little buttons and options to consider. Picking a printer (and setting its properties) is much easier than it used to be on both platforms!

Macintosh. On the Macintosh you can specify which kind of printer you want to use—as well as which particular printer, if you have more than one on a network—by selecting it from the Printer popup menu, which lists every printer you've set up on that machine. If your printer doesn't appear in this list, click the Printer button at the lower left of the Print dialog and choose Add Printer from the drop-down list in the Printer dialog that appears (see Figure 15-2).

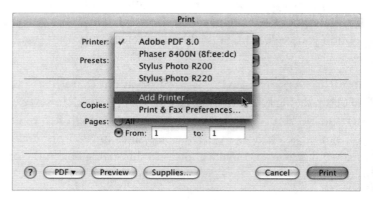

Figure 15-2
The Mac OS X Print Driver dialog box

If you are working with just a single PostScript laser printer, you hardly need to worry about the Printer dialog box. Just set it once and forget it, except when you want to switch between PostScript printers on the network. I'll discuss the other features you see in the Print Driver dialog box later in this chapter in "Page Setup, Printer, and Properties."

Windows. In Windows you also choose a printer from the drop-down menu in the Print dialog box (see Figure 15-3). The only printers that appear listed here are those that you have already set up in Windows. (You can add a new printer with the Windows Add Printer utility. I'll step you through one example of this process later in this chapter.)

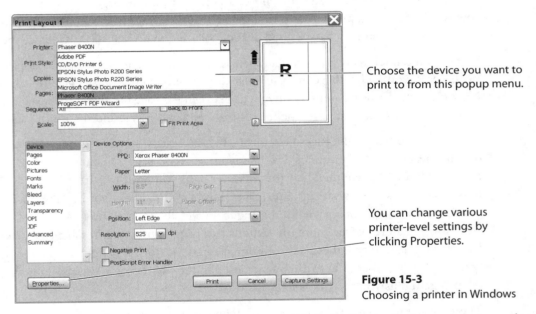

Choose the device you want to print to from this popup menu.

You can change various printer-level settings by clicking Properties.

Figure 15-3
Choosing a printer in Windows

Once you've chosen a device, it behooves you to click the Properties button to ensure that the printer settings conform to your wishes. The Properties dialog box controls the way the printer driver works. Note that there are several features that appear in both the Properties dialog box and QuarkXPress's Print dialog box; in these cases, ignore the settings in the Properties dialog box and use XPress's instead. (I discuss these settings in more depth in "Page Setup, Printer, and Properties," later in this chapter.)

The Pages You Want

There are several other settings in the Print dialog box that stick around no matter what option you choose: Print Style, Copies, Pages, Sequence, Scale, Collate, Spreads, Back to Front, and Print Area. I'm going to hold off on the Print Style popup menu until later in this chapter—for now, suffice it to say that it's a way to save various Print dialog box settings so you can choose them quickly later. Here's the rundown on the other controls.

Copies. I might as well start with the simplest choice of all. How many copies of your layout do you want printed? Let's say you choose to print a multiple-page layout, specifying four copies. The first page prints four times, then the second page prints four times, and so on. In other words, you may have a good deal of collating to do later (see "Collate," below).

Pages. You can tell XPress to print all the pages in your layout, or just a selection of pages. In the past, you had to have an XTension to print noncontiguous pages in your layout. Now it's easy: just type commas or hyphens between the page numbers. For instance, typing "1, 4-6, 9" prints the first page, the fourth through sixth pages, and the ninth page.

The values you type in the Pages field must either be exactly the same as those in your layout or must be specified as absolutes. If your layout starts on page 23, you can't type "1" in the From field; it must be either "23" (or whatever page you want to start from) or "+1" (the plus character specifies an absolute page number—in other words, "the first page"). Similarly, if you are using page numbering in an alphabetical system (such as "a," "b," "c," etc.) or using a prefix (see more on sections and page numbering in Chapter 4, *Building a Layout*), you have to type these sorts of numbers into the slots. It's annoying, but if you don't type the page number exactly the way it's used in the program (or use absolute numbers), the program tells you that "no such page exists."

There's one more potential problem with typing page numbers into the Pages field: if you have used prefixes such as "A-" then your page numbers appear as A-1, A-2, A-3, and so on. This means you can't type a range of page numbers. (If you type A-1-A-6, XPress will just get confused.) Fortunately, you can change the separation characters that XPress pays attention to in the Preferences dialog box (see Figure 15-4). You can change the hyphen and the comma characters to just about any other symbols you want, except letters and numbers.

> ***Tip: From Beginning or End.*** *You can print all the pages in a layout by typing "All" into the Pages field (or choosing it from the popup menu to the right of the field). On the other hand, if you only want to print the first four pages, you can type the cryptic "+1-+4" (remember that the plus sign means "absolute page number," no matter what page-numbering scheme you're using). To print from page 15 to the end of the layout, type "15-end".*

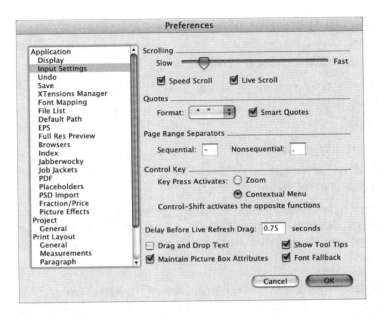

Figure 15-4
Range Separators

Tip: Capture Settings. It seems to happen to me at least once a day: I go to the Print dialog box, I spend time setting up the options in the various panes, and then I remember a change I forgot to make on the layout pages. In this situation in the past, you'd have to press Cancel and lose all the work you did in the Print dialog box. Fortunately, now you can click the Capture Settings button. This closes the dialog box but remembers the values and options you have chosen.

Unfortunately, this feature doesn't remember all the settings. For instance, it won't remember values you type in Page Range or Copies, and it won't remember which color plates you *don't* want to print (see "The Colors Pane," later in this chapter).

Sequence. This gives you slightly more control over which pages in your layout get printed. You have three choices: All, Odd, or Even.

- **All.** This is the default position for printing pages from QuarkXPress. It means "all pages that you have selected above." In other words, if you have selected a page range from 23 to 28, having All Pages selected won't counteract your desires; it'll just print all those pages.

- **Odd/Even.** These two choices are mutually exclusive. I sometimes joke about this feature when I'm working on jobs with several strangely designed pages: "Just print the odd ones, and leave the rest." The only real value I've ever gotten out of this feature lies in the following tip, "Printing Double-Sided Layouts."

Tip: Printing Double-Sided Layouts. You can print double-sided pages with the following technique.

1. Print all the odd-numbered pages (select Odd).

2. Place these pages back into the printer, face down (or face up, depending on how your printer feeds the paper).

3. Select Back to Front.

4. Print all the even-numbered pages (select Even).

If everything is set up right, and if your layout has an even number of pages, the second page should print on the back of the first, and so on.

You can use this same technique to print layouts when photocopying onto two sides of a page (if your photocopier handles automatic two-sided copying, ignore this). Print the odd-numbered pages first, then the even-numbered pages, and then ask your local FedEx Kinko's person what to do next.

Scale. This is fairly self-explanatory. Want to print at half final size? Enter 50 here (you don't have to type the percent sign). You can enter any whole number (no decimal points) between 25 and 400 percent. This is especially nice when printing proofs of a larger-format layout, or when trying to create enormous posters by tiling them. You could create a 4-by-4-foot poster in QuarkXPress and then enlarge it to 400 percent, so that when that last sheet printed out of your printer and you'd tiled all 439 sheets together, you'd have a 16-foot-square poster.

Collate. I said earlier that when you printed multiple copies of your layout you would receive x copies of the first page, then x copies of the second page, and so on, leaving you to manually collate all the copies. You can have QuarkXPress collate the pages for you instead, so that the full layout prints out once, then again, and again, and so on.

The problem with Collate is that when you do it takes much longer to print your complete job. This is because the printer has to reprocess the entire layout for each new set of copies. How long this takes depends on the number of fonts and pictures you use, among other things. For a long layout, the time difference becomes a toss-up: do you take the time to collate the pages yourself or have the printer take the time to process them?

Spreads. This is a powerful but potentially dangerous feature, so it should be used with some care. Turning on Spreads in the Print dialog box tells QuarkXPress to print spreads as one full page rather than as two or three pages. For example, printing a two-page, facing-pages spread with registration marks normally results in one page printing with its set of crop marks, then the next page, and so on. When Spreads is turned on, the pages abut each other and sit between the same crop marks (see Figure 15-5).

Two pages printed as a spread; this only works for center spreads, or when you've set up panels of a brochure or poster as individual pages.

A reader spread printed as two pages. This is what your printer generally wants. Note the bleed for images that cross the page break.

Figure 15-5 Printing spreads versus printing individual pages

I think there are two good uses for the Spreads feature.

- If you're building a folding brochure (like a tri-fold) and you lay out each panel on a separate page, you need to turn on the Spreads option in order for the panels to print out next to each other. (Note that the primary problem with doing this is that the third panel in a tri-fold brochure typically needs to be slightly more narrow so that it folds inside the other panels—and XPress won't let you have different-sized pages within a layout.)

- Turning on the Spreads feature is a good way to proof a layout on a desktop printer so you can see what two pages will look like next to each other in the final, bound layout.

The Spreads feature is not an imposition feature. That is, it won't create printer spreads, which are required when the layout will be bound (however, see the next tip).

*Tip: **Roll Your Own Printer Spreads.*** *Page imposition is a tricky business, and there's lots of software out there to help you do it. QuarkXPress itself does not perform any kind of imposition, including basic printer spreads (where pages 1 and 16 print together, then pages 2 and 15, and so on). Fortunately, there are some great page-imposition tools out there. On the high-end, there's Creo's Preps and Dynagram's InPosition XTension. More appropriate for the smaller design shop is A Lowly Apprentice Production's Imposer or Imposer Pro (see Appendix A, XTensions and Resources).*

However, sometimes you just want to do a quick little booklet at just as little cost. You can use the Spreads feature in conjunction with the Page Layout palette to "strip" together pages which will be double-sided and saddle-stitched. Just follow these steps.

1. *Create your layout as usual, but don't use facing pages or automatic page numbers (see Chapter 4, Building a Layout). Make sure you have an even number of pages.*

2. *When you're finished, use the Page Layout palette to move the last page to the left of the first page. Then move the second-to-last page (which has now become the last page) up to the right of the second page (which is now the third page). Then, move the next last page to the left of the next single page, and so on.*

3. *When you're done, every page should be paired with another page, and the last pages in the layout should be the middle pages. For example, in an 8-page booklet, the final pages would end up being the spread between pages 4 and 5.*

4. *Make sure the Spreads feature is selected in the Print dialog box when you print the layout page.*

*Tip: **Printing Spreads in a Layout.*** *Don't waste paper or film when you print contiguous spreads from a single layout; if for no other reason, it's expensive. If you have a multiple-page spread crossing pages 45 through 47, have your service bureau print the pages from 1 through 44 and 48 through the end as single pages, and then print the three-page spread on a separate pass.*

Back to Front. The problem with talking about printing from QuarkXPress is that each PostScript printer model is slightly (or not-so-slightly) different from the next. For example, when you print a multiple-page layout on your laser printer, does the first page come out face up or face down? Some printers do one, some the other, and some give you a choice. If the pages come out face up, you'll love the Back to Front feature. Selecting Back to Front prints the last page of your page selection first, then prints "backwards" to the first page. The stack of pages that ends up in the output tray will be in proper order.

Note that you can't select this feature when you are printing spreads or thumbnails (if you want a good brain twister, try to think of how pages would print if you could select these together).

Fit in Print Area. When you turn on the Fit in Print Area checkbox, XPress calculates the Reduce or Enlarge setting for you, so that your layout fits snugly on whatever paper size you're using at the orientation you specify. This is much faster than trying to figure out the proper percentages to get a tabloid page onto a letter-sized page, or vice versa.

By the way, Fit in Print Area is grayed out whenever you've turned on the Thumbnails option.

Print Status

As soon as you click Print, XPress displays the Print Status dialog box, which not only tells you what page it's printing, but also what color plate, tile, and EPS/TIFF images it's working on (see Figure 15-6). Remember that no program can know how long a page will take to print on a PostScript printer, so there's no way to show how much longer the print job will take. Instead, the status bar in the Print Status dialog box only displays the percentage of pages that have been printed (for example, if you have two pages in your layout, the status bar is 50-percent full after the first page, even if the second page takes 10 times longer than the first one to print). Nonetheless, this is a nice intermediate step, and often makes me feel better when I'm waiting for those long jobs to print.

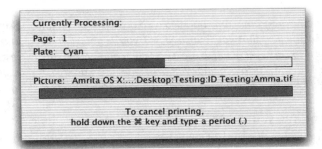

Figure 15-6
Print Status dialog box

THE DEVICE PANE

The first of the options panes, Device is chosen by default when you open the Print dialog box. Here, you select the appropriate PostScript Printer Description (PPD). A PPD is just a reference file, installed when you install the software that comes with your printer. It describes the device's options, such as whether it's color or black and white, what paper sizes it accepts, its resolution, and so on. The available options in the Device pane will vary from printer to printer, since they're dependent on specific information about the printer that's contained in the PPD.

Specifying the type of PostScript printer you'll be printing to with this popup menu lets QuarkXPress optimize the way it prints your layout. It also determines several other aspects of the print job, including activating or deactivating the roll-fed printer specifications features (see below). I wish I had a dollar for every time I solved someone's printing problem simply by getting them to pick the correct printer from this popup menu. Believe me: The choice you make here is crucial to success in printing. However, if you choose a non-PostScript printer in the Print driver, this popup menu will likely be grayed out.

Printer Description Files. If the type of printer you're using is not listed on the menu, you probably don't have a PPD file for it. In XPress 3.x, you could use either a PPD or a PDF file (that's Quark's Printer Description File, *not* the Acrobat file type of the same acronym). However, PDFs are now a thing of the past, and XPress now only reads PPDs.

The proper PPD file for your device probably came with the printer, but you can often find updated PPD files at the Web site of your printer's manufacturer.

If you can't find a PPD specifically designed for your printer, you can usually select a printer that is similar to the one you have from the Printer Description popup menu. For example, I print to my Ricoh PC 6000/PS using the LaserWriter II selection since both printers are old 300-dpi desktop laser printers of comparable speed, and so on. On the other hand, an Epson Stylus color inkjet printer is not the same as an Agfa SelectSet 9000.

> *Tip: Managing Your PPDs.* Some programs come bundled with dozens of PPDs, and they install them all on your hard drive. So, the next time you launch XPress, you've got a Printer Description popup menu a half-mile long! If you're never going to use a particular printer, you can delete its PPD file from your hard drive. (On both the Macintosh and Windows, PPDs are scattered over a number of different folders; try doing a systemwide search for ".ppd" to find the ones you're looking for.)

If you don't use a PPD now, but you might in the future, you can "hide" it using QuarkXPress's PPD Manager (under the Utility menu; see Figure 15-7). To hide a PPD, click the checkmark in the Include column. To make it active again, click in the column again. Note that this doesn't actually move or change the PPD file at all—it still appears normally in other programs—it just tells XPress not to include the PPD on the Printer Description popup menu in the Print dialog box.

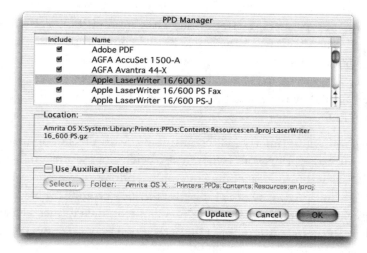

Figure 15-7
PPD Manager

Here are a couple more PPD-management tricks.

- If you have a lot of PPDs, you could break them down into separate folders or directories on your hard disk. When you want to switch from one folder's PPDs to another, you can click the Select button.

- If you add, remove, or change a PPD while XPress is running, you can update the PPD list by clicking the Update button. Note that XPress automatically updates the list each time you launch the program (if there's anything to update).

> *Tip: Editing Your PPDs.* One of the best things about PPDs is that they're editable. In fact, they're just text files that you can edit with any word processor. Because XPress gathers so much information about your printer from the PPD, customizing it is sort of like setting print preferences in QuarkXPress. For instance, you can change the name of your printer (how it appears on the Printer Description popup menu), the default halftone settings, or even the printer's default paper size. Be careful when messing with PPDs, however; little errors can cause jobs not to print. Always work on a copy of the file, and don't edit it unless you feel comfortable with this kind of thing.

Paper Size. Only the paper sizes that your printer can handle will be displayed in this drop-down menu, although you can choose Custom and specify any size you wish. Beware: this may confuse the printer, resulting in paper-feed errors or rejected jobs. Stick to genuine paper sizes for best results. If the Paper Size popup menu is grayed out, then QuarkXPress knows that the printer either prints only on one size of paper or is a roll-fed device that can print any size you want. If you choose Custom from the Paper Size popup menu, you can enter your own values in the width, height, page gap, and paper offset fields. Unless you have a printer with unusual media options, you'll probably just pick an existing media size from the paper-size options and let it go at that.

Paper Width. The Paper Width specification is not an actual control so much as a description of the device you'll be printing to. Whatever the case, and whatever the measurement style, just replace the default number with the proper paper width.

Paper Offset. This feature controls the placement of your layout on the paper or film. The printer's default paper offset, even when set to zero, is almost always large enough so that you don't have to worry about changing the value of Paper Offset here. If you want it farther from the edge for some reason, change this value.

However, the Paper Offset setting shouldn't exceed the layout height subtracted from the paper width (that is, if you have a 10-inch-tall layout printing on 14-inch paper, your offset certainly should not be more than 4 inches, or else you'll chop off the other end of the page).

Page Gap. This specification determines the amount of blank space between each page of the layout as it prints out on the roll. Initially, this value is zero. I recommend changing this to at least 1/4 inch ("1p6") so you can cut the pages apart easily. If you're printing with the Spreads option turned on, this gap between pages is placed between the spreads, not between the pages within the spread.

Paper Height. When QuarkXPress prints to a roll-fed printer, it has to tell the printer exactly how long each page will be. That is, while the Paper Width field tells XPress how wide the paper is, the Paper Height field tells XPress how much paper has to roll in order to image a page correctly. When the Paper Size popup menu is set to Custom (it is by default for roll-fed imagesetters), the Paper Height setting is changed to Automatic. I generally leave this as is, since XPress is usually better at calculating measurements than I am. Again, if you know what you're doing and you think you need to tweak this, go ahead, but go carefully.

Position. When you select a paper size that is larger than your layout, XPress lets you specify where on the page you want your layout to sit. You've got four choices: Left Edge, Center, Center Horizontal, and Center Vertical (see Figure 15-8). Left Edge is the default (it's the way QuarkXPress has always worked); the other three choices are self-explanatory. I find this control a matter of personal preference most of the time, though using one of the Center settings is critical if you want to print something on both sides of a piece of paper and have the two sides align.

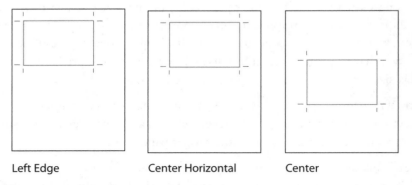

Left Edge   Center Horizontal   Center

Figure 15-8 Page positioning

Resolution. If you have selected a specific PPD, the resolution value is displayed but cannot be changed. However, if the appropriate PPD for your target device is not available, you can choose one of the generic PPD options, such as Generic Imagesetter or Generic Color. With no "official" PPD to guide it, the Resolution field now changes from a drop-down menu to a type-in field.

Negative Print. If you were generating film directly out of QuarkXPress, this would allow you to output negative film. This option usually makes sense only if you print separations, although it does make for an interesting composite output.

PostScript Error Handler. When you print to a PostScript printer, your computer writes a little program in PostScript language and sends it down the network to the printer. If there are any errors in the PostScript, or if the PostScript file contains an instruction that the printer can't fulfill, you get a PostScript error.

The problem is that sometimes your page won't print and you'll have no idea why. Fortunately, the PostScript Error Handler (on the Device pane of the Print dialog box) can come to the rescue.

If you think you're getting a PostScript error, switch on this feature. QuarkXPress adds some extra code to the PostScript file that is sent to the printer. As soon as anything goes wrong, this code catches the error and prints out the page up to the point of the error. Then it prints a second page with a little PostScript information (if you don't know PostScript programming, this probably won't help you much) and a gray box; the box specifies where on the page the error occurred. With this in hand, you can often quickly figure out if the PostScript error is based on a corrupt graphic or font or on some other page element.

Most PostScript printer drivers also include an error handler. For instance, on the Macintosh you can turn on the driver's error handler by clicking the Printer button in the Print dialog box. In Windows, you can turn it on by clicking Properties in the Print dialog box. I find that Quark's built-in error handler is usually more useful in identifying problems, so I use it instead of these.

THE PAGES PANE

Under Page Options, you have control over the orientation of printing, as well as thumbnail, page flip, and tiling controls.

Orientation. Remember back to college when you had orientation day? The idea was to make sure you knew which way you were going while walking around the school grounds. Well, this Orientation is sort of the same, but different. The idea is to make sure QuarkXPress knows which way you want your layout to go while it's walking through the printer. You have two choices: Portrait and Landscape. I've included some samples in Figure 15-9 so you can see what each one does.

The left column is "portrait" or "tall"; the right column is "landscape" or "wide."

Document size: 8.5 x 11 inches (Laser printer output)

Document size: 11 x 8.5 inches (Laser printer output)

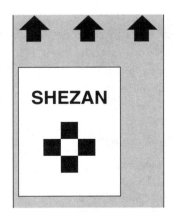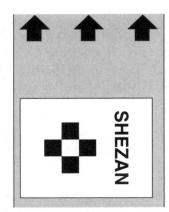

Figure 15-9
Page orientation

Document size: 8.5 x 11 inches (Roll-fed printer output)

Include Blank Plates. As I write, my white-paper recycling bin overfloweth. I go through so much paper that I feel guilty every time I drive through a forest (which is difficult to avoid in the Pacific Northwest). Therefore, whenever I have the chance to save a tree here and there, I jump at it. QuarkXPress gives me just this chance with the Include Blank Plates control on the Pages pane of the Print dialog box. When you turn on Include Blank Plates (it's on by default), QuarkXPress prints as it always has: every page, no matter what is (or isn't) on it. When you turn off Include Blank Plates, QuarkXPress won't print a page if there isn't anything printable on it. This includes pages whose only objects are colored white, or are set to Suppress Printout. I've gotten in the habit of always turning this off when I print.

Thumbnails. Selecting Thumbnails shrinks each page of your layout down to about 12 percent of its size and lines up each page next to the other. It then fits as many as it can onto each printed page. This is great for an overview of your file, though the output you get is usually too small to really give you much of an idea of anything except general page geometry (see "Tip: Faster, Larger Thumbnails," below). Note that on PostScript printers, it takes just as long to print this one sheet of many pages as it does to print every page individually, so plan your time accordingly. If you just want to look over the pages, it would probably be faster to see them onscreen in Thumbnails view. Remember that you don't have to print all your pages when you select Thumbnails. I often find it helpful to just print one or two pages at a time to see how they're looking.

> *Tip: Faster, Larger Thumbnails.* I find the size that Thumbnails usually gives me pretty useless; it's just too small! And if I have pictures on the pages, the job takes too long to print. So I use this feature in conjunction with two others: Rough, and Reduce or Enlarge. Rough is nearby on the Output popup menu, on the Pictures pane. Just make sure this is selected, and your thumbnails print with "X"s through the pictures and with simplified frames. You can find the Scale option in the top half of the Print dialog box. Change the scale factor to 200 percent, and your thumbnails are printed at 24 percent instead of a little over 12 percent. This is just about the right size for most letter-size pages.

> *Tip: Two Thumbnails per Page.* If you want your thumbnails much larger, you can up the scaling factor to 375 percent and turn the page orientation to Landscape on the Pages pane of the Print dialog box. With this value, you can get two letter- or legal-size pages on one page. You can get two tabloid-size pages on one letter-size landscape page with an enlargement of 300 percent. If your layout is made of two-page spreads, then you can print letter- and legal-size pages up to 400 percent (the maximum allowed for enlargement), and tabloid-size pages up to 350 percent.

Note that both the Macintosh and Windows printer drivers offer the ability to print more than one layout page per printed page. However, XPress seems to conflict with the drivers on both platforms, causing either strange printing or PostScript errors most of the time. It's too bad, but I just stick with XPress's own Thumbnails feature.

Page Flip. QuarkXPress can mirror pages at print time if you choose Horizontal, Vertical, or Horizontal & Vertical from the Page Flip popup menu. Flipping an image is used mainly for creating either wrong- or right-reading film from imagesetters, or film with emulsion side up or down. The differences? Let's look at what happens when you print onto film.

As the film moves through the imagesetter, the side of the film that is coated with a photographically sensitive emulsion is exposed to a laser beam. If Page Flip is set to None (it is by default), the film is imaged right-reading, emulsion up (or wrong-reading, emulsion down, if you prefer). This means that when you are holding the film so that the type reads from left to right and graphics are oriented correctly ("right-reading"), the emulsion of the film is facing you. If you select either Horizontal or Vertical from the Page Flip popup menu, the film emerges right-reading, emulsion down (which is how most printers want it, especially in North America). To look at it a different way, this means that when you hold the film with the emulsion away from you, the text and graphics look correct ("right-reading").

If you want to know why you'd ever care whether the emulsion is up or down, check with your print service provider (and then talk to a screen printer; you'll see they need different film output for similar but different reasons). Providing film in the right format could reduce the reproduction generations at the printer—saving time and money, and improving quality.

Note that setting the Page Flip popup menu is exactly the same as turning on "Flip Horizontal" or "Flip Vertical" in the Macintosh printer driver (see "Page Setup, Printer, and Properties," below, for more information on setting values in the printer driver).

Page Tiling and Overlap. What's a person to do with a 36-by-36-inch layout? Printing to paper or film is—well, almost impossible without a large-format printer. You can break each page down into smaller chunks that will fit onto letter-size pages. Then you can assemble all the pages (keep your Scotch tape nearby). This process is called *tiling* and is controlled on the Pages pane of the Print dialog box. The three options for tiling are Off, Auto, and Manual.

- **Off.** Off is off. No shirt, no shoes, no tiling. QuarkXPress just prints as much of the page as it can on the output page, starting from the upper-left corner.

- **Auto.** Selecting the Auto tiling feature instructs QuarkXPress to decide how much of your layout to fit onto each printed page. You do have some semblance of control here; you can decide how much overlap between pages you would like. Remember that you have a minimum of 1/4-inch border around each page (at least on most laser printers), so you'll probably want to set your overlap to at least 1/2 inch to get a good fit. I generally use a value of 4 picas, just to be safe.

  Note that QuarkXPress does not make an intelligent decision as to whether it would be more efficient to print the pages in Landscape or Portrait orientation, so you'll want to be careful to set this appropriately on the Pages pane of the Print dialog box.

  Note that the Overlap amount might vary slightly when the Absolute Overlap checkbox is off (it's off by default). This is because XPress tries to center the tiled layout on the printed pages (see Figure 15-10). When you turn on Absolute Overlap, XPress just gives up and places the upper-left corner of the layout in the upper-left corner of the first page.

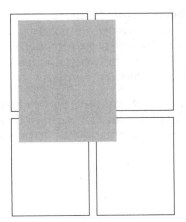 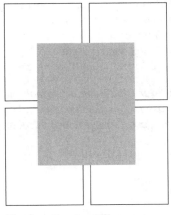

Note that the overlap is not shown in this illustration.

Absolute Overlap On   Absolute Overlap Off

Figure 15-10 Tiling documents

- **Manual.** Most people seem to overlook the value of Manual tiling, skipping over it to Auto tiling. But there are times to trust a computer and times not to, and when it comes to breaking up my pages into manageable sizes, I generally prefer to make the choices myself.

  When Manual tiling is selected, QuarkXPress prints only as much of the page as fits on the page selected, starting at the ruler coordinate "0,0." You can then move the "0,0" coordinate to some other place on the page (see the section on rulers in Chapter 3, *Working with Items*, for more on this) and print the page again. In this way you can manually perform the same task as Auto tiling does, or you can be specific about what areas of the page you want to print. Note that if you have a six-page layout and print using Manual tiling, you get (for example) the upper-left corner of each of the six pages before the printer stops. If you want only one page or a smaller range of pages, use the From and To specifications at the top of the Print dialog box.

  I should point out that where you place the "0,0" point is usually not where QuarkXPress starts printing. It actually tries to give you a little extra room so that the area you selected prints on the imaged area of the printer. For example, if you're printing to a desktop laser printer, QuarkXPress actually moves your starting point a couple of picas up and to the left. This is another area where QuarkXPress tries to be helpful, but ends up just being confusing and difficult to predict.

Tip: Printer as Magnifying Glass. You can use the Manual Tiling and Enlarge features to blow up a particular area of the page for inspection (when 800-percent magnification on the screen still doesn't suit you). Change the enlargement factor in the Scale option to 400 percent (or whatever enlargement you desire), then move the "0,0" point of the rulers to the area you want to inspect. Now print that page with Manual Tiling on, and—mirabile dictu! A super-size sectional.

Tip: Assembling Your Tiled Pages. This really has nothing to do with the use of QuarkXPress, but when it comes to assembling tiled pages, I find it invaluable. The idea is simple: when fitting two tiled pages together, use a straight-edge to cut one, then use the other blank border area as a tab.

THE COLORS PANE

A descendant of the Output tab in QuarkXPress 6/6.5, the Colors pane lets you specify output options.

Mode. You're given the choice of Composite (all colors print combined) or Separations (a separate page is generated for each printing ink). If you are printing to a non-PostScript printer, your only choice is Composite.

Setup. When you print to a black-and-white printer like a desktop laser printer, you can pick either Grayscale or Black & White. When you choose a PostScript color printer (or a simulation, like Acrobat PDF), the Setup popup menu lets you tell XPress how to send color information to the printer. The choices are Grayscale, Composite RGB, Composite CMYK, Composite CMYK and Spot (which has replaced DeviceN, but accomplishes the same thing), and As Is.

Which of these you choose depends on your workflow, your printer, and the output you're trying to achieve.

- **Grayscale Versus Black & White.** Choosing Grayscale is the same as turning on Print Colors as Grays in the old version of the program. Unfortunately, you don't have too much control over which shades of gray go with which color, so subtle differences in colors (such as between a pink and a light green) may blend together as one shade of gray. But it's still better than printing the file out as a page of solid black, which is what you get when you set the Print Colors popup menu to Black & White (see Figure 15-11).

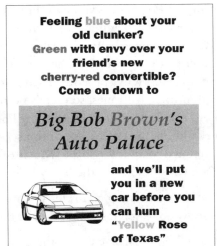

Print Colors set to Black and White Print Colors set to Grayscale

Figure 15-11 Print Colors as Grayscale versus Black & White

- **Composite CMYK/RGB.** Desktop color printers should generally be considered RGB devices, so you should send composite RGB data to them. In this case, even CMYK data gets translated to RGB before the page is printed. If you choose Composite CMYK, then XPress will separate all your RGB data (including any RGB TIFF files) into CMYK mode before sending them, causing some images to appear washed out.

- **As Is.** When you choose As Is, XPress doesn't bother with any color transformations; RGB images and colors are sent as RGB, CMYK images and colors are sent as CMYK—XPress just leaves it to the printer to sort it all out.

- **Composite CMYK and Spot.** You should use this option (called DeviceN in the previous version) when you want to create composite color PostScript, but have applied spot colors to images (like TIFF or JPEG), used spot colors or multi-inks (including hexachrome colors), or imported duotones into your layout. Where RGB defines three "inks" and CMYK defines four inks, this option lets XPress define any number of inks. Then, the PostScript RIP can later determine whether the inks should be separated onto separate plates or combined to create a composite color.

Halftoning. XPress offers you two choices on the Colors pane's Halftoning popup menu: Conventional and Printer. The difference is simple: Conventional means that QuarkXPress includes halftone settings (angle, frequency, and spot function) when sending PostScript to the printer. Choosing Printer means that XPress won't send halftone information at all. Why should you care? Some devices—like color inkjet printers—don't print with normal halftones, so there's no reason to specify values like halftone frequency and so on. And keep in mind that many PostScript printers ignore the settings you create here. In addition, the RIPs at your print service provider will introduce their own halftone angles, frequency, and dot shape. Much of these settings are a holdover from the olden days when RIPs did less of the heavy lifting than they do now.

Note that the Halftoning control is not an option when you're printing color separations. There's really no reason it should be, since the feature was designed mostly for color printers.

Resolution. Don't change this number with the expectation that it has any major significance to how your job prints. It doesn't determine the resolution at which your job prints. However, it does determine some important issues when you're printing bitmapped images. Low-resolution, 72-dpi black-and-white images can be smoothed with Quark's proprietary bitmap-smoothing algorithms, which depend on knowing the resolution of the printer. Also, bitmapped images that have a very high resolution may print significantly faster when you include the right printer resolution. For example, QuarkXPress internally reduces the resolution of a 600-dpi line-art image when it knows it's printing to a 300-dpi printer. The printer doesn't need any more than that anyway, and you save time because QuarkXPress only has to download half as much information (and the PostScript interpreter has to wade through only half as much).

Frequency. I talked at some length about halftones and halftone screens back in Chapter 11, *Image Tuning*. The Frequency setting on the Colors pane of the Print dialog box is where you get to specify the halftone-screen frequency of every tint in your layout (except for those graphic images that you have set using the Halftone feature on the Style menu, and EPS graphics that have their screen specified internally). This includes gray boxes, tinted type, screened colors, and so on.

The default value for the halftone screen (the one that QuarkXPress uses unless you specify something else) is determined by the PPD you've chosen in the Printer Description popup menu. On most laser printers, the value is 60 lpi (lines per inch). You can type your own setting from 15 to 400 lines per inch. Raising the screen frequency nets you "smoother" grays, but you'll find you have fewer gray levels to work with (I talk about this trade-off in the book *Real World Scanning and Halftones*).

Tip: A Colorful Shade of Gray. A couple of caveats to this tip before I get to it: This is helpful primarily if you're printing proofs that won't be reproduced, and if you don't need a wide spectrum of gray values in your output. That said, I think a great screen frequency to use for printing to a 300- or 600-dpi printer is 106 lpi. Go ahead and try it. I think you'll like the tone of the gray.

Color plates. The window at the bottom of the Colors pane is the color plates list, which identifies which colors can or will print. The color list has three states, reflecting your printing options.

- When you're printing to a black-and-white printer, and the Separations checkbox is turned off on the Colors pane of the Print dialog box, the color plates list displays only the black plate. After all, the printer can only print black.

- When you're printing to a color printer, the Separations checkbox is turned off, and you've selected a composite color setting from the Print Colors pop-up menu, the color plates list displays the process colors (cyan, magenta, yellow, and black) plus any spot colors you've used.

- When the Separations checkbox is turned on, the color plates list displays either just the process colors or the process colors plus all your spot colors, depending on the status of the Plates popup menu (see Figure 15-12).

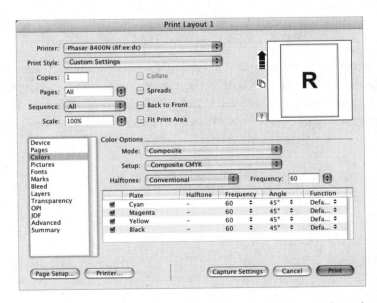

Figure 15-12
Color plates listed in the Colors pane

I'm going to hold off describing the various controls on the color plates list until "Color Separations," later in this chapter. For now, suffice it to say that this is where you can suppress printing of colors, as well as set color-specific halftone information.

THE PICTURES PANE

Pictures are often the single most time-consuming part of printing a page; but if you're only printing rough proofs, you may be able to cut corners. You have several options for Output and Data in the Pictures pane, and if you're in a hurry, some of the options may speed things up considerably. Why wait by the printer when you could be working?

Normal. What can I say about Normal? It's how you'd usually want your normal layouts to print out. This is the default setting in the Print dialog box, and the only times you change it are when you want special printing effects like those listed below. You get just what you created—no better, no worse.

Low-Resolution Output. If you select Low Resolution from the Output popup menu, QuarkXPress prints your layout using the picture-preview image built into the layout rather than the source picture file. If you've imported a huge, high-resolution TIFF or EPS, Low Resolution mode prints the layout using the low-resolution (36- or 72-dpi) screen image that QuarkXPress creates when you import the picture.

This is a godsend if you have to make many proofs to a low-resolution desktop printer. I can't tell you how much time I've wasted either sending layouts with high-resolution pictures to low-resolution devices (it takes forever for them to print), or manually hiding the pictures somewhere on my hard disk so QuarkXPress can't find them, then telling it to print anyway (that was the old trick for making QuarkXPress use the internal low-res image).

Rough. If your layout has many illustrations or special frames in it, you may want to print your proof copies with Rough selected. This feature automatically replaces each picture in your layout with a big "X," and every complex frame with a double line of the same width (see Figure 15-13). Clearly, the pages print significantly faster than with Normal or Low Resolution.

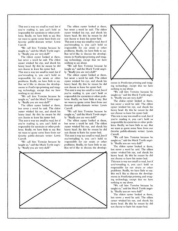

Picture boxes and complex frames are simplified.

Figure 15-13
Page printed with Rough selected

Data Format. This only pertains to how bitmapped images (like TIFF and JPEG) are sent to the printer. While sending the information in ASCII format is more reliable over some networks, binary is almost always fine and has the benefit of creating a much smaller PostScript file (the images are half the size of ASCII).

The third choice, Clean 8-bit, is a good compromise. It is as small as binary, but it strips out the particular binary characters that cause some networks to go into conniptions. I generally use the Clean 8-bit setting unless I'm on a strictly Macintosh-based network, in which case I use Binary. On the other hand, you may need to use ASCII format if you are printing from a PC. Consult the documentation for your printer to see if it requires ASCII.

Overprint EPS Black. I explored overprinting and trapping back in Chapter 14, *Color*, but there is one overprinting control that you can only set in the Print dialog box: Overprint EPS Black. When you turn on this checkbox, every object colored black in EPS images overprints its background regardless of whether you set it to overprint in the original illustration program. Note that this control ignores the Overprint Limit on the Trapping pane of the Document Preferences dialog box, so even an EPS object that is only 10-percent black will overprint.

I find this feature most useful when working with EPS files built in programs that don't let you specify overprinting. For instance, my friend and colleague Phil Gaskill recently laid out a textbook that contained hundreds of molecular diagrams built in a scientific illustration application. The people who wrote this program didn't expect anyone to place these graphics over colored backgrounds, so there was no control for overprinting at all. All those thin lines would have been a trapping nightmare if it weren't for the Overprint EPS Black feature.

Full Resolution TIFF Output. When you print a document that includes TIFF or JPEG images, QuarkXPress may downsample the image data behind the scenes. The program figures that you'll never need more resolution in your images than two times the halftone screen frequency, so it cuts off the data at that point. If you have a 200-dpi image reduced to 50 percent on your page (which makes it a 400-dpi image; see Chapter 10, *Pictures*), and you've specified an 80-lpi screen in the Frequency field on the Colors pane of the print dialog box, QuarkXPress chops off the image resolution at 160 dpi (two times the frequency). Typically, that's okay. In fact, it's great if you're proofing high-resolution images on a laser printer. However, every now and again, this feature can jump up and bite you.

For example, if you reduce an image considerably in a picture box, you can sometimes get mottling or jaggy artifacts from the downsampling. Or, if you're purposely printing at a very low screen frequency because your color printer requires it (some do), your images may look really weird because QuarkXPress has downsampled them so much.

Fortunately, you can turn on the Full Resolution TIFF Output checkbox and none of your bitmapped images will get downsampled at print time. Note that this feature (and solution) only affects TIFF images. EPS pictures don't get downsampled because QuarkXPress can't touch the data that's encapsulated in them. Also, XPress always turns on this option when you set the Halftoning popup menu to Printer on the Colors pane, because there's no halftone screen to use as a reference.

THE FONTS PANE

The Fonts pane is simplistic, and its primary purpose is to control downloading of font information in the outgoing print stream. There's no good reason to *not* download fonts; when networks ran at glacial speed and printers were short on memory, we pared every little bit out of the files we sent to printers. But we have more elbow room these days, and it's important to avoid font substitution. Hence, the default choice in this pane is to download all fonts.

You may find that turning on the option to Optimize Font Formats speeds printing a bit. And note that none of these options are available if you have selected a non-PostScript printer.

THE MARKS PANE

Many years ago, it was necessary for skilled craftsmen called film strippers to align the individual pieces of film for the printing plates. Registration marks were crucial to the exact positioning required. Now, it's rare that a job has to be stripped by hand; most printing companies either output prepunched imposed films, or (more commonly) go direct to printing plates with no intermediate film.

However, when you print composite lasers to show to your client, check your work, or submit to the printing company as a guide to your job, you will often find marks and page information helpful, even if they only serve to help you trim out a page for a presentation of how the final job will look.

The Marks options control crop marks (or trim marks), registration marks, and page information around your document (see Figure 15-14).

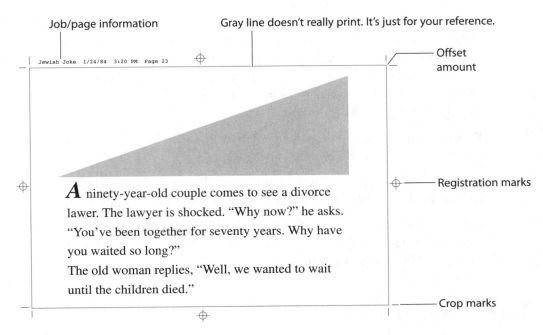

Figure 15-14 The Registration feature places items around your page.

- **Crop marks.** Crop marks specify the page boundaries of your document. They are placed slightly outside each of the four corners so that when the page is printed and cut to size, they will be cut away. These are also called "trim marks" or "cut marks."

- **Registration marks.** Registration marks are used primarily for color-separation work, but you get them even if you just need crop marks on a one-color job.

- **Page and job information.** The page and job information that is printed in the upper-left corner of the page includes the file name, a page number, and a date and time stamp

- **Color bars and step wedge.** When you print color separations (again, more on that in "Color Separations," later in this chapter) along with registration marks, QuarkXPress also adds a color bar and a grayscale step wedge to your output. This lets your lithographer take densitometer readings from the film and final output, as well as ensure that colors are registering well.

To make QuarkXPress add all these marks to your printed page, you need to select either Centered or Off Center from the Mode popup menu in the Marks pane. These features refer to the placement of registration marks. If you select Centered, each registration mark is placed exactly in the center of each side of the printed page. When you choose Centered or Off Center, this activates the marks function, and you can then specify the width, length, and offset values for marks.

Width. Think of this as line weight. You may find that the default .003 inch width is a bit anemic on your printer. Feel free to experiment.

Length. How long do you want your trim marks to be? (Keep in mind that if the marks fall outside the printable area of your printer, they'll still be trimmed off.)

Offset. By definition, trim marks image outside the trim. But with the default offset value, they will intrude on any artwork in the bleed. Set the offset to more than your bleed value (typically .125 inch) to avoid this.

THE BLEED PANE

The Bleed control is a good example of how a little feature can sneak into a product and cause havoc when people don't take the time to understand it. I know people who just ignored the Bleed control and lost a *lot* of money throwing away their film output. Fortunately, the control isn't difficult to understand; you just need to remember to use it.

The term "bleed" refers to an object that prints all the way to the edge of your page. In prepress, it's very important for bleeding objects to print past the page boundaries by at least 1/8 inch, because paper trimmers aren't perfect. If the object only extends to the edge of the page boundary and the paper cutter slips by a few points, the object won't sit at the edge of the paper anymore (ugly). Extending the object past the boundary is kind of like setting a trapping value for the bleed (see "Trapping," in Chapter 14, *Color*).

Back in XPress 3.x, to make something bleed off a page, you simply placed it so that it was partially on the pasteboard. As long as it touched the page, the object would print (see Figure 15-15). I'm not sure why Quark changed this, but now, by default, XPress crops out everything beyond 1 point past the edge of the page. In other words, you can extend a picture box 1/2 inch past the page boundary, but when you print the page, the bleed only extends by about a point.

Keyline represents the side of the page.

This object bleeds off the page.

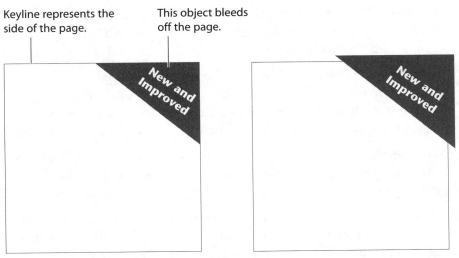

How the page looks when Bleed is set to zero   After increasing the Bleed setting

Figure 15-15 Bleeding objects

Fortunately, the Bleed pane of the Print dialog box lets you extend this puny bleed to whatever you want (see Figure 15-16). The Bleed Type popup menu offers three choices for extending your bleeds: Page Items, Symmetric, and Asymmetric.

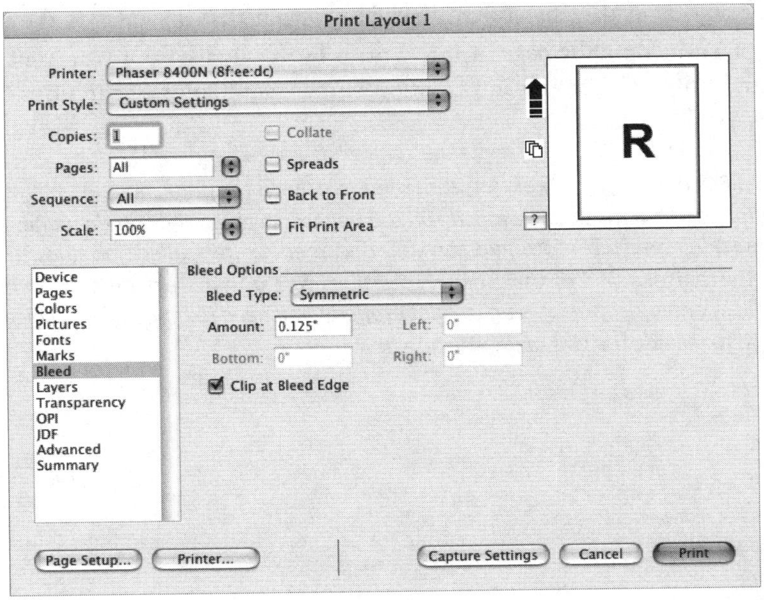

Figure 15-16
The Bleed pane

- **Page Items.** When you choose Page Items, XPress acts like it did back in those heady XPress 3.x days: Anything touching the page gets printed. That is, the bleed amount is automatically extended to include the bounding box of any object on the page.

- **Symmetric.** Choosing Symmetric lets you specify a single bleed setting, which XPress uses on all four sides of every page. This is the setting I use most often. In fact, I've gotten into the habit of setting this to at least "1p6" even when I'm not bleeding objects. Later in the chapter, you'll see how to set this as your default value.

- **Asymmetric.** The Asymmetric setting lets you choose a different bleed amount for each of the four sides of the page. The only time I find myself using this is when I'm putting job slug information outside the print area (see "Tip: Job Slugs," below).

When you choose either Symmetric or Asymmetric from the Bleed Type popup menu, XPress offers one additional choice: the Clip at Bleed Edge checkbox. This feature acts like the Page Items setting: When you turn it off, XPress automatically extends the bleed amount to include all objects that are inside the bleed area. For instance, if you specify a half-inch symmetric bleed, and you happen to have a 5-inch-wide text box on the paste-board that is within a half-inch of the page, then the *whole* text box prints out. Again, this might be useful for job slugs, but I tend to leave this checkbox turned on so I'm not surprised at print time.

There's one other aspect of the Bleed feature you should know about. When you set the Bleed value, any object on the Pasteboard that falls within that distance of the page gets printed, whether it's touching the page or not. This is especially useful if you want to create your own registration marks or job information slugs (see "Color Separations," later in this chapter).

> **Tip: Job Slugs.** *Bleeds are typically objects that print mostly on the page, but bleed slightly off it. But you can also create items that are mostly off the page, or even entirely off the page. This is ideal for adding additional job information on your documents, often called "job slugs." (Of course, those of us in the moist Pacific Northwest know our slugs well, and these page items rarely look like slugs at all.) In order for your job slug to print properly, you need to make sure the bleed setting is large enough to include the text or picture boxes.*

THE LAYERS PANE

The Layers pane (see Figure 15-17) lets you specify which layers will print and which will not. A noble feature, indeed, but you can control the same thing by setting the visibility of each layer in the Layers palette (see more about the layers palette in Chapter 3, *Working with Items*). I'd much rather turn on and off layers in the Layers palette because I get immediate visual feedback of what my document will look like when printed. It's just too easy to make a mistake in the Layers pane of the Print dialog box.

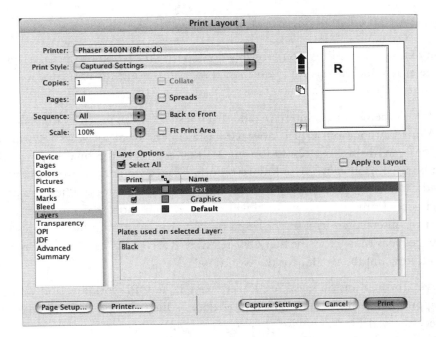

Figure 15-17
The Layers pane

By the way, if you make a change to the printing status of one or more layers in the Print dialog box, you can turn on the Apply to Layout checkbox. This tells XPress to update the Layers palette to match what you've set in the Print dialog box (nonprinting layers get their Suppress Output option turned on; you can tell because the layer name appears italic in the palette). Again, I have to stretch my imagination for a use for this.

> *Tip: Find the Mysterious Color. Here's one use for the Layers pane of the Print dialog box: Let's say the Colors pane tells you that you're using a spot color somewhere in your document, but you can't figure out where. You can click on each of the layers listed in the Layers pane to see what ink plates are being used there. By narrowing down on which layer the spot color appears, you might find it easier to discover the offending object.*

THE TRANSPARENCY PANE

Remember that, while transparency effects are fun and beautiful (well, in the right hands), they require an imaging model that goes beyond what PostScript supports. So, as mentioned in the transparency flattening section of Chapter 14, *Color*, QuarkXPress has to process the content so the outgoing print stream contains PostScript-legal objects. See Chapter 14 for in-depth coverage of transparency and the appropriate settings to use here.

THE OPI PANE

If you don't know what OPI is, you probably don't need this. If you use an OPI workflow, chances are that someone has told you the appropriate settings to use. But, just so you know, I discuss it here.

OPI stands for Open Prepress Interface (and that doesn't tell you much). Originally developed by Aldus Corporation, OPI is now used as a generic term for workflows in which pages are designed using low-resolution images that represent the final high-resolution images to be used in imaging. The low-resolution images are derived from the high-res images and carry within them references to their high-res ancestors. When the prepress operator chooses Print or File from the File menu and then chooses Export, the outgoing print stream is intercepted by a server-based process that substitutes the high-res images for the low-res stand-ins. How the high/low-res swap is accomplished depends on the particular workflow, and the vendor for the workflow.

OPI Active. Turning this on says "Yes, I'm working in an OPI workflow, and we need to create an appropriate print stream going out the door." Once this option is turned on, other options become available (otherwise, they're grayed out).

TIFF Options. Even if you don't include the low-res images, there are references to them in the PostScript data that's sent when you choose Print from the File menu. Some workflows require that you include the low-res files—this is something only your IT person or team leader can tell you, because it varies depending on your workflow.

EPS Options. As with the TIFF options, your choice here will be governed by the needs of your particular OPI system.

THE JDF PANE

If you're not using the Job Jackets feature in QuarkXPress 7, you can ignore this pane. But if you are, you can use this option to generate a JDF (Job Definition Format) file to be stored in the same directory as a PostScript file you create from the layout. (If you print directly to a printing device, no JDF file is generated). To generate the JDF file, turn on the Output JDF option, and choose a Contact from the Include Job Jacket Contact drop-down menu.

A JDF Job Ticket is really an XML-based file (wow, two mystery acronyms in one sentence!) that can be read by JDF-aware devices and processes. It's like a Job Ticket held inside the PostScript file. This may not mean much to you now, but watch this acronym: It's likely to become more relevant to your work as time goes by.

THE ADVANCED PANE

For a pane called Advanced, this doesn't present you with much complexity—just an option to choose between PostScript Level 2 and PostScript Level 3. If you're printing to a non-PostScript device such as an inkjet printer, this option will be grayed out and there's nothing for you to do here.

If you can choose, what should you choose? If your printer supports it, go for the gold—Level 3. Check the documentation for your printer to see which level of PostScript it supports. Note that if your printer only supports Level 2, choosing Level 3 won't improve output; it may result in a failure to print.

THE SUMMARY PANE

For a one-stop overview of all the settings you've chosen in the Print dialog box, scroll through the log window to see everything broken down by topic. This might be a good place to take one last look at everything without tediously clicking through the options in the left column and investigating all the fields and radio buttons in each pane as it appears on the right.

Page Setup, Printer, and Properties

When you print your document, QuarkXPress interacts with whatever printer driver you have selected. The driver controls some aspects of the print job and XPress controls others. I've been discussing in some detail the settings you can make in QuarkXPress's Print dialog box. Now I want to take a quick break to discuss some options you have in the printer driver itself.

Of course, printer drivers are completely different on the Macintosh and in Windows, so I need to cover them one at a time. Also, note that there are many different versions of these drivers, and the one you use may well appear differently than the ones I show here. Don't fret about it too much; with a little exploration, you'll find that many of the features are the same.

Macintosh: Page Setup and Printer

In QuarkXPress for Macintosh, you can access the printer driver settings by clicking the Page Setup and Printer buttons in the Print dialog box (see Figure 15-18). In most cases, the settings you make in these two dialog boxes apply to this one print job only, and you'll have to change them again next time you print.

After making changes to either the Page Setup or the Printer dialog box, when you leave the dialog box (by clicking OK, Cancel, Print, or Save, depending on what you're doing), XPress returns to the normal Print dialog box.

Page Setup. The Page Setup dialog box is split into three or more "pages," each found in the Settings popup menu. However, all the features here—including settings for Scale, Orientation, and Paper Size—are duplicates of settings in QuarkXPress's Print dialog box. Because XPress either ignores the settings you make here or overrides them, I just don't pay any attention to this dialog box.

Printer. If the dialog box you get when you click the Printer button looks familiar, that's because it's the same dialog box you get when you choose Print from almost any other Macintosh application (see Figure 15-19). However, in this case, after you click Print or Cancel, you're dropped back into QuarkXPress's Print dialog box.

The Printer dialog box lets you control a number of aspects of the print job, including which printer to use, how many document pages per printer page you want to be laid out, and which printer tray to pull paper from (if the printer has more than one). This Print Driver dialog box lets you print the PostScript file to disk instead of to a printer, too. Many of these driver features are also ignored over overridden by XPress's own print features.

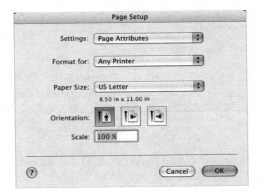

Click these buttons to access the printer driver dialog boxes.

Figure 15-18
The Macintosh printer driver settings and Page Setup dialog box

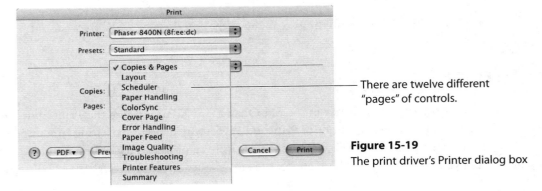

There are twelve different "pages" of controls.

Figure 15-19
The print driver's Printer dialog box

Windows: Properties

You can adjust printer driver settings in Windows by clicking the Properties button in the Print dialog box (see Figure 15-20). There are a number of different settings here, spread out over four or five different panes (depending on the version of the PostScript driver you're using), but there's one theme that runs through them all: Almost none of them apply to working with QuarkXPress. (On the other hand, if you're working with a non-PostScript driver, many of the controls will affect your output; but again, I'm not talking about non-PostScript devices here.)

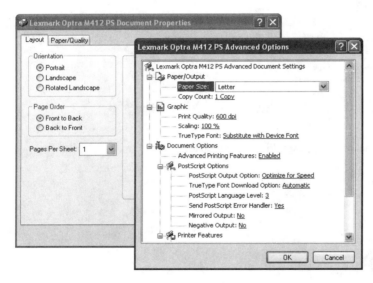

Figure 15-20
The Properties dialog box in Windows

The controls fall into three categories.

• Most are duplicates of settings in QuarkXPress's Print dialog box. These get overridden by XPress, so you should ignore them.

• Some cause PostScript errors or strange things to occur.

• Some just don't do anything at all, even though they look like they should.

OUTPUT STYLES

One of my favorite features in the old QuarkPrint XTension was the Print Styles feature, which let you save collections of Print and Page Setup dialog-box settings under one name. Fortunately, the folks at Quark built this feature right into QuarkXPress, so no additional XTension is necessary. There are two great benefits to output styles. First, you can easily change the default settings for XPress's Print dialog box. If you have one printer and you're tired of selecting the same PPD from the Printer Description popup menu or turning off the Include Blank Pages option every time you print, this is the feature for you. And QuarkXPress 7 goes beyond just print styles, adding EPS, PDF and PPML (Personalized Print Markup Language, for variable data publishing). That's why it's now called Output Styles rather than its old name, Print Styles.

Output Styles are also great for service bureaus or anyone else who prints to a number of different devices from one copy of XPress, because you can build dozens (hundreds? Sorry, I've never tried) of different print styles.

Building an output style. You can make a new output style by choosing Output Styles from the Edit menu (see Figure 15-21). Output styles are like application preferences in one way: Changes you make here apply to the program as a whole, not just to documents you may have open. Once the Output Styles dialog box is open, click New and choose the type of style you want to make (print, PDF, EPS, PPML) from the New drop-down menu options, or select a style and click Edit or Duplicate. At this point XPress displays the Edit Output Style dialog box, which looks awfully similar to the Print dialog box.

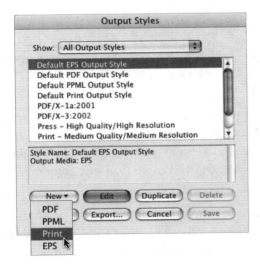

Figure 15-21
Creating a new Print Output Style

Go ahead and make changes to the Edit Output Style dialog box, then give the collection of settings a name. I tend to make the name as descriptive of my settings as possible. Finally, click OK to leave the Edit Output Style dialog box, then click Save to leave the Output Styles dialog box, saving your work. That's it!

There are a few things you cannot change in the Edit Output Style dialog box. For instance, you can't specify a page range, the number of copies, or the settings in the Page Setup,

Printer, or Properties dialog boxes. This is unfortunate, because these often need to be changed every time you print. But, then again, since you do have to change these options every time you print, perhaps there's no point in trying to establish their settings here.

Selecting an output style. Once you have built an output style, you can select print styles from the Print Style popup menu in the Print dialog box, and PDF styles from the PDF Style popup in the Export PDF dialog. It's as easy as that (see Figure 15-22).

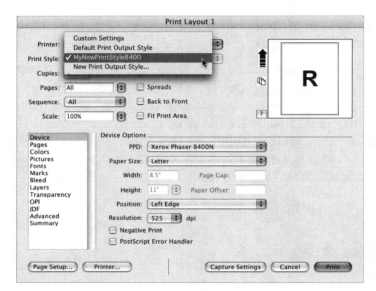

Figure 15-22
Choosing a custom Print Style (created in Output Styles) in the print dialog box

Moving output styles around. Output styles are application-wide and are stored in the XPress Preferences file. If you lose this file or if you need to delete it because it has become corrupted, your print styles are lost. (It's a good idea to keep a regular backup of the XPress Preferences file.) If you use the same print style from more than one computer, you can move it in one of two ways.

- You can copy your XPress Preferences file from one computer to the next. This copies all your preferences, even including Hyphenation Exceptions and kerning table edits, which may be more than you hoped for. This doesn't work cross-platform.

- You can select an output style in the Output Styles dialog box and click Export to save the output style to disk. (Oddly, in QuarkXPress 6.5, you could select multiple print styles to export, but that doesn't work with output styles.) Then, in a different copy of QuarkXPress, you can click Import in the same dialog box to append the style. This does work when moving the file from Mac to PC (or vice versa), as long as the file name includes the three-letter ".qpj" file-name extension.

COLOR SEPARATIONS

I come now to the last area of the Print dialog box, which as a subject deserves a whole section of the book to itself: Color separation. The concept behind color separation is simple, and QuarkXPress does a pretty good job of making the practice just as easy, but the truth is that this is a very complicated matter which, in the space of this book, I can only touch on briefly.

The Basics of Color Separation

A printing press can only print one color at a time. Even five- and six-color presses really only print one color at a time, in quick succession, as the paper passes through the units of the press. As I discussed in Chapter 14, *Color*, those colors are almost always process colors (cyan, magenta, yellow, and black), or they may be spot colors, such as those you choose from the Pantone Solid swatch book.

Colors that you specify in your QuarkXPress documents may look solid on the screen, but they need to be separated and printed onto individual plates for printing. Each of the four process colors is printed as a tint or a halftone (if you don't understand the fundamentals of halftoning, I *really* recommend that you look at Chapter 11, *Image Tuning*). By overlapping the screened tints, you can create a multitude of colors.

If you print color separations for a job with only process colors, you output four pieces of film for every page of the document. Each spot color requires adding another plate to the lineup. These days, most printing companies go directly to plate without intermediate film, but it's still important to understand the concept that there is a relationship between the colors you use in your layout and the printing plates that are generated. Even though you will probably never be called upon to generate separated film from QuarkXPress, you may want to print separated output on your desktop printer to check your work. Wonder why that spot color keeps showing up in your output colors list? Separated lasers will show you where the villain is (or where it *isn't*, since QuarkXPress won't print blank plates).

Printing Color Separations

To print color separations, select Colors in the Print dialog box, and choose Separation from the Mode popup menu. This activates the color plates list, giving you a choice of which color plates you want to print and at what halftone settings. As long as the printer type is a black-and-white printer (like a laser), by default the color plate list is set to print all the colors, which include the four process colors plus any spot colors you have defined (see Figure 15-23).

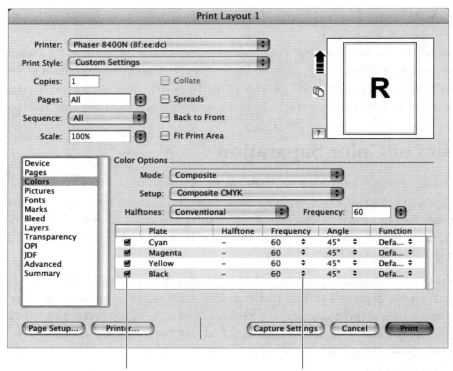

The checkmark indicates that the plate will print. Click on it once to turn it off.

If you have more than one color selected on the list, you can turn them all off (or on) with this popup menu.

Figure 15-23 Making separations via the Colors pane

Even if all the color plates are set to print, QuarkXPress only prints plates for the colors that are actually used in your document. If you create custom spot colors, but don't use them in your document, they still appear on the color plates list. But don't worry: They won't print.

> **Tip: Convert to Process.** *It's driven service bureau owners stark raving mad. It's caused thousands of dollars in wasted film output. It's one of the greatest problems affecting humankind today. (Well, okay, maybe that last one was a little extreme.) I'm talking, of course, about people leaving the Spot Color checkbox turned on in the Edit Colors dialog box when they really meant to build process colors. The result: Every color they create is a spot color, and therefore prints out on its own plate.*
>
> *But fear no more! When you print separations, XPress offers you two choices under the Setup popup menu in the Colors pane of the Print dialog box: Process & Spot or Convert to Process. If you want all your spot colors to separate into CMYK, select Convert to Process. Note that this only changes your spot colors to process colors at print time; the colors in the document are actually still specified as spot colors.*

The Rosette

Even if you're not directly generating film or plates, it's good to know some of the inner workings of the art of placing ink on paper. When the process-color plates are laid down on top of each other, the halftones of each color mesh with each other in a subtle way. Each plate's halftone image is printed at a slightly different angle, and possibly at a different screen frequency as well. The result is thousands of tiny rosette patterns (see Figure 15-24). If this process is done correctly, our eyes blend the separate colors together to form one smooth, clean color. However, if the angles or screen frequencies are slightly off, or if the registration (alignment) of the plates is wrong, then all sorts of chaos can ensue. Both of these problems can come about from error on the press, but more likely they indicate problems with the output (film- or plate-making) process.

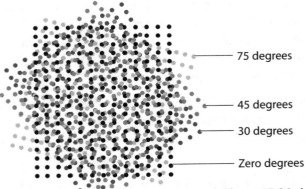

75 degrees

45 degrees

30 degrees

Zero degrees

Figure 15-24 A simulated process-color rosette

The most common effect of the above problems is a patterning in the color called a *moiré pattern* (that's pronounced "mwah-ray"). There's almost no good way to describe a moiré pattern; it's best to just see a few of them. They might be pretty subtle, but it would behoove you to learn to identify them and learn how to make them go away. Figure 15-25 shows an outlandish example of this patterning caused by the screen frequency and angles being set completely wrong.

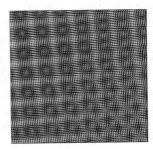

Figure 15-25
Moiré patterning

Making sure you didn't get moirés was a major undertaking in the color prepress industry during the 1990s, and resulted in screening technologies that are built right into the image-setters. Balanced Screens and High Quality Screening (HQS) are two examples of this, available from major imagesetter vendors Agfa and Heidelberg. In the early days, it was crucial that desktop users specify the correct angles and lines per inch, but current RIPs ignore this information, and your choices in QuarkXPress are usually overridden by the settings in the RIP.

Screening and moiré problems are discussed in much more depth in a book that I co-wrote with Steve Roth, Conrad Chavez, and Glenn Fleishman, *Real World Scanning and Halftones*.

The Color Halftone Settings

QuarkXPress lets you change the halftone settings for each color in your document in the Colors pane of the Print dialog box. If you're working with the right PPD file, you rarely need to do this, but when you need this flexibility, it's great to have the opportunity. Keep in mind that your desktop printer may ignore your settings. But if you're after a special effect, it's worth experimenting to see if your printer responds.

There are four halftone settings you can control on the color plates list: Halftone, Frequency, Angle, and Function. To make a change, select a color (or select more than one color with the Shift or Command/Ctrl key), and choose from one of the popup menus at the top of the list.

- **Halftone.** As I mentioned back in Chapter 14, *Color*, each spot color you create is assigned a matching process color—whatever halftone settings are applied to the process color are also applied to the spot color. The Halftone column on the color plates list lets you change the associated color at print time. For instance, if you see an "M" next to a Pantone color, you know that this Pantone color will use the halftone settings for Magenta. If you want, you can then change this to C, Y, or K. Personally, I think if you're going to make this kind of change, you should do it in the Edit Color dialog box instead.

- **Frequency.** The values in the Frequency column are pulled from your printer's PPD file. They may not always match the Frequency field at the top of the dialog box. In fact, it's not uncommon to find different frequency values for each process color. There's a level of faith here—you've got to trust that whoever built the PPD knew what they were doing.

- **Angle.** The angle column lists the halftone angle at which each color will print. As I said earlier, the angles are usually zero, 15, 45, and 75 degrees, but they may be radically different (again, depending on the PPD file). Note that just because you specify a particular angle doesn't mean you're going to get it. Due to some technical issues, some angles are actually impossible to set on digital printers. (Unfortunately, 15 degrees is one such angle; screening systems such as Balanced Screens actually catch the call for 15 degrees and change it to an appropriate number on the fly.)

- **Function.** The last column on the color plates list is labeled Function, which refers to PostScript's spot function. This controls the shape of the halftone spot for each color. It's quite rare that you need to change this unless you're building low-lpi special effects. I discussed the various spot shapes that XPress can build back in Chapter 11, *Image Tuning*.

WORKING WITH AN IMAGING CENTER

Whether you're sending your XPress documents to a service bureau or to a commercial printer, it's important to include the right information and files. Imaging centers have developed standard etiquette and rules, spoken only in hushed voices (and usually after the customer has left the shop). In this section I bring these rules out into the open and take you through, step by step, how to best send files to your service bureau, and how to ensure that you'll receive the best-quality output from them.

The first thing to remember when dealing with service bureaus is that they don't necessarily know their equipment or what's best for your file any better than you do. That's not to say that they are ignorant louts, but I am of the opinion that really good imaging centers are few and far between, and you (the customer) have to be careful and know what you're doing. The principal relationship I talk about in this section is that of you, the customer, and a service bureau to which you are sending your QuarkXPress files to be output. I'll talk first about sending the actual XPress document, and then about sending either a PostScript or a PDF file. Many of my suggestions may be totally wrong for the way your particular service bureau functions, so take what works and leave the rest. Some prefer PDF files, for instance, while others opt for the XPress files.

Tip: Some Questions for Your Service Bureau. Here is a list of questions that you may want to ask when shopping for an imaging center.

- *What imagesetters or platesetters do they have available, and what resolutions do they support?*
- *Do they have dedicated equipment just for film or platesetting, and do they calibrate it using imagesetter linearization or other software? If they're using other software, do you need a component on your system when making files to output with them?*
- *Do they have an in-house color-proofing system? Does it realistically mimic the halftone appearance of a printed piece (as the Kodak Approval system does), or is it a continuous-tone proof to show color only (such as the MatchPrint inkjet proofers)?*
- *Do they have a customer agreement that lists what they're responsible for and what the customer is responsible for?*
- *Do they have a job ticket for output that lets you fill in all the details of your particular project?*

There are no right or wrong answers to any of these questions. However, asking them not only tells you a lot about the company, but also teaches you a lot about the process they're going through to output your files.

How to Send Your File

You have three basic choices in transporting your document to a service bureau or printer: sending the file itself (and all of its support files and the necessary fonts), sending an Adobe PDF, or (rarely these days) sending a PostScript file. While printers are increasingly willing to accept PDFs, most still want the application files. Don't assume: Ask the printer what they prefer, and solicit their guidance as you prepare your files for submission.

Sending QuarkXPress Files

These days, I prefer to send PDF files to imaging centers. However, I know that most places still prefer to receive the actual QuarkXPress file, which gives them the control to fix certain aspects of the job if something goes wrong. And the truth is that many QuarkXPress users don't want to be responsible for checking all the buttons and specifications necessary to print PostScript or generate PDFs. If you find yourself in either of these situations, you'll need to know what to do in order to optimize your chances of success. Let's look at the steps you need to take.

Check your fonts. I can't tell you how important it is to keep track of which fonts you've used and where they are on your disk. Ideally, the printer should have the fonts necessary for output, but let's be realistic: what printer owns every single font on earth? And there are a *lot* of fonts! I generally send my own fonts along with my job to ensure that the job images correctly.

Look over your document. Take the extra time to carefully peruse your entire document. If you need to, zoom in to 200 percent and scroll over the page methodically. Also, look over the Usage dialog box to see what fonts and pictures you used. Many problems with printing occur not with the printing at all, but with that one extra word that slipped onto its own line, or the one image that was "temporarily" set to Suppress Printout and then was never switched back.

Print a proof. If you can print the document on a desktop laser printer, chances are the file will print at your service bureau. That's not a guarantee, but it's usually a pretty good bet. When you print this proof, go over it, too, with a fine-tooth comb. You might have missed something in the onscreen search. Print out separated lasers to troubleshoot more subtle problems: Are objects overprinting when you want them to knock out? Does the type look correct in separations?

Include your illustrations. If you have imported pictures into your document using Get Picture, you need to include the original files on the disk with your document. Remember that QuarkXPress only brings in a representation image for the screen, and then goes to look for the original at print time. You can use the Usage dialog box to see which graphic images you imported, whether they're set to Suppress Printout, and whether they are missing, modified, or present.

The idea is to send your service bureau a folder rather than just a file. Give them everything they could ever think of needing, just in case. The Collect for Output feature can really help this process along (see "Collect for Output," below).

Checklists for Sending QuarkXPress Files

I find checklists invaluable. Not only do they improve your method by encouraging you to do the appropriate task in the right order, they're satisfaction guaranteed every time you can check an item off the list, which in itself is a boon to flagging spirits as a deadline looms. Below are examples of checklists I use before sending files to a service bureau.

Fonts

- What fonts did you use in your document? Are you sure they are PostScript or OpenType fonts rather than the Macintosh system dfont-flavored fonts? (By the way, TrueType fonts are not evil; many years ago, RIPs couldn't process them, but that hasn't been a problem for a long time. You may still find printers that say they'd rather you not use TrueType fonts because of those old experiences. If they balk, consider sending a PDF instead.)

- Does your service bureau have your fonts? (If not, send them.)

Document Check

- Check for boxes and lines set to Suppress Printout.

- Check for text-box overflows.

- Check for missing or modified pictures in the Usage dialog box.

- Check for widows, orphans, loose lines, bad hyphens, and other typographic problems.

Proof

- Print a proof on a laser printer or use Acrobat Distiller to distill the file (if that can handle it, then the service bureau probably can).

- Check the proof carefully to make sure it's what you want. If you're working with clients, have them look over the proofs and sign off on them.

Relevant Files

- Did you include EPS, TIFF, PDF, and JPEG files?

- Did you include the document itself? (Don't laugh; sometimes this is the one thing people *do* forget after a long day.)

Collect for Output

To make the above process significantly easier for y'all, Quark has included a cool feature called Collect for Output. Selecting this command from the File menu copies your document and all the picture files necessary for its output to a folder of your choice—it doesn't move or remove the original files. XPress also gathers all the necessary fonts and creates a report containing detailed information about your document, including fonts and pictures you used and trapping information. Then all you have to do is get the folder to your printer by FTP, messenger, or carrier pigeon.

Using Collect for Output is simplicity itself. When you choose it from the File menu, it prompts you to find a folder, and asks you to specify a name for the report (see Figure 15-26). I typically just use QuarkXPress's default name; it's simply the name of your document with "report" stuck on the end. Then, when you click Save, QuarkXPress copies your document and extra files, wherever they might reside, to that target folder. If you haven't saved your file before selecting Collect for Output, QuarkXPress asks you if you want to save first.

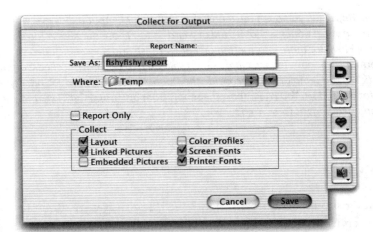

Figure 15-26
Collect for Output

Note that to avoid potential copyright problems, QuarkXPress won't copy fonts to the folder unless you specifically ask it to. The legal ramifications of sending these files are between you, your service bureau, and your font vendor. I don't blame Quark for wanting to stay out of this one!

Collecting files for output often takes longer than manually copying each file, as QuarkXPress does a very thorough search for each file it needs. This may take a bit longer, but the process does give you the satisfaction of knowing you haven't forgotten to copy that little bitty logo illustration hidden at the bottom of page 32.

Also note that you may need lots of space on your hard drive to do this. I recently worked on a job in which the combined size of the document and all the pictures in it was over 500 MB. When I went to Collect for Output, not only did it take almost forever to do, but I ran out of hard-drive space halfway through the procedure. If you're working with big files like this, it may be easier and less painful for you to simply copy files yourself.

> **Tip: Catching All the Fonts and Pictures.** *You can find out what fonts and pictures you used by looking in the Font Usage and Picture Usage dialog boxes. Unfortunately, you can't print these lists out. However, all this information is in the report that QuarkXPress builds when you use Collect for Output. Better yet, XPress offers a checkbox called Report Only in the Collect for Output dialog box, which lets you get the report even if you don't have enough space on your hard drive (or time on your hands) to do a full Collect for Output.*
>
> *After saving the report to disk, you can open it in a word processor or import it into a new QuarkXPress document and find the names of the fonts and the graphics (as well as a lot of other information).*

> **Tip: Formatting the Report.** *If you open the report that Collect for Output builds in a word processor, the first thing you'll notice is that it's full of weird codes. Those are XPress Tag codes (see Chapter 7, Copy Flow, for more information on XPress Tags), and they're included so that you can quickly format the report. In fact, QuarkXPress ships with a document called Output Request Template (it's in the Templates folder, inside the QuarkXPress folder), which has style sheets predefined for this report. You can import the report from disk using Get Text, and each paragraph, including headings, is formatted for you.*

TROUBLESHOOTING

After all of this, printing should be a breeze, right? Well, I wish it were. Too often, I get phone calls from my service bureau saying, "Your job wouldn't print." Back in the good old days, a service bureau would offer to fix it for you. Now life has gotten busy for them, and they usually expect you to do the fixing. Here are some tips that I've found, over the years, to work.

Graphics Look Awful

One of the most common problems with print jobs from QuarkXPress has never had anything to do with QuarkXPress itself. The problem is with the people sending their files. Remember that QuarkXPress does not actually embed any EPS, PDF, DCS, JPEG, or TIFF files that you have imported. It only brings in a low-resolution representation of the screen image, and maintains a link with the original file. If that file changes or is missing when QuarkXPress tries to print it, the graphic will look different from what you expected, because only the low-res proxy inside the XPress document will print, not the real thing.

Two notes to write on your forehead follow.

- If you're going to send your QuarkXPress document, then send a folder, not a file. The folder should include the document, all linked images that you used, and possibly the fonts, too. Use the Collect for Output feature, which I discussed earlier in this chapter.

- PDF files contain the images and embedded fonts, but usually they are not easily editable. Sometime that's not a benefit, if there's a problem with the PDF, but if you've built a perfect layout and made a bulletproof PDF, it's a great way to submit jobs.

Because QuarkXPress downsamples TIFF images to two times the halftone screen frequency, sometimes you can get strange mottling or jaggy images, especially if you've scaled down an image considerably (see "The Pictures Pane," earlier in this chapter).

General Fixes

QuarkXPress sometimes causes PostScript errors at print time. Almost all these errors are the result of printer-memory problems (called VMerror), and almost all of them can be avoided with a few tricks.

Reset the printer. My favorite technique for avoiding memory problems is simply to turn off the printer, wait a few seconds, and turn it back on again. This flushes out any extraneous fonts or PostScript functions that are hogging memory. It's sort of like waking up after a good night's sleep, but different.

Rotate your own graphics. If you've scanned in big bitmapped graphics, and need to rotate them, you should use Photoshop or another image-manipulation program rather than doing it in QuarkXPress. Rotating large bitmapped images in QuarkXPress may or may not choke the printer, but it certainly slows it down a lot, because the rotation is actually performed by the RIP, not by QuarkXPress. (Note that I'm not talking about object-oriented, vector artwork here, such as that from Illustrator or FreeHand.)

Take care in selecting your fonts. If you play with a lot of different fonts trying to find one you like, you may inadvertently leave remnants of old fonts lying around. For example, a space character may be set to some font that you don't use anywhere else. Nonetheless, QuarkXPress must download that font along with every other font you use. This takes up memory that could be used for something else. Try using the Usage dialog box to see which fonts are sitting around in your document. Then purge the ones you don't need.

Print fewer pages at a time. I have successfully coached long documents out of a printer by printing two to ten pages at a time rather than all 500 pages at once. This is obviously a hassle, but it's better than not getting the job printed at all

Remove enormous graphics. One of the great promises of desktop publishing was that I could print an entire page with every graphic and text block perfectly placed. Remember that promises are often broken. Case in point: Large graphics (and even small graphics) sometimes choke old printers. These files often print all by themselves, but when placed on a page they become the chicken bone that kills the giant. Yes, using every trick possible, you might get the page out, but is it worth the time? RIPs are much more robust these days than in the early years of desktop publishing, but it is still possible to build a file that won't RIP. Don't build in unnecessary complexity.

Make sure you're current. Someone recently called and asked me why her file wouldn't print (this question is, by the way, almost impossible for anyone to answer over the telephone). I suggested a few things, and then asked what version of QuarkXPress she was using. It turned out she was using an older version of the program, and as soon as she updated, the printing problem went away. This is not uncommon. They don't talk about it much, but the engineers at Quark are constantly trying to make their program print better. For instance, QuarkXPress 4 was a disaster in some respects, but Quark quickly released free patches for 4.01 and then 4.02, which fixed most of the really egregious printing errors.

What's amazing to me is that there are people who say, "QuarkXPress has a lot of trouble printing," but when pressed they admit that they only heard that someone else had trouble with XPress 4 when it first came out. Those first impressions sure do die hard.

Save As. Logically, it makes no sense that resaving your document under a different name should help a file print, but it has been known to work.

Selective printing. You can try to pinpoint what page element is causing the error by printing only certain parts of the page. For example, select Rough in the Print dialog box to avoid printing any pictures or complex frames. If the page prints, chances are that one of the graphic images is at fault. You can also use Suppress Printout to keep a single image from printing.

If the page still doesn't print after you print a rough copy, try turning off one layer at a time, or suppress the printing of one text box at a time, or changing the fonts you used. If you are printing color separations, try printing a single plate at a time. And so on.

Reimport. If the problem turns out to be a graphic you've imported, you might try reimporting it. That failing, open the graphic in its originating application and resave it.

Check printer type. Make sure you have the correct printer type selected in the Device pane of the Print dialog box. Picking the wrong PPD is the single most common problem people have when printing.

Document Settings

If you use custom kerning or tracking tables, hyphenation exceptions, or custom frames, QuarkXPress will bark at your service bureau as soon as they open your file. "The preferences are different," XPress says, and asks if you want to use the document's preferences or just the ones in the current copy of the program. The appropriate answer is almost always "Document Preferences." If your service bureau tells XPress to use XPress Preferences instead, then your painstaking work may be screwed up and your page won't print as it's supposed to.

One problem: in version 3X, the keystroke for Keep Document Settings was Command-period or Esc. In every later version, this same keystroke "clicks" Use XPress Preferences instead. That could be an "oops" if you're not paying attention.

Fonts Come Out Wrong

Don't forget that you have to have the fonts loaded for every font in the document when you print. "Every font" means the fonts you selected, those that were imported, and those that are stuck somewhere in an EPS document. Also, watch out for EPS files nested inside of EPS files nested inside of EPS files. Depending on which application created each EPS file, QuarkXPress may or may not be able to dig deep enough to find every font you used.

Registration Problems

Imagine the Rockettes kicking their legs to chorus-line stardom in perfect synchronization. Then imagine the woman at one end having no sense of rhythm, kicking totally out of sync with the others. This is what happens when one color plate is misregistered to the others. When a sheet of paper is rushed through a printing press and four colors are speedily applied to it, there's bound to be some misregistration—sometimes up to 1 or 2 points. However, you can help matters considerably by making sure that your film and plates are always as consistent as possible.

Whenever I am told that a job printed great "except for one plate that was off-register," I immediately ask if that plate was run at a different time than the others. The answer is almost always yes. I realize it's expensive and time-consuming to print four new plates every time you want to make a change to a page, but it is a fact of desktop life that you can almost never get proper registration when you reprint a single plate. Why? The weather, temperature, alignment of the stars—all sorts of reasons contribute to this massive hassle. You'll find that direct-to-plate environments are much less prone to these difficulties that the older method of generating film to create plates. There are fewer intervening steps, and more automated handling to minimize environmental influences.

JOB FINISHED

As I said way back at the beginning of the book, don't give up until you get it to work. If you run into difficulty, there is almost always a workaround. Working through to that solution almost always teaches a valuable lesson (as Grandma used to say, "It builds character."). However, remember that the solution is sometimes to just print the job in pieces and strip them together traditionally. It feels awful when you have to clean off your drafting table and dust off your waxer, but efficiency is often the name of the game.

And when the last page comes out of the imagesetter, don't forget to thank your computer, QuarkXPress, the printer, and yourself for a job well done.

CHAPTER SIXTEEN
PDF

The idea of a paperless office has long been a dream of Shangri-la, a place where no one would have to be burdened with paper cuts and filing cabinets. Instead, all documents would be electronic, easily read on any computer platform, easily stored on disk or somewhere on the Internet. Adobe has done its part in bringing us closer to this utopia with its Acrobat format, which lets you build and edit Portable Document Format (PDF) files from almost any program. These PDF files, in turn, can be viewed on any computer that has a reader program (which is free from *www.adobe.com* and available for Macintosh, Windows, Linux, and even Palm operating systems).

While the PDF format was originally designed for archiving or viewing documents that were meant for paper output, it has grown to incorporate features suitable for Web or multi-media publishing, too (see Figure 16-1). Plus, PDF files are now widely used to send files to output providers, such as when advertisements are sent to magazines and newspapers (because PDF is more flexible and often more robust than the EPS format).

There are many reasons why you would create a PDF file of your XPress layout. Perhaps you want to send a draft or final version to a client for approval. Instead of sending your actual QuarkXPress layout to a client or a publication for printing, you can simply email the more-compact and less-volatile PDF file. Most printing companies accept print jobs as PDF files. (If you are printing colors—especially spot colors—make sure the printer has experience with printing color separations from PDF files.) If the PDF file will be viewed primarily on screen, you can create a more robust experience by adding hyperlinks so that the user can navigate to different sections in the document.

Note that this chapter includes information about creating Acrobat PDF files for either the Web or print.

Acrobat's tools let you navigate through the document quickly.

Bookmarks act like a table of contents.

Anything you can design on your page can be included in the Acrobat PDF file.

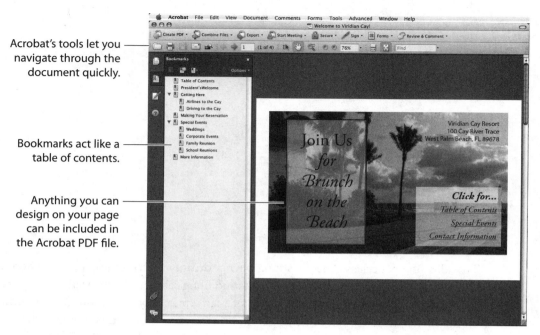

Figure 16-1 Acrobat features

Viewing PDFs on the Web. Several popular Web browsers allow you to view PDF files within your Web browser window, but this still requires that you have the Reader program (or Acrobat) somewhere on your hard disk. You can also configure your Web browser to view PDFs directly in Acrobat Reader or Acrobat. In this case, the Web browser downloads the whole PDF file to disk and then opens it with the Reader or Acrobat application.

CREATING A PDF FILE

There are three ways to make an Acrobat PDF file from a QuarkXPress file: using the Mac OS X print driver, exporting directly using the built-in Jaws software, or using Acrobat Distiller.

Mac OS X print driver. Mac OS X can write Acrobat PDF files to disk from any OS X application, using an OS-level interpreter (not supplied by Quark or Adobe). The process is simple: First, click the Printer button at the bottom of the Print dialog box to open the print driver's dialog box. Click the Save as PDF button and then tell the operating system where to save the file. Finally, after you click OK (which returns you to the XPress Print dialog box) click Print to create the PDF file on disk.

"Printing" a PDF does a reasonable job on text and simple page items such as lines. However, it doesn't do well with graphics, especially EPS files. Also, there's currently no way to control font embedding, image compression, or any of the other important features you get with the other methods. While this is a quick way to get a PDF from an application that can't otherwise create one, such PDFs are usually not suitable for commercial printing.

The Jaws solution. If you really want a good-quality PDF file, you'll be much better off using the Export Layout as PDF feature (in the File menu). This forces XPress to silently write a PostScript file to disk and then turn it into a PDF using the Jaws PDF engine. (Jaws is PostScript and PDF technology that Quark licensed from Global Graphics—it is not a true Adobe technology, like Acrobat Distiller, but it works well most of the time.) QuarkXPress 7 does allow the creation of PDF/X-1a and PDF/X-3 files, and also allows you to create and save custom PDF-creation options. I discuss this feature in more depth in "Export Layout as PDF," below.

Acrobat Distiller. Although QuarkXPress can write PDF files directly to disk (via the Jaws engine), you may find that Acrobat Distiller (part of the Adobe Acrobat Professional product) creates somewhat smaller PDFs. And your printer may require you to use a particular target PPD (PostScript Printer Description) when generating PostScript and Distilling to ensure that proprietary information is included in the resulting PDF needed by the printer's particular workflow.

If you want to use Distiller rather than the Jaws engine, select Create PostScript File for Later Distilling in the PDF panel of the Preferences dialog box (see Figure 16-2). Now, when you select Export Layout as PDF from the File menu, XPress writes only the PostScript to disk and lets you process it with Distiller later. If you have set up a "hot folder" in Distiller (a folder that Distiller watches for incoming files), you can choose this same folder in XPress's Preferences dialog box and skip the step of telling XPress where to write the PostScript file.

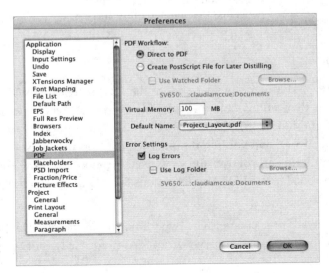

Figure 16-2
PDF Preferences

Note that it's a good idea to visit the PDF Export Options dialog box before saving the PostScript to disk. This lets you control what does and doesn't get into the PDF file (hyperlinks, for example). I cover PDF export options in an upcoming section.

INTERACTIVE PDF FEATURES

QuarkXPress allows you to create hyperlinks to facilitate navigation in the XPress layout and in an exported PDF. Hyperlinks are a great way to help your reader navigate a PDF for a more pleasant reading experience. Interactive components can help you find your way around a long, complex layout while you're working on it, even though the layout might be destined purely for print. But you might consider how helpful they can be in a file repurposed for online viewing.

A hyperlink is just a hot spot that takes you to a destination. There are three flavors of hyperlink destinations: Page hyperlinks take the reader to a designated page; anchors take the reader to a specific element or bit of text; URL hyperlinks launch the user's default browser and open a Web page. All of these features can truly bring a document to life.

To create an anchor destination, select a box or a range of text, and click the Anchor icon in the Hyperlinks palette. Give the anchor a name (Figure 16-3) so you can invoke it later with a hyperlink. Then go to the spot in the layout that will be the "jumping off point" and create a hyperlink that references the anchor.

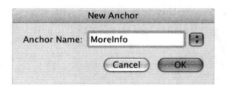 Make it easy on yourself and give sensible, memorable names to anchors. You'll be thankful you did when you create the hyperlinks that jump to those anchors.

Figure 16-3 Naming an anchor

It isn't necessary to create Page destinations; just choose the box or text that will be the hyperlink hot spot area, and then choose New Hyperlink from the Hyperlinks palette drop-down menu (or click the link icon). Choose Page in the Type option in the New Hyperlink dialog box (Figure 16-4), and you're presented with a drop-down list of all the pages in the layout. You don't have control over the view magnification when the end user jumps to the page; that's controlled in the PDF Export options (see "Export Layout as PDF," later in this chapter).

To create a hyperlink to a Web address, create a new hyperlink, and in the New Hyperlink dialog box, choose URL (a Web address, like http://www.quark.com) for the type of hyperlink.

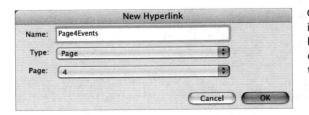

Creating a Page destination is simple—just create a new hyperlink, choose the Page option, and then select the target page.

Figure 16-4 New Hyperlink dialog box

There's more: As you'll see later in the section "Export Layout as PDF," you can export lists and indexes as active hyperlinks in a PDF. Think of these as multipurpose navigation tools. A list that will become a table of contents in a printed book can also become live, clickable bookmarks in the exported PDF.

CREATING PDF OUTPUT STYLES

While QuarkXPress offers a good starting list of supplied PDF output styles, you will probably want to create some custom styles. You'll find that creating an optimal export style entails some experimentation to find the proper balance of resolution and compression settings for different types of jobs. For example, in a huge annual report with images serving as ghosted background shots, you may be able to aggressively compress and resample the image content as you make the PDF without negatively impacting the printed piece. By contrast, a product catalog with industrial equipment pictures containing complicated dials and labels might require that you use no compression or resampling, lest you lose important detail when the catalog is printed.

To create a custom PDF output style, start as if you were exporting a PDF: Choose Export Layout as PDF from the File menu. Click the Options button at the bottom of the dialog box, and the PDF Export Options dialog box appears (Figure 16-5). Work your way through the list of options (explained in detail in the following section). When you're satisfied with your recipe, choose New PDF Output Style from the PDF Style drop-down menu at the top of the dialog box. Give your new style a name, and it will be available in future sessions. Click OK to return to the Export as PDF dialog box, and then give your PDF a name and save it.

Another way to create a custom PDF output style is to choose Output Styles from the Edit menu and click the New button in the Output Styles dialog box. The New button then becomes a drop-down menu. Select PDF from the drop-down list, and you're taken to the Edit PDF Style dialog box. Choose your settings, give the style a name, and then click the OK button, which returns you to the Output Styles dialog box. Click the Save button, and you're done. This method has the advantage of being available even when you have no layout open.

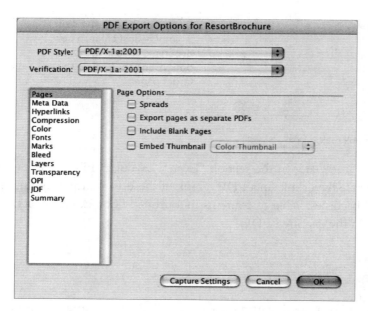

Figure 16-5
The PDF Export Options dialog box

To edit or delete an output style, choose Output Styles from the Edit menu, then select the name of the desired style from the list of styles. Click the Edit or Delete button. In addition, you can export styles for other users: Select a style from the list and click the Export button. Name and save the exported style. Unfortunately, you can't simultaneously select multiple output styles for export; you have to export them one at a time. Importing an output style is just as easy: Choose Output Styles from the Edit menu, click the Import button, navigate to the new style, click Open in the Import dialog box, and then click Save in the Output Styles dialog. This makes it easy to standardize custom PDF styles across a workgroup.

EXPORT LAYOUT AS PDF

In order for Jaws or Acrobat Distiller to generate a PDF file, QuarkXPress needs to write PostScript to disk. There are two ways to do this: you can use the Print dialog box to print to a file, or you can use the Export Layout as PDF feature. I discussed how to write PostScript to disk in Chapter 15, *Printing*. Suffice it to say that using Export Layout as PDF is easier and gives you more control. Plus, you can't take advantage of any of QuarkXPress's inter-active features—like hyperlinks—unless you use Export Layout as PDF, so we'd better focus on that here.

Choose Layout as PDF from the Export submenu (under the File menu). In the Export as PDF dialog box (see Figure 16-5), tell the program where to save the PDF file. XPress writes a PostScript file to disk, and then uses Jaws to "distill" this file into a PDF file. If you have turned on the Create PostScript File for Later Distilling option in the PDF panel of the Preferences dialog box, then XPress leaves the PostScript file where it is and lets you process it with Acrobat Distiller.

To get the most of XPress's PDF features, click the Options button to open the PDF Export Options dialog box . Here you're presented with a comprehensive list of preferences.

> **Tip: Set Up PDF Preferences.** *If you find yourself visiting the PDF Export Options dialog box often and making the same or similar changes each time, you should consider changing the default settings for this dialog box in the PDF pane of the Preferences dialog box. There you can choose between going directly to PDF or distilling later. You can even choose a watched folder to throw your PostScript into (of course, this requires that you own the retail Acrobat product to process those PostScript files with Distiller), and you can set up the configuration for the default naming conventions for PDFs (Project_Layout.pdf, Layout_Project.pdf, Project.pdf or Layout.pdf).*

Pages. Here, you can choose whether to export pages in spreads; to export each page as a separate PDF (requested by some printers to simplify the process of imposition); or to include blank pages. You're also given the option to embed thumbnails in the PDF, but there's never a reason to turn on this option: Adobe Acrobat generates thumbnails on the fly whenever you open a PDF, and embedded thumbnails add to the heft of a PDF.

Meta Data. Add a title (which is internal information within the PDF and can be different from the file name), as well as a subject, author name, and relevant keywords. While all this information is "under the hood" in the PDF, it can be useful when you're performing a search among a large number of PDFs.

Hyperlinks. In the Hyperlinks tab (see Figure 16-6) you can choose to include interactive features in your PDF—hyperlinks that let the viewer bounce from place to place within (and without) your document. If you're creating a layout that you're sending off to be printed, you might as well turn off the Include Hyperlinks checkbox because no one will need them. However, if someone will be viewing the PDF file onscreen, these hyperlinks can be very helpful.

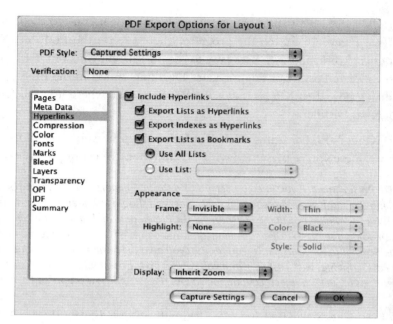

Figure 16-6
The PDF Export Options dialog box showing the Hyperlinks options

You can also make several other choices in the Hyperlinks tab of this dialog box, including whether your indexes will turn into hyperlinks and what hyperlinks will look like onscreen in the Acrobat Reader.

- **Export Lists as Hyperlinks.** If you have used the Lists feature to create a list (like a table of contents) in your layout, you can turn those list items into hyperlinks automatically by turning on Export Lists as Hyperlinks. For instance, when this is on, a viewer looking at your table of contents could click on a page number and be transported to that page. (I discuss lists and indexes in Chapter 9, *Long Documents*.)

- **Export Indexes as Hyperlinks.** Page numbers in your layout's index can also be exported as hyperlinks, which is very helpful, and appreciated by users. Of course, you have to have used the Index feature to make your index first!

- **Export Lists as Bookmarks.** One of my favorite interactive tools in PDF documents is the Bookmarks feature—sort of a table of contents that can be visible all the time in the Acrobat Reader application. QuarkXPress can create bookmarks for you automatically, based on any or all lists in your layout. Again, you have to use the Lists feature for this to work. You have two choices here: Use All Lists or Use List. If you have only one list specified in your layout, then these choices are the same, of course.

Tip: Hidden Lists and Bookmarks. Unfortunately, at the time of this writing, the bookmarks only appear in your PDF file if you actually build the list in your layout and you export that page (the page with the list on it) to PDF. This is pretty annoying, because sometimes you want bookmarks in your PDF document, but you don't actually want to display the list as one of your pages. The only way around this, as far as I can tell, is to build the list as the last page of your layout, export the whole layout as PDF, and then use the Acrobat application to delete that last page.

- **Appearance.** When the Include Hyperlinks checkbox is turned on, XPress automatically includes all the links you have added using the Hyperlinks palette (see "Interactive PDF Features," earlier in this chapter). However, while hyperlinks appear underlined and in a different color on-screen in QuarkXPress, they are often invisible in PDF files—that is, there is no visual indication that text or pictures are hot links. If you want your PDF file's hyperlinks to be visible, you need to set the Frame popup menu to Visible and then set the Width, Color, and Style popup menus to indicate how the hyperlinks should appear.

  The Appearance section of the PDF Export Options dialog box offers one other setting: the Highlight popup menu, which tells XPress how you want the link to appear when you click on it. You have four options: None, Invert, Outline, and Inset (which looks like a button that gets pressed in).

- **Display.** The last setting here, the Display popup menu, lets you tell XPress what view percentage you want Acrobat Reader to use when it jumps to the new page (this only affects hyperlinks to other pages within your layout, like those from an index or bookmark). The options are Zoom, Fit Window, Fit Width, and Fit Length. You're on your own on this one; What you select will depend entirely on your layout and your audience's needs.

Compression. Since raster images occupy most of the space in a hefty PDF, Compression settings can be a juggling act between maintaining image quality and slimming your PDF. Your choices here will be governed by the use intended for your PDF: A PDF for print should be much higher resolution (and be less aggressively compressed) than a PDF destined for online viewing.

The Compression options may look complex, but you're actually being asked the same question three times: "How much do you want to compress, and what resolution do you want?" QuarkXPress allows you to choose separate options for three types of image content—color, grayscale, and monochrome (bitmap/line art scans). Depending on the nature of your content, you might choose to use different settings for each type of image.

You're offered two different ways to reduce the size of image content: Compression and Resolution.

Reducing resolution discards pixels. An image with 72 pixels per inch (ppi) contains less than a third of the information of an image with 300 ppi. (The Compression dialog box labels resolution as "dpi," which, frankly, is incorrect—it should be "ppi" instead. But we all know what it means.)

Compression is a method of expressing the same image content in a more economical way, either by averaging the values of large expanses of similar color (JPEG) or by encoding the information in a more compact language (ZIP). JPEG compression is more appropriate for photographic images, and ZIP compression is better for flat-color content such as maps or cartoon art. The list of permutations—Automatic ZIP/JPEG High, Manual JPEG High, Manual ZIP, and so on—looks daunting, but I'll make it easy for you. If you want no compression, choose None (and accept that your PDF may be rather large) or choose one of the Automatic ZIP/JPEG flavors. The Automatic options allow QuarkXPress to selectively apply JPEG or ZIP compression to different types of image content appropriately, optimizing the results.

But here's a caveat: If you choose Automatic ZIP/JPEG High, you're asking for high compression, not high quality. It's labeled correctly, but easy to misread. High compression equals more aggressive compression, and thus, more loss of image detail in the interest of a smaller PDF. For example, the PDF in Figure 16-7 was generated with the Automatic ZIP/JPEG Low setting and weighs in at 3.7 MB. The PDF shown in Figure 16-8 was created with the Automatic ZIP/JPEG High and is a svelte 428 K. Both PDFs retain the original image resolution of 300 ppi, but the highly compressed PDF shows unattractive rectangular artifacts and loss of detail.

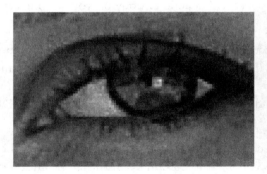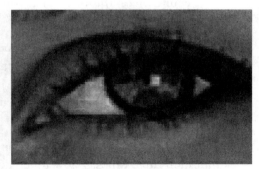

Figure 16-7 Low Compression = higher quality **Figure 16-8** High Compression = lower quality

Compress Text and Line Art is turned on by default, and you should leave it turned on. There's no erosion of detail in text and vector content—it's always sharp, and this function doesn't contribute much to the file size of a PDF.

The Color Output section of the dialog box is very important, because it can drastically affect your layout's colors. If you want QuarkXPress to generate color separations, then choose Separations from the Type popup menu. If you have a one-page layout with black, cyan, and a spot color, you'll get three black-and-white pages. However, if you turn on the Produce Blank Pages checkbox, you'll get five pages: cyan, magenta, yellow, black, and the spot color—but the second and third pages will be blank.

Unless your printing company specifically asks for separations, however, it's probably best to choose Composite from the Type popup menu, and then choose CMYK (or Composite CMYK and Spot, which has replaced DeviceN; see Chapter 15, *Printing*) from the Print Colors popup menu. In this case, the printers will actually do the color separations from this file. If the PDF file is destined for the Web, you should also use Composite, but you can use RGB colors or Grayscale instead.

Fonts. The default choice, Select All, is appropriate: You want font information embedded in the PDF for proper display and printing.

Marks. Usually, a printer doesn't require you to include marks in a PDF submitted for print, but if you have any doubt, ask.

Bleed. If your layout contains artwork that bleeds, be sure to include the setting here. The default setting is Symmetric (same amount of bleed on all four sides), and you'll rarely use the Asymmetric option. For no bleed, choose Page Items. If you turn off Clip at Bleed, items that extend beyond the bleed limit will image. The default, Clip at Bleed, crops any oversized content at the bleed edge. Since anything that far beyond the trim will be, well, trimmed off in the printing and binding process, there's no advantage to keeping it all. And extraneous image content can add a bit to PDF file size.

Layers. If you're using layers to isolate content for different versions of the layout, you can selectively show and hide layers for export.

Transparency. If QuarkXPress is forced to rasterize any vector content, you want it to be rasterized at a value matching the resolution of the ultimate imaging device. For a desktop printer, that might be 300–600 dpi. A commercial RIP (Raster Image Processor) attached to an imagesetter or platesetter may range from 1800 to 2400 dpi or above. Ask your printer what's appropriate, but if you have to guess, enter 2400 dpi (see Figure 16-9).

If you don't have the OPI XTension loaded, the Output tab gives you the chance to use OPI anyway. However, if you're going to use an OPI workflow, you'll want the OPI XTension loaded, so you can just ignore this checkbox.

OPI. When the OPI XTension is active, XPress displays the OPI tab of the PDF Export Options dialog box, which lets you specify whether to include your TIFF and EPS images. I cover OPI workflows in Chapter 15, *Printing*.

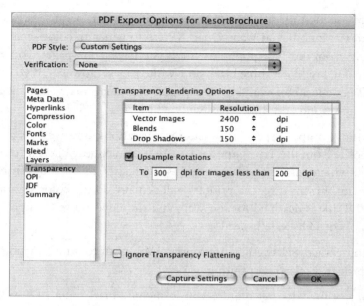

Figure 16-9
Transparency settings

Tip: PDFs of Books and Multiple Layouts. Please note that there is no way to make a single PDF of multiple layouts (like books in a Book palette) or multiple layouts at the same time. Instead, if you need this, you'll have to save each of them individually and then combine them into a single PDF using Acrobat Professional.

PDF FOR PRINT/ADVERTISING

Because it's crucial to ensure both file fidelity and successful imaging, a PDF for print or for advertising submission needs to play by some very specific rules. Start, of course, by building your layouts to the correct size, adding bleed where necessary, and ensuring that your graphics are in the correct color space and of adequate resolution: A PDF of bad content is still a bad PDF. Just making a PDF doesn't cure problems with the job.

That said, you're faced with a list of seven PDF output options when you choose Export Layout as PDF from the File menu. How do you pick the appropriate format for sending your important job to the printer? First, ask your printer how you should create PDFs for job submission. Follow the provided specifications and all should be well. However, if your printer doesn't offer guidelines, you're on your own. Fortunately, QuarkXPress offers a reliable format for PDF export for times like these.

Glancing down the list of output options, you'll see some options that don't sound very promising: Screen – Medium Quality, and Screen – Low Quality clearly are not appropriate for commercial printing. Default PDF Output Style sounds suspicious, since it offers only Medium Quality. Print – Medium Quality doesn't sound like it would do the job, either. Initially, you'll find that the most tempting is Press – High Quality/High Resolution. It contains the word "Press," so it must be perfect, right?

Wrong. While the *content* of a Press PDF is fine for print as far as image resolution and font embedding, its *format* may be an issue in some imaging workflows. A PDF created with the Press – High Quality option is compatible with Acrobat 5.0 and later (so far, this sounds good, doesn't it?). Since the current version of Acrobat is several numbers higher, you'd think this wouldn't be a problem. However, some older workflows and some aging imaging devices don't handle Acrobat 5.0-flavored PDFs correctly. These are perfectly legal PDF files, but they may not behave correctly in all scenarios. As imaging devices and processes are updated, this won't be an issue, but you don't want to take any risks with that innocent little PDF you're sending off into the world.

Fortunately, QuarkXPress 7 offers an ideal format for PDFs intended for commercial printing. PDF/X is a subset of PDF designed specifically for reliable print job submission and that was developed by the American National Standards Institute's (ANSI) Committee for Graphic Arts Technologies Standards (CGATS). Newspapers and advertisers needed a reliable format for the safe, blind exchange of files, and PDF/X is the result. (Tidbit: the "X" in PDF/X stands for "exchange.")

But notice that there are two X-flavored PDF choices in the Export Layout as PDF options. What's the difference?

PDF/X-1a:2001. Despite its somewhat ungainly moniker, this option is your best choice if the printing company hasn't given you any guidance. You will find that many printers and publications stipulate that files submitted for print should meet the PDF/X-1a:2001 requirements to ensure successful imaging and printing. The PDF/X-1a:2001 specifications include:

- **Color Space Limitations.** A PDF/X-1a file can contain only CMYK, grayscale, and bitmap (black and white) images, as well as spot-color images such as duotones and tritones. RGB geometric content (such as color boxes and lines) is also forbidden. Bonus: if your layout contains RGB images or geometry, QuarkXPress converts the content to CMYK in the outgoing print stream, resulting in a legal PDF/X-1a file with CMYK images and other elements.

- **Font Embedding.** Fonts must be embedded and subset. Subsetting ensures that the embedded fonts are tagged with a unique name that prevents efforts by any subsequent device or process to substitute its own fonts. The goal is to prevent font substitution in the interest of faithfully rendering the text as it exists in the original application file.

- **Trim and Bleed Boxes.** The coordinates of trim and bleed areas must be correctly defined internally, in the PDF. It's up to the originating application to accomplish this, and other processes (such as imposition or trapping) need to honor the definitions of trim and bleed for the file to image correctly.

PDF/X-3:2002. This option is appropriate only if you are participating in a fully color-managed workflow. While color management is a powerful solution to the need for color consistency among devices and across platforms, it is strenuous to implement and maintain. If you are working with an enlightened printer who supports color-managed files for submission, seek your printer's input for correct color profile embedding guidelines. Don't assume that a PDF/X-3:2002 will be expected—or correctly handled—by an unsuspecting print service provider.

COMMON PDF FILE PROBLEMS

Despite your best efforts to ensure that you have built a healthy QuarkXPress file, step carefully as you export a PDF to make sure that your hard work pays off in the best PDF possible. There are a few little speed bumps along the way. Here are some of the lurking dangers.

Font Embedding Issues

Three species of fonts are currently available—PostScript (often called Type 1), TrueType, and OpenType. All font formats are fully supported by QuarkXPress 7, and for the most part, the different formats coexist peacefully. Understandably, it's important to embed fonts in PDFs to maintain file fidelity to your original QuarkXPress file, so failure to embed a font is a showstopper, and a resulting PDF would be unusable. While the default font-handling option in QuarkXPress is to embed and subset fonts (XPress uses the term "download," but it's just a different term for the same concept), it is possible to encounter fonts that do not allow embedding. Such fonts are exceedingly rare, but it's worth knowing that there are resistant fonts.

How can you know if a font has not embedded correctly? Use a dedicated preflight program or use the preflight tools in Adobe Acrobat (note that these tools are not available in the free Adobe Reader).

Image Issues

Assuming your original images are healthy, and that you haven't done terrible things to them such as enlarging them to 300 percent in the QuarkXPress layout and then rotating them at 2.1 degrees, only your PDF Export options can mess things up. If you inadvertently choose an option that's appropriate for online viewing, the resulting PDF will not fare well in print.

Since there is no way to interrogate a PDF in order to discover which output style was used to create it, you have two choices: pay close attention as you rush to create your PDF or use the analytical tools in Acrobat or a preflight application to uncover image problems in the PDF. The first method is arguably wiser—and certainly less expensive!

Choosing the wrong Color option will alter the appearance of images in your PDF (e.g., choosing Composite RGB when you should be choosing Composite CMYK instead). Selecting an inappropriate compression or resolution setting will erode your perfectly good images on the way to creating a PDF.

Mistreatment at the Printing Company

It's unavoidable: your printer *will* have to do something to your PDF. Trapping must be performed, and it's likely that your job will require imposition for printing plates. And if you are submitting an advertisement as a PDF, your file will need to be placed into an existing page for the final publication. During any one of these processes, it is possible for font embedding to be compromised if the software handling your file does not correctly maintain the embedding and subsetting applied during the export from QuarkXPress.

How can you prevent this? Well, truthfully, you can't. Hopefully, you can trust your printer to coddle your PDF. But it's vital that you carefully examine the contract proofs provided before your job actually goes to press (you do look at the proofs, don't you?). Check closely for jumbled text, incorrect fonts, and missing characters. Don't accept an assurance that "it will all be just fine when we crank up that million-dollar press at three o'clock in the morning and run your job." Insist on a new proof and give it the same eagle-eye treatment before signing off on the job.

Checking Your PDF Files for Problems

Of course, you should examine PDF files before submitting them to your printer. Compare them to the original QuarkXPress file to make sure nothing has shifted or disappeared. But some more subtle problems, such as image-color space or inadequate resolution, may be more challenging to catch. If you want to perform more detailed forensics on your PDF files before sending them, consider using a dedicated preflight program such as one of Markzware's FlightCheck products, or the built-in preflight capabilities in Adobe Acrobat 6.0 or later. All of these programs provide methodical tools to check font embedding, image properties, and even page dimensions.

THE FUTURE OF PUBLISHING

One of the basic elements of democracy has long been "freedom of the press," but freedom of the press has always been reserved for those who own one. Now, for the first time in history, most people who want to can publish their own work on the Internet and the World Wide Web. And because QuarkXPress has been the tool of choice for most publishing professionals, it makes sense that people would look to this program to take them into the brave new world.

In this chapter, I've briefly summarized the various tools that ease the transition from print to screen. Of course, the future of publishing depends less on which tools you use than on *what* you create. Happy XPressing!

CHAPTER SEVENTEEN

Going Online with QuarkXPress

Since you're a QuarkXPress user, you probably create, or will create, your share of print documents. Today, however, most companies also want to use the Web as an additional advertising or information distribution medium. Using the Internet has become an integral part of our lives. Checking the weather or keeping informed with up-to-date news items can be accomplished with a few clicks of the mouse. Want new product information? Check the company's Web site. Lost your manual for that new digital camera? Download a PDF of the manual.

With faster connections now available to more people, not only can you publish your content, but you can add more graphics to your designs to make your pages more appealing. Of course, there are limitations to publishing on the Web (and to multimedia in general).

- Few people want to read a lot of text on screen.

- You can't take a computer with you in the bathtub.

- Availability of electricity, much less a good connection to the Internet, is limited around the world.

- It's difficult to protect the copyright of your work because it's so easy to copy the digital files of anything published on the Web.

Nonetheless, people have been clamoring to build Web pages for the past several years, and there's no reason to think this trend will stop. And because there are more than a million people around the world who already publish with QuarkXPress, the question has inevitably arisen: How can I get content out of XPress and onto other people's screens?

The Web versus multimedia. Most of what I'm talking about in this chapter revolves around publishing for the World Wide Web. However, anything you can put on the Web can be put on a CD-ROM or a kiosk or a disk. The differences are a range of primarily distribution (how many people will be able to access your work?) and file size (larger files may be inappropriate for the Web, depending on your audience). So, when I talk about getting stuff online, don't think I'm just talking about the Internet.

Repurposing content. As you'll soon see, QuarkXPress is not the world's best Web-page generator, although it is greatly improved from version 5. So why did Quark put all that time and energy into adding so many Web tools? For a simple reason: They saw too many of their customers mocking up Web page designs using QuarkXPress, Illustrator, and Photoshop, then printing the designs out and telling the Web folks to recreate the whole thing using other tools. It's a sadly common workflow, and it's incredibly inefficient.

The Web tools in QuarkXPress let you cut out a major step in the process because you can quickly build a mock-up of a Web page or Web site using the XPress tools you already know how to use, and the Web folks can use your work as a first draft. Sure, you can build a finished Web page or a Web site in XPress, but in most cases you'll want to tweak your results in a more sophisticated program, like Adobe Dreamweaver or Adobe GoLive.

HTML and PDF. There are two primary methods of putting interactive XPress pages onto the Web: creating HTML and creating PDF files (see Chapter 16, *PDF*). Each of these has its limitations and strengths, and you might find yourself using different methods for different situations. There's one thing that they have in common, though: they both require a radically different approach to laying out pages and presenting material than print-based publications do. You can't just plop a for-print brochure into one of these formats and call it quits. As I've said before, *how* to design is outside the purview of this book, but knowing what you can and cannot achieve with each method is essential to making the switch to online publishing.

Note that while XML is also often considered a "Web format," it's really more of a way to encode your content so that it can be formatted in a number of different ways, including print. I'll discuss QuarkXPress's XML tools in more detail in Appendix C, *XML Tools*.

> **TIP: Getting Online.** There are more than a thousand Internet books on the market, so I'm just going to defer to them to cover many of the basics—like how to get an Internet account, use a Web browser, build a Web page from scratch, place your Web pages on a Web server so that people can see them, optimize your graphics for the Web, and so on. For instance, Elizabeth Castro's HTML for the World Wide Web: Visual QuickStart Guide, also from Peachpit Press, is a good reference for HTML codes. Instead, this chapter will focus on getting your XPress pages into an interactive, screen-ready form.

HTML AND WEB BROWSERS

Almost everyone who surfs the Web is looking at pages built with HTML (HyperText Markup Language). HTML is like QuarkXPress's XPress Tags language (see Chapter 7, *Copy Flow*); it is code-based (formatting is handled using special codes like <b> and </b> in the text) and it's generally linear—it describes the first paragraph, then it describes the second paragraph, and so on (see Figure 17-1).

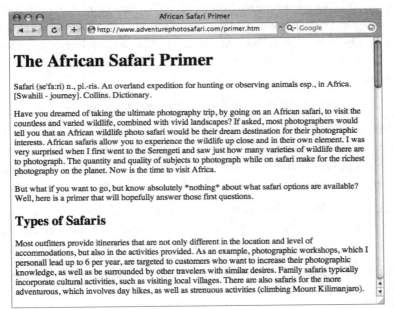

A basic HTML page viewed in a Web browser

HTML source code. Note the similarity to XPress Tags.

Figure 17-1 HTML pages

Originally, HTML was based on the idea that the viewer rather than the publisher of the information should determine the look of the page. In this model, you just add codes specifying where the headings are, what words should be emphasized, and so on; then your audience configures their browsers to display your headings and emphasized words in certain ways. One person will see headings in Helvetica, another person sees them in Times Roman. Over the past few years, however, HTML has grown to include additional formatting that lets you—the author/publisher—control how you want the page to look.

In order to view an HTML file properly, you need a Web browser—basically just a program that interprets the HTML codes ("make this <i>italic</i>") into WYSIWYG text ("make this *italic*"). The two primary Web browsers are Microsoft's Internet Explorer and Mozilla Firefox. If you are using Macintosh OS X, Apple's Safari is also a serious contender in the browser wars.

However, it turns out that HTML has some severe design limitations.

- Different Web browsers interpret the codes differently, so line spacing, fonts, font sizes, and column widths (and more!) may be completely different from what you expect. While it's not hopelessly impossible to control typography on the Web, it does take some work. But you can forget about kerning or tracking your type!

- You might think that Futura displays well and matches your design, but if that font is not available on a user's computer, then another font is substituted and may change the look of the page.

- Color consistency is impossible, so what you see on one screen may be quite different from what you see on another.

There are a host of other problems, too, but given a proper understanding of the limitations, you can begin to gain mastery over the medium. The key is to remember that you just can't design and produce pages in the way you've become accustomed to over the years.

Exporting Your Content

If you're reading this chapter, chances are that you want one of two things from QuarkXPress: either to export final Web pages that look just like what you see in XPress, or to export your content (text and perhaps graphics, too) so you can use it in another Web design program. XPress gives you some of the tools you want, but not all.

It comes down to page geometry (*geometry* is the part of the HTML code which says *where* something should be on a page). The basic Export HTML feature (which I'll cover later in this chapter) exports your page with geometry, so that your final HTML looks almost exactly like what you see in XPress. There is no way to export your whole document (text and graphics) without the accompanying geometry—a major oversight in my opinion.

Save Text as HTML. You can, however, export a single text story as HTML without page geometry by selecting the Content tool, clicking in the story, and then choosing Save Text from the File menu (or press Command-Option-E or Ctrl-Alt-E; read more about exporting text in Chapter 7, *Copy Flow*). From here, you can select HTML from the Format popup menu. The result is a text file with HTML codes that you can import into another program.

Note that the HTML created using Save Text is styled using Cascading Style Sheets (CSS), which are much fancier ways of styling text. While most Web programs (Dreamweaver and so on) support CSS, some older programs do not. I haven't found any way to get simple, non-CSS tags out of XPress.

Note that you can use this Save Text method from both Web and regular print layouts. (I cover the difference between these two formats soon.)

Use an XTension. Before version 5, everyone who wanted to export HTML from QuarkXPress used a commercial XTension such as Extensis BeyondPress or Gluon's WebXPress. As it turns out, many people will still want to continue using these XTension because they let you do things that QuarkXPress can't do by itself. For instance, both can export all your text and graphics from a regular XPress document, without reformatting it as a Web document.

More importantly, they can export all your stories and graphics as linear HTML, without page geometry. Unfortunately, at the time of this writing, BeyondPress doesn't work with QuarkXPress 5, 6, or 7, and it's pretty unlikely that Extensis will update it.

Gluon's WebXPress now works in QuarkXPress 7, and it offers a number of other cool features, like XML, eBook format, and Palm HTML export. It can also create a Web page with a table of contents page. This is a great XTension for converting your XPress documents (you don't have to convert your file to a Web layout first).

WEB DOCUMENTS AND FILE STRUCTURE

While people have been writing HTML code by hand for years, the trend is increasingly toward using WYSIWYG ("What You See Is What You Get") editors that write the HTML for you, such as Adobe Dreamweaver or Adobe GoLive. These programs make it easy to add JavaScript and advanced features of HTML, which XPress does not. If you plan to do extensive Web development and site management, you might want to use one of these programs in conjunction with QuarkXPress. For example, you would design the page in XPress, adding the text and graphics, export as HTML, and then modify and manage the page in Dreamweaver.

So, what is the advantage of even using QuarkXPress? First, you can design your Web page using the familiar Text Box and Picture Box tools, and moving the boxes around to your liking. You can even preview the page in a browser before exporting to make sure that your design displays properly. Second, you can easily convert existing XPress content to a Web document.

Setting Up Folders

Before you begin building your site, you need to develop an outline of the site. The outline is similar to a storyboard for a multimedia project or a movie, giving you an idea of the scope of the project and a start for setting up the file structure you need for the site. At a minimum, each site should have a single folder containing your HTML files and images. Depending on the complexity of your site, you may also have subfolders to help you organize the files (see Figure 17-2). Don't put your QuarkXPress documents inside the same folder as the HTML files—it makes it harder to manage them later.

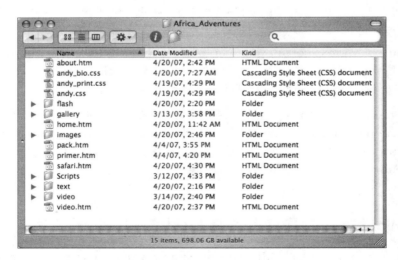

Figure 17-2
Site folder containing HTML pages and folders

It's a good practice to keep all your graphics in one or more folders within your site. For example, within your site folder you would create a subfolder with a name such as "images." You might also want to create separate folders for different areas within the site. For example, you might have a product section, or a series of press releases. Creating separate folders for each of these areas makes it easier to manage the files. Once you create a

Web site, the number of pages within that site seems to grow exponentially in time, so organizing your site before you begin building your pages makes your file maintenance job much easier. When you complete all the pages, you transfer the site folder to the Web server, and then you are ready to go!

> **TIP: Naming Files and Folders.** *Naming your files for use on a Web server is different from naming your files for print. Some Web servers are case-sensitive; some require that you use only lowercase file names. Your best bet is to use lowercase characters for all your files. Here are some other rules to follow:*

- HTML pages need either the .htm or .html extension at the end of the file name. Generally it doesn't matter which extension you use; just be consistent. There are exceptions based on your Web server. Check with your Web Administrator if you are unsure.

- Don't use spaces within your file names. Use the underscore or dash character to simulate a space to separate words. For example, use *info_page.htm* instead of *info page.htm*. The space character is translated to "%20" and some Web browsers have trouble with this sort of thing.

- Use letters and numbers, but not characters such as %, ★, or /.

- Use the same rules for naming folders within the site—use lowercase and don't use spaces. (But don't use a file name extension like .htm or .html in folder names.) If you can, keep your folder and file names as short as possible. The folder name becomes part of the URL (the address of the page). For example, the address of a page might be *http://www.63p.com/foldername/info.htm*.

CREATING WEB PAGES

As I said earlier, Web layouts are totally different than regular print files. To create a new Web document, choose Project from the New submenu (under the File menu; or press Command/Ctrl-N) and choose Web from the Layout Type popup menu. Or, if you already have a project open, you can add a Web layout by selecting New from the Layout menu and picking Web from the Layout Type popup menu. The New Project and New Layout dialog boxes let you define the basic parameters of your Web page (see Figure 17-3). Remember that you can always change these settings later if you want to change your page design. Let's take a look at these settings.

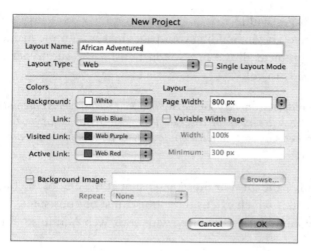

Figure 17-3
The New Web Layout dialog box

> **TIP: Converting to a Web Layout.** *If you have an existing XPress print document, you can use the Layout Properties dialog box (in the Layout menu) to turn it into a Web layout space. I suggest first using the Layout menu to duplicate the print layout, then converting the duplicate into a Web layout. That way, you still have the original print layout space, just in case.*

Because of the differences between Web and print layouts, you need to pay special attention to what happens to your text boxes. Print layouts can contain more text styling options than HTML documents—for example, drop caps, tracking, and kerning. To solve this problem, XPress turns on the Convert to Graphic on Export on all text boxes when you change a print layout into a Web layout. (I cover this feature in "Building the Web Page," later in this chapter.)

This conversion ensures that the resulting Web page resembles your print page as closely as possible, but it means the entire page is a series of graphics. This may or may not be what you want. Remember, graphics take longer to download than text, so people with slow connections may have to wait to see your pages. If you don't want your text to be converted to a graphic, you will later need to turn off this option in the Modify dialog box for each of the text boxes.

Of course, some features (particularly those that are marked with an asterisk in the Edit Style Sheet dialog box) simply have no equivalent in HTML. For example, tabs are not supported in HTML. Any tabs you have in your document are converted to spaces.

Page Width. In the print world, you could create documents as small as a postcard or as large as a poster (four feet square). Your Web pages can be any size, too, but realistically, you're limited to the width of the computer monitor that displays your page. Common screen sizes include 640 x 480, 800 x 600, 1,024 x 768, and 1,600 x 1,200 pixels. People don't usually mind scrolling up and down, but few people like scrolling to the left and right, so your pages need to fit the width of their screens. Your best bet is to pick a size that appeals aesthetically and contributes to onscreen readability. I usually use 800 pixels as the starting point for the page width, though sometimes I go for the lowest common denominator: 600 pixels.

You can also choose Variable Width Page, which means your page can expand or contract as the browser window changes. When you use Variable Width Page, your Web page width is based on a percentage of the width of the browser window—usually between 90 and 100 percent. This may sound appealing, but I find that it usually just gets you in trouble. XPress just doesn't give you enough tools for managing how images and other page elements should flow when the browser window changes. If you're laying out Web pages in XPress, I recommend leaving Page Width set to an absolute value.

Page Colors. You can control the background color of the page, the color of the text, and the color of the links on the page. The default colors are based on standard browser defaults—a white page with black text, blue text hyperlinks, and so on. You can override any of these colors using the popup menus. There are the normal XPress colors, plus ten common Web colors (see the next tip) in the list (see Figure 17-4). However, if you don't like these colors, you can choose New from the list to choose any color you want from XPress's standard Edit Color dialog box (see Chapter 14, *Color*, for more on choosing colors). Any color you create using this "Other" method, shows up in your document's Colors palette, so you can use it there, too.

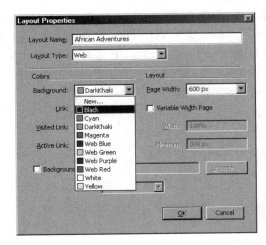

Figure 17-4
Web-safe color popup menu

TIP: Web-Safe Colors in XPress. In the "bad old days," most people had 8-bit color monitors which could only display 256 colors at any one time, and colors would often get dithered (which looked kind of mottled and ugly). In order to counteract this, people tried to pick colors from a palette of 216 "Web-safe" colors, which wouldn't dither on screen. Today, every computer is sold with a 24-bit color card, few colors are ever dithered on screen, and many designers simply choose whatever RGB color they want. However, if you really care about using Web-safe colors, XPress can give 'em to you.

When you have a Web document open, XPress automatically displays a bunch of Web colors in the Colors palette, like Web Navy and Web Maroon. However, these are not necessarily Web-safe colors. If you want to add a Web-safe color to your document, you can select Web Safe Colors from the Model popup menu in the Edit Color dialog box (see Chapter 14, *Color*) for more on how to create and edit colors. Or, use my favorite method.

1.   Pick any RGB color in the Edit Color dialog box.

2.   Change the percentage values in each of the Red, Green, and Blue fields to the nearest 20-percent mark—0, 20, 40, 60, 80, or 100 percent. For instance, if the Red field reads 24 percent, change it to 20 percent. If the Blue field reads 71 percent, change it to 80 percent.

3.   Save the color (you might include "Web safe" in its name to remind you).

That's all there is to it.

Background Image. A background image is generally a small graphic that "tiles" behind the contents of your page by repeating itself to the width and height of the browser window. To add a background image, turn on the Background Image checkbox, and then use the Select or Browse button to direct XPress to your image on the hard disk.

By default, the Repeat popup menu is set to None, which means the image will not be repeated (tiled). This only makes sense when you have a single large image you want behind your Web page. That's pretty rare. Instead, select "Tile" from the Repeat popup menu to repeat the image on the page horizontally and vertically (like the tiles on a bathroom floor). Or you can choose "Horizontal" to repeat the image across only the top of the page, or "Vertical" to repeat the image down the left side of the page.

Setting Up File Paths

Once you have a Web document open, you need to tell QuarkXPress where you're going to be putting your HTML files. The reason has to do with file paths. If XPress doesn't knows where your HTML files will be saved, it cannot correctly create links to graphics or write proper HTML codes for your hyperlinks—the path names would work as you are testing your pages on your local hard drive, but would break when you transfer your HTML files to the Web server. Therefore, it's essential that you take this site management step.

QuarkXPress has pretty limited site management tools, so you have to pay attention to where you put your files. While some other Web programs have sophisticated features to manage HTML and graphic files, XPress offers just two features: Image Export Directory and Site Root Directory. These both live in the General tab of the Preferences dialog box—but only for Web layouts (they're not relevant for regular print layouts; see Figure 17-5).

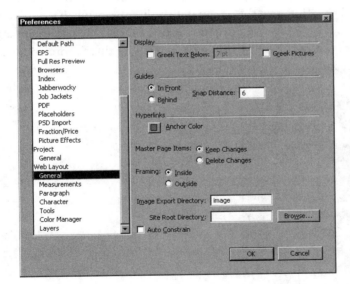

Figure 17-5
Web Layout preferences

Choose Preferences from the Edit menu (or press Command-Option-Shift-Y or Ctrl-Alt-Shift-Y), and select the General category under Web document. First, set the Site Root Directory by clicking Select (Macintosh) or Browse (Windows), to locate the site folder you made on disk. Next, if you have already created a folder (in your site folder) in which you want your graphic files saved, then type the name of this folder for your images in the Image Export Directory field. The default name is "image," but you can change it to whatever you want. If the folder you enter does not yet exist, then XPress creates it when you export your HTML.

If you will be creating a number of XPress Web documents for a single Web site, you can set up the Image Export Directory and the Site Root Directory while no documents are open. This way, the preferences are picked up by all subsequent new Web documents.

> **TIP: Single Document Sites.** *While some folks create a different Web document for each Web page, I find that it makes more sense to keep all or most of a site's pages together in the same document. Each page in the Web document gets saved as a separate HTML file. This way, you can maintain consistency in the look and feel of your pages by using the document's master pages, style sheets, and colors.*

Page Properties

Once you have set up the Web document's file paths, and before you start building the elements on your page, you should take a moment to visit the Page Properties dialog box (choose Page Properties from the Page menu or press Command-Option-Shift-A or Ctrl-Alt-Shift-A; see Figure 17-6). Note that this menu item only appears when you have a Web document open. All the settings you made when you first created the document are displayed in this dialog box (you can change them, too), along with three more options: Page Title, Export File Name, and Meta Tag Set.

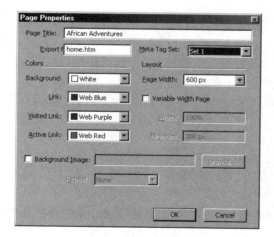

Figure 17-6
The Page Properties dialog box

If you have a multi-page Web document, each page will get exported as a separate HTML document, so you need to open and change the Page Properties dialog box for each and every page.

Page Title. Every HTML page must have a title, which appears in the Web browser window's title bar (see Figure 17-7), and often is listed in Web search engines. If someone bookmarks your Web page in their browser, the title is what appears in their list of bookmarks, so it's important that you type a descriptive word or phrase into the Page Title field of the Page Properties dialog box. If you forget to title the page, it is left blank, which—to be blunt—looks dumb and unprofessional.

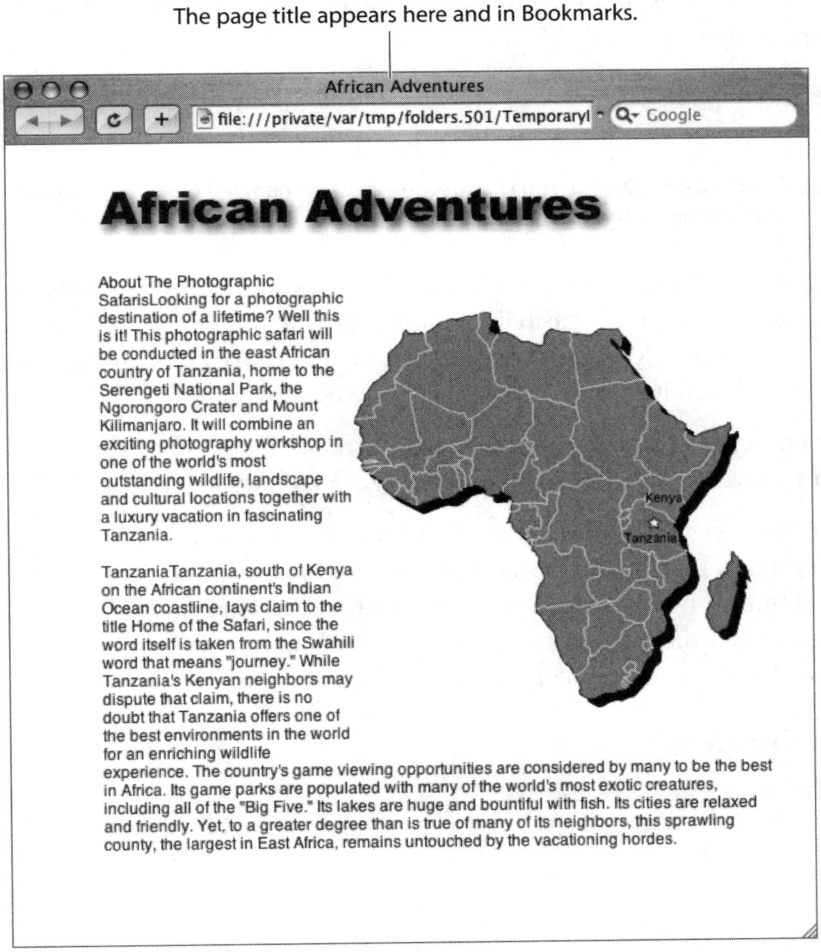

The page title appears here and in Bookmarks.

Figure 17-7 The page title appears in the browser window.

Export File Name. The Export File Name option is where you set the file name for the HTML file that XPress creates when you export to HTML. (See "TIP: Naming Files and Folders," earlier in this chapter for more on how to name HTML files.) If you don't enter a name, XPress creates file names such as Export1.htm, Export2.htm, and so on. Trust me, these are not good names for your HTML pages!

By the way, if you enter a file name without a three-letter extension, XPress adds ".htm" to the file name. If you want the ".html" extension or some other extension instead, enter the full name in the Export File Name field.

If you have a multi-page Web document, make sure that the Export File Name is different for each page.

> **TIP: Quick Name Changes.** You can change the export file name of the page in the Page Layout palette. Just select the name and then type the name you want.

Meta Tags. Many search engines use meta tags for keywords and descriptions of the page. If you want to increase the probability of users finding your page, you should always include some meta tags. Meta tags are one of those things that can't hurt and may help a user find your page, so it is worth the time it takes to set them up.

Applying meta tags to your document is a two-step process: First you have to create a meta tag set, and then you use Page Properties to apply the tags to the Web page.

1. Choose Meta Tags from the Edit menu. Here, you can either edit the default "Set 1" or define a new one (see Figure 17-8). Unless you are very familiar with the meta tag format, I think it is easier just to edit the default set. Later, if you want to create more sets (perhaps for different pages in your site), you can duplicate this set or create a new one. Go ahead and name the sets anything you want.

Figure 17-8
The Meta Tags dialog box

2. After selecting a set and clicking Edit, select the first line in the Edit Meta Tag Set dialog box (the one called "keywords"; see Figure 17-9), and then click Edit. Type a series of words or phrases, separated by commas, in the Content text area. Enter all the words or combination of words that a user might enter in a search engine to locate your page. Try to think outside the box. For example, if you offered services using QuarkXPress you might enter something like: Quark, QuarkXPress, XPress, Quark Xpress, Quark Express, and any other variations of the spelling of the name that someone might use.

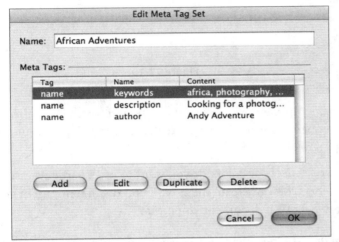

Figure 17-9
The Edit Meta Tag Set dialog box

3. Click OK, then select the second line ("description") and click Edit (or just double-click on the line). Enter a short (a sentence or so) description about the contents of the page in the Content field. Then click OK.

4. If you want, you can add more meta tags by clicking the New button, selecting an option from the Meta Tag popup menu, selecting a type of meta tag from the Name popup menu, and then typing the value of the meta tag in the Content field. For

instance, you might select "name" from the Meta Tag popup menu, "author" from the Name popup menu, and then type your name in the Content field. When you export the HTML, this information is saved at the beginning of the HTML file, so people looking at the HTML code will see your name (see Figure 17-10).

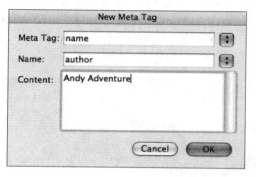

Figure 17-10
Adding custom meta tags

5. When you're done setting up the meta tag set, click OK and Save to save the set in your document. Then open the Page Properties dialog box and choose your set from the Meta Tag Set popup menu.

Meta tag sets act just like style sheets or colors: If you want to use a particular set of meta tags in a bunch of documents, you can create them while no documents are open. Then they'll be available in every new Web document you create.

> **TIP: Learning More About Meta Tags.** *There are over a dozen cool meta tags that Web browsers understand. Most of these are listed in the Name popup menu when you click Add in the Edit Meta Tag Set dialog box. For instance, you can choose "name" from the Meta Tag popup menu, "copyright" from the Name popup menu, and in the Content field, type something like: "© 2007 Eddie Poole" (without the quotation marks). The © is HTML code for "display the copyright symbol," although because it's a meta tag, nothing is displayed anyway.*

Similarly, you can use the ROBOTS meta tag to stop the little programs called robots or spiders that many search engines use to find new Web pages they can add to the database. If you don't want your page added (perhaps it contains private information, or is simply a listing of products), you can use meta tags to tell the robots to go away. Create a new meta tag in your meta tag set; choose "name" from the Meta Tag popup menu, "ROBOTS" from the Name popup menu, and then type "noindex" in the Content field (don't include the quotation marks, of course). If you create a similar meta tag but with "nofollow" in the Content field, then robots and spiders won't follow any of the links that are listed on that Web page.

To find out more about meta tags and what sort of values you can use, look at *www.webreference.com* or some other online HTML guide.

BUILDING THE WEB PAGE

Once you define the properties for your Web page, you are ready to start drawing text and picture boxes and importing your content. The Web layout looks similar to a print layout within XPress, though the ruler is set to pixels and you'll see the Web Tools palette under the regular Tool palette. (If you don't see this palette, select Show Web Tools from the Tools submenu, under the Window menu.) These tools are for creating forms and drawing image maps, which are covered later in this chapter.

You can use almost every feature in XPress to build your Web page, though some features are grayed out because HTML doesn't support them. For instance, you cannot rotate a text box because there's no such thing as rotated text in HTML. However, if you choose to convert the text box to a graphic (see "Converting Text to a Graphic," below) then suddenly you can rotate it. Similarly, you can put text on a Bézier line, but XPress will automatically convert the object to a graphic upon export.

Text Boxes

Here are some other restrictions to creating text boxes in Web documents.

- The box must be rectangular. If you create any other shape, XPress converts the box (and the text inside it) to a graphic.

- You cannot apply fractional point sizes to text. If you enter a fractional size, XPress rounds the point size to the nearest whole size. For example, 12.5 points becomes 13 points.

- Text runaround is turned off for all text boxes unless you convert them to a graphic (see the next section).

- You cannot link text boxes across pages. In fact, when you are in a Web document, you can only view one page at a time, and the Pasteboard is not available. This is an icky limitation, and I'm hoping that they'll let you do this in future versions of the program.

If you set up your documents to have a variable page width, you also need to turn on the Make Variable Width checkbox (on the Text tab of the Modify dialog box; see Figure 17-11) for each text box that you want to stretch when the Web browser window changes width.

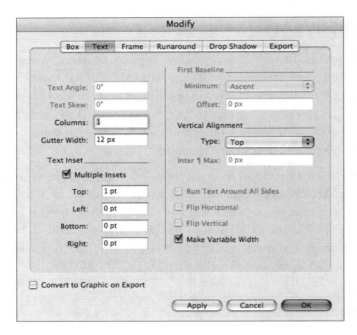

Figure 17-11
Make Variable Width option in the Modify dialog box

Converting Text to a Graphic

As I said earlier, character formatting and text box attributes that are not supported in HTML—such as kerning, tracking, baseline shift, and so on—are disabled in Web documents. If you want to include any of those features, you first need to convert the text box to a graphic. Select the text box and then choose Modify from the Item menu (or press Command/Ctrl-M). Then, turn on the Convert to Graphic on Export checkbox in the Modify dialog box (see Figure 17-12).

Once that option is checked, then all typographic controls are enabled for that text box. As the feature's name indicates, this doesn't convert your text box to a graphic until you export the HTML. After you turn on this option, you can tell XPress how you want to export the graphic, that is, what file format, color palette, alternate text, and so on.

GIF or JPEG. By default, when you turn on the Convert to Graphic on Export checkbox, QuarkXPress converts the text box as a GIF image. This is almost always a better choice for text than JPEG. GIF is suited for text and line art with solid colors, and JPEG is best for photos and continuous tone graphics. However, you can change the file format in the Export tab of the Modify dialog box (see Figure 17-13), if you really want to. A third option, PNG, is not fully supported by all browsers (especially in earlier versions), so I usually avoid it. (If you want to know more about these file formats, check out one of the many other books on the market that discuss Web graphic file formats, including a book I coauthored, Peachpit's *Real World Photoshop*.)

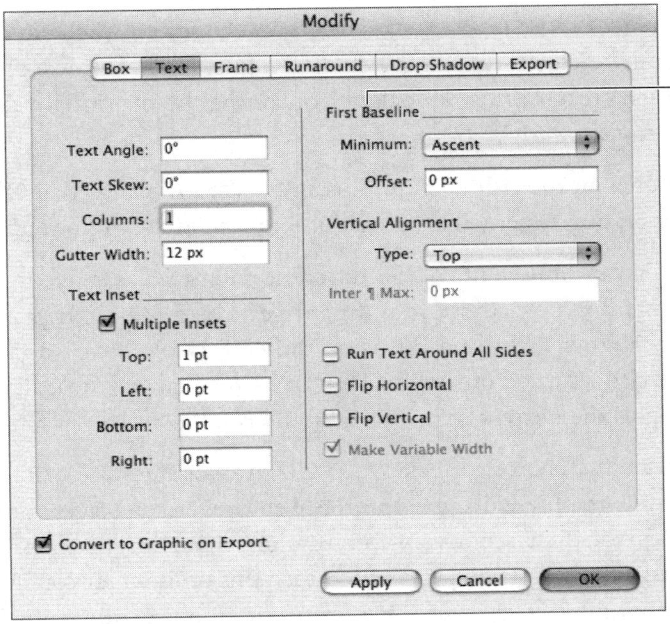

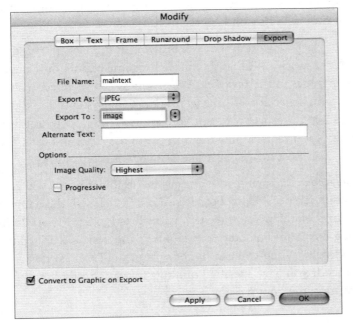

Features such as First Baseline become active when Convert to Graphic is on.

Figure 17-12
Modify dialog box with Convert to Graphic on Export turned on.

Figure 17-13
Export tab

Color Palettes. When you select GIF as the export format, you can choose among the Web-safe palette, a system palette, or the Adaptive palette in the Export tab of the Modify dialog box. As I mentioned earlier, the Web-safe colors will not dither on 8-bit color monitors, but there are very few of those types of screens around anymore. While in the "old" days I would have recommended always using Web-safe colors, today I almost always use the Adaptive palette, which creates a custom palette containing the majority of the colors in your text, whether or not they are Web-safe colors.

The two other color palettes in the Palette popup menu—Windows and Mac OS—limit your colors to the one operating system. These are dumb; pretend they're not even there.

By the way, because GIFs can only contain 256 different colors, XPress needs to know what to do with colors that don't exactly fit into the image's color palette. If you turn on the Dithering checkbox, XPress will use a diffusion dither for colors that don't fit the palette exactly. If you leave this turned off (which is what I almost always do), all colors in the exported graphic snap to the nearest color that is in the palette.

Use Interlacing. You have the choice to make your GIF images interlace or not. When you turn on Interlacing, the graphic will appear in the Web browser in stages, almost like a venetian blind opening. You first see a very-low-resolution version, then it becomes increasingly more detailed. The only time you want to turn this on is when you have a relatively large image that is used for navigation. That is, turn it on if it would really help the viewer to see a low-resolution version as quickly as possible. I leave it off for most images. Having it on makes your file size a tiny bit larger.

Alternate Text. Alternate Text displays in the Web browser in three cases: when the user rolls over an image, if the browser can't find the image for some reason, or if the user has disabled the viewing of graphics in the browser. Alternate text is also an accessibility feature: The alternate text you enter for an image is spoken in systems for the visually impaired. Not all images need alternate text, but you should always include this text for graphics that are important for understanding the purpose of the page, and for any navigation buttons on the page. For most images, just one or two words will suffice.

Export To. The default folder for saving your images is the folder name you created in the General panel of the Preferences dialog box. If you did not change the name, XPress uses the name "image" for the folder. You'll see that name listed in the Export To fields of the Export Modify dialog box. You can enter a new folder name for the selected image by typing a new name in the field. When you export your page as HTML, XPress creates the folder in the root directory. If you have specified multiple folders already, you'll see all the folder names (up to seven) in the popup menu.

TIP: Use Photoshop Instead. Now that you know how to convert text to a graphic in XPress, I am going to recommend that you use a graphics program such as Adobe Photoshop or Adobe Fireworks to create your graphics instead. Even though XPress gives you tremendous control over your type, it has limitations for exporting text as an image. First, you can't create anti-aliased text. For graphic headings, the smooth edges that anti-aliasing produces makes for better looking text on the screen. In Photoshop, you can wrap the text to give the appearance of text on a path. In Fireworks, you can attach text directly to a path.

Defining CSS Font Families

Of course, you probably don't want to convert all your text boxes to graphics. If you don't make the text boxes into images, when choosing fonts for your Web layout you'll need to pick a font that is available to your users. You might love your specially designed typeface for your print job, but you need to stick to common fonts for your Web projects. To control the font usage in your document, you can define a set of fonts that will be used if the original font is not available on the user's machine. For example, you might use Futura as the font for a heading, but if the person looking at your Web page doesn't have Futura, then you should specify a second (maybe Helvetica) or third (maybe Arial) choice. This is called making a CSS font family. It's easy (see Figure 17-14).

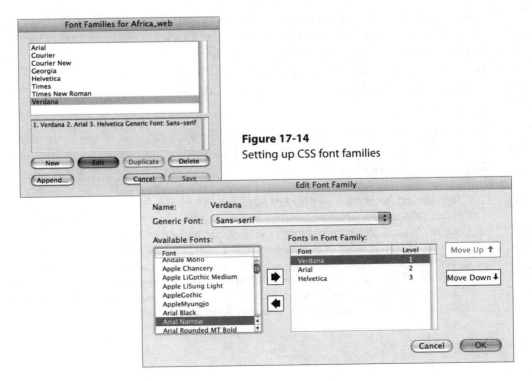

Figure 17-14
Setting up CSS font families

1. Choose CSS Font Families from the Edit menu, then click New.

2. Choose the font you want to use as the primary font from the Available Font list and then click the right arrow to move it to the Font Family list.

3. Add alternate fonts to the list in the same manner.

4. Finally, choose a generic font from the Generic Font popup menu (like Serif or Sans Serif). That "font" will be used if none of the other fonts in your list are available.

You can use the up or down arrows to change the order of the fonts in the list. Use the left arrow to remove a font from the list.

Picture Boxes

When you create pages for print, you typically import either TIFF or EPS graphics. You can import those file types into a Web layout, too, and XPress converts those files to either GIF or JPEG when you export the page. Unfortunately, you don't get as much control over the conversion process as you do in Photoshop or Fireworks. For instance, you can't optimize the image to reduce its file size, and you're limited to QuarkXPress's default optimization settings.

The only settings you can change are in the Export tab of the Modify dialog box (select the picture box and press Command/Ctrl-M). If you choose JPEG, you can select the image quality, but you have no way to preview the final results until you view the page in the browser. In comparison, Photoshop and Fireworks let you preview the results of your optimization choices and tweak the settings to get the best combination of both file size and image quality.

As with text boxes, you can choose the folder for exporting the image in the picture box. Choose an existing folder name from the Export To popup menu, or type a new folder name in the Export To field.

> **TIP: Use Full Resolution on Your EPS Files.** Sure, XPress can automatically convert your document's TIFF and EPS pictures into GIF or JPEG files upon export. However, because EPS graphics contain "encapsulated" data, XPress can't really get in and convert them properly, so you end up with GIF or JPEG versions of the low-resolution screen previews you see in XPress. Yuck! If you're going to repurpose your XPress pages, make sure you change the Preview Resolution on each EPS graphic to Full Resolution (see more on this in Chapter 2, QuarkXPress Basics) or stick with TIFF files. (Though to be painfully honest, you'll often get a better result if you convert images yourself in Photoshop and import them into XPress as GIF or JPEG.)

TIP: Don't Crop GIFs and JPEGs. *If you use another program such as Photoshop or Fireworks to create your GIF or JPEG images, make sure the picture box you draw for the image is the exact size as the image (or larger than the image). That way, XPress just uses the original GIF or JPEG image. However, if you rotate, scale, or crop the image in any way, XPress has to re-export the image with the settings in the Export tab of the Modify dialog box. That means further image degradation, and often larger image sizes (XPress doesn't do as good a job at compressing as Photoshop and Fireworks do). You can ensure the picture box is the same size as the picture by using the Fit Box to Picture feature in the Style menu.*

TIP: Be Careful with Transparency. *You can import a TIFF image with an embedded clipping path into a Web document and use the Clipping feature to make the background appear transparent (see Chapter 11, Image Tuning, for more on clipping paths). However, when you export your page as HTML, you need to be careful. The GIF format handles transparency like this just fine, but JPEG does not (there's no such thing as transparent pixels in a JPEG image). So, if your TIFF is being exported as a JPEG, XPress has to fake the effect by merging whatever is behind the image into the image itself. If the image is on top of a flat colored background, it usually works okay (though there may be some color shift). If it's on top of a pattern or text or another image, then watch out! In some cases, the result is pretty icky (see Figure 17-15).*

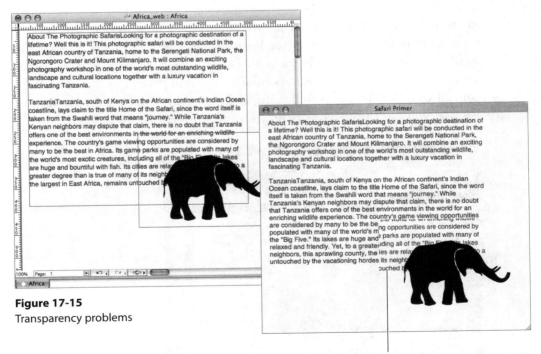

Figure 17-15
Transparency problems

When it comes to HTML, you should never trust that what you see in XPress will be what you get in a Web browser!

Note that what was transparent is now opaque, obscuring some of the text.

Tables and Lines

While lines are always automatically converted into graphics when you export HTML, a table made with the Table tool can be a graphic or a regular HTML table. The difference, like text boxes, determines what you can do with the tables. For example, you cannot use dashes or dotted lines for the table grid unless you turn on the Convert Table to Graphic on Export checkbox in the Modify dialog box.

PREVIEWING YOUR PAGES

As you build your Web pages, you'll want to preview them in a Web browser, because what you see in your XPress document is not necessarily the way it'll look in the browser. Plus, not all browsers display the page the same way, so you might want to see the page in several different browsers.

First, you need to let XPress know what browsers you have and which one you want to use as the default. Choose Preferences from the QuarkXPress application menu (Mac OS X) or the Edit menu (Windows), or press Command-Option-Shift-Y (Ctrl-Alt-Shift-Y) and then select the Browsers panel (see Figure 17-16). You may see a browser listed in the Available Browsers list if XPress located your default browser when you installed the application. If not, click the Add button, then locate a Web browser on your hard drive. Add all your Web browsers to this list, and then select the Default checkbox next to the browser you want as the primary browser (the one you use most often).

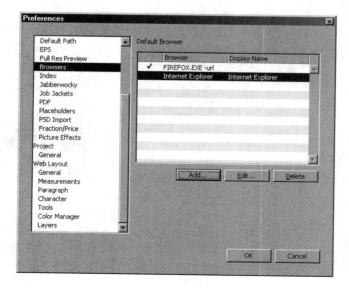

Figure 17-16
Adding browsers to the preferences

Then, to preview your document in a Web browser before you actually export it, click the HTML Preview button near the bottom corner of the document window. You may see a brief message explaining the page is being exported as HTML, and then your default browser is opened and the page is displayed. If you want to preview the page in one of your other browsers, press and hold down the HTML Preview button, and then choose another browser from the popup menu (see Figure 17-17). This Preview HTML menu is also available in the context-sensitive menu (Control-click on Macintosh, right-button click on Windows).

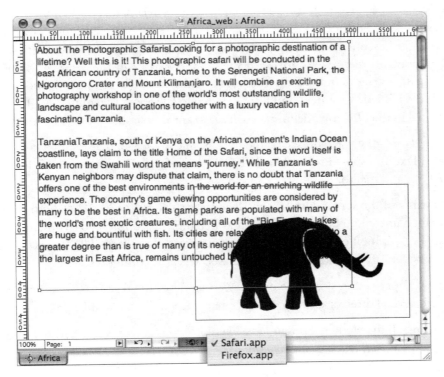

Figure 17-17 Popup menu from HTML Preview button

Note that when you preview your page in the browser, your local links (links to other Web pages on your hard drive) won't work. You'll have to wait until you export your page to check the links. Links to other pages in this document will work.

> **TIP: Refresh the Page.** *If you make changes to a graphic on the page, such as cropping or changing the box size, the new image may not appear properly the next time you preview the page in the Web browser. Generally, pressing the Refresh button loads the new graphic properly. If not, quit the browser and try to preview again.*

HYPERLINKS

What is a Web page without links? Links let your users explore your site, jumping from Web page to Web page. You can also add links to files that your users can download, or you can add links to send an email. Links can also be added to take your users to another site all together.

About URLs

A hyperlink uses a URL to link you to somewhere. (URL stands for Uniform Resource Locator, an awkward name but descriptive of what it stands for.) The URL provides a standard method of locating something on the Internet. You can think of it as the linked item's address. The URL contains the method to access the item, the name of the server or domain, the directory path to the item, and the file name of the item. (It can also include a named anchor in the HTML document, but I'm not going to talk about that quite yet.) These items are separated in the URL by a delimiter such as a comma, a slash, a colon, or a number sign.

- The *method* is the way you access the item. On a Web page, that method is the HyperText Transport Protocol, or HTTP. Some of the other methods are FTP, HTTPS, and mailto.

- The name of the server could be an IP address such as 129.30.104.4 and the domain name could be in a form such as mycompany.com, mygovernment.gov, or myorganization.org. The domain name is normally preceded by "www.", but it can be left off depending on how the Web server is configured.

- The directory is the path name on the Web server of the resource. If an item is located several directories deep, the path name might look like this: products/images/.

A URL using all the elements might look like this:
http://www.mycompany.com/products/home.htm.

> *TIP: Use Relative Links. Not all the URL components need to be included when you specify a hyperlink. For example, if you are linking to a page that resides in the same directory as the page you're linking from, you can simply type the name of the linked file. For example, instead of typing the super-long URL http://www.moo.com/products/cows/prices.htm, you could just type prices.htm (as long as the two Web pages are in the same directory). This is called using a relative URL—a Web address that is specified relative to the current document.*

Anytime you leave out the method (the *http://* part, for instance), the Web browser assumes that you're using a relative URL. So, if you type */fish/index.html* the Web browser looks for a file called *index.html* inside a directory called *fish* inside the same directory that the current Web page is in.

When specifying relative URLs, you can also use the "../" (period period slash) format to indicate "the directory that contains the directory this document is currently in." For example, *../dogs/prices.htm* means "the file called *prices.htm* that is inside the folder *dogs* which is inside the *products* folder" (which contains both *cows* and *dogs*). This seems really complex at first, but once you use it a few times it's really logical; and it's good to get in the habit of using relative URLs like this instead of absolute URLs, whenever possible.

The Hyperlinks Palette

The Hyperlinks palette (see Figure 17-18) is where you create the links for your page, and also apply them to text and pictures. Choose Hyperlinks from the Window menu to access the palette. Once the palette is open, making a hyperlink is easy.

Figure 17-18
The Hyperlinks palette

1. Click the New Hyperlink button (at the top left, it looks like a chain link) in the Hyperlinks palette.

2. Type a name for your link. This name is internal to your XPress document only and displays in the Hyperlinks palette.

3. Choose the type of link from the Type popup. Your choices here are: URL, Page, or Anchor. The dialog box changes based on which option you choose from the list. I cover the Anchor type later in this chapter.

   If you choose URL, then type the URL for the link. There's a popup menu to the right of the URL field that lists several common methods for the URL (see Figure 17-19). You can either use those or type them yourself (they're just there to save you some typing). This popup menu also lists the other hyperlinks in the palette; this is useful if you want to make a new link similar to an earlier one you made.

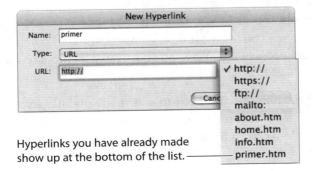

Hyperlinks you have already made show up at the bottom of the list.

Figure 17-19
Making a new hyperlink

If you have multiple pages in your document, you can easily link to other pages in your document. Choose Page from the Type popup menu, and then choose the page you want for the link from the Page popup menu.

4. Optionally, you can add a target for your link in the Target field or select one of the preset targets from the popup menu to the right of the field. The target is the window you want the link to open in. Your options here are: none, _blank, _self, _parent, or _top. Blank opens a new browser window, self and none replace the current page with the new page. Parent and top are used when your page contains frames. If you type any other word in the Target field, the Web browser will open a new window and name it whatever you typed; the name doesn't appear on screen anywhere, but if you later use that target again, the Web browser knows which window you're talking about.

    *Tip: **Add a Target.** To add a target to either text or a graphic, select the object first, then click New from the Hyperlinks palette. If you click New when nothing is selected, the target field is not available. You are then adding a link that can be used for a variety of objects. Selecting the object first applies the link and the target (if wanted) to just the selected object.*

5. Click OK.

If text, a picture box, or a line was selected when you made your new hyperlink, the link is automatically applied to that text or object. Otherwise you have to apply it manually. If you want to create a hyperlink that you'll use later and don't want to apply it to anything right now, then make sure nothing is selected on your page.

    *TIP: **Show Your Links.** When viewing the Hyperlink palette you can choose to see either the name of the link or the actual link. Use the Show popup menu to choose either Name or Link. You can also isolate the type of links you want to display in the palette. Click each icon (URL, Anchor, or Pages) to show or hide those types of links.*

Applying Hyperlinks. Once you add your links to the Hyperlinks palette you can begin creating links on the page. Links can be added to text, images, or lines. To apply a hyperlink, select the word, phrase or image on the page, and then click the link in the Hyperlinks palette. If you selected an image for the link, a small link icon is added to the top right part of the picture box. If you selected text for the link, it is underlined and changed to the link color. (The link color was defined when you created your Web document or else it was set with Page Properties.)

Editing and deleting Hyperlinks. If you need to edit the hyperlink, select the link in the Hyperlinks palette (make sure nothing is selected, or this will apply the hyperlink) and then click the Edit button (it looks like a pencil). You can also Command/Ctrl-click on the hyperlink to edit it.

If you want to delete a link from the palette, select it, then click the Delete Hyperlink button. If you're just trying to remove the link from some text or an object, you need to select that text or object name in the Hyperlinks palette first (you can just select the text or object on the page, too), and then click the Delete Hyperlink button. That removes the hyperlink from that object.

> **TIP: Contextual Hyperlinks.** *You can also add, edit, and remove hyperlinks in the Hyperlink submenu in the context-sensitive menu (Control-click on the text on the Mac; right-button click on Windows). This is often much faster than managing links in the Hyperlinks palette.*

> **TIP: Reapplying Hyperlinks.** *When you select an object or some text on your page that has a hyperlink, it gets highlighted in the Hyperlinks palette. To remove the hyperlink, just click the Delete Hyperlink button in the palette. To apply a different hyperlink, just click a different link in the palette. Or, alternately, Command/Ctrl-click the object's name in the palette (the part that is already highlighted) and choose a different URL (either type a new one in or select one from the popup menu).*

Creating Named Anchors

Creating a link to a new page is easy: you just link to the URL of the page. When the user clicks the link, the top of the new page is displayed. But what if there is much more information on the Web page than can fit on one screen? How do you jump to a specific section within a long page? The trick is using named anchors. A named anchor is invisible HTML code that can be inserted on a page. Once there's an anchor in place, you can link to that page *and* that anchor. When the user clicks the link, the browser jumps to the page and then jumps down to the anchor.

You can have as many anchors on your page as you want. And you can link to the anchor from within the same page, or you can link to the anchor from another page.

Using named anchors is a two-step process. First, you create the anchor, and then you create the link to the anchor. To create the anchor, place the cursor in some text (preferably at the beginning of a paragraph) or select a picture box or line. Then, click the New Anchor button in the Hyperlinks palette (it looks like an anchor or—if you squint—a smiling cyclops). A pink arrow covers the first letter if you were in a text box; an anchor icon is added to the image or line if you had one of those selected. The Hyperlinks palette adds the anchor to the list (see Figure 17-20).

Figure 17-20
A named anchor in the Hyperlinks palette

Once the anchor is created, you can add the link: Select some text, a picture box, or a line and then click the anchor name in the Hyperlinks palette.

This works as long as the named anchor is on the same page or in the same document as the link. If you're linking to a named anchor in some HTML file that isn't being generated from this document, then you'll need to write out the URL and add the name of the anchor preceded by a number sign. For example, if the named anchor was on a page named *info.htm*, and the anchor name was *staff*, then the link would be: *info.htm#staff*.

ROLLOVER IMAGES

Web page designers love rollovers. A *rollover* is an image on a Web page that changes in some way when the user moves the cursor over it. For example, it may appear to change color or shape; maybe it lights up to indicate that it's a hotspot. Then, when the cursor is moved away, the image returns to its original form. A rollover indicates interactivity to the user, usually signifying a link to another page. XPress 7 includes both single-position, "basic" rollovers and two-position rollovers. I cover the latter in the next section.

Before adding a rollover to your XPress document, you need to create the graphics for each state of the rollover: the original image on the page (the "off" state), and the image you see when the cursor is over the image (the "on" state). You can use programs like Adobe Photoshop or Adobe Fireworks to create the two rollover images. Actually, in those programs you can even create a four-state rollover (the other two states involve what happens when you actually click on the image), but XPress only supports a simple rollover with two images.

You should probably put these images in the same folder where you're keeping your Web graphics (like your images folder). You can save these images in any normal file format XPress can read (TIFF, JPEG, GIF, EPS, and so on)—XPress will convert non-Web formats to GIF or JPEG upon export—but if you know these images are going to be used for rollovers, I suggest saving them as GIF or JPEG in the first place.

Creating the rollover. Once you have both images on disk, you're ready to create the rollover in XPress. First, draw a picture box and import your graphic. I suggest you use the Fit Box to Picture feature in the Style menu (or in the context-sensitive menu) to ensure the box size is exactly the same as the picture. (This was imperative in XPress 5, but is only suggested in version 6 and 7.)

Next, choose Create Rollover from the Basic Rollover submenu (under the Item menu) to open the Rollover dialog box (see Figure 17-21). Here, you have a choice as to how to import the two rollover images.

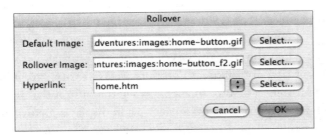

Figure 17-21
The Rollover dialog box

- You can use the Select (Macintosh) or Browse (Windows) buttons to locate the on state images on disk (what XPress calls the Rollover state). You can also set the off ("default") state in this dialog box if you got excited and jumped into this dialog box before using Get Picture.

- You can also just click OK without setting the Default and Rollover state images in the dialog box. In this case, to set the rollover image, select Rollover Image from the Basic Rollover submenu (under the Item menu). The default image should be replaced by an empty picture box, which you can fill using Get Picture, just like any other picture box. To switch back to the default image, choose Default Image from the same submenu.

Finally, if the rollover is to be a hyperlink, you can type the link in the Create Rollover dialog box, or tell XPress where to find the HTML file (if it's already on disk). If you forget this step you can just use the Hyperlinks palette to apply a hyperlink later. (As usual, there are several ways to do the same thing in XPress.)

If you later want to change your rollover image back to a regular picture, you can select Remove Rollover from the Basic Rollover submenu (under the Item menu). Similarly, you can edit the rollover by choosing Edit Rollover.

> **TIP: Rollover with Context.** *The Create Rollover, Edit Rollover, and Remove Rollover commands also live in the context-sensitive menu. If you Control-click (Macintosh) or right-click (Windows) on a rollover picture box, XPress gives you the option to edit or remove the rollover. Otherwise, it lets you turn the box into a rollover. This also lets you switch your view from Default Image to Rollover Image, so you can see them. (You couldn't do this in version 5, which was a real pain in the behind.)*

Two-Position Rollovers

Now that you understand basic rollovers, you can move on to what XPress calls a two-position rollover. Everyone calls these things something different, but here is what happens. In a basic rollover, a new image replaces the original image when a user moves the mouse pointer over the original image. In a two-position rollover, a separate image elsewhere on the page is replaced when the user rolls over the original image. Let's say you have navigation buttons on your page for linking to product pages in your site. When the user rolls over each button, you want a picture to appear *below* the button that represents the linked page. For example, a button for the shoes page would display a picture of some shoes; the button for watches would display a picture of a watch, and so on.

As with basic rollovers, you need to create the two images you want to use as the rollover images. Again, both images need to be the exact same size as the picture box. Let's say you have a grayscale and a color version of the same image. Here is how you can create the two-position rollover that swaps them.

1. Draw a text box and type "Show Color Photo" into it. Format the text and the text box to your liking. (Of course, you could also create a button in Photoshop that says the same thing and import the button into a picture box. If you do that, skip step 2.)

2. Check Convert to Graphic in the Modify dialog box for this text box.

3. Draw a picture box elsewhere on the page and import the grayscale image into it. This picture is the one that displays as the page loads.

4. With the picture box still selected, choose Create 2-Position Target from the 2-Position Rollovers submenu (under the Item menu). Don't panic. Your original image disappears, and you see a target icon in the top right corner of the box.

5. Import the second picture (the color one, in this example) into the picture box. You now have two pictures contained in the same picture box (though you can only see one at a time).

6. From the Web Tools palette, select the Rollover Linking tool. Click the text box with the Rollover Linking tool, and then click the picture box. This action links the two boxes together.

Finally, preview the page in a browser to test the rollovers: You should see your text button and the grayscale image. When you move the cursor over the text button, the image in the picture box switches to the color image. Cool, eh?

Viewing the rollover images. XPress displays the first image in your picture box. If you want to see the rollover image instead, choose it from the Show submenu (in the 2-Position Rollovers submenu under the Item menu or in the context-sensitive menu).

Removing the target image. If you decide you want to remove the rollover action, select the target image, and then choose Remove Target from the 2-Position Rollovers submenu (under the Item menu or in the context-sensitive menu). Select the image name that appears when you select the submenu. Once you remove the target image, the rollover no longer works.

> **TIP: Appearing and Disappearing.** You don't have to have an image in the picture box in either the default or the rollover state when creating basic or two-position rollovers. For example, you could leave the default position blank (no picture imported) and just put a picture in the rollover state. In this case, when the cursor rolls over the trigger (either the rollover itself or the link to the two-position rollover), the image suddenly appears out of nowhere!

CASCADING MENUS

Cascading menus are menus that pop up when the user moves the mouse pointer over them. The advantage to using them is that you can squeeze a lot of links into a small amount of space. If you are not sure as to how they work, check out the *www.quark.com* page. As you move over the Products button, for example, a menu "cascades" down, listing all of the Quark products.

Once you create the cascading menus, you then attach them to either a text or picture box. (Though if you use a text box, you must turn on the option to export the contents as a graphic.)

Creating the Menus

Before you can place a cascading menu on your Web page, you have to create the menus. Choose Cascading Menus from the Edit menu and then click New to create the first menu.

Formatting the menu. The Menu Properties tab of the Edit Cascading Menu dialog box lets you specify what the cascading menu will look like and how it will act. Type a name for your menu and choose from the options in the Menu Properties tab of the dialog box to format your menu (see Figure 17-22).

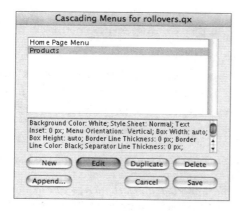

Figure 17-22
Creating a cascading menu, part 1

- **Background Color.** Choose a color from the popup menu to define the color of the menus. This menu is just like the popup menu for choosing the background color of your page.

- **Style Sheet.** To control the look of the text in the menu, you can define a character style sheet for the text. All character style sheets you have previously defined display in the popup menu.

- **Text Inset.** Just like text inset for a text box, the Text Inset option moves the text the amount you specify from the left side of the menu.

- **Menu Orientation.** Choose Vertical to drop the menu down from the bottom of the box, choose Horizontal to push the menu from the right side of the box.

- **Box Size.** The default setting for Box Size is Auto, which uses the contents of the largest menu item to control the size of the menu. If you are not happy with the menu size, you can enter your own values.

- **Border.** Choose the outside border size and color for the menu. Set the value to zero if you don't want a border around your menu.

- **Separator.** Choose the size and color for the separator line between the items in the menu.

- **Opening Animation.** You can choose the animation direction for the menu (which direction it moves) from the popup menu: Top to Bottom, Bottom to Top, Left to Right, or Right to Left.

- **Speed.** If you choose an option other than None from the Opening Animation direction, you can then choose the speed (in milliseconds) of the menu animation. If you enter zero, there is no time delay between the time the user moves over the menu and when it displays. (Don't make this number too large or else your users will think the menu isn't responding.)

- **Offset.** By default, the cascading menu appears at the same position as the box where it is attached. This means that the first item in the menu covers the text or picture box. Generally, you will want your menus to appear either below (for vertical menus) or to the left or right (for horizontal menus) of the attached box. Use the Measurements palette to determine the height of the box (for vertical menus) and type that value in the Y field. If you are using horizontal menus, type the width of the box in the X field. Then, your menus appear either below or to the side of the box.

Adding menu items. Once you've told XPress how you want the cascading menu to look and behave, select the Menu Items tab in the Edit Cascading Menus dialog box to add the menu items (see Figure 17-23). First, choose Menu Item from the New popup button to create a new item in your menu. Type the text you want to appear in the Menu Item Name field and then enter a link in the Hyperlink field. If you want to add a submenu to one of your menu items, select the item and then choose Submenu Item from the New popup button. Add the name and link for that item as you did for the menu item.

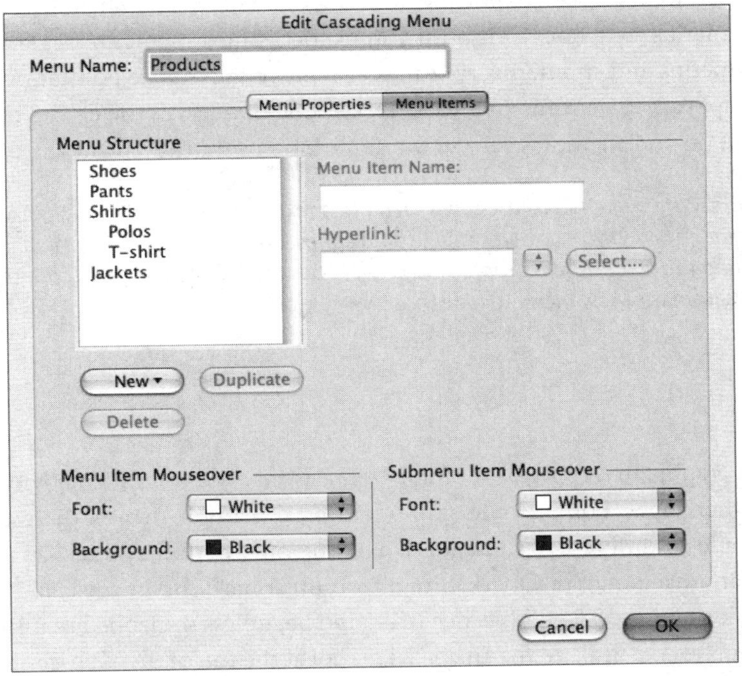

Figure 17-23
Creating a cascading menu, part 2

Note that there is no good way to change the order of the items in your menus other than deleting them and adding them again in the right order, so plan out your menus before you start adding the items.

The other options in the Menu Items tab of the Edit Cascading Menu dialog box are options to change the background color and font color of the menus and submenus as the users move the cursor over them. Generally, you'll want to change the background color of the menus to give your users visual feedback as to which menu item is selected. Of course, you would want to choose a contrasting color to the background for the font color. Again, the color popup menus are the same as other color menus.

Attaching the Menus

Once you create the cascading menus, then you can attach them to either a picture box or a text box. However, as I noted earlier, if you use a text box, you must first turn on the Convert to Graphic on Export option (in the Modify dialog box). Select the box, choose Cascasding Menu from the Item menu (or the context-sensitive menu), then select the menu you want to use from the submenu list.

Cascading menus, like the other Web interactive elements, don't work in XPress. To test your menus, click the Preview in HTML button at the bottom of the document window or export the HTML to disk (see "Exporting Your Page as HTML," later in this chapter). Your links on the menus may not work until you export your document, but you should be able to see the menus and submenus appear as you move the mouse pointer over them. By the way, there appears to be some bug in XPress's code that leaves the cascading menus visible if you scroll on and then off them without clicking in the Web browser.

> **TIP: Hide Visuals.** When you add a cascading menu to a text box, a small icon (looks like a sub-menu) appears in the box. If you have a small text box, the icon for the cascading menu plus the icon for converting the text box to a graphic may cover your text. To see your text, choose Hide Visual Indicators from the View menu to hide those pesky icons.

IMAGE MAPS

An image map is a graphic that contains multiple hotspots that add user interactivity, usually as hyperlinks to other pages. For example, you might have a simple map of the world, and want to direct people to different Web pages depending on where they click on the map. In order to make an image map in QuarkXPress, you must have the ImageMap XTension active in the XTensions folder. When it's active (it should be, unless someone has turned it off with XTension Manager), you'll see the Image Map tool at the top of the Web Tools palette.

Actually, there are three Image Map tools, each of which let you draw a different shape: a rectangle, a circle, and a Bézier box. To get a different tool, click and hold on the tool in the palette (see Figure 17-24).

Applying an image map to a picture is easy: Select the picture box, and then use one of the Image Map tools to draw the shape of each hotspot area over the picture. Remember that holding the Shift key as you drag with the Oval or Rectangle tool creates circles or squares. By the way, when you export your HTML, XPress always converts your nice ovals and Bézier shapes into polygons with straight edges, so don't get too particular about how perfectly you draw these shapes.

Once you have the hotspots drawn on the image, you can then apply your hyperlinks for those areas. Adding hyperlinks to these hotspots is exactly the same as adding them to pictures; just select the hotspot before clicking on the link in the Hyperlinks palette.

Figure 17-24
The Image Map tools

> **TIP: Draw Inside the Box.** *While you can draw hotspots that extend outside the boundaries of the picture box, you shouldn't. It won't do any good anyway; XPress always crops your hotspots down to fit within the picture box when you export the file.*

Deleting image maps. To remove one hotspot in an image, select it and then press Delete or Backspace. To delete all of the hotspots in an image, choose Delete All Hot Areas from the Item menu.

HTML FORMS

Go to almost any large site, or even a small site, and you'll see a page with a form. It could be as simple as a text entry field to enter your email address or search the site, or as complex as a survey or a form to place an order. Unfortunately, it's sort of a pain to make forms in most programs. But not QuarkXPress! It's positively easy to make a form in this program, and it's one of the best reasons to use XPress for authoring your pages.

How forms work. Here's how forms work: Once the user fills in the form fields (checkboxes, menus, text entry fields, and so on), he or she clicks a button that submits the data to the Web server. Sitting on the server is a program that can be run using the CGI (Common Gateway Interface), and this program processes the data, does something with it (such as send an email with the posted information or create a new record in a database), and then passes a result page back to the user.

The key to making all this work is the program sitting on the server (often called a "cgi script"), which is usually written in a programming language like Perl, C, or PHP. You'll need to ask your Web administrator how to access the appropriate CGI script on your server before putting a form on a Web page. Usually, it's a URL address, like *../cgi–bin/processdata*.cgi.

You also need to know exactly what data the CGI script is expecting. For instance, if the script is going to put the form data into a database, you probably need to know the exact names of each field in the database. Once you have that information, you can use XPress to create the page and the fields of the form.

Just to be clear, QuarkXPress cannot make CGI scripts that will run on your Web server. Those have to be made separately; XPress just gives you the tools to create the Web page that can send data to those little programs.

Define the Form

The first step in creating a form on your page is to draw a form box with the Form Box tool—all the form items on your page must fit inside that form box. The Form Box tool is the second tool in the Web Tools palette (see Figure 17-25). A small icon at the top right of the box indicates that the box is a form box.

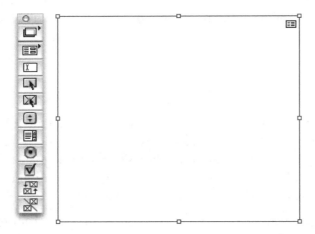

Figure 17-25
Making a form box

TIP: Fast Forming. *You actually don't need to use the Form Box tool to make a form box. If you use any of the form tools on your page, XPress automatically makes a form box for you. The size of this form box is determined by the pixel dimensions in the Preferences dialog box (double-click the Form Box tool and then click the Modify button to change these dimensions). You can also make any box into a form box by selecting Form from the Content submenu (under the Item menu, or in the context-sensitive menu).*

By the way, you can have more than one form box on your page, with each one acting as a separate form, with different Submit buttons, and so on.

After making a form box, you need to give XPress some details about the form, like where and how to send the data on the form. This is all handled on the Form tab of the Modify dialog box. With the form box selected, choose Modify from the Item menu (or press Command/Ctrl-M), and then select the Form tab (see Figure 17-26). Here you must specify six settings: Name, Method, Target, Encoding, Action, and Form Validation. Some of these—like Method and Encoding—are technical and depend on the settings in your CGI program, so you'll need to discuss them with your Web server administrator.

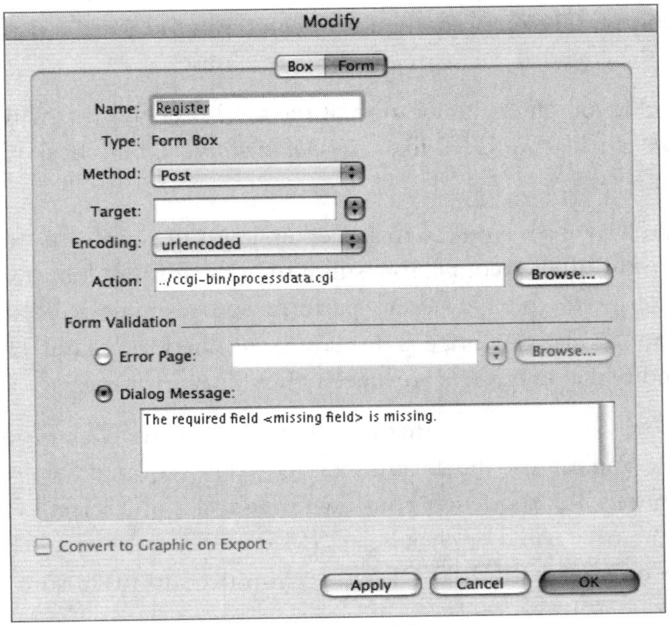

Figure 17-26
Form tab of the Modify
dialog box

Name. The first field on the Form tab is where you can enter a name for your form. The default value for this field is FormBox1. The name of a form is important if you are going to add some JavaScript (in some other program) that references or validates the form. If you have multiple forms on the page, each form must have a unique name. Don't use spaces or special characters when naming your forms.

Method. The Method popup menu tells the CGI how the form is processed. The default value—Post—is generally what you will use. The Post option specifies that the Web browser should send the form data to the CGI as a separate HTTP transaction. The Get option specifies that the Web browser should append the form data to the URL.

Target. Server scripts usually reply to a form's being submitted with a response in the form of a URL. You can set a target window for that response. If you don't set a target, the form page is replaced by the reply page. However, you can use any target window (see "Hyperlinks," earlier in this chapter for more on target windows).

Encoding. When data is passed from a form to a Web server, the data is passed as a string of characters. The Encoding popup menu lets you specify how to pass that string: urlencoded (the default), form-data, or plain. With the urlencoded option, spaces are replaced by the + symbol, and nonnumeric characters are replaced with the % symbol followed by the hexadecimal value of the character. Plain leaves the text as it was typed. Form-data is used if you are sending attached files to the server (see "The File Select Tool," below). Generally, if you are using a CGI to process the form, you'll want to use the urlencoding option. The CGI parses the encoded data string before processing.

Action. In the Action field, you enter the location of the CGI program that will be used to process the form. This is usually a URL like *../cgi-bin/myscript.cgi*, but check with your Web server administrator.

Form Validation. As you'll soon see, you can make certain items in your form "required," meaning that the viewer must fill them out before submitting the form. When you do this, XPress adds some JavaScript to the HTML to perform some simple validation. If a required field is left empty, an error message is displayed, and the form is not submitted. The Form tab of the Modify dialog box lets you specify how that error message appears.

The default setting, Dialog Message, means that in case of an error, the Web browser will display an alert dialog box. You can use the default message ("The required field <missing field> is missing (see Figure 17-27)) or enter your own message. If you select Error Page, you'll also need to type the page name or click Select (Macintosh) or Browse (Windows) and navigate to the page on your hard disk. Of course, you need to make sure that this URL actually exists on your Web site, too!

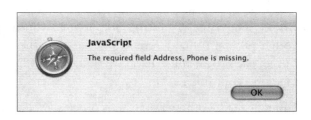

Figure 17-27
Error message in browser

The File Select Tool

Hiding behind the Form Box tool (if you click and hold on that tool) is the File Select tool, which lets you add a file selection feature to your form. Very few forms actually require this feature, which lets a user upload a file from their hard drive to the Web server (but only when the CGI script is set up to accept it). However, it's nice that XPress lets you do it, just in case.

To add a file selection field in your form, drag out a box with the File Select tool (it should be wide enough to display the file name once the user selects one, plus the width of the Browse button itself). Then, while this form item is selected, choose Modify from the Item menu (see Figure 17-28). In the Form tab of the Modify dialog box, give the item a unique name and if the user must select a file before submitting the form, turn on the Required checkbox.

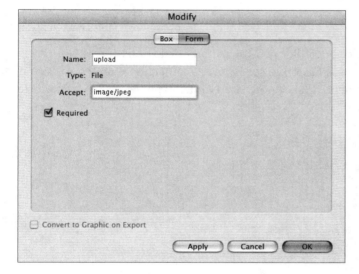

Figure 17-28
File Selection tool options

The Accept field is supposed to let you determine what kinds of files the Web browser will accept, but very few (if any) browsers actually pay attention to this information yet. Just in case you still want to try, you have to type the file type in a MIME format. For instance, if you only want to let the user select JPEG files, you could type "image/jpeg" here. For more than one MIME type, separate them with commas. Or, to accept all file types, leave this field blank. But as I said, I haven't seen this actually work yet, so I leave it blank.

By the way, if you're making a form that lets you upload a file, you'll need to change the form method to "Post" and the encoding to "form-data".

Text Fields

If you are gathering text information in your form, you need to create a text field for each piece of information. For example, you might have a name field and an email field. To add a text field inside your form box, select the Text Field tool and drag out a box. By default, the height of the box is preset for you (one line high), but you can make the field any width you want. Next, you should make a text box next to the text field box and type in a label for the field (or else no one will know what to type in the field; see Figure 17-29).

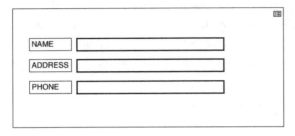

Figure 17-29
Text boxes with labels next to text fields

After making a text field, select it, open the Modify dialog box (press Command/Ctrl-M or Command/Ctrl-double-click on it; see Figure 17-30), choose the Form tab, and fill out a few options for that field. The options are Name, Type, Max Chars, Wrap Text, Read Only, and Required.

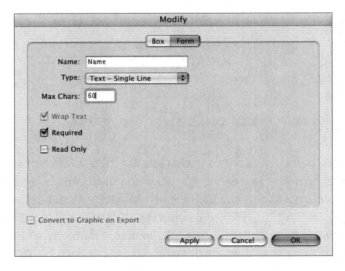

Figure 17-30
Text field options

Name. You need to choose a unique name for your text field. This name is passed along with the information in the form in order for the CGI script to know what to do with it. If the script is going to put this in a database, then the Name field should probably match the database field name.

Type. You can choose among four types of text fields in the Type popup menu: Text – Single Line, Text – Multi Line, Password, and Hidden Field. If you're asking for something like a name or an email address, choose Text – Single Line. However, if you're asking for a bunch of text (like for comments or descriptions), you should choose Text – Multi Line. If you chose Password, then the Web browser will automatically replace whatever the user types with asterisks. Note that this type of field only hides what is entered on the screen; the data that is passed to the form is not secure or encrypted.

You can use hidden text fields for entering data that needs to be sent to the Web server but that shouldn't be displayed in the browser. For example, if you created a form that sends an email to you, you might add a hidden field that contains your email address. Of course, the information in an hidden field can still be seen if you view the source in the browser (so it's invisible on the Web page, but not secure).

By the way, form items cannot typically overlap each other; XPress just won't allow it. However, hidden text fields *are* allowed to overlap if space is tight, since they won't actually be visible on the Web page.

Max Char. To limit the number of characters the user can enter into the field, type a number in the Max Char field. If the width size of the field is smaller than the Max Char size, then the data scrolls as the user types in the field. Unfortunately, when you turn this on, QuarkXPress automatically overrides the width setting of your text entry field; the program has some magic formula for setting the size, which is sort of annoying.

Wrap Text. When you set the Type popup menu to Text – Multi Line, XPress offers you the option of wrapping text in the text entry field. When the Wrap Text checkbox is turned off, the result is a text entry field that has horizontal and vertical scroll bars. You need the horizontal scroll bars because the text that the user enters can extend past the boundaries of the frame. When you turn on the Wrap Text option, however, you only get a vertical scroll bar. In most cases you'll want to turn Wrap Text on.

Read Only. If you turn on the Read Only option, the Web browser won't let the user change the text in the field. Why would you want to do this? Trying to come up with a good reason strains my brain.

Required. As I noted earlier, if you turn on the Required checkbox for a text entry field, the Web browser won't allow the form to be submitted with that field left blank. There's no way to do any kind of special checking that the data is the correct type (like saying "make sure it's a valid credit card number")—just that the user has typed something.

> **TIP: Start with Default Text.** *If you want some default text in the text entry field, you can simply type it in the field. Whatever is in the field when the HTML is exported becomes default text. As long as the Read Only checkbox is not turned on, the user can select that text and change or delete it.*

Lists and Popup Menus

A list or popup menu provides a way to offer choices to the user in a compact form. For example, you could place a popup menu in your form that lists all the states or countries. Or you might display a list of ten software applications and ask the user to select one or more items from that list. The opportunities are infinite! (Well, maybe not infinite. Maybe just a lot.)

Making menus. QuarkXPress thinks of both popup menus and lists as menus, and requires that you create a menu "set" before making a popup menu or a list. Fortunately, making a menu set is easy.

1. Select Menus from the Edit menu. The Menus dialog box (see Figure 17-31) looks a lot like the Style Sheet dialog box, and works much the same way. Click New to create a new menu, or select an existing menu and then click Edit. If you have a similar menu in another Web document, you can click Append and import that list into the current document.

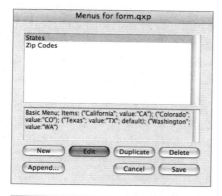

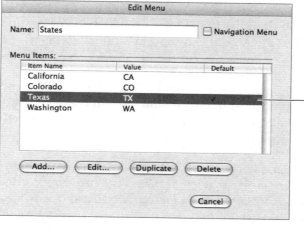

Click in this column to make this menu item the default item in the list.

Figure 17-31
Menus and Edit Menu dialog box

2. Type a name for your menu. The name is internal to XPress and not used in the exported HTML, so you can give it a descriptive name—you can use spaces in this name.

3. Your menu can be set up so that each menu item has a hyperlink to a different Web page. For example, a popup menu might help the user navigate around your Web site. In this case, turn on the Navigation Menu checkbox in the Edit Menu dialog box.

4. Click Add to add a menu item. In the Menu Item dialog box (see Figure 17-32), type the value you want to appear in the menu in the Name field. This information is what the user sees in the list. If you turned on the Navigation Menu option in the previous step, then you should type the URL associated with this menu item in the URL field. Otherwise, in the Value field, type what you want the form to send to the Web server if the user selects this option. For example, you might type "Washington" in the Name field and the two-letter abbreviation "WA" in the Value field. If the user selects Washington from the menu, then the value WA will be sent to the server.

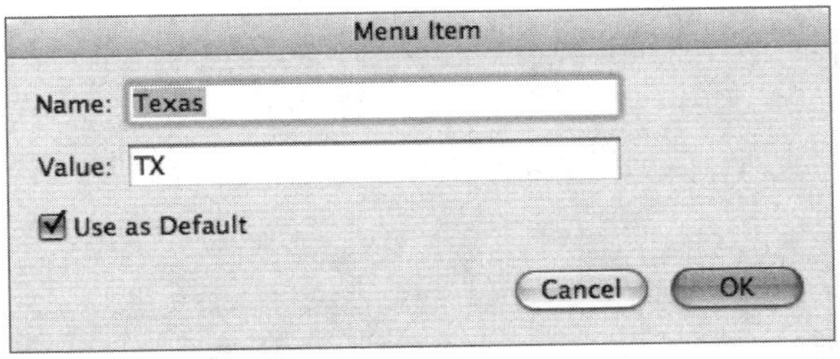

For non-navigation menus

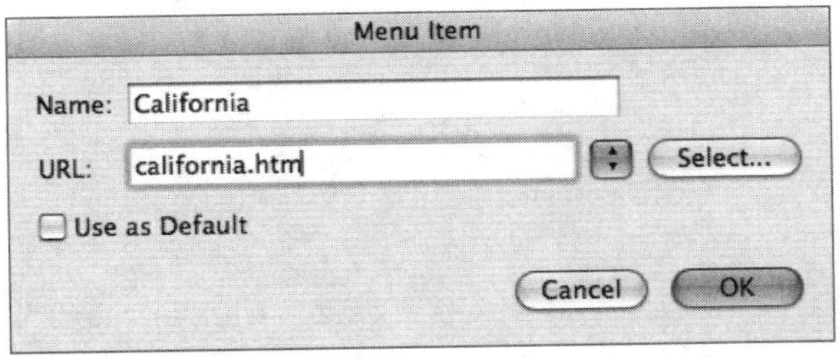

For navigation menus

Figure 17-32
The Menu Item dialog box

5. If you want this menu item to be the default selection (the one that shows up selected when the Web page first appears), click Use as Default. You can also set the Default menu item in the Edit Menu dialog box by clicking in the Default column.

6. Repeat this process until you have added all the items you want to your menu, then click OK, and then Save.

TIP: Rearrange Menu Items. *As you build your menu, you might decide to change the order the items appear in the Edit Menu dialog box (which, in turn, determines how the items appear in the popup menu or list in your browser). To rearrange a menu item, drag the item in the list either up or down.*

Drawing out menus. To add a popup menu or list to your form, select the Popup Menu tool or the List Box tool from the Web Tools palette and click inside the form box. At this point, you cannot control how large the list or popup menu will be, so just position it so that it has room to grow to the right. Once you add one of these items to your form box, you need to visit the Form tab of the Modify dialog box (press Command/Ctrl-M; see Figure 17-33).

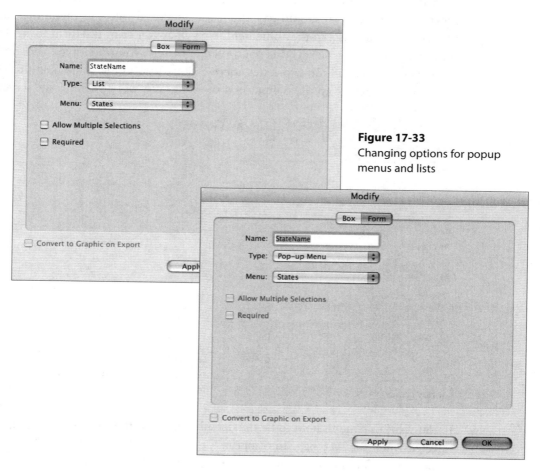

Figure 17-33
Changing options for popup menus and lists

- **Name.** The first item in the Form tab of the Modify dialog box is always Name. Get in the habit of always naming your items instead of using the default names that XPress generates. The name is used when you reference the field using JavaScript, and it appears in the data that is sent to the CGI script. Even if you are not going to use scripting now, you may in the future and the names will already be in place. When you pick a name, don't use spaces or special characters.

- **Type.** If you used the List Box tool to draw the box, then List appears in the Type popup menu. If you used the Popup Menu tool, then Popup Menu appears in the list. However, you can always change the type of list here if you picked the wrong tool. (I tend to do that a lot.)

- **Menu.** Here, pick the name of the menu you created in the Edit Menu dialog box. However, remember I said you had to build the menu set first? Well, I sort of lied. If you want to create a new menu set, you can click New in this dialog box. The Edit Menu dialog box appears, and you can follow the instructions for making a menu set that I discussed earlier.

- **List options.** When the Type popup menu is set to List, XPress gives you two more options to think about: Allow Multiple Selections and Required. As I've said before, Required means that the user has to select something from the list before the form is submitted. Allow Multiple Selections tells XPress whether you want people to be able to choose more than one item in the list. Unless you have a good reason for the user not to select more than one item in the list, just turn on the Allow Multiple Selections checkbox. In fact, if you only want them to choose one, then a popup menu might be a better way to go anyway.

  TIP: Multiple Selections. *For users to select multiple items in a list on a Web page, they need to hold a modifier key. Holding the Shift key selects multiple items in a row, the Command key (Macintosh) or the Ctrl key (Windows), selects discontinuous items in the list. You might want to provide this information next to your lists to remind folks.*

Checkboxes and Radio Buttons

Another method of providing selection options for your users is to use either checkboxes or radio buttons. The advantage to these is that the user sees all the options on the Web page. Checkboxes allow the user to choose multiple items; radio buttons allow only one choice.

To add a checkbox or radio button, select either the Radio Button tool or the Check Box tool from the Web Tools palette. Both these tools work the same: Draw a box on the page wide enough to include the checkbox or radio button, plus a label. The box looks and acts just like a text box, except that there's either a radio button or checkbox on the left side. Now, with the Content tool selected, type a label in the box (see Figure 17-34). You can format this label using XPress's normal text formatting tools.

Figure 17-34
Radio buttons and
checkboxes on the page

You'll need to modify these buttons using the Form tab of the Modify dialog box to make them operational.

Radio buttons. Radio buttons are social creatures; they only make sense in groups because the idea of radio buttons is that when you click on one, the other radio buttons automatically deselect. So the first thing you need to do after drawing out two or more radio buttons is open the Modify dialog box and type in their group name (see Figure 17-35). Here is a potential "gotcha." Each radio button in your group must have *exactly* the same group name. If you rename the group, make sure you enter that same name for each radio button. If one radio button has a different group name than the rest, it won't work with the group.

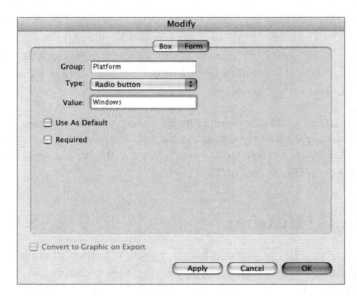

Figure 17-35
Radio button options

TIP: Apply Group in a Group. The best way to ensure that all the radio buttons in a group have exactly the same Group name is to select them all when you apply the Group name in the Modify dialog box.

Note that each radio button in your group needs a unique value that describes the button. That value is what is sent to the CGI script on the Web server—the user doesn't see it. For example, in a form asking what operating system you're using, you might see four radio buttons labeled Macintosh, Windows, Unix, and Linux. However, behind the scenes (in the Modify dialog box), the values might be set to 1, 2, 3, and 4. If you click the Unix button, the number 3 would get sent to the CGI script, along with the name of the group.

If you want one of your radio buttons to be pre-selected when the user first sees the form, turn on the Use as Default option in the Modify dialog box.

Checkboxes. Checkboxes don't require a group name. Instead, each item must be named uniquely in the Form tab of the Modify dialog box. As with radio buttons, the data you type in the Value field is what is sent to the CGI on the Web server, along with the checkbox's name. Note that if the user does not turn on the checkbox, then that information is not sent to the CGI script.

Checkboxes have two other options: Initially Checked (which tells the browser to turn the checkbox on by default) and Required (which means the checkbox must be turned on before the form is submitted. Required checkboxes are good for agreement forms (like "Click here to acknowledge that you have read this contract").

Buttons

Perhaps the most important element in a form is the button that actually sends the form information to the Web server, called a submit button. You can create two kinds of buttons in QuarkXPress: text buttons and image buttons.

Text buttons. True to their name, text buttons have text in them—usually something like "Find," "Submit," or "Send." To make a text button, select the Button tool and click once within the form box. The button always starts off small and scraggly; it expands as you type in it. (Just like in a text box, you have to use the Content tool to type in a text button.) The name you type doesn't matter, as long as it conveys the message to click this button to send the form.

As it turns out, your button can do one of two things: It can submit the file, or it can reset the form back to its original default state. By default, the button is a submit button. If you want a reset button, then choose Modify from the Item menu (or press Command/Ctrl-M) and change the Type popup menu to Reset. Of course, it's a good idea to change the Name field in the Modify dialog box, no matter what kind of button you've got (see Figure 17-36).

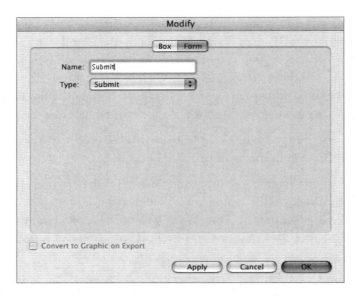

Figure 17-36
Button options

Image buttons. While text buttons are like text boxes, image buttons are like picture boxes. You can use the Image Button tool to drag out an image button box to any size you choose, and then use Get Picture to import a picture into it. Image buttons are always submit buttons (that is, when the user clicks on it, the Web browser immediately submits the form to the CGI script). But they have another interesting side effect: Along with any other data in the form, the image button includes the X and Y coordinates of where the user clicked.

For example, you could make an image button that fills an entire form box (so that it's the only item in the form), and import a picture of a city street map. When the user clicks on the picture, the X and Y coordinates of the click would be sent to a custom CGI script, which could (perhaps with the help of a database) return the nearest restaurants to that place on the map.

EXPORTING YOUR PAGE AS HTML

When you have completed your Web page, and have previewed it in the browser, you are then ready to export the document to disk as an HTML page.

- If you haven't done it already, create a folder on disk to store your HTML files.

- Verify that you've defined the Site Root Directory in the General panel of the Preferences dialog box.

- Check the Page Properties dialog box for each page of your document to verify that you have set the Title and export file name.

Finally, choose HTML from the Export submenu (under the File menu) or from the context-sensitive menu (Control-click on the Macintosh, or right-button click on Windows). In the Export HTML dialog box (see Figure 17-37), navigate to (and open) the folder you defined as the Site Root. This is where you want your HTML files to be saved. You can save the HTML files anywhere, but if they're not inside your Site Root directory, then some links may be messed up.

Figure 17-37
Export HTML dialog box

Before you actually click the Export button, take a look at three options here: Pages, Launch in Browser, and External CSS File.

Pages. If you have more than one page in your Web document, then XPress lets you choose which pages you want to export as HTML files. Remember, each page in the document becomes a different HTML file. To choose specific pages, separate the page numbers by commas or hyphens. For instance, "3, 6, 9-10" will export four HTML pages.

Launch Browser. I almost always want to see how the HTML file turned out after exporting it, so I turn on the Launch Browser checkbox. When this is on, XPress immediately launches the default Web browser and opens the HTML file. However, if you export more than one HTML file, the Web browser only opens the first one.

External CSS File. QuarkXPress uses an HTML feature called Cascading Style Sheets (CSS) to format your text. CSS styles are very much like style sheets in QuarkXPress: they're named groups of typographic formatting. When you export your document as HTML, XPress automatically turns your document style sheets into CSS styles with the same names. Any text that has no specific style sheet is given a default CSS style name, like Text1 or Text2. Note that to make CSS work cleanly, every text character in your document must be given both a paragraph style sheet and a character style sheet. All local formatting shows up as separate CSS styles like "Text1." (See Chapter 7, *Copy Flow*, for more information on style sheets in your QuarkXPress documents.)

If you leave the External CSS File checkbox turned off, QuarkXPress saves your CSS style definitions in your HTML files. That is, each file has its own CSS definitions. However, if you turn on this option, XPress saves the CSS definitions in a separate file (in the same folder as your HTML files). The benefit of external CSS files is that you can quickly use a text editor to change the definitions of that single file (or replace the file with another one that has the same names but different definitions). When you do this, *all* the HTML files that reference that external CSS file are updated immediately. It's very slick.

Turning this feature on is also good when you're going to send the HTML file off to a Web geek in another department. That way, he or she can quickly apply the proper corporate formatting to the text instead of being bogged down with whatever styles you thought looked cool.

Tables in HTML

One of the trickiest problems in HTML is positioning text or graphics precisely around a page. There are two methods for specifying page geometry: complex tables and absolute positioning in Cascading Style Sheets. You don't have to think about this much because it's all handled behind the scenes when you export the HTML, but the more you know about how this works, the more efficient you can be.

Tables in HTML were originally meant to be a means of presenting information in an organized manner. For example, tables were used to display financial data or statistics in rows and columns. However, tables can be used to position things on your page. For example, in a Web document, XPress creates a table the size of the page. When you draw a text or picture box, XPress converts it to a cell within the table. These tables have nothing to do with the Table tool in the Tool palette; these HTML tables are just for positioning things on your page.

The complex tables technique breaks down when you place one object on top of another on your page because cells of a table can't overlap each other. In this case, XPress uses the absolute positioning feature of Cascading Style Sheets (CSS), which tells the Web browser exactly where on the page to place the object. The problem with this is that some older Web browsers can't deal with these tags and the page ends up looking wrong. Fortunately, this is pretty rare these days, as most people have more modern browsers.

> **TIP: Seeing the Table.** *If you want to see the complex table that XPress generates in HTML files, you can open the HTML file in an HTML editing program like Adobe GoLive or Adobe Dreamweaver. Another option is to open the HTML in a text editor (like BBEdit on the Macintosh), search for any text that says "BORDER=0" and replace it with "BORDER=1". Then you can save the file and open it in a Web browser, which will show you the table lines. This won't look pretty; it's just for educational purposes.*

> **TIP: Make Tables Simpler.** *Knowing what is happening "behind the scene" helps you create pages that display properly in all browsers. Let's say you are creating a page containing two columns of text and you want to use two separate text boxes instead of one text box with two columns. You should make sure the two boxes begin at exactly the same position down on the page. Of course that is true even for print, but on a Web page, uneven text boxes cause unnecessary code to be inserted. XPress inserts small transparent spacer images into empty cells to make the table cells match the boxes in your document. Take the time to align your boxes with the Space/Align command from the Item menu (see Chapter 3,* Working with Items) *or use the Measurement palette to verify that the Y values of the boxes are the same).*

> **TIP: Printing Your Web Document.** *Unfortunately, you cannot print your Web document to a printer from within QuarkXPress. Instead, when you select Print from the File menu, XPress exports the current page as a temporary HTML file, launches your default Web browser, opens the HTML file there, and then prints from that program. That means you can't print more than one Web page in your document at a time, and it means you can't use any of QuarkXPress's regular Print dialog box features. Is this annoying to you? It should be.*

IMPORTING HTML

QuarkXPress not only exports HTML codes to disk, but it can also import HTML into a text box. You must have the HTML Text Import XTension active in order to do this (which it should be, unless someone turned it off in the XTensions Manager dialog box).

Importing an HTML file works exactly the same as importing a Microsoft Word document; you select a text box with the Content tool and then choose Get Text from the File menu. Note that if you're using QuarkXPress for Windows and the HTML file has a .html file name extension (instead of .htm), you will probably have to select Display All Files from the File Type popup menu (in the Get Text dialog box).

Unfortunately, XPress isn't very smart at importing HTML files and there is a *lot* that it just ignores. For starters, the HTML Text Import XTension currently doesn't understand

Cascading Style Sheet (CSS) tags. That's sort of a problem, because XPress exports all its HTML with CSS tags. That means XPress cannot import the HTML that it exports. Well, it can, but all the formatting is stripped away. Similarly, it ignores all images and turns HTML tables into tab-separated text.

What *can* it import properly? It understands very basic HTML codes, such as <B> (bold text), <HR> (a horizontal rule, which becomes a Rule Below in XPress), and
 (a soft return). Codes to make ordered and unordered lists work pretty well. The best part is that the headings are mapped to style sheets in your document. For example, if you have a paragraph style called H1 in your document, the import filter will automatically apply that style sheet to paragraphs that have the <H1> code in the HTML.

Clearly, Quark has a way to go with this import filter. But, nevertheless, it is nice that you can import basic HTML files.

> **TIP: Importing HTML Codes.** *If you want to import the actual HTML codes instead of XPress interpreting them into formatted text, turn off the Convert Quotes checkbox in the Get Text dialog box, and then hold down the Command key (Macintosh) or Control key (Windows) when you click the Open button. I'm not sure why you'd want to do this, but ain't it good to know that you can?*

XPRESS PAGE AS PICTURE

Trying to replicate in HTML exactly what you see on your XPress page is tricky. However, I find that I've often got an element of an XPress page that I want to duplicate exactly on the Web (like a logo built in XPress, or a particularly well-designed headline). One of my favorite methods of converting QuarkXPress pages into a form that Web browsers can understand is one of the simplest and yet least used: Simply transform the whole page—text, pictures, and all—into a picture (see Figures 17-38 and 17-39).

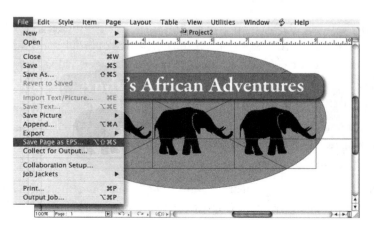

Save your XPress document as an EPS file...

Figure 17-38
Converting pages to pictures (part 1)

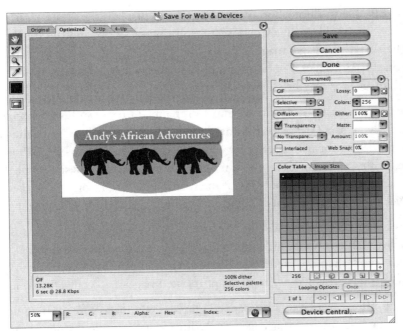

...and open it in Photoshop.

Export the rasterized Photoshop image as a GIF file using Save for Web...

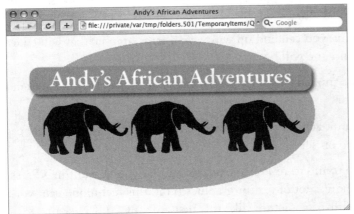

...and place it in your HTML Web document.

Figure 17-39
Converting pages to pictures (part 2)

1. Reduce the size of your document so that it's just bigger than the objects on the page (select Document Setup from the File menu). You may want to copy the page items to a new document before doing this.

2. Save the QuarkXPress page as an EPS (select Save as EPS from the File menu; see "Page as Picture," in Chapter 10, *Pictures*). Note that there are XTensions available that let you save just a portion of your XPress page as an EPS; if you have one of these, you can skip the first step and just save the area you're interested in using the XTension.

3. Open this EPS file in Photoshop. When Photoshop displays the Open Generic EPS dialog box, you should probably choose a resolution of 72 ppi and the RGB color mode. The size of the page/image is up to you (I usually just leave it the same size). Turning on the Anti-aliased option typically provides a better-looking result, but your final image size may be slightly larger.

4. Once the image is rasterized (turned into a bitmapped image) in Photoshop, you can crop it and save it as a GIF or JPEG image, depending on the content of the page. Typically, the JPEG format is better for natural, scanned images, while GIF is good for images with solid colors. (If you don't know how to save in these two file formats or why you'd want to, check out one of the many other books on the market that discuss Web graphic file formats, including Peachpit's *Real World Photoshop*.)

5. You can place this file on the Web as is, but it won't be interactive in any way. However, you can easily add links to the page by importing the graphic back into XPress and giving the page/picture an image map. You can then save this image as an HTML file, and XPress will write the appropriate image-map codes for you.

By turning your XPress page into a bitmapped graphic, you make sure your audience will see everything that you see on your page—including fonts, lines, and page geometry. But there are a number of problems with this technique.

- If you're not careful, you can end up with a very large graphic that will take so long to download that no one will bother.

- Small text sizes are unreadable when rasterized at such low resolution, even if they're anti-aliased.

- Your audience cannot zoom in or out, change the fonts, or even print the page very well (what they see on screen is exactly what they'll get on paper).

Nonetheless, if you're trying to re-create a masthead that you've built in XPress, or even just a simple page without a lot of text or graphics on it, this technique can work surprisingly well (I've made full-page pictures like this that are only 20 K in size).

THE FUTURE OF PUBLISHING

One of the basic elements of democracy has long been "freedom of the press," but freedom of the press has always been reserved for those who own one. Now for the first time in history, almost anyone can publish his or her own work on the Internet and the World Wide Web. And because QuarkXPress has been the tool of choice for most publishing professionals, it makes sense that people would look to this program to take them into the brave new world.

In this chapter, I've briefly summarized the various tools that ease the transition from print to screen. Of course, the future of publishing depends less on which tools you use than on *what* you create. Happy XPressing!

APPENDIX A

XTensions and Resources

When you set up that grill you bought for barbecuing your chicken and vegetables, it's unlikely that you're going to find all the best grilling instruments in the box. So what do you do? You drive back to the store and fill up your shopping cart with a big fork, a spatula, a baster, cleaning equipment, and so on. If you're into carpentry and you buy a table saw, you know you're also going to buy a cross-cut blade separately.

And, after you pull your copy of QuarkXPress out of its packaging, one of the first questions you should ask yourself is: "What other tools do I need to get my job done?"

As any QuarkXPress demon knows—and as I've tried to make clear throughout the book—QuarkXPress is not an island. I don't use QuarkXPress for everything, and I don't expect you to, either. And even if you do, there are many add-on XTensions from Quark and other developers that increase your power and efficiency in making layouts.

Utilities and software. Part of being efficient in electronic publishing, I believe, is using the right tool for the job. Don't use a pair of pliers on a hex nut; don't use a pair of scissors to prune your roses; don't use QuarkXPress when other programs do something better. I rely on dozens of utilities and other software programs to get my work done, including Adobe Photoshop, Microsoft Word, CE Software's QuicKeys, FileBuddy, Adobe Illustrator, Design Science's MathType, Adobe GoLive, TypeTool, Bare Bones's TextWrangler, Quicksilver, VueScan—the list goes on and on.

In this appendix, I primarily talk about XTensions and information resources, but I'm not trying to minimize the importance of these other tools. You can find more information, what these tools are and where to get them at *www.peachpit.com/Quark7.*

XTENSIONS

I first covered XTensions and how they can add functionally to QuarkXPress back in Chapter 2, *QuarkXPress Basics*. Throughout the book, I have mentioned several commercial vendors and their products, but there's no way I could cover them all (there are more than 300 XTension developers alone). More important, I haven't told you where you can get them.

Remember that Quark XTensions that worked in any previous edition of QuarkXPress do not work with version 7—they must be updated for the new version. Unfortunately, some XTension developers have shown little interest in updating some of their XTensions. Check with the developer to see if an XTension you rely on has been updated.

Quark's Freebies

There's no reason not to get—and use—the free XTensions that Quark publishes. The best way to find them is to download them from its Web site (*www.quark.com*).

Where these XTensions used to be called Bob, Son of Bob, and other Bob'ish names, Quark now uses slightly more conservative names, such as TypeTricks (which includes many type-related features like Make Fraction, Make Price, Word Space Tracking, and so on) and Jabberwocky (my personal favorite: It lets you fill any text box with random text). TypeTricks and Jabberwocky now ship with QuarkXPress 7—Quark often releases a feature as an XTension first, then builds the XTension into the next version of the software, as with PSD Import (natively import Photoshop files) and QuarkVista (apply filters, adjust pictures, and render transformations). As this book goes to press, the only free XTension for version 7 is Quark XPert Tools Pro (previously from ALAP) for Mac and Windows. There are many good features in this bundle that I can honestly say that every QuarkXPress user should have them installed on their machine. Here is a list of XTensions:

- **XPert Align.** Align items with other items or to the page.

- **XPert BoxTools.** Adjust the size and placement of items, text, and graphics.

- **XPert FindChange.** Find any type of item.

- **XPert Guides.** Create and edit on-screen guides.

- **XPert ImageInfo.** Access information about pictures and modifying pictures in QuarkXPress projects.

- **XPert ItemStyles.** Save item attributes such as color, frame style, line width, picture scale, and text inset as style sheets that you can apply to any item from a palette.

- **XPert Layers.** Locate, select, and modify items by layer and work with QuarkXPress items.

- **XPert PageSets.** Save settings in the New Document dialog box as a style.

- **XPert Paste.** Paste an item to the same X-Y coordinates of the original on a different page or spread.

- **XPert Pilot.** See thumbnail previews of pages and spreads in an open project.

- **XPert Print.** Print or export QuarkXPress pages and spreads as EPS files.

- **XPert Scale.** Scale QuarkXPress documents, items, groups, and contents, similar to the way drawing programs scale objects.

- **XPert TextLink.** Use a palette to link and unlink text boxes and text paths.

- **XPert Toolbars.** Create custom palettes for quick access to any QuarkXPress function.

- **XPert Type.** Access common text formatting options and make changes.

My Recommendations

I have put together a list of what I feel are some of the most useful XTensions available for XPress 7, what they do, and where to buy them. I hope you will find them as useful as I do.

Quark Print Collection. This XTension was previously known as ALAP Imposer Pro, which is now a Quark product. It enables you to impose native XPress layouts (or PDF files) quickly and simply. You can also create custom printer marks, which could include slugs, color bars, and logos. It's available from *www.quark.com*.

Quark Interactive Designer. This XTension allows you to combine sound, video, and animation with the page layout and design tools of QuarkXPress. The final layout is exported as Adobe Macromedia Flash (SWF). This XTension needs an entire section of its own. It's available from several different vendors. However, you can purchase this XTension from *www.apple.com* for a lower price.

QX-Tools Pro 7. OnOne Software has completely rebuilt this XTension package for XPress. Some of the new features include QX-Underline (underlining that skips descenders), QX-Superselect (compound text selection based on any characteristic), QX-Tips&Tricks (tips and tricks for streamlined productivity) and updated versions of QX-FindChange, QX-Viewer, and QX-Shortcuts. The package is available from *www.ononesoftware.com* for the full version or the upgrade. You can also try before you buy with a 30-day free trial.

FlightCheck Pro v6.02. FlightCheck is the essential tool for print shops, creative designers, prepress departments, customer service reps, and graphics professionals within the digital print and publishing industries. It helps you prepare your XPress documents and other document types for commercial printing. You can purchase FlightCheck directly from *www.markzware.com* for the full version or the upgrade.

LiveKeys 2.0. This XTension from Badia gives you the freedom to make QuarkXPress shortcuts work just the way you want. You can customize all menu shortcuts, assign keyboard shortcuts to tools and special commands, manage style sheet shorts, and a lot more. This very useful XTension can be purchased directly from *www.badiaxt.com*. Try before you buy with the free LiveKeys Light version.

BarCoder XT. This XTension from Vision's Edge allows you to create UPC, EAN, and ISBN bar codes. All you do is enter the bar code's numbers, choose options such as bar height, color, and background transparency, and how the bar code should print. BarCoder then generates an EPS file and places it in your XPress layout. It's available from *www.visionsedge.com*.

Where to Find and Buy XTensions

Now you know there are XTensions out there, but how do you find them? While you can often buy XTensions directly from the developer, it's usually easier to use one of several companies that specialize in distributing XTensions. Here are two of the larger distributors.

- **The Power XChange.** The Power XChange sells plug-ins and XTensions for all kinds of programs, including XPress and Acrobat. The Power XChange is a combination of two companies: XChange and The World Wide Power Company. You can find them in the USA at 800-940-0600 or at 303-940-0600, or on the Web at *www.thepowerxchange.com* or *www.thepowerco.com*

- **XCite and XChange.** If you live in Europe, check out XCite, which also sells XTensions and plug-ins for various programs. You can find them at *www.xcite-international.com*. Similarly, you should check out the XChange UK (*www.xchangeuk.com*) and the XChange in France (*www.xchangefr.com*).

There are many other distributors in other countries, as well as mail-order companies and so on. If you're looking for a demo version of an XTension, you can try the above distributors, but you might also search Web repositories such as Version Tracker (*www.versiontracker.com*).

PUBLISHED RESOURCES

I have a love-hate relationship with computer magazines. On the one hand, I love getting magazines such as *Step Inside Design*, *Publish*, and *Macworld*. On the other hand, the stacks of publications in my office are becoming life-threateningly high. Nonetheless, there is a lot of information about publishing in QuarkXPress (and publishing in general) in these magazines.

One solution to the paper problem is Jay Nelson's *Design Tools Monthly*. Each month he combs all the rags for great publishing-related news and tips, and then presents it to you in a short newsletter. It's much more expensive than the magazine subscriptions, but it sure is cheaper than the time it takes to read those magazines (plus, you get a cool CD of goodies each month). You can find DTM in the USA at 303-543-8400 or on the Web at *www.design-tools.com*.

World Wide Web. As much information as there is in print, there's exponentially more on the Web. Here are a couple of places you should know about immediately.

- Quark's site at *www.quark.com* is full of great information. Every XPress user should check in here at least once a month to see what's new.

- PlanetQuark at *www.planetquark.com*: This new Web site has quickly become the best location for QuarkXPress-relevant tips and tricks on the Web.

- While they're not specifically about QuarkXPress, I also bookmark and check several other sites regularly: Pariah Burke's *www.quarkvsindesign.com*, Anne-Marie Concepción's *www.senecadesign.com*, and for all things creative visit *creativepro.com*.

GET IT WHILE IT'S HOT

It's so easy to just launch QuarkXPress and start using it that I find it's hard to stop and think about how life could be made easier with the addition of some other tools or information. Of course, if you work by the hour, then it's a benefit to your bank account for you just to keep your blinders on and be as inefficient as possible. For the rest of us, it's worth it to take the time now to save much more time down the road. Enjoy!

APPENDIX B
Scripting

I don't know why, but some people just like doing things the hard way. Like those people who insist on doing long division on the back of an envelope rather than using a calculator. Or like folks who scroll around their layouts using the scroll bars instead of using the Grabber Hand. Yes, it's weird, but they seem happy enough; so why bother them by telling them there's an easier way to do it?

Well, I don't know about you, but doing repetitive tasks in QuarkXPress drives me crazy. Stepping through a layout to make a tiny formatting change to one little character on each page, searching for all the paragraphs in my 100-page story that start with a numeral and then applying the proper style sheet to them, changing the border around every picture in my layout one at a time. Each of these just seems like another one of those monotonous, robotic tasks that I do every day when working on my computer.

I'm here to tell you that the days of monotony, the weeks of dull mechanical routines, the months of dreary, unchanging keystrokes are over! There are two things that can alleviate all these woes: macros and scripting. In this appendix, I'll discuss editing and running scripts and the new scripts that ship with QuarkXPress 7. For more detailed information on writing a script, download the Web bonus Appendix D, *Scripting Basics*, at *www.peachpit.com/Quark7*.

Macintosh only. Before I get started, there's one other thing you need to know: Scripting in QuarkXPress is Macintosh only. I feel pretty confident that the folks at Quark will update XPress for Windows to be scriptable as quickly as they can. Until then, if you only use Windows, you won't be able to script. However, you will be able to use macros if you buy a separate macro utility.

Editing and Running AppleScripts

The Macintosh version of QuarkXPress 7 ships with an XTension called Script (it's in the XTensions folder), which not only allows XPress to be scriptable, but also adds a Scripts menu to the menu bar (see Figure B-1). You can add or remove the scripts listed in this menu by moving files in and out of the Script folder, which you should be able to find in the QuarkXPress folder on your hard drive.

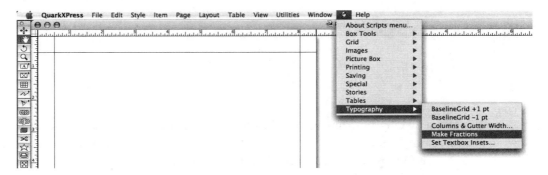

Figure B-1 The Scripts menu

The Scripts menu lets you run scripts, but it won't let you write or edit them. For that, you need to use an application such as Script Editor (for AppleScript scripts), UserLand Frontier (for UserTalk or Frontier scripts), or CE Software's QuicKeys. I think the best place to start is Apple's free Script Editor, which ships on all Macintosh systems. In OS X, it's in the AppleScript folder, inside the Applications folder.

Note that scripts that are in the Scripts menu should be *compiled*, but not self-running applications. The difference has to do with how they're saved in Script Editor's Save As dialog box.

> *Tip: Hard-Core Scripting.* If you really get into scripting, you will find yourself spending a lot of time writing or debugging scripts and you will want to take a look at some of the other scripting applications on the market. For instance, Late Night Software's Script Debugger is a full-featured tool that helps you write and debug scripts, and is better than the rather spartan (but free) Script Editor. UserLand Frontier is also a very powerful script editor, though it primarily uses its own scripting language rather than AppleScript.

Also, the more complicated a script, the more it requires a way for the user to interact with it—buttons, text fields, dialog boxes, popup menus, and so on. If you're interested in building user interfaces for your scripts, take a look at Apple's own AppleScript Studio or Late Night Software's FaceSpan.

Tip: Hiring a Scripter. Even though scripting is extremely powerful, it's just a fact of life that most people don't want to learn the ins and outs of scripting. Fortunately, there are a number of scripters for hire. In case you're looking for such a person, I've compiled a small list of freelance scripting consultants on the Real World QuarkXPress Web site: www.peachpit.com/Quark7.

GETTING SCRIPTING INFORMATION

It's nearly impossible to learn how to script QuarkXPress without extra documentation. Fortunately, Quark ships some information about AppleEvent scripting along with the Macintosh version of QuarkXPress, although it's not immediately obvious. It's an Acrobat PDF file called Apple Events Scripting, which can be accessed directly from the Scripts menu by selecting the Special submenu, and then choosing Open Apple Events Scripting PDF (see Figure B-2).

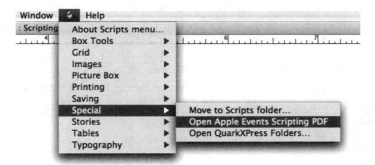

Figure B-2
Locating the Apple
Events Scripting PDF

Books. Fortunately, since the last edition of this book, several good books have been published on AppleScripting. Most are somewhat general, such as *Danny Goodman's AppleScript Handbook* and the *AppleScript for Applications Visual QuickStart Guide*. Those are great, but if you're going to script QuarkXPress, you owe it to yourself to find a copy of *AppleScripting QuarkXPress* by Shirley Hopkins; it's very good and comes with a CD-ROM with lots of example scripts.

Examples. The best way to learn how to script QuarkXPress is by first looking at and deconstructing other people's scripts. If you can find a script that already does what you want, then use it. If the script isn't quite right, then edit it to make it work for you. Quark has provided a number of scripts in the Scripts folder, inside the QuarkXPress folder. You can open these in Script Editor to see how they work or edit them to suit you.

Scripting Dictionary. All scriptable applications have a built-in scripting dictionary that outlines the various things that can be scripted in that program. One way to see this information is by choosing Open Dictionary in the File menu of the Script Editor utility. The dictionary is often most helpful as a quick reference when your books or documentation isn't around.

The Web. The World Wide Web is one of the best sources for AppleScript information. There are a number of great sites out there that offer both tutorials on scripting and scripts that you can download, use, and learn from. The best place to start is Apple's own scripting site *http://www.apple.com/applescript*.

QUARK-PROVIDED SCRIPTS

Quark provides a number of scripts that install with the application. These scripts are generally pretty basic, and they are definitely a time-saver for some of those repetitive, time-consuming tasks. There are a couple of scripts that you will find surprisingly fun and very useful. Let's take a look at what XPress 7 has to offer for scripts.

On the XPress menu bar, locate the Script icon that looks like a paper scroll and click to expand the menu. Ten submenus are located in the Script menu, and each contains one or more scripts. Some of these scripts require you to enter some type of information within a dialog box, and others don't require any user interaction.

Script Menu Items

Box Tools scripts work with text and picture boxes.

- **Add Crop Marks.** This script adds registration crop marks to any single box with default parameters of 0.5-point line width, 24-point line length, and a 6-point offset.

- **Easy Banner.** This unique script places a banner with your choice of text (up to 25 characters) and banner color (see Figure B-3).

- **Make Caption Box.** This script places a text box with a caption beneath the text or picture box you select. You will be prompted to enter the caption text.

- **Shrink or Grow at Center.** This nifty script resizes your text or picture boxes from the center to the outside edges, at a value you specify. When using this script with a picture box, you also have the option to scale the images by selecting one of six options (see Figure B-4).

Figure B-3
Box Scripts—Add Crop Marks
and Easy Banner

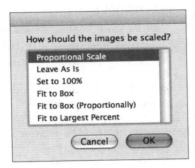

Figure B-4
Image Scaling Options

Grid script works with text or picture boxes.

- **By Dividing a Box.** This script takes a box and divides it into a grid of smaller boxes. You will be prompted to enter the number of columns and rows. Then you will be asked for gutter measurements and whenever you want guides attached to the boxes.

Images scripts work with images placed into picture boxes.

- **Contents to PICT file.** This script extracts a copy of the image in the selected box and saves it as a PICT file to the location of your choice.

- **Copy To Folder.** This script places an exact copy of the selected image to the location of your choice.

- **Fldr to Selct PBoxes.** Once you start using this script, you'll wonder how you ever lived without it. This script places the images from a specified folder into selected picture boxes in your layout. This script is great for creating catalogs of your stored images.

Picture Box scripts work only with picture boxes.

- **Crop Marks & Name.** This script places crop marks around the selected picture box and places a text box (similar to placing a caption) below the picture box that contains the file name of the image placed in the picture box.

- **Place Name.** This script creates a text box below the selected picture box that contains the file name of the image placed in the picture box.

- **Set All Bkgnd None.** This script changes the background color to none on one or more selected picture boxes.

- **Set All Bkgn.** This script changes the background color on one or more selected picture boxes to any color in your color palette you choose.

Printing scripts refer to the output of projects using OPI or Open Prepress Interface. This is the method of placing low-resolution images within your layout, which will then be swapped at the RIP for high-resolution images that are stored on an OPI file server on your network.

- **OPI Don't Swap Image.** This script indicates that you do not want the OPI swap to occur for the selected image.

- **OPI Swap Image.** This script indicates that you want the OPI swap to occur for the selected image.

Saving refers to additional Save as options.

- **Each Page as EPS.** This script enables you to save each page of your layout to an individual EPS file.

Special refers to specialized scripts that are not application driven.

- **Move to Scripts folder.** This script enables you to select an AppleScript from the folder of your choice.

- **Open Apple Events Scripting PDF.** This script opens the QuarkXPress AppleScript documentation provided by Quark. It's an Acrobat PDF file called Apple Events Scripting.

- **Open QuarkXPress Folder.** This script opens the folder of your choice within the QuarkXPress application folder (see Figure B-5).

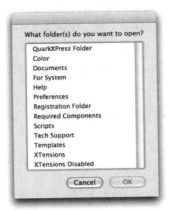

Figure B-5
Folders within QuarkXPress
application folder

Stories scripts refer exclusively to text boxes.

- **Link Selected Text Boxes.** This script links any and all selected text boxes, whether or not they contain any text. You cannot do this with the standard linking tool in XPress. This wonderful script saves you lots of time when it comes to flowing text and merging individual text boxes.

- **To or From XPress Tags.** This script enables you to export selected text as XPress Tags or allows you to import text into your current project with XPress Tags.

- **Unlink Selected Boxes.** This script allows you to unlink individual boxes from anywhere within a text chain without breaking the chain. Any text in the box that has been removed from the chain will remain as part of the text chain.

Tables script only works with tables.

- **Row or Column Color.** This script enables you to alternate the background colors of rows or columns from available colors in your color palette. You will be asked to select the starting row or column and how many rows or columns you want between fills. You will then choose a color and a shade percentage for that color. You can apply this script to as many varying columns or rows as you desire.

Typography scripts work for Typography settings.

- **BaselineGrid -1 pt.** This script decreases the layouts' baseline grid by 1 point. To view the baseline grid, select Baseline Grid from the View menu. These settings can also be changed in the Preference palette.

- **BaselineGrid +1 pt.** This script increases the layouts' baseline grid by 1 point. To view the baseline grid, select Baseline Grid from the View menu.

- **Columns & Gutter Width.** This script adds columns to any existing single text box. To use this script, select a text box and then select the script. You will be prompted to enter the number of columns you would like and the column gutter width.

- **Make Fractions.** This script creates fractions from numbers within a single story or throughout the entire layout—your choice.

- **Set Textbox Insets.** This script enables you to set new text box insets for any text box.

Take a look at Figure B-6. This figure combines several scripts to create the effects shown here. I first created a picture box the size of a full catalog page. I selected the picture box and used the By Dividing a Box script under the Grid script, which converted one picture box into 20 evenly sized and spaced picture boxes.

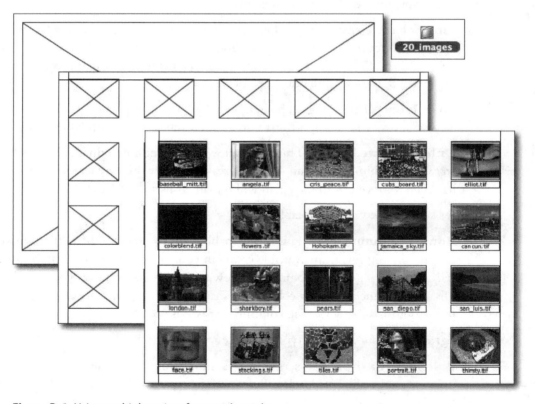

Figure B-6 Using multiple scripts for superb results

I then selected all of my new picture boxes and applied the Fldr to Selct PBoxes script, which directed me to choose a folder of images. The script then placed the images individually into each of my selected boxes. And last but not least, for each selected picture box, I applied the Place Name action from the Picture Box scripts.

By using a combination of Fldr to Select PBoxes script and Place Names script, XPress allowed me to view all of the images that I was using for a new project on a single page without having to think about creating a group of picture boxes for the images or text boxes for the image names. This just goes to show that there are a lot of hidden features in every application, and sometimes we just have to dig a little to find them.

THE FUTURE OF SCRIPTS

Clearly, AppleEvent scripting gives you extremely powerful control over your environment in QuarkXPress (and other programs). As more people learn about it, I'm expecting that I'll hear of some amazing applications online and in the press. I recently sat next to a publisher of a magazine who wanted to start putting stuff online. His problem was that he had no good way of automating the process from a database to QuarkXPress to output (like Acrobat). As soon as I started talking about scripting, his eyes lit up. That's one man out of thousands who wants to hire a scripter. Any takers?

APPENDIX C
XML Tools

Take this test to determine whether you should read this appendix. Rate your true feelings about style sheets between one ("I don't even know what they are") and ten ("I am totally in love with style sheets and I scream epithets at my colleagues when they don't use them properly"). If you score five or less, go back and read Chapter 7, *Copy Flow*, until you appreciate style sheets more. If you rate above five, you're on the right track. If your feelings tend toward 11, then read this chapter.

Before I get into the details of what XML is, let me explain why your feelings about style sheets will determine your success with XML. First, it's almost impossible to be efficient with XML if you haven't been somewhat religious about using style sheets in your layouts. In fact, layouts that don't really require style sheets (like ads and one-page flyers) are usually inappropriate for XML anyway. XML is all about magazines, newspapers, books, and other documents that have the same kinds of elements week after week, month after month, or file after file.

Second, it takes a certain kind of person to make both style sheets and XML work properly. Someone who enjoys intricate details, problem solving, and precision. Someone who prefers databases over design and production over prettiness.

I'm not saying that designers shouldn't pay attention to this stuff; they are an important part of the process. But they're going to have to work with a production or IT person who really understands XML and who can lay the groundwork for these kinds of documents. The more designers can speak the language of XML, the better the communication will be, and the more successful the undertaking will prove.

Theory and practice. While I will discuss the basics of making and handling XML files in this appendix, I won't get into the nitty-gritty details of how the software works, for two reasons. First, the documentation for the XML functions in XPress 7 takes up over 140 pages, and we just don't have the space in this book to do it justice.

Second, and perhaps more important, many people who want to get into an XML workflow with XPress won't be using the XML tools that come from Quark. For instance, today some companies that are creating XML from their QuarkXPress layouts use a third-party system, such as Easypress's Atomik (*www.easypress.com*) or AiEDV's BatchXport (*www.aiedv.ch*). These systems typically offer more (or different) control than the technology that comes with XPress.

However, programs like Atomik and BatchXport are designed for automating the XML export process significantly more than avenue.quark allows. If you're trying to export the past five years of your magazine articles in XML format, you're going to want as much automation and batch processing as possible.

So, while some folks will be using XPress's tools, it doesn't make sense to really focus on them. Instead, it's more important to look at why XML is important and what sorts of things you need to know in order to start using XML workflows.

> *Tip: Check Out the Docs. Whether or not you're using the XTensions that come with QuarkXPress, if you're interested in learning more about XML, you should read through the "Guide to avenue.quark" that comes with the downloadable XML QuarkXTensions—it's an Acrobat PDF file in a folder called Documents on the QuarkXPress XMLXTensions disk image. While much of what it talks about overlaps what I discuss in this appendix, it's a good "next step" after reading this.*

SEPARATING CONTENT AND FORM

The basic concept of XML (eXtensible Markup Language) is that your content (the words and pictures that make up your layouts) and the form that content takes should be two separate things.

For example, let's say you have a magazine article written in Microsoft Word and four different QuarkXPress layouts. You could use Get Text to pour the article into all four templates to get four very different looks (perhaps one in color, one in black and white, one Web layout, and one for print). If you were careful in your use of style sheets (again, see Chapter 7, *Copy Flow*), then the text would automatically be formatted properly (and differently) for each template.

In this simple example, the Word document is the content, and each XPress template is a form the article can take. XML takes this idea even further, letting you do things that you can't do with proprietary formats like Microsoft Word. If your article were in XML format, you could not only flow it into several different layouts (in XPress and even in other programs, like Adobe InDesign), you could even create an "abstract" version for display on a cell-phone screen. Or you could archive it in a database, transform it automatically into HTML and put it on the Web, or convert it to Braille for the blind.

If you had a thousand articles in XML format, you could quickly process them to pull out just the titles and bylines. In fact, XML makes no sense for a single short article, but makes lots of sense when dealing with a large amount of data, many different layouts, or many different looks for the same layout.

XML is simply a way to describe your content so that it can do all these things relatively quickly. No wonder so many companies around the world want to start using XML.

The call from above. So what do you do when your boss storms in and says, "The vice-president of executive whims has declared that we're going to an all-XML workflow?" First, take a deep breath. Then think about the following issues.

- Using XML is a long-term, major decision. It requires a *lot* of planning. I highly recommend that you work with a company that specializes in XML in order to choose or create a DTD and workflow (I'll explain DTDs later in this appendix).

- It is possible for people who don't know anything about XML to import and export XML from QuarkXPress, but not without careful behind-the-scenes planning. The primary XML XTensions from XPress, avenue.quark, and XML Import, don't give you all the tools you need to create XML files, so there's no way to just jump in.

- The underlying concepts of QuarkXPress and XML are at odds in many ways. While XPress is all about formatting content (text and graphics) and putting it anywhere you want on a page, XML is all about sticking to a strictly defined linear structure. QuarkXPress is like techno-grunge music; XML is like a Bach cantata. Where making a page in QuarkXPress is like drawing with crayons, XML is the equivalent of filling out your tax forms—one lets you draw outside the lines of the coloring book, the other forces you to do it right, or else.

- There are some things you can do in XPress that are hard (or impossible) to export into XML. Notoriously difficult is exporting anything that you might consider content but isn't (like dividing lines or text converted to outlines).

- XML is all about breaking down your layouts into logical components, but the logic is often complex. In an XPress layout, the "title" style sheet will always look the same. However, it's not unreasonable for "title" to mean very different things within the same XML document, depending on whether it falls after a tag called <book>, one called <heading1> or one called <real_estate_insurance>. (I'll cover tags and other XML terminology in the next section.)

- If you can't get your production folks to use style sheets, you might as well give up now.

- A lot of systems on the market focus more on getting XML out of XPress than getting it back in again. If you're going to use a third-party program, make sure you ask the vendors about XML Import.

If your boss still wants to work with XML after you discuss these issues (and you've waited a week to see if the VP will have spontaneously changed his or her mind), then you'd better keep reading and see how all this XML stuff works.

XML Basics

In HTML (HyperText Markup Language), you can make a paragraph look like a heading by putting <H1> at the beginning and </H1> after it. Adding this label is called *tagging* the paragraph with the <H1> ("heading 1") tag. Similarly, you can make a word bold by tagging it with <B> (and </B>, which ends the tag). Most HTML tags or codes tell a Web browser what your content should look like.

XML (Extensible Markup Language, which is a descendent of SGML, the Standard Generalized Markup Language) is a way of applying *any* kind of tag to your content—you can even make up your own bizarre tags. Most XML documents focus entirely on what your content is—what it means—rather than what it should look like. For instance, your XML might include tags like <author>, <title>, and <publisher> (yes, tags are always surrounded by angle brackets). Later, you can use an XML processing program to convert these tags into something else by *mapping* tags to HTML tags, or XPress Tags, or some other kind of formatting. (No, this kind of processor utility isn't included.)

It's important to emphasize that XML tags may have nothing to do with how something will get formatted. For instance, you might tag all the names of companies in your document with an <inc> tag, whether they show up in a heading or the middle of a paragraph. This way you could later use an XML-aware database to search for all the companies mentioned in your document.

Note that XML, also like HTML, is always written as plain text files, so you can open and edit them in any text editor like BBEdit or Windows Notepad.

Syntax and Structure

XML is extremely flexible, but it also requires a strict syntax. For instance, every tag must have a closing tag (that's the one with the slash in it), and multiple tags must be fully nested. For instance, you might find this in an XML file: <software><layoutapps>QuarkXPress </layoutapps></software>. In this case, the <layoutapps> tag is *nested* inside the <software> tag, and you must close it before you close the <software> tag.

As you can see, it's pretty easy to write XML. What's difficult is writing XML in a form that can later be read and understood by an XML processor (software that can read the XML and do something with it, like map the tags to HTML properly). In order for this to happen, your XML must conform to a set of rules, called a DTD (Document Type Definition).

A DTD (please don't call it a DDT; that's an insecticide) defines both the names of the tags and how the file will be structured. For instance, the DTD for this book might define the following tags and structure.

- <paragraph>

- <heading1>

- <heading2>

- <heading3>

- <chapter_title>

- <chapter>, which must include a <chapter_title> followed by a collection of one or more chunks of text tagged with <paragraph>, <heading1>, <heading2>, and <heading3> (not necessarily in that order)

- <book>, which must include one or more <chapter> tags

Of course, the actual structure of this book is more complex than that (it also includes illustrations, lists, tips, and so on), but it's good to start simple. If you were trying to export XML from a book that was already laid out in XPress, you might use the already-defined style sheets to determine the XML tags for paragraphs, headings, and so on. More on that later in this appendix.

> **TIP:** Chapter 2 of Quark's "Guide to avenue.quark" PDF has a good discussion about creating and using DTDs.

Choosing a DTD. The DTD is an extremely important part of the XML workflow, but it's a complex document that takes time and planning to create. While you can use a custom DTD for your documents, there are a number of industry-standard DTDs which might work for you. The best reason to use an already-defined DTD (besides not having to pay someone to write a new one) is that if two companies write to the same DTD, they can exchange data.

For instance, if two scientific journals use the same DTD, they can be assured that their content will be transportable. If a database company wants to pay you for your journal's content, it'll be much easier (and cheaper) for everyone if the content is already in a form that the database company can understand. You can find a number of industry-standard DTDs at *www.xml.org* (this, and other links, are available on the *Real World QuarkXPress* Web site, too).

Well-formed versus valid XML. Any properly tagged XML document can be called *well formed*. However, only XML documents that conform to the strict rules of a given DTD can be called *valid*. There are utilities that can confirm whether an XML file is well formed, and others that can compare an XML file with a DTD to see if it's truly valid.

By the way, a DTD only defines the form of an XML file, not the meaning of the tags. That means you could have a valid XML file that has the wrong kinds of data in it—like putting someone's name inside a tag that is reserved for a credit card number. Describing and confirming *meaning* is a much more difficult challenge. XML *schemas* can help some by providing information about what kind of data should be allowed for a piece of tagged data (see *www.schema.net*).

How to Read a DTD

In order to really understand XML, it helps to be able to read a DTD. The DTD may be in its own separate file, but it's often included at the top of an XML file (especially XML files exported from QuarkXPress). Again, this information is all plain text, so you can see it in any text editor. (Special thanks to Deborah Lapeyre of Mulberry Technologies for her help with this appendix.)

DTDs have four basic parts (called declarations): document type, comments, elements, and attributes. There are others (like entities, notations, and processing instructions), but I don't need to get into those details here.

Document type. The DOCTYPE declaration is always at the top of the DTD and it tells you the name of the top level element. It then either points to an external DTD file or includes the definition of the DTD inside square brackets: [and].

Element. Each tag you can use must be defined by an element declaration which first gives the name of the element and then (in parentheses) describes what makes up this element. For example:

```
<!ELEMENT firstname (#PCDATA) >
```

This declares a tag called <firstname> which must consist of "Parsed Character DATA," which is basically text (anything that can be typed). Here's another example:

```
<!ELEMENT author (surname, firstname?) >
```

This declares a tag called <author> which consists of two other elements: surname and firstname.

In an Element declaration, every little symbol means something. Here, the question mark after *firstname* means that this element is optional, and the comma between the "child" element names means that if there is a <firstname> tag, it must follow the surname.

If you replace the comma with a vertical bar (surname | firstname), it would mean the author tag could include either <firstname> *or* <surname>. See Table C-1 for information on what the various codes mean. These codes can also be placed outside parentheses, too, like this:

```
<!ELEMENT authors (firstname, surname)+ >
```

Table C-1 DTD codes

Symbol	What it means
+	Required, and may repeat (one or more)
?	Optional, but can't repeat (zero or one)
*	Optional, and may repeat (zero or more)
no mark	Required, and cannot repeat (exactly one)
,	"Followed by"
|	"Or"

In this example, the <authors> tag may include one or more groups of text that is tagged with <firstname> and followed by <surname>.

> **Tip: Everything is Case-Sensitive.** *Note that the names of tags and attributes are case-sensitive, so a <video> tag is different than a <Video> tag. Similarly, the ELEMENT, #PCDATA, and other items that you see in all capital letters here must be typed that way. That detail has gotten more than one person in hot water.*
>
> *Just to make the process even tougher, remember that in general every element and attribute name must begin with either a letter or an underscore. That means A123 is a valid name, but 123A is not. Names may then contain upper- or lower-case letters, numbers, the colon, underscore, hyphen, and period. Nothing else. No asterisks, no commas, no percent signs. Hey, I told you that XML was strict.*

Attribute. An attribute lists additional information that is associated with an element. For example, you might want a <book> element to have a "pub_date" attribute which never shows up in print (or on the Web, or whatever), but is useful to parse or search in a database. You will see attributes declared like this:

```
<!ATTLIST book pub_date CDATA #IMPLIED >
```

Attribute declarations are always lists that have four parts: the element name, the attribute name, the attribute type, and whether or not it's required. In the example above, the *pub_date* attribute is declared to be associated with the <book> element, the attribute is CDATA (which is sort of like #PCDATA; it just means any kind of text), and it's optional.

You can see any XML reference guide for the various sorts of attribute types. Here are the four options for the fourth "column."

- #REQUIRED means this attribute must be present whenever the tag appears in the XML file.

- #IMPLIED means the attribute is optional.

- #FIXED is always followed by some value (a "fifth column"); if the attribute is missing, then it's assumed to be this value, but if it is present then it must be set to this value.

- Some default value. If the attribute is present, it can specify any value, but if the attribute is missing, then this value is assumed.

For example, here's an element and two attributes in a list:

```
<ELEMENT clothing (#PCDATA) >
<ATTLIST clothing size (large | small) "small"
 model CDATA #REQUIRED>
```

Here, the XML tag <clothing> can specify an attribute called "size" and that attribute can equal either "large" or "small." However, if the attribute is missing from the XML document, then "small" is assumed. The second attribute, "model", can be any text and must be present.

You can specify attributes inside an XML document like this:

```
<clothing size="large" model="FunkyChicken">
T-shirt</clothing>
```

Comments. As you can tell, DTDs can be dense, so when people write them they add comments that are ignored by XML parsers (software that can read and process XML tags) but will remind them of what things mean when they later want to read or edit the DTD. Comments are always surrounded by these tags: <!— and —>. Note that you cannot use double hyphens within a comment. For example, you may see a comment like this:

```
<!- This section declares the various elements within chapters. ->
```

In general, if a comment doesn't mean anything to you, you can ignore it.

An Example of DTD and XML

Now that you know a bit about DTDs and XML, read through the following file, which includes a DTD followed by XML. The first line simply describes what version of XML we're using, what character set encoding we're using, and says this file is "standalone"— that is, it contains the DTD and doesn't depend on any external files.

Of course, this is a very simple example. Real world situations require more complexity, but, again, we've all got to start somewhere.

```
<?xml version="1.0" encoding="UTF-8" standalone="yes" ?>
<!DOCTYPE report [
<!ELEMENT report (meta, title, body) >
<!ATTLIST report xmlns:HTML CDATA #FIXED
 "http://www.w3.org/TR/REC-html40" >
<!ELEMENT meta (author, subject) >
<!ELEMENT author (surname, firstname?)>
<!ELEMENT surname (#PCDATA)>
<!ELEMENT firstname (#PCDATA)>
<!ELEMENT subject (#PCDATA)>
<!ELEMENT title (#PCDATA | inc)*>
<!ELEMENT body ((para | figure | blockquote)*, section*)>
<!ELEMENT para (#PCDATA | inc)*>
<!ELEMENT figure (HTML:img, caption)>
<!ELEMENT HTML:img EMPTY>
<!ATTLIST HTML:img src CDATA #REQUIRED>
<!ELEMENT caption (para+)>
<!ELEMENT blockquote (para+, caption?)>
<!ELEMENT section (title, (para | figure |
 blockquote)*)>
<!ELEMENT inc (#PCDATA)>
]>
<report>
<meta>
<author>
<surname>Schultz</surname>
<firstname>Howard</firstname>
</author>
<subject>Global Domination</subject>
</meta>
<title>Our Great and Grand Test</title>
<body>
<para>First body paragraph, which tells all about our plans to take over the
world by selling coffee.</para>
<para>Second body paragraph, which discusses <inc>Superbucks</inc> and other
stores. </para>
<figure><HTML:img src="beans.gif"></HTML:img>
<caption>
<para>The caption to the illustration goes here.</para>
</caption></figure>
<para>Here is the first paragraph that follows the
conclusion of a figure. It will be followed
by a second, blank paragraph</para>
<para></para>
<blockquote>
<para>First para in a block quote </para>
```

```
<para>Second para in a block quote</para>
</blockquote>
<section>
<title>This is a section</title>
<para>1st section para</para>
<para>2nd para of this section.</para>
</section>
</body>
</report>
```

Quark's XML Tools

For many publishers, XML is like a miracle that lets them repurpose their data in a myriad of ways. In the future, this kind of repurposing will become increasingly important, as people begin to shift their ideas of page-layout programs away from "here's where it all ends up" to "this is one end out of many."

Even though these tools are in flux (as is the whole industry), it's worth taking a quick look at what these XTensions do and how they're cool.

Before You Start

Although some programs let you export XML even without a DTD, QuarkXPress won't let you export XML without one. If you just want to start playing with these tools, you can use a DTD that is installed in the Templates folder, inside the QuarkXPress folder. This DTD is part of the XML tutorial that Quark ships. XPress's XML Import can infer a DTD from any well-formed XML file.

A problem with Quark's tools is that they simply cannot be approached without a reasonable amount of training (both in XML and in the tools themselves). This is very different than any other aspect of XPress. I've long said that the best way to learn any aspect of XPress is just to play around with it—even color management can be learned this way. However, Quark's XML XTensions will drive you insane before you figure them out on your own, unless you're already an XML-savvy person.

Another problem is that these XTensions don't give you much room for error—when you make a mistake, you can rarely undo it. Therefore, train your fingers to save (or better, Save As) often, so you can always revert to an earlier version when something goes wrong.

avenue.quark and Other XTensions

QuarkXPress has three XTensions that handle XML tasks: avenue.quark, XML Import, and Item Sequence. When avenue.quark first shipped, it was extremely limited in functionality and sold separately. It quickly gained a less-than-stellar reputation and the third-party market for XML XTensions grew quickly. However, in XPress 7 these XTensions are much better than they were originally, and you shouldn't write them off.

> **Tip: Finding Quark's XML XTensions.** *You won't find Quark's XML XTensions on your XPress installation CD. Instead, you need to download them from Quark. As of this writing, the URL is www.quark.com/products/xpress/xtensions/xml_xtensions.html*
>
> *The single download contains three XTensions:*
>
> • **avenue.quark.xnt** *for exporting XML from an XPress layout*
>
> • **XML Import.xnt** *for importing XML into an XPress layout*
>
> • **ItemSequence.xnt** *makes "named sequences" for easier XML tagging and export*

avenue.quark. XPress's primary XML tool is avenue.quark (an XTension that editors hate to see at the beginning of a sentence because it's written in all lower-case characters). This XTension lets you tag the content in your layout relatively quickly through a combination of dragging text boxes around and automatically matching your layout's style sheet names to the tags specified in a DTD.

avenue.quark's basic workflow is straightforward.

1. While your layout is open, select XML from the New submenu (under the File menu).

2. In the New XML dialog box, choose a file that has an embedded DTD (see Figure C-1). The files that show up here are in the Templates folder, inside the QuarkXPress folder.

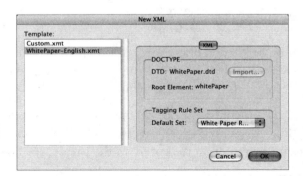

Figure C-1
The New XML dialog box

3. After the XML Workspace palette opens (see Figure C-2), you can set up tagging rules that map your layout's style sheets to the tags in the DTD. You do this by selecting Tagging Rules from the Edit menu (see Figure C-3).

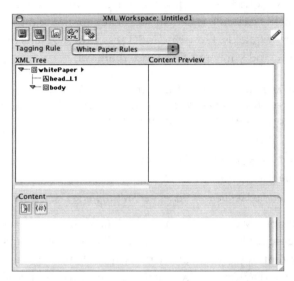

Figure C-2
The XML Workspace palette

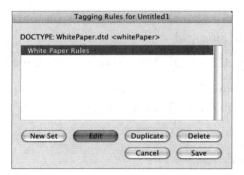

Figure C-3
Tagging Rules

4. Hold down the Command/Ctrl key and drag a text box on top of an element in the XML Workspace palette. XPress applies the tags to the story according to the tagging rules and shows you the result in the palette (see Figure C-4).

5. You can preview the XML document by clicking on the XML Preview button (the one that has an icon of a little set of eyeglasses), or save the XML document to disk by clicking the Save button (the button in the corner of the palette; see Figure C-5).

That's basically it. There is a host of other features that lets you insert various XML elements, which are accessed primarily by Control-clicking/right-clicking on the XML tree in the palette. If you need more information about these, check out the avenue.quark documentation.

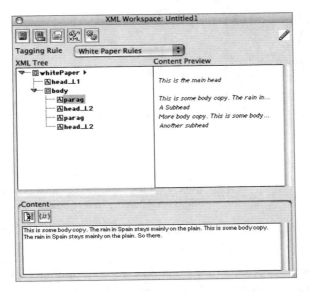

Figure C-4
A tagged story

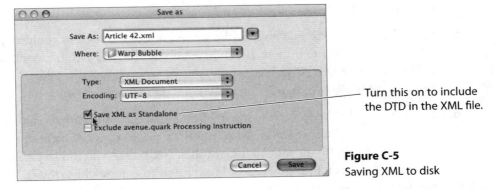

Turn this on to include the DTD in the XML file.

Figure C-5
Saving XML to disk

XML Import. While most QuarkXPress users focus on how to get XML out of their layouts, most XML people look at the problem from the opposite perspective: They expect that people's content will *start* as XML and that the main problem is how to import it into various templates. Quark's XML Import XTension does a pretty good job of getting XML into an XPress layout, based on "placeholders" that you add to the layout. Here's how you do it.

1. While a QuarkXPress layout is open, open the Placeholders palette (select Placeholders from the Window menu).

2. Click the first button in the Placeholders palette. This lets you select an XML or XMT (XML template) file with an embedded DTD. The DTD's tree shows up in the palette (see Figure C-6). You can also select a "well-formed" XML file (one without a DTD), in which case XPress will construct what it thinks is the correct DTD.

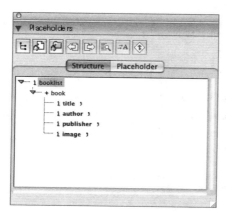

Figure C-6
Adding placeholders to text boxes

3. Drag various elements from the Placeholders palette into text boxes in your layout. Parent elements automatically bring their child elements with them.

4. Apply formatting to the placeholders in the text box. You can double-click on a placeholder to select it and then apply whatever regular text formatting you wish. Save your file!

5. Click the Select XML File button (the second button) in the Placeholders palette to choose an XML file to import. If you have a folder full of XML files with the same DTD, click the Select XML Folder button instead and choose that folder. You can select the same XML file as in step 2, if that XML file contains the content you want to import.

6. Click the Toggle Placeholders/Content button (that's the one with the little magnifying glass icon). The placeholders are automatically replaced by the content in the XML file (see Figure C-7). If you chose a folder full of XML files, you can step through them by pressing Next and Previous XML File buttons (the ones with arrows). You can turn this button on and off to switch between the placeholders and the imported content.

The Joy of Pi
David Blatner
Walker & Company
image:cover123.jpg

The QuarkXPress 4 Book
David Blatner
Peachpit Press
image:cover124.jpg

Real World QuarkXPress 6
David Blatner
Peachpit Press
image:cover125.jpg

QuarkXPress Power Shortcuts: Productivity Shortcuts for QuarkXPress 4 and 5
David Blatner
Pearson Education
image:cover126.jpg

Figure C-7
Importing XML in place
of the placeholders

7. When you're ready to import an XML file, click the last button in the palette, the Convert Placeholders to Text button. This action can't be undone; that's why you saved your file after formatting the placeholders!

At this point, the layout is just like any other QuarkXPress file. Note that the imported XML doesn't retain any of its tags, so you can't easily turn around and export it to XML again.

Item Sequence. It's a hassle to drag one text box into the XML Workspace palette at a time, and often people don't have all the parts of a story in a single text box anyway. Enter the Sequences palette! You can open this palette by selecting Sequences from the Window menu (see Figure C-8).

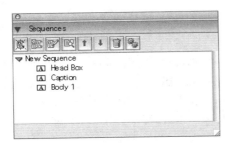

Figure C-8
The Sequences palette

1. To create a new sequence, click the New Sequence button (that's the first one on the left).

2. Now select a text or picture box and click the Add Item button (that's the second button). This box is added to the current sequence in the palette. Repeat this until the sequence includes all the boxes you want to be tagged with XML.

3. You can change the name of any item in the sequence (or the sequence itself) by selecting it and clicking the Edit Name button (that's the third one). If you want to change the order of items in the sequence, just select it and use the Up and Down buttons in the palette.

4. When you're ready to tag the content with XML, hold down the Command/Ctrl key and drag the sequence name on top of the top element in the XML Workspace palette.

Of course, if you had to create a sequence for each new layout, it would drive you batty. Fortunately, you can make a sequence once and then save the XPress layout as a template— the sequence is saved with the file. Then, when you flow text or graphics into this template, the sequences are already built and ready to tag.

Tip: Exporting XSLT. *Something really interesting happens when you export HTML from a Web layout in which you have inserted placeholders (with the Placeholders palette): You get an XSLT file instead of HTML. XSLT is a way to transform XML data into HTML to serve Web pages on the fly. For instance, let's say you have 100 magazine articles saved in XML, and you want to display them on your Web site using the same layout. You could build the template in XSLT and then use an XML/XSL-aware processor to create the HTML whenever the user requests one of the articles.*

This can work beautifully, but whether the XSLT files that QuarkXPress generates would function in this workflow is unclear. At the time of this writing, I have not heard of anyone making use of these files, and some XML experts think it's unlikely that most Web browsers could use them. If you prove them wrong and can serve up HTML based on one of the XSLTs, please let me know!

THE OPEN STREET

For folks who create structured documents that they need to repurpose with different formatting or for different media, there is little doubt that XML is the best thing since that little slicer thing that cuts up hard boiled eggs. On the other hand, folks who like to draw outside the lines and make shorter documents, like ads, will likely find XML almost completely useless.

A QuarkXPress layout has always been like a dead-end road for your content—once your text and graphics hit the page, it's been hard to get them out again. XML changes that, turning XPress into just one stop on a through street. XML lets your data flow in and flow out. In a perfect world, your data would begin as XML before it even gets close to QuarkXPress. It's not always as easy as it sounds, but XML is certainly a powerful workflow when you use it correctly.

Index

Real World QuarkXPress 7 Macintosh Keystrokes

Interface

Environment dialog box	⌥-Help or ⌘-⌥-⌃-E
Change document window	⇧-🖱 on title bar
Interrupt screen redraw	⌘-🖱 (period)
Force screen redraw	⌘-⌥-🖱 (period)
Select through objects	⌘-⇧-⌥-🖱
Select multiple objects or points	⇧-🖱
Deselect all objects	Tab (with Item tool)
Context-sensitive menu	⌃-🖱

Dialog Boxes

OK	Return or Enter
Cancel	⌘-Period or Esc
Apply	⌘-A
Continuous Apply	⌘-⌥-A or ⌥-🖱-Apply
Yes	⌘-Y
No	⌘-N
Next field	Tab
Previous field	⇧-Tab
Next tab in dialog box	⌘-⌥-Tab
Previous tab in dialog box	⌘-⌥-⇧-Tab
Undo/Reset changes	⌘-Z or F1
Redo changes [1]	⌘-⇧-Z

Palettes

Show/Hide Tools	F8
Show Tools/Next tool [2]	⌘-⌥-Tab or ⌥-F8
Previous tool	⌘-⌥-⇧-Tab or ⌥-⇧-F8
Keep a tool selected	⌥-🖱 in Tool palette
Toggle Item/Content tool	⇧-F8
Tool preferences	🖱🖱 tool in Tool palette
Show/Hide Measurements	F9
Go to Measurements first field	⌘-⌥-M
Font field in Measurements	⌘-⌥-⇧-M or ⇧-F9
Next Font in list [3]	⌥-F9
Previous Font in list [3]	⌥-⇧-F9
Show/Hide Page Layout	F10
Show/Hide Style Sheets	F11
Show/Hide Lists	⌥-F11
Show/Hide Colors	F12
Show/Hide Trap Information	⌥-F12
Edit Color or Style Sheet	⌘-🖱 in palette

Indexing

Highlight text field in Index palette	⌘-⌥-I
Add text to index	⌘-⌥-⇧-I

Tabs and Rulers

Open Tabs dialog box	⌘-⇧-T
Delete all Tab Stops	⌥-🖱 in Tab ruler
Delete all Guides [4]	⌥-🖱 in ruler
Set Tab Stop in dialog box	⌘-S

Menus

QuarkXPress

Preferences dialog box	⌘-⌥-⇧-Y
Hide QuarkXPress	⌘-H
Hide Others	⌘-⌥-H
Quit	⌘-Q

File

New Project	⌘-N
New Library	⌘-⌥-N
Open	⌘-O
Close	⌘-W
Close all documents	⌘-⌥-W
Save	⌘-S
Save As	⌘-⌥-S
Revert to last Auto Save	⌥-Revert to Saved
Import Text/Picture	⌘-E
Save Text	⌘-⌥-E
Append	⌘-⌥-A
Save As EPS	⌘-⌥-⇧-S
Print	⌘-P
Output Job	⌥-⌘-P

Edit

Undo	⌘-Z or F1
Can't Redo	⇧-⌘-Z
Cut	⌘-X or F2
Copy	⌘-C or F3
Paste	⌘-V or F4
Paste in Place	⌘-⌥-⇧-V
Select All	⌘-A
Find/Change	⌘-F
Close Find/Change palette	⌘-⌥-F
Style Sheets dialog box	⇧-F11
Colors dialog box	⇧-F12
H&Js Settings dialog box	⌘-⌥-J or ⌥-⇧-F11

Style

Character	⇧-⌘-D
Alignment Left	⇧-⌘-L
Alignment Centered	⇧-⌘-C
Alignment Right	⇧-⌘-R
Alignment Justified	⇧-⌘-J
Leading	⇧-⌘-E
Format	⇧-⌘-F
Tabs	⇧-⌘-T
Rules	⇧-⌘-N

Legend

⌘	Command	⌥	Option
⇧	Shift	⌃	Control
🖱	Click	⋯🖱	Click and drag

[1] This is editable in the Preferences dialog box.

[2] If Tool palette isn't showing, this keystroke acts like Show Tools.

[3] Next and previous font are by font menu order, so the movement may seem random.

[4] Option-clicking when the pasteboard is touching the ruler deletes pasteboard guides; with the page touching, it deletes page guides.

Item

Modify (Item Specifications)	⌘-M or ⌘-🖰
Frame	⌘-B
Runaround	⌘-T
Clipping	⌘-⌥-T
Duplicate	⌘-D
Step and Repeat	⌘-⌥-D
Delete	⌘-K
Super Delete (Marvin)	⌘-⌥-⇧-K
Group	⌘-G
Ungroup	⌘-U
Lock/Unlock	F6
Bring to Front	F5
Space/Align	⌘-, (comma)
Move Forward	⌥-F5
Send to Back	⇧-F5
Send Backward	⌥-⇧-F5
Edit Shape	⇧-F4
Edit Runaround	⌥-F4
Edit Clipping Path	⌥-⇧-F4
Change to Corner Point	⌥-F1
Change to Smooth Point	⌥-F2
Change to Symmetrical Point	⌥-F3
Change to Straight Segment	⌥-⇧-F1
Change to Curved Segment	⌥-⇧-F2
Drop Shadow	⌥-⇧-⌘-D

Page

Go to Page	⌘-J
Toggle displaying master pages	⇧-F10
Display next master page	⌥-F10
Display previous master page	⌥-⇧-F10
Go to first page	⌘-Home or ⌃-⇧-A
Go to last page	⌘-End or ⌃-⇧-D
Go to previous page	⇧-Page Up or ⌃-⇧-K
Go to next page	⇧-Page Down or ⌃-⇧-L
Web Page Properties	⌘-⌥-⇧-A

Layout

Layout Properties	⌥-⇧-⌘-P
Cycle through layouts	⌘-' (apostrophe)

View

Fit in Window	⌘-Zero
Fit pasteboard in Window	⌘-⌥-Zero
Actual Size	⌘-1
Thumbnails	⇧-F6
Show/Hide Guides	F7
Snap to Guides	⇧-F7
Show/Hide Baseline Grid	⌥-F7
Show/Hide Rulers	⌘-R
Show/Hide Invisibles	⌘-I

Utilities

Check Spelling: Word	⌘-L
Check Spelling: Story	⌘-⌥-L
Check Spelling: Layout	⌘-⌥-⇧-L
Word Count	⌘-L
Add word (in Spelling)	⌘-A

Add all suspect words to dictionary	⌥-⇧-Done
Suggested Hyphenation	⌘-⌥-⇧-H
Font Usage	F13
Picture Usage	⌥-F13

Window

Tools	F8
Measurements	F9
Page Layout	F10
Style Sheets	F11
Colors	F12
Trap Info	⌥-F11
Lists	⌥-F12

Moving

Scroll up one screen	Page Up or ⌃-K
Scroll down one screen	Page Down or ⌃-L
Scroll with Grabber Hand	⌥-🖰
Live scroll toggle	⌥-🖰 Scroll Box
Previous spread	⌥-Page Up
Next spread	⌥-Page Down

Moving Selected Items

(Also applies to moving pictures in picture boxes with Content tool.)

Nudge an object in 1-point increments (with Item tool)	Arrow keys
Nudge an object in 1/10-point increments (with Item tool)	⌥-Arrow keys
Move object with constraint	⇧-🖰
Center align (horizontally) two or more items to each other	⌘-[
Center align (vertically) two or more items to each other	⌘-]
Left align two or more items to each other	⌘-Left Arrow
Right align two or more items to each other	⌘-Right Arrow
Top align two or more items to each other	⌘-Up Arrow
Bottom align two or more items to each other	⌘-Bottom Arrow
Center align (horizontally) one or more selected items relative to the page	⌘-⇧-[
Center align (vertically) one or more selected items relative to the page	⌘-⇧-]
Left align one or more selected items relative to the page	⌘-⇧-Left Arrow
Right align one or more selected items relative to the page	⌘-⇧-Right Arrow
Bottom align one or more selected items relative to the page	⌘-⇧-Down Arrow
Top align one or more selected items relative to the page	⌘-⇧-Top Arrow

Zooming and Magnification

Toggle 100%/200%	⌘-⌥-🖰
Zoom in	⌃-🖰 or ⌃-🖰
Zoom out	⌃-⌥-🖰 or ⌃-⌥-🖰
Fit in Window	⌘-Zero
Actual Size	⌘-1
Custom magnification	⌃-V

Real World QuarkXPress 7 Macintosh Keystrokes *(continued)*

Text

Moving Through Text
(Hold down Shift key to select while moving.)

Character by character	Left/Right Arrows
Line by line	Up/Down Arrow
Word by word	⌘-Left/Right Arrow
Paragraph by paragraph	⌘-Up/Down Arrow
Start of line	⌘-⌥-Left Arrow
End of line	⌘-⌥-Right Arrow
Start of story	⌘-⌥-Up Arrow
End of story	⌘-⌥-Down Arrow
Next table cell	⌃-Tab
Previous table cell	⌃-⇧-Tab

Selecting Text

One word	🖰🖰 in word
One word and punctuation	🖰🖰 between word and punctuation
One line	🖰🖰🖰
One paragraph	🖰🖰🖰🖰
Entire story	🖰🖰🖰🖰🖰 or ⌘-A
Drag-and-drop text (or copy text)	⌘-⌥-····🖰 (or ⌘-⇧-⌥-····🖰)

Deleting Text

Previous character	Delete (Backspace key)
Next character	⌦ or ⇧-Delete
Previous word	⌘-Delete
Next word	⌘-⌦ or ⌘-⇧-Delete
Highlighted characters	Delete

Character Formats

Character format	⌘-⇧-D
Increase point size (presets)	⌘-⇧-> (period key)
Decrease point size (presets)	⌘-⇧-< (comma key)
Increase point size 1 point	⌘-⇧-⌥->
Decrease point size 1 point	⌘-⇧-⌥-<
Other Size	⌘-⇧-Backslash (\)
Plain Text	⌘-⇧-P
Bold	⌘-⇧-B
Italic	⌘-⇧-I
Underline	⌘-⇧-U
Word Underline	⌘-⇧-W
Strikethrough	⌘-⇧-Slash (/)
Outline	⌘-⇧-O
Shadow	⌘-⇧-S
All Caps	⌘-⇧-K
Small Caps	⌘-⇧-H
Superscript	⌘-⇧-=
Subscript	⌘-⇧-Hyphen
Superior	⌘-⇧-V
Increase Scaling 5 percent [5]	⌘-]
Decrease Scaling 5 percent [5]	⌘-[
Increase Scaling 1 percent [5]	⌘-⌥-]
Decrease Scaling 1 percent [5]	⌘-⌥-[
Increase Kern/Track 10 units	⌘-⇧-]

[5] *These keystrokes scale in the direction (horizontal or vertical) that you last selected from the dialog box.*

Decrease Kern/Track 10 units	⌘-⇧-[
Increase Kern/Track 1 unit	⌘-⌥-⇧-]
Decrease Kern/Track 1 unit	⌘-⌥-⇧-[
Increase "wordspacing" 1 unit (with Type Tricks XTension)	⌘-⌥-⇧-⌃-]
Decrease "wordspacing" 1 unit (with Type Tricks XTension)	⌘-⌥-⇧-⌃-[
Baseline Shift down 1 point	⌘-⌥-⇧-Hyphen
Baseline Shift up 1 point	⌘-⌥-⇧-=

Paragraph Formats

Paragraph Format	⌘-⇧-F
Left Alignment	⌘-⇧-L
Right Alignment	⌘-⇧-R
Center Alignment	⌘-⇧-C
Justified Alignment	⌘-⇧-J
Forced Justification	⌘-⇧-⌥-J
Leading	⌘-⇧-E
Tabs	⌘-⇧-T
Rules (above and below)	⌘-⇧-N
Increase Leading 1 point	⌘-⇧-"
Decrease Leading 1 point	⌘-⇧-;
Increase Leading 1/10 point	⌘-⌥-⇧-"
Decrease Leading 1/10 point	⌘-⌥-⇧-;
Copy Paragraph Format	⌥-⇧-🖰-any paragraph
Apply No Style before applying style sheet	⌥-🖰-on style sheet in Style Sheet palette

Special Formatting Characters

One Symbol Character	⌘-⌥-Q
One Zapf Dingbats Character	⌘-⌥-Z
Soft Return (New Line)	⇧-Return
Discretionary New Line	⌘-Return
Discretionary Hyphen	⌘-Hyphen
Nonbreaking Hyphen	⌘-=
Nonbreaking Space	⌘-5 or ⌃-5
New Column	Enter
New Box	⇧-Enter
En space	⌥-Space
Nonbreaking En space	⌘-⌥-Space or ⌘-⌥-5
Flex Space	⌥-⇧-Space
Nonbreaking Flex Space	⌘-⌥-⇧-Space
Punctuation Space	⇧-Space
Nonbreaking Punctuation Space	⌘-⇧-Space
Breaking em dash	⌥-⇧-hyphen
Nonbreaking em dash	⌘-⌥-=
Current page number	⌘-3
Previous text box page number	⌘-2
Next text box page number	⌘-4
Indent to Here	⌘-Backslash (\)
Right Indent Tab	⌥-Tab

Find/Change Characters

Tab	\t or ⌘-⌃-Tab
New paragraph	\p or ⌘-Return
New line	\n or ⌘-⇧-Return
New column	\c or ⌘-Enter
New box	\b or ⌘-⇧-Enter
Previous text box page number	\2 or ⌘-2

Current page number	\3 or ⌘-3
Next text box page number	\4 or ⌘-4
Wildcard	\? or ⌘-?
Punctuation Space	\. or ⌘-period
Flex Space	\f or ⌘-⇧-F
Backslash	\\ or ⌘-\

Pictures and Lines

Changing the Picture

Increase size by 5 percent	⌘-⌥-⇧-> (period key)
Decrease size by 5 percent	⌘-⌥-⇧-< (comma key)
Center picture in box	⌘-⇧-M
Fit picture to box	⌘-⇧-F
Fit picture maintaining ratio	⌘-⌥-⇧-F
Move picture 1 point	Arrow keys
Move picture $^{1}/_{10}$ point	⌥-Arrow keys
Negative	⌘-⇧-Hyphen
Halftone Specifications	⌘-⇧-H
Contrast Specifications	⌘-⇧-C

Changing the Picture Box

Resize Picture Box	····▸ Handle
Constrain to square or circle	⇧-····▸
Maintain aspect ratio	⇧-⌥-····▸
Scale picture with box	⌘-····▸
Maintain ratio of box and picture	⌘-⇧-⌥-····▸

Bézier Editing

Edit Shape toggle	⇧-F4
Delete Bézier point	⌥-▸-point
Delete active point while drawing	Delete
Add point	⌥-▸-segment
Change to Smooth point	⌃-····▸ or ⌥-F2
Change to Corner point	⌃-▸ or ⌃-····▸ on handle or ⌥-F1
Change smooth to corner while drawing	⌘-⌃-····▸-handle
Edit path while still drawing	⌘-····▸
Retract curve handles	⌃-▸-point
Expose curve handles	⌃-····▸-point
Select all points in active box	⌘-⇧-A or ▸▸-point
Select all points in active path	▸▸-point
Constrain active point/handle to 45° movement	⇧-····▸-point/handle

When Importing Pictures

Import Picture	⌘-E
Low-resolution screen image	⇧-Open
TIFF line art to grayscale	⌥-Open
TIFF grayscale to line art	⌘-Open
TIFF color to grayscale	⌘-Open
Don't import spot colors in EPS	⌘-Open
Force reimport of all pictures	⌘-Open in Open dialog

Lines

Increase width (presets)	⌘-⇧-> (period key)
Decrease width (presets)	⌘-⇧-< (comma key)
Increase width 1 point	⌘-⌥-⇧->
Decrease width 1 point	⌘-⌥-⇧-<
Other width	⌘-⇧-Backslash (\)
Constrain resizing at 45°	⇧-····▸
Constrain resizing to angle	⇧-⌥-····▸

Function Keys

F1	Undo
⌥-F1	Change to corner point
⌥-⇧-F1	Change to straight segment
F2	Cut
⌥-F2	Change to smooth point
⌥-⇧-F2	Change to curved segment
F3	Copy
⌥-F3	Change to symmetrical point
F4	Paste
⇧-F4	Edit Shape
⌥-F4	Edit Runaround Shape
⌥-⇧-F4	Edit Clipping Path Shape
F5	Bring to Front
⇧-F5	Send to Back
⌥-F5	Bring Forward
⇧-⌥-F5	Send Backward
F6	Lock/Unlock
⇧-⌥-F6	Thumbnails view
⌘-F6	Font Usage
F7	Show/Hide Guides
⇧-F7	Snap to Guides
⌥-F7	Show/Hide Baseline Grid
F8	Show/Hide Tools
⇧-F8	Toggle Item/Content tool
⌥-F8	Next Tool
⇧-⌥-F8	Previous Tool
F9	Show/Hide Measurements palette
⇧-F9	Edit font name field
⌥-F9	Next font in list[6]
⇧-⌥-F9	Previous font in list[6]
F10	Show/Hide Page Layout palette
⇧-F10	Go between master pages and pages
⌥-F10	Next master page
⇧-⌥-F10	Previous master page
F11	Show/Hide Style Sheets
⇧-F11	Edit Style Sheets
⌥-F11	Show/Hide Lists
⇧-⌥-F11	Edit H&Js
F12	Show/Hide Colors palette
⇧-F12	Edit Colors
⌥-F12	Show/Hide Trap Information palette
⇧-⌥-F12	Trapping Preferences
F13	Font Usage
⌥-F13	Picture Usage

[6] *The previous/next font is determined by font name, so you may not get the font you expect.*

al World QuarkXPress 7 Windows Keystrokes

Interface

	F1
...ronment	⌃-About QuarkXPress
...errupt screen redraw	Esc
...rce screen redraw	⇧-Esc
...elect through objects	⌃-⇧-Alt-ϰ
Select multiple objects or points	⇧-ϰ
Deselect all objects	Tab (with Item tool)
Context-sensitive menu	Right-ϰ or ⇧-F10

Dialog Boxes

OK	Enter
Cancel	Esc
Apply	Alt-A
Continuous Apply	Alt-ϰ-Apply
Yes	Y
No	N
Next field	Tab
Previous field	⇧-Tab
Next tab in dialog box	⌃-Tab
Previous tab in dialog box	⌃-⇧-Tab
Undo last change	⌃-Z
Undo all changes in dialog box	⌃-⇧-Z
Redo change[1]	⌃-Y

Palettes

Show/Hide Tools	F8
Show Tools/Next tool[2]	⌃-Alt-Tab or ⌃-F8
Previous tool	⌃-Alt-⇧-Tab or ⌃-⇧-F8
Keep a tool selected	Alt-ϰ Tool
Toggle Item/Content tool	⇧-F8
Tool preferences	ϰϰ Tool
Show/Hide Measurements	F9
Go to Measurements first field	⌃-Alt-M
Font field in Measurements	⌃-Alt-⇧-M or ⇧-F9
Next Font in list[3]	⌃-F9
Previous Font in list[3]	⌃-⇧-F9
Show/Hide Page Layout	F4
Show/Hide Style Sheets	F11
Show/Hide Lists	⌃-F11
Show/Hide Colors	F12
Show/Hide Trap Information	⌃-F12
Apply and then exit dialog	Enter
Edit color or style sheet	⌃-ϰ in palette

Tabs and Rulers

Open Tabs dialog box	⌃-⇧-T
Delete all Tab stops	Alt-ϰ in Tab ruler
Delete all Guides[4]	Alt-ϰ in horizontal or vertical ruler
Set Tab stop in dialog box	Alt-S

Legend

⇧	Shift	⌃	Ctrl
ϰ	Click	⁻⁻ϰ	Click and drag

Indexing

Highlight text field in palette	⌃-Alt-I
Add text to index	⌃-Alt-⇧-I
Edit index entry	ϰϰ on index entry

Menus

File

New Project	⌃-N
New Library	⌃-Alt-N
Open	⌃-O
Close	⌃-F4
Close all documents	Alt-W then press A
Save	⌃-S
Save As	⌃-Alt-S
Revert to last Auto Save	Alt-Revert to Saved
Import Text/Picture	⌃-E
Save Text	⌃-Alt-E
Append	⌃-Alt-A
Save As EPS	⌃-Alt-⇧-S
Page Setup	⌃-Alt-P
Print	⌃-P
Output Job	⌃-Alt-P
Exit	⌃-Q

Edit

Undo	⌃-Z
Redo	⌃-Y
Cut	⌃-X
Copy	⌃-C
Paste	⌃-V
Select All	⌃-A
Find/Change	⌃-F
Close Find/Change	⌃-Alt-F
Preferences dialog box	⇧-⌃-Alt-Y
Style Sheets dialog box	⇧-F11
Colors dialog box	⇧-F12
H&Js settings dialog box	⌃-⇧-F11

Style

Character	⌃-⇧-D
Alignment Left	⌃-⇧-L
Alignment Centered	⌃-⇧-C
Alignment Right	⌃-⇧--R
Alignment Justified	⌃-⇧-J
Leading	⌃-⇧-E
Format	⌃-⇧-F
Tabs	⌃-⇧-T
Rules	⌃-⇧-N

[1] This shortcut is editable in the Preferences dialog box.

[2] If Tool palette isn't showing, this keystroke acts like Show Tools.

[3] Next and previous font are alphabetical, so you may not get the font you expect.

[4] Alt-clicking when the pasteboard is touching the ruler deletes pasteboard guides; with the page touching, it deletes page guides.

Item

Modify (Item Specifications)	⌃-M or ⌃-↖↖
Frame	⌃-B
Clipping	⌃-Alt-T
Runaround	⌃-T
Duplicate	⌃-D
Step and Repeat	⌃-Alt-D
Delete	⌃-K
Super Delete (Meltdown)	⌃-Alt-⇧-K
Group	⌃-G
Ungroup	⌃-U
Space/Align	⌃-, (comma)
Lock/Unlock	F6
Bring to Front	F5
Move Forward	⌃-F5
Send to Back	⇧-F5
Send Backward	⌃-⇧-F5
Edit Shape	F10
Edit Runaround	⌃-F10
Edit Clipping Path	⌃-⇧-F10
Change to Corner Point	⌃-F1
Change to Smooth Point	⌃-F2
Change to Symmetrical Point	⌃-F3
Change to Straight Segment	⌃-⇧-F1
Change to Curved Segment	⌃-⇧-F2
Drop Shadow	⌃-Alt-⇧-D

Page

Go to Page	⌃-J
Toggle displaying master pages	⇧-F4
Display next master page	⌃-⇧-F4
Display previous master page	⌃-⇧-F3
Go to first page	⌃-Page Up
Go to last page	⌃-Page Down
Go to previous page	⇧-Page Up
Go to next page	⇧-Page Down
Web Page Properties	⌃-Alt-⇧-A

Layout

Layout Properties	⌃-Alt-⇧-P
Navigating among layouts	Alt - ' (apostrophe)

View

Fit in Window	⌃-Zero
Fit pasteboard in Window	⌃-Alt-Zero
Actual Size	⌃-1
Thumbnails	⇧-F6
Show/Hide Guides	F7
Snap to Guides	⇧-F7
Show/Hide Baseline Grid	⌃-F7
Show/Hide Rulers	⌃-R
Show/Hide Invisibles	⌃-I

Utilities

Check Spelling: Word	⌃-W
Check Spelling: Story	⌃-Alt-W
Check Spelling: Layout	⌃-Alt-⇧-W
Word Count	Alt-L
Add word (in Spelling)	Alt-A
Add all suspect words to dictionary	Alt-⇧-Close
Suggested Hyphenation	⇧-⌃-Alt-H
Usage dialog box	F2

Window

Tools	F8
Measurements	F9
Page Layout	F4
Style Sheets	F11
Colors	F12
Trap Info	⌃-F12
Lists	⌃-F11

Moving

Scroll up one screen	Page Up
Scroll down one screen	Page Down
Scroll with Grabber Hand	Alt-⁛↖
Live scroll toggle	Alt-⁛↖ Scroll Box
Next spread	Alt-Page Down
Previous spread	Alt-Page Up

Moving Selected Items
(Also applies to moving pictures in picture boxes with Content tool.)

Nudge an object in 1-point increments (with Item tool)	Arrow keys
Nudge an object in $^{1}/_{10}$-point increments (with Item tool)	Alt-Arrow keys
Move an object with horizontal and vertical constraint	⇧-⁛↖

Zooming and Magnification

Toggle 100%/200%	⌃-Alt-↖
Zoom in	⌃-spacebar-↖ or ⌃-spacebar-⁛↖
Zoom out	⌃-Alt-spacebar-↖
Fit in Window	⌃-Zero
Actual Size	⌃-1
Custom magnification	⌃-Alt-V

Text

Moving Through Text
(Hold down Shift key to select while moving.)

Character by character	Left/Right Arrows
Line by line	Up/Down Arrow
Word by word	⌃-Left/Right Arrow
Paragraph by paragraph	⌃-Up/Down Arrow
Start of line	⌃-Alt-Left Arrow or Home
End of line	⌃-Alt-Right Arrow or End
Start of story	⌃-Alt-Up Arrow or ⌃-Home
End of story	⌃-Alt-Down Arrow or ⌃-End
Next table cell	⌃-Tab
Previous table cell	⌃-⇧-Tab

Real World QuarkXPress 7 Windows Keystrokes *(continued)*

Selecting Text

One word	⇡ ⇡ in word
One word and punctuation	⇡ ⇡ between word and punctuation
One line	⇡ ⇡ ⇡
One paragraph	⇡ ⇡ ⇡ ⇡
Entire story	⇡ ⇡ ⇡ ⇡ ⇡ or ⌃-A

Deleting Text

Previous character	Backspace
Next character	Delete or ⇧-Backspace
Previous word	⌃-Backspace
Next word	⌃-Delete or ⌃-⇧-Backspace

Character Formats

Character format	⌃-⇧-D
Increase point size (presets)	⌃-⇧-. (period)
Decrease point size (presets)	⌃-⇧-, (comma)
Increase point size 1 point	⌃-Alt-⇧-. (period)
Decrease point size 1 point	⌃-Alt-⇧-, (comma)
Other Size	⌃-⇧-\ (backslash)
Plain Text	⌃-⇧-P
Bold	⌃-⇧-B
Italic	⌃-⇧-I
Underline	⌃-⇧-U
Word Underline	⌃-⇧-W
Strikethrough	⌃-⇧-/ (slash)
Outline	⌃-⇧-O
Shadow	⌃-⇧-S
All Caps	⌃-⇧-K
Small Caps	⌃-⇧-H
Superscript	⌃-⇧-Zero
Subscript	⌃-⇧-9
Superior	⌃-⇧-V
Increase Scaling 5 percent	⌃-]
Decrease Scaling 5 percent	⌃-[
Increase Scaling 1 percent [5]	⌃-Alt-]
Decrease Scaling 1 percent [5]	⌃-Alt-[
Increase Kern/Track 10 units	⌃-⇧-]
Decrease Kern/Track 10 units	⌃-⇧-[
Increase Kern/Track 1 unit	⌃-Alt-⇧-]
Decrease Kern/Track 1 unit	⌃-Alt-⇧-[
Baseline Shift down 1 point	⌃-Alt-⇧-9
Baseline Shift up 1 point	⌃-Alt-⇧-Zero

Paragraph Formats

Paragraph Format dialog box	⌃-⇧-F
Left Alignment	⌃-⇧-L
Right Alignment	⌃-⇧-R
Center Alignment	⌃-⇧-C
Justified Alignment	⌃-⇧-J
Forced Justification	⌃-Alt-⇧-J
Leading	⌃-⇧-E
Tabs	⌃-⇧-T
Rules (above and below)	⌃-⇧-N
Increase Leading 1 point	⌃-⇧-"
Decrease Leading 1 point	⌃-⇧-;
Increase Leading 1/10 point	⌃-Alt-⇧-"
Decrease Leading 1/10 point	⌃-Alt-⇧-;
Copy Paragraph Format	Alt-⇧-⇡-any paragraph
Apply No Style before applying style sheet	Alt-⇡-on style sheet in Style Sheets palette

Special Formatting Characters

One Symbol Character	⌃-Alt-Q
One Zapf Dingbats Character	⌃-Alt-Z
Indent to Here	⌃-Backslash (\)
Soft Return (new line)	⇧-Enter
New Column	Enter on key pad
New Text Box	⇧-Enter on key pad
Discretionary New Line	⌃-Enter
Flush Right Tab	⇧-Tab
Nonbreaking Hyphen	⌃-=
Discretionary Hyphen	⌃-Hyphen
Nonbreaking en dash	⌃-Alt-⇧-Hyphen
Breaking em dash	⌃-⇧-=
Nonbreaking em dash	⌃-Alt-⇧-=
Nonbreaking Space	⌃-5
En Space	⌃-⇧-6
Nonbreaking En Space	⌃-Alt-⇧-6
Flex Space	⌃-⇧-5
Nonbreaking Flex Space	⌃-Alt-⇧-5
Punctuation Space	⇧-Space
Previous text box page number	⌃-2
Current text box page number	⌃-3
Next text box page number	⌃-4

Find/Change Characters

Tab	\t or ⌃-Tab
New paragraph	\p or ⌃-Enter
New line	\n or ⌃-⇧-Enter
New column	\c or ⌃-Keypad Enter
New box	\b or ⌃-⇧-Keypad Enter
Previous text box page number	\2 or ⌃-2
Current page number	\3 or ⌃-3
Next text box page number	\4 or ⌃-4
Wildcard	\? or ⌃-?
Punctuation Space	\. or ⌃-. (period)
Flex Space	\f or ⌃-⇧-F
Backslash	\\ or ⌃-\ (backslash)

[5] *These keystrokes scale in the direction (horizontal or vertical) which you last selected from the dialog box.*

Real World QuarkXPress 7 Windows Keystrokes (continued)

Pictures and Lines

Changing the Picture

Increase size by 5 percent	⌥-Alt-⇧-. (period)
Decrease size by 5 percent	⌥-Alt-⇧-, (comma)
Center picture in box	⌥-⇧-M
Fit picture to box	⌥-⇧-F
Fit picture maintaining ratio	⌥-Alt-⇧-F
Move picture 1 point	Arrow keys
Move picture 1/10 point	Alt-Arrow keys
Negative	⌥-⇧-Hyphen
Halftone Specifications	⌥-⇧-H
Contrast Specifications	⌥-⇧-C

Changing the Picture Box

Resize Picture Box	⌖-handle
Constrain to square or circle	⇧-⌖-handle
Maintain aspect ratio	Alt-⇧-⌖-handle
Scale picture with box	⌥-⌖-handle
Scale picture and constrain box shape	⌥-⇧-⌖-handle
Maintain ratio of box and picture	⌥-⇧-Alt-⌖-handle

Bézier Editing

Edit Shape toggle	F10
Delete Bézier point	Alt-⌖-point or Backspace
Delete active point while drawing	Backspace
Add point	Alt-⌖-segment
Change to Corner point	⌥-⇧-⌖-handle or ⌥-F1
Change to Smooth point	⌥-⇧-⌖-handle or ⌥-F2
Change smooth to corner while drawing	⌥-⌖-point, then ⌥-F1
Edit while creating item	⌥-⌖
Retract curve handles	⌥-⇧-⌖-point
Expose curve handles	⌥-⇧-⌖-point
Select all points in active box	⌥-⇧-A or ⌖⌖-point
Select all points in active path	⌖⌖-point
Constrain active point/handle to 45° movement	⇧-⌖-point/handle

When Importing Pictures

Import Picture	⌥-E
Import at 36 dpi	⇧-Open
Import color TIFF as grayscale or grayscale TIFF as line art or EPS without adding spot colors	⌥-Open
Force reimport of all pictures	⌥-Open in Open dialog

Lines

Increase width (presets)	⌥-⇧-. (period)
Decrease width (presets)	⌥-⇧-, (comma)
Increase width 1 point	⌥-Alt-⇧-.
Decrease width 1 point	⌥-Alt-⇧-,
Other width	⌥-⇧-\ (backslash)
Constrain to 45° or 90°	⇧-⌖
Constrain to existing angle	⇧-Alt-⌖

Function Keys

F1	Help
⌥-F1	Change to Corner point
⌥-⇧-F1	Change to Straight segment
F2	Usage dialog box
⌥-F2	Change to Smooth point
⌥-⇧-F2	Change to curved segment
F3	Maximize or minimize window
⇧-F3	Fit Spread
⌥-F3	Change to symmetrical point
⌥-⇧-F3	Next master page
F4	Show/Hide Page Layout palette
⇧-F4	Toggle between master pages and document pages
⌥-F4	Close
Alt-F4	Quit
F5	Bring to Front
⇧-F5	Send to Back
⌥-F5	Bring Forward
⌥-⇧-F5	Send Backward
F6	Lock/Unlock
⇧-F6	Thumbnails view
⌥-F6	Previous Document
⌥-⇧-F6	Next Document
F7	Show/Hide Guides
⇧-F7	Snap to Guides
⌥-F7	Show/Hide Baseline Grid
F8	Show/Hide Tools
⇧-F8	Toggle Item/Content tool
⌥-F8	Next Tool
⌥-⇧-F8	Previous Tool
F9	Show/Hide Measurements palette
⇧-F9	Edit font name field
⌥-F9	Next font in list[2]
⌥-⇧-F9	Previous font in list[2]
F10	Edit Shape
⇧-F10	Context (right-button) menu
⌥-F10	Edit Runaround
⌥-⇧-F10	Edit Clipping Path
F11	Show/Hide Style Sheets
⇧-F11	Edit Style Sheets
⌥-F11	Show/Hide Lists
⌥-⇧-F11	Edit H&Js
F12	Show/Hide Colors palette
⇧-F12	Edit Colors
⌥-F12	Show/Hide Trap Information palette
⌥-⇧-F12	Trapping preferences

Peachpit Press
1249 Eighth Street • Berkeley, CA 94710
510/524-2178 • FAX: 510/524-2221
http://www.peachpit.com/Quark7/
©2008 David Blatner. All Rights Reserved.